PERSONNEL MANAGEMENT

PERSONNEL MANAGEMENT

Kendrith M. Rowland
Gerald R. Ferris

*University of Illinois
at Urbana-Champaign*

Allyn and Bacon, Inc.
Boston   London   Sydney   Toronto

Library of Congress Cataloging in Publication Data

Rowland, Kendrith Martin.
   Personnel management.

   Bibliography: p.
   Includes indexes.
   1. Personnel management.   2. Personnel management
—Addresses, essays, lectures.   I. Ferris, Gerald R.
II. Title.
HF5549.R653   658.3   81-14995
ISBN 0-205-07740-4   AACR2

Printed in the United States of America.
10 9 8 7 6 5 4 3 2 1   87 86 85 84 83 82

CONTENTS

v

PREFACE

Organizational scientists write books for a number of different reasons, perhaps most typically because it is something they have wanted to do for a long time ("I have had this book in me for nearly ten years"), or because they feel there is a real need for it ("Why hasn't something like this been done before?"). *Personnel Management* falls into the second category, and some elaboration will serve to clarify this point.

First of all, this book was not "written" by us. Rather, it is a collection of contributed chapters by experts in the field. Thus, we like to depict our role as planning and organizing—perhaps "orchestrating"—the efforts of others in the accomplishment of a meaningful outcome. Rather than regard this book as a collection of readings, we prefer to think of it as a text that just happens to include seventeen original chapters written by twenty-four people. This book, therefore, is intended to answer a need in the field of personnel management; that is, to present a forum for the exchange of current thinking and future perspectives on the field. To date, nothing quite like this has ever been done.

Second, and consistent with the emerging trends in the field, we have included topics we believe represent legitimate areas of concern for the field, but ones not likely to be found in most personnel management texts today. Job and organizational stress, for example, is a prominent concern for many organizations and management groups. Behavioral scientists, in turn, are beginning to give more attention to this topic. The fact that stress is infrequently discussed in personnel management texts does not suggest to us that it is an inappropriate area of attention for the personnel function.

Organizational exit, while a relatively new term, does not constitute a new and original topic. Organizational scientists and practitioners have acknowledged and avidly discussed the problems of absenteeism and turnover for some time. We see absenteeism and turnover, however, as but one side of the coin, representing only the voluntary side of exit. An equally important side of organizational exit is involuntary exit, the processes by which individuals leave organizations against their will, and, in like manner, the responsibilities of the organization for addressing these matters.

Motivation also represents a continuing concern for behavioral and organizational scientists. The focus given the topic in this book, in contrast to that usually given it in the organizational behavior literature, is more utilitarian than descriptive (in a sense, more managerial). Motivational strategies are discussed as ways to meet persistent human resource problems in organizations.

Third, we would like to say something more about the rather distinctive format of this book. While some may not view it as a text, because it lacks a tight, integrative framework, our primary purpose was to address a number of different and perhaps more critical concerns expressed by instructors of courses in personnel management, especially the more advanced courses. We found, for example, that a good many instructors felt constrained by the structure of the conventional text, and, as a result, were turning to readers to allow them more flexibility. A reader permits flexibility, but often, unfortunately, at the expense of comprehensiveness. To meet the dual needs for flexibility *and* comprehensiveness, we decided to use the contributed chapters format as an appropriate alternative.

Further, to depart significantly from a mere rendition of the selected topics in each chapter, we established essentially two guidelines for the contributing authors. In order to ensure comprehensiveness and provide grounding in the basics, we asked that considerable attention be paid to state-of-the-art concepts, issues, and information. In addition, we asked that a part of each chapter be devoted to a discussion of new perspectives on the area and the identification of important issues for practice and research in the future.

Fourth, we were naturally interested in the overall, content quality of the final product. With many texts, it is not reasonable to assume that the author can be an expert in each (or even several) of the areas covered. Thus, some weaknesses in content coverage are bound to occur. For the topics addressed in this book, we believe we have convened some of the most knowledgeable people in the field. Thus, the student and professional practitioner should receive a thorough grounding in each area. The flexibility and comprehensiveness of the chosen topics and format, plus the strengths of the contributing authors in their respective areas of expertise, seemed to us an ideal (and an unbeatable) combination.

The content of the book is organized into eight parts. Part One, entitled "Foundations," includes in Chapter One (Rowland and Ferris) perspectives on the field of personnel management and two major components of the field: personnel practice and personnel research. Chapter Two (Arvey and Shingledecker) focuses on research methods in personnel management.

Part Two is entitled "Personnel and Job Planning." In Chapter Three (Dyer), consideration is given to human resource planning, a personnel activity that attempts to link the organization to its external environment. Job analysis, one of the most fundamental activities of the personnel function, is described in Chapter Four (Sparks). Conceptually, the activities of this section of the book set the stage for a series of interactions between the individual and the organization.

The title of Part Three is "Organizational Entry," which is the processes by which individuals attain organizational membership. Chapter Five (Schwab) reviews the processes of job search by the individual and recruitment by the organization. The employment interview, the most widely used device in the selection process, is discussed in Chapter Six (Hakel). Finally, Chapter Seven (Sharf) provides an in-depth analysis of the legal constraints on personnel testing and other employment practices.

"Evaluation and Reinforcement of Work Performance" is the title of Part Four. Chapter Eight (Kavanagh) examines the performance evaluation process and new perspectives on this much neglected topic, while matters of pay and compensation, which affect the employment relationship, are reviewed in Chapter Nine (Mahoney). In Chapter Ten (Mitchell), the topic of work motivation is discussed and some strategies for increasing it are suggested.

Part Five is "Personnel Training and Development." Chapter Eleven (Lacey, Lee, and Wallace) provides perspectives on both general training and development concepts and issues, while Chapter Twelve (Boehm) deals with the specific uses and benefits of the assessment center technique in selecting and developing managers.

Part Six, "Careers and the Work Environment," focuses on several important topics in personnel management. Career planning and development is a popular personnel activity today. This topic is discussed in Chapter Thirteen (Milkovich and Anderson) from the standpoint of both the individual and the organization. An equally important topic is the antecedents and consequences of job and organizational stress, which is reviewed in Chapter Fourteen (Beehr and Schuler). The final chapter in this section, Chapter Fifteen (Fossum), considers union-management relations, with special emphasis on the collective bargaining process.

Having gone full circle from planning for human resources, to recruiting and selecting them, evaluating and rewarding them, and then developing them, Part Seven, "Organizational Exit," focuses on the processes by which individuals leave organizations. Chapter Sixteen (Steers and Stone) discusses both voluntary and involuntary exit and a number of relevant issues for personnel practice and research.

"Overview," Part Eight, is the final section of the book. Chapter Seventeen (Strauss) presents perspectives on the field and the practice of personnel management in organizations from the past and present, but gives primary attention to the future.

In closing, we would like to acknowledge the major contributions of others. To Mike Meehan, Managing Editor of Allyn and Bacon, we owe a debt of gratitude for believing in us and our ideas for this "impossible" book. To the contributing authors, we extend a word of special thanks for giving their best and timely efforts in the preparation of their respective chapters. To Carol Halliday and Howard Weinstein, a word of special thanks also; Carol, for her careful (and patient) typing skills, and Howard, for helping us with the references.

The "orchestration" analogy used earlier clearly applies. The individual authors contributed substantially to this being a quality piece, much as musicians are the integral components in a celebrated orchestra. However, they cannot bear the responsibility of weaknesses in the planning and organizing of this book, an occasional editorial quirk, Chapter One, and any other potential "sour notes" that are detected. These, of course, must be borne by us as the conductors (or, in this case, coeditors).

K. M. R.
G. R. F.

PERSONNEL MANAGEMENT

PART ONE
FOUNDATIONS

The processes by which we seek to advance the field of Personnel Management (PM) are theory-building, research, and practice. Good theory, supported by appropriate research methods, is the fundamental building block of professional practice. Theory is shaped by professional practice, and theory is deficient if it fails to adequately explain and support practice. In turn, practice is not good (or professional) if it fails to adequately use and test theory. In a sense, the link between theory and practice is research.

In Chapter 1, Rowland and Ferris present their perspectives on the field of personnel management, both in terms of practice and research. They review and then propose some tentative explanations concerning the changing image and role of the personnel function in organizations and the field in general. In the latter part of the chapter, they lay some groundwork for the topics covered in Chapter 2. They suggest that the field may be plagued by the lack of good theory because of a preoccupation with method in research. They also discuss some different modes of scientific inquiry for the field. The current emphasis on method and inductive theory-building is not without merit, but an exclusive reliance upon such a mode of inquiry will likely result in little new ground-breaking theory and thereby have detrimental consequences for the advancement of the field.

In Chapter 2, Arvey and Shingledecker touch on some important philosophy-of-science issues which provide the essential tools for better theory-building. They also discuss traditional, as well as some less traditional, methods for investigating and understanding organizational phenomena. The presentation takes the reader through the basic psychometric issues in laboratory and field research, including a discussion of some currently popular designs and analytical tools. Arvey and Shingledecker argue for more longitudinal research in the future in order to more thoroughly understand the antecedents of the phenomena of interest and seek to establish more definitive causal statements. These arguments lead to a discussion of some data analytic tools in field research for establishing these causal statements, such as cross-lagged panel correlations and path analysis.

CHAPTER ONE

PERSPECTIVES ON PERSONNEL MANAGEMENT

Kendrith M. Rowland and Gerald R. Ferris

Kendrith M. Rowland is Professor of Business Administration at the University of Illinois at Urbana-Champaign. He received his DBA from Indiana University. Professor Rowland has served in several administrative capacities at the University of Illinois, including Assistant Dean of the College of Commerce and Business Administration, and Associate Head of the Department of Business Administration. His research interests span a number of areas in both organizational behavior and personnel management. He is the author of numerous journal articles and is coeditor of the book, *Current Issues in Personnel Management*. Prior to his academic career, Professor Rowland served as a psychiatric social worker and as a corporate communications and training director in industry.

Gerald R. Ferris is Visiting Lecturer of Personnel Management and Organizational Behavior at the University of Illinois at Urbana-Champaign. He received his Ph.D. from the University of Illinois at Urbana-Champaign. Professor Ferris formerly was Associate Director of Organizational Research at the Institute for Personality and Ability Testing, and he still consults with that organization and others in a number of personnel management areas. Professor Ferris' research interests include the performance appraisal process, the employment interview, and determinants of employee absenteeism. He is the author of several journal articles and coeditor of the book, *Current Issues in Personnel Management*.

Organizations can be viewed as collections of people and activities, separated by function, that share a common mission. Among the functions in organizations are manufacturing, marketing, and personnel. Each function is included in an area of formal inquiry in most college and university business curricula. The personnel function represents the applied component of the field of Personnel Management (PM). It is usually identified as a staff function, much as production planning or quality control are viewed as staff functions to manufacturing.

The personnel function, as part of the general management process, is concerned with the development, implementation, and evaluation of organizational policies and practices bearing on the employment relationship. That is, while the focus of general management is on the management of the organization's many resources, the specific focus of the personnel function is on the management of its human resources.

There is some evidence to suggest that changes in the field of PM and the role of the personnel function are occurring (e.g., Meyer, 1976). These changes, it is proposed, reflect the current philosophical climate of American society—a climate that is embedded in what is identified as the Quality of Work Life (QWL) Era. The QWL era translates for organizations into a greater emphasis on the individual employee and improving his or her work environment to enhance job satisfaction and productivity.

A brief excursion into the past will be used to demonstrate how the personnel function has evolved over the years from a nearly total concern with productivity to a greater, and some would say more balanced, concern with satisfaction and productivity.

HISTORICAL ANTECEDENTS

The history of the personnel function is divided into five eras, each with a different philosophical orientation or climate.

Industrial Revolution Era

Between the late 1700s and mid-1800s, this country began to change from an agricultural to an industrial society. During this time, major changes occurred in the processes by which goods were produced. With the emergence of factory-centered production, production in the home declined. Machinery and factory methods to facilitate production were introduced, thus resulting in the decline of many skilled crafts. People were brought together into work settings and structurally organized by division of labor and hierarchy of authority, both considered useful mechanisms for increasing production efficiency. Along with advantages in efficiency, the Industrial Revolution Era brought with it such problems as long hours and low wages for many employees (including children), and later other equally serious problems, such as monotony, boredom, and alienation, largely the result of routine, unchallenging work that was piecemeal in nature and coordinated by others. The personnel function did not exist in any formal way during this era. At times, some personnel-type activities were assumed by the owner-manager or delegated back to the community.

Scientific Management Era

About 1900, an era emerged that became well known for its explicit emphasis on technical, man-machine efficiency to increase productivity. It is usually identified as the Scientific Management Era and is associated with the efforts of Frederick Taylor, Frank and
Lillian Gilbreth, and others. This approach sought to make the production of goods
more efficient by identifying the ''one best method'' for performing each job (Taylor,
1911).

    In accordance with the scientific management philosophy, the approach was to en-
gineer the job and then fit the employee to it. Scientific management was a prominent
philosophy until the 1920s, but it began to decline when employers realized that many
of the problems in organizations were human problems, even after they had engineered
the job for maximum efficiency.

Industrial Psychology Era

A new era began to emerge between 1910 and 1920, which directly addressed the weaknesses of the scientific management approach, and changed the focus from the job to
the individual. This period is labeled the Industrial Psychology Era. With the work of
Hugo Munsterberg (1913) on the selection of railway motormen for the city of Boston,
and Robert Yerkes on the development of psychological tests for the United States Army
during World War I, a concern for some of the traditional personnel practices arose.
When an improper job-person match occurred, industrial psychologists introduced
training as the remedy, the purpose being to ''change'' the person rather than the job.
This approach, while it focused on the individual, still had a fairly strong orientation to
technical efficiency; that is, the proper selection and training of an employee for a given
job.

Human Relations Era

The next era is identified as the Human Relations Era. It gave considerable emphasis to
improving social relationships between supervisors and employees in work groups. This
era grew out of the research of two Harvard professors, Elton Mayo and Fritz Roethlisber-
ger, at the Hawthorne plant of the Western Electric Company in the late 1920s and early
1930s. While the original intent of these researchers was to investigate the effects of
physical factors (e.g., ventilation and illumination) on productivity, their results suggested that social factors played an equally important role in influencing employee satisfaction and productivity. A characterization of the philosophy of this era is the phrase,
''Happy workers are productive workers.'' This era continued through the 1950s. It was
supported and shaped to a considerable extent by the social welfare and egalitarian perspectives that emerged during the depression of the 1930s and World War II.

Quality of Work Life Era

It appears that the current Quality of Work Life (QWL) Era began in the 1960s. While
the primary objective of the earlier eras was to maximize production by (1) restructuring
the production process (i.e., division of labor and hierarchy of authority), (2) increasing

technical or man-machine efficiency, (3) selecting or modifying the person to achieve a better job-person fit, and (4) improving human relationships at work (i.e., to build co-operation and loyalty), our society now began to witness a broader set of concerns. These concerns, in part, had to do with the possible or experienced adverse effects of organizational policies and practices on the well-being of employees or potential employees, especially minorities, and on an assortment of work-related conditions. These concerns were emphasized and legitimized by federal laws regarding equal employment opportunity (Civil Rights Act, Title VII), safety and health (Occupational Safety and Health Act), and the protection of retirement income (Employee Retirement Income Security Act).

These concerns, also with major implications for work organizations, were related to questions about national goals and policies on such critical issues as employment/unemployment, inflation/recession, pollution, and energy, to name a few. What were the nation's goals on these issues? What priorities, if any, had been placed (or were being placed) on them? What policies should guide the nation in the accomplishment of its goals?

With the advent of much legislation in regard to the management of human resources in organizations, and the concomitant compliance required by government regulations and guidelines, additional programs and monitoring activities were created for the personnel function. In summary, organizational efforts toward improving productivity continued, but these were supplemented with efforts toward providing equal employment opportunity, job enrichment, protection of privacy and freedom of speech, reduction of stress, drug abuse, alcoholism, and so forth, all of which demonstrated considerable interest in the employee as an individual.

Recent proposals for pressing on with these efforts have received a great deal of attention and acceptance (e.g., Hackman and Suttle, 1977; Lawler, 1980). However, few have examined the implications of this type of response to the QWL philosophy and the possibility that the consequences may not always be as positive as depicted. For example, in reviews about the rise and decline of bureaucratic organizations, an underlying assumption is that decline was a response to changing conditions in the environment, particularly the lack of commitment by employees to work and their organizations. In that context, much of the thrust of organizations was to respond to a *crisis of commitment* (Beer, 1980). The matter of commitment involved not only an "economic contract"; it also involved a "psychological contract" (Schein, 1971). The consequence, perhaps, was a psychology of entitlement.

On the other side of the QWL philosophy, of course, is the issue of productivity and the accomplishment of essential organizational goals, including survival. During the past decade, our nation has witnessed a declining rate of productivity. According to recent sources (*Work in America,* 1979; *Wall Street Journal,* 1980), many reasons exist for this decline. Some of these can be classified as people-centered reasons, such as changing value systems concerning the meaning and importance of work, and efforts, in response to federal legislation, to integrate and upgrade the labor force through a variety of equal opportunity/affirmative action programs. It is possible, in this regard, to consider the emergence of another type of crisis, a *crisis of adaptability* at the organizational level (Beer, 1980). The connotation here is that productivity must increase for organizations to remain competitive with other organizations in this country and abroad, and to begin to address some of the problems of world population growth in the face of currently available natural resources.

The choice, in a simplistic frame, is to address either the crisis of commitment or the crisis of adaptability, or, perhaps as a third alternative, to address some combination of both. A major implication of a focus on commitment alone is that organizations may maximize the well-being of the individual employee, but potentially "goodwill themselves to death." So far, the QWL philosophy has emphasized (and perhaps rightly so) the crisis of commitment, but our nation has paid a price for it—productivity has fallen off. Thus, the answer to the productivity problem is probably not an escalation of the present approach, unless it can build such a level of commitment to the collectivity that the individual employee is willing to forego the opportunity to maximize self-interest in exchange for ensuring the viability of the larger unit. This point makes reference to the distinction between the concepts of *individualism* and *collectivism* (e.g., Wagner, 1982; Lazarsfeld and Menzel, 1961). In this country, the dominant ethic is individualism. In fact, this ethic forms the very basis of our capitalistic society. The claim that the individualism ethic is at least partially responsible for some of the organizational problems today receives support from the successes of many Japanese organizations operating in a society with a predominantly collectivist ethic.

Therefore, in regard to the suggested trade-off between commitment at the individual level and adaptability at the organizational level, the answer may well be to view the two not as mutually exclusive choices, but rather as interactive and interdependent. That is, within an attitudes (A) → behavior (B) → attitudes (A) framework, two potential courses of action for the management of human resources are possible. One course of action would be to first build commitment, which in turn would hopefully lead to adaptability (increased productivity). The alternate course of action would be to "push" for adaptability. This presumably would impact positively on employee attitudes (increased commitment) if the outcomes were seen as reenforcing to fundamental (survival) goals. Conceptually, these two approaches are driven by two popular models: one, that attitudes cause behavior (e.g., Costello and Zalkind, 1963), the other, that behavior causes attitudes (Bem, 1972; Weick, 1979).

The extremes of either of these two courses of action, it seems, should be avoided. Rather, an interactive, complementary approach might be based on a contingency perspective; that is, matching the course of action to be taken with the situation at hand. Major problems exist with respect to a contingency perspective, however, because of the uncertainties encountered when every course of action "depends on the situation." This perspective may be salvageable, but the task, of course, is to better specify the conditions under which the outcomes of certain decisions are more or less advantageous. There is a final problem: whether the decision to change from one course of action to another in a pluralistic, political environment can be accomplished in a timely fashion.

EVOLUTION OF PERSONNEL DEPARTMENTS

As noted in the review of the history of the personnel function, personnel departments did not always exist. The first personnel departments were established about 1910, during the early years of the Industrial Psychology Era. The first college course in personnel management (i.e., a course essentially for managers of personnel departments) was offered through an evening program at Columbia University in 1920 by Ordway Tead. Professor Tead also coauthored the first personnel management textbook in the same year (Tead and Metcalf, 1920).

The principal activities of personnel departments during the Industrial Psychology Era were the selection, training, and compensation of factory and office employees. These activities were expanded during the Human Relations Era to include the development and implementation of a variety of fringe benefits and social programs (now combined perhaps under the rubric of employee relations), such as team sports, long-service and retirement awards dinners, and picnics to celebrate special company achievements or holidays. This era also saw the growth and expansion of unionization, and activities by personnel departments to cope with this significant development in labor-management relations.

Often these activities were the responsibility of a small staff of generalists. As time went on, organizations grew larger and began to face legal and quasi-legal constraints in the management of their employees, especially those protected by union contracts. There arose a need for some division of labor and specialization within personnel departments. The scope of personnel activities expanded to encompass the selection, training, and compensation of managers, contract negotiations and grievance handling, and eventually the administration of a wide range of new and improved employee benefit programs. These activities often required additional skills, and sets of activities that used to take little time, now required the full-time attention of several people.

With the emergence of the QWL era and more employment legislation, the activities of personnel departments and the number of specialists responsible for those activities expanded still further. Government compliance requirements in regard to equal employment opportunity and affirmative action were added to virtually every personnel activity. This led, in turn, to the introduction and use of human resource information systems for record keeping and for anticipating future staffing requirements at all levels in the organization. Formal human resource planning activities, which began in the late 1950s, became more sophisticated and at times made effective use of these information systems. Organization development programs, including job enrichment and team-building activities to increase job challenge and work coordination, were established in many organizations to complement existing programs and activities in the management development area. The new benefit programs of the 1950s were refined and altered to meet changing conditions.

A consequence of the evolution of personnel departments, and the growth and diversity of activities conducted by personnel practitioners, is the terminology problem. There is considerable confusion about what one should label this function and the field that supports it.

THE TERMINOLOGY PROBLEM

Some common terms that attempt to define the function and the field are *employee relations, personnel,* or *personnel management.* More recently, the term *human resource management* has come into popular usage. At times, the term *industrial relations* is used, but typically this refers to such activities as grievance handling, collective bargaining, or, in a generic sense, union-management relations. With the exception of the latter, these terms are often used interchangeably. For the purposes of this book, the terms *personnel* and *personnel management* are generally used.

PERSPECTIVES ON THE FIELD

Having provided a brief, historical perspective on the personnel function, our attention is now directed to a number of alternative perspectives on the field of Personnel Management (PM). One of these perspectives has to do with the organization of the field itself. Is there, for example, any useful way of looking at the field? Can it be divided somehow to help one's understanding of it? From our perspective, which is offered as but one of several alternatives, the field of PM can be divided into two components: personnel practice and personnel research. Personnel practice is equated with the efforts of personnel department staffs to effectively perform the personnel function in organizations. In turn, personnel research is equated with the conceptual and methodological tools employed by college and university faculty and personnel researchers in large organizations (e.g., AT&T) in the area of PM. Both personnel practice and personnel research contribute to, and draw from, the composite field of PM.

Clearly, the focus of the field (as identified here and by others) is on people, and especially people as employees in work organizations. As a result, the field is problem-centered. However, the personnel research component of the field recognizes and encourages investigations of people-oriented topics that appear to have limited relevance to the solving of people problems in work organizations. In fact, such investigations often create new problems or redefine old ones for practice and research. On the other hand, when and where good personnel practice and personnel research come together, useful approaches to solving such problems are often found.

The following perspectives attempt to deal somewhat independently and nontraditionally with the two components of the field: first personnel practice and then personnel research. Also, a time dimension is added to allow some brief speculation concerning the future of PM. However, major emphasis on the future of PM is provided in Chapter 17.

PERSPECTIVES ON PERSONNEL PRACTICE

Most observers would agree that the professional practice of the personnel function has changed since the 1960s, since the beginning of what has been called the QWL era.

Like other eras before it, the QWL era arose out of a variety of major developments in the social, economic, technological, political, and demographic environments of American society, and continues to be supported by them.

The External Environment

Reactions to major developments occurring in the external environment are often transformed through the legal environment into federal laws. The legal environment, in a sense, serves as the filter and ultimate mechanism for merging fact and value in society. The federal laws bearing on the employment relationship enacted prior to 1960 are quite different from those enacted during the 1960s and 1970s. Prior legislation (during the Human Relations Era) dealt extensively with wages and hours of work and union-management relations within the organization and the policing of those relations; that is, the rights of employees to organize and bargain collectively vis-à-vis the rights of the employer and the union. Among these laws are the Fair Labor Standards (Wages and Hours) Act of 1938, the National Labor Relations (Wagner) Act of 1935, the Labor-Management Relations (Taft-Hartley) Act of 1947, and the Labor-Management Reporting and Disclosure (Landrum-Griffin) Act of 1959.

Although amendments to these laws continue, the federal laws enacted during the 1960s and 1970s deal more directly with the rights of the individual (or classes of individuals, such as minorities and women) on a wide range of issues vis-à-vis the rights of the employer. The most basic and important federal laws bearing on the employment relationship enacted during the 1960s and 1970s are, as noted earlier, the Civil Rights Act of 1964 (Title VII), the Occupational Safety and Health Act of 1970, and the Employee Retirement Income Security Act of 1974.

Organizations as Open Systems

To indicate that the environment has a major impact on organizations and professional practice suggests the acceptance of a few related premises. One of these is that organizations, as proposed by Katz and Kahn (1978), are open systems: open, in that they are responsive to external pressures; and systems, in that a response by one element in the organization/environment relationship usually leads to a variety of other responses by the same or other elements in that relationship. Another premise is that, because of the flood of federal legislation during the past two decades on many broad organization-to-individual and organization-to-society issues, most organizations are now more permeable to external pressures than ever before. Never, it seems, has the environment been closer to, or more involved with, the core technology of organizations (Thompson, 1967). What could be closer to the ''inner workings'' of organizations than legislation regarding the ways in which organizations should or should not manage their human resources? Finally, not only is the organization more permeable to environmental pressures, the environment continues to change at a rather rapid pace.

Buffering Strategies as an Organizational Response

How, then, can managers begin to adequately plan, organize, and control? A conceptual answer to this question at the organization/environment level is offered by Thompson (1967). He suggests that organizations develop a number of strategies to deal with the uncertainty created by the environment, among them, the strategies of forecasting and buffering. Forecasting, by definition, represents an attempt to anticipate change before it occurs. Buffering, on the other hand, is associated with the design of structural devices (i.e., larger or more specialized organizational units) and technological work-flow devices (i.e., new or more complex procedures). These buffering devices serve in both proactive and reactive ways to shield the organization from the pressures of the environment and to give managers a little time to try to make sense of them. Once the strength or potential impact of these pressures is reasonably understood and resources for coping with them are reallocated or secured, the nature of the buffering devices (especially the reactive ones) may change from one of initial defensiveness to one of compromise or confrontation. There is the subsequent danger, of course, that once these devices are designed and in place, they will become inflexible to further change and represent a nonproductive drain on resources.

The notion of buffering is a particularly appealing one. A closer look suggests that, in fact, many organizations have apparently used this strategy in responding to the actual or potential pressures of the legal environment. Legal requirements concerning the rights of employees in the employment relationship are shielded by larger, more specialized personnel departments involved in an ever-wider range of activities. In addition, the legal and/or public relations departments of organizations are often engaged in boundary-spanning activities (Aldrich, 1979) to supplement and support the activities of the personnel department and facilitate the overall buffering process. This process may include a number of more proactive political activities, such as joining industry or association lobbying efforts and supporting selected candidates for public office, or more direct economic activities, such as entering into joint ventures or mergers (Pfeffer and Salancik, 1978).

Designing buffering devices for the personnel function (or any function), in turn, draws on the resources of the organization and places greater responsibility on that function to meet its organizational obligations; for the personnel function, to protect or shield the organization from "errors" of commission or omission in the management of its human resources. This carries with it an increased amount of visibility and risk for the function. No wonder personnel people are seen at times as "heroes" and at other times as "traitors," and have designed a few internal buffering devices of their own. Janger (1977), for example, indicates that one way to attempt to control the "uncontrollables," and thereby reduce the risk of errors, is to centralize personnel policy making and planning activities at the corporate level, while continuing to support decentralized decision making at the unit level, where more sensitivity to, and information regarding, critical interpersonal and intergroup relationships presumably exist.

A Model of the Organization/Environment Relationship

Presented in Figure 1–1 is a model of the organization/environment relationship. It is an adaptation of a model proposed by Leavitt (1965) for approaching intraorganizational change. This model is a fairly simple one and includes four interdependent variables: task, structure, technology, and people. Leavitt proposes that the interdependencies of these variables must be accounted for and reasonably balanced in order to avoid or reduce negative consequences for the organization. By interpreting the variable

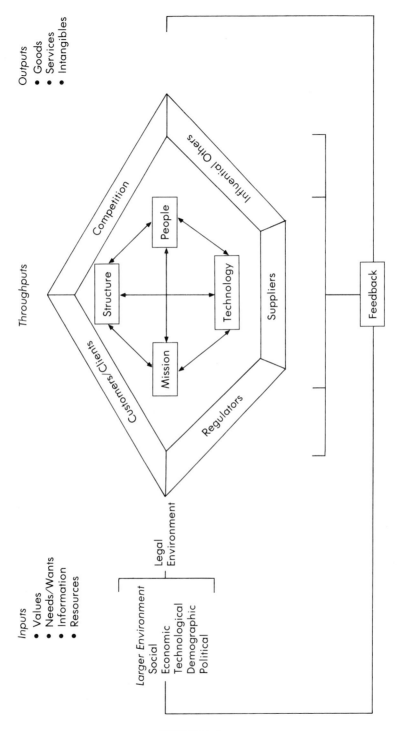

FIGURE 1–1
A Model of the Organization/Environment Relationship

"task" to mean the task *of* the organization, it is replaced with the variable "mission," which connotes a primary organizational goal or set of goals. This permits consideration of (and to some extent, assessment of) the condition of the ongoing relationship between the organization and its external environment (i.e., its effectiveness), as well as the condition of the organization itself (i.e., its efficiency). Finally, to accommodate Leavitt's task (job) variable, it is incorporated into the technology (work flow/equipment) variable.

Borrowing once again from Thompson (1967), the concept of "task environment" is used. Task environments are viewed as elements of the larger environment, but more immediately critical to the organization's well-being. They affect the day-to-day decisions of managers and, in a structural sense, serve to define the organization, establish its mission, and determine its domain or boundaries. For illustrative purposes only, five critical task environments are identified: customers/clients, competitors, regulators, suppliers, and influential others.

In general, it is believed that people in the external environment (i.e., the general public) with values, needs, information, and resources act as initiators and organizers of inputs to the creation and control of the organization. Rules and procedures for the interpretation and use of such inputs are developed within the legal environment in the form of laws. These laws prescribe the content and process of relationships in the throughput milieu—relationships among the task environments and between the task environments and components of the organization. The outputs as goods, services, and intangibles are fed back to the environment as potential contributions to the well-being of the general public. Within this context, coalitions of individuals, including managers (entrepreneurs), seek opportunities for self-expression and fulfillment.

An Assessment

There is considerable evidence regarding the growing interest in, and importance of, the personnel function, especially in terms of budgets, numbers of professional practitioners, and activities performed. Surveys published by the Bureau of National Affairs (1979, 1980), for example, indicate that (1) median personnel department budgets for companies in several industries are increasing at or above the rate of inflation, (2) median ratios of professional practitioners per 100 employees for these same companies and industries are being maintained at 0.5 or 0.6, and (3) additional activities are being assumed by personnel department staffs.

Further evidence of an increasing investment by organizations in the personnel function is reflected in a survey conducted by Information Science, Inc. (*Wall Street Journal*, October 16, 1979). In this survey, chief executives reported that they devoted 40 percent of their time to personnel matters, up from 25 percent five years ago. In addition, they reported that the pay for their chief personnel executives was equal to or more than the pay for their top legal, administration, and manufacturing executives.

There is also some evidence of an increasing acceptance of the personnel function and personnel practitioners. This evidence can be found in several well-known journal articles. In these articles, illustrations are provided to support the contention that the personnel function is becoming more central in the overall management of many organizations. But why? As indicated earlier, it is more than a generalized internal concern about human resources. It is in large part the result of external pressures on organizations. Organizations, in turn, allocate resources to the personnel function to cope with these pressures. With the acquisition of resources, the function and those who possess the necessary knowledge and skills to maintain an acceptable organization/environment relationship gain influence and power (Hickson et al., 1971; Pfeffer, 1977; Pfeffer and Salancik, 1978). A notable example is the strategically important relationship that the personnel function maintains with powerful federal regulatory agencies, such as the Equal Employment Opportunity Commission (EEOC).

The usual criteria for assessing the "goodness" of the personnel function are efficiency and effectiveness. Effectiveness is typically associated with an assessment of the function. Unfortunately, in the assessment of effectiveness, who conducts the assessment and what specific criteria are used or should be used are problematic (Cameron, 1978), since the biases of special interest groups vying for influence and power, for example, can render the reliability and validity of the results questionable, at best.

Efficiency, by contrast, is typically associated with an internal, value-free assessment of the function. While efficiency can be viewed as maximizing outputs relative to inputs, or "doing things right," effectiveness can be viewed as "doing the right things." The personnel function can be judged as efficient but ineffective, effective but inefficient, and inefficient and ineffective.

The effectiveness of the personnel function is often judged by the organization in terms of efficiency criteria. Were personnel requisitions promptly filled? Was the union contract settled with a minimum of new and costly benefits? Were the rates of absenteeism and turnover maintained or reduced? The long-run effectiveness of the personnel function, however, both in terms of the organization and the environment, often depends on its being somewhat inefficient, at least in the short-run. For example, preparing job descriptions, conducting orientation meetings, providing career, retirement, and outplacement counseling, and processing complaints, grievances, and suggestions are essentially inefficient activities, but critical to long-run effectiveness. A continual trade-off goes on between efficiency and effectiveness in most organizations. Both are necessary. The ongoing problem, of course, is to determine an optimal mix. The discussion here is analogous to the earlier one concerning whether organizations, as implied within the QWL philosophy, should emphasize (and to what extent) a course of action that responds to the crisis of commitment or the crisis of adaptability.

Operationally, by what means is an assessment of the personnel function made? A popular approach is the *personnel audit,* which usually includes a procedural audit and a functional audit. The procedural audit focuses on the activities performed by members of the personnel department and the amount of time spent on each. The procedural audit, by definition, is internal to the personnel department, and thus represents a measure of the function's efficiency. The functional audit seeks to measure the function's effectiveness. It attempts to assess how well the function, as it performs its various activities, is serving the organization and helping the organization achieve its short-run and long-run goals.

It is proposed that the increasing acceptance of the personnel function and professional practitioners will lead to a changing, more positive image for both, and the taking on of an influential "internal consultant" role on matters of human resource management and organization planning. It will lead to a broader set of responsibilities and a greater emphasis on activities at the organizational level, such as organization design and development. Further, the entry point for external consultants in these and other related areas will be through the personnel department.

Finally, as a sign of increasing maturity, it is proposed that as personnel practitioners assume increasingly visible roles in organizations, they will develop a higher level of professionalism through such organizations as the American Society for Personnel Administration (ASPA). A variety of accreditation programs are now available to practitioners, educators, and college students through the Personnel Accreditation Institute, which was established in 1975. A greater and more sophisticated sharing of information and the results of often jointly conducted investigations are taking place between personnel practitioners and personnel researchers in the popular journals of the field, among them, *Personnel Administrator, Personnel Journal,* and *Personnel.* Professional associations for specialists with their own publications, some of them of recent origin, are in abundance. These associations include the American Society for Training and Development (ASTD), the American Compensation Association (ACA), and the Human Resources Planning Society (HRPS).

PERSPECTIVES ON PERSONNEL RESEARCH

Statements concerning the changing nature of the field of PM usually refer to the current and projected future status of personnel practice. Only a few systematic attempts have been made to analyze the research component of the field and thus to consider the possibility that what is occurring with respect to personnel practice may not necessarily be occurring with respect to personnel research. That is, can the attention that the professional practice of personnel is now enjoying be assumed also to apply to personnel research? To pursue this matter further, a number of issues regarding the field and personnel research are addressed.

Most of these issues, it seems, are embedded in the traditional notion that the field of PM is applied, practical, or practitioner-oriented, the implication being that it is not terribly rigorous, and perhaps even atheoretical. This would argue against the field encompassing a legitimate area for the investigation and study of personnel problems. Is it possible, in other words, to distinguish between personnel research and the professional practice of personnel? If not, then the changes occurring in personnel practice should produce fairly comparable changes in personnel research.

The increasing interest in, and importance of, the personnel function has led to the expansion of PM curricula in many colleges and universities. This, in turn, has increased the demand for those pursuing PM careers in academia. In a recent Academy of Management analysis of job openings and applications in the PM area, there were over 3.5 jobs for every applicant. However, it is unclear whether this is only a result of the increased demand for practitioners (so more course offerings and faculty are needed), or whether the personnel research component of the field is taking on an increased importance.

In addition to the matter of the internal differentiation of the field, a related question can be raised: Is the personnel research component of the PM field distinct from other academic areas?

Personnel Research and Industrial Psychology.   One can consider, for example, the overlap between personnel research and industrial psychology (personnel psychology). The claim can be made that, while the overlap here is considerable, it is not complete. That is, while such topics as selection and training are researched by industrial psychologists, such topics as human resource planning and career planning and development are not.

Conversely, if one makes the claim that there is a great deal of overlap between PM and industrial psychology, recent criticisms levelled at industrial psychology can be extended to include the personnel research component of the PM field. Gordon, Kleiman, and Hanie (1978), among others, conclude that the field of industrial psychology is not much more rigorous than dictated by common sense, and, therefore, it needs to raise its scientific caliber. Two complaints, which serve to perpetuate the common-sense nature of the field, are made. First, there is virtually no theory-guided research in the field. Instead, the field is characterized by the approach to research that simply describes relationships among observable phenomena, often referred to as inductive or "dust bowl" empiricism. There are too many "one-shot" studies or incomplete efforts to understand a particular phenomenon. Programmatic research efforts, it is proposed, will remedy this state of affairs by focusing more on hypothesis formulation than hypothesis testing.

A second criticism refers to the preoccupation with method in industrial psychology (and personnel research). Perhaps the belief is that a focus on method compensates for a lack of theoretical development. Accompanying this belief may be another one: that good methodology leads to the demonstration of systematic empirical relationships through which understanding and prediction result. Unfortunately, a preoccupation with method can lead to a restriction in the areas of "legitimate inquiry." That is, topics of a more complicated nature are ignored, even though they are of real consequence.

In a similar vein, Argyris (1976) argues that industrial psychology is too concerned with individual differences, measurement, and prediction. He believes that the focus on prediction has been pursued to the virtual exclusion of understanding. He claims that industrial psychologists have not focused heavily on explaining phenomena because of the applications orientation of the field. That is, typical problems that serve as the focus for research are generated from practical problems in the profession (e.g., selection of personnel, and so forth). Thus, the interest of personnel practitioners and researchers is in predicting relevant outcomes, not necessarily in truly understanding the processes involved.

Personnel Research and Organizational Behavior.   Another issue examines the relationship between the personnel research component of PM and Organizational Behavior (OB). An initial requirement here is to clarify the focus within OB. Clearly, the macro aspects of OB do not apply or share any common ground with personnel research as it is currently conceptualized. However, when restricting the domain of OB to only micro topics, the overlap with personnel research seems more reasonable, even though others speak of the differences between the two. Strauss (1970), for example, claims personnel is applied and essentially atheoretical. He suggests that personnel might be viewed as "the practical application of OB" (p. 147). Strauss may be referring here to personnel practice, not personnel research. However, despite his discussion of the distinctions between personnel and OB, Strauss concludes that personnel and OB should be viewed as a single course of study.

Recently, the Personnel/Human Resources Division of the Academy of Management shed some light on the nature of personnel research in its domain statement. Unfortunately, hopes that this statement would suggest steps leading to a conceptual demarcation between the personnel research component of the PM field and other academic areas are not met. It is stated early (in a quote from Inkeles) that, "Any attempt to set limits to a field of intellectual endeavor is inherently futile" (Personnel/Human Resources Division Domain Statement, p. 1). While the general validity of this statement is not questioned, it appears to offer too easy an escape from the need to conceptually establish the limits of a particular area of scientific inquiry. Most distressingly, the claim is made that personnel research draws upon a number of disciplines, such as psychology and sociology, as well as related fields—"most notably organizational behavior, which draws upon some of the same disciplines" (p. 2). Such a statement suggests that personnel research derives its existence from OB and that OB somehow preceded it chronologically. The available evidence, however, does not support this conclusion.

Cummings (1978) recently attempted a reconceptualization of OB, justifying it as a separate field of inquiry. He sees OB as being the more fundamental discipline, with personnel research viewed as more applied in orientation. In this regard, he shares an opinion similar to Strauss' (1970). Also, he sees OB as more concept-oriented, perhaps also emphasizing its greater theoretical development. Personnel research, on the other hand, is seen as technique-oriented. Expanding on this notion, one useful distinction between personnel research and OB is the nature of the particular topics covered and the way they might be appropriately conceptualized.

It seems that most PM topics share one characteristic—they are process-oriented; that is, they involve the processing of individuals through a series of specifically defined steps or stages. Thus, the technique orientation is obvious. Personnel activities are designed to improve and facilitate the management of human resources. These are process activities by nature and, therefore, represent a set of skills or techniques to be perfected. This point, however, can be most clearly sorted out in the context of the practitioner-researcher distinction. Any professional field is concerned to some degree with specific skills. When speaking of the PM field, one usually makes associations to professional practice and the activities or techniques that comprise that profession. OB, on the other hand, has no easily identifiable professional counterpart, and thus exists primarily as an academic-oriented field. However, when viewing the personnel research component of the field, skills or techniques similar to those employed by OB researchers are required. These research skills include sound research methodology and statistical expertise, as well as firm grounding in theory. From this perspective, the research component of PM and micro OB can be viewed as quite similar. However, it seems that both fall somewhat short in the assumptions made concerning the phenomena they investigate.

Paradigms and Philosophy of Science

The perspectives on personnel research include a consideration of the assumptions made about the phenomena to be studied. This involves a discussion of some philosophy of science issues and the nature of scientific paradigms.

Much of the interest today with paradigms in the natural and behavioral sciences can be attributed to Kuhn (1970), who calls attention to issues involved in "within paradigm" research, the nature of paradigm shifts, and scientific revolutions. More recently, and with specific relevance to the organizational sciences, Burrell and Morgan (1979) address the nature of sociological paradigms and the way they can be brought to bear on systematic inquiries of organizational phenomena. They discuss general philosophy of science issues, such as ontology (i.e., does something exist in an objective sense or is it constructed cognitively?), epistemology (i.e., ways of knowing or gaining knowledge —is there something in the real world to be observed and studied, or is it personally experienced?), and views on human nature (i.e., determinism versus free will), and demonstrate how the assumptions one makes about reality often dictate the methodological approaches taken to study a given phenomenon.

If PM and the other areas discussed here are to advance, it is suggested that alternative ways of viewing phenomena must be sought. This may mean a shift to a different paradigm. The main paradigm utilized in personnel research is what Burrell and Morgan (1979) refer to as the functionalist paradigm, which assumes that all phenomena can be objectively measured and dictates a positivistic, deterministic approach to understanding. Burrell and Morgan mention that the functionalist paradigm contains a predominance of the research in the behavioral sciences. An alternative, such as the interpretive paradigm, might provide a different perspective on PM. The interpretive paradigm assumes that all phenomena are socially constructed rather than existing as objective realities, and dictates a different set of methodologies or ways of trying to understand phenomena, such as phenomenological and ethnographic approaches. (Some of these issues are further elaborated on in Chapter 2.)

Silverman, who is an advocate of the action research frame, has discussed and employed a phenomenological approach to his study of the employment interview, in which the experiences of individuals involved are examined (Silverman and Jones, 1976). Phenomenological approaches also have been suggested for the investigation of organizational climate, although this topic is usually identified as falling within the domain of OB and not PM.

These and other perspectives might better serve the purpose in conceptualizing PM, and determining its ontological status, as well as its legitimate epistemologies. An argument for more qualitative research methods has been advanced recently by Morgan and Smircich (1980).

Dependent Variables in Personnel Research

If no other means can be found to distinguish an area of inquiry from others, it is suggested by Heneman (1980) that one look to its dependent variables. In light of the earlier discussion concerning the conceptual distinctiveness of personnel research, this suggestion might prove to be a plausible one. In the "domain statement" of the Personnel/Human Resources Division, however, the dependent variables believed to be of interest to personnel researchers are not presented as the exclusive property of the area. The implication here, of course, is that Heneman's argument is invalid. In an examination of the dependent variables of interest to researchers in personnel and OB, as shown in Table 1-1, it appears that there is considerable overlap. The personnel research vari-

TABLE 1–1
Dependent Variables of Interest to P/HR and OB

P/HR Domain Statement	*Cummings and Dunham (1980)*
Productivity and performance	Attitudes (including satisfaction)
Employee motivation	Involvement in work organization and job
Employee ability	Behavior
Attendance (absenteeism)	Participation
Length of service (turnover)	Performance
Occupational health and safety	
Job satisfaction	
Organizational commitment	

ables are those listed in the "domain statement," while the OB variables are those discussed by Cummings and Dunham (1980).

A more detailed discussion of the major dependent variables of interest to the personnel research area can be found in later chapters.

Table 1–1 leaves the impression that personnel research and OB are not conceptually distinct areas, but rather closely related. However, it is proposed that Table 1–1 provides only a "surface" representation of the dependent variables in the two areas. A more in-depth assessment suggests that the orientation and, therefore, the levels of priority currently assigned these variables are different. Perhaps the dependent variables of primary interest to personnel researchers are those associated with the activities of the personnel system—such people-processing activities as recruiting, selecting, evaluating, training, and compensating. Next in priority are those variables among the outputs of the system (attitudes and behavior) which, in a problem-solving context, impact on the effectiveness of the organization's human resources. In some respects, the dependent variables of primary interest to personnel research are also the variables of primary interest to industrial psychology. The variables of primary interest to OB, on the other hand, tend to be only those associated with the outputs of the personnel system. Both industrial psychology and OB, in contrast to personnel research, place less emphasis on the processing and problem-solving aspects of human resource management in organizations. Thus, the orientation and priority assigned the dependent variables listed in Table 1–1 may represent a way of distinguishing personnel research from industrial psychology and OB.

Two further issues, alluded to earlier, seem to be inhibiting progress in gaining a better understanding of organizational phenomena. One is a methodological issue; the other a design issue.

A persistent problem in personnel research (as well as in industrial psychology and OB) is the quality of the data. In about 85 percent of the studies where performance is evaluated, for example, one finds subjective ratings rather than objective or "hard" measures of performance being used. Researchers often talk about the need for "hard," objective measures of performance, such as the actual number of units produced, sales volume, and so forth, but in practice they either ignore such indicators or, perhaps more accurately, find that such data are not available or maintained in personnel files. It seems that for the future, researchers should be more concerned with identifying "hard" criterion measures as evaluation devices. The pursuit of "hard" *unobtrusive* measures (e.g., Webb et al., 1966) is also worthy of additional interest and development.

Another important problem is the way the understanding of behavior in organizations is approached. One quickly gains the impression from an examination of the research designs frequently used that explaining behavior in organizations is quite simplistic. Studies often examine the relationship between two variables, such as employee job satisfaction and absenteeism, and, if a relationship is found, the investigator appoints one of the variables as causal and the other as outcome. The fact that the study is cross-sectional in nature (as opposed to longitudinal), and only correlational, is overlooked. A more representative means of approaching the investigation of behavior in organizations seems to be to take account of the dynamic and multidimensional nature of both behavioral and organizational phenomena. Multivariate investigations, which simultaneously examine several dependent variables while isolating the specific contributions of certain independent variables, are taking place. But much more is needed in the future. It becomes even more crucial that researchers engage in such research designs when one considers the complex interrelationships of dependent variables in organizations (Cummings and Dunham, 1980).

In addition to clarifying and perhaps expanding the repertoire of dependent variables in personnel research, organizational scientists need to take account of other relevant issues as well. Staw and Oldham (1978) suggest a refocus of research toward more fruitful ventures, instead of merely identifying additional determinants of behavioral and organizational outcomes. One of the important points they make concerns the extent to which a researcher's own values and beliefs have led him or her to label certain outcomes as "good" or "bad." For example, both researchers and practitioners have labored under the belief that absenteeism and turnover are persistent problems in organizations—very costly, and thus negative in nature. Hence, research typically is directed at identifying the antecedents of these outcomes, and practitioners and line managers are encouraged to eliminate them. A given level of absenteeism or turnover, however, may be functional in certain situations and, in fact, contribute to organizational efficiency and effectiveness.

Discussed earlier were notions of efficiency and effectiveness with respect to the operation of the personnel function. At present, while the focus is on personnel research, indices of efficiency and effectiveness are still a major overarching concern (whether research or applied). Thus, a linkage between a concern for efficiency and effectiveness can be discussed from both an applied and a research standpoint. The possible exception, typically in the realm of personnel research, is the existence perhaps of an intervening step between programs, processes, or interventions in organizations and the ultimate impact on organizational efficiency or effectiveness. That is, much personnel research being microanalytically oriented examines effects of interventions on individual attitudes and behavior. While the next step often is not taken, the inference is made that these employee attitudes and behavior impact directly or indirectly on the efficiency and effectiveness of the organization. It is these "intermediate dependent variables" that have tended to be the focus of both personnel and organizational behavior research. As Table 1–1 depicts, the intermediate dependent variables typically examined by these two areas are virtually identical. However, the independent variables investigated by personnel and organizational behavior researchers tend to be different. While personnel researchers often consider policies, programs, and interventions on the aforementioned dependent variables, organizational behavior researchers consider the effects of such variables as leadership style, task characteristics, and so forth. Thus, it seems that Heneman (1980) was incorrect when he claimed that a particular discipline can be defined and differentiated by its dependent variables. Rather, it appears to be the case here that personnel research and organizational behavior (at least micro OB) may be more accurately differentiated by examining the differential nature of their independent variables.

A major problem with research in these areas is an almost exclusive focus on "intermediate dependent variables." Even though existing conceptual models typically include the second linkage, that from "intermediate dependent variables" to efficiency and effectiveness indices, this linkage is rarely tested empirically. Instead, it is assumed to exist almost as an implicit element of the model. One recent investigation addressed this issue by showing relationships between employee absenteeism and organizational efficiency (Moch and Fitzgibbons, 1980). There exists a further problem, however, in the form of a fundamental inconsistency between the way theoretical models are designed and illustrated, and the way effectiveness is defined. By graphically depicting a conceptual linkage between some given "intermediate dependent variable(s)" and organizational effectiveness, the assumption is that this linkage can be determined internally. However, by definition, effectiveness can be determined only from an external perspective (Pfeffer and Salancik, 1978). This tends not to be the case for efficiency, which can be determined internally. This analysis seems to point to several weaknesses in both personnel and organizational behavior research.

A Conceptual Integration

After examining the relationships of personnel research to several other academic areas, and viewing it from several different perspectives, one is still left with the question posed earlier concerning the distinctiveness or independent existence of personnel research and the possibility of developing a more convenient way of conceptualizing it.

Perhaps the most fundamental criticisms of personnel research, which serve to distinguish it from other related areas such as OB, are the relative lack of theory, and an almost totally inductive approach, methodologically—a characteristic shared by industrial psychology. As was noted, this lack of theory, along with a preoccupation with method, tends to cast personnel research and industrial psychology in a fairly similar position.

In discussing similarities and differences between OB and other disciplines, Cummings (1978) concludes that there is virtually complete redundancy between OB and organizational psychology, bearing in mind that the macro side of OB is essentially labeled Organizational Theory and thus discussed under a separate heading.

Thus, viewed in this sense, personnel research and industrial psychology seem somewhat similar, and OB and organizational psychology appear redundant. Perhaps the major distinction then between these two clusters is the difference in the use of theory. The case can be made that there is a preoccupation with method to varying degrees in OB, as well as organizational psychology. But where will this conceptualization lead? Can the distinctions of fields (or areas) be maintained separately as before, or might one observe what can be done with the two clusters just discussed? It is interesting that OB and personnel research, which appear to be in different clusters, are often regarded as separate academic areas, offered in many cases in separate departments with distinctly separate curricula. Industrial and organizational psychology, which tend to reflect different orientations and therefore occupy separate clusters, are nearly always offered in the same department (a department of psychology) and as part of the same general program referred to as I/O Psychology.

While the differences justifying the separate clustering have been discussed, the similarities also might be important. In this case, a bond seems to exist where, *physically,* the specific curricula are offered. Industrial and organizational psychology share a common link of being offered in a psychology department, even though they are dissimilar in subject matter. Personnel research and industrial psychology, while more similar conceptually, are offered in different programs and departments in most colleges and universities.

This distinction is also apparent with respect to personnel research and OB. The common link of where the curricula are located is not shared, since there is some confusion as to where personnel management courses should be offered. At some institutions it is part of the industrial relations curriculum, while at others it is part of the business administration curriculum. Furthermore, the claim could be made that personnel research and OB are viewed as less distinct when they share existence in the same department.

The ultimate task, however, remains: to attempt a conceptual identification, classification, or integration of PM. In the interest of parsimony, one might choose the path Cummings (1978) has taken with respect to OB. That is, after analyzing differences between OB, organizational psychology, organizational theory, and PM, Cummings suggests deleting labels that may be causing more confusion than clarification, and identifying a general field of Organizational Sciences. Extending this a bit, and taking account of the similarities many of these fields share, a threefold classification consisting of Organizational Theory, Organizational Research, and Organizational Service might be suggested. For categorization purposes, it would seem much easier to simply classify the field into theory, research, and service. Maintaining distinctions among fields in the organizational sciences seems somewhat artificial and does not seem to contribute substantially to the advancement of knowledge or the understanding of phenomena. One of the hallmarks of a science is parsimony. If the goal is to develop a science of organizations and behavior in organizations, personnel researchers should begin to establish parameters, while keeping redundancy at a minimum.

Implications of the Reconceptualization

Clearly, it is one thing to propose a different way of conceptualizing a system or field and quite another for that conceptualization to be accepted and implemented in practice. This proposed reconceptualization of the organizational sciences area with specific reference to PM will undoubtedly raise some serious questions and evoke a variety of reactions. For one thing, this way of thinking eliminates a set of categories or subspecialties that has served the field for many years and with which professionals and academicians have come to identify. This is by no means a minor point. The divisions of the Academy of Management, for example, have been around for some time, and academicians are accustomed to thinking about the Personnel/Human Resources Division, the Organizational Behavior Division, the Management and Organization Theory Division, the Managerial Consultation Division, and so forth. Eliminating such categories and, instead, assigning topics according to Organization Theory, Research, or Service would not be readily or easily accepted.

How would one divide subject matter under this new conceptualization? Take, for example, the topic of personnel selection, which typically has been associated with PM. Categorizing this under the new framework would be a relatively simple matter. If someone were conducting a research investigation on the relative predictability of a specific personality measure and work performance of salespersons across industries, such an effort would be classified as Organizational Research. If, however, the attempt was to conduct a validation study for an organization in a consulting capacity, this would be labeled Organizational Service. Of course, all subject matter will not be this easily distinguishable, but, in general, confusion will be reduced and parsimony will be increased. The purpose of the particular effort should be the determining factor in categorization; that is, whether the effort is directed at contributing to organizational theory, research, or service.

SUMMARY

Many issues have been raised in this chapter about the field of personnel management. Historically, PM has experienced a rather rocky existence in organizations, although evidence has emerged to indicate that perhaps this trend is changing. The control or maintenance of strategic links with external government regulatory agencies is proposed as a major causal factor promoting the increased power and prestige held by PM within organizations today. However, this proposal may be tenuous, at best, in light of changes in the federal administration and expected budget cutbacks for such agencies as the EEOC. Further speculation about the future of PM will be withheld until Chapter 17, where Strauss takes a more probing look into the future.

A second major component of this chapter addressed a previously neglected issue—the status of the personnel research component of PM. Most publications discussing the status of PM actually refer solely to the professional practice of PM and neglect the research side of PM, which exists in academia and a few large organizations. This discussion departs rather significantly from the first part of the chapter in both content and style. However, this probably captures reality when one considers the popular distinction between practice and research.

Discussion Questions

1. It has been said that the status of the personnel function in organizations is changing and that personnel practitioners will become more influential in organizations. To what factors can this be attributed?

2. Develop a ten-year projection of the personnel function and of the field of personnel management, and identify the important issues that are likely to emerge.

3. Federal regulatory agencies play an important role in determining the activities of the personnel function. What implications will the current administration have on the future impact of these agencies on the personnel function and organizations in general?

4. Historically, what criticisms have been leveled at personnel research? Are these criticisms well founded?

5. Define what is meant by a paradigm, and discuss why there might be a need for a shift to a different paradigm in personnel research.

CHAPTER TWO

RESEARCH METHODS IN PERSONNEL MANAGEMENT

Richard D. Arvey and Pamela Shingledecker

Richard D. Arvey is Professor of Psychology at the University of Houston. He received his Ph.D. in Psychology from the University of Minnesota. Before joining the faculty at Houston, Professor Arvey held the position of Senior Associate at Personnel Decisions, Inc., and later served on the faculty of the Department of Industrial and Personnel Management at the University of Tennessee. Professor Arvey has been active in research in a number of areas and has published over forty journal articles. He is author of the book, *Fairness in Selecting Employees.* He has consulted also with a number of organizations, including Ford Motor Company, Southwestern Bell Telephone Company, and the Exxon Corporation.

Pamela Shingledecker is a doctoral student in Industrial/Organizational Psychology at the University of Houston. She has taught courses in introductory psychology, statistics, and industrial/organizational psychology. She has served as an intern with Atlantic Richfield Company and is currently the John F. MacNaughton Research Fellow with the University of Houston Interviewing Institute. Her research interests include union-management relations, sex roles in organizations, organizational effectiveness, and discipline in organizations.

A distinguishing feature of the field of personnel management is a frequent reliance on data and research findings as an information base in making decisions. That is, personnel specialists make efforts to gather and use data as well as establish valid relationships among relevant variables to aid in the decision-making process.

This chapter concerns the different research methodologies and strategies that are available to, and used by individuals in, personnel management. Its objectives are twofold: first, to present in a rather straightforward descriptive fashion the predominant and frequently used research methodologies; and second, to discuss some of the relevant issues associated with research and conducting research in organizations. To a great extent, it is a presumptuous effort for one short chapter—books have been written on practically each separate topic area discussed here. Thus, limited space forces this presentation to be somewhat abbreviated.

A POINT OF VIEW

Before proceeding, it may be wise to discuss briefly some of the philosophical underpinnings of our research strategies and methodologies. To a large extent, psychological research of the nature we discuss here is conducted using a "scientific model" or scientific frame of reference. This framework is characterized by a set of assumptions about the world and the way to acquire and communicate knowledge about the world. Burrell and Morgan (1979) present the set of assumptions that appear to characterize an objectivist approach to social science:

1. *Ontological assumptions.*   Most individuals adopting the traditional scientific model assume that "reality" is of an objective nature; that is, that the real world is comprised of real structures and exists independently of individual perception and/or appreciation of it. An alternative perspective is that there is no reality outside of the individual's perceptions and labels of the world.
2. *Epistemological assumptions.*   Individuals adopting scientific models seek to explain and predict what happens in the world by searching for causal relationships and regularities between variables. The growth of knowledge is cumulative by adding to the stock of knowledge hypotheses that have been eliminated and new insights gained through rigorous, controlled research methods. An alternative view is that "knowledge" is essentially individualistic and that the social world can be understood only from the point of view of the individuals who are directly involved in the activities to be studied.
3. *Human nature.*   At one extreme, human nature may be characterized as completely determined by the situation or environment; at the other, behavior is viewed as voluntary and the result of free will. Social science methodologies vary in their assumptions, both implicit and explicit.
4. *Methodologies of studying social behavior.*   Most traditional research strategies utilize a nomothetic approach: the process of testing hypotheses in accordance with the "canons of scientific rigour" (Burrell and Morgan, 1979, p. 6). They are occupied with the construction and use of quantitative techniques for the analysis of data, and use surveys, questionnaires, tests, and other instruments as their tools. An alternative approach is to make efforts to gain firsthand experience and knowledge of the subject under investigation.

Most of the methods described in this chapter are indeed characterized by implicit assumptions that there is an objective reality, that it can be studied using scientific methodologies, and that these methodologies are predominantly quantitative in nature.

''Good research is characterized by careful sampling, precise measurement, and sophisticated design and analysis in the test of hypotheses derived from tentative general laws'' (Behling, 1980, p. 483). The point to keep well in mind, however, is that alternative approaches do exist that may have a good deal of viability for researchers and practitioners in personnel management.

QUANTITATIVE METHODOLOGIES

Essentially, individuals use two major quantitative methodologies in their efforts to be objective and scientific in the field of personnel management. First, personnel specialists gather *descriptive* data. They are interested in the existing status or state of the employee population in the organization. For example, in efforts to learn about the current state of morale or job satisfaction, a personnel specialist may employ survey research or questionnaire methods to assess these opinions. An interview strategy might also be utilized. In any case, the focus is on the assessment of existing and current states.

A second major research methodology involves efforts to assess *relationships* among variables. The focus is not so much on the assessment of the current state of a variable (although it is typically required), but instead the relationships among two or more variables of interest. For example, a personnel specialist might be interested in how a different incentive system will affect the pay satisfaction of employees. He or she is interested in the relationship between two variables: incentive systems and pay satisfaction. In assessing this relationship, the personnel specialist might decide to experiment by trying out different incentive systems with different groups of employees and later assessing the differences among these groups in terms of their pay satisfaction. Another relationship the specialist might be interested in assessing is the correlation between test scores of applicants and their later job performance. To assess this relationship, the specialist might correlate these two variables. These two examples illustrate the two major research strategies used to assess relationships among variables: experimental designs and correlational designs.

MEASUREMENT

Because both the descriptive and relational approaches to research demand that variables be measured in some quantitative way, some fundamental properties of measurement systems will now be discussed. There are essentially five defining properties of measurement systems:

1. *Definition and operationalism of the concept to be measured.* One of the basic tenets of measurement is that one must tie down precisely what it is that must be measured. The concept must be defined in a certain context.
2. *Observations of the phenomenon.* In order to measure something, the phenomenon must be observed. For example, if an individual is interested in measuring job performance of employees, supervisors could be asked to *ob-*

serve and be aware of their subordinates' performance levels. Moreover, one could ask the employees themselves to act as observers.

3. *Quantification of the observations.*   Measurement also involves some systematic quantification of the observations. For example, in measuring job performance one could use "objective" quantification techniques, such as simply recording the frequency of events (e.g., number of units produced), or use more "subjective" devices, such as asking supervisors to rank or rate their employees on a job performance scale. Guion (1965) and Saal, Downey, and Lahey (1980) have detailed the problems with both the objective and subjective means of quantifying job performance data.

4. *Reliability of measurement.*   In order to have any meaning or usefulness, a variable must be measured reliably. Reliability concerns the *consistency* of measurement. Will a research obtain the same results or rank ordering of people (or objects) when a concept is measured twice? If a measure does not even correlate well with itself (e.g., exhibit consistency), how can one expect it to demonstrate relationships with other variables? There are various methods that can be employed to assess the reliability of a measurement system:

   a. *Test-retest.*   This method consists of correlating scores after measuring the concept twice. For example, if one were interested in assessing the reliability of an "Attitude toward Female Managers" scale, the scale could be administered to fifty employees, then a week later readministered to the same employees. These two sets of scores could be correlated to yield an estimate of reliability. Estimates obtained by using this method tend to give inflated values because of a memory factor—employees remember their previous responses and tend to respond in a similar fashion.

   b. *Equivalent forms.*   An alternate method of estimating reliability is to construct two separate forms of the same measuring device. For example, one could build two different versions of the "Attitude toward Female Managers" scale previously mentioned. The scales would have different items, but would be similar in context. The estimate of reliability is derived by correlating employees' responses to the two forms of the scale. Equivalent forms should exhibit equal means, equal variances, and equal intercorrelations (Campbell, 1976), and are thus difficult to construct.

   c. *Internal consistency estimates.*   It is also possible to determine how consistent one part of a measuring device is with another part; that is, how internally consistent a measure is. For example, one could correlate the scores derived from summing all the odd-numbered items on an attitude scale with the scores derived from the summation of all the even-numbered items. Obviously, this is called an *odd-even estimate.* Additionally, one could compute an estimate derived from correlating scores based on the first half with scores based on the second half of a scale (called a split-half method). Finally, there are estimates based on correlating each item of a scale with every other item. For example, the Kuder-Richardson formula and Cronbach's alpha coefficient are two such estimates (Guilford, 1965).

d. *Conspect reliability.*   Another form of reliability is associated with situations in which the scores obtained from two different observers are correlated. For example, supervisory ratings of job performance given by two different supervisors rating the same individuals might yield an estimate of inter-rater or conspect reliability. While it is likely that different supervisors appraise employee performance differently, it is usually desirable that some degree of agreement be achieved among the raters.

5. *Validity of measurement system.*   In addition to assessing the reliability of a measuring device, it is also important to determine whether the device is measuring what one thinks is being measured. It is possible to employ a very reliable measure of the wrong concept. Establishing the meaning of a measure has been traditionally given the name of *construct validity.* There is much confusion concerning the meaning of construct validity among researchers, and no attempt will be made here to go into a great deal of detail about the various discussions and points of view (see Campbell, 1976; Cook and Campbell, 1976, for more elaboration). Basically, construct validity has to do with assessing

   a. whether the measure demonstrates relationships that fit logically into the theoretical network of relationships between the measure and other variables (Cronbach and Meehl, 1955), and

   b. whether *other* concepts or measures represent possible ''confounds''; that is, establishing whether variance on the measuring device represents something unintentional or unwanted.

Campbell (1976) has indicated the kinds of studies that may be useful contributions to the assessment of construct validity. Among these, he mentions the following:

1. Factor analyses of the components making up the measure
2. A wide range of reliability estimates
3. Correlations with other variables theorized to measure the same theory
4. Correlations with other variables that might account for or rule out potential sources of variance in the instrument being validated

One interesting approach to the establishment of construct validity is to utilize the multitrait-multimethod approach described by Campbell and Fiske (1959). Suppose a researcher was interested in assessing the construct validity of his or her measurement of a particular concept (e.g., job satisfaction). The researcher had measured the concept by asking employees to respond to a five-item opinion questionnaire, and then summed their responses to these items. These same employees were also asked to indicate their opinions about the working conditions in the organization (using five items to assess these sentiments), and their opinion about their supervisors (again using five items). Thus, the researcher had used the same *method* to assess three different variables (opinions of job satisfaction, working conditions, and supervision). The individual also decided to try a different approach (method) to measure these same variables (traits). Consequently, the researcher interviewed the employees and asked them questions designed to assess their feelings and sentiments about their job satisfaction, working conditions, and supervisors. Then these sets of scores were correlated; and the results are those shown in Figure 2–1.

The correlations may be divided into different blocks. For example, the triangles in the upper left and lower right corners of the matrix are referred to as the *hetero-trait-monomethod triangles* because they refer to correlations between different variables using the same assessment method. The two triangles in the lower left corner of the matrix are referred to as the *heterotrait-heteromethod triangles* because they refer to correlations between different concepts assessed using different methods. The circled correlations are referred to as *convergent validity coefficients* because they represent the correlations between two different measures of the same concept. A requirement for the construct validity of a variable is that it demonstrate convergent validity. More formally, convergent validity is demonstrated when the correlation between the same concept using different methods is significantly different from zero and reasonably high. Thus, in this example, the measures of job satisfaction and working conditions demonstrate convergent validity, while the attitudes toward supervision measures do not.

One can also assess the degree of discriminant validity for a measure. The basic notion behind this concept is that a measure can be invalidated because it correlates too highly with other measures that are conceptually different and from which it is intended to differ. In the example given, a measure of job satisfaction should *not* correlate well with a measure of employee sentiments toward their supervision. In more formal terms, discriminant validity is demonstrated by the following:

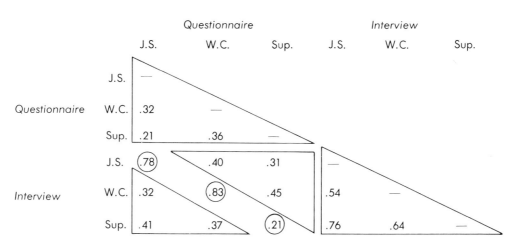

FIGURE 2–1
Correlations between Job Satisfaction, Working Conditions, and Supervision Variables Using Questionnaire and Interview Methods

1. A convergent validity correlation value should be higher than the values lying in its corresponding columns and rows in the heterotrait-heteromethod triangles. The logic behind this requirement is that a measure of a trait or concept should correlate more highly with another measure of the same concept than with other variables having *neither* concept or method of assessment in common. Reviewing the example, the measure of job satisfaction and working conditions meet this criterion; however, the supervision scale does not.

2. A convergent validity coefficient should be higher than its corresponding values in the heterotrait-monomethod triangles. The logic is that a measure of a concept should correlate more highly with an independent effort to measure the same concept than with measures designed to get at different concepts that happen to use the same assessment method. Reviewing the pattern of correlations shown in Figure 2–1, the job satisfaction and working conditions variables meet this criterion, while the supervision variable does not. In fact, all of the correlations in the interview monomethod triangle are fairly high, suggesting that this particular mode of assessment is not particularly diagnostic.

To summarize the findings of this hypothetical study, one can say that the measurement of employees' feelings of job satisfaction and working conditions demonstrate reasonably good convergent and discriminant validity and therefore construct validity. The third variable, attitudes toward supervision, fails to meet these criteria in both assessment procedures. In essence, the patterns of correlations exhibited by measures permit an assessment of the construct validity of a measure or measurement system.

Eventually, a researcher must make an assessment of the degree to which the measuring instrument measures what it is intended to measure. As Campbell (1976) indicates: "If an investigator never sticks his neck out with regard to what he thinks his instrument is measuring, he will never establish surplus meaning or rule out competing explanations as to why his measure acts the way it does in the empirical world" (p. 203).

DESCRIPTION

Descriptive data are used by personnel specialists to obtain a snapshot view of the current state of the organization and its members. Assessment of the existing state may be utilized to determine the current level of organizational and employee effectiveness. Assessment is also useful in determining how the organization and organizational members stand on specific issues prior to or after some intervention or change. Unlike relational research, descriptive data do not examine the effect of the change or compare differences. Descriptive data only reflect the existing state at a particular time.

Both objective and subjective data can be utilized for descriptive purposes. Personnel specialists are frequently interested in gathering objective data on such variables as turnover, absences, accidents, grievances, and productivity. Subjective data are typically gathered to assess the attitudes and perceptions employees have with regard to themselves, other employees, their jobs, and the organization.

Objective Data

Objective data are often referred to as *hard data* because they are thought of as free from the biases that enter into subjective judgments. Much of the data considered to be objective is easily obtained and verified. There is little confusion surrounding data involving variables such as test scores, grade point averages, wages, and annual profit. However, because most objective data are obtained from organizational records, the quality of these records is a concern. When the researcher is not a part of the organization, interpretation of organizational records may be particularly difficult. Researchers must make an attempt to assess or control the accuracy and consistency of record keeping in the organization.

A more difficult problem for the researcher is the operational definition of the variable of interest. What is meant by an absence, turnover, or a grievance? When investigating absenteeism, are both excused and unexcused absences relevant? If not, how can they be distinguished accurately? It seems appropriate to separate turnover as a result of firing from voluntary turnover. But should an employee who left a job because his or her spouse was transferred be placed in the same category as someone who left for a better job? When investigating grievances, should a personnel specialist consider only those grievances formally filed with the labor board, or should comments dropped in the employee suggestion box also be included?

If researchers do not explicate their definition of the variables of interest, it will be difficult to develop a cumulative understanding of the variables and their relationship with other variables. Although the collection of objective data in most cases is more straightforward than the collection of subjective data, clarification of the variable of interest is imperative.

Subjective Data

Subjective data are utilized by researchers in personnel management for two basic reasons. First, in many instances there are no objective methods for assessing the variable of interest, and researchers must rely on subjective evaluations for assessment. For example, measuring the productivity of an assembly-line worker by counting the number of products he or she produces an hour is a relatively straightforward objective process; however, measuring the productivity of a middle-level manager is a more difficult, ambiguous assessment problem. When productivity cannot be measured objectively, performance ratings may be utilized for assessment. A second reason that researchers utilize subjective methodologies is to gain some insight into the attitudes and perceptions of organizational members. The most common methodology employed to assess employee attitudes and perceptions is survey research. The following is a discussion of issues related to the utilization of subjective data in descriptive research with an emphasis on survey research.

Ratings

The most popular method for quantifying subjective judgments is the rating scale (Guion, 1965; Saal, Downey, and Lahey, 1980). There are few practitioners or researchers in the field of personnel management who have not used ratings of some form. Whenever ratings are made, however, there is a potential for errors in human judgments. There are three major errors common to rating scales:

1. *Halo error.* This is the tendency to rate a person or object in about the same way on all traits or dimensions because of an overall (global) impression (Guion, 1965). This may occur when the rater has insufficient information to evaluate a specific dimension and therefore relies upon the global impression. It may also occur when the rater has sufficient information to evaluate the specific dimension, but allows the global impression to alter that evaluation (Nisbett and Wilson, 1977). An example of the former is found when an interviewer fails to obtain information about an applicant's ability to supervise others and rates the applicant as capable because the applicant has made a favorable impression on other dimensions. The latter occurrence of halo error is illustrated when a disgruntled employee responds negatively to all survey questions about the organization even though there is evidence (to him or her) that some areas are satisfactory.

2. *Leniency.* The most common definition of leniency error implies a tendency on the part of the rater to give markedly skewed distributions of ratings in either a favorable or unfavorable direction (Guion, 1965; Bernardin et al., 1976; Saal and Landy, 1977; DeCottis, 1977). Although the avoidance of leniency is desirable, what appears to be leniency may be a reflection of reality (Saal, Downey, and Lahey, 1980). If organizational policies of recruitment, selection, and training are effective, supervisory evaluations of subordinates would be expected to be favorably skewed.

3. *Central tendency.* Saal, Downey, and Lahey (1980) point to a distinction between central tendency error and restriction of range error. Central tendency is characterized by ratings restricted around the center or midpoint of the scale, whereas range restriction is characterized by the restriction of rating variability along any point of the scale. Both central tendency and restriction of range create problems in interpretation of ratings because it is difficult to distinguish a high from a low rating when variability is reduced. Yet researchers must examine these errors differently. When examining central tendency error, some reference to the scale's midpoint must be made.

Questionnaire Development in Survey Research

Although the survey is an important tool in psychological research, the formulation of the questions comprising the survey still remains somewhat of an art, dependent on rules of thumb and past experiences of the researcher (Bouchard, 1976). The type of questions asked should be based on the purpose of the survey. In all cases, however, questionnaires should be developed to minimize bias and data distortion and to maximize the probability of accurate, valid responses. A useful step in the early stages of questionnaire development would be to involve some of the potential respondents in the construction of the questionnaire. Regardless of how meticulous the researcher is in structuring and wording questions, the respondents are the best indicators as to whether a particular question is appropriate.

Question Structure.   Structuring the question is dependent upon the type of information desired, the education level of the respondents, and the need for quantification. Dillman (1978) describes four basic question structures.

1. *Open-ended questions* provide no answer choice for the respondents; they must create their own answers. Open-ended questions are used to allow respondents to freely express themselves or to elicit recall information, when listing all the possible responses would be impossible. These questions are very demanding in that they require respondents to recall information, organize that information, and verbalize it. Statistical analysis is difficult because few people respond in the same fashion and the data are difficult to organize and/or aggregate.
2. *Close-ended questions with ordered choices* offer choices that represent a continuum or gradation of a single dimension or concept. The rating scale typifies this type of question. Questions with ordered choices are less demanding of the respondent and are more amenable to quantification and statistical analysis. However, the response range is narrow and the researcher must thoroughly specify the dimensions of interest. These questions are also susceptible to the biases associated with rating scales.
3. *Close-ended questions with unordered choices* offer choices to the respondent, but no single dimension underlies them. The respondent chooses from among discrete categories the one that best reflects his or her situation. A typical question might be: ''Are you the most satisfied with your pay, your working hours, or your benefits?'' The respondent must select the element with which he or she is most satisfied by comparisons. The researcher might also ask the respondent to rank-order the dimensions. These questions can become demanding as the list of choices increases and the respondent must compare too many dimensions. As with questions with ordered responses, the researcher must thoroughly specify the relevant choices.
4. *Partially close-ended questions* are in response to the possibility of the researcher overlooking possible choices of the respondent. These questions attempt to combine the positive qualities of both the open-ended and close-ended questions. Respondents are given choice alternatives, but they are also allowed space to expand or offer other alternatives. These questions can be used to assess the quality of the close-ended questions. A large number of respondents creating their own response could be an indication that the researcher did not thoroughly cover the relevant categories in the questions.

Writing Questions.   Those who have been involved in survey research recognize the great effort and frustrations involved in writing questions. Whenever possible, it is desirable to use questionnaires, such as the various job satisfaction scales, that have already been validated. Frequently, however, researchers must devise their own questionnaires. There are many excellent references available (Payne, 1951; Erdos, 1970; Dillman, 1978) that present rules of thumb and suggestions for writing questions. The primary concern is that the questions be interpreted by the respondent in the same way that the researcher meant the questions to be interpreted. Presented here are several of the questions that Dillman (1978) suggests the survey researcher ask.

1. *Will the words be uniformly understood?* Whenever possible, short simple words should be substituted for lengthy complex words.
2. *Are the questions too vague or too precise?* Questions should not be so vague that the respondents interpret them differently, and not so specific that the respondents cannot answer.
3. *Is the question biased?* The question should not be "loaded" to imply a socially desirable response or an opinion that is held by the researcher.
4. *Is the question objectionable?* Personal questions should be worded so that respondents are not offended or embarrassed by the question or their response.
5. *Is the question too demanding?* Questions that require respondents to perform mathematical calculations or complex rankings should be avoided.
6. *Are the answer choices mutually exclusive?* Response categories should not overlap.
7. *Is an appropriate time referent provided?* Specification of a time limit standardizes the respondent's frame of reference.

These are but a few of the issues to be considered in writing questions, and other references should be consulted for thorough question writing. Although rules of thumb are useful in formulating questions, they cannot replace the utility of involving potential respondents in question-writing and pilot-testing.

Administering the Questionnaire.   Survey administration provides the opportunity to enhance the participation and motivation of the respondents. The administration process should encourage the respondents not only to participate but also to respond honestly and accurately. This process begins prior to the actual survey administration by giving the participants advance notice that the survey will be given and why. If the survey is to be administered in person rather than by mail or phone, the setting must be properly prepared. Space for writing, pencils, and aids for those who cannot read should be available. A survey form that appears simple, short, clear, and professional can encourage participation. The purpose of the survey, an assurance of confidentiality, and some incentive to participate are useful in the introduction, whether it is presented in a cover letter or orally. The incentive may be monetary or an explanation of how the survey will be beneficial to the respondents. Although the survey administrator may attempt to increase participation, standardization of the process is important. The administrator should avoid biasing survey responses or treating respondents differently.

Interpreting Survey Results.   The confidence placed on survey results is a function of the researcher's thoroughness in data collection, including sample selection, question development, and survey administration. The answers given can be no better than the questions asked. When the response rate is low or the incidents of nonresponse and "don't knows" are high, the researcher must interpret the results with caution. Even when the response rate is high, the researcher must always be aware of the biases present when subjective judgments are made and interpret them accordingly.

EXPERIMENTAL DESIGN

Earlier, this chapter indicated that a major methodology used by individuals in personnel management is to establish relationships among two or more variables. It was suggested that one common method of establishing relationships is to conduct experiments in field and laboratory settings. In fact, the use of experimental designs is not only helpful in establishing relationships among variables, but it is also paramount in establishing cause and effect relationships.

A "true" experiment involves the random assignment of subjects to various groups. Traditionally, one such group receives a pretest on some variable and then some "treatment," whereas another group receives a pretest but no treatment or some kind of placebo. Subsequently, the two groups are compared on a posttreatment test or variable (usually the same measuring instrument as the pretest). The independent variable is, in this case, the treatment (received treatment, did not receive treatment); while the dependent variable is the change in the measurements on the pre- and posttest measures. Obviously, several levels of the independent variable could be "manipulated" so the design is not limited to simply a treatment/no treatment paradigm.

Cook and Campbell (1976) outlined three necessary conditions for assuming that the relationship between two variables is causal and goes in a particular direction (e.g., A→B). The first condition is temporal; A must precede B. A second condition is that the treatment must demonstrate a relationship (co-vary) with the dependent variable. Usually, statistics are the determinants of the relationship observed. A third condition is that there must be no plausible alternative explanations of B other than A. For example, a researcher might have conducted an experiment and found a relationship between types of incentive systems and employee satisfaction with pay. However, a viable explanation for the relationship may have been that a seasonal drop in employment levels was responsible for the relationship observed. Cook and Campbell (1976) indicate that such possible alternatives represent threats to the "internal validity" of an experiment; they represent doubts about whether a relationship between A and B can be reasonably inferred. Some of the various "threats" to internal validity detailed by Cook and Campbell (1976) are the following:

1. *History.*   This is a threat that occurs when some event took place between the pre- and posttest which was responsible for the change in B.
2. *Maturation.*   This is a threat when the posttest change is the result of the subject growing stronger, older, etc., when this maturation process is not the treatment variable of interest.
3. *Testing.*   This represents a threat when an effect might be the result of simply taking a test several times. For example, subjects may improve their scores

on a numerical abilities test because of taking the test several times. They could practice during the time interval, study the kinds of problems they had most trouble with, etc.

4. *Instrumentation.* A change between pretest and posttest measurement may be caused by some change in the measuring instrument rather than the treatment of interest.

5. *Statistical regression.* If subjects are classified into treatment groups on the basis of their scores on the pretest (e.g., high or low scores), their scores on the posttest could be the result of the natural tendencies for these scores to "regress toward the mean" for unreliable variables. This change could not, of course, be the result of the treatment, but rather statistical regression.

6. *Selection.* Differences observed in the posttest measure could have been caused by preexisting differences between the individuals receiving the treatment compared to those who did not.

7. *Mortality.* This represents a threat when one effect may be observed because of the fact that some people dropped out of particular treatment groups during the course of an experiment. The different experimental groups may then be composed of different individuals, which could account for the observed effect.

8. *Interactions with selection.* Some of the preceding threats may interact with selection to produce spurious treatment effects. For example, a selection-maturation interaction may occur when different experimental groups comprised members who mature at different rates.

These threats to internal validity are essentially controlled by using a traditional randomized experiment in which one group receives the "treatment" and another is utilized as a control group; subjects are randomly assigned to the groups.

> When respondents are randomly assigned to treatment groups, each group is similarly constituted (no selection, maturation, or selection-maturation problems); each experiences the same testing conditions and research instruments (no testing or instrumentation problems); there is no deliberate selection of high or low scores on any tests except under conditions where respondents are first matched according to, say, pretest scores and then randomly assigned to treatment conditions (no statistical regression problem); each group experiences the same global pattern of history (no history problem); and if there are treatment-related differences in who drops out of the experiment, this is interpretable as a consequence of the treatment and is not due to selection. Thus, randomization takes care of most, but not all, the threats to internal validity (Cook and Campbell, 1976, p. 230).

In many situations, particularly in personnel contexts, it is virtually impossible to assign subjects or employees at random to different treatment groups. In circumstances in which it is not possible to achieve randomization, Cook and Campbell (1976) describe several "quasi-experimental" research designs. Space does not permit a full discussion of all these designs. However, there are three "quasi-experimental" designs that may be particularly useful to personnel and human resources managers: the nonequivalent control group design, the time series design, and the control group time series design.

Nonequivalent Control Group Design. This design is represented symbolically as follows:

Experimental group: O   X   O
Control group: O   O

where "O" indicates a measurement and "X" signifies a treatment. This design looks much like the traditional pretest/posttest control group design previously described; however, in this design subjects are *not* assigned randomly. The groups are preformed or preselected on some basis. For example, a researcher might have conducted an experiment to determine whether job enrichment increased employee productivity. In the efforts to conduct the study, one preexisting intact work group was used as the group receiving the job enrichment "treatment," whereas a different work group was utilized as the control group. If the two groups have similar means and standard deviations on the pretest, this design provides fairly satisfactory control over most threats to internal validity. The main threats to internal validity arise from interactions between such variables as selection and maturity, or selection and history. In the absence of randomization, the possibility always exists that some critical difference not reflected in the pretest is operating to contaminate the posttest data. For example, in the preceding illustration, it could be that the experimental group of employees were an especially "motivated" group compared to the control group employees. This preexisting difference could interact with the treatment and produce the observed differences. Also, statistical regression is another possible threat to the internal validity of the design.

Time Series Design. Symbolically, this design looks like

Experimental group: $O_1\ O_2\ O_3$ X $O_4\ O_5\ O_6$

A series of measurements is made both before and after the treatments. Obviously, one looks for a change in scores, after the treatment, that is relatively stable over the ensuing measurements. The major threat to this design is *history;* that is, the coincidence (with X) of some influential event that has the effect hypothesized to be a result of X.

Control Group Time Series Design. A design that attempts to control for the main weakness of the time series design is one in which a control group is added:

Experimental group: $O_1\ O_2\ O_3$ X $O_4\ O_5\ O_6$
Control group: $O_1\ O_2\ O_3$ $O_4\ O_5\ O_6$

This design has the effect of controlling for the effects of contemporary *history.* If the control group fails to demonstrate a gain from O_4 to O_5 while the experimental group yields a gain, the plausibility of some contemporary event accounting for the gain is greatly reduced since both groups experienced this event.

External Validity

In addition to threats to the internal validity of a research outcome, Campbell and Stanley (1963) have warned that there are also threats to the external validity of a research design. External validity has to do with how *generalizable* a particular set of research findings are. Can the results of the experiment generalize to other subject populations, other settings, work groups, industries, and so forth? It may be that the research results are "true" for the specific work group and employee population that were used in the study, but these results fail to generalize to another job setting.

Campbell and Stanley (1966) indicate the following as threats to the external validity or generalization of a study:

1. *Interactions of selection and the experimental variable.* When subjects who might be unusually susceptible to the effects of the experimental variable are selected, the results might not be generalizable to a larger group. Thus, if an experimental group consisted of extremely dissatisfied employees, the treatment may not "work" for satisfied employees.
2. *Reactive or interactive effect of pretesting.* Simply giving a pretest may limit the generalizability of the experimental findings. A pretest could alert subjects to issues, problems, skills, and so forth, that they might not ordinarily notice.
3. *Reactive effects of experimental procedures.* The experiment itself may produce effects that limit the generalizability of the findings. If subjects are aware of the fact that they are in an experiment, they may alter their normal behavior and react differently.
4. *Multiple-treatment interference.* When subjects are exposed repeatedly to two or more treatments, the effects of previous treatments are not usually erasable. Thus, it is difficult to segregate the effects of subsequent treatments from those previous treatments.

Any research design that is used should be examined for potential threats to generalizability as well as internal validity.

Types of Experimental Research

Experimental paradigms used by individuals in personnel management are typically employed in two kinds of settings: field and laboratory.

Experiments in Field Settings. Utilizing "true" and quasi-experimental designs in actual ongoing organizational settings is somewhat rare in personnel and industrial/organizational psychology. Cook and Campbell (1976) specify some of the major obstacles faced by researchers conducting experiments in organizational settings. These include the following:

1. *Difficulty in gaining and maintaining access to research populations in field settings.* Many organizations simply do not like researchers "tampering" with their employees. Occasionally, there is an underlying fear that the research project will "stir up" the waters and make employees more sensitive to ongoing problems that they otherwise might have ignored.

2. *Withholding the treatment from control group members.* If the treatment holds promise for increasing productivity, morale, or other important organizational variables, it may represent a problem if it is withheld for research purposes. Organizational members granting permission to conduct the experiment may not understand the necessity for a no-treatment control group. In fact, control group members may grow to resent not receiving the treatment.

3. *Problems in achieving randomization.* In many organizational settings, it simply is not possible to assign employees at random to different experimental conditions.

4. *Refusals to participate in the planned experiment.* Field studies are especially vulnerable to problems in subject participation. For example, union management may not feel the experiment is within the best interests of their membership. Participants may refuse to participate, or, in some cases, sabotage the experiment.

5. *Natural attrition.* Members of organizations move in and out of the experimental process. Sometimes employees leave the company, get transferred, promoted, and so forth, which are all *naturally* occurring attrition problems.

6. *Treatment contamination.* One difficult problem in conducting research in field settings is that in many instances employees are aware of the different treatments. Thus, once they are aware of, for example, different incentive plans, they may compete against each other or at least discuss the various components of the different treatment conditions.

7. *Informed consent.* More recently, researchers have been required to obtain "informed consent" information from subjects, which is typically a signed statement that the subject understood that he or she would be participating in a study and that he or she knew something about it. This requirement, while defensible from ethical and sometimes legal standpoints, often makes it difficult to conduct research in field settings.

Typically, experiments in the field are said to have far greater generalizability in their research findings than those findings obtained in laboratory settings. Specifically, it is asserted that field studies are represented by a broader and more representative sampling of subjects, behaviors, and research settings characteristic of organizations than what is studied and sampled in laboratory studies. However, Dipboye and Flannegan (1979) have recently questioned this assumption. They examined published laboratory and field studies and found that the field research was considerably limited in its sampling of subjects, behavior, and settings, and that "in some respects laboratory research provides as firm a basis for generalization to the general population of working people and organization as does field research."

Laboratory Studies. In determining relationships among variables, researchers often turn to laboratory studies. Laboratory studies are experiments conducted outside of organizations, typically in a university setting, and frequently utilizing undergraduate students as subjects. The advantage of such studies rests predominantly in the level and type of control a researcher has in insuring that external variables are not responsible for the research findings; that is, the internal validity of the findings is usually much stronger. On the other hand, the external validity or generalizability of the research findings is often said to be not as strong as that derived from research conducted in field settings. Some individuals have even advocated the abandonment of laboratory experimentation because it is too artificial.

Fromkin and Streufert (1976) and others (Cozby, 1977; Wood, 1977) have described some of the factors that may influence subjects and their participation in laboratory experiments which represent artifacts in the experimental process. These are as follows:

1. *Demand characteristics.* In some experiments, subjects' awareness of their role in the experiment and their desires for the study to "work out right" are such that they make efforts to be "good" subjects. In essence, subjects are able to guess what the experimenter wants and then respond according to these hunches in order to contribute to the body of scientific knowledge. Orne (1959) suggests that the kinds of cues or information (e.g., "scuttlebutt," subject recruitment information, instructions, etc.) that reveal the experimental hypothesis are "demand characteristics." Fromkin and Streufert (1976) argue that before tossing out the laboratory paradigm because of this factor, it might be profitable to estimate or attempt to circumvent this effect.

2. *Evaluation apprehension.* Subjects may often look at an experiment with some apprehension or anxiety because of "expectations that the psychologist may undertake to evaluate his (the subject's) emotional adequacy, his mental health, or lack of it" (Rosenberg, 1969, p. 281). Thus, the subject may be especially concerned about doing well or winning a positive evaluation from an experimenter. In general, evaluation apprehension is heightened by:
   a. cues in the introduction and instructions, which provide hints about an impending examination of personal adequacy; or
   b. experimental procedures, which seem surprising, mysterious, or excessively ambiguous (Fromkin and Streufert, 1976).

Fromkin and Streufert (1976) indicate that apprehension evaluation may be minimized by assuring subjects that: (1) the purpose of the study is more statistical, mathematical, or technical in nature in contrast to a study of individual personalities; and (2) the experimenter is *not* interested in individual responses but in normative, aggregate, or nomothetic aspects of responses.

3. *Experimenter expectancy.* The basic proposition behind this concept is that the researchers' expectations regarding the outcome of the study tend to affect subjects' responses in such a way as to confirm the experimenters' expectations. These shifts in responses may be the result of verbal and nonverbal cues displayed by the experimenters. Experimental designs have been developed in an attempt to control for these possible biasing factors. For example, the individuals or research assistants actually conducting the experiment may be kept "blind" with regard to the hypothesis or the specific condition being investigated.

Fromkin and Streufert (1976) argue that their review of the systematic research reveals that these three artifacts are not as prevalent in laboratory settings as once claimed, and many times operate in field settings on similar levels. Thus, they argue, laboratory studies should not be relegated to a position of lower status relative to alternative research strategies.

CORRELATIONAL DESIGNS

Experimental designs attempt to establish causality by manipulating variables and making some observations on a dependent variable, whereas correlational designs attempt to clarify relationships among variables that already exist in nature (Cronbach, 1957; Wiggins, 1973). Although correlation is a necessary condition for establishing causality, it is not a sufficient condition. Thus, causal interpretations with correlational designs should be made with caution, since a correlation between variables only indicates that a relationship exists.

A simple correlation coefficient (r) indicates the degree and direction of covariance between two variables. The correlation coefficient ranges from $r = +1.0$ for a perfect positive relationship, through $r = 0$ for no relationship, to $r = -1.0$ for a perfect negative relationship. A positive correlation indicates that as one variable increases in value so does the other variable. For example, age and job satisfaction are positively correlated if satisfaction increases with age. Conversely, a negative correlation indicates that as one variable increases, the other variable decreases. Unemployment and turnover are negatively related if turnover decreases as unemployment increases. In most instances, researchers are interested in relationships that include more than two variables. A personnel specialist, for example, might be interested in how a person's race, sex, and job performance are related to job level. When there is more than one predictor variable, more complex multivariate designs are utilized.

Correlational designs are most frequently utilized when predictive accuracy, rather than causation, is of primary concern. For example, causation is not relevant for the personnel specialist interested in predicting future performance from test scores. Predictive accuracy is the primary concern. Correlational designs are also utilized when there exists a complex network of variables not easily isolated into meaningful parts for experimental manipulation. When complex interactions are expected, researchers may utilize correlational designs in exploratory fashions to identify naturally occurring relationships, and then attempt subsequent experimental manipulations. Likewise, experimental findings can be confirmed using correlational designs to test whether the relationships hold when experimental controls are not present. There are also a few correlational designs that allow some attempts to make causal statements about the relationships among variables by examining their correlational patterns. The following discussion focuses on the most common multivariate correlational design, linear multiple regression, and those correlational designs that address causality: path analysis and cross-lagged panel correlations.

Linear Multiple Regression. The general purpose of multiple regression analysis is to explain a portion of the variance of a criterion (Y) or a dependent variable by estimating the contribution to this variance by two or more predictors (X) or independent variables (Kerlinger and Pedhauzer, 1973). There are also multiple regression techniques that examine curvilinear relationships; however, this discussion will be limited to linear multiple regression.

Multiple regression procedures result in a linear equation that maximizes the correlation between the predicted score and the actual score. This multiple correlation coefficient (R) reflects the accuracy with which the criterion scores can be estimated (or predicted) from the predictors. Likewise, R^2 reflects the proportion of variance in the criterion variable that is explained by the predictors (Weiss, 1976).

The resulting linear equation is an additive composite of the weighted predictor scores with the weights chosen so as to maximize R. The equation is typically presented in the following form:

$$Y' = a + b_1X_1 + b_2X_2 + \ldots + b_kX_k$$

The predicted criterion is Y', the intercept is a, the weights are b, and the predictors are X. The regression weights occur in two forms. The raw score weights, b-weights, are applied to the raw scores of the predictor variables. The standard score weights, beta weights, are applied to the standard or Z-scores of the predictor variables. These beta weights are used to test the significance of each predictor. The variable with the highest beta weight contributes the most to predicting variance in the criterion variable.

When investigators wish to reduce a larger set of predictor variables into a smaller subset, stepwise multiple regression procedures are appropriate (Weiss, 1976). There are several types of stepwise regression. The feature common to all stepwise regressions is that a mathematical procedure determines the order in which the predictor variables enter the equation. The variable that accounts for the most variance in the criterion enters the equation first, and then variables are ordered according to the unique variance they add to the criterion.

When researchers have some theoretical or conceptual knowledge concerning the expected relationships among variables, hierarchical regression may be appropriate. In hierarchical regression, the researcher decides the entry order of the predictor variables rather than allowing the statistical procedure to order the variables which might capitalize on sampling error.

A major criticism of multiple regression is that it is susceptible to sample-specific characteristics; that is, the unique features of the data derived from the specific sample contribute heavily to the relationships observed (Wiggins, 1973; Weiss, 1976). If results are influenced by (determined largely by) sample characteristics, it is unlikely that they will generalize to other samples. Thus, cross-validation is recommended. Cross-validation involves the "checking-out" of a relationship on an independently drawn but similar sample. Cross-validation procedures vary, but most utilize a hold-out sample to test the generalizability of the regression equation results from the original sample. Another possible technique to determine the generalizability of multiple regression findings is to apply what is known as "shrinkage formulae." These are mathematical formulae that estimate "true" relationships without sample error. Shrinkage formulae have been open to criticism, yet they have been found to be comparable to true cross-validation procedures in estimating the cross-validated R (Schmitt, Coyle, and Rauschenberger, 1977).

Path Analysis. Path analysis is a specific application of multiple regression methodology in which causal relationships are examined (Kenny, 1979). Because causation implies correlation, a set of correlation coefficients or regression weights can be examined for possible patterns of causality. Although causation cannot be thoroughly demonstrated by path analysis, not finding hypothesized relationships implied by a causal model may rule out a causal interpretation. Utilizing *a priori* research and knowledge, researchers specify alternative causal models implying different patterns of relationships. Models inconsistent with the regression analysis results are rejected and consistent models are retained for further analysis (Feldman, 1975).

Equations are typically presented in the form of a path diagram.

$$X_2 = P_{24}X_4$$
$$X_1 = P_{14}X_4 + P_{13}X_3 + P_{12}X_2$$

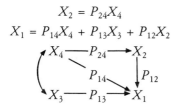

Rather than independent and dependent variables, hypothesized effects are referred to as *endogenous variables;* hypothesized causal agents are referred to as *exogenous variables.* Causal links are presented by arrows from the causal agent to the effect, and path coefficients (P_{ij}) are computed to estimate the strength of the relationship. Path coefficients can be represented by either the regression coefficients or standardized betas. When no lines are drawn, the correlation is hypothesized to be zero. In the above model, X_3 and X_4 are purely exogenous variables, and no prediction is made about their relationship with each other as indicated by the curved two-tailed arrow. X_4 directly affects X_2 and X_1 and also indirectly affects X_1 through X_2. X_3 directly affects X_1 and is unrelated to X_2. X_2 directly affects X_1.

Cross-Lagged Panel Correlations. Lazarfeld's "16-Fold Table" was developed to provide information about the direction of causality from repeated measurement of two dichotomous variables. The cross-lagged panel correlation is a modification of Lazarfeld's method that may be applied to continuous variables (Campbell and Stanley, 1966; Cook and Campbell, 1976). Like path analysis, one may use cross-lagged panel correlations to examine causality with correlational data. Data are measured at two points in time and cross correlations are calculated and compared. The highest cross correlation indicates the direction of causality. This interpretation is based on the notion that effects should correlate higher with a prior cause than with a subsequent cause.

A simple form of cross-lagged data is shown below:

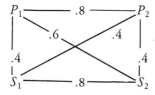

The question asked in this example is, "Does productivity (P) cause job satisfaction (S) or does job satisfaction cause productivity?" Three sets of correlations are typically examined.

1. *Test-retest correlations,* $r_{P1,P2}$ and $r_{S1,S2}$, are examined for reliability of measurement.
2. *Synchronous correlations,* $r_{P1,S1}$ and $r_{P2,S2}$, are examined for evidence of shared variance and stability.
3. *Cross-lagged correlations,* $r_{P1,S2}$ and $r_{P2,S1}$, are examined for directionality. The higher correlation is assumed to represent the direction of causality.

In the preceding example, the reliability and stability of measurement are verified by the similarity between both the test-retest correlation and the synchronous correlations, before inferences can be made. Because the correlation between productivity at time 1 and satisfaction at time 2 is higher, productivity is considered the causal factor. This is a highly simplified example, and the analytic procedures, in actuality, are far more complex. For a recent critique of the cross-lagged panel correlation method, refer to Rogosa (1980).

Moderator Variables. The term *moderator* has been used with some frequency in personnel-oriented research over the past few years. Basically, a moderator is a variable that acts to enhance prediction in some nonadditive fashion. There are various models and approaches to moderator variables. The major approaches are the following:

1. *The moderator as a subgrouping variable.* Occasionally, it is possible to enhance predictability by dividing or subgrouping subjects into relatively homogenous groups (e.g., males-females; blacks-whites, etc.). The correlation coefficient between prediction and criterion variables may differ according to the subgroup. This is alternatively labeled *differential validity.* There was a substantial controversy for some time concerning whether differential validity was a real phenomenon in the selection of black and white applicants (Schmidt, Berner, and Hunter, 1973; Katzell and Dyer, 1977; Arvey, 1979).

2. *Ghiselli's "D" technique.* Earlier, Ghiselli (1956) proposed a technique whereby a moderator variable was correlated with an absolute difference score between standardized predictor (Z_p) and standardized criterion (Z_c). A high difference score would indicate a substantial amount of error in prediction. In essence, the magnitude of D served as an index of predictability; the smaller the D, the better the predictability. A high positive correlation between the moderator variable and D would indicate that a high score on the moderator predicted high deviation scores or errors in prediction. A low score on the moderator would be associated with a low deviation score between the predictor and criterion standardized scores, and therefore an accurate prediction using the predictor.

3. *Moderated regression.* A more contemporary use of the term *moderator variable* is in connection with regression techniques. The hypothesized moderator variable is

put into the regression equation first as a variable by itself. For example, if Z were the hypothesized moderator, X was an independent variable, and Y the predicted criterion variable, the equation would be:

$$Y = a + bX_1 + b_2Z$$

Subsequently, the moderator variable would be added into the equation in interaction with the X variable:

$$Y = a + b_1X + b_2Z + b_3X_1Z_1$$

The multiplicative term represents the moderator effect. Its contribution is assessed by reviewing the subsequent change in R^2 or proportion of variance accounted for in the second equation compared to the first equation without the interactive term included.

In general, the search for reliable moderator variables that cross-validate has been disappointing (Zedeck, 1971). Ghiselli (1972) suggests that moderators may be "fragile and elusive" (p. 270). The most prominent example of the failure to detect real moderators is the differential validity issue with regard to race as a subgrouping variable. The evidence is quite strong that the differences between minority and nonminority correlations are very small (Linn, 1978).

QUALITATIVE RESEARCH

Up to this point the present chapter has presented the major models associated with quantitative approaches to research methodologies. Specifically, it has presented elements of both experimental and correlation designs. In recent years there has been a number of criticisms of the natural science model and the quantitative approaches associated with it. Behling (1980) has identified five general objections to the application of this model.

1. *Uniqueness.* Each organization, group, and person differs to some degree from all others; the development of precise general laws in organizational behavior and organization theory is thus impossible.
2. *Instability.* The phenomena of interest to researchers in organizational behavior and organization theory are transitory. Not only do the "facts" of social events change with time, but the "laws" governing them change as well. Natural science research is poorly equipped to capture these fleeting phenomena.
3. *Sensitivity.* Unlike chemical compounds and other things of interest to natural science researchers, the people who make up organizations, and thus organizations themselves, may behave differently if they become aware of researchers' hypotheses about them.
4. *Lack of realism.* Manipulating and controlling variables in organizational research changes the phenomena under study. Researchers thus cannot generalize from their studies because the phenomena observed inevitably differ from their real world counterparts.

5. *Epistemological differences.*   Although understanding cause and effect through natural science research is an appropriate way of "knowing" about physical phenomena, a different kind of "knowledge" not tapped by this approach is more important in organizational behavior and organization theory (pp. 484–485).

Behling (1980) goes on to discuss these objections in greater detail and finds that none of the barriers are insurmountable. Yet, there has been a trend to recognize and incorporate more qualitative research methodologies as mechanisms for studying behavior in organizations. These alternative research strategies may be identified as "qualitative" because of the greater reliance on more subjective data sources and means of analyzing such data. As indicated by Morgan and Smircich (1980), qualitative research is best represented as an *approach* that emphasizes: (1) more involvement of the researcher with subjects, (2) greater recognition of the inherently dynamic nature of employees and the employment process, and (3) the inadequacies of surveys, questionnaires, and analytical statistical models to tap into these processes accurately.

There are three qualitative research methodologies that will be discussed briefly: the interview, observation, and participant observation.

The Interview.   The interview is a frequently used method in organizational research. Researchers utilize the interview in the exploratory stages of an investigation, during the major stages of an investigation, and during the wrap-up phase of the investigation as an aid to data interpretation (Bouchard, 1976). Data collected in the interview process are often more rich than observational or survey data in terms of providing a context for why people feel, think, or act in the way they do. Because the interviewer can probe the interviewee for additional information, a more complete understanding of the object of investigation can be obtained.

The interview may vary in the degree of structure provided. In the most highly structured interview, both the questions and responses are specified and the interviewee chooses the appropriate response. This type of interview is actually an oral survey and may be administered either face to face or by telephone. An unstructured or nondirective interview specifies neither the questions nor the responses. This type of interview is typically used in clinical settings in which the interviewer merely guides the discussion. Most research interviews fall somewhere between the highly structured and highly unstructured interview, with questions prepared in advance supplemented with probing as the interviewee responds.

A major concern with the interview process is that participants feel free to respond truthfully and accurately. The interview situation must be prepared in such a way that participants trust the interviewer to protect their anonymity. Interviewers must also convey that they are willing to listen and use the information in the best interests of the participants. Little information will be obtained if participants view the researcher as a "tool" of management who is there only in order to achieve the goals and objectives of the organization. Thus, interviewers should attempt to establish rapport with the interviewee, yet also maintain a professional image. Whenever possible, it is useful to notify participants in advance, explaining how they were chosen, what the information will be used for, and how their information will be kept confidential.

Whenever information is collected face to face, the potential for social desirability bias is also great. Participants search for cues that will indicate what the interviewer ''wants to hear'' and respond accordingly. Although this process cannot be avoided entirely, interviewers can minimize data distortion by maintaining a neutral stance. Interviewers should also be aware of their own biases and their possible influence in the data-collection process. As with any measurement device, the quality of the interviewer as an instrument affects the quality of the data.

Observation. Learning by observation is a naturally occurring event in almost everybody's life. For example, few children learn to walk by verbal instruction; instead, they learn through observation. Researchers attempting to learn about organizations may also find the observation process to be a useful learning strategy. While self-reports of organizational behavior may be honest representations by the respondents, observers are often able to see things that respondents neglect or take for granted (Bouchard, 1976). Because the observer is an outsider and not actually involved in the organizational process, he or she is possibly able to present a more objective view of events that have taken place.

A potential problem with the use of the observational methodology is a measurement interaction effect (Campbell and Stanley, 1966). When observers are present, organizational members may behave differently from the way they would without the observers' presence. However, given enough time, employees may adapt to the observers and likely ignore their presence (Bouchard, 1976). The limitations of the observer are also a potential problem. The observer cannot possibly ''see'' everything that occurs. In addition, what an observer does observe and record is selected and reduced through the perception process. As with any data-reduction process, errors will result. Observers should be thoroughly trained in observing and recording data so that these errors may be minimized.

Participant Observation. Ethnography or participant observation has long been recognized as an anthropological research strategy. This methodology is based on the notion that events can be adequately interpreted only when the views of both insiders and outsiders are taken into account (Hader and Lindeman, 1933). The participant observers take the role of both an insider and outsider by temporarily becoming members of the group under investigation. The amount of their participation may vary from total participation where others are not aware of their role as observers, to open participation and observation, with members of the group aiding the observational process as informants. Ethical issues should be considered if researchers intend to conceal their observational role.

Because the participant observer actually becomes a part of the event under investigation, objectivity is also a major concern with this strategy. Bouchard (1976) suggests several ways in which objectivity can be increased.

1. Support interpretations with data from other sources.
2. Separate facts from interpretations.

3. Examine all conflicting positions.
4. Avoid overidentification with a particular subgroup.
5. Be aware of one's own biases and the biases of group members.
6. Be aware of changes in attitudes throughout the process. Changes in attitudes and emotions may be a cue to a problem in objectivity.

ETHICAL ISSUES IN CONDUCTING RESEARCH IN ORGANIZATIONS

Conducting research in organizational settings must also be done in such a manner that it does not violate any ethical or legal standards imposed by the profession or by the court systems. The protection of human subjects in research designs should be a high-priority item. Thus, researchers should be aware of the American Psychological Association's (1973) ethical standards in this regard. Some of the kinds of standards indicated by this document are the following:

1. Ethical practice requires the investigator to inform the participant of all features of the research that reasonably might be expected to influence willingness to participate and to explain all other aspects of the research about which the participant inquires. Failure to make full disclosure gives added emphasis to the investigator's responsibility to protect the welfare and dignity of the research department.
2. Ethical research practice requires the investigator to respect the individual's freedom to decline to participate in research or to discontinue participation at any time. The obligation to protect this freedom requires special vigilance when the investigator is in a position of power over the participant. The decision to limit this freedom increases the investigator's responsibility to protect the participant's dignity and welfare.
3. The ethical investigator protects participants from physical and mental discomfort, harm, and danger. If the risk of such consequences exists, the investigator is required to inform the participant of that fact, secure consent before proceeding, and take all possible measures to minimize distress. A research procedure may not be used if it is likely to cause serious and lasting harm to participants.
4. Information obtained about the research participants during the course of an investigation is confidential. When the possibility exists that others may obtain access to such information, ethical research practice requires that this possibility, together with the plans for protecting confidentiality, be explained to the participants as a part of the procedure for obtaining informed consent.

Recently, the legal system has also imposed on researchers the need to be sensitive about minority employees and issues associated with discrimination in research. The Civil Rights Act of 1964, Title VII, which forbids organizations to discriminate on the basis of sex, race, religion, or natural origin, and the ensuing litigation, has made it critical that researchers be aware of minority group issues in conducting research in organizational settings. Researchers should be alert to some of these factors.

1. *The use of race, sex, age, and other legally sensitive demographic data in conducting survey research.* While it may be useful for research purposes to col-

lect these data on subjects, employees may not be aware of the ultimate uses of the data and suspect discriminatory intent or action.

2. *Separate or differential treatment for minority and nonminority group employees.* A training program designed only for blacks or women, for example, may be inherently suspect even if data indicate that the treatment is most effective for these subgroups of individuals. Researchers must be sensitive to the political aspects of their research and treatment efforts and be prepared to deal with them.

3. *The use of legally prohibited classification variables as predictors.* Even if race, for example, might be empirically demonstrated to be the best predictor of job performance, the researcher should be aware of the illegal nature of such a scheme if race were used as a predictor. The issue becomes somewhat blurred when race is used as a "moderator," because ultimately the variable is included in a linear prediction model and might qualify as a "predictor" in this instance.

4. *The problems inherent in conducting research with different minority groups in an employee population.* Enough has been said about data-collection problems (e.g., interviewing) when dealing with minorities, so this issue will not be discussed here.

In sum, researchers must be aware of the ethical and legal nature of their research procedures and methodologies.

A FINAL WORD

This chapter has been relatively brief. However, the reader should have a feel by this time that conducting research in organizations is no easy task. Personnel managers must tiptoe through methodological "swamps" and analytical "traps" to gather data for decision making. We believe, however, that it is well worth the effort to conduct research and to use the data appropriately. One must learn more about organizational processes and employee behavior if enhanced efficiency and increased satisfaction are to be achieved. These changes will probably not occur happenstance; they must be aided by accurate information and correct inferences about relationships.

Discussion Questions

1. How might a personnel specialist approach a problem that exists in his or her organization if he or she decides to use "subjective" or nonobjective methodologies? Give an example. Do you think these methodologies will be effective in dealing with the existing problem?

2. What is meant when we say that a "threat to internal validity was controlled"? Specifically, what is meant by "a threat" and how might it be "controlled"? Give an example.

3. Think about the popular "Pepsi" vs. "Coke" advertisement. Can you think of any possible explanations for the outcomes of the study or studies? Is it a "true" experiment? Does the study have adequate external and internal validity? Why or why not?

4. Indicate the major factors that distinguish between correlational and experimental designs. Is one methodology to be preferred over the other? Why or why not?

5. What ethical issues are important when we do research with members of an organization? Do we need to have the same concerns as academic researchers? Who should we be "safeguarding"—the organization or the individual employee?

PART TWO

PERSONNEL AND JOB PLANNING

In the overall sequencing of personnel activities, the first logical activity is to forecast the organization's human resource needs and develop programs for meeting those needs. The forecasting side of human resource planning (HRP) seeks information from the environment, especially the demographic environment, and attempts to integrate that information into the organization's business plan and to determine the availability or nonavailability of required talent. If shortages or surpluses of required talent exist, or are anticipated in the future, the programming side of HRP initiates programs, including programs of recruitment, transfer, and outplacement. Historically, few organizations have systematically engaged in HRP or fully exploited its potential. In Chapter 3, Dyer proposes that HRP is coming of age. He presents a conceptual model for HRP and then discusses in detail the components of that model. He also suggests directions for HRP practice and research in the future.

Often a concurrent personnel activity is job analysis. Nearly every subsequent internal personnel activity is dependent to some extent on the accurate analysis of job and human requirements for work performance. Job analysis provides informational inputs to the selection of personnel, the validation of selection instruments, the design of training and development programs, and the identification of criterion dimensions in performance evaluation. Although job analysis represents an important personnel activity, it is not adequately undertaken in most organizations. Sparks, in Chapter 4, provides a detailed discussion of the substance and process of job analysis, current and anticipated future issues in job analysis, and relevant legislation.

CHAPTER THREE

HUMAN RESOURCE PLANNING

Lee Dyer

Lee Dyer is an Associate Professor in the New York State School of Industrial and Labor Relations at Cornell University. He received his Ph.D. in Labor and Industrial Relations from the University of Wisconsin. Professor Dyer has a well established reputation as a researcher and consultant in the area of human resource forecasting and planning. His other areas of interest include compensation policies and practices, management development, and organizational change and development. He is the author or coauthor of over thirty articles and six books and monographs. In addition, Professor Dyer has been a consultant to many organizations, including Corning Glass Works, Mobil Oil Company, and several public school systems.

"Personnel Directors are the New Corporate Heroes." With this article in *Fortune* magazine, Meyer (1976) vividly captured the bullish spirit surrounding personnel in the mid-1970s. The field had been thrust into the limelight by the need to respond to legislation regarding equal employment opportunity, safety and health, and pensions. Increasing attention was being paid to labor costs as wages, salaries, and fringe benefits rose, and productivity declined. For the first time, top managers seemed to be hearing personnel's longstanding plea that the management of human resources be given at least as much attention as that typically paid to the management of money and machines (*Business Week,* February 26, 1979).

Being a hero, however, is not easy. With the limelight came a corresponding responsibility to show that the personnel department could indeed contribute to the

Financial support in the preparation of this chapter was provided by The Research Fund of the New York State School of Industrial and Labor Relations, Cornell University. Grateful appreciation is expressed to Lori Walter for research assistance and to John Fossum, George Milkovich, and Donald Schwab for helpful comments on earlier versions of the manuscript.

organization's "bottom line." Thus, throughout the seventies many personnel people found themselves struggling as never before to turn a disparate collection of often reactive, and sometimes superfluous, activities into an integrated set of proactive, goal-oriented programs. This sense of urgency led, in turn, to a heightened interest in human resource planning (HRP).

BACKGROUND

As Figure 3–1 (Dyer, 1980) shows, the personnel department contributes to organizational effectiveness and efficiency by helping to attain objectives pertaining to productivity, staffing levels, compensation and personnel program costs, policy commitments (e.g., no layoffs), and legal obligations (e.g., affirmative action goals and timetables). Key results leading to these objectives include performance levels and personnel flow (accession, movement, and loss) rates, and, perhaps, attendance, grievance, and accident and illness rates. Personnel management attempts to affect these results by influencing employee capabilities, perceptions, attitudes, and, eventually, behaviors through a wide variety of policies and programs. The entire drama takes place within an environment that often exerts a significant effect on both the policies and programs undertaken and the results attained.

HRP is the process through which organizational goals, as put forth in mission statements and business plans, are translated into human resource objectives concerning staffing levels and flow rates and, from these, into an integrated set of personnel policies and programs. HRP helps to assure that organizations are neither over- nor under-staffed, that the right employees are placed in the right jobs at the right times, that organizational and environmental change is anticipated and adjusted to with a minimum of cost, and that there is direction and coherence to personnel activities (Vetter, 1967; Frantzreb, 1979a).

HRP is not new, although a survey in the mid-1960s showed efforts at that time to be only scattered and fragmentary (Janger, 1966). Ten years later, a similar survey found that 86 percent of the responding companies were involved in HRP, and over one-half regarded it as a major personnel activity (Janger, 1977). In recent years, HRP specialists have emerged in many organizations and have assumed reasonably well defined roles (Walker and Wolfe, 1978). In 1977, a professional society of human resource planners was established, and it has expanded rapidly in terms of both membership and activities.

The HRP literature has also expanded rapidly in recent years. Much of the early writing in the area was descriptive and exhortatory, although over time it has become increasingly conceptual, analytical, and empirical. Statisticians and operations researchers have been heavy contributors, especially to the development of computer-based modeling techniques. Personnel scholars have been less frequently involved; nevertheless, in recent years a number of personnel-oriented articles and books have begun to appear (for annotated bibliographies, see Frantzreb, 1977c and 1978; Walker, 1980).

It seems likely that HRP applications and research will continue to develop rapidly in the 1980s. What follows is an attempt to describe the current state of the area and to suggest directions that future developments might take.

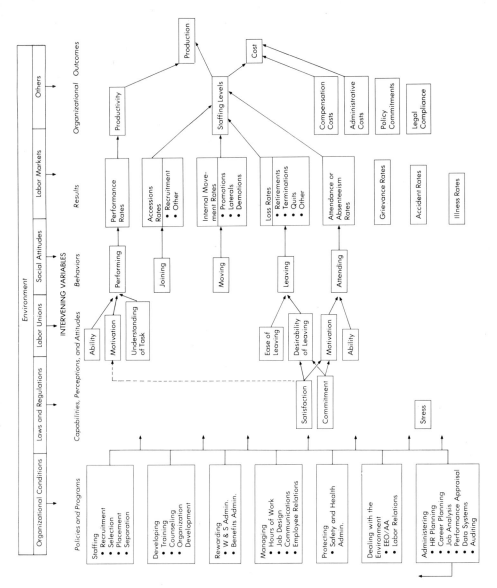

FIGURE 3-1
Toward a Conceptual System of Personnel Management

54

A CONCEPTUAL MODEL

Conceptual models of HRP abound (Frantzreb, 1979c). A careful review of these models seems to suggest that the process is best viewed as involving the three interrelated phases shown in Figure 3–2: (1) setting HRP objectives, (2) planning personnel programs, and (3) evaluation and control.

HRP objectives are of two types. The first involves future staffing needs, or the number and types of employees an organization will require to meet its goals during a planning period. Staffing level objectives emerge from an analysis of financial and production or output goals, adjusted for targeted changes in productivity, organizational structure, and the like. The second set of HRP objectives pertains to desired personnel

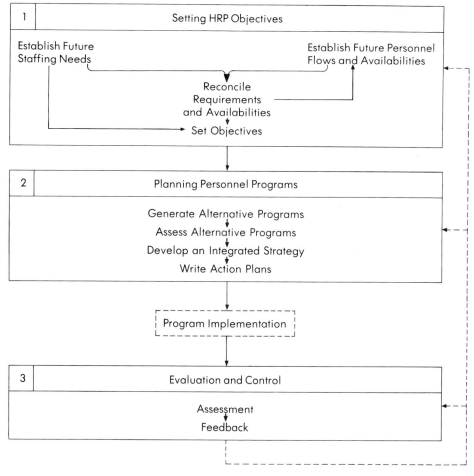

FIGURE 3–2
Conceptual Model of the Human Resource Planning Process

flows; that is, to the combination of accessions, internal moves, and losses (see Figure 3–1) that will result in personnel availabilities to match anticipated needs.

With objectives established, it is possible to *plan personnel programs.* As Figure 3–2 shows, for each objective, alternative personnel programs (recruiting, promoting, training, compensation, etc.) are considered and assessed for their likely effects. Those eventually decided upon are merged into an integrated strategy and often written up in the form of action plans.

Over time, staffing level and flow rate objectives are monitored for continuing applicability, and programs are analyzed in terms of their results. These assessments are fed back into the processs and necessary adjustments are made, thus completing the third phase: *evaluation and control.*

Unfortunately, the foregoing model obscures the rich variety of HRP applications found in actual practice. For example, HRP can be strategic or operational. As shown in Table 3–1, strategic plans tend to be long-term and general, while operational plans are short-term and specific. Further, both types may be wide or narrow in scope—involving an entire organization or only selected units or employee groups. Finally, both types may be carried out on a recurring basis (e.g., annually) or only sporadically (e.g., when new facilities are brought on line). As an example, Corning Glass Works develops focused strategic plans (FSPs) for new businesses as they show promise of significant growth, and comprehensive operational plans (COPs) for the entire corporation annually. In both cases, only managerial and professional personnel are included (Dyer, Shafer, and Regan, 1980).

Irrespective of variations encountered, it is argued here that the HRP process will be strengthened by giving consideration to each of the three phases indicated in Figure 3–2. Accordingly, attention is now turned to a more detailed examination of these, beginning with the establishment of HRP objectives.

SETTING HRP OBJECTIVES

The importance of HRP objectives lies in the fact that they serve as both targets and standards: targets for subsequent steps in the planning process and standards for judging the value of the plans made. As pointed out earlier, an initial set of HRP objectives emerges from analyses of future staffing needs, while subsequent objectives stem from attempts to reconcile anticipated personnel availabilities with these needs.

Establishing Future Staffing Needs

Business plans[1] determine future staffing needs. Through business planning, management charts an organization's future in terms of financial objectives, product mix, technologies, resource requirements, and the like (Walker, 1980). Once the direction of the business is set, the human resource planner assists in developing workable organiza-

---

[1]The term *business plans* is used here in a generic sense. It is realized that governmental and not-for-profit institutions also develop long- and short-range plans from which staffing needs are derived.

TABLE 3–1
Variations of HRP Process

Type of HRP	Impetus	Time Frame	Major Concerns	Involvement	Output
Strategic	• Strategic "business" plan: Long-range objectives re: profits, product mix, market shares, etc. • Anticipated environmental change (legislation, labor markets, labor union strategies)	2–5 years	Productivity, organizational redesign, adequacy of human resources (back-ups, bench strength, potential), employment stability	Heavy line (top), some staff (i.e., finance, personnel)	Policy directions
Operational	• Operating "business" plan/budget • Anticipated or actual personnel problems	1–2 years	Labor costs, personnel expenditures, staffing levels, personnel flows, employee development and motivation, labor peace	Some line (all levels), heavy staff (mostly personnel)	Program plans

tional structures and in determining the numbers and types of employees that will be required to meet financial and output goals.

This is no easy task. The expertise of many levels of management and several functional specialists may be required (Frantzreb, 1976; Walker, 1978). Further, existing methodologies are at best crude. Research has so far failed to develop adequate means of determining whether organizations are currently under- or over-staffed, let alone techniques to establish appropriate staffing levels for new businesses or emerging technologies.

As a consequence, *managerial estimates* often are relied upon. Estimates of total staffing needs may be made by top management in the unit or employee group at issue (top-down), or initial estimates may be made by lower level managers whose figures are refined and consolidated through group discussions at successively higher levels (bottom-up).[2] A variant is the *delphi technique* through which independent estimates of future staffing needs are elicited by means of successive iterations of questionnaires. At each iteration, estimates are sought and clarifying data may be provided. The expectation is that four or five iterations will result in a convergence of estimates. Managerial estimation procedures were described by Walker (1980) and the delphi technique by Milkovich, Annoni, and Mahoney (1972).

Practices apparently vary concerning the amount of guidance and assistance managers receive when making estimates of future staffing needs. Minimal guidance may come in the form of checklists of factors to be considered or questions to be asked (Walker, 1980). Managers may also be provided the results of time study analyses or a set of predetermined staffing guides (Ettelstein, 1977; Niehaus, 1979). In certain circumstances, statistical projections may be derived.

Four frequently discussed statistical forecasting techniques are summarized in Table 3-2. Two of these—*regression analysis* and *productivity ratios*—use such work load indicators as sales volume, production levels, value added, productivity rates, and budgets to forecast future staffing needs. The third technique—*personnel ratios*—relies on relative patterns of employment levels in various units or among selected occupational groups, while the fourth—*time series analysis*—simply extrapolates past staffing levels, giving no consideration to future business plans.

The various statistical projection techniques tend to be limited in practice. All, for example, rely on past data, which restricts their use to situations where a relevant history exists. Regression analyses, productivity ratios, and (usually) personnel ratios are feasible only where analyses uncover systematic and reliable historical relationships among workload indicators and staffing patterns, and where work-load indicators are forecast with tolerable accuracy. Further, because of the heavy reliance on historical data, statistical techniques work best in relatively stable organizations that anticipate little change in product mix, productivity levels, technology, or organizational design. Unfortunately,

[2]HRP may be organized around jobs or, where large numbers of jobs are involved, job categories (or, as they are sometimes called, states). Generally, the literature suggests that if more than twenty or thirty jobs are at issue, aggregations are called for, but Dyer, Shafer, and Regan (1980) have presented a case in which sixty-six job categories were used successfully.

TABLE 3–2
Statistical Techniques Used to Project Future Staffing Needs

Name	Description
(1) Regression analysis	Past levels of various work-load indicators, such as sales, production levels, and value added, are examined for statistical relationships with staffing levels. Where sufficiently strong relationships are found, a regression (or multiple regression) model is derived. Forecasted levels of the retained indicator(s) are entered into the resulting model and used to calculate the associated level of human resource requirements. For applications, see Drui (1963) and Bright (1976).
(2) Productivity ratios	Historical data are used to examine past levels of a productivity index $(P) = \dfrac{\text{Work load}}{\text{Number of people}}$. Where constant, or systematic, relationships are found, human resource requirements can be computed by dividing predicted work loads by P. An example is provided by Wikstrom (1971, pp. 18–23).
(3) Personnel ratios	Past personnel data are examined to determine historical relationships among the number of employees in various jobs or job categories. Regression analysis or productivity ratios are then used to project either total or key group human resource requirements, and personnel ratios are used to allocate total requirements to various job categories or to estimate requirements for nonkey groups. See Wikstrom (1971, pp. 24–29).
(4) Time Series Analysis	Past staffing levels (instead of work-load indicators) are used to project future human resource requirements. Past staffing levels are examined to isolate seasonal and cyclical variations, long-term trends, and random movement. Long-term trends are then extrapolated or projected using a moving average, exponential smoothing, or regression technique. For an example using exponential smoothing, see Drandell (1975), and for one using a regression technique, see Burack and Mathys (1979, pp. 155–157).

these are the very organizations in which managerial estimates may be most accurately made without the use of statistical techniques.

Available evidence suggests that the art of establishing future staffing needs is in its infancy. To date, research on the subject has been neither voluminous nor particularly rigorous (Bowey, 1977; Bartholomew and Forbes, 1979). Judgmental techniques undoubtedly predominate in practice, but statistical techniques dominate the research literature. Yet to be examined are the decision-making models that managers use, the relative use and value of decision aids, such as staffing guides and statistical forecasts, and the accuracy of results attained. And yet, these are researchable issues (Mintzberg, Raisinghani, and Theoret, 1976; Mintzberg, 1979), lending some ground for optimism in the decade ahead.

Notwithstanding current shortcomings in practice and research, each organization engaged in HRP must somehow decide upon (or implicitly assume) desired staffing levels for each job or job category in the unit or occupational group involved. However developed, these numbers (plus the productivity rates and labor costs they imply) become the objectives for the next step in the process.

Establishing Future Human Resource Flows and Availabilities

Given a set of staffing needs, how can adequate numbers of the right types of people be made available on a timely basis to meet them? As shown in Figure 3–3, future personnel availabilities are a function of the personnel levels in various job categories at the beginning of the planning period adjusted to reflect: (1) losses resulting from retirement, termination, resignation, and other reasons; (2) gains and losses resulting from internal moves into or out of job categories through promotions, lateral moves, or demotions; and (3) accessions through recruitment or other means.

Sometimes future personnel availabilities are estimated using historical flow (i.e., loss, movement, and accession) rates and then compared with established personnel requirements to identify anticipated shortages or surpluses in various job categories. Where such gaps appear, simulation techniques may be used to test variations in historical flow rates (within predetermined policy and budgetary constraints) and ultimately to derive one or more sets of flow rates that will create a match between availabilities and needs. Alternatively, the analysis may begin with the established staffing needs and certain policy and/or budget constraints, and work backward to derive an acceptable set of flow rates. Either approach may be done judgmentally or statistically.

Although not shown in Figure 3–3, flow analyses, particularly regarding accessions, may involve extensive studies of anticipated environmental conditions in such areas as legislation, labor markets, and societal norms and values. Some large corporations (e.g., General Electric) maintain specific staff groups to conduct such studies (see Frantzreb, 1980). Also not shown is the possibility that the analyses may occasionally indicate that established staffing needs cannot be met within existing constraints. Should this happen, top management must decide whether to change the business plans (e.g., delay a planned expansion) or to alter the constraints. Apparently such reconsiderations are rare, although they may become more widespread as analyses of future flows and availabilities increase in frequency and sophistication.

From Figure 3–3 it is apparent that an organization's current work force provides the base from which estimates of future flows and availabilities are made. Judgmental analyses require extensive data about each employee, including name, job title, performance rating, promotability rating, years of service, years on present job, geographic location, previous jobs held, training programs attended, special skills possessed, and career interests. Some statistical analyses begin with nothing more than a simple count of people in each job category. Others additionally include a record of certain employee characteristics (e.g., age or length of service) that are expected to be related to one or more flow rates (e.g., retirements or resignations).

Judgmental analyses of flows and availabilities may be done using executive reviews, replacement analysis, or vacancy analysis. *Executive reviews* tend to focus on spe-

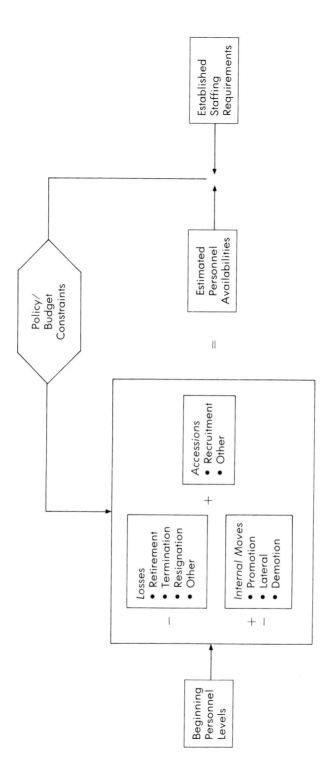

FIGURE 3-3

Model of the Process Used to Establish Personnel Flows and Availabilities

cial groups of employees, particularly those at the very highest levels and those judged to have the potential to reach these levels. These reviews are carried out through one or more meetings at which executives thoroughly discuss each person under review to determine which are likely to (or should) leave the organization, be promoted, or be reassigned during the planning period. Determinations are made on the basis of the data previously mentioned: performance, long-term potential, career aspirations, and the like. As the deliberations proceed, anticipated moves (flows) emerge and judgments can be made concerning the overall adequacy of current personnel in light of established needs. Executive review procedures have been described by Saklad (1976) and Dyer, Shafer, and Regan (1980).

Replacement analysis is similar to the executive review procedures except that the "technology" tends to be more formal and greater numbers of employees may be involved. It begins with the development of replacement charts showing for each job under consideration the incumbent and one or more replacements who could fill the job should it become vacant. By examining replacement charts, managers can systematically determine likely vacancies resulting from retirements, terminations, and so forth, and plan out desired internal moves. They also can assess the general condition of the organization in terms of such indices as the percentage of jobs with replacements who are ready to move now, the ratio of replacements to incumbents, and the number of jobs that have no backups. Replacement analysis is widespread, and its use is well described by Frantzreb (1977a).

Executive reviews and, especially, replacement analysis often are conducted with no explicit consideration given to changes in staffing needs. Further, they provide only qualitative information concerning future personnel flows. A judgmental method designed to overcome these shortcomings is *vacancy analysis.* Here, beginning staff levels are arrayed by job categories (states), and from these numbers are subtracted anticipated losses to yield what is called effective supply. Effective supply is matched against established staffing needs to yield a preliminary estimate of anticipated vacancies. Each vacancy is then considered to determine whether it is likely to be filled internally and, if so, from which job categories. The internal adjustments having been made, the remaining vacancies are calculated and judgments are made as to whether these will be filled from other units within the company or from outside. For an example of vacancy analysis, see Dyer, Shafer, and Regan (1980).

Statistical techniques for forecasting and/or analyzing future personnel flows and availabilities include Markov analysis, simulation, renewal analysis, and goal programming. These are summarized in Table 3-3.

Markov analysis is used to track past patterns of personnel movements and to project these patterns into the future. The theoretical and mathematical underpinnings of Markov analysis are complex (Bartholomew and Forbes, 1979), but it is one of the more straightforward statistical techniques to use (Niehaus, 1979).

Markov analysis begins with the development of a transition matrix that models the unit or employee group under consideration, as shown in part A of Figure 3-4. The percentages represent average rates of historical movements between job categories (states) from one period to another (often one year and the next). In this case, a five-year historical analysis revealed, for example, that in any given year about 10 percent of the middle managers moved to top management, while 80 percent stayed in middle management,

TABLE 3–3
Statistical Techniques Used to Establish Future Human Resource Flows and Availabilities

Name	Description
(1) Markov Analysis	Projects future flows to obtain availability estimates through a straightforward application of historical transition rates (see Figure 3–4). Historical transition rates are derived from analyses of personnel data concerning losses, promotions, transfers, demotions, and, perhaps, recruitment. See Vroom and MacCrimmon (1968), Forbes (1971), Heneman and Sandver (1977).
(2) Simulation (based on Markov Analysis)	Alternative (rather than historical) flows are examined for effects on future human resource availabilities. Alternative flows reflect the anticipated results of policy or program changes concerning voluntary and involuntary turnover, retirement, promotion, etc. See Gillespie, Leininger, and Kahalas (1976), and Milkovich and Krzystofiak (1979).
(3) Renewal Analysis	Estimates future flows and availabilities by calculating: (1) vacancies as created by organizational growth, personnel losses, and internal movements out of states, and (2) the results of decision rules governing the filling of vacancies. Alternative models may assess the effects of changes in growth estimates, turnover, promotions, or decision rules. See Bartholomew and Forbes (1979).
(4) Goal Programming	Optimizes goals—in this case a desired staffing pattern—given a set of constraints concerning such things as the upper limits on flows, the percentage of new recruits permitted in each state, and total salary budgets. See Patz (1970), and Niehaus (1979).

5 percent were demoted to lower management, and 5 percent left the unit. Using these data, future personnel flows can be projected by multiplying the staffing levels at the beginning of the planning period by the computed probabilities, and future availabilities determined by summing the columns.

An example involving a one-period projection is shown in part B of Figure 3–4. Projections made in this way—here 100, 190, and 490 for top, middle, and lower management, respectively—can be compared with established staffing requirements and anticipated shortages and surpluses, and their causes noted. Assuming no growth or contraction, the present analysis shows parity at the top, and shortages of 10 and 110 people at the middle and lower levels, respectively. From these data, changes in flow rates that might help match availabilities with needs can be suggested. For example, to fill the anticipated shortage of middle managers, the organization might plan to recruit ten people from outside, or to increase slightly (to 7 percent) the proportion of lower-level managers to be promoted and to offset the effects of this by recruiting more heavily at the lower level.

Markov analysis has long been discussed as a method of estimating personnel availabilities (Vroom and MacCrimmon, 1968; Rowland and Sovereign, 1969). A number

(A)

	M₁	M₂	M₃	Exit
Top Management (M₁)	.80			.20
Middle Management (M₂)	.10	.80	.05	.05
Lower Management (M₃)		.05	.80	.15

(B)

	Beginning Personnel Levels	M₁	M₂	M₃	Exit
Top Management (M₁)	100	80			20
Middle Management (M₂)	200	20	160	10	10
Lower Management (M₃)	600		30	480	90
Forecasted Availabilities		100	190	490	

FIGURE 3-4
Elements of a Markov Analysis

of authors, however, have suggested that its virtues have been oversold (Heneman and Sandver, 1977; Niehaus, 1979). Research into the applicability and accuracy of Markov analyses is not extensive, and the results so far are mixed (c.f., Forbes, 1971; Mahoney and Milkovich, 1971; Gillespie, Leininger, and Kahalas, 1976; Ledvinka and LaForge, 1978).

As described, Markov analysis leaves to the analyst or decision-maker the task of judgmentally generating possible alternative flows that might match personnel availabilities with established staffing needs. A straightforward extension, however, permits this to be done statistically, and for the options to be tested using computer *simulation* techniques.

Such techniques, which are usually based on Markov analysis, represent a step away from forecasting *per se* and into decision making and *a priori* control. Various possible flows are specified and the expected numbers of employees in the various states are calculated. The analysis may be repeated several times until desired staffing levels are realized. Mass (1978) provided an interesting discussion of simulations and some hypothetical results by testing the cumulative effects of differing strategies of recruitment and flows into and out of training programs. Gillespie, Leininger, and Kahalas (1976) reported an application in a certified public accounting firm.

By far the greatest use of simulation to date, however, has been in the specialized area of affirmative action planning. Here affirmative action goals are analogous to established staffing levels in the more general case. Various combinations of flow shares for minorities and women are modeled to determine which (if any) are likely to yield full utilization of these groups (Churchill and Shank, 1976; Ledvinka and LaForge, 1978; Chew and Justice, 1979; Milkovich and Krzystofiak, 1979).

As described, simulations do not consider costs. An analysis may yield two or more sets of flow rates that will meet staffing needs, but without cost data there are no reasonable grounds for choosing one over another. Recently, Ward and Eastman (1979) have described a technique used by Western Electric to cost out various flow options, and it is reasonable to expect that future simulations may be extended to include such estimates.

Markov analysis, and simulations based on it, are known as supply-push models because promotions and other internal movements are estimated by applying historical transition rates in various job categories without considering whether vacancies exist in other job categories, or whether individuals are ready to move. Since these features do not reflect reality in many cases, some researchers have begun to experiment with renewal, or demand-pull, analysis.

Renewal analysis, like vacancy analysis, is driven by job vacancies. Vacancies are created by organizational growth, personnel losses, and internal movements out of various job categories. Growth (or shrinkage) is factored in by setting job category sizes equal to established staffing requirements. Then, a computer program is used to: (1) remove from each job category individuals expected to be lost, (2) fill vacancies at the top according to established rules, (3) repeat (1) and (2) for the next category down, and so forth until all vacancies are eliminated (or it becomes obvious that they cannot be). While simple conceptually, renewal analysis is theoretically and mathematically complex (Bartholomew and Forbes, 1979). Most of the basic work on it has been done in Great Britain, and Bowey (1977) provides a brief review of the research. An application, installed at the Bank of America, is described by Ceriello and Frantzreb (1975).

The success of renewal analysis depends in large part on the accuracy of estimated loss rates. Considerable research has been conducted, again mostly in Great Britain, to develop improved methods of projecting losses, and especially voluntary turnover (Bowey, 1977; Clark and Thurston, 1977; Bartholomew and Forbes, 1979). Most such studies treat length of service as a key independent variable (c.f., Uyar, 1972).

Goal programming, the fourth statistical technique, optimizes one or more goals (called objective functions) subject to a series of linear constraints. The usual goal is to meet established staffing requirements as closely as possible (i.e., to minimize the deviations between requirements and estimated personnel availabilities). Another possible goal is to minimize staffing costs. Typical constraints include upper limits on the percent of flows from each job category, upper limits on the number of new recruits permitted in each category, and total salary budgets. Usually, loss and some flow rates (up to established limits) are given, and are incorporated in the form of embedded transition matrices (see Niehaus, 1979). Once goals are established and constraints are set, the resulting linear equations are solved simultaneously, yielding an optimal set of promotion, transfer, demotion, recruitment, and/or layoff rates. Straightforward examples of goal programming are provided by Patz (1970) and Niehaus (1979). Applications of the technique to affirmative action planning problems can be found in Kahalas and Key (1974), Flast (1977), and Niehaus (1979).

Goal programming is a powerful and flexible technique. One great advantage is its ability to "look ahead" and calculate a set of flows in earlier time periods that will smooth out the effects of significant events (e.g., a steep drop in staffing requirements) in later periods. Markov and renewal analyses lack this capability. Goal programming also can be used to play "what if" games by altering goals and/or constraints in various runs. Obviously, however, the technique is mathematically complex. In one apparently straightforward application, the analysis involved 1,150 constraints and 1,275 variables (Draper and Merchant, 1978).

Although goal programming is particularly complex, all statistical methods of estimating personnel flows and availabilities involve significant data manipulations that may be feasible only with the aid of computers. Fortunately, personnel departments are increasingly gaining access to, and expertise with, computers, and new software programs are appearing regularly. Almost certainly the use of statistical modeling of the sort discussed in this section will expand considerably in the next few years.

Whether done judgmentally or statistically, or by using a combination of the two, analyses of future personnel flows and availabilities in the context of staffing requirements ultimately result in objectives that drive the second phase of the HRP process. Sample objectives include the following:

1. Controlling the flow rates decided upon, including retirements, terminations, layoffs, resignations, transfers, promotions, lateral movements, demotions, and inflows through recruitment
2. Controlling the flow shares of women and minorities (to meet affirmative action goals and timetables)
3. Meeting desired replacement ratios (i.e., number of ready replacements per position)

PLANNING PERSONNEL PROGRAMS

Objectives are intended to spur action. Programming is the name given to the process of translating HRP objectives into action plans. Responsibility for programming is generally shared between personnel specialists and line managers. The former typically conduct the preliminary analyses, while the latter provide additional insights and enhance acceptance of the decisions arrived at (c.f., Bell, 1974; Martin, 1978). The recommendations of staff and line managers may have to be taken to top management for approval prior to implementation.

Programming is the most critical, yet the least well developed, phase of the HRP process. The lack of development stems from a curious paradox: organizations continuously program (e.g., when budgeting and problem solving), but personnel scholars have tended to address the issues involved in programming only peripherally. Milkovich and Mahoney (1976) are an exception to this generalization. They have adapted the normative decision-making literature (MacCrimmon and Taylor, 1976) to the programming process, and their framework is used here. Specifically, discussion is focused on the following key elements (see Figure 3–1):

1. The generation of alternative programs that might be used to meet each of the established objectives
2. The assessment of the various alternatives generated based upon anticipated benefits and costs and feasibility analyses

3. A decision to pursue various programs judged to be mutually reinforcing and capable of being implemented during the planning period

Generating Alternative Programs

The generation of alternatives has not been widely discussed in either the decision making (Alexander, 1979) or the HRP literatures. Preliminary studies, however, suggest a clear dichotomy between the approach that is generally advocated and the one that is usually used. Those who approach the subject normatively encourage decision-makers to generate as many alternatives as is feasible, given the problem at hand. In programming, this would mean that several personnel programs would be considered potentially equivalent or complementary options for meeting each HRP objective (Milkovich and Mahoney, 1976; Martin, 1978).

At least two studies have shown, however, that the usual practice is to restrict the search for options, either by not considering ones that are much different from those previously tried, or by eliminating many possible alternatives through early, informal evaluation (Mintzberg, Raisinghani, and Theoret, 1976; Alexander, 1979). In HRP, it appears that heavy reliance is placed on past experience, practices in other organizations, or prepackaged approaches offered by consulting firms (Walker, 1978, 1980).

If the normative approach generally yields superior results, it becomes important to determine how a greater number of alternative programs can be generated in practice. Several approaches have been considered. One is to involve additional people through such techniques as brainstorming or problem-solving groups. A second approach is to obtain options from the published literature; for example, useful lists of program options to deal with employee shortages and surpluses have been provided by Martin (1978) and Ward and Eastman (1979). A third approach is to use a model or heuristic to guide the search process.

Milkovich and Mahoney (1976) advocated the latter approach, as did Alexander (1979) who pointed out that ". . . models . . . may be a repertoire of available solutions. Such models can include extra-organizational experience or applications, and theoretical knowledge, or they can enable the design of alternatives using or modifying given (often unique) or ready-made solutions'' (p. 388). Most useful in the generation of alternative personnel programs are models that specify: (1) the key factors that affect established objectives, and (2) the ways in which various personnel programs affect these key factors (Milkovich and Mahoney, 1976, 1978).

Unfortunately, personnel theory and research have thus far not progressed to a point that would permit building a fully explicated model of the type needed, although one such effort has been previously discussed (see Figure 3–1 and Dyer, 1980). That model suggests that the major objectives outlined earlier are primarily affected by the extent to which employees join, stay with, and move around in the organization, and the extent to which they effectively perform. The model further suggests that each of these four factors is determined by employee ability and motivation.

Ability to join, stay, and move, in turn, is affected by the availability of employees as ''candidates'' and by the choices that the organization makes among available candi-

dates. For example, employees can be promoted to a new job only if they are first identified as promotable and then are chosen as the ones who will advance. Ability to be an
effective performer is affected by somewhat different factors: employees skills (vis-á-vis
job requirements) and the degree of understanding employees have about the behaviors
and/or results that are expected.

Figure 3–1 also suggests that employees' motivations to join, stay, move, and perform effectively are important. Motivation is affected by the rewards available and by
employees' perceptions of: (1) the attainability of the behavior(s) in question, and (2)
the attractiveness and the attainability of the rewards offered. (See Mitchell's further
discussion of this topic in Chapter 10 of this book.) To continue the earlier example,
employees are motivated to be promoted to new jobs when they feel that: (1) there is
some chance that the promotion can be obtained, and (2) the inducements are attractive
and will be forthcoming if the promotion is in fact received.

Organizations use a wide variety of personnel programs to identify employees as
available or unavailable to join, stay, or move; choose wisely among those identified as
available; enhance the match between employee skills and established job requirements; clarify job expectations; offer rewards consistent with desired behaviors; and influence employee perceptions of the attainability of organizationally desired behaviors
and of the desirability and attainability of the rewards offered. Figure 3–1 lists the most
common of these programs; none will be unfamiliar to students of personnel management.

Individuals responsible for generating alternative personnel programs can gain
guidance from general models of personnel (Dyer, 1980), and the more "micro" theoretical literature. Examples of the latter include March and Simon (1958) on voluntary
turnover; Campbell and Pritchard (1976) on the motivation to join, stay, and perform;
and, working from the program side, Mahoney (1979) on compensation and its effects
on the decision to join, stay, and perform. Further guidance is available in the empirical
literature, in many personnel management texts (c.f., Heneman et al., 1980), and in
the subsequent chapters of this book.

Assessing Alternative Programs

Once a list of possible personnel programs for each HRP objective has been built,
the next task is to narrow the list retaining the one(s) offering the greatest possibility
of success within existing constraints. Conceptually, the task resembles a classic goal-
programming problem: each objective is specified, constraints are delineated, and a
solution that will meet the objective without violating the constraints is generated. In
practice, the analysis is complicated in many cases because neither the objectives nor
the constraints can be easily quantified. Further, at this point the classic optimize-
satisfice dilemma (March and Simon, 1958) is encountered. Is it necessary or desirable to pursue optimal programs, or is it enough to identify those that meet some
standard of acceptability? Many observers (c.f., Murray and Dimick, 1978) have suggested that satisficing is the best that can be achieved because of the ambiguities inherent in personnel work.

Little systematic evidence is available concerning the criteria used by organizations to assess alternative programs. Two views seem to prevail in the literature. The first focuses on the rational aspects of decision making, emphasizing such criteria as cost effectiveness, technical feasibility, and ease of program implementation (Cheek, 1973). The second focuses on the forces inhibiting rationality (e.g., the lack of cost effectiveness data) and talks instead of affordability; pressures from employees, labor unions, regulatory agencies (e.g., EEOC, OFCCP, OSHA); and managerial norms and values (c.f., Murray and Dimick, 1978).

Cost effectiveness is at once an appealing and a problematic criterion. Few organizations would deny the desirability of favorable benefit-cost ratios, but many apparently put little effort into the types of research necessary to make such analyses a reality. Greater attention has been paid to costs than to benefits (Murray and Dimick, 1978). Researchers have demonstrated the use of comparative cost analyses in program selection (c.f., Sands, 1973; Davis and Pinto, 1975), and many organizations accumulate cost data through budgeting exercises and from accounting records. Program benefits, on the other hand, remain elusive since they are difficult to specify, let alone quantify.

Benefits specification is hampered by the lack of models or research linking program activities with outcomes. This problem was mentioned earlier in connection with the generation of program alternatives. At present, only a small number of a program's potential benefits may be known, although over time theoretical and empirical advances, as well as accumulated experience, should improve this situation.

An early development with respect to benefits specification was Weber's (1971) use of theory and research to build a computerized behavioral model to test the effects of recruiting, promotion, and salary decisions on a variety of outcomes, including voluntary turnover, job performance, and salary costs. A more recent development is the work of Huber, Ullman, and Leifer (1979), who used organizational experience to empirically link variations in program characteristics to variations in organizational outcomes. (While these authors treated structural characteristics as independent variables, the methodology appears readily adaptable to the study of personnel programs.)

A promising approach to the quantification of program benefits has been offered by Cheek (1973), who suggested that an estimate be made of each benefit's probable occurrence and the probable dollar effect (Winter and Rowland, 1980). These estimates may be derived from past experience, pilot programs, or from the collective judgments of personnel specialists, financial analysts, and line managers.

Just as it is important to know more about the criteria that personnel people use in assessing program alternatives, so, too, is it important to discover how the criteria are applied in decision making. Most discussions of this issue tend to be prescriptive. Martin (1978), for example, outlined the key issues he feels managers should address. And Cheek (1973) described an evaluation system in which each program is first rated as either high, medium, or low on each of several criteria (including, as mentioned earlier, cost effectiveness, technical feasibility, and ease of implementation). Following this, a heuristic is used to combine these ratings to yield an assessment of the program's overall desirability. When all programs have been rated in this manner, they are ranked on a program priorities schedule. Cheek's (1973) methodology would appear to offer advantages over less well-specified approaches, although this hypothesis has yet to be tested.

Developing a Strategy and Writing Action Plans

At this point in programming, two tasks remain. One is to combine the previously selected programs into an integrated strategy; the other is to codify responsibilities in the form of action plans.

The issue in strategy formulation is to attain as many objectives as possible within existing constraints (money, people, managerial tolerance, political realities, legislation, etc.). Ideally, there should be no important objective without a program, no program without an important objective, and all programs should mesh into an integrated, compatible whole. Almost certainly this must be a judgmental, rather than a statistical, process. Subjectivity is involved in setting priorities and meshing programs. Further, much of the decision making at this point will be done by top management, which may introduce into the picture a broader set of considerations, constraints, and values. A decision tool that may be useful at this juncture is a program by objectives matrix (Huber et al., 1979).

Once a programming strategy is adopted, it may be reduced to a set of action plans (Martin, 1978). Action plans are documents that specify the following for a given period: (1) objectives, (2) programs or actions planned, (3) time frames and deadlines, (4) person(s) responsible for program or action implementation, and (5) resources (money, staff, facilities, data) to be made available.

The use of action plans has been pioneered by organization development (OD) specialists, and is probably uncommon in HRP or in the personnel management field more generally. Nonetheless, it would appear to be a useful process to help assure that planned programs are indeed taken seriously. At a minimum, action plans should prove useful to the various personnel functions as they set out to plan the details of their own specialized activities. They also may help in the process of evaluation and control.

Summary

Milkovich and Mahoney (1976) have called programming the "weakest link" in the HRP process. Clearly, the issues involved are less sharply focused than in the objective-setting phase, and the methods and techniques are less well advanced.

Further, the process described is normative; it is not known how many, if any, organizations follow the steps outlined, nor whether it would be advantageous to do so. Some authors reject the notion of sequential phasing in decision making (MacCrimmon and Taylor, 1976). And research on organizational policy making (none in personnel) shows a tendency to intermingle phases, particularly the generation and assessment of alternatives (Mintzberg, Raisinghani, and Theoret, 1976). Decision-makers, it appears, are likely to search for and assess options simultaneously, which at once suppresses the number of options considered and the sophistication of the assessment made. Thus, rather than following the sequence shown in Figure 3–1, it may be that programming involves little more than creeping incrementalism (Lindblom, 1959). Or it may be an even more complex process than is suggested in Figure 3–1, consisting instead of a multistage, iterative process, involving progressively deepening investigations of alternatives (Mintzberg, Raisinghani, and Theoret, 1976).

Either way, it is unlikely that programming will ever be a highly rationalized process. Further, to some extent the results are always bound to be less than perfect—goals will change, theory will remain inadequate, measures and data will be missing or contaminated with error, and decision-makers will be bounded in their rationality (Huber, Ullman, and Leifer, 1979). Nonetheless, the *raison d'etre* of HRP is to move the personnel function to a more proactive, integrative posture. Thus, it is essential to develop better theory and research concerning key linkages between programs and their results and to devise improved heuristics or decision aids to guide program choice, as well as to direct continuing efforts toward the improvement of the decision-making process.

EVALUATION AND CONTROL

Evaluation and control constitute the third phase of the HRP process (see Figure 3–2). Typically, evaluation and control are performed by the personnel department with human resource planners taking responsibility for monitoring the various processes and for feeding back the results to key decision-makers on a timely basis.

As Walker (1974) suggests, the nature of evaluation and control should match the degree of sophistication in the rest of the HRP process. In fledgling applications, evaluation may be qualitative rather than quantitative, with very little emphasis placed on control.

Franztreb (1977b) and Walker (1974) suggest that under these circumstances, planners should attempt to assess:

1. The extent to which they are tuned into the organization's personnel problems and opportunities and the extent to which their priorities are sound
2. The quality of their working relationships with the personnel and financial specialists and line managers who supply their data and use HRP results
3. The quality of the communications that flow between the parties involved
4. The extent to which forecasts, plans, and recommendations are being heeded by organizational decision-makers
5. The perceived value of HRP among various constituents

More formal or advanced evaluation and control procedures involve: (1) a set of standards, (2) means of comparing results against the standards and for determining the causes of observed deviations, and (3) channels through which deviations and their causes can be communicated and corrective action set in motion (Carlson, 1976). In

HRP, the standards are set forth in the form of HRP objectives and program action plans. Key comparisons include the following:

1. Actual staffing levels against established staffing requirements
2. Productivity levels against established goals
3. Actual personnel flow rates against desired rates
4. Programs implemented against action plans
5. Program results against expected outcomes (e.g., improved applicant flows, reduced quit rates, improved replacement ratios)
6. Labor and program costs against budgets
7. Ratios of program results (benefits) to program costs

Recipients of feedback data might include top management, line managers, personnel managers and specialists, and the human resource planners themselves. Top management or line managers might be apprised of over- or understaffing. Such deviations may be acceptable because of changing business requirements, but an effective evaluation and control procedure would raise and attempt to encourage a discussion of the issue. Personnel managers might be apprised of the failure to implement scheduled personnel programs or the failure of implemented programs to attain desired results within established budgets. Human resource planners could use evaluation data to help in future efforts to establish staffing requirements, model personnel flows, and plan personnel programs. Benefit-cost analyses, for example, would be beneficial in future rounds of programming.

Anecdotal evidence suggests that human resource planners have only recently begun to evaluate their work (Frantzreb, 1977b). Ackerman (1979) describes the use of a line management committee structure for this purpose, and Dyer, Shafer, and Regan (1980) outline a relatively decentralized approach. In the latter case, quarterly data are collected on a number of quantitative and qualitative indicators, including staffing levels, loss rates, interdivisional transfer rates, intradivisional movement rates, recruiting rates, women and minority utilization and flow rates, and performance problems. In quarterly reviews, the data are compared with preestablished standards, and deviations are either declared acceptable or corrections are planned.

Mahoney and Milkovich (1972) have demonstrated the use of Markov analysis in evaluation and control. Using data covering several years, these authors compared actual personnel flows in three organizations with the flows that might be expected based on established personnel policies and labor union agreements. In all three cases, significant deviations from expectations were observed. A natural follow-up to this study would be to determine the extent to which the deviations observed resulted in favorable or unfavorable effects on such HRP objectives as meeting staffing requirements and productivity targets, and controlling labor costs.

Future advances in the design and implementation of evaluation and control procedures will no doubt come through the systematic application of control (Lawler, 1976) and communications (Porter and Roberts, 1976) theories. Realistically, however, developments in this area probably must await more extensive applications in the other phases of the HRP process.

ORGANIZING AND MANAGING HUMAN RESOURCE PLANNING

A paucity of information precludes an extended discussion of the issues involved in organizing and managing HRP. Nonetheless, experience and some literature do suggest three important areas for consideration: (1) fitting HRP to the organization, (2) introducing and sustaining HRP, and (3) designing data systems support.

Fitting HRP to the Organization

Although every HRP application can be conceptualized in terms of the model shown in Figure 3-2, applications in practice vary in terms of: (1) results expected; (2) horizon, scope, and frequency; (3) phase emphasized (e.g., staffing requirements, personnel flows and availabilities, personnel programs, evaluation and control); and (4) techniques used. A major challenge is to blend together the optimal combination in each case.

So far, few attempts have been made to codify the key variables involved, to investigate the compatibility of components and techniques, or to identify matches between key variables and process alternatives. Some guidance, however, is provided by Walker (1974), who lists such key variables as objectives, business planning horizon, number of employees, geographic dispersion, stage of organizational development, technology, the experience of key executives, and the nature of the economic, social, and political environment. Walker then goes on to illustrate four "stages" of HRP, ranging from formative to futuristic, and to match HRP stages with organizational conditions. As presented, Walker's approach is relatively abstract. Nevertheless, human resource planners must continue to grapple with the issue of fit and future conceptual work, research and experience almost certainly will yield data to fill in the details.

Ideally, it eventually will be possible to specify and diagnose the key variables in any given situation and to design a HRP effort that will fit, giving full weight to results desired, as well as to compatibility of the various phases and techniques.

Introducing and Sustaining HRP

Accumulating evidence suggests that HRP efforts are difficult to introduce and sustain (c.f., Wikstrom, 1971; Bell, 1974; Bright, 1976; Frantzreb, 1979b). Such efforts typically represent a major organizational change, and, unless the change process is well-managed, difficulties can arise. A vast literature exists on the management of organizational change through organization development (OD), and some attempts have been made to apply this material to HRP (c.f., Patten, 1978; Burack and Mathys, 1979).

In practice, HRP is partly technical and partly political (Hills, 1978). Several constituencies—top management, line management, personnel people—must be served, and it is helpful to have license if not support from them all. One suggestion is to assure that organizational needs, and not merely the planners' needs, are being met. Another is to focus on important rather than trivial issues. Generally, however, planners are advised to begin with manageable projects, perhaps with pilot programs, and build visible successes that can serve as springboards for escalation (Bell, 1974; Bright, 1978). This is sometimes referred to as a strategy of opportunism.

Of course, opportunism must be tempered with caution. Frantzreb (1979) discusses a fascinating case in which division personnel managers attempted to surreptitiously use corporate human resource planners to gain control over regional hiring quotas. When the regional managers resisted, the planners were caught in the middle at considerable expense to their credibility.

Planners often are advised to develop close ties with financial and operations planners, and to involve line managers in planning as early and as frequently as they can (c.f., Bright, 1978; Frantzreb, 1979a). Bell (1974) provided a discussion guide that can be used to fashion this involvement during the early stages of a planning process. Many writers advise that the support of top management is an absolute "must." Dyer et al. (forthcoming), however, present a case in which planning was started with minimal participation by line managers and with no attempt having been made to gain support from the top. The strategy in this situation was to minimize the visibility of the planning process *per se,* relying instead on the usefulness of the resulting data to eventually foster acceptance and generate commitment and support.

Designing Data Systems

HRP creates a seemingly insatiable demand for data. And, indeed, data deficiencies are often cited as the most serious impediments to effective HRP. Frantzreb (1979c), for example, described a situation in which data problems caused a project to extend to twice the estimated time of completion and to 150 percent of the estimated cost.

One problem is access. Some of the data required by personnel planners (e.g., past or forecasted sales or production levels) are not personnel data and may not be readily available. Further, planners may not control personnel data systems, and thus their data requests may not receive high priority. A second problem concerns data format. Personnel records typically are individualized. While this is adequate for the more judgmental methods of estimating personnel flows and availabilities, it can cause difficulties for users of statistically-oriented techniques. Individualized personnel records may not be easily translatable into summary statistics concerning historical or even present flow rates, especially if these records are not computerized.

Data deficiencies create a planning dilemma. If encountered, is it preferable to begin planning or to wait until the data situation can be improved? The former option is risky since the results may be highly inaccurate, but the latter choice may lead to interminable delays. While no definitive resolution can be offered, many authors (c.f., Bell, 1974) suggest that planning should begin as soon as the data base is even marginally adequate. Management may not tolerate the building of elaborate data systems with no obvious application. HRP, however, tends to create a strong data demand that makes needed improvements in data systems particularly apparent.

A complete discussion of personnel data systems is beyond the scope of this chapter. A general discussion of the subject can be found in Bassett (1976). From a planning perspective, Walker (1974) and Burack and Mathys (1979) discussed possible evolutionary steps that data systems may follow. Bell (1974) modeled a fully developed data system, and Burack and Mathys (1979) provided a checklist of key data inputs and three case studies of data system development. MacCrimmon (1971) made an explicit linkage between various types of HRP applications and corresponding data needs, and Niehaus (1979) presented an excellent discussion of computerized data support systems.

TOWARD THE FUTURE

As an emerging area, HRP obviously is an easy target for criticism, as well as a fruitful area for significant contributions in the years ahead. Many criticisms and suggestions for further work have been indicated or implied throughout this chapter. What follows is a more explicit elaboration of particularly pressing issues.

1. An easy and early step toward the demystification and clarification of HRP would be taken by adopting the view that it is a broad-based process whose major contribution is to direct and integrate personnel programs toward the accomplishment of organizational goals. Confusion is engendered when HRP is treated as synonymous with staffing planning or, worse, defined in terms of a given method or technique (e.g., Markov analysis or replacement planning).
2. Conceptual models and heuristic devices are needed to facilitate advancement in HRP research and practice. Models of the overall process abound, and more are unnecessary. Helpful, however, would be:
   a. Models of the various components of the objective-setting phase, with special emphasis on the two key components: staffing needs and personnel flows and availabilities.
   b. Further specification of conceptual systems of personnel, with special emphasis on the identification of important personnel programs, intervening variables, outcomes, and environmental influences, and the relationships among these variables. These would aid immeasurably in program planning.
   c. Heuristic devices to specify the organizational variables that are important to the success or failure of HRP and the most appropriate: (1) form (in terms of horizon, scope, and frequency), (2) phase emphasis, and (3) methods and techniques associated with each—in short, models addressed to the issue of "fit."
3. Research is needed to test the usefulness of the various HRP methods and techniques, both statistical and judgmental, with special emphasis on external, as well as internal, validity. Political issues involved in getting various methods and techniques adopted should be addressed, as well as various change strategies that might help to overcome problems at the implementation stage.
4. Research also is needed to clarify and "model" the decision strategies and rules applied by managers when using judgmental methods and techniques to establish staffing requirements and personnel flows and availabilities, and when

generating and deciding among alternative programs. The decision-making literature may prove helpful here.

5. The determinants (or at least correlates) of flow rates are yet another area in need of serious study. Some progress has been made with respect to voluntary turnover, but not other flows. An intriguing issue concerns the degree and nature of interactions among flow rates; what, for example, are the implications of reducing turnover by 20 percent, or slowing down promotion rates?

6. Some serious attention needs to be paid to evaluation and control. One important issue concerns standards: What are acceptable accession, loss, and movement rates, and performance levels? Another concerns evaluation methodologies: To what extent are benefit-cost analyses applicable? When should other standards be applied? A third issue concerns feedback: What are the most effective and efficient means of communicating HRP results? Control and communications theory should direct this research.

7. Finally, the issue arises as to the personnel activities that can and cannot be planned and budgeted using HRP. And, by implication, the need exists to address the planning and budgeting of residual activities in some other way.

SUMMARY AND CONCLUSION

HRP is an emerging activity that shows considerable promise as a means of making the practice of personnel management more proactive, integrative, and effective in contributing to organizational goals. HRP comes in many forms; essentially, however, any application can be viewed as a process involving three phases: (1) setting HRP objectives, (2) planning personnel programs, and (3) providing for evaluation and control.

Objectives are set by first establishing staffing needs, and then by estimating and reconciling or directly establishing personnel flows that will match personnel availabilities with established staffing needs. Objectives emerge from the established staffing requirements, the desired flow rates, and the assumptions that were made throughout the process.

The heart of the HRP process involves the planning of personnel programs to meet the objectives set. This phase involves the following aspects: generating alternative programs, assessing and deciding among these programs, combining programs into an integrated strategy, and writing action plans.

Following the implementation of action plans, the entire process and its results are evaluated and the results are used to recalibrate the present effort and to guide future attempts at HRP.

HRP has been the subject of some conceptual and empirical work, and the number of applications appears to be increasing dramatically. At this point, however, much remains to be done to assure that HRP achieves a meaningful identity and its full potential as a legitimate and useful contributor to the practice of personnel management.

Discussion Questions

1. Explain the purposes of human resource planning (HRP). What could a company do with a fully functional HRP process that it could not do otherwise?

2. Describe the three major phases of HRP. Explain the relationships among them.

3. Define human resource requirements and human resource availabilities. Explain how they are related.

4. List three HRP objectives. Develop program options for each and discuss the major factors that should be considered in selecting among the program options.

5. The installation of HRP is a major organizational change. Do you agree or disagree? What are the implications of your position on this matter for human resource planners?

CHAPTER FOUR

JOB ANALYSIS

C. Paul Sparks

C. Paul Sparks is Personnel Research Coordinator for the Exxon Company, U.S.A. He received his B.S. and M.A. degrees from Ohio State University and did additional graduate work at Tulane University. After serving as Assistant Chief of Personnel Research in the U.S. Army's Adjutant Generals Office, he joined the consulting firm of Richardson, Bellows, Henry, & Co., and eventually rose to the presidency of this firm. Mr. Sparks is a Fellow and Past President of the Industrial and Organizational Division of the American Psychological Association and is currently a member of its Committee on Tests and Assessments. Mr. Sparks is also an Adjunct Professor of Psychology at the University of Houston and a licensed psychologist in the state of Texas.

Job analysis is the process of determining the characteristics of an area of work according to a prescribed set of dimensions. A job analysis is *not* a job description, although it may lead to a job description. A job analysis is *not* a job evaluation, although it may provide data for such an evaluation. The end product of the analysis of a job is a set of data that can be interpreted according to some prescribed classification matrix. This matrix may be one described in relevant literature, or it may be one developed by the analyst or researcher. The choice will most likely depend on the objectives of the job analysis.

All methods of job analysis begin with a set of *job descriptors*, the units of analysis. These will determine in large part the uses to which the end product can be put. The smaller the unit of analysis, the greater is the opportunity to differentiate among jobs. The larger the unit, the easier is the task of developing job families. The smallest unit for descriptive purposes is the *task*, a specific statement of what the individual does; e.g., answers the telephone. One should note that this task description does not imply any purpose nor suggest use of any skills or knowledges other than those required to answer the telephone. The value of such a limiting description might have been challenged some years ago. In today's equal employment and affirmative action climate, this simple task might make a large difference in the ability of a deaf person or a language-handicapped person or a motor-impaired person to handle the job.

The next step above the task is the *position*. A position is a group of tasks performed by the same person. Some jobs have many persons who perform identical tasks in identical settings; e.g., soldering fittings in an assembly plant. However, many positions with the same job title and with incumbents who are considered interchangeable have similar but not identical tasks. Where these positions are sufficiently similar they are said to form a *job*. A group of similar jobs is said to form an *occupation*. The reader is referred to Shartle (1959) for a more detailed description of these terms. Their use within the framework of today's job analysis techniques and systems will be discussed later in this chapter.

A great deal has been written on the subject of job analysis. Unfortunately, this literature is extremely fragmented. The sources in which this literature appears range from journal articles likely to be found in most university libraries to private publications of agencies and institutes. These latter may be available if one knows what to ask for or where to make the request. The disciplines and specialties involved with job analysis are many, including psychology, education, industrial engineering, management, economics, labor relations, and occupational medicine. Zerga (1943) published a bibliography of 401 items covering the period 1911 to 1941, inclusive. His compilation was apparently made with little critical evaluation. Sources ranged from industrial publications to refereed journals. Zerga's frame of reference was essentially the same as that of this chapter, with due allowance for technical, social, and political developments since 1943. He cites Uhrbrock's (1934) definition as "very satisfactory" and then quotes him as follows: "Job analysis is a 'method' of gathering pertinent facts about a worker and his work. The method to be used varies, depending upon the objective of the study. Different sources are consulted, and different records result, depending upon whether one is using job analysis to devise a training program, develop a safety plan, prepare employment specifications, or revise a wage payment plan" (p. 249).

Prien and Ronan (1971) published a review of research findings on job analysis. It is an extremely well organized article and contains a large number of references from the 1950s and 1960s. They state, "The primary references report research designed to order and structure the domain of work using various techniques and focusing on different and specific job description formulae" (p. 372). Prien and Ronan specifically excluded studies "primarily of concern to the engineering psychologists, the industrial engineer or focused primarily on such topics as job evaluation, motivation, work organization or job redesign" (p. 372).

Pearlman (1980) reviews the personnel literature on the development of job families. His article contains an excellent set of references, the majority of which are from the 1970s. While the article focuses on personnel selection, many of the methodological treatments are applicable to other uses of job analysis. It is perhaps surprising that so few books have been written on job analysis. All the recent books between 1970 and 1980 (e.g., Berwitz, 1975; Mintzberg, 1973; Ronan and Prien, 1971; Salvendy and Seymour, 1973; Stone and Yoder, 1970; Youngman et al., 1978) have focused on one or a small number of the many facets of job analysis. The exception is McCormick (1979), which endeavors to cover many aspects of the field with examples of forms and techniques used, and with attention to the application of job analysis results. This chapter is the author's attempt to cover the subject broadly, but with sufficient references for the reader who wishes to delve more deeply into a particular area.

USES OF JOB ANALYSIS

As mentioned previously, the choice of a job analysis technique most likely depends on the objectives of the analysis. The researcher or analyst should be aware of the many uses of the data that can be generated.

Writing Job Descriptions

Organizations need job descriptions for a variety of purposes. Job titles seldom convey such information, except for jobs that are well known and that differ little from organization to organization. A description based on good job analysis data can convey to applicants information on which to make a rational decision as to the extent of their interest and the likelihood of success on the job. It can convey to recruitment sources, employment agencies, and the like, information that will enhance referral of appropriate candidates and minimize referral of inappropriate ones. Where job posting and bidding are utilized, a good description can help avoid arguments as to whether a bidder is qualified.

Training Program Development

Training programs generally proceed from some perceived need. Without a sufficiently sensitive job analysis, the training program may waste valuable time and money. Few training programs distinguish between the "need to know" and the "nice to know" aspects of the subject matter or skill being taught. A job analysis permits the establishment of Training Performance Objectives (TPO's) which are fitted to job requirements.

Job-Related Interviews

In the employment office, the trained interviewer frequently has the most meager specifications when trying to determine the fit between the candidate and the job. The net result is usually an attempt to assess the personal characteristics of the candidate at the expense of skills and knowledges pertinent to the job. If the candidate is referred for an interview by an operating supervisor who does know the requirements of the job, this supervisor is ordinarily untrained in interviewing. A file of job requirements based on job analyses permits employment interviews that are demonstrably more job-related, a very important consideration in terms of federal and state guidelines on employee selection.

Test Development, Selection, and Validation

Preemployment tests are used as an aid to selection for many jobs. These may be achievement, aptitude, or skill. Such tests typically exist or can be built to measure differing levels of performance. Job analysis provides information on which to base a choice of tests, both as to the type and content and to the performance levels required. Sometimes the job analysis effectively provides validation of the test through content comparison with the job analysis data.

Performance Appraisal

Many jobs have a merit pay component, with salary differences based on job performance. Even where pay is not involved, personnel actions such as promotion, selection for training, layoff, and discharge may be related to performance. Counseling for improved performance is a typical personnel practice. Performance appraisal should be based on demands of the job, not on personality traits or characteristics, unless these are demonstrably job-related. A performance appraisal program tied directly to job analysis is the best assurance of job-relatedness.

Job Evaluation

Most job families are hierarchical in nature; that is, job titles and pay increase with additional experience, competencies, responsibility, and so forth. It is vitally important to organizations that equity be established and maintained within job families and across different job families. An appropriately based job analysis program provides the building blocks for the creation of pay grades and job classification systems.

Other

Depending in part on the type of job analysis performed and on the results of that analysis, the data may contribute to several other aspects of personnel management. For example, the organization may decide on a program of job enrichment. Job restructuring can be accomplished most effectively by analyzing duties and tasks of adjacent jobs that might provide the enrichment possibilities. As another example, human resource planning might be enhanced through better knowledge of critical skill requirements that might be in short supply.

DEVELOPING JOB INFORMATION

The foundation of any job analysis program is information. The analyst must first decide what information is to be collected. This will depend in large part on the objectives of the program. The next step is a decision on how the information is to be collected—both the physical means and the agents. Finally, a decision must be made on how to record the information, including definition of any scaling or classifying systems that might be employed.

Establishing Objectives

Some types and methods of job analysis provide data that can be used to satisfy more than one objective. However, it is always wise to try to match the use to be made of the end product with the technique or method employed. For example, recent research (Cornelius, Carron, and Collins, 1979) used the same clustering technique to analyze the similarities and differences among seven foremen jobs in a chemical processing plant, but used three different methods in developing information about the jobs. The seven jobs were grouped according to degree of similarity in three different ways. Each of the three would have been preferred for a different purpose—one as a basis for hiring foremen from outside the organization, one as a basis for establishing a supervisory training program, and one to develop job families for test validation. The discussion of specific techniques later in this chapter will hopefully shed more light on these relationships.

Choosing Descriptors

Among the more common descriptors are education or training requirements normally used as job qualifications; level in the organizational hierarchy; number of persons supervised; dollar assets employed in the job; working conditions; tools or instruments used; aptitudes, skills, or knowledges required; physical demands reflecting need for strength or agility; tasks performed; and behaviors demonstrated. Some of these can be observed directly. Some cannot be observed but can be based on quantified or quantifiable data. Some require prior research, judgment of presumably knowledgeable persons, or some form of inference. Almost all eventually rest on a foundation of tasks performed or behaviors demonstrated.

Task statements focus on operations that can be observed, for example, "types from hand-written copy." Task statements generally culminate in a definition of the *job-oriented content* of the job(s) being analyzed. On the other hand, behavior statements generally culminate in a definition of the *worker-oriented content* of the job(s) being analyzed and focus on the demands made of the worker or the anticipated outcomes, for example, "communicating outside the immediate work area." These distinctions often become fuzzy in actual practice, but they are helpful in deciding on the accumulation of basic data. One might remember the story of the two masons, one of whom said, "I'm laying bricks," while the other said, "I'm helping build a cathedral."

Frequently, information on several descriptors will be collected in the same job analysis. The U.S. Department of Labor, Manpower Administration (1973) published a volume entitled *Task Analysis Inventories: A Method for Collecting Job Information.* This publication provides forms for use in inventorying twenty-two separate and highly diverse occupations. In spite of the title of the reference, the items encompass much more than tasks. All areas are not included for all the occupations, but the basic list is as follows:

What the Worker Does
Education and Training Requirements
Licensure, Certificates, Rating, etc.
Communication Responsibilities
Area of Responsibility
Work Aids Used
Machines and Equipment
Techniques Used
Specializations
Products
Services
Registry and Association Requirements
Union Affiliations
Environmental Setting

The list certainly points up the variety of possible descriptors and also gives some hints as to problems of collecting the information.

Collecting Descriptor Data

Problems associated with the collection of descriptor data can be subsumed under three main headings: (1) methods of collecting data, (2) agents for collecting data, and (3) cataloging and scaling data.

Methods. Obviously, methods will vary with the type of descriptor data to be collected. However, for any one type there may be more than one method. The choice may depend upon such factors as cost, the availability of competent collecting agents, accessibility of workers, and the type of data analysis contemplated. Among the more common are the following:

1. *Observation of the worker doing the job.* This method is best suited to jobs where performance of tasks is the principal component of the job and the end products are readily apparent. It is poorly suited to jobs where the end products depend heavily on the integration of cognitive or artistic skill. To note that the worker uses a drill to bore holes in a steel plate may be an apt description of a machinist's task. To note that an advertising specialist puts words on paper with a felt-tipped pen may be accurate, but it fails to communicate properly the nature of the job.
2. *Interview with the job incumbent.* This method is applicable to a wide variety of jobs, including jobs at different levels of the organizational hierarchy. It is extremely time-consuming and costly. It also suffers from the fact that the interviewer is not likely to be able to separate the idiosyncratic facets of the job, as performed by the incumbent, and the basic activities of the job as performed by a number of incumbents. Since the only remedy for this is to interview multiple incumbents, the inefficiency of the method becomes apparent.

3. *Conference with experienced personnel.* This method is also applicable to a wide variety of jobs. It lessens the risk of recording idiosyncratic behavior, but the seeming consensual agreement may be, at best, generalizations at a higher level than specific behavior.
4. *Open-ended or unstructured questionnaire.* This method is most often used with professional, staff, or managerial personnel. The job incumbent or some other knowledgeable person writes a narrative in response to a topical outline or a series of questions.
5. *Structured questionnaire.* This method may be used with jobs of all types and at all levels. The content of the questionnaire may be varied to fit the objectives of the analysis. The response mode may be varied to obtain information along a variety of dimensions, a point to be discussed later in some detail. The questionnaire is most often completed by job incumbents, although others (e.g., supervisors) may complete it on another's job. Commercially prepared, standardized questionnaires are available, some of which are applicable to a variety of jobs.
6. *Diary maintained by the worker.* This method is generally used for jobs that have very little structure. The job incumbent simply maintains a chronological record of activities or events.
7. *Other.* Observation of the worker doing the job may be recorded on film. An analysis of the physical movements, strength, or agility required by a job might better be studied from a film record than from written notes maintained by a live observer. Records of activities performed may be a source of job information. A great amount of detail concerning the job of a delivery-salesperson can be ascertained from an inspection of the transactions performed. Information pertaining to certain jobs may often be found in the compensation, safety, or training departments.

Obviously, these methods may be used in combination. One method may frequently be the starting point in preparation for the use of some other. A limited number of interviews or observations may be the first step in preparation of a questionnaire that will be administered to a larger number of job incumbents. A conference of experienced personnel may be used to develop topics or questions for use in an open-ended questionnaire.

Agents.   Much attention has been given to the subject of the type of person required to obtain the descriptor information. Three classes of individuals come immediately to mind: job analysts, job incumbents, and job supervisors. Each provides advantages but also has disadvantages. Method constraints must also be taken into consideration. A diary can hardly be maintained by anyone other than the job incumbent.

1. *Job analyst.* The job analyst is trained in the systematic recording and interpretation of the information collected. However, where the number of jobs to be analyzed is large, the time and expense required for complete coverage may be almost prohibitive. Sometimes personnel specialists or operating employees

available in-house are used as analysts. Preferably they should at least be trained by a skilled analyst.

2. *Job incumbent.* The job incumbent is likely to have the best information on what he or she is doing. However, the incumbent may not be in a position to properly evaluate the relative importance of the many tasks and behaviors that make up the job. Some researchers have also been concerned with the possibility that the incumbents would tend to inflate their jobs. Employers who have union contracts have frequently been concerned that having incumbents describe their jobs might result in a freezing of the job content or in jurisdictional disputes over the work to be done by different classes of workers. The use of job incumbents is certainly the most efficient way to obtain multiple descriptions of the same job.

3. *Job supervisor.* The job supervisor should be in a position to know relatively well what job incumbents do and the relative importance of the different activities. There are exceptions; for example, a generalist who supervises technical or professional specialists or an engineer who supervises craft workers. It has been suggested that supervisors, even when appropriate, may tend to give idealized job descriptions; that is, how the job should be performed rather than how it is actually performed.

Cataloging and Scaling.   At some point in the analysis, the data that have been accumulated must be brought together in some kind of summary fashion. This simply means that the data collected must be organized according to some structure. This will be illustrated in detail as specific job analysis instruments and formats are discussed later. Here the concern is the fact that the analyst or reporter must be provided appropriate response options. The objectives of the analysis and the method employed are important considerations.

Data collected are generally characterized as either *qualitative* or *quantitative*. In some instances, what looks like quantitative data may be the interpretation of the analyst or reporter of qualitative data, but it nevertheless lends itself to mathematical manipulation.

A narrative description of the activities performed may be all that is required to meet the objectives of the analysis. A further step might be augmenting the listing of activities with a description or notation of the context in which the activities are performed. A still further step might be use of the description to rate the job along certain dimensions. For example, the job might be rated in terms of the amount of education required for satisfactory performance. In other words, essentially qualitative information is used to classify the job, either directly or by translation to some set of scales through a judgmental process.

Many times the information necessary to analyze a job quantitatively is recorded directly by the reporter or analyst. This is particularly true where structured questionnaires are used. The task analysis inventory technique recommended by the U.S. Department of Labor, and discussed earlier, simply provides that the analyst mark an ''X'' in a box to show that the task or tool (or whatever) is part of the job being analyzed. The job can then be compared with other jobs by counting the overlap of ''Xs.'' This simplistic approach is frequently considered insufficient to show job similarity or difference. Two jobs may have activities "A" and "B" in common, but activity "A" may command 60 percent and "B" may command only 10 percent of time spent on one job, while the situation is reversed on the other job. To counter the "yes-no" approach, most inventories or checklists provide scales that will enable differentiation. Among the more common are frequency, time required, criticality, training time, supervision required, complexity, and difficulty.

TECHNIQUES FOR STRUCTURING INFORMATION

It was noted in the introduction to this chapter that a group of similar positions formed a *job* and that a group of similar jobs formed an *occupation*. A definition of *similarity* is necessary. Two processes may be used to establish similarity. One is rational and has a long history. Jobs look alike or seem to have the same skill or knowledge requirements, or they do not. Educational or training programs, pay scales, and selection techniques have all been instituted or developed based on such rational determinations. The other process is statistical and has a quite recent history. It begins with quantified or quantifiable data, which are manipulated by statistical analysis to cluster jobs by either overt manifestations, such as activities, or covert manifestations, such as attributes required. The statistical programming may be of several different kinds and new ideas are being advanced almost daily. The great strides taken through use of computers, particularly in terms of storage capacity, makes feasible the use of techniques that were almost impossible only a few years ago, even though the techniques themselves were known.

Standardized Instruments

One technique for structuring job information is to use a standardized instrument and analyze it in different ways. Two such instruments stand out as having a substantial research base. One is the *Position Analysis Questionnaire* (PAQ) developed by Ernest J. McCormick and his associates at the Occupational Research Center, Department of Psychological Services, Purdue University (McCormick, Jeanneret, and Mecham, 1972). The other is the *Occupation Analysis Inventory* (OAI) developed by Joseph W. Cunningham and his associates at the Center for Occupational Education, North Carolina State University (Pass and Cunningham, 1977).

Position Analysis Questionnaire (PAQ). The PAQ is a structured job analysis questionnaire containing 187 job elements. These elements are worker-oriented and so might be characterized as behavior statements. McCormick (1979) describes the PAQ as organized in six divisions and gives examples of two job elements from each division:

1. *Information input.* (Where and how does the worker get the information he or she uses in performing the job?)
   Examples: Use of written materials
   Near-visual differentiation

2. *Mental process.* (What reasoning, decision-making, planning, and information-processing activities are involved in performing the job?)

   Examples: Level of reasoning in problem solving

   Coding / decoding

3. *Work output.* (What physical activities does the worker perform and what tools or devices does he or she use?)

   Examples: Use of keyboard devices

   Assembling / disassembling

4. *Relationships with other persons.* (What relationships with other people are required in performing the job?)

   Examples: Instructing

   Contacts with public, customers

5. *Job context.* (In what physical or social contexts is the work performed?)

   Examples: High temperature

   Interpersonal conflict situations

6. *Other job characteristics.* (What activities, conditions, or characteristics other than those described above are relevant to the job?)

   Examples: Specified work pace

   Amount of job structure

Each job element is rated on one of six different types of rating scales. These scales by type are: Extent of Use, Importance to the Job, Amount of Time, Possibility of Occurrence, Applicability, and a Special Code (used in the case of a few specific job elements). Each scale, except for Applicability, which is dichotomous, has five steps ranging from some version of very low to some version of very high, plus a provision for noting that the element does not apply to the job being rated. In addition to the 187 standard elements, the PAQ contains seven items relating to amount of pay/income, which are optional and are used for research purposes only.

The PAQ is scored on a number of basic job dimensions that have been derived through factor analysis. Results provide a quantitative profile for the job analyzed. In addition, McCormick and his associates have used the PAQ to derive job-related aptitude requirements for determining job-related selection tests (McCormick, DeNisi, and Shaw, 1979; McCormick and Mecham, 1970) and job evaluation points for determining pay scales and job classifications (Robinson, Wahlstrom, and Mecham, 1974). PAQ Services, Inc., has recently been formed to provide data-processing services and conduct further research.

The PAQ has been a favorite with job analysis researchers who have been directly associated with McCormick. Its structure lends itself readily to many types of study, both applied and theoretical. For example, Taylor and his associates (Taylor, 1978; Taylor and Colbert, 1978; Colbert and Taylor, 1978) used the standard PAQ dimensions to develop job families, then used the same dimensions to empirically develop another set of job families, and, finally, used these empirically developed job families as the foundation for a validity generalization study of selection tests. Arvey and Mossholder (1977) used the PAQ in development of an analysis of variance procedure for determining similarities and differences among jobs.

Occupation Analysis Inventory (OAI).   The OAI started from a somewhat different orientation than the PAQ. Cunningham and his associates were interested in the possibility of occupational clustering for the development of occupational education programs. However, there appears to be no reason why the OAI cannot be used for other purposes. It has been used to estimate "the human ability requirements of job classifications in a state competitive civil service system" (Cunningham, Phillips, and Spetz, 1976).

The OAI consists of 602 work elements grouped into five categories. The categories and major subcategories are:

1. *Information Received*
   Information Content
   Sensory Channel
2. *Mental Activities*
3. *Work Behavior*
   Physical Work Behavior
   Representational Work Behavior
   Interpersonal Work Behavior
4. *Work Goals*
5. *Work Context*

One reason for the large number of elements in the OAI is the inclusion of many *job-oriented* elements or activities associated with a particular occupation. This is more easily understood by noting the representation of jobs studied according to their coding in the *Dictionary of Occupational Titles* (U.S. Department of Labor, 1965). The number in the sample, the three-digit DOT code, and the category are listed below (Boese and Cunningham, 1975):

327	000–199	Professional, Technical, and Managerial Occupations
355	200–299	Clerical and Sales Occupations
181	300–399	Service Occupations
44	400–499	Farming, Fishery, Forestry, and Related Occupations
507	500–999	Operatives, Skilled Trades, and Related Occupations
1414	—	Total

Ratings on the OAI's 602 elements for each of the 1,414 jobs selected to represent these occupations were factor analyzed to develop basic dimensions. An example of the final product is shown below:

Factor A-1: Electrical and electronic information: Information obtained from operating, diagnosing, and observing electrical devices or from relevant drawings, displays, and written materials.

Like the PAQ, the OAI has been subjected to systematic analysis to determine both its psychometric properties and the extent to which it can be used as a proper foundation for application in settings other than the job description.

Standardized Formatting

Job information may be obtained by a variety of methods, as has been discussed previously. Regardless, it can be summarized in standardized fashion. One way of accomplishing this is to have the analyst interpret the information according to a standard format; that is, the analyst uses specified scales and uses the job information as evidence of appropriate placement along the scale. The results of some methods of information collecting are easier to handle in this way than others. Some form of task description is the easiest.

Functional Job Analysis (FJA). The basic concept of FJA was developed by Sidney A. Fine and his associates during research performed in preparation for the 1965 edition of the *Dictionary of Occupational Titles.* Much of the later work on FJA was performed at the W. E. Upjohn Institute for Employment Research (Fine and Wiley, 1971). Scales were developed for three primary classifications: data, people, and things. These were considered to exist in a hierarchy from a low level of the triad to a high level. In addition, the total job could be partitioned off into these three primaries. The FJA system also includes four other scales (Fine, 1973), but they are separate characterizations. These are worker instructions, reasoning development, mathematical development, and language development.

Each step of the functions scales is carefully defined to maximize consistency of level assignment. For example, the lowest level of the *Data Function Scale* is *Comparing.* This is defined as "Selects, sorts, or arranges data, people, or things, judging whether their readily observable functional, structural, or compositional characteristics are similar to or different from prescribed standards." An intermediate level of the *People Function Scale* is *Persuading,* defined as "Influences others in favor of a product, service, or point of view by talks or demonstrations." The highest level on the *Things Function Scale* is *Setting Up,* defined as "Installs machines or equipment; inserts tools; alters jigs, fixtures, and attachments; and/or repairs machines or equipment to ready and/or restore them to their proper functioning according to job order or blueprint specifications. Involves primary responsibility for accuracy. May involve one or a number of machines for other workers or for worker's own operation" (Fine, 1973).

A complete listing of the steps in each of the scales is given here. Note that alternatives are provided for some of the steps.

Data Function Scale

1. Comparing
2. Copying
3A. Computing
3B. Compiling

4. Analyzing
5A. Innovating
5B. Coordinating
6. Synthesizing

People Function Scale

1A.	Taking instructions—helping	4A.	Consulting
1B.	Serving	4B.	Instructing
2.	Exchanging information	4C.	Treating
3A.	Coaching	5.	Supervising
3B.	Persuading	6.	Negotiating
3C.	Diverting	7.	Mentoring

Things Function Scale

1A.	Handling	2B.	Operating—controlling
1B.	Feeding—offbearing	2C.	Driving—controlling
1C.	Tending	3A.	Precision working
2A.	Manipulating	3B.	Setting up

While Fine and his associates use these scales to interpret data collected by means of task statements, any compilation of job information could be used if it provided sufficient detail for making reliable and valid judgments.

Job Element Method.   This method was developed by Ernest S. Primoff of the U.S. Civil Service Commission (Primoff, 1971), now the Office of Personnel Management. It was developed as a basis for the establishment of standards for the selection of candidates for employment in the federal government. Its use has been extended into state and local government agencies as well. The method uses a set of carefully defined criteria and systematic procedures for determining critical worker requirements and then examining for them. Job elements are the various knowledges, skills, abilities, and other personal characteristics (KSAOs) necessary for workers to perform the job. KSAOs are identified by persons familiar with the job, usually incumbents and their supervisors. Initially, KSAOs are proposed and listed with little critical evaluation. The evaluation comes through the application of four rating scales. The rating factors and the rating scale categories are:

Barely acceptable workers now on the job:
+   (2)   All have
v   (1)   Some have
o   (0)   Almost none have
To pick out acceptable workers the element is:
+   (2)   Very important
v   (1)   Valuable
ȯ   (0)   Does not differentiate

Trouble likely if the element is not considered:

+ (2) Much trouble
v (1) Some trouble
o (0) Safe to ignore

Practicality. Demanding this element we can fill:

+ (2) All openings
v (1) Some openings
o (0) Almost no openings

A specific application of the *Job Element Method* is the J-coefficient, whereby the important or critical job elements are translated directly into selection characteristics (Primoff, 1972). These elements are identified by constructing index scores from the rating values obtained from application of the scales just discussed. For example, an overall item index is constructed by multiplying the superior worker's value by the practicality value and adding the trouble value.

Work Elements Inventory. This inventory was developed by Melany E. Baehr and her associates at the Industrial Relations Center, University of Chicago (Baehr, Lonergan, and Potkay, 1967). It is defined on the form used to profile the results as "A standardized and quantitative measure for defining the basic dimensions of jobs in terms of underlying work behaviors and for assessing the relative importance of these dimensions for overall successful performance." A job description instrument, the *WEI*, with factorially determined job dimensions, is scored and the results are profiled for the job on a standard score scale according to degree of importance to the job. The overall dimensions and their subscales are:

Organization
  Setting Objectives
  Improving Procedures
  Promoting Safety
  Developing Technical Ideas
Leadership
  Decision-Making
  Developing Teamwork
  Coping with Emergencies
Personnel
  Developing Employee Potential
  Supervisory Practices
  Self-Development
Community
  Community-Organization Relations
  Handling Outside Contacts

Baehr and her associates have used the same technique to construct other inventories; see *Skills and Attributes Inventory* (Baehr, 1971).

Physical Abilities Analysis (PAA). A special subset of abilities and job demands is physical proficiency. Edwin A. Fleishman has devoted many years to this area (Fleishman, 1964, 1975, 1979). His research and that of his associates has isolated nine abilities that form the basis for evaluating physical requirements of tasks. The importance of this research is growing daily with increased attention to employment of women in nontraditional physically demanding jobs, employment of the handicapped, and job protection for older workers. The nine abilities are listed here with a brief description of each as used by Fleishman:

Dynamic strength. This is defined as the ability to exert muscular force repeatedly or continuously over time.

Trunk strength. This is a derivative of the dynamic strength factor and is characterized by resistance of trunk muscles to fatigue over repeated use.

Static strength. This is the force that an individual exerts in lifting, pushing, pulling, or carrying external objects.

Explosive strength. This is characterized by the ability to expend a maximum of energy in one or a series of maximum thrusts.

Extent flexibility. This involves the ability to extend the trunk, arms, and/or legs through a range of motion in either the frontal, sagittal, or transverse planes.

Dynamic flexibility. This contrasts with extent flexibility in that the ability involves the capacity to make rapid, repeated flexing movements, in which the resilience of the muscles in recovering from distention is critical.

Gross body coordination. This is the ability to coordinate the simultaneous actions of different parts of the body or body limbs while the body is in movement. This ability is frequently referenced as agility.

Gross body equilibrium. This is the ability to maintain balance in either an unstable position or when opposing forces are pulling.

Stamina. This is synonymous with cardiovascular endurance and enables the performance of prolonged bouts of aerobic work without experiencing fatigue or exhaustion.

In analyzing a job by PAA, the analyst uses a seven-point scale which is anchored at the top with a maximum performance task and at the bottom with a minimum performance task. Other tasks well known to the raters are used to describe other levels on the scale. The physical tasks of the job are compared with these scaled examples and are slotted in appropriately.

Job Evaluation Methods. Another special subset of job analysis problems is related to pay. No specific technique is described here but almost all provide a standard format with thoroughly defined factors to be considered and scales for each factor so that differing requirements can be reflected. The study of job evaluation methods is certain to escalate significantly in the near future. (Mahoney reviews this topic further in Chapter 9.) The Equal Employment Opportunity Commission (EEOC), charged with enforcement of Title VII of the Civil Rights Act of 1964, has suggested that one reason for lower pay for jobs held predominantly by women is bias in evaluation of jobs. EEOC contracted with the Committee on Occupational Classification and Analysis, Assembly of Behavioral and Social Sciences, National Research Council to determine whether appropriate job measurement procedures existed or could be developed to assess the worth of jobs. An interim report (Treiman, 1979) has been prepared, but the final report is not yet available as of this writing. Blumrosen (1979) has prepared an exhaustive summary of various factors involved in comparing jobs. Her basic thesis is that much wage discrimination against minorities and women is the result of job evaluation.

Statistical Programming

The increasing availability of sophisticated software statistical packages and the computer hardware capable of handling large amounts of data has led to new techniques for determining similarities and differences among jobs. While these depend on some kind of numerical input (binary input will generally suffice), the data origination is not normally an essential consideration, if data input can be scaled. In other words, a narrative job description can be used if it can be analyzed to provide quantitative information along appropriate scales.

Air Force Comprehensive Occupational Data Analysis Program (CODAP)

This program has been developed over a period of many years by Raymond E. Christal and his associates at the Personnel Research Division, Air Force Human Resources Laboratory, Lackland Air Force Base, Texas (Christal and Weissmuller, 1976; Archer and Giorgia, 1977). The system is beginning to be used outside the Air Force (Trattner, 1979), and training programs in the use of CODAP are being offered across the country. The heart of the program is a task analysis. Tasks and duties involved in a particular job are developed by incumbents, supervisors, or experts. The Trattner study is an excellent example of CODAP in operation and it has the added advantage of being readily accessible in most libraries.

After the listing of tasks included in the occupation had been prepared, job incumbents were first asked to indicate whether or not they performed the task listed. They were then asked to indicate the relative amount of time spent in performing that particular task relative to other tasks performed. A scale was used rather than actual amounts or percentages of available time. The scale used was

1. Very much below average
2. Below average
3. Slightly below average
4. About average
5. Slightly above average
6. Above average
7. Very much above average

Each task rating of each job incumbent was summed across all tasks, and each task rating was then divided by that sum to give an estimated percentage. The total of these percentages thus accounted for the total job. These relative time data were then fed into the computer for development of a group job description. The computer ranked the tasks in terms of the percentage of the group who performed the task and then displayed the data in terms of:

Average Percent Time Spent by Members Performing
Average Percent Time Spent by All Members
Cumulative Sum of Average Percent Time Spent by All Members

Finally, an average percent overlap was computed—the average percentage of time spent in performance of the same tasks for the individuals in the group being studied.

Ward and Hook Hierarchical Grouping Procedure. (Ward and Hook, 1963; Feild and Schoenfeldt, 1975). This is an iterative clustering method that can be used to develop the most parsimonious explanation of the number of groups that can be formed from a large number of observations. The essence of the technique is the successive clustering of individuals into groups that contain members who are more like that group than they are to members of any other group. Use of the technique does require some judgment by the user in determining where to stop the iterative process. The technique is discussed here because of its widespread use in job analysis. For a more complete discussion of cluster analysis, the reader is referred to Tryon and Bailey (1970).

Analysis of Variance. Statistical technique discussion is beyond the scope of this chapter and it is noted that there are no other chapters specifically devoted to the subject. Analysis of variance is mentioned because it has been proposed as one method of determining the degree of similarity among jobs (Arvey and Mossholder, 1977). Essentially, an analysis of variance compares variations among ratings for a job with those of other jobs. In other words, given that ten incumbents of Job X will vary somewhat in the actual tasks and duties of their position, is that difference lesser or greater than that found when Job X is compared to Job Y? The proposal of Arvey and Mossholder has been attacked as being incomplete, and other proposals are proliferating.

Factor Analysis. This statistical technique has a longer history of use with job analysis. It begins with a matrix of correlations showing the relationships between items or scales for different positions or jobs. For example, the profiles of machinists, welders, laboratory technicians, clerks, typists, bookkeepers, etc., could each be correlated with each of the others. A factor analysis of the resulting matrix would probably group these into some appropriate classes which could be compared on the basis of their factor loadings.

Pearlman (1980) has expressed the concern that preoccupation over alternative methods of job family development may hinder more substantive questions of purpose. This would seem to be particularly true in the litigious atmosphere that prevails today. Different techniques can and sometimes do give different answers. Expert witnesses for plaintiff and defendant can be expected to espouse different methods.

EVALUATING ADEQUACY OF RESULTS AND END PRODUCTS

Once the job analysis is completed and the descriptions, profiles, classifications, and so forth, can be determined, the adequacy of the end product should be evaluated before the results are put to use. Several points should be considered.

Psychometric Properties

The end result of a job analysis is a measurement. As such, it is subject to evaluation in terms of its psychometric adequacy.

Reliability. Reliability is a measure of the consistency of the results obtained. Two different analysts should obtain the same results from an analysis of the same job, or an analyst should obtain the same results from an analysis of the same job on two different occasions, unless the job has changed in the meantime. Techniques for establishing and documenting the extent to which a job analysis is reliable do exist and they vary with the type of result developed as the final product. The methods involved are highly technical and beyond the scope of this chapter. More important, even where the extent of reliability can be statistically shown, there is no professional consensus on what constitutes an acceptable level of reliability.

Validity. Validity is a measure of the accuracy of the results obtained. It is quite possible for two analysts to agree completely and for both to be wrong as a result of incomplete information, biased interpretation, and so forth. There is almost no way of statistically showing the extent to which a job analysis result is accurate or valid, particularly as one moves from simple operational type jobs to those demanding complex skills or a high degree of interaction with others. The most common method of ensuring accuracy is the use of multiple reporters or interpreters. Here, again, there is no professional consensus on what is an acceptable accuracy level.

Comprehensiveness. A job analysis result may be both reliable and valid, for what it covers. The description of a secretarial job in terms of the skill demands of shorthand, typing, filing, and so forth, may be highly accurate, but it is certainly not complete unless it includes such activities as answering the telephone, accepting and relaying messages, and so on. Some systems, for example CODAP, provide an indication of the percentage of the job covered by the tasks finally selected as the basic description. At a less sophisticated level, job incumbents can be asked to estimate the percentage of the total job that is covered by the descriptive elements.

Relating Results to Objectives

Earlier it was pointed out that the first step in development of job information should be the establishment of objectives; this plays a significant role in choosing descriptors, collecting descriptor data, and structuring the information obtained. Does the final product meet the needs that prompted the job analysis? The answer to this question is obviously judgmental, but it should be asked.

GOVERNMENTAL REGULATIONS AND CASE LAW

Job analysis is increasingly subject to governmental regulations and the interpretation of those regulations by the federal courts. These have been mentioned occasionally in previous texts. Here, the subject will be explored in depth since the impact is and will continue to be severe.

Governmental Regulations

The principal regulation involved today is the *Uniform Guidelines on Employee Selection Procedures (1978), 43 FR 166* (August 25, 1978). This was augmented on March 2, 1979, with the publication of ninety *Questions and Answers to Clarify and Provide a Common Interpretation of the Uniform Guidelines on Employee Selection Procedures,* and on May 2, 1980, with publication of three additional Q's and A's. Additional guidance will undoubtedly be forthcoming. The *Guidelines* are the product of a long and arduous process which began on August 24, 1966, with publication by the Equal Employment Opportunity Commission (EEOC) of *Guidelines on Employment Testing Procedures.* Between 1966 and 1978, numerous guidelines were published—an additional one by EEOC and others by the Office of Federal Contract Compliance Programs in the Department of Labor, the Civil Service Commission (now the Office of Personnel Management), and the Department of Justice. The new (1978) *Uniform Guidelines* have been agreed upon by the Equal Employment Opportunity Commission, the Office of Personnel Management, and the Departments of Justice and Labor, and are available for adoption by any federal agency having an equal rights enforcement responsibility. The *Uniform Guidelines* are an interpretation by the agencies of laws and executive orders which prohibit discrimination in employment practices on grounds of race, color, religion, sex, or national origin.

One might wonder at this amount of detail since the *Guidelines* refer to *Employee Selection Procedures.* Part of the answer is found in the *Guidelines* definition of *Selection Procedure:* "Any measure, combination of measures, or procedure used as a basis for any employment decision. Selection procedures include the full range of assessment techniques from traditional paper and pencil tests, performance tests, training programs, or probationary periods and physical, educational, and work experience requirements through informal or casual interviews and unscored application forms."

The other half of the answer is found in Section 2B of the *Guidelines* themselves where *Employment Decisions* are defined: "Employment decisions include but are not limited to hiring, promotion, demotion, membership (for example, in a labor organization), referral, retention, and licensing and certification, to the extent that licensing and certification may be covered by Federal and equal employment opportunity law. Other selection decisions, such as selection for training or transfer, may also be considered employment decisions if they lead to any of the decisions listed above."

The linchpin between the two is that any selection procedure or employment decision that has an adverse effect on any of the protected groups (they appear to be discriminated against) must be justified by a showing of *job-relatedness* or *business necessity.* Federal enforcement agencies generally require demonstration of job-relatedness through a formal study that shows *validity* for the selection procedure. The *Guidelines* specify the collection of information about the job, generally in the form of *job analysis,* as one of numerous conditions for an acceptable validity study. Given the many opportunities to find evidence of possible discrimination, a job analysis is almost a requirement.

Section 14A of the *Guidelines* states: "Any method of job analysis may be used if it provides the information required for the specific validation strategy used." To obtain the full impact of this highly permissive statement, one must refer to the definitions of job description, job analysis, work behavior, observable, knowledge, skill, and ability as they appear in the *Guidelines:*

L. *Job description.* A general statement of job duties and responsibilities.
K. *Job analysis.* A detailed statement of work behaviors and other information relevant to the job.
Y. *Work behavior.* An activity performed to achieve the objective of the job. Work behaviors involve observable (physical) components and unobservable (mental) components. A work behavior consists of the performance of one or more tasks. Knowledges, skills, and abilities are not behaviors, although they may be applied in work behaviors.
O. *Observable.* Able to be seen, heard, or otherwise perceived by a person other then the person performing the action.
M. *Knowledge.* A body of information applied directly to the performance of a function.
T. *Skill.* A present, observable competence to perform a learned psychomotor act.
A. *Ability.* A present competence to perform an observable behavior or a behavior which results in an observable product.

The emphasis in this kind of job analysis is clearly on what the worker does. This, of course, may be determined in different ways, as discussed previously. The *Guidelines* clearly prefer direct observation. Developing all of the work behaviors in a job other than the most simple is forbidding; to do so by observation only is virtually impossible. Some resolution of this dilemma is necessary and it will probably be through the courts.

There is no authoritative guidance on how far to fractionate a job into its component parts. In one exceptionally thorough job analysis, the researchers combined some work behaviors that typically appeared in sequence. "Attend roll call, view TV line-up, take notes on orders and instructions, review Daily Bulletin," was listed as one job duty (Barrett, et al., 1975). Other analysts might well separate these and count them as four, particularly if there might be differences among them in importance. Earlier, there was a discussion of possible definitions of *job.* To have some kind of defensible employment procedure, as well as meet some recordkeeping requirement of the *Guidelines,* it is necessary to develop some system for combining positions, and even jobs, so that appropriate numbers of persons are available for validation studies and for application of results. Otherwise, selection is reduced to random behavior or to individual matchings of persons and jobs. In both of these situations utter chaos could be expected with each administrative or technological change.

Court Decisions

Job analysis is playing an increasingly important role in court decisions. The vast bulk of these are decided under authority of Title VII of the Civil Rights Act of 1964. However, there is increasing attention to other antidiscrimination laws, most notably the Equal Pay Act of 1963 and the Age Discrimination Act of 1967. Initially, court rulings were mainly concerned with whether or not some systematic job analysis existed. Recently, rulings have also been concerned with the methodology of the particular system or technique employed, and whether it satisfied the intended purpose or objective.

The seminal case, *Griggs* v. *Duke Power Co.* (1971), did not actually mention job analysis as a technique. Instead, the U.S. Supreme Court, in a unanimous decision, ruled that preemployment tests and other standards which disproportionately disadvantaged Negroes were illegal, absent a showing of job-relatedness. The Court also ruled that the EEOC *Guidelines on Employee Selection* (1970) were entitled to "great deference" as the interpretation of the law (Title VII) by its enforcement agency. In *Albemarle Paper Co.* v. *Moody* (1975), the U.S. Supreme Court wrote, "We granted certiorari because of an evident circuit conflict as to the standards governing awards of backpay and *as to the showing required to establish the 'job-relatedness' of pre-employment tests*" (emphasis added). Having reaffirmed that the EEOC *Guidelines* (1970) were "entitled to great deference" the Court in a six-to-two decision wrote, in part, "measured against the *Guidelines,* Albemarle's validation study is materially defective in several respects: . . . . The study in this case involved no analysis of the attributes of, or the particular skills needed in, the study job groups." Chief Justice Burger dissented, complaining about the "wooden application of EEOC *Guidelines.*" Justice Blackmun wrote, "I cannot join, however, in the Court's apparent view that absolute compliance with the EEOC *Guidelines* is a *sine qua non* of preemployment test validation." Nevertheless, as was noted earlier, the EEOC (1978) strengthened its job analysis requirements.

Not all cases have gone against employer defendants. In *Arnold* v. *Ballard* (1975), the District Court relied heavily on a job analysis (see Barrett et al., 1975) in approving a high school education requirement. In *EEOC* v. *E. I. duPont de Nemours & Co.* (1978), the company's job analysis was used, in part, to support a preemployment testing program and to show that persons available for hire did not have qualifications in a racially balanced fashion. Many other cases could be cited, but these examples should provide some indication of the importance of job analysis in employment cases. Similar rulings, pro and con, are being decided based, in part, on job analysis with respect to equal pay, age discrimination, and handicapped discrimination.

THE FUTURE OF JOB ANALYSIS

Many personnel practices (e.g., validation of preemployment tests) are impractical or impossible for the small- or medium-sized employer. Constraints of money, talent, and number of employees get in the way. This is not true of job analysis. Given that validation of preemployment tests by a larger employer, a consortium, or a test publisher requires a job analysis, the smaller employer may in effect "borrow" the validation study by a showing of job comparability. Also, job analysis as a basis for developing performance appraisal content or specifications for interviewers requires no specific number of jobs or employees.

Court decisions under the Equal Pay Act and the Age Discrimination Act were mentioned earlier and a reference was made to discrimination against the handicapped (Rehabilitation Act of 1973). Each of these three areas will require further attention to job analysis, albeit a different kind of attention to each.

It is a well-documented fact that women earn less than men, on the average, even after such factors as education, experience, jobs held, full-time vs. part-time work, and so forth, are taken into account. As mentioned earlier, attempts are being made to narrow that gap. One proposed villain is the job evaluation plans used by business and industry. A job evaluation is of necessity based on a job analysis. The Equal Pay Act is clear that equal pay for the sexes must eventuate when jobs held by both sexes are identical or nearly so. The rub comes when the jobs are different but are held to be comparable. A resolution in terms of "comparable worth" would have a seriously disruptive effect on personnel practices and on the economy. One can be reasonably certain that some form of job analysis and job evaluation research will be forthcoming—something that will narrow the gap in earnings but without a full commitment to equality based on comparability.

The 1978 amendments to the Age Discrimination Act raised the minimum legal retirement age from sixty-five to seventy. Some states have abolished altogether the concept of a legal minimum. Many observers predict this as a piece of national legislation in the near future. The effect of this on job analysis will be felt most strongly in the use of the job analysis to develop defensible performance appraisal bases so that employees unable to perform satisfactorily can be terminated or retired on job performance terms and not on the basis of age. For physically demanding jobs, such job analyses may be necessary to provide underpinning for medical disability retirements or terminations.

Regulations issued under authority of the Rehabilitation Act of 1973 require employers to take affirmative action to employ the handicapped and to advance them consistent with their capabilities. These regulations state emphatically that the handicapped must be evaluated in terms of their ability to perform the essential tasks of the job and must not be turned away because of inability to perform acts which have little or no consequence. The regulations also provide that an employer must provide "reasonable accommodation" to the individual's handicap. Job analyses to identify the essential tasks must obviously have a large component of "criticality" in the resulting job description.

It should be obvious from the foregoing that no one system of job analysis offered to date can meet all of these described needs. Already many employers are performing two or three different ones and trying to meld them. Research is underway which attempts to compare different systems on the extent to which they each meet different needs and on the cost effectiveness of each. Perhaps a completely new and different system will be developed, but seventy years of research and practice will not be discarded lightly.

Research will undoubtedly continue on ways to cluster jobs in the most meaningful fashion. Percentage of overlap is a very crude statistic and other approaches have had their share of professional criticism. Also, more research can be excepted on measurement of the reliability and validity of results obtained from various job analysis systems and techniques.

An area of research that will certainly receive added attention is the extent to which job incumbents can perceive the underlying characteristics of their jobs. The area is particularly pertinent in terms of job design or redesign. The reader is referred to Taber, Beehr, and Walsh (1978) for a comparison of manufacturing employees' perceptions of their jobs through a survey of work attitudes and job evaluation ratings made by outside observers. In a completely different situation, Hogan and Fleishman (1979) had subjects rate tasks whose metabolic costs were known on the effort required to complete the task. Successful replication of studies such as these has numerous possibilities.

IN CONCLUSION

Job analysis bids fair to get great attention in the decade of the eighties. This is not to say that there has not been attention during earlier decades; witness the literature citations throughout the chapter. But the antidiscrimination laws of the sixties and seventies, the enforcement agency regulations of the seventies, the court decisions of the seventies and resolution of those cases moving forward, will combine to give increased impetus. Money will be more readily available for research. Employers will hire additional staff personnel and consultants with job analysis expertise in order to achieve a defensible position.

Discussion Questions

1. Distinguish "equal pay for equal work" and "equal pay for work of comparable value," citing the implications of the distinction for the administration of compensation systems.

2. How can a small employer with little or no staff expertise available comply with rules and regulations that require or imply the need for job analysis?

3. Is job specialization (as opposed to job breadth) more characteristic of larger or smaller employers and, if there is a difference, why and what implications does this have for the formulation of job families?

4. If a physical ability testing program results in proportionately fewer female hires then female applicants, can the employer continue to use the testing program and, if so, on what basis?

5. Discuss the problems encountered in using task analysis as a job analysis method for studying professional, technical, and managerial jobs.

PART THREE
ORGANIZATIONAL ENTRY

One of the earliest and most persistent concerns of the field of personnel management is the selection and placement of employees. With the onset of the Industrial
Psychology era (see Chapter 1), Munsterberg's (1913) work on the selection of
railway motormen for the city of Boston helped elevate job-person matching to
prominence. More recently, a broader area has been defined. It is referred to as
"organizational entry." This area considers the processes by which individuals attain organizational membership from the standpoint of both the individual and the
organization. Federal legislation imposes a dominant, external influence on these
entry processes. Thus, an analysis of organizational entry processes is not complete
without consideration of the various influences or constraints under which they
operate. The three chapters in this section provide a thorough coverage of contemporary organizational entry processes.

A logical first step in the entry process involves individuals' choices relative to
employment search, and organizations' attempts to procure human resources. In
Chapter 5, Schwab discusses these processes from a somewhat different perspective than typically employed. Taking a labor economics/decision-making approach
to job search and recruitment, Schwab focuses on present-day concerns and identifies critical issues that organizations and personnel practitioners must address relative to procuring ample supplies of qualified employees.

The most widely used personnel selection device is the employment interview,
despite its recognized lack of objectivity and uncertain psychometric properties. In
Chapter 6, Hakel reviews behavioral science research on various psychological factors involved in the interview process, and discusses, from a practical/applied
standpoint, issues and points of concern in actually conducting interviews. Hakel
also identifies some ways in which practitioners can improve the utility of the interview as a decision-making tool, as well as bring it more closely into line with equal
employment opportunity guidelines.

Beginning in the early 1900s, and extending through the mid-1960s, this country experienced the so-called "testing boom." Personnel testing enjoyed increased
usage in organizational decision making, only to decline suddenly with the advent
of equal employment opportunity legislation. In Chapter 7, Scharf reviews the

landmark court cases and legislative enactments that serve to form the contemporary legal climate in this country with respect to testing and other related employment practices. He also discusses and provides illustrative examples of the issues and implications of test validation requirements specified under the law. The case-law approach taken by Scharf is instructive in that it not only defines the current state of affairs in this area, but also identifies trends for the future.

CHAPTER FIVE

RECRUITING AND ORGANIZATIONAL PARTICIPATION

Donald P. Schwab

Donald Schwab is Professor and H. I. Romnes Faculty Fellow in the Graduate School of Business and the Industrial Relations Research Institute at the University of Wisconsin-Madison. He received his Ph.D. from the University of Minnesota, with emphasis in Industrial Relations and Psychology. Professor Schwab is a well-known researcher, being the recipient of over ten research grants and the author of over fifty journal articles and papers presented at professional meetings. Additionally, Professor Schwab is the coauthor of four books, including *Managing Personnel/Human Resources: Strategies and Programs.* Professor Schwab has been active in professional associations and has served on the editorial review boards of several behavioral science journals.

This chapter is concerned with how organizations obtain new employees from external labor markets and how individuals seek and choose among organizational opportunities. From a demand perspective, questions addressed include: How do organizations seek out and attempt to attract persons to become employees? How do organizations evaluate and choose among employees? What are the consequences of alternative inducement and evaluation strategies for obtaining and maintaining an adequate work force?[1] From the supply side, questions of interest are: How do individuals seek out organizations? How do they react to organizational attempts to recruit them? How do they evaluate the inducements (or attributes, in decision science jargon) offered by organizations? What

---

[1]Questions involving the organization's evaluation of job applicants might be viewed as the exclusive purview of selection—a topic considered in detail by Hakel and Sharf in Chapters 6 and 7. On close examination, however, the distinction between recruiting (attracting applicants) and selection (choosing among applicants) becomes tenuous. Selection, at least self-selection, goes on during recruiting, and recruiting goes on during the evaluation process. As a result, the present chapter will review, though briefly, some issues that might ordinarily be thought of as within the jurisdiction of selection.

are the consequences of alternative search and evaluation strategies for obtaining jobs and the characteristics of the jobs obtained?

These topics go together logically because the major outcome—employment —depends on the results of a series of decisions made by both the organization through recruiting and the individual seeking employment. Figure 5–1 illustrates this sequence of decisions as they are typically made and identifies the domain of the theory and research presented here.[2] It begins with both the individual and the organization having decided to search. The individual searches for employment opportunities and the organization searches for employees. Third-party intermediaries such as employment services, public or private, may be used during this phase. For the process to terminate successfully, individuals and organizations must identify a possible employment relationship. Organizations usually attempt to generate applications and then evaluate individuals in terms of their predicted suitability for the job in question. Individuals attempt to obtain an offer(s) with acceptable attributes. In some markets it is customary to obtain more than one offer for simultaneous consideration, while in others it is expected that an applicant will accept or reject an offer on receipt.

When an offer is extended and accepted, the process of decisions leading to initial employment ends. However, the new employee is followed in this review to outcomes such as employee satisfaction, tenure, and performance. These outcomes are examined only if they can be attributed to some decision or behavior prior to organizational entry. Thus, research on satisfaction as a function of the realism of the organization's recruiting practices is germane and is included; research on satisfaction as a function of activities following employment (e.g., supervisory practices) is neither germane nor included.

One should keep in mind that the decisions made in Figure 5–1 occur in an economic and political environment. Perhaps most significant is the labor market. A tight labor market, characterized by low levels of unemployment, puts the job seeker at a relative advantage, while a loose labor market is advantageous to the employer. Also of importance is public regulation, including that affecting the inducements organizations offer (e.g., minimum wage laws), and especially equal employment opportunity regulation aimed directly at organizational recruiting and selection practices. Unfortunately, little of the research takes cognizance of these economic and political variables.

The issues identified for inclusion in Figure 5–1 obviously exclude some interesting related questions. For the organization, there are questions about whether additional employees are needed, and, if so, whether they should be recruited internally or externally. (See Dyer's discussion of these issues in Chapter 3.) For the individual, there are questions pertaining to vocational preparation and choice.[3] Also omitted is the decision people make about whether to seek employment in the first place—the labor force participation decision.[4] The decision to exclude these and other related issues was made

[2]The process shown is certainly not descriptive of all situations. Steps in either party's sequence may be skipped. For example, an university may identify a research professor as an attractive prospective employee. Following an evaluation, the professor may be offered a job without having gone through any search activities.

[3]For reviews of that literature, see Crites (1969) and Holland (1976).

[4]See, for example, Marshall, King, and Briggs (1980, pp. 198–206).

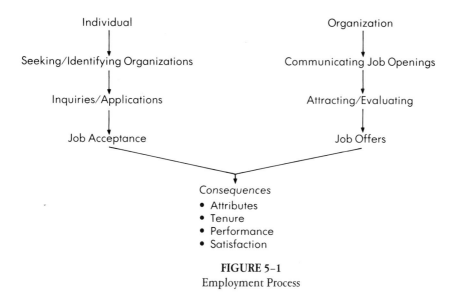

FIGURE 5-1
Employment Process

because of space limitations and not because they lack relevance to the principal purposes of this chapter.

The chapter is organized to address the major issues identified in Figure 5-1. In the next section, participation theories are briefly described and tentatively evaluated. The focus is then directed to the empirical research generated from the organization side. Recruiting methods (e.g., newspaper advertising), the effectiveness of these methods in terms of attracting applicants, and the consequences of the use of these methods on human resource outcomes, such as employee performance and satisfaction, are reviewed. The next major section addresses the process from the perspective of the employment seeker. Included are individual search methods and their effectiveness, and individual reactions to organizational recruiting and inducement (e.g., wages) policies. An attempt is made to identify fruitful areas for additional investigation.

CONCEPTUAL FOUNDATIONS

Not surprisingly, economists have contributed most directly to theories of participation. However, this theorizing has been limited in two important respects. First, until recently, economic theorizing has been limited to employment decisions under conditions of certainty. This is a serious shortcoming, because recruiting and employment search occur largely because of imperfect information and hence the uncertainty that exists in actual labor markets. More recently, theorizing has partially ameliorated this conceptual shortcoming. Second, economic theory has dealt with the employment problem almost exclusively from the supply (employment seeker) side. On the demand side, employers have been assumed to view employees as constituting a homogeneous group. As a consequence, available theory tells little about how employers might try to develop recruiting strategies aimed at achieving organizational goals.

Employment Decisions with Certainty

The point of departure is microeconomic labor market analysis in its classical and neo-classical forms. (See also Mahoney's Chapter 9 in this book.) As articulated in Smith's (1963) *Wealth of Nations* (first published in 1776), freely functioning labor markets serve to move employees through employment opportunities toward the equalization of *net-advantage* (utility). Jobs more advantageous are hypothesized to attract more pro-spective employees and hence drive wages down; jobs less advantageous are hypothe-sized to attract less prospective employees and hence drive wages up. Thus, wage varia-tion between jobs is seen as the principal mechanism through which net-advantage tends toward equality (though the latter is not likely to be attained because of exoge-nous shocks to markets). Components of jobs besides wages contributing to net-advan-tage are working conditions, necessary training, responsibility, and the probability of success in the occupation. These persist in explanations of market behavior to this day (e.g., Fogel, 1979; Rees, 1973). Neoclassical economists, beginning with Clark (1900), modified this explanation only by implicitly or explicitly assuming elements of net-advantage were equal except for wage. Other things being equal, wage differentials were expected to allocate persons to needed jobs.

These explanations have been remarkably durable because many economists believe them to be predictive of how people are allocated to occupations (e.g., Hicks, 1963). However, as noted, they have a major shortcoming in regard to understanding the employment process. Both explanations, especially the neoclassical one, assume that labor market participants are knowledgeable about the available market opportu-nities (e.g., Cartter, 1959). In decision science terminology, they assume that job decisions are made under conditions of certainty. Specifically, the models assume that prospective job seekers are: (1) aware of all employment alternatives (perfectly knowl-edgeable at the *extensive* margin, in Rees's (1966) terms), and (2) aware of all attrib-utes (e.g., the wage level) associated with each alternative (complete knowledge at the *intensive* margin). The job seeker is expected to simultaneously order all job alterna-tives according to some global criterion (net-advantage or utility) as a function of some model that weights the value of each job alternative according to an importance hierarchy for the attributes.

Introduction of Risk and Uncertainty

The formulation of job choice (in which search was assumed away) was first challenged vigorously by the research of institutional labor economists in studies of local labor mar-kets (e.g., Myers & Shultz, 1951; Reynolds, 1951). Reynolds, in particular, argued that the traditional views were deficient in several serious respects. Job seekers that he ob-served had limited knowledge about alternative employment opportunities, even in a local labor market. Moreover, they had limited knowledge of the intensive margin, often no more than a global sense (perhaps not accurate) of whether the employer was "good" or "bad," what the wage rate was, and what the type of work offered was. As a further complication, job seekers often could not consider multiple employment opportunities simultaneously. Rather, because of market constraints, job seekers had to make sequential decisions, first having to reject one alternative before considering another.

Several theories are available that can be used to account for some of these issues. Although only partly stimulated by this research, and not always aimed particularly at employment decisions, these theories have direct implications for decision making when the alternatives and/or attributes of a decision problem are not known with certainty.

Expectancy theory, as formulated by Vroom (1964), introduces two forms of risk into a general model of choice. This model can be directly applied to employment decisions as follows: The force to choose the jth job (F_j) is a function of the product of the expectancy (subjective probability) that the jth job will be offered (E_j), and the summed products of the valences (utilities) of job attributes (V_k) and perceived instrumentalities of the jth job for the attainment of these attributes (I_{jk}).

$$F_j = f[\sum_{k=1}^{n}(V_k \times I_{jk})E_j]$$

The job seeker is expected to behave rationally; that is, make the employment decision with the greatest positive or lowest negative force (where unemployment and labor force withdrawal are possible alternatives).

Expectancy theory thus deals with risk at the intensive margin, or the lack of perfect knowledge about the attributes that will be obtained if a job is accepted, through instrumentalities. It also deals with the risk of obtaining a job offer through expectancies. However, expectancy theory does not account for imperfect knowledge at the extensive margin (i.e., knowledge of the job alternatives available). All job opportunities are assumed to be considered simultaneously so that the employment process retains its emphasis on choice, as in classical and neoclassical economic theory.

Two other conceptual formulations address job seekers' lack of extensive knowledge. Interestingly, in economic theory, interest in job search has developed more from a general concern with imperfect and costly information (see especially, Stigler, 1962) than from the empirical research of the market institutionalists. Although there are variants, job search theory typically assumes that the job seeker knows the market wage distribution.[5] Search is assumed to occur sequentially with random draws from the wage distribution. Offers are usually assumed to be generated one at a time. The task addressed by job search theory is to establish a *reservation wage* that, if accepted, will maximize discounted life-time earnings. This wage is developed as a function of the incremental (marginal) cost of search (both direct and opportunity), and benefit (the wage to be received on the accepted job). The reservation wage, in turn, is hypothesized to influence the wage subsequently received on the new job and the duration of time spent searching. Obviously, job search theory frees (but only partially) prior economic theory from the restrictive assumptions regarding knowledge at the extensive margin.

Decision scientists, most notably Simon (1979), have also developed theoretical models with direct implications for job search and choice. Underlying this orientation is

[5]Alternative formulations of job search theory are discussed by Lippman and McCall (1976).

a concern, not only with the implications of imperfect knowledge, but also with the difficulties of combining multiple attributes into some overall utility for a particular alternative (*bounded rationality*). A noncompensatory model is proposed where minimum standards of acceptability are established for each essential attribute.[6] An illustration for a two-attribute situation is shown in Figure 5-2. Any job offer obtained, which exceeds the minimum reservation wage *and* minimal type of work, would be accepted; otherwise, rejected.

Evaluation

All of the models discussed emphasize the importance of organizational attributes in choices that job seekers make. This is a significant contribution. It should at least alert one to the need to study recruiting in combination with other personnel functions that influence organizational attributes. Thus, for example, recruiting effectiveness cannot be studied adequately in the absence of knowledge about the role of wage and salary administration.

The theories differ substantially in what they hypothesize about organizational characteristics or attributes. Classical economic theory is the only one that explicitly develops a typology of characteristics important in job choice.[7] Moreover, the actual relative importance is not hypothesized *a priori,* because of expected individual differences and because of the compensatory manner in which attributes are assumed to combine in determining net-advantage or overall utility (Rottenberg, 1956).

Neoclassical and job search theories have tended to treat wage as the only organizational attribute considered by job seekers. Although the *ceteris paribus* assumption is

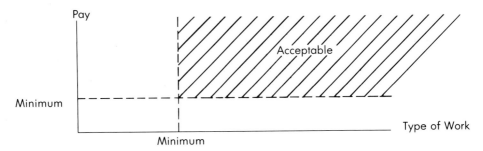

FIGURE 5-2
Satisfactory Job Opportunities

[6]In the case of job choice these may consist of only the wage and type of work, due in part to the job seeker's difficulty in obtaining information about other job attributes prior to employment.

[7]Surprisingly, psychological theory is also devoid of *theorizing* about the importance of attributes in *job choice.* (There are, of course, psychological typologies regarding the importance of attributes once in the organization—most visibly Herzberg's two-factor typology (Herzberg, 1966.) A subsequent section shows that the lack of theory has not prevented a great deal of psychological research on the relative importance of attributes in organizational research.

often explicated, these theories are not helpful in identifying important attributes. Although expectancy and bounded rationality theories clearly assume multiple attributes, they are in the terminology of Campbell and his associates (1970), pure *process* theories. As such, they specify how people combine and utilize information to make decisions (choose a job), but do not specify the attributes or their importance, *a priori*, as would a *content* theory.

As already noted, the theories are generally not helpful for understanding or manipulating organizational recruiting practices. Classical and neoclassical theories assume intensive and extensive knowledge so that recruiting as a means of conveying information is simply not considered. The expectancy formulation, though still a theory of choice, introduces risk at the intensive margin and in terms of the probability of a job offer. It, therefore, not only identifies a role for recruiting, but it can be used to hypothesize how that role affects the probability of job choice.

Job search theory deals with lack of knowledge at the extensive margin, but not at the intensive margin, since wage is treated as the only salient attribute and it is assumed known once a job offer is found. Decision models based on a satisficing strategy recognize imperfect knowledge about both intensive and extensive margins. Thus both implicitly acknowledge a role for recruiting. Unfortunately, both require further elaboration to incorporate recruiting into their premises or to make predictions about the effects of recruiting.

ORGANIZATIONAL RECRUITMENT

The previous section noted that there has been a paucity of theory directly applicable to organizational recruiting activities. This lack of conceptualization, however, has not prevented empirical investigation of recruiting. Two general questions have been given substantial attention: What methods do organizations use to attract prospective employees? How do organizations initially evaluate individuals generated through the recruiting process?

Recruiting Methods

Organizations can obtain recruits through several different methods. One method is reactive, simply letting job seekers initiate the process by applying at the organization. Others are more proactive, including advertising and the use of labor market intermediaries (e.g., employment services). The results of a recent Bureau of National Affairs (BNA, 1979) survey of recruiting methods used by a sample of organizations ($n = 188$) for five occupational groups is shown in Table 5–1.

As Table 5–1 shows, organizations tend to use multiple methods for all occupational groups. This is most descriptive of professional/technical recruiting; least so for sales. There are also substantial differences in the use of specific methods by occupation. Employee referrals, walk-ins, high schools, and the public employment service are all used

TABLE 5–1

Organizational Recruiting Methods by Occupation

Source	Office/ Clerical	Plant/ Service	Occupation Sales	Professional/ Technical	Management
Employee Referrals	92	94	74	68	65
Walk-ins	87	92	46	46	40
Newspaper Advertising	68	88	75	89	82
Local High Schools or Trade Schools	66	61	6	27	7
U.S. Employment Service (USES)	63	72	34	41	27
Community Agencies	55	57	22	34	28
Private Employment Agencies	44	11	63	71	75
(company pays fee)	(31)	(5)	(49)	(48)	(65)
Career Conferences/ Job Fairs	19	16	19	37	17
Colleges/Universities	17	9	48	74	50
Advertising in Special Publications	12	6	43	75	57
Professional Societies	5	19	17	52	36
Radio-TV Advertising	5	8	2	7	4
Search Firms	1	2	2	31	54
Unions	1	12	0	3	0

Note: Figures are percentages of companies providing data for each employee group.

Source: Reprinted by special permission from *Personnel Policies Forum*, copyright 1979, by the Bureau of National Affairs, Inc., Washington, D.C.

more extensively for office/clerical and plant/service than sales, professional/technical, and management. However, private agencies and colleges/universities are more likely to be used to recruit the latter groups. Special publications, and especially search firms, are reserved almost exclusively for recruiting professional/technical and management employees.

Method Effectiveness. Of course, use of a method tells only a small part of the story. Which methods are most likely to yield an adequate number of applicants of high quality? The BNA (1979) asked its participating sample of personnel executives to give a judgment regarding the "most effective source for each (occupational) group." The responses to this question are shown in Table 5–2.

Except for plant/service employees, newspaper advertising was endorsed more frequently as most effective in every occupational group. Walk-ins are relatively highly endorsed for office/clerical and plant/service. Private employment agencies obtain similarly high endorsements for sales, professional/technical, and management.

Of some surprise are the relatively few endorsements obtained by employee referrals. A similar survey of roughly 600 employers by the U.S. Department of Labor (1976) found that employee referrals were viewed as most successful (32.5 percent), followed by newspaper advertisements (29.6 percent). A survey of over 1,000 employers in Great Britain found that "recruitment through personal contacts" (which would include referrals among others) was the most "satisfactory" external recruiting method (*Department of Employment Gazette*, 1975).

Surveys of this sort are potentially limited because they measure managerial *perceptions* of effectiveness. These perceptions may or may not correspond to actual effectiveness. Moreover, it is not clear how effectiveness is defined by those who provide the information. A survey of the Chicago labor market (Rees and Shultz, 1970) asked employers to elaborate on their reasoning for the reported perceptions of effectiveness. Quality of applicants was the most frequently reported reason for preferring a method, although cost and convenience were also criteria reported (Ullman, 1966).

There have been few attempts to assess effectiveness against a "hard" criterion. In one exception, Hill (1970) obtained performance data on clerical employees in three insurance organizations. Although the results were not statistically significant (at $p < .05$), performance ratings on persons who were referred by other employees were higher than those who obtained employment through other methods in all three organizations.

Studies using employment survival as the criterion of effectiveness are partially summarized in Table 5–3. It shows one-year survival rates as a function of recruiting method. In all seven samples, survival rates are higher among persons who were referred by other employees compared to gate applications, want-ad users, or users of private employment agencies.

A number of explanations have been offered for these results. Ullman (1966), for example, suggested that employees who are referred have a more accurate perspective of the job and hence are more likely to remain on it. Stevens (1974) alternatively suggested that market intermediaries, such as employment agencies, may pressure the applicant to accept an option that might otherwise be rejected. "The result may be simply a redis-

TABLE 5–2

Organizational Judgments of Most Effective Recruiting by Occupation

Source	Office/ Clerical	Plant/ Service	Sales	Professional/ Technical	Management
			Occupation		
Newspaper Advertising	39	30	30	38	35
Walk-ins	24	37	5	7	2
Employee Referrals	20	5	17	7	7
Private Employment Agencies	10	2	23	25	27
U.S. Employment Service (USES)	5	6	0	1	1
Local High Schools or Trade Schools	2	2	0	0	0
Colleges/Universities	1	1	8	15	2
Community Agencies	1	3	0	1	2
Unions	0	2	0	0	0
Career Conferences/ Job Fairs	0	1	2	2	1
Professional Societies	0	1	1	0	2
Search Firms	0	0	2	5	17
Radio-TV Advertising	0	1	0	0	1
Advertising in Special Publications	0	0	3	5	8

Note: Figures are percentages of companies providing data for each employee group as indicated in Table 5–1. Columns may add to more than 100 percent because of multiple responses or less than 100 percent because of nonresponses.

Source: Reprinted by special permission from *Personnel Policies Forum*, copyright 1979, by the Bureau of National Affairs, Inc., Washington, D.C.

TABLE 5–3
One Year Survival Rates as a Function of Recruiting Method

| Source | Method* | | | |
	Employee Referrals	Gate Applications	Want Ads	Private Agencies
Decker and Cornelius (1979)				
Bank Employees	69%	57%	67%	52%
Insurance Agents	70	64	57	62
Abstract Service	96	90	79	94
Gannon (1971)				
Bank Employees	74	71	61	61
Reid (1972)†				
Engineering and Metal Trades	39	25	16	—
Ullman (1966)				
Clerical, Company 1	25	—	12	—
Clerical, Company 2	72	—	26	38

*Some studies reported results from additional methods not included here.
†Value for gate applications was referred to in the study as "notice/off-chance."

tribution of unemployment from the present to the future" (p. 13). Hill (1970) noted that the apparently positive effect of employee referrals may reflect criterion contamination. The same employees who recommend initial employment may influence subsequent assessments of performance and hence chances of survival.

Evaluation and Needed Research

To date, recruiting research has done little more than document the methods organizations use to attract job seekers and identify managerial perceptions of the value of these methods. A few studies have assessed performance and survival as a consequence of recruiting method. While the latter clearly represent an improvement over prior methodologies, they too have serious limitations.

A major deficiency occurs because these studies have not explained the reasons for the differential consequences of alternative method usage. Perhaps as Ullman (1966), and more recently Wanous (1980), suggest, the differential consequences stem from the information provided by alternative sources. Employee referrals, for example, may provide relatively "realistic" previews of the job. Thus employees who obtain a job through this method may be more aware (and hence presumably more tolerant) of the employment conditions they experience once in the organization. This explanation clearly emphasizes the importance of the employees' psychological adjustment. If true, it would have direct implications for designing the information content of recruiting programs.

A different explanation involves the hypothesis that job seekers recruited from alternative methods constitute samples from different applicant populations. Job seekers who use referrals may differ, not because they have acquired different information during recruiting, but because they come from a different population than job seekers recruited through other methods.

The latter hypothesis, if valid, has very different implications for recruiting practice. Specifically, it suggests that organizations should focus on identifying the method(s) that taps into the population with the most satisfactory *base rate*(s) (i.e., the percentage of applicants who would be successful if hired). Methods differ greatly in their potential for doing this. For example, employee referrals are essentially constrained to the group that constitutes current employees' existing acquaintances. Advertising, alternatively, is potentially flexible in the populations it taps. Illustrative of this possibility is Martin's (1971) description of how Hughes Aircraft directed written advertisements to different populations of potential applicants. By monitoring responses to different ads (by assigning each a unique return box number), Hughes was able to determine response rates as a function of advertising content and geographical location. A simple extension of this methodology would also allow an assessment of subsequent human resource outcomes, such as survival rates.

A second limitation of available research has been its failure to account for the potential interaction between recruiting method and the labor market. Response rates to recruiting appeals vary substantially as a function of the unemployment level (e.g., Martin, 1971). Quality of applicants probably also varies in response to varying levels of unemployment. However, it is unknown whether response rates and applicant quality vary uniformly across method as the market becomes relatively loose or tight. Only if they do, can generalizations be made from studies done cross-sectionally in labor markets with specific (though usually unreported) unemployment levels.

Finally, research has not accounted for potential interactions between recruiting method and the attributes offered to induce applicant participation. Suggestive of such an interaction is Ullman's (1966) discussion of the Chicago labor market study. He reported that firms preferring applicants from newspaper advertisements (versus referrals) were generally low paying and otherwise unattractive in terms of attributes offered. Perhaps current employees of such organizations were providing accurate job previews to their acquaintances so that self-selection worked adversely among those joining through referrals. Newspaper advertisement respondents, alternatively, may not have been aware of the organization's unattractive attributes. In any event, such evidence combined with the theoretical importance of attributes clearly suggests the need to incorporate them in future studies of recruiting method effectiveness.

EVALUATION OF APPLICANTS

Once the applicant has made contact with the organization through whatever method, evaluation typically takes place in two stages. Stage one usually involves the personnel department and ordinarily consists of an initial screening only. Formal selection techniques, such as psychological tests, are administered during this stage. Candidates who successfully pass this stage are then typically sent to the employing department (second stage), which makes the final hiring decision, usually on the basis of a personal interview(s) only.

Conventional descriptions of personnel activities make a sharp distinction between recruiting and selection. The former is usually depicted as generating applicants, with only passing reference to quality (that is, quantity is emphasized). Selection, in this scheme, is viewed as the primary function to sort among those applicants.

This arbitrary distinction breaks down in practice. As already suggested, organizations are likely to attempt to identify and recruit from applicant populations with high probabilities of job success. In addition, information acquired about applicants throughout the recruiting process is often used evaluatively in the decision to make employment offers. This section briefly considers research on criteria used by organizations in making employment decisions.[8] In the next section, evidence is reviewed suggesting that the evaluative components of the recruiting process impact on applicants' reactions to the organization as a potential employer.

Major Independent Variables

Job Applicants. Most of the research on organizational evaluation criteria has focused on characteristics of applicants. One stream of research has focused on variables that may serve as job qualifications. These include academic qualifications, work experience, and psychological test scores. After reviewing this research, Schwab and Olian (1980) concluded that "however qualifications are manipulated, they account for a large percentage of variance explained in overall suitability ratings on employment recommendations."

Research has also focused on personal characteristics of applicants, particularly those having equal employment opportunity implications.[9] Sex is the single most studied characteristic of this sort. Schwab and Olian (1980) found nine studies in which males, *ceteris paribus,* were evaluated more favorably than females, an equal number in which there were no differences, and two in which females were evaluated more favorably. Some studies have also found interactions between sex and the type of job sought. Although statistically significant results are typical, sex, acting as a main effect or in interaction with job type, has accounted for very little variance in evaluations.

Less research has been performed on race and age of applicants. Regarding race, Schwab and Olian (1980) found only five studies; none of these studies found evidence that blacks received lower evaluations than whites. Only two studies were found dealing with age, so generalizations are unwarranted.

Most recently, research has been performed on whether or not applicant nonverbal communication (e.g., gesturing) during interviews influences organizational assessments of employment suitability. Imada and Hakel (1977), Dipboye and Wiley (1977), and McGovern and Tinsley (1978) found that employer representatives are influenced by nonverbal communication, although just which nonverbal components are most in-

---

[8]This section is based on a paper by Schwab and Olian (1980).
[9]See also a review by Arvey (1979).

fluential is yet to be established. This research is especially interesting because it suggests that job seekers may acquire such skills (in contrast, for example, to the acquisition of academic credentials) and thereby improve their employment prospects. It is also interesting since nonverbal communication is unlikely to represent an important qualification for many jobs.

Decision Makers.   There is little research to suggest how variables other than applicant characteristics might influence evaluations of employment suitability. Several studies have focused on the organizational representative making the employment recommendation. Most convincing here is strong evidence that decision makers exhibit wide differences in applicant preferences (see, e.g., Rowe, 1963; Mayfield and Carlson, 1966). Unfortunately, little is known about what accounts for these differences. (See Chapter 6 in this book for further details.)

Hiring Environment.   There has been a noticeable absence of research on how variables that transcend both the applicant and decision maker may influence employment decisions. For example, what impact do equal employment opportunity regulations or affirmative action plans have on such decisions? Do employment decisions vary systematically as a function of the state of the labor market? How do organizational selection policies influence recruiters' assessments of suitability? These questions are of obvious significance, but Schwab and Olian (1980) were unable to find any research regarding them.

Evaluation and Needed Research

In reviewing the research on organizational evaluations of applicants, one cannot help but suspect that the methodological *tail* has wagged the substantive *dog*. Research has been almost exclusively experimental. As a consequence, it has dealt primarily with applicant variables that are easily manipulated experimentally. To a lesser extent, characteristics of the decision makers have been investigated.

What is most urgently needed is research on how environmental variables influence organizational evaluations of applicants. Organizational characteristics should be studied in much greater detail. For example, does variance in the level of organizational attributes influence its employment standards? Do high wage organizations attract and choose more highly qualified applicants, as has been suggested by some labor economists (e.g., Reynolds, 1951)? How do policies regarding the employment of women and minorities affect actual employment decisions? Only one study (Rosen and Mericle, 1979) has addressed this issue. Are the employment requirements necessary to pass through the initial screening, as conducted by the personnel department, the same as those necessary to be offered a job by the employing unit?

Until questions of this sort are addressed, one will not likely find out if the error variance component, which is so large in most studies, truly represents individual differences among decision makers or organizational differences that have simply been uncontrolled in prior research. A potentially helpful literature to suggest research strategies is available in marketing on organizational buying behavior (for a review, see Sheth, 1977). The analogies between the two types of decisions appear quite extensive.

In all probability, research accounting for organizational variance in applicant evaluations will have to move from the laboratory into the field. In the process, investigators would be well advised to study applicants other than new entrants, which have been overrepresented to date. They would also be well advised to incorporate the sequential nature of employment decisions as they actually occur in the usual employment process.

THE INDIVIDUAL'S DECISION TO PARTICIPATE

To a considerable extent, research on individual participation decisions parallels that of research on organizational recruitment. Some of this research has focused on the methods used by job seekers in finding employment possibilities. Another stream has focused on how applicants evaluate and choose among job opportunities.

Applicant Search

Research on applicant search has been conducted largely within an economic orientation. Many studies have been performed in local labor markets. They have tended to examine the methods job seekers use to obtain employment, the duration of unemployment as a function of personal characteristics and behaviors, and the outcomes obtained after reemployment, especially wages. A number of more aggregative studies have focused more narrowly on the methods of search employed. Studies have also been recently conducted on the consequences of search intensity.

Search Methods.   As noted earlier, job seekers often have little information about organizational opportunities (extensive knowledge), or about the attributes associated with these opportunities (intensive knowledge). As a consequence, much research has been directed at how job seekers acquire information about organizations and jobs. Some of this research has simply documented the methods used by job seekers. Most, however, has also attempted to identify the method that led to job attainment.[10]

Much of the evidence on methods used by job seekers comes from studies of local labor markets. Stevens (1977) summarized twenty-two such studies on thirty samples of job seekers conducted between World War II and 1970. Overwhelmingly, they indicate that job seekers obtain jobs based on information acquired through informal methods. Friends/relatives were cited as the source of information a median 34 percent of the time (range, 9–59). The median for direct application was 32 percent (range, 9–52). The public employment service median of 6 percent (range, 0–23) was a distant third.

---

[10]The measurement problems here are obvious and probably quite serious. In addition to memory difficulties (the studies are exclusively retrospective), there is the problem of ascribing to a single method credit for a job which likely was obtained using multiple methods.

More recent studies tend to confirm the heavy reliance that job seekers place on informal methods in obtaining employment. Partial results of a nation-wide survey reported by Rosenfeld (1975) are shown in Table 5–4.[11] They indicate some differences in method usage by occupation. White collar job seekers are more likely to obtain employment through private employment services than blue collar job seekers. They are less likely (with the exception of clerical workers) to obtain employment through the public employment service. For all occupational groups, however, direct applications and friends/relations account for about one-half to three-fourths of successful job sources.

Search Intensity.   In addition to the methods used to acquire information, it is probable that the effort job seekers expend in their search activities also influences employment seeking success. This is the issue of search intensity.

Evidence suggestive of the probable importance of search intensity has been generated in several places. Dyer (1973), for example, found that delaying active search following job loss was positively associated with duration of unemployment among middle-age managerial and professional job losers. He also found that perceived financial security was positively related to unemployment duration, which may suggest a two-stage process: financial security reduces search intensity which, in turn, increases duration of unemployment.

Studies stimulated by job search theory have examined the duration of unemployment as a function of unemployment benefits. Although the results are not entirely unambiguous, it appears that increases in benefit levels increase the duration of unemployment (for reviews, see Fields, 1977; Welch, 1977). One explanation for this conclusion is

TABLE 5–4
Method by which Current Job Was Obtained by Occupation

Occupation	Direct Application	Friends/ Relatives	Ads in Paper	Private Service	Public Service	Other
Professional	30.7	20.3	9.0	5.6	1.6	32.8
Managerial	24.3	25.3	16.5	10.9	2.5	20.5
Sales	42.8	23.8	16.8	4.3	2.2	10.1
Clerical	25.4	22.9	14.5	15.1	6.7	15.4
Craft Workers	41.1	28.2	9.5	1.5	4.2	15.5
Operatives Nonfarm	41.5	29.2	10.8	1.2	7.0	10.3
Laborers	40.1	36.1	6.4	.5	5.9	11.0
Service	38.7	29.1	14.8	1.3	5.7	10.4

Source: C. Rosenfeld. "Job Seeking Methods Used by American Workers." *Monthly Labor Review* (1975): 39–42.

[11]See also Schiller (1975).

that benefits allow job seekers to hold out for better employment conditions.[12] However, another explanation is that the increased benefits associated with nonwork (unemployment) simply result in a reduction in search intensity, thus resulting in an extended period of unemployment.

Research in vocational counseling is also suggestive of the value of search intensity. In general, this literature has begun to suggest that client job seeking may be more effective in obtaining employment than counselor attempts to obtain placement (e.g., Zadny and James, 1977). Moreover, programs designed to facilitate client search appear to benefit from components that encourage greater intensity of search. One such component, in a project described by Azrin, Flores, and Kaplan (1975), involved family, counselor, and fellow client encouragement to search out many alternatives. Although the program confounded this treatment with job seeking skill-building (e.g., recommendations for dress and grooming), 90 percent of participating clients were employed within two months compared to 55 percent of a nonparticipatory control group.

Finally, two studies have addressed the question of search intensity directly. Felder (1975), and more recently Barron and Gilley (1979), operationalized intensity as the average numbers of hours spent searching each week. Both found that men searched more intensively than women. Barron and Gilley also reported that search intensity was negatively related to unemployment benefits and to other nonwage income. These findings offer direct support for the hypothesis that financial resources reduce search intensity. Felder also found that intensity was negatively related to prior unemployment. In expectancy theory terms, prior unemployment may reduce expectancies about obtaining employment and, hence, the force to search.

Evaluation and Needed Research

The research on methods used by job seekers is very limited in scope, despite the large number of investigations performed and the impressive range of samples studied. True, a great deal is known about the methods used and about the methods that result in employment. However, a number of important questions remain.

Virtually nothing is known about the duration of unemployment associated with alternative methods (do some methods produce jobs more rapidly than others?), or about the job attributes obtained as a function of alternative methods. Suggestive that methods may influence these variables are studies by Felder (1975) and Reid (1972). Both found, for example, that male users of the public employment service tended to remain unemployed longer than users of alternative methods. Both also found that the methods used are related to the attributes obtained in the new job. Interestingly, both studies found that persons who obtain jobs with the help of friends or relatives are more likely to experience a wage reduction (compared to their last job) than users of alternative methods.

---

[12]Largely because of methodological difficulties this linkage has not been empirically demonstrated or refuted (Welch, 1977).

Other problems include the fact that none of the research has taken costs into account in addressing the efficiency of alternative methods (Stevens, 1977). Moreover, the research has not identified the types and quality of information provided, although there is evidence that market information is related to employment success (Parnes and Kohen, 1975). Finally, little is known about what leads people to use alternative methods, and nothing about whether some alternatives are more productive for some persons than for others.

As a consequence, it is premature to recommend methods people should use to maximize their job-obtaining chances, which is, after all, of major concern to job seekers. Nor is it appropriate yet to suggest ways that various methods could be made more effective. The latter is a major concern of public policy, especially with respect to the public employment service.

Research on search methods would provide an incomplete picture of applicant job search, even if it adequately addressed the preceding issues. In addition to the methods used to acquire information, it is probably important to take search intensity into account as well. Although admittedly tentative, that evidence suggests that intensity is predictably related to personal characteristics, and, particularly, to situational variables of individuals. Less is known about the consequences of intensity, although it probably influences the duration of unemployment.[13] In any event, search intensity should be incorporated with method usage in subsequent research on job applicants.

APPLICANT CHOICE

Much of the literature reviewed thus far has used, as dependent variables, data on whether or not job seekers obtained employment and/or the time required to attain employment. Left out, therefore, is a very important element in the employment process; namely, the decision to accept or reject a specific job offer. Fortunately, research has been conducted on the latter issue. Indeed, two separate literatures have emerged. One focuses on how job seekers react to various job attributes or combinations of attributes. It has potential implications for the theories of choice discussed earlier. The second has examined how job choosers respond to alternative recruiting practices. Embedded in it is the recognition that market information is less than perfect. The information medium (i.e., recruiting procedures) thus may potentially influence applicants as well as the message (i.e., attributes) being offered.

The Message

Investigations of applicant preferences for, and reactions to, jobs have taken three general forms.[14] Most frequently, applicants are asked to rank order or provide ratings of

---

[13]It should be noted that Felder (1975) found intensity to be inversely related to duration of unemployment, although not at a statistically significant level. Again, using a more representative sample, Barron and Mellow (1978) found that search intensity (as measured by hours searching) did increase the probability of reemployment during a subsequent time period. On the other hand, a study in Pennsylvania found that intensity (as measured by number of employer contracts) did not reduce the duration of unemployment.

[14]This section is based on a paper by Schwab, Rynes, and Aldag (1980).

their preferences for an investigator-chosen list of attributes. A second type has incorporated attribute ratings with one or two other perceptions reflecting risk, typically within an expectancy theory framework. The dependent variables in such studies are usually an overall utility rating of jobs or actual job choice. A third form has made inferences about attribute preferences using a policy-capturing approach.

Ranking and Rating. As noted, many studies have asked applicants to rank or rate a set of job attributes. Lawler (1971) found forty-nine such studies, although not all asked for responses from job applicants. Since his review, a number of additional such studies have been reported (e.g., Allen, Keaveny, and Jackson, 1978; Brief, Rose, and Aldag, 1977; Singer, 1974; Weaver, 1975; Ullman and Gutteridge, 1973).

By far the most ambitious investigation has been reported by Jurgensen (1978). He has obtained rankings of self-preferences from job applicants at the Minneapolis Gas Company since 1945 and on preferences applicants ascribe to others since 1949. Summary results of this study are shown in Table 5–5, which reports median ranks by sex and self-preferences versus those ascribed to others.

Before much emphasis is placed on the findings, it is important to recognize that the ranking/rating methodology is of dubious validity. While the limitations are many (see, e.g., Lawler, 1971, for a review), two seem especially vulnerable to errors of social desirability. For example, Opsahl and Dunnette (1966) hypothesized that the relatively low rank of pay in many such studies reflects social desirability. The much higher rank of pay ascribed to others than to self in the Jurgensen (1978) data (see Table 5–5) is consistent with this hypothesis.

TABLE 5–5
Median Ranks of 10 Job Attributes Obtained from Applicants to the Minneapolis Gas Company

| | Sex and Preference Source | | | |
| | Men | | Women | |
Attribute	Self	Others	Self	Others
Advancement	3.3	3.8	5.3	4.3
Benefits	6.8	5.2	8.0	5.9
Company	4.5	6.8	4.6	7.1
Co-Workers	6.0	7.7	5.2	7.3
Hours	7.6	5.4	6.9	5.0
Pay	5.6	2.1	6.0	2.1
Security	2.5	3.6	4.9	5.4
Supervisor	6.3	7.4	5.3	7.0
Type of Work	3.3	4.9	1.5	3.5
Working Conditions	7.9	6.9	6.5	6.8
(N)	(39,788)	(32,810)	(16,833)	(15,138)

Source: Adapted from C. E. Jurgenson. "Job Preferences (What Makes a Job Good or Bad?)." *Journal of Applied Psychology* 63 (1978): 267–276. Copyright 1978 by the American Psychological Association. Reprinted by permission.

The second major criticism is theoretically based. If attributes are combined in some compensatory fashion to form an overall utility value for a job alternative (e.g., as hypothesized in classical economic theory), then the importance of any attribute could change as a function of the level of that attribute in combination with the levels of other attributes. If true, to ask for the value of specific attributes in the abstract is a vacuous exercise.[15]

Expectancy Models.   Recall that expectancy theory hypothesizes that choice is a function of the applicant's assessment of the attributes (valence), of the perceived likelihood that a job will provide these attributes (instrumentality), and the probability of obtaining the job offer (expectancy). Tests of expectancy theory could thus be used to address applicant evaluations of job attributes in two ways. First, valence responses could be used as direct estimates of the importance of attributes. These responses, of course, are essentially identical to ratings as previously discussed, with all of the potential problems already identified.

Second, the predictability of the model might be used as an indirect test of the importance of attributes; that is, one might argue that the valence responses accurately reflect job seeker assessments of attributes if they accurately predict job seeker choices. Unfortunately, that argument is not necessarily valid. That a model is predictive does not necessarily mean that it is isomorphic with the decision process used by the job seeker. For example, high predictability could result from the relationship between instrumentalities and choice; valences may contribute little or nothing.

Studies testing expectancy theory have usually found that valences combined with instrumentality assessments of attributes are highly predictive of the dependent variable. However, a summary of selected measurement characteristics of these investigations (see Table 5–6) shows that they have ordinarily used an overall attractiveness rating/ranking of jobs or occupations as the dependent variable. As a consequence, the causal direction is unclear and the strength of the relationship may be substantially inflated because of response biases (e.g., Schwab, 1980). Moreover, studies that have investigated specific components of the theory have found that valence did not increase predictability over that provided by instrumentality alone (Lawler, et al., 1975; Mitchell and Knudsen, 1973; Muchinsky and Taylor, 1976; Oldham, 1976; Sheard, 1970). Thus, expectancy theory evidence generated so far provides little reassurance that asking subjects for assessments of the importance on valence of attributes provides much information.

Policy Capturing.   A recently employed methodology asks participants only for an overall evaluation of each job alternative. However, the attributes for each alternative are systematically varied by the investigator. For example, one job might be described as consisting of a high salary, rapid promotion, and low security. Another job might be described as having a moderate salary, slow promotion, high security, and so forth. Evaluations of the jobs, in total, are analyzed statistically as a function of the attribute levels contained in the job descriptions. This procedure is usually referred to as *policy captur-*

---

[15]In economic jargon, this issue has to do with the marginal rates of substitution between attributes. See either Reynolds (1951) or Rottenberg (1956) for an elaboration of this issue.

TABLE 5-6
Measurement Characteristics of Expectancy Theory Predictions of Job Attractiveness and Choice

Reference	Independent			Dependent	
	Valence	Instrumentality	Expectancy	Overall Attractiveness	Job Choice
Bartol (1976)	Yes	Yes	No	Yes*	No
Hill (1974)	Yes	Yes	No	Yes	No
Holmstrom and Beach (1973)	Yes	Yes	No	Yes	No
Lawler et al. (1975)	Yes	Yes	Yes	Yes	Yes
Mitchell and Knudsen (1973)	Yes	Yes	No	Yes*	No
Muchinsky and Taylor (1976)	Yes	Yes	No	Yes	No
Oldham (1976)	Yes	Yes	Yes	No	Yes
Pieters, Hundert, and Beer (1968)	Yes	Yes	No	No	Yes†
Sheard (1970)	Yes	Yes	No	Yes	No
Vroom (1966)	Yes	Yes	No	Yes	Yes
Wanous (1972)	Yes	Yes	No	Yes	No

*Dependent variable was stated choice of occupation.
†Choice made before expectancy theory perceptions obtained.

ing because the decision maker's policy is inferred from the variance in job evaluations attributable to variation in attribute levels.

The procedure is intuitively appealing in light of the compensatory model hypothesized in classical economic theory. Presenting multiple levels of attributes allows decision makers to take into account trade-offs that may occur as one confronts various combinations of attributes associated with different alternatives. It also appears to ameliorate some of the other methodological problems associated with the rating/ranking of attributes. Social desirability as an undesirable influence is less likely because participants are only asked to evaluate jobs in a global way. Evaluations of alternatives (rather than attributes) also appear to conform more closely to the decisions job seekers must actually make in the labor market.

A study by Zedeck (1977) is illustrative of this method. He had subjects (two samples) evaluate sets of job descriptions in terms of whether they would be willing to accept the positions described. Six attributes (see Table 5-7) were varied across five levels (e.g., in one sample salary ranged from $10,000 to $14, 800 per year) that were arbitrarily assigned numerical values.[16] He then regressed the evaluation scores of jobs on the attribute scores for each subject.

On average, the policy-capturing methodology explained 53 percent (sample 1) and 67 percent (sample 2) of the variance in overall job ratings. However, he also found that individuals apparently differ in the models they use to make job decisions. Moreover, Einhorn (1971) and Fischer (1976) found that individuals may not combine information about attributes in a linear fashion.

Participants in Zedeck's second sample were also asked to provide direct importance assessments of the attributes. One method asked for a simple ranking (from 1 to 6); the other asked subjects to allocate 100 points among the attributes according to their importance. A composite ranking (across all subjects) of attribute importance yielded by the three methods is provided in Table 5-7. Security was the most important variable in the policy-capturing model (i.e., it made the largest contribution to explained variance in overall job ratings). However, security ranked fifth in importance in the two methods that assessed importance of attributes directly. Likewise, while responsibility ranked one and two in the direct methods, its contribution to variance in overall ratings using policy capturing was fourth.

Clearly then, policy capturing may result in different evaluations of attribute importance than does rating/ranking. Moreover, given the limitations identified with rating/ranking, and the apparent methodological attractiveness of policy capturing, the latter estimation procedure is probably superior.

The Medium

Research on whether the recruiting medium impacts on job seekers has been based on the premise that organizational recruiting practices may influence evaluations of jobs and organizations independently of the attributes offered.[17] Two sources of influence

[16]Jobs were described to make the attributes empirically orthogonal of each other. This is important for interpreting the weights obtained from the analysis.

[17]The discussion in this section relies primarily on a review by Rynes, Heneman, and Schwab (1980).

TABLE 5–7
Attribute Importance as a Function of Method

| | Rank Orders | | |
Attribute	Policy Capturing	Ranks	Points
Flexibility	6	6	6
Salary	2	2	1
Security	1	5	5
Advancement	4	1	2
Responsibility	3	3	3
Growth	5	4	4

Score of 1 is most important and score of 6 is least important.
Source: S. Zedeck. ''An Information Processing Model and Approach to Study of Motivation.'' *Organizational Behavior and Human Performance* 18 (1977): 47–77.

are potentially involved. One consists of the administrative procedures necessary to attract and process job applicants. Examples include behaviors of organizational representatives, such as recruiters, written communication with applicants, and the realism of recruiting practices. The second involves those organizational activities used to evaluate applicants for the job offer decision. Examples of the latter include applicant reactions to psychological testing and other methods used to obtain information on which the employment decision will be based.

Administrative Issues. Most of the research aimed at administrative concerns has been on how organizational representatives, especially the recruiter, impact on job applicants. Some has focused on how the organizational representative's knowledge of either the (1) jobs offered, or (2) applicants' qualifications, influences applicant evaluations. Not only did Rynes, Heneman, and Schwab (1980) find a good deal of anecdotal evidence on this point, but they found experimental evidence that recruiter knowledge of jobs offered influenced applicant subjective probabilities of receiving and accepting a job offer.

Characteristics of organizational representatives have also been investigated. Rynes, Heneman, and Schwab (1980) found a number of studies that purportedly investigated personality characteristics of recruiters. Unfortunately, most of this research has not defined or measured personality in a very rigorous fashion. Fewer studies have examined demographic characteristics of organizational representatives, although recruiter age has been examined in several studies.

The few studies on recruiting procedures have tended to find that such procedures are influential in terms of applicant responses. For example, Arvey and associates (1975) found that delays in responding to applications lowered applicant responses to the recruiting process. Ivancevich and Donnelly (1971) claimed that contacts with applicants after acceptance (but before they reported to work) influenced the rate at which they actually reported for work.

A current issue investigated in this respect is the ''realistic job preview'' (RJP). Evidence reviewed elsewhere suggests that RJPs lead to higher postemployment satisfaction levels and survival rates (Wanous, 1977, 1980). At issue here, however, is whether RJPs influence reactions to the recruiting procedure, specifically whether or not RJPs have an adverse impact on self-selection. While Rynes, Heneman, and Schwab (1980) found that most studies of RJPs did not adequately address this issue, studies by Reilly, Tenopyr, and Sperling (1979) and Farr, O'Leary, and Bartlett (1973) found evidence of an adverse self-selection effect. On the other hand, a study by Wanous (1973) did not. Clearly, more research will have to be conducted on RJPs before this question is answered.

Evaluative Issues. Investigations of applicant responses to the way organizations evaluate them has concentrated on the selection interview and psychological testing. The most tenable general conclusion obtained by Rynes, Heneman, and Schwab (1980) is that applicants prefer evaluation procedures with high "face" validity. Thus, for example, there is evidence that work samples are preferred to paper and pencil tests among applicants who would perform manual jobs (Schmidt et al., 1977).

Evaluation and Needed Research

A substantial amount of research has been performed on both the message and the medium. With respect to the former, however, few generalizations seem warranted. There are several reasons why no generally accepted hierarchy of attributes has emerged, and probably will not emerge. First, as noted, differences in methodology appear to yield markedly different estimates of attribute importance. Until an appropriate methodology is recognized, all findings will be suspect.

Second, individuals probably differ in their assessments of attributes. Both expectancy theory and policy-capturing studies suggest this possibility. If true, researchers would be well advised to focus on the predictability of individual preferences. Such studies should include pertinent labor market variables as well as personal characteristics.

Longitudinal research on attribute preferences would also be appropriate. Search theories hypothesize that the evaluation of attributes may vary over time. Moreover, there is some empirical support for this hypothesis with respect to job seeker evaluations of wages (e.g., Felder, 1975; Kasper, 1967).

Finally, more attention needs to be given to the decision models job seekers use to choose among jobs. Expectancy theory and policy capturing, by implication at least, assume that the evaluation of any one job is independent of the evaluation of other jobs. However, Soelberg (1967) has suggested that job seekers compare alternatives, which would mean that evaluations are not independent. If true, none of the methodologies that have been used extensively to date may be appropriate.

Turning to the medium, Rynes, Heneman, and Schwab (1980) concluded that organizational recruiting practices do impact on applicant reactions including, in some cases, their decisions to accept or reject an offer. This conclusion must be tempered in several respects. First, the evidence has overwhelmingly been obtained on new entrants, usually students graduating from college. It seems probable that new entrants are more responsive to recruiting efforts than experienced workers, who are presumably more knowledgeable about employment conditions. Second, research has been limited to examining a restricted number of recruiting procedures. It may be that the most influential aspects of recruiting are yet to be identified. In this vein, it is recommended that more emphasis be given to studying procedural elements of the recruiting process (as was done by Arvey et al., 1975) as opposed to characteristics of organizational representatives.

Finally, no research on recruiting (the medium) has been conducted within a methodological framework that also obtains variation in job attributes (the message). It may be that recruiting practices are colinear with organizational attributes (and hence potentially redundant), or that the medium and the message interact. In any event, our knowledge of applicant responses to organizational recruiting will be limited until researchers examine attributes with recruiting simultaneously.

CONCLUSIONS

Each year, millions of jobs are filled from the external labor market. To accomplish this, organizations must usually engage actively in recruiting, and individuals must search out, and choose among, employment opportunities. A good deal is known about some portions of these parallel decision sequences, but much remains to be learned.

Well known are the methods individuals use to seek employment and the methods leading to employment. Also well known are the methods organizations use to recruit and the methods personnel managers believe to be effective. It is also known that organizational recruiting procedures influence employment acceptance rates and post-employment outcomes such as survival rates. Finally, little is known about some of the criteria both organizations and individuals use to make their final employment decisions, although much of the decision variance remains unexplained.

The major unknown in the process has to do with explaining the reasons for what is known. It is especially important to explain why some recruiting methods yield better results than others. Is it because different methods provide different information? If so, what are the differences? Or is it because of systematic differences in the users of alternative methods? If the latter, what are these differences? What role do labor market and legislative factors play in influencing both organizations and employment seekers? Answers to these sorts of questions will do much to contribute to an understanding of personnel management and will provide much intellectual excitement for the field.

Discussion Questions

1. Discuss the kinds of labor markets where choice models would likely be most relevant versus those where search models would probably be applicable.

2. Both job attributes (the message) and recruiting procedures (the medium) have been found to influence job seekers' choice decisions. How do you think these sources of influence combine to influence decisions?

3. Why does the importance assigned to attributes seem to vary as a function of the method for obtaining the information? In your judgment, what is the best method for obtaining such information?

4. What are the two or three most important research needs for improving the effectiveness of organizational recruiting practices? Why are they important?

5. Design an organizational recruiting program to attract highly qualified college graduates into a professional job (e.g., engineering). Specify assumptions about organizational characteristics that you feel it would be important to know about before you develop your recruiting program.

The material in this manuscript was prepared with support from the Graduate School, University of Wisconsin-Madison and from Grant No. 21-55-78-32, Employment and Training Administration, U.S. Department of Labor, under the authority of Title III, part B, of the Comprehensive Employment and Training Act of 1973. Researchers undertaking such projects under government sponsorship are encouraged to express freely their professional judgment. Therefore, points of view or opinions stated in this document do not necessarily represent the official position or policy of the Department of Labor. The author gratefully acknowledges the critical comments of Lee Dyer, Tom Mahoney, Judy Olian, and Sara Rynes on earlier drafts of this manuscript.

CHAPTER SIX

EMPLOYMENT INTERVIEWING

Milton D. Hakel

Milton D. Hakel is Professor of Psychology at Ohio State University. He received his Ph.D in Psychology from the University of Minnesota. Professor Hakel is currently the editor of the journal *Personnel Psychology*, and serves on the editorial boards of several other behavioral science journals. Professor Hakel has published extensively and has been awarded research grants from many different federal agencies, including a Fulbright-Hays Research Grant in 1978. He is also the author of the forthcoming book, *Personal Judgment and Personnel Decisions*. Professor Hakel is perhaps best known for his research on the employment interview.

In 1915, Walter Dill Scott became the first person to document the relatively poor reliability of judgments made by interviewers. Thirty-six sales applicants were independently interviewed by six sales managers. After each manager had interviewed all candidates, the candidates were rank-ordered independently. Scott analyzed the agreement and found it was very poor. The candidate ranked first by one interviewer was ranked thirty-second by another. In general, there was little agreement about whether a candidate belonged in the upper or lower half of the distribution. The overall picture emerging from his data was very discouraging. In a companion report published a year later (Scott, 1916), a similarly gloomy result emerged from a study relating interviewers' judgments to measures of job performance, one of the first validity studies.

Although Scott's research methods left a great deal to be desired, his conclusions have stood the test of time.

In 1960, England and Patterson suggested a "moratorium on books, articles and other writings about 'how to interview,' 'do's and don'ts about interviewing' and the like until there is sufficient research evidence about the reliability and validity of the interview as an assessment device to warrant its use in such work."

In 1963, Dunnette and Bass surprised no one by saying, ''The interview is a costly, inefficient and usually non-valid procedure, often used to the exclusion of far more thoroughly researched and validated procedures. The interview should be retired from its role as an assessment tool and be retained only as a public relations, recruiting and information disseminating device.'' Three years later, Dunnette (1966) was moved to suggest that interviewers also do a poor job of public relations.

Little has happened in the last few years to encourage optimism about the reliability and validity of interviews as they are usually conducted. Given the typical organization's practices with regard to interviewing, the lack of interviewer training, and the lack of guidance for interpreting applicants' responses, the calls for a moratorium and/or for retiring the interview are still warranted. The interview is, after all, basically a subjective method.

Thus, the predominant view of the interview among academic researchers and psychometrists has been quite negative, and both the substance and the limits of this view will be examined in some detail. There are also many other perspectives on interviewing that will be covered.

Despite its subjectivity, the interview is the single most important means of gathering information for making personnel decisions. For most managers and practitioners, hiring without using the interview is unthinkable. For most job applicants, the prospect of being hired without being interviewed is likewise unthinkable. If given a choice between being interviewed and taking a test, most applicants would choose the interview. Most people have faith in the process. The interview is the place to ''put your best foot forward.'' ''If you can just get in to see the interviewer, you can tell your whole story and once the interviewer understands 'the *whole* story,' a job offer is sure to result.'' A face-to-face exchange of information is much more satisfying than filling out forms or test answer sheets. An applicant believes that he or she can persuade others of the appropriateness of his or her conduct, and that ''extenuating circumstances'' are *really* extenuating. Unfortunately, the applicant's trust in the process and faith in the interviewer are probably naive and misplaced. The picture looks bleak indeed.

Research conducted during the 1960s and 1970s, however, offers some hope for improved interviewing practices. The research findings make it possible to take a new perspective on employment interviewing. But before presenting recommendations for interviewing practice, one should look first at the previous state-of-the-art, examining four outcome issues: reliability, validity, fairness, and utility. Then research on the interviewer's decision-making processes will be surveyed. This will be followed by recommendations for practice.

OUTCOME RESEARCH

Evaluative research on interviewing has focused on reliability and validity as principal outcomes. Both of these topics will be briefly surveyed; in addition, fairness and utility will be covered, in all cases noting both substance and limitations.

Reliability

Several comprehensive reviews of the research literature have been written. Wagner (1949) located 125 articles concerning interviewing, but only 24 of them dealt with the results of empirical research. He reported reliabilities ranging from .23 to .97, with a median value of only .57. Ulrich and Trumbo (1965) reported trait-rating reliabilities ranging from .15 to .90 and concluded that ratings yield, with but few exceptions, reliabilities considerably below the level generally regarded as necessary for individual assessment and prediction. They recommended that the interviewer's attention be confined to assessing applicants' social skills and motivation, a recommendation which was based on the absence of techniques superior to the interview for making these assessments. Thus the interview takes its place in the selection process, not on its merits, but by default. Mayfield (1964) presented similar conclusions. Recent research has not focused on reliability, and the few incidental reports result in no substantial change in the estimate of typical reliability.

Validity

The comprehensive reviews show similar results for studies of validity. Wagner (1949) reported a median validity coefficient of .25. Mayfield (1964) concluded that even when interrater agreement is high, validities based on job behavior criteria are usually very low. He also concluded that predictions based on interview inferences rarely have been more, and usually have been less, accurate than predictions based on tests alone. Finally, he noted that validities for interview-based trait ratings are consistently high for only one trait—intelligence, and intelligence is more reliably measured by tests. Little has been reported in the years since these reviews to change the overall picture. Both reliability and validity are lower than desired. This gives the substance of the state-of-the-art, and there are some limitations.

Unfortunately, these conclusions come from studies in which the research designs are little better than the design used by Scott (1915) in the initial investigations of reliability and validity. Most of the studies conducted on employment interviewing have been poorly conceived, poorly conducted, and therefore generally inconclusive. Mayfield noted, for example:

1. Practically no experimental investigations of the employment interview have been conducted. The typical study simply compares interview-based ratings with estimates or ratings of job behavior. Thus, the typical investigation shows nothing of the process leading to either set of ratings.
2. Most studies have failed to record, in any systematic way, the behavior of the interviewer during the interview.
3. Most studies have failed to record, in any systematic way, the behavior of the interviewee during the interview.
4. Most studies have failed to record the nature and method of information transmission during the interview.
5. Most studies have failed to examine in any way the process of impression formation and decision making as it occurs during the interview.

If the studies are taken at face value, then the emerging conclusions regarding reliability and validity are indeed discouraging. Proper interpretation of research data is a fine art, however. Averaging the results of several fallible studies will give a fallible average. That average may properly typify the usual results, but it would be wrong to conclude on the basis of such an average that all interviews are unreliable and invalid.

When one sees a familiar number, it is easy to believe that its meaning is clear. It is easy to forget the circumstances that gave rise to the number, and all of the qualifiers and caveats that belong to it. Interpreting reliability and validity averages is analogous to the problem faced by an employment interviewer in trying to interpret a job applicant's grade point average. Because grades are reported on a numerical scale, it is easy to make comparisons among applicants. But these relative comparisons can be quite misleading, especially when one tries to compare students who attended different schools. As every student knows, grades are influenced by many factors, only some of which are under the control of the individual student. Interviewers probably assign too much importance to the grade point average as an indicator of the applicant's intellectual ability (Hakel, Dobmeyer, and Dunnette, 1970) and neglect to emphasize the other factors that influence grades: the applicant's motivation, difficulty of courses, grading standards of instructors, institutional standards and practices concerning pass-fail courses and withdrawing from courses where one is doing poorly, the abilities and motivations of other students in the course, the quality of the course, the department and the institution, and blind chance.

This analogy is useful because, although most readers will have experience with grade point averages, few aside from psychometrists have sufficient acquaintance with correlation coefficients used to report reliability and validity. Thus, it is easy to take reported findings at face value. Yet, problems beset the interpreter of reliability and validity averages: deficient research designs, small sample sizes, variations in information gathered, variations in the judgments to be made, problems in measuring the judgments themselves, problems in measuring criteria, and blind chance. All of these factors influence the observed results, and therefore the interpretation of reliability and validity studies.

A final problem in interpreting averages relates to the way people process information. When contemplating an average, one easily forgets that there is variability about that average. Interview reliabilities as high as .90 and .97 have been observed; at the other extreme, reliability coefficients have been observed that cannot be differentiated from chance correlations. The point is that there *is* variability in results and that it doesn't make a great deal of sense to talk about *the* reliability or *the* validity of the interview unless one takes into account the variability of results and the nature of the studies used to compile those averages.

Fairness

During the 1970s, fairness became an overriding issue in the evaluation of selection techniques. It has been most obviously an issue in the use of tests where mean differences between blacks and whites are interpreted as evidence of unfairness. The essential issue is whether the selection device gives unwarranted advantages to members of one group or another (Chapter 7 on personnel testing and the law by Sharf presents more information on this concern, showing that what would seem to be a simple issue is, in fact, very complex.) The issue must be resolved in terms of actual job performance, rather than in terms of predictions of job performance or differences on predictor measurements.

The issue of fairness has just begun to be raised regarding the interview (Arvey, 1979). Here, and with tests, the issue must be resolved in terms of effectiveness in predicting job performance; that is, with regard to validity. No such studies have been reported, nor have there even been studies of the interview *in use* reporting black-white or male-female differences in interviewer predictions of potential job performance.

The question of the interview's fairness, however, deserves complete and thorough analysis. The interview is far more susceptible to bias, error, and other problems in selection than is testing or the statistical use of biographical information. It is evident that if one's intent is to discriminate *against* the members of one group, or to discriminate *for* the members of another group, the simplest way to do so is through the employment interview. While it is technically feasible to do so, it would be quite difficult to construct a test to be intentionally discriminatory. The interview deserves close scrutiny.

Federal guidelines make it clear that the interview is to be accorded the same status and receive the same scrutiny as any other selection technique. It is to be treated by the same standards applied to tests. Thus, in recent years there has been a growing number of court cases concerning interviewing practices. Arvey (1979) concluded that the interview is highly vulnerable to legal attack and that one can expect more litigation concerning it in the future. He reviewed nine cases where interviewing practices were at issue. In addition, he reviewed pertinent research and reached several conclusions:

1. The mechanisms and processes that contribute to bias in the interview are not well specified by researchers.
2. Findings based predominantly on resume research (simulation) show that females tend to receive lower evaluations than males, but this varies as a function of job and situational characteristics.
3. Little evidence exists to confirm the notion that blacks are evaluated unfairly in the interview.
4. There is little research investigating interviewer bias against elderly and handicapped individuals.
5. Evidence concerning the differential validity of the interview for minority and nonminority groups is nonexistent.

It is possible to gather data pertinent to the fairness of the interview, but with the exception of simulation studies (where generalizability may be questionable), this has not yet been done. As litigation develops and continues during the 1980s, it would be useful to have well-designed research pertinent to the interviewing practices under examination. It is unfortunate that judges and juries will have to rely on only the specifics of the case, without access to a large body of validated findings in making their judgments.

Is the interview unfair? It clearly has the potential to be so. Except for a few simulation studies, however, there are no pertinent research data.

Utility

Interviews cost American organizations over a billion dollars a year. The people who do the millions of interviews held each year must feel that they are worthwhile. But do the benefits compensate for the costs? Do they exceed the costs?

In principle, the utility of any selection technique is measurable as the ratio of benefits to costs. In a formal utility analysis, calculating the direct costs of interviewing is relatively simple: recruitment brochures, application forms, salaries for interviewers and the supporting staff, rent on facilities, and a value for applicants' time. Indirect costs, such as opportunity foregone in order to conduct interviews, are difficult to estimate. When seeking to evaluate the benefit part of the equation, however, real difficulties emerge. One should be able to assess the productive contribution of those who are hired (''positives''), as well as estimate the contributions that would have been made by those who were not hired (''negatives''). In the group that is hired, there will be some proportion that fails, at least in a relative sense (''false positives''). In the group that is not hired, there will be some proportion who would have succeeded if they had been placed on the job (''false negatives''). The goal in selection is to minimize false positives and false negatives. Occasionally it is possible to compute the costs of those who fail once they have been hired. The easiest case occurs when someone quits, or is fired, and then it is possible to estimate the cost of replacing that individual. The more difficult case is someone who stays, but who is not performing at a satisfactory level. Union contracts, seniority clauses, civil service rules, and other similar devices, such as tenure in universities, protect less than fully competent performers from being singled out and dismissed because competency is not always clearly definable and measurable. How does one estimate the difference between actual production and potential production if each person had performed in a fully competent manner?

Performance varies on a continuum, and for convenience it is thought of as successful or failing. For any individual, on some days, his or her performance will be higher on that continuum and, on other days, lower. Earlier in a career, it is likely to be far lower than it will be later on. How does one establish a point to demarcate success from failure among those who have been hired? The measurement and estimation problems are even more difficult in the case of those not hired. To perform a complete utility analysis, one must be able to estimate the same kinds of costs for people who were not employed by the organization.

Formal utility analyses are rarely done. However, the other kind of utility analysis, the implicit and informal analysis made everyday by managers, suggests that interviewing is worth far more than the billion dollars a year spent on it. Despite its poor reliability and validity, when compared with other selection techniques, the interview is the most widely used selection procedure. There are ways to improve it and those will be discussed after surveying several reasons for the interview's poor reputation.

In summary, the outcome research seems negative. Interviewers' judgments tend to be less reliable and less valid than desired for sound psychometric practice. Fairness is a concern that needs a great deal more attention, and utility is difficult to evaluate. Some of the reasons why this is so will now be explored by reviewing research on how interviewers make judgments.

HOW INTERVIEWERS MAKE JUDGMENTS

Overview

With the 1964 publication of *Decision Making in the Employment Interview,* Edward Webster revolutionized thinking about the interview. Webster noted that the interviews' reliability and validity were lamentable and that they would remain so forever unless research was begun on the factors that influence interviewers' judgments. Collectively known as the McGill studies, because of the university at which they were done, the research by Webster and his students revolutionized the approach to the interview. Because of the pivotal importance of these studies, they will receive relatively greater prominence in this section.

Research on how decisions are made is needed before one can begin to redesign the interview to improve those decisions. Such research began with the McGill studies and has been continued by dozens of other researchers. Over a hundred experimental investigations have been conducted in the last fifteen years, and a voluminous but fragmented literature is available. It forms the basis for the ideas presented here, and readers desiring more detail are referred to two excellent review articles: Schmitt (1976) and Arvey (1979), and also to original sources. The topic areas surveyed here are first impressions, favorability and order of information, stereotyping, trait attributions, and other effects and biases. First, however, some comments should be made on the difficulty of interviewing and the seeming randomness of interviewers' decisions.

Task Difficulty

Interviewing is a complex and difficult cognitive and social task. It is not merely "sitting around and talking to people." The combination of social and cognitive demands (managing a smooth social exchange, while instantaneously processing information for relevance and favorability) make interviewing uniquely difficult among all managerial tasks. There are many motivational, social, cognitive, and informational factors that influence the success of interviewing, and when these are taken into account, the disappointing reliability and validity discussed earlier are easier to understand. Most important, when some of these factors are accounted for in the design of an interview approach, at least reliability has been improved.

Randomness in the Interview

The typically observed low reliability for the interview, coupled with the fact that 90 percent or more of the labor force is employed, has led statistically sophisticated observers to wonder whether the interview-based selection is truly a random process. Whether one is offered employment in a given firm seems often to be a chance phenomenon.

Success in the interview is influenced by ephemeral things, like firm handshakes and smiles, the interviewer's mood, the time of day, and characteristics of preceding job applicants.

Selection decisions are not random, however. If selection decisions were truly random, given the assumption that applicant pools for the various jobs were random selections from the labor force, there would be no sex differences or race differences in membership in various occupational categories. But there are well-documented disparities relating to race and sex in occupational membership. These disparities seem to go beyond those attributable to the nature of the supply of labor. These differences have generally been taken as evidence of adverse impact and unfair discrimination, and they need to be interpreted properly. Specifically, they need to be allocated to valid prediction of job effectiveness and to systematic bias. A great deal of research of a far more complex nature than has been done in the past is needed to do this allocation correctly. And once the nature and magnitude of bias has been established, it should then be possible to devise interviewing procedures that are free of such bias or to devise corrections for it. The "decision-making" research of the last fifteen years is a good start, but there is a long way still to go.

First Impressions, Favorability, and Order of Information

It is abundantly clear that whatever information occurs first has a disproportionate influence on the final outcome of interviews. Many lines of evidence support this conclusion, and they begin with the doctoral dissertation by Springbett (Webster, 1964). It is reviewed here in detail to provide a model of typical experimental research on the interviewing process. Springbett investigated the relation between interviewer's final hire or reject decision and the kind and order of information presented during an interview. He experimentally manipulated the applicant's appearance, the favorability of personal history and biographical information, and, counterbalancing these factors, the order in which information was presented. Experienced interviewers from the Canadian Armed Forces and from industry served as interviewers and independently rated three applicants. Springbett found that early impressions, whether positive or negative, played the dominant role in the final decision. The order in which information was presented influenced its effectiveness in shaping the overall results. For example, one step in the interview process was to review the application form and rate it. If it was presented first, final decisions were almost always directly predictable from the rating of the application form itself. When the application form was presented later in the interview process, it still had a significant impact, although its impact was smaller.

Finally, the interview appears to be a search for negative information as indicated by Springbett's finding that only one unfavorable preliminary rating resulted in a reject decision in 90 percent of the cases. If the first impression was poor, very little happened subsequently to improve it. To understand this last finding, one needs to know that Springbett had his subjects make two preliminary ratings followed by a final decision at the end of the interview. Interviewers received an initial chunk of information (the application form or a physically present job applicant or a personal history statement) and then made a rating based on it alone. This was followed by another chunk of information (one of the chunks not already presented), making the second rating, then the third chunk of information and a final rating. This methodology is easily criticized on the grounds that interviewers do not ordinarily make intervening ratings, but rather they simply receive information for a period of time and then make a single summary evaluation.

Current research shows that first impressions are critical, but perhaps not quite so important as one might infer from Springbett's finding alone. The requirement to make preliminary evaluations clearly interferes with the course of the decision-making process. For example, an unpublished study by Hakel, Leonard, and Siegfried (1972) showed that interview decisions change over the course of the interview and that evaluations may improve, as well as deteriorate. The problem in Springbett's and other research—the obtrusiveness of requiring preliminary ratings—was eliminated in this study by having independent groups of interviewers make one final evaluation after a fixed amount of information had been presented. What differed for each group was the amount of information given. Thus, the first impression was also the final impression, and the groups varied in the amount of information that went into the final impression.

Other research clearly confirms that the order of information, as well as its favorability, is critical in decision making. Studies of both persuasion and impression formation show that primacy and recency are important factors influencing the impact of information. Whatever information is presented first (primacy) has a distinct advantage. Whatever information is presented last (recency) also has a distinct advantage. There have been many studies of the comparative efficacy of primacy and recency and such studies have been extended to the interview. Haccoun (1970) found that both first and last positions are strategic and that the best way to minimize the unfavorable effect of negative information is to "sandwich" it between chunks of primary and recent favorable information.

A widely cited finding of the McGill studies is that interviewers make their decisions within an average of four minutes from the beginning of the interview. This finding has been cited enough times by enough different authors (including the present one) to have achieved the status of immutable fact. It is a finding, however, that has never been replicated. Moreover, it did not come from a formal research study, but rather from pilot work conducted by Springbett. The finding is based on a total of twenty interviews conducted by eight different interviewers. In each interview, the interviewer started a stop watch at the beginning of the interview and was instructed to turn it off, surreptitiously of course, at the point at which he or she felt no further information would emerge that would change one's mind about the decision. A surreptitious rating was made at this point and it was subsequently compared with the final decision made at the end of the interview. In nineteen of twenty cases, this rating was the same as the final rating made after the interview. The interviews lasted an average of fifteen minutes, while the average "decision time" was four minutes. The finding is certainly consistent with a view of the interview as being subjective, haphazard, and capricious. It ought to be replicated.

The net importance of these studies and others in the published literature is that the sequence of information elicitation during the interview should be standardized. Standardization should enhance both reliability and fairness, and may also improve validity (and thus utility, too).

Stereotypes

Several research studies show that stereotypes are important in an interviewer's decision making. For any particular job, it appears that interviewers have a stereotypical conception of an ideal applicant, a notion advanced by Springbett and studied by Sydiaha and Rowe (Webster, 1964). Decision making after the interview, and information search during the interview, are conducted in concert with this stereotype. At the end of the interview, the current applicant is compared with the ideal applicant stereotype, and if there is enough similarity, a favorable recommendation is made. On the other hand, if there are marked discrepancies on even only one factor of the stereotype, a low recommendation or even a rejection recommendation is the result.

Although there is no direct evidence, it is possible to construe the information seeking that an interviewer does during the interview as being governed by the stereotype. The stereotype, being multifaceted, is used as a point of reference, and the interviewer will seek information in most or perhaps even in every facet, jumping from one facet to the next. A serious fault of stereotypical information gathering during the interview comes from using the stereotype as a substitute for specific information from the applicant; that is, using it to generalize or to "fill in the gaps." Stereotypes and a related concept, the implicit personality theory, are summarizations of descriptions of behavior and inferences about people's characteristics. Sometimes these associations are accurate, but other times they are erroneous. The difficulty for the interviewer, or any other judge of people, resides in knowing when it is accurate or erroneous.

Despite the likelihood of error, characterizations of others involve abstraction, whether they are called stereotypes, implicit personality theories, caricatures, or any other name. Behavior prediction and decision making would be impossible without such abstract conceptualizations to "make sense of" the behavior of others.

During the interview, stereotyping and implicit theorizing can be a problem if, as mentioned, the interviewer uses the stereotype to "fill in the gaps" not covered by facts and comments from the applicant. Knowing that Applicant A was fired from two jobs raises serious questions that ought to be probed. Unfortunately, many interviewers will refrain from probing and will simply make a direct inference from this fact that the person will also be a problem in the current job. Knowledge that Applicant B was a member of a social fraternity and earned zero percent of his college expenses calls forth certain stereotypical inferences about other characteristics of Applicant B. Knowledge that Applicant C was once a college professor causes certain other inferences to be made. Such inferences may be stimulated by all different kinds of information: biographical and demographic facts about applicants, the applicant's dress and grooming (Do blondes have more fun? Is it super-gauche to wear white socks? Are wide ties a sign of mental disturbance?), and the applicant's verbal and nonverbal behavior. (Are weak handshakes a sign of weak character?)

The content and categories that make up stereotypes and implicit personality theories seem to be meaningful in specific cases, but in fact the categories are very broad. It seems nonsensical, indeed idiotic, to describe someone as an introverted extrovert (or as an extroverted introvert, if you prefer). Yet that description is perhaps most accurate for most people. Every person emits some behaviors that are best characterized as introverted, and at other times behaviors that are best characterized as introverted. When all of the behaviors are summed, the individual falls somewhere in the middle. Thus, although the characteristic may be bipolar (introversion—extroversion, friendly—hostile, excitable—calm, good—bad), most people will fall somewhere in the middle.

Trait Attributions

Much contemporary research in social psychology is directed toward understanding the conditions under which people attribute various traits and dispositions to others (Kelley, 1973; Fischhoff, 1976). Much of that research is concerned with questions about attributions of causality. (Did the individual cause the event? Or was it caused by factors in the environment?) Some of the attribution research concerns trait attribution, the naive perceivers' opinions and theories about the personal causes of behavior. Did Person A score high on the examination because Person A is intelligent? Because the examination was easy? Because Person A was lucky? Because Person A was highly motivated? Except in very rare circumstances (namely, properly done formal experiments), the significance of any particular behavior or outcome is ambiguous. While a given behavior may imply a particular trait or mental state, such as sweaty palms implying nervousness, the opposite implication does not follow. (It is not true that nervousness will be exhibited via sweaty palms.) Answering a particular differential calculus problem correctly may imply that one has considerable mathematical ability, but knowing that someone has a high amount of mathematical ability does not imply that he or she will be able to solve a given calculus problem correctly. Implications from behaviors to traits are unidirectional. They are irreflexive. This is a fundamental point and most people understand it, but despite its intuitive obviousness, it seems to be ignored whenever people have to make decisions about others.

As discussed in the preceding section, interviewers' judgments are mediated by stereotypes and implicit personality theories. Facts about an applicant are interpreted within the framework provided by a stereotype. This interpretational and inferential framework might lead to accurate evaluations on the average, but the frame of reference itself is irreflexive. One will be able to make accurate behavioral predictions only to the extent of the correlation between the reference frame and the specific outcomes being predicted.

An often recited dictum in personnel psychology is that the best predictor of future behavior is past behavior. Following this dictum literally implies a selection strategy that omits mediating characterizations and abstractions. As an interviewer, one would collect information about the applicant's past effectiveness and the similarity between those behaviors and the behaviors called for on the new job. One would omit all of the inferential steps in the ordinary decision-making chain and concentrate instead on making a thorough sampling of past behavior.

The best way to make proper attributions and to avoid errors caused by stereotyping is to use a standardized interview guide, developed specifically for the job in question. All questions on the guide should be asked of every applicant, and, of course, the questions should be devised to elicit information pertinent to the many kinds of behaviors and dispositions that might be important for effective job performance. Use of an interview guide will insure that all applicants are given the opportunity to provide comparable information. Using the guide will assure that comparative judgments will be made on a fair and impartial basis.

Other Effects and Biases

The research literature presents a veritable rogues' gallery of biases and other assorted effects through which interview decision making can go wrong. Individually, these studies lead to pessimism about the possibility of reengineering the interview. Collectively, their impact is almost devastating.

It has been shown that the preceding applicants create a context in which the current applicant is evaluated. Depending upon this context, an applicant may be seriously overrated or underrated. This shift in evaluation is known as the "contrast effect," because an unwarranted rating is given on the basis of the contrast between the current applicant and preceding applicants. The existence of the effect is beyond doubt, but its magnitude and practical importance are a matter of some debate. Published studies have shown that the magnitude of the effect varies anywhere from .5 percent of the variance to 80 percent of the variance.

The applicant's nonverbal behaviors (smiling, eye contact, gesturing, posture) can have a significant impact on the interviewer's evaluations. Imada and Hakel (1977) showed that when the application form facts and the verbal behavior of the applicant were held constant, variation in nonverbal behavior accounted for up to 40 percent of the variance in ratings. This study, together with another by Washburn and Hakel (1973), conclusively showed that nonverbal behavior can have important influences. As in the case of the contrast effect, the magnitude of this influence is open to debate.

The halo effect is another problem in the way interviewers process information and make ratings. The halo effect is thought to occur when an applicant possesses a characteristic that is so outstanding, either in a positive or a negative direction, that the characteristic generalizes to other characteristics and "creates a halo" around the applicant. A societal manifestation of the halo effect occurs in the use of champion athletes or other public figures in testimonial advertising. For example, the typical world class gymnast knows no more than anyone else about the chemistry and physiology of personal hygiene. Yet, because of the gymnast's excellence in one area, one grants expert status, and defers to that person's word on topics about which one is equally well informed. On the negative side, knowledge that a person has served time in prison for conviction of a felony casts a negative halo about all of that person's characteristics.

Like anyone else, interviewers can fall prey to the halo effect. It is difficult to point out specific cases in which halo occurs, but after the fact, in analyzing thirty or so sets of ratings done after the interview, the presence of halo is usually indicated by high intercorrelations among the ratings or by reduced variance among ratings within persons. As noted earlier, most applicants are appropriately evaluated somewhere in the middle on most traits. From a statistical standpoint, someone who is truly high on every trait is extremely rare, as is someone who is truly low on every trait. Yet, when postinterview ratings are analyzed, the proportion of people given all high ratings or all low ratings is extremely large. Definitive research is needed.

Consideration of the interviewer's task, however, provides some suggestions about why halo is observed. The interviewer is hired and paid to make decisions about people, and to do so effectively. It seems to follow that the interviewer should be confident about his or her choices. After all, if the interviewer is not confident of having selected the appropriate people, why should anyone else be? One simple but obviously fallacious way to show that all of the good applicants have been hired and that all of the bad applicants have been rejected is to give high ratings to the good ones and low ratings to the bad ones. Extreme ratings are given in spite of the fact that few selectees are good on every dimension and few rejectees are truly low on every dimension. Thus, the within-person variances are reduced and the trait intercorrelations are increased because of the demand on the interviewer to be decisive.

An additional explanation for halo comes from consideration of the kinds of feedback an interviewer is likely to encounter. Springbett (Webster, 1964) was the first to associate feedback with the relative overweighting of unfavorable information. Of the several outcomes in making a selection decision, the interviewer is most likely to get feedback about those people he or she hires who subsequently fail on the job. The effect of this negative feedback is to make the interviewer especially sensitive to facts or impressions that might indicate potential failure. These specific negatives in turn generalize to other traits. Of the other possible outcomes, the interviewer might get reinforcement for having hired those employees who succeed, but only under extremely unusual circumstances will one get feedback from other firms on the subsequent job performance of those people one did not hire. The net effect is to create overdependence on unfavorable information. This, combined with the emphasis on decisiveness, can lead to the creation of halo as observed in ratings.

Many books and articles report the interview to be predominantly a search for negative information. This conclusion stems from work by Springbett and others showing the relative importance of unfavorable information. Sackett (1979) cast a new perspective on this general problem. As part of an investigation of hypothesis confirmation and self-fulfilling prophesy biases in impression formation, groups of employment interviewers and student subjects selected fifteen questions out of a list of thirty that could be asked in an interview. Unknown to the subjects, the items had been previously scaled for the likelihood that each was intended to elicit positive or negative information. A positive question would be one like, "Tell me about your greatest achievement," and a negative question would be one like, "Tell me about a failure." Sackett found that the interviewers, versus the students, were much more likely to select positive questions for use in the interview, and this finding seemed to create a contradiction. If interviewers ask positive questions, why is it that negative information is weighted so heavily? The resolution to this paradox lies in the applicant's answers. Interviewers are much more likely than students (playing interviewers) to give a low rating to any piece of information (Bernstein, Hakel, and Harlan, 1975). Thus, if an interviewer and a student role-playing an interviewer both ask the same positive questions, the interviewer will regard the applicant's answer as being more negative than will the student.

A summary of research findings is presented in Table 6–1. Studies already discussed and additional findings are included, together with references to original sources.

TABLE 6-1

Experimental Studies of Decision Making in the Interview

Variables	Studies	Conclusions
1. Negative-positive nature of information	Springbett (1958) Bolster and Springbett (1961) Hollmann (1972) Constantin (1976) Tucker and Rowe (1979) London and Poplawski (1976) Sackett (1979)	Springbett, and Bolster and Springbett found that negative information was weighted too heavily. Hollmann concluded negative information was weighted appropriately, but positive information was not weighted heavily enough. Constantin found that job-relevant unfavorable information resulted in lower ratings of applicants than job-irrelevant negative information, and favorable information resulted in higher ratings regardless of its relevancy. Tucker and Rowe reported that after receiving unfavorable information concerning an applicant, fewer internal attributions were made of past successes, and, after receiving favorable information concerning an applicant, fewer internal attributions of past failures were made. Sackett found that interviewers preferred positive to negative questions and showed no systematic use of confirmatory or disconfirmatory questioning strategies.
2. Temporal placement of information	Blakeney and Mac-Naughton (1971) Johns (1975) Peters and Terborg (1975) Farr (1973) Springbett (1958) Anderson (1960) Crowell (1961) Farr and York (1975)	Blakeney and MacNaughton reported negligible primacy effects. Peters and Terborg found that a favorable-unfavorable information sequence resulted in better applicant ratings than an unfavorable-favorable sequence. Farr and York reported recency effects of information favorability when interviewers made repeated judgments and primacy effects when a single judgment was required of each interviewer.
3. Interviewer stereotypes	Sydiaha (1959, 1961) Bolster and Springbett (1961) Rowe (1963) Mayfield and Carlson (1966)	Interviewers seem to have a common "ideal" applicant against which interviewees are evaluated, although this generalized applicant may be the effect of halo (Hakel and Dunnette). Mayfield and Carlson also suggested that the "ideal" applicant may be at least partially specific or unique to the interviewer, and Hakel, Hollmann, and Dunnette found evidence for two clusters of stereotypes. Rothstein and Jackson reported that judgments regarding the likelihood that tar-

142

	Hakel, Hollmann, and Dunnette (1970) London and Hakel (1974) Hakel (1971) Rothstein and Jackson (1980)	gets would exhibit certain behaviors were unique for each target, not based on a global desirability stereotype.
4. Job information	Langdale and Weitz (1973) Wiener and Schneiderman (1974)	Job information is used by interviewers and serves to decrease the effect of irrelevant information for both experienced and inexperienced interviewers.
5. Individual differences	Dobmeyer (1970) Valenzi and Andrews (1973) Rowe (1963)	There are wide individual differences and little or no configurality in cue utilization by interviewers. In addition, interviewers did not give accurate verbal statements of their cue utilization policies.
6. Nonverbal cues	Washburn and Hakel (1973) Imada and Hakel (1977) McGovern and Tinsley (1978) Tessler and Sushelsky (1978) Hollandsworth et al. (1979) Sigelman, Elias, and Danker-Brown (1980) Sterrett (1978)	Washburn and Hakel, Imada and Hakel, and McGovern and Tinsley found that nonverbal behavior significantly affects ratings of applicants. Tessler and Sushelsky reported that eye contact had a negative effect on applicant ratings when the applicant was perceived as occupying a high status position. Hollandsworth et al., and Sigelman, Elias, and Danker-Brown reported that verbal behavior contributed more to interview impressions than nonverbal behavior. Sterrett found no significant difference in ratings of applicants displaying various intensities of body language.

143

TABLE 6–1 Continued

Variables	Studies	Conclusions
7. Attitudinal and racial similarity	Baskett (1973) Rand and Wexley (1975) Ledvinka (1971, 1972, 1973) Sattler (1970) Wexley and Nemeroff (1974) Peters and Terborg (1975) Frank and Hackman (1975) Haefner (1977)	Baskett reported that applicants perceived similarity to the interviewer, resulting in higher judgments concerning their competency and recommended salary, but no greater likelihood of recommended employment. Subsequent investigators have confirmed the effect of attitude similarity on interview ratings. Ledvinka reported that black interviewees were more likely to elicit responses of job rejection from black interviewers than were white interviewers in exit interviews. Haefner found that race had no effect on hiring decisions.
8A. Sex and competence	Zikmund, Hitt, and Pickens (1978) Heneman (1977) Muchinsky and Harris (1977) Haefner (1977)	Zikmund, Hitt, and Pickens, and Heneman found that highly competent males were evaluated more positively than highly competent females. Muchinsky and Harris reported that females were rated more suitable than males at low and average levels of scholastic achievement for a female sex-typed job; females of average scholastic achievement were rated as more qualified than males for a male sex-type job.
8B. Sex and physical attractiveness	Heilman and Saruwatari (1979) Dipboye, Arvey, and Terpstra (1977) Dipboye, Fromkin, and Wiback (1975)	Heilman and Saruwatari found attractiveness to be an advantage for men, but not for women except when seeking nonmanagerial positions. Dipboye, Arvey, and Terpstra found that attractive males were rated significantly higher than attractive females, but ratings given to moderately attractive males and females did not differ.
8C. Sex and presentation style	Dipboye and Wiley (1977) Dipboye and Wiley (1978)	Interviewers were equally as willing to hire a moderately aggressive female as a moderately aggressive male; moderately aggressive applicants were preferred over passive applicants

144

Topic	References	Findings
8D. Sex and type of job	Cohen and Bunker (1975) Rose and Andiappan (1978) Renwick and Tosi (1978)	Sexual discrimination of a type that assigns individuals to sex role congruent jobs was suggested. Rose and Andiappan reported that subjects favored applicants for managerial positions whose sex matched those of the prospective subordinates. Renwick and Tosi found that applicants' field of specialization and graduate degree played a more influential role in selection decisions than sex or marital status.
9. Disability	Rose and Brief (1979) Stone and Sawatzki (1980) Krefting and Brief (1976)	Rose and Brief find that disabled applicants were evaluated no differently than nondisabled applicants. Stone and Sawatzki report that physical or psychiatric disability did not affect interview evaluations, but psychiatric disability lowered applicants' selection chances while physical disability did not.
10. Age	Haefner (1977) Rosen and Jerdee (1974)	Younger applicants were preferred to older ones.
11. Contrast effects	Carlson (1968, 1970) Hakel, Ohnesorge, and Dunnette (1970) Rowe (1967) Wexley et al. (1972) Wexley, Sanders, and Yukl (1973) Landy and Bates (1973) Latham, Wexley, and Pursell (1975) Heneman et al. (1975) London and Poplawski (1976)	The majority of these studies found that an applicant's rating was at least partially dependent on the other individuals being rated at the same time. Landy and Bates, and Hakel, Ohnesorge, and Dunnette found the contrast effect to be minimal, and Latham, Wexley, and Purcell found a workshop successful in the elimination of several rating errors including that of contrast effects. Heneman et al. found that interviewee order has an effect on validity. London and Poplawski concluded that individuals seemed to be evaluated on their own merit, although a negative group stereotype may result in a contrast effect working in favor of the individual who does not meet that stereotype.
12. Interviewer experience	Carlson (1967a)	Reliability of interview data was not greater for experienced interviewers, but the stress for quotas impaired the judgments of inexperienced interviewers more than it did the experienced interviewers in the sense that inexperienced interviewers were more likely to accept bad applicants.

Continued

TABLE 6–1 Continued

Variables	Studies	Conclusions
13. Type of information	Carlson (1967b)	Personal history information had a greater effect on interview judgments than photographs of the interviewee. A photograph had its greatest effect on the final rating when it complemented personal history information.
14. Accuracy of interviewer as measured by number of factual questions he is able to answer	Carlson (1967a)	More accurate raters used a structured guide, were more variable in their ratings, and tended to rate lower.
15. Structure of interview	Schwab and Heneman (1969) Carlson, Schwab, and Heneman (1970) Heneman et al. (1975) Latham et al. (1980) Tucker and Rowe (1977)	Structured interviews resulted in greater inter-interviewer reliability than interviews conducted without a guide. Tucker and Rowe concluded that there was very little to gain by delaying the inspection of the application form in the interview.
16. Expected interview length and applicant quality	Tullar, Mullins, and Caldwell (1979)	Interviewers required more time to make a hire/no hire decision when viewing a high-quality applicant and when they expected the interview to last for a longer period of time.
17. Interviewer and applicant values	Vecchiotti and Korn (1980) Harlan, Kerr, and Kerr (1977)	Students rated idealistic values high, while campus recruiters ranked business related values high (Vecchiotti and Korn). High school students indicated that they would prefer to discuss motivators as opposed to hygiene factors in an interview, and interviewers indicated that this preference is wise (Harlan, Kerr, and Kerr).
18. Interviewer behavior	Schmitt and Coyle (1976) Rogers and Sincoff (1978)	Schmitt and Coyle reported that perceived interviewer personality, manner of interview delivery, and adequacy of job information affected interviewee evaluation of the interviewer and the company, and reported likelihood of job acceptance. Rogers and Sincoff reported that stature, age, and fluency affected subjects' perceptions of interviewers.

19. Rater characteristics	Bernstein, Hakel, and Harlan (1975) Dipboye, Fromkin, and Wiback (1975) Muchinsky and Harris (1977) London and Poplawski (1976) Dipboye, Arvey, and Terpstra (1977) Simas and McCarrey (1979) Gorman, Clover, and Doherty (1978)	Bernstein, Hakel, and Harlan found no important differences in ratings made by students and those made by interviewers other than students are more lenient in their ratings. Dipboye, Fromkin, and Wiback reported that students were more lenient in their ratings than professionals. Muchinsky and Harris and London and Poplawski found that females give higher ratings than males. Dipboye, Arvey, and Terpstra found males and females equally biased. Simas and McCarrey reported that highly authoritarian subjects rated male applicants more favorably than female applicants. Gorman, Clover, and Doherty questioned the usefulness of interview simulations.
20. Rating instrument	Vance, Kuhnert, and Farr (1978)	Behavioral rating scales proved superior to graphic rating scales.
21. Validity	Latham et al. (1980) Landy (1976) Heneman et al. (1975)	Latham et al. reported the behaviorally-based interview questions derived from job analysis resulted in high reliabilities and validities. Landy reported that police officer performance could be predicted from averaged interview factor scores, but not from averaged overall recommendations of interviews.

Note: Additions to the literature published since Schmitt's article have been abstracted by Tracy McDonald.
Source: Adapted from N. Schmitt. "Social and Situational Determinants of Interview Decisions: Implications for the Employment Interview." *Personnel Psychology* 29 (1976): 90–92.

Most of this section has dealt with the question of why interviewers make decisions poorly. Described here are only some of the reasons why this happens, and there are many more possible reasons for the generally discouraging outcomes in research. Research is experimental, and social psychology has identified many additional problems in the way people form impressions and make decisions. The net picture emerging from these investigations is that people are poor information processors, when compared with mathematically-based information processing and decision-making rules. People are relatively insensitive to probability or frequency information. They overweight some information and give too little weight to other information. They usually are reluctant to revise opinions or impressions when they receive additional data. Thus, the general psychological literature suggests that interviewers are not unique in making decisions poorly, but rather that they are typical. Just as there is variation in the adequacy with which investment counselors give advice to stockholders, there is variation in the adequacy with which employment interviewers make decisions. Some investment counselors undoubtedly use better methods in making forecasts than others. The same is true among employment interviewers. This now leads to a consideration of the practical side of interviewing—the ''state-of-the-art'' procedures for interviewing.

EFFECTIVE INTERVIEWING PRACTICES

Interview Guide

An interview guide is an outline or a program for conducting an interview. There are many possible variations in the format and the content, but the essential element is that a given guide will be used for all interviews with candidates for a particular job. From the standpoint of reliability, use of an interview guide guarantees that every candidate has a chance to offer responses to the same questions. Thus, when an interviewer wishes to make comparative evaluations of several candidates, he or she has comparable samples of information. In contrast, the laissez-faire style of interviewing results in haphazard sampling. The advantages of comparable sampling become more apparent upon considering that many organizations have more than one interviewer. Obviously, an interview guide will facilitate the comparison of applicants interviewed by different interviewers, resulting in greater fairness to all applicants. If the questions that make up the guide have been carefully selected to elicit job-related information from applicants, then both the validity and the utility of interview judgments should be improved.

Table 6–2 shows an abbreviated interview guide for choosing among applicants to become selection interviewers. The guide is presented here to illustrate several specific features, as well as the general format. It is purposely incomplete to prevent its thoughtless adoption for use in actually choosing future interviewers. The omitted questions, dealing with specific education and work experience, are easily constructed and should be constructed in a way that guarantees their pertinence for the specific job, location, and organization in question.

TABLE 6–2
An Abbreviated Interview Guide for Use in Evaluating Selection Interviewer Applicants

Opening

- Give a warm, friendly greeting—smile.
- Names are important—yours and the applicant's. Pronounce it correctly and use first and last names consistently. Tell the applicant what to call you and then ask the applicant for his or her preferred form of address.
- Talk briefly about yourself (your position in the company and then your personal background, hobbies, interests, etc.) to put the applicant at ease so that she or he might reciprocate with personal information.
- Ask the applicant about hobbies, activities, or some other topic that you believe will be of interest to "break the ice."

Structure the Interview

- State the purpose of interview: "The purpose of this interview is to discuss your qualifications and to see whether they match the skills needed to work as a selection interviewer. First, let's talk about your work experience and next your education and training. Then I will give you a preview of what the interviewer's job is really like. Finally, there will be a chance to ask about anything you want. How's that?"
- Since you plan to take notes, mention this to the applicant: "By the way, I will be taking some notes during the interview so that I don't miss any pertinent information that may come from our discussion. Okay?"

Work Experience: Most Relevant Job

- Use this comprehensive opening question: "Let's talk about your work experience. How about starting with the job that you feel gave you the best preparation for working as a selection interviewer. Tell me all about the job: how you got it, why you chose it, your actual job duties, what you learned on the job, the hours and your attendance record, the pay, why you left (or are leaving), and things like that."
- Probe and follow up to cover each of these items thoroughly: how the applicant got the job, reasons for choosing it, job duties, etc.
- Summarize the major facts and findings from the applicant's most relevant job. For example: "Let me summarize what we have covered to make sure that I've got it right. You worked as a _____ where most of your time was spent doing _____ and _____, and you used these skills, _____ and _____. You chose the job because of _____ and your reasons for leaving it are _____ and _____. Anything else to add?"

Other Work Experience

- If time is available, discuss other jobs the applicant has held that might be pertinent. Get a brief overview of each job the applicant has held. Emphasize jobs held in the last five years or less, since older experience is less likely to be relevant for your decision.
- Ask the work experience questions you specifically prepared for this applicant when you planned the interview.
- Summarize your major findings about all jobs. When the summary is satisfactory to the applicant, go on to discuss education and training.

Continued

TABLE 6–2 Continued

Education and Training

- Use this question to start the discussion: "Now let's talk about your education and training—schools, courses, likes and dislikes, things like that. Let's start with this: What did you learn in school that might be helpful for you in working as a selection interviewer?"
- Probe to get specific answers to these questions: "What training have you had in interviewing techniques? What courses have you had in psychology or personnel management?" and so on.
- Ask the education and training questions you specifically prepared for this applicant when you planned the interview.
- Summarize the applicant's education and training, just as you summarized work experience. When the applicant is satisfied with your summary, go on to discuss the Job Preview List.

Job Preview List

- Introduce the Job Preview List: "As a selection interviewer, you have many responsibilities and duties. Here is a list of some major factors."
- Give the applicant the Job Preview List. Discuss it point by point. Be sure that you describe the job realistically. Don't "paint a rosy picture."

Selection Interviewer Job Preview List

1. Conduct screening and final evaluation interviews with all applicants for nonexempt factory and clerical positions.
2. Administer and score screening tests and weighted application blanks.
3. Maintain records and compile reports on all applicants for Affirmative Action purposes.
   .
   .
   .
10. Recommend two candidates for each position for interviews by the hiring manager.

Applicant's Questions

- Turn the interview over to the applicant: "As I mentioned at the start, you would have a chance to ask anything you would like. We've just had a short preview of what the job would be like, but here is a chance to ask anything you want about the company, training, and so on."
- Respond fully and frankly to all of the applicant's questions, and note any further information that the applicant volunteers that will aid you in making your evaluation.

Closing the Interview

- Conclude with a warm, friendly close—smile.
- Outline the next steps in the decision process.
- Tell the applicant when to expect a decision.
- Thank the applicant.

Continued

TABLE 6–2 Continued

After the Interview

- Take time to write summary notes immediately. Describe the applicant's behavior and the impressions he or she created. Cite facts and specific incidents from the interview or from the person's work or educational history.
- Wait a day and then complete the Evaluation Form.

Opening the Interview.   Many how-to-do-it books on conducting interviews contain advice to open the interview with a period of small talk to establish rapport. The essential idea is to create a warm and relaxed atmosphere in which the applicant feels comfortable. The applicant's comfort will create a climate more conducive to the open exchange of information. This open exchange is important because the applicant may let down his or her guard and let slip some information that might be unfavorable. After all, popular knowledge counsels that the applicant's job is to put one's best foot forward. Many interviewers talk about recent events or the applicant's hobbies or outside interests (the poor interviewers talk about the weather or difficulty in getting to the interview). A different tactic supported by research on the facilitating effects of self-disclosure is one in which the interviewer takes a few moments to describe, first, his or her own position in the company, and second, hobbies and interests. This disclosure by the interviewer sets up a norm of reciprocity. The basic idea is that the interviewer will model open and candid behavior and that, in the presence of such a model, the applicant will also be open and candid.

Structuring.   The next point of importance in the interview guide is a step known as structuring. It consists of giving a statement of the purpose of the interview, as well as an outline of the topics to be covered and their sequence. In most interviews the structure is implied or assumed, but making it explicit has several advantages. First, it builds the interviewer's ''control position,'' thereby making it easier to guide applicants who talk too much and to encourage talking from applicants who talk too little. Second, it is a courtesy to the applicant, informing him or her of the sequence of events. Third, it helps to build the perception that the interview has been planned beforehand, that the applicant's comments and ideas will be heard and appropriately interpreted, and that the interviewer regards this interview as an important rather than as a casual activity.

Comprehensive Question.   A comprehensive question for opening the discussion of work experience is shown next in the guide. As in the structuring statement, the comprehensive question sets out an outline and a possible sequence of topics for discussion. The comprehensive question should create an open discussion and should encourage the applicant to do most of the talking. All how-to-interview books counsel that the applicant should do most of the talking, some of them suggesting that the applicant should talk as much as 90 percent of the time. Using the comprehensive question to open the discussion can help in achieving a realistic talk ratio in favor of the applicant of 2 to 1, or 3 to 1.

There are many additional ways to achieve this goal. The interviewer's style of questioning will certainly influence applicant responsiveness. Closed questions that can be answered with a simple yes or no (questions beginning with "are . . ." or "do . . .") encourage applicants to give brief direct answers. Open questions (what, why, how, who, when) and directives (tell me . . .) encourage the applicant to give fuller, more complete responses. Verbal reinforcements such as "uh huh" and "I see," accompanied by head nods, may keep an applicant talking. The interviewer's nonverbal behavior, consisting of facial expression, eye contact, posture and body orientation, and gesturing may also be used to keep the applicant talking or to close off a particular line of conversation.

The phrasing of questions and comments also influences the effectiveness of probing. Especially when one uses a comprehensive question to begin the discussion of a topic area, it is essential that the interviewer follow up and probe all of the items included in that list. Techniques such as restatement, echoing, paraphrasing, and reflection are all ways of getting the applicant to elaborate on what has been said. The calculated pause, which depends upon maintaining eye contact for its effectiveness, is another excellent tactic for getting a more complete answer. It is not used very often, however, because it involves violating the social norm of keeping a conversation going.

One of the greatest difficulties in conducting the interview is staying on track. It is quite easy to ask two questions at the same time, get an answer to only one of them, and think that both have been answered. It's quite easy to forget to cover some particular topic or question. Thus, the topic list in the interview guide following the comprehensive question is an important interviewing aid. A complete guide should list all the standard topics that should be queried. There should also be space to insert preplanned questions that are developed from examining the applicant form or resume.

It is quite desirable to take brief notes during the interview. This can be done unobtrusively if the interviewer jots down only one or two key words and maintains eye contact while writing. At first the words are more of a scrawl than usual, but with a little practice the script becomes recognizable. Having the key words jotted down makes it possible after the interview to go back and completely document what was said.

Summarize. Summarizing is a technique that has several important functions. Successful summarization demonstrates that the interviewer has listened and reported accurately. It allows the applicant to clarify, amplify, or add information that might have been omitted, thus improving the applicant's impression of the interview's fairness. Finally, summarizing may uncover new information that might prove to be decisive.

A similar cycle of asking a comprehensive question, probing, and following up on specific aspects, and then summarizing, is the best means for gathering information about each additional topic.

Realistic Job Preview. After work history and educational background and other job-related credentials have been discussed, the conversation can turn to recruiting the applicant by giving a preview of job duties. There are many ways an interviewer might conduct this preview. It is probably most common for the interviewer simply to ask the applicant if there are any questions about the job or the company. This casual approach can be contrasted with what is probably the best approach to giving job information, the realistic job preview, described in the following section. (A complete treatment of recruiting strategies is given by Schwab in Chapter 5 of this book.)

Closing. Finally, the close ought to outline the next steps in the decision process and tell the applicant when to expect a decision. This is a matter of common courtesy and resembles the "structuring" previously described.

An interview guide is probably the best aid a personnel manager can use to insure effective interviewing, but it is not the only one.

Realistic Recruitment

Wanous (1980) has described the traditional approach to providing preemployment information about the job duties and the company as involving overt attempts to sell the applicant on the advantages of joining the organization. This involves the selective presentation of information favorable to the company, and sometimes the deliberate enhancement or distortion of facts to make them appear to be more positive than they really are. This traditional "hard-sell" approach emphasizes persuasion and attempts to recruit employees by emphasizing positive factors and omitting negative ones. Wanous argues that this approach leads to voluntary quit rates and to rates of job dissatisfaction that are unnecessarily high, and that these rates can be reduced through a strategy of using realistic job previews and realistic recruitment.

Realistic recruitment involves presenting *all pertinent* information *without distortion.* There are many methods for doing so, ranging from discussions as shown in the interview guide, to booklets and films, to job visits and tours. The realistic preview may take place prior to any formal contact with the applicant, or during the interview, or after a job offer is made. The realism is intended to affect job satisfaction and thus reduce the likelihood of voluntary turnover. It may have its influence through a "vaccination" effect, preventing people from developing unrealistically high expectations. It may encourage self-selection, and thereby lead to a better match between the individual's needs and the organization's climate. It may also promote a greater feeling of personal control, which in turn builds greater commitment to the organization.

The results of thirteen experimental studies reviewed by Wanous (1980) generally support the effectiveness of realism in influencing applicant recruitment, job satisfaction, and tenure. Realism does not hurt recruitment; giving full information without distortion does not "scare away" applicants. Job offer refusal rates are the same or slightly higher for realistic as compared with traditional recruitment. Some studies show attitude, performance, or survival advantages for employees given realistic job previews. In sum, the literature suggests that realistic recruitment is a useful tool. It is a fine complement to a sound selection and placement system.

Multiple Interviews

One way to offset some of the fallibility of a single interview is to do two of them, or even three or four. Having several interviewers hold multiple, independent interviews has a number of advantages: idiosyncratic biases of a particular interviewer might be cancelled by another interviewer's opposite bias, the longer the "test," the more reliable the "score," the average of several independent ratings or a consensus decision will be more reliable than a single rating or decision, interviewers who are potential peers for the applicant might add a critical perspective to that held by an interviewer who would be the applicant's supervisor, and perceived fairness of the interview process might be higher if the applicant is interviewed by persons of both sexes and/or of different races.

There are some disadvantages to multiple interviewing. From the applicant's viewpoint, the redundancy in answering the same question for two or more people may be boring. This problem can be alleviated by designing multiple interview guides in which the content of questions overlaps little or not at all. Some overlap is desirable, though, to check on the consistency of the applicant's answers. The second major disadvantage is cost—the additional time spent interviewing and the time spent in meeting to evaluate the applicant. This cost needs to be balanced against the increased reliability and the greater perception of fairness.

Training in Interviewing Skills

The first compelling illustration of the use of training to improve the effectiveness of interviewing was reported by Wexley, Sanders, and Yukl (1973). Subsequent studies have supported this conclusion, but a great deal more research is needed to show the specific relationships between various training procedures and improved outcomes of interviewers' judgment processes.

The training approach that looks most promising for use in training questioning and decision-making skills is behavior modeling, or as it is named by Goldstein and Sorcher (1974), "applied learning." Evaluative research on the applied learning process is generally favorable (Kraut, 1976). It has been adapted for training interviewers in the use of the interview guide shown in Table 6-2, and also in evaluating applicants and making selection and placement decisions.

The typical applied learning workshop involves a presentation of a set of "learning points" or "key behaviors"—essentially a small set of verbal guides for handling a specific situation effectively—followed by a model or demonstration, either live or filmed, that exhibits those learning points. This is followed by rehearsal or role playing by the participants in the workshop. When the trainee's performance shows mastery of the learning points, social reinforcement is given by trainers and peers. This writer frequently supplements these basic elements with videotape recordings of the rehearsal sessions, so that the trainee may learn from self-observation as well as peer and trainer feedback.

Although behavior modeling training is labor intensive, commitment to the development and maintenance of a reliable, valid, and fair interviewing program requires substantial investment. Providing interview guides, using realistic job previews, and conducting multiple independent interviews will amount to little without sound training in their use.

CONCLUDING COMMENT

Time will tell whether the pessimism evident in Scott's (1915, 1916) early reports and England and Patterson's (1960) and Dunnette and Bass's (1963) reviews will still be warranted at the end of the 1980s. Recent research suggests many ways in which typical interviewing practices could be improved, but typical practices change slowly.

Discussion Questions

1. As noted in the introduction, England and Patterson have suggested a moratorium on "how to do it" advice on interviewing. In view of the findings of the last twenty years of research, is this call for a moratorium still warranted?

2. What are the advantages and disadvantages of interviewing and testing?

3. Compare and contrast the research focused on outcomes with the research focused on the decision-making process. What are the advantages and disadvantages of each approach?

4. As shown in Table 6–1, the interview literature is comprised of many specific findings, each of which is only a small part of the whole. To what extent are these findings a trustworthy basis for attempting to design improved interviewing procedures?

5. What results would you expect to find in a field study that compared the traditional, laissez-faire approach to interviewing with a structured interview similar to the guide presented in Table 6–2? Be sure to comment on reliability, validity, fairness, and utility.

CHAPTER SEVEN

PERSONNEL TESTING AND THE LAW

James C. Sharf

James C. Sharf is a Vice President of Richardson, Bellows, Henry, & Co., Inc., and specializes in the development, validation, and implementation of corporate selection procedures. He received his Ph.D. in Organizational Psychology from the University of Tennessee. After receiving his degree, Dr. Sharf joined the faculty of the School of Business Administration at the American University in Washington. In 1975, he joined the Equal Employment Opportunity Commission (EEOC) as its Staff Psychologist. During his four years with the EEOC, Dr. Sharf represented the Commission on many interagency deliberations and assisted in the development of the 1978 *Uniform Guidelines on Employee Selection Procedures*. Dr. Sharf has published numerous articles on fair employment practices and has been active in professional organizations.

Writing about personnel testing and the law from the viewpoint of a consulting industrial psychologist is difficult without appearing to be writing about the law and personnel testing. As will become apparent to even the casual reader, it would be merely an academic exercise to talk about contemporary personnel testing in the abstract without identifying the legal context in which personnel decisions are made. In today's environment, the practitioner tends to take the more rational principles of measurement and evaluation as a known quantity and concentrates on understanding the less rational, inductively reasoned precedent of case law built primarily around Title VII of the Civil Rights Act of 1964.

This chapter picks up personnel testing at the point when it became subject to fair employment laws, and attempts to define the intent of Congress as articulated in Title VII. While the egalitarian assumptions of the law presume that all people are equally qualified for all jobs, personnel testing has been built on the reality that people differ in abilities, many of which are related to performance on the job. This tension between testing and the law is most clearly seen in issues distinguishing the Congressionallydefined rights of the individual compared to the EEO enforcement agencies' advocacy for the rights of the class (any given class) to its "fair share" of jobs.

The first part of this chapter focuses on the legal assumptions about the statutorily-defined rights of the individual contrasted with the EEO enforcement agencies' advocacy of the rights of the class. The threshold question of when there is sufficient evidence to create a *prima facie* presumption of employment discrimination is examined in detail.

Competence to do the job is the employer's rebuttal to the *prima facie* presumption of discrimination in showing that: (1) the required competence is related to job performance, and (2) the competence is not equally possessed by all candidate populations, hence differences in selection rates or so-called "adverse impact" of the selection procedure in the first place. Validation strategies by which measures of employees' competencies are operationally defined are described and illustrated with case studies.

Finally, the advocacy of the EEO enforcement agencies to the *end* of equal employment is described and highlighted through identification of issues related to the *Uniform Guidelines on Employee Selection Procedures*. The points of contention between the "numbers game" of the *Uniform Guidelines* and the professional community's standards defining the *means* of equal employment opportunity are highlighted. Since many of the issues of fair employment are as yet unresolved, the objective of this chapter is, in a large sense, to educate the student of contemporary personnel management about the key questions, so that the developments in case law and professional practice can be astutely followed in the next decade.

ASSUMPTIONS: INDIVIDUAL VERSUS CLASS

The language of Title VII of the Civil Rights Act of 1964 expresses Congressional intent in prohibiting employment discrimination:

> It shall be an unlawful employment practice for an employer: (1) to fail or refuse to hire or to discharge any *individual,* or otherwise to discriminate against any *individual* with respect to his compensation, terms, conditions, or privileges or employment because of such *individual's* race, color, religion, sex, or national origin; or (2) to limit, segregate, or classify his employees or applicants for employment in any way which would deprive or tend to deprive any *individual* of employment opportunities or to otherwise adversely affect his status as an employee, because of such *individual's* race, color, religion, sex, or national origin (emphasis added).

While the statute explicitly prohibited discrimination against individuals, very early in the history of Title VII it became clear that, while an individual case could be won on its merits, the individual case all too frequently failed to address the underlying employment practices that may have contributed to patterns of exclusion. Since courts recognized that individual instances were generally symptomatic of classwide discriminatory employment patterns and practices, it followed that plaintiffs began to develop cases for members of classes, all of whom had been adversely affected by a given employment practice. Necessarily, such arguments were based on statistical analyses of employment data (Copus, 1976).

Because of historical patterns of employment discrimination prior to the passage of Title VII, however, early case law developed without any clear precedent as to what employment patterns and practices were *prima facie* evidence of discrimination: No matter how the plaintiff chose to portray an employment practice, the employment statistics generally tended to support a presumption of discrimination (Morris, 1977). Central to pattern and practice arguments was the role of employment statistics. As one circuit court judge was to note in a voting discrimination case some years earlier, "Statistics often tell much and the courts listen" (*Alabama* v. *United States,* 1962).

Statistical Descriptions of Employment Practices

Statistical arguments were not original to Title VII cases, the courts having had prior experience in zoning, jury selection, voting, and school discrimination cases. In jury selection, for example, the courts generally examined the composition of the jury as a sample drawn from the population to test the hypothesis that the sample was representative of the population. The reasoning of such arguments rested on the assumption that, but for discrimination, the sample would resemble the population from which it was drawn. If the hypothesis that the sample was representative of the population was rejected on the basis of sampling statistics, the courts then sought an explanation for the results.

As Justice Marshall noted in *Castaneda* v. *Partida* (1977), a jury selection case, "In every other case of which I am aware, where the evidence showed both statistical disparity and discriminatory selection procedures, this Court has found that a *prima facie* case of discrimination was established, and has required the State to explain how ostensibly neutral selection procedures had produced such non-neutral results." Until 1977, however, the critical question never was asked concerning with which population the sample was to be compared.

In March, 1977, Chief Justice Burger wrote a dissent in *Castaneda* focusing on statistical comparisons: "The decision of this Court suggests, and common sense demands that *eligible* population statistics, not gross population figures provide the relevant starting point . . . a *prima facie* case is established only where the challenger shows a disparity between the percentage of minority persons in the *eligible* population and the percentage of minority individuals on the grand jury" (emphasis added).

Under Title VII, according to Shoben (1978), plaintiffs had successfully argued until 1977 that disparities in selection rates or disparities in workforce/labor market and even workforce/population comparisons for classes covered by Title VII were presumptive evidence of discrimination without any attention given to defining who in the labor market or in the population was qualified to perform a given job.

The use of such statistical arguments in establishing a presumption of employment discrimination under Title VII had been assured in 1971 when the Supreme Court in *Griggs* v. *Duke Power Company* (1971) noted: ". . . good intent or absence of discriminatory intent does not redeem employment procedures (which) operate as 'built in headwinds' . . . Congress directed the thrust of the Act to the consequences of employment practices, not simply the motivation." With the *Griggs* emphasis on consequences of employment practices, plaintiffs had been able to establish a *prima facie* presumption of discrimination on the simplistic argument that, but for the effects of discrimination, an employer's workforce would reflect parity with the race and/or sex composition of the labor market. It also was similarly successfully argued that selection rates for various classes covered by Title VII should be the same (i.e., if one out of five white males was hired, similarly one out of five black males should have been hired).

The *Uniform Guidelines on Employee Selection Procedures* (1978), adopted by the Equal Employment Opportunity Commission (EEOC), the Office of Personnel Management (formerly the U.S. Civil Service Commission), the Department of Labor's Office of Federal Contract Compliance Programs, and the Department of Justice, have operationally defined this egalitarian presumption in the so-called "four-fifths rule." According to this rule of thumb, if a selection rate (number hired/number applied) for any class covered by Title VII (race, color, religion, sex, and national origin) is less than four-fifths of the best selection rate, a rebuttable presumption of discrimination known as a *prima facie* case is established. As will be seen, this simplistic rule of thumb has raised at least as many questions as it has answered.

Through the first decade of Title VII, however, the precedent of case law was built on a presumption of discrimination based on well-intended but incomplete reasoning. The respondent's bar had failed to ask the right questions regarding which population was appropriate for comparisons, or who among the applicants was qualified.

Critical Distinctions in Employment Discrimination

The crucial distinction between employment discrimination and other types of discrimination such as zoning, voting, school, and jury selection was to become the role of qualifications; that is, the question of who was eligible in the population from which the selections had been made.

Just as Chief Justice Burger's dissent in *Castaneda* pointed out that it would be illogical to argue that a jury should reflect parity with the general population instead of the qualified population of voting age citizens, it was overly simplistic to presume that but for discrimination there would be no disparity between selection rates, or no disparity between workforce/labor market comparisons.

The well-intended, but critical flaw to Title VII *prima facie* reasoning was the simplistic, egalitarian assumption that all people are equally qualified for all jobs. This very presumption was noted by David Copus (1975), former Director of National Programs Division at the EEOC and lead attorney on the AT&T case for the government:

> The most widely-known and well established principle of Title VII law was first laid down by the Supreme Court in *Griggs* . . . (and) most frequently applied when an employer or union attempts to explain the absence of women or minorities from certain jobs by claiming that few if any women or minorities possess the skills, abilities, or other qualifications which are required for the job. In order to sustain such a claim of differential distribution of qualifications, the employer or union must shoulder the 'heavy burden' of proving that there is, in fact, 'a fit between the qualifications and the job' . . . In short, absent compelling proof to the contrary from the defendant, *Title VII assumes that Anglo males, females, and minorities are equally qualified for all jobs*. The implication of this conclusion for statistical proofs is immense (emphasis added).

In 1977, the Supreme Court handed down a number of decisions neither complementary to the egalitarian assumptions of Title VII enforcement personnel nor to the
precedent in the first decade of Title VII *prima facie* case law. In *International Brotherhood of Teamsters* v. *United States* (1977), while the Court agreed that as a general rule
of thumb, "Where gross statistical disparities can be shown, they alone in a proper case
constitute *prima facie* proof of a pattern or practice of discrimination," they also noted:
". . . Statistics are not irrefutable. . . . Their usefulness depends on all of the surrounding facts and circumstances. . . . Like any other kind of evidence, they may be
rebutted."

Role of Qualifications in Workforce/Labor Market Comparisons

Teamsters and *Hazelwood School District* v. *United States* (1977) were the "one-two
blow" to the previous simplistic Title VII *prima facie* arguments. In both cases, the Supreme Court was asked to find a *prima facie* case of discrimination based on work-
force/labor market comparisons. In May, 1977, in the *Teamsters* case, the Court built
on Chief Justice Burger's earlier dissent in *Castaneda* and invited respondent employers
to challenge the incorrect assumption that all people are equally qualified for all jobs:

> Petitioners argue that statistics, at least those comparing the racial composition of an
> employer's workforce to the composition of the population at large, should never be
> given decisive weight in a Title VII case because to do so would conflict with PP 703(j) of
> the Act (which) provides: "Nothing contained in this subchapter shall be interpreted to
> require an employer . . . to grant preferential treatment to any individual or to any
> group because of the race . . . or national origin of such individual or group on account
> of an imbalance which may exist with respect to the total number or percentage of per-
> sons of any race . . . or national origin in any community, state, section or other area, or
> in the available workforce in any community, State, section, or other area." The argu-
> ment fails in this case because the statistical evidence was not offered or used to support
> an erroneous theory that Title VII requires an employer's workforce to be racially bal-
> anced. Statistics showing racial or ethnic imbalance are probative in a case such as this
> one only because such imbalance is often a telltale sign of purposeful discrimination; ab-
> sent explanation, it is ordinarily to be expected that nondiscriminatory hiring practices
> will in time result in a workforce more or less representative of the racial and ethnic com-
> position of the population in the community from which employees are hired. Evidence
> of long-lasting and gross disparity between the composition of a workforce and that of
> the general population thus may be significant even though PP 703(j) makes clear that
> Title VII imposes no requirement that a workforce mirror the general population. . . .
> Considerations such as small sample size may, of course, detract from the value of such
> evidence . . . and evidence showing that the *figures for the general population might
> not accurately reflect the pool of qualified job applicants would also be relevant* (empha-
> sis added).

Then in the *Hazelwood* case, decided in June, 1977, the Supreme Court noted:

> There can be no doubt in light of the *Teamsters* case that the District Court's compari-
> son of Hazelwood's teacher workforce to its student population fundamentally miscon-
> ceived the role of statistics in employment discrimination cases. The Court of Appeals

was correct in the view that a proper comparison was between the racial composition of Hazelwood's teaching staff and the racial composition of the *qualified* public school teacher population in the relevant labor market. . . .

In *Teamsters,* the comparison between the percentage of Negroes on the employer's workforce and the percentage in the general area wide population was highly probative, because the job skill there involved—the ability to drive a truck—is one that many persons possess or can fairly readily acquire. When special qualifications are required to fill particular jobs, *comparisons to the general population (rather than to the smaller group of individuals who possess the necessary qualifications) may have little probative value* (emphasis added).

These Supreme Court opinions directed lower courts to look beyond mere statistics in determining when there is sufficient evidence of disparity in an employer's employment figures to create a presumption of discrimination. This point was concisely stated by a well-known District Court Judge, John Sirica, in *Dendy* v. *Washington Hospital Center* (1977):

The phrases "prima facie case" and "discriminatory effect" are terms of art without specific meaning. Lacking any pretense of scientific exactness, they merely serve as guideposts to assist in singling out employment practices for which it is appropriate to ask employers to offer justifications. The precise point at which statistical data casts sufficient suspicion on an employment practice to require explanation by an employer is not fixed by any rule of thumb.

It appears likely, henceforth, that the presumption of discrimination is to be regarded as a sliding scale, depending on the level of job skill involved. As stated in *Teamsters,* where the job skills are minimal, or readily learned by most, it may well be successfully argued by plaintiffs that all are equally qualified and a presumption of discrimination will be made by showing a disparity between an organization's workforce and the race and/or sex composition of the general population, or a disparity in selection rates without regard to which applicants are qualified for the job in question.

Above low-skilled, entry-level jobs, plaintiffs are going to have increasingly uphill burdens in establishing *prima facie* cases because of the Supreme Court's invitation to respondent employers to challenge the plaintiff's statistical assumptions. Plaintiffs will have to be better prepared in developing their cases relative to data concerning who in the labor market is qualified.

First, in the *Teamsters* decision, the Supreme Court noted that PP 713(b) of Title VII makes no presumptions that an employer's workforce should necessarily reflect parity with the labor market, although it did note that nondiscriminatory hiring practices over time will produce a workforce ". . . more or less representative of the population in the community from which employees are hired." Second, in *Teamsters* the Supreme Court also noted that once a *prima facie* case had been established by statistical workforce disparities, the employer must be given an opportunity to show ". . . that the claimed discriminatory pattern is a product of pre-Act hiring rather than unlawful post-Act discrimination, or that during the period it is alleged to have pursued a discriminatory policy it made too few employment decisions to justify the inference that it had engaged in a regular practice of discrimination."

Finally, it is likely that in above low-skilled, entry-level jobs, the courts will begin to allow employer arguments regarding qualifications to refute the *prima facie* case, instead of relegating qualification arguments solely to rebutting a *prima facie* case once the legal burden has been shifted by the plaintiff. A recent post-*Teamsters* case has more correctly identified the proper use of workforce/labor market and selection rate comparisons under Title VII.

Workforce/Labor Market Case Study

In January, 1980, in *EEOC* v. *United Virginia Bank,* the Fourth Circuit rejected the simplistic, egalitarian argument that a *prima facie* case of discrimination existed because of disparities between the employer's workforce and the *general* labor market. The *United Virginia Bank* case was noteworthy in three respects:

1. Lower courts are beginning to respond to the 1977 teachings of the Supreme Court in *Teamsters* that "... Figures for the general population might not accurately reflect the pool of qualified job applicants ..." and *Hazelwood* that "When special qualifications are required to fill particular jobs, comparisons to the general population (rather than to the smaller group of individuals who possess the necessary qualifications) may have little probative value."
2. The Court of Appeals construed the burden of defining the qualified labor market to be on the plaintiff, who in this case was the EEOC, in establishing the *prima facie* case initially.
3. In rejecting the plaintiff's *prima facie* arguments, the court assumed that the employer's qualifications were job-related, rather than relegating the burden of defending the job-relatedness of those same qualifications had the *prima facie* case been established. In this case, the Court of Appeals reasoned:

> At trial, the EEOC presented the following as evidence of discrimination: (1) the principal part of its case was a statistical comparison of black employees at UVB with black people in the total area workforce; (2) a statistical comparison of black and white applicant to hire ratios; (3) specific policies which allegedly discriminate against blacks, for example, credit checks and a high school education requirement; and (4) individual instances of discrimination, mainly relating to an alleged failure to hire qualified black applicants when openings were available.

> The centerpiece and keystone of the EEOC's case, both in the district court and on appeal, is that the proper statistical comparison in this case is between the percentage of black employees working in various job classifications at UVB and the percentage of black people in the local labor force. . . .

> The fundamental problem with the EEOC's statistical evidence lies in the fact that UVB's workforce was compared with the workforce as a whole. As the district court correctly recognized, this comparison was improper. It is clear that: "When special qualifications are required to fill particular jobs, comparisons to the general population (rather than to the smaller group of individuals who possess the necessary qualifications) may have little probative value. *Hazelwood School District* v. *U.S., Teamsters* v. *U.S.* . . ."

The EEOC, however, rigidly continues to argue that all the black local labor force is qualified for the office and clerical positions at UVB. This is simply not true. Tellers must be able to deal with the public, handle and account for money, and operate adding machines, typewriters and other office machines. The district court found that the entire percentage of black people in the local labor force would not provide an appropriate statistical group for comparison with UVB black employees. Since this determination was a factual one, it will not be disturbed unless clearly erroneous. . . .

The EEOC failed to present any evidence as to the percentage of persons in the labor force qualified to hold the various positions at UVB . . . the burden was on the EEOC to prove discrimination and to produce evidence to support its position. The SMSA report constitutes the only evidence which even remotely speaks to qualifications. Without these figures, the EEOC's case is virtually without any statistical evidence to support it.

Further problems emerge when an attempt is made to compare the SMSA percentages with the UVB employees. When the EEOC prepared its figures for black employees and applicants, it made no effort to exclude employees hired prior to the effective date of Title VII (July 2, 1965). Thus, the figures EEOC presents are weighted against UVB to the extent that white employees hired prior to the time Title VII was in effect were included in the employment figures. . . . It is therefore clear that the June 9, 1975, employment list as a whole was improperly used against UVB because the EEOC made no attempt to factor out the pre-Act hires. . . . Taking all of these things into consideration, we are of the opinion that the statistical evidence we have just discussed does not suffice to prove a *prima facie* case of discrimination. . . .

It is simply not realistic to say that every member of the labor force has the qualifications to be a bank teller, for example. It is even more unrealistic to say that every member of the labor force has the qualifications to be a bank manager or official. Despite the examination of employee records covering a period of nine years, the EEOC did not present evidence of one person who was qualified to be a bank official or manager, who had applied for the job and who was denied employment. . . .

Another set of statistics argued by the EEOC deals with the number of applicants compared with the smaller number of hires . . . (a simple comparison of the total applicant flow, with no attempt to prove the qualifications of the applicants, may have little meaning if any. (Hazelwood . . . points this out.) The evidence shows that in 1973–74 . . . 12.4 percent of the white applicants were hired and 4.4 percent of the black applicants. The EEOC argues that this is *prima facie* evidence of discrimination since whites had a nearly three times better chance of being hired than blacks. Once again, however, the EEOC, in not carrying the burden of proof which is on the plaintiff, has not produced any evidence as to the relative number of blacks and whites, although the applications were apparently at hand, who were qualified for the jobs at UVB. The EEOC again asks us to find that all black people in the local labor force are qualified for the jobs available at UVB. To repeat, for the reasons stated in our discussion of the general hiring statistics, we reject this argument. . . .

The burden of proof was on the EEOC, and it failed to present any evidence of the post-Act hires or on the percentage of black people in the labor force qualified to work at

UVB in various job categories. We have taken the time to show that even on the sparse evidence in the record, the EEOC has not proved its case and we note that failure of proof is the primary basis for our decision.

QUALIFICATIONS AND EMPLOYMENT

The legitimate uses by an employer of qualifications in general, and measures of competence in particular (such as employment tests), were addressed by Congress in adopting the Tower Amendment to Title VII which ". . . allows employers to give and to act upon the results of any professionally developed ability test provided that such test, its administration or action upon the results is not designed, intended or used to discriminate because of race, color, religion, sex or national origin."

First of all, it is significant to note that neither the courts nor the enforcement agencies have limited their definition of "tests" to only pencil and paper measures (Holley and Feild, 1975). Rather, they have included almost all aspects of the personnel decision-making process, from background checks to supervisory performance appraisals. Second, although the wording cited above might have been interpreted by the courts to require a showing that a selection procedure is illegal only where it was implemented with *intent* to discriminate, the courts have in fact ruled that *use* of a selection procedure is prohibited if it results in biased effects.

Writing the unanimous Supreme Court opinion in *Griggs* v. *Duke Power* (1971), Chief Justice Burger stated:

> Nothing in the Act precludes the use of testing or measuring procedures; obviously they are useful. What Congress has forbidden is giving these devices and mechanisms controlling force unless they are demonstrably a reasonable measure of job performance.

> Congress did not intend by Title VII . . . to guarantee a job to every person regardless of qualifications. In short, the Act does not command that any person be hired simply because he was formerly the subject of discrimination, or because he is a member of a minority group. Discriminatory preference for any group, minority or majority, is precisely and only what Congress has proscribed. What is required by Congress is the removal of artificial, arbitrary and unnecessary barriers to employment when the barriers operate invidiously to discriminate on the basis of racial or other impermissible classification.

> Congress has not commanded that the less qualified be preferred over the better qualified simply because of minority origins. Far from disparaging job qualifications as such, Congress had made such qualifications the controlling factor so that race, religion, nationality and sex become irrelevant. What Congress has commanded is that any tests used must measure the person for the job and not the person in the abstract.

With this strong statement emphasizing the role of job qualifications, the Supreme Court has reaffirmed what Title VII commands. *Job-related standards are the foundation upon which fair employment practices are built.*

Accordingly, the courts have looked at whether the use of a selection procedure disproportionately disqualifies a group on the basis of race, color, religion, sex, or national origin. The courts then look for evidence that selection procedures having such results are job related; that is, whether the procedure measures the person for the job.

Burden of Job-Relatedness Proof under Title VII

The Supreme Court stated these rules as follows in *Albemarle Paper Company* v. *Moody* (1975):

> In *Griggs* v. *Duke Power Co.*, this Court unanimously held that Title VII forbids the use of employment tests that are discriminatory in effect unless the employer meets "the burden of showing that any given requirement (has) . . . a manifest relation to the employment in question." This burden arises, of course, only after the complaining party or class has made out a *prima facie* case of discrimination—has shown that the tests in question select applicants for hire or promotion in a racial pattern significantly different from that of the pool of applicants. . . . If an employer does then meet the burden of proving that its tests are "job related," it remains open to the complaining party to show that other tests or selection devices, without a similarly undesirable racial effect, would also serve the employer's legitimate interest in "efficient and trustworthy workmanship." Such a showing would be evidence that the employer was using its tests merely as a "pretext for discrimination."

Differences in selection rates, generally referred to as *adverse impact,* are not sufficient for drawing the conclusion of illegal discrimination—for adverse impact is based, in addition, on the court's finding that the selection procedure is not job-related. *Job-related* refers to what the industrial psychologist calls validity—a showing, for example, that a selection test is related to performance on the job.

It would be well to remember that implicit in any personnel decision is the notion of predicting performance; that is, prediction of how an individual will perform in a new situation. The impact of Title VII in the long run will be to remove this prediction from an implicit hunch (as has often been the traditional practice) to more rigorous efforts to develop and to document that personnel decisions, whether made with tests or otherwise, are in fact job-related.

While the term *testing* is used as a generic label in the *Uniform Guidelines,* covering virtually all aspects of employment decision making as used by the industrial psychologist or personnel specialist, the term *test* is a shorthand for a number of objective means of gathering information about people. As used by Ghiselli (1966) in a comprehensive text, *The Validity of Occupational Aptitude Tests,* five major categories of pencil and paper tests include intellectual abilities, spatial and mechanical abilities, perceptual accuracy, motor abilities, and personality.

The profession also recognizes a second major objective means for the assessment of occupational skills by having candidates perform content-oriented tests, which are generally referred to as *work samples.* Probably the best known work sample for selection purposes is the typing test, where the clerical candidate performs that part of the job dealing with typing. Because of the specificity of such work samples, however, few principles have been developed by the profession governing the generalizability of such assessment procedures across similar, but not necessarily identical, jobs that might be found in the same job family.

The assessment center is a third major category of objective selection procedures enjoying wide popularity, particularly for exempt jobs. Typically included in the assessment center are a number of objective selection procedures including pencil and paper tests, structured interviews, role playing and group exercises, and work samples in the form of so-called "in-basket" simulations. (For a comprehensive discussion of the assessment center, see Chapter 12.)

After adverse impact is shown for any aspect of the employment decision-making process, a validation study showing the job-relatedness of the selection procedure is the typical rebuttal by a respondent. If an employer cannot convince the court that his or her selection procedure, which has an adverse impact, is job-related, the court then concludes the employer's selection procedures were illegal and may award attorneys' fees and back pay for the plaintiffs who suffered economic harm from the discrimination.

Although there are several ways of demonstrating adverse impact (as will be discussed), employers have often adjusted their selection rates so as not to show adverse impact by hiring equal proportions/quotas of various classes covered by Title VII under the assumption that there will be no basis for having to demonstrate job-relatedness if there is no adverse impact. Such adjustments may prove to be shortsighted in several ways. Even though adverse impact may not be shown with respect to qualification rates, this is no defense to illegal discrimination if actual selection figures reflect disproportionate numbers of members of classes not selected. More importantly, such adjustments in selection rates by themselves may not tell the employer who can perform the job.

The long-range approach of meeting an employer's business and fair employment objectives will not be met by quota-based hiring, but by improving the job-relatedness of standards used in making personnel decisions. This means that employers should expect to use more objective employment selection procedures, and to perform validation studies showing that such objective standards are job-related, thereby meeting their own business necessity of hiring the most competent person for the job, as well as complying with the objectives of the fair employment laws.

Validation Strategies

There are essentially two major ways an employer can demonstrate that one's selection procedures are job-related. These methods involve primarily two types of validation strategies: criterion-related and content validities. Without going into great detail, in the criterion-related validation study, an effort is made to show statistically that a relationship exists between the scores of a group of persons on a test and their subsequent respective performances on the job. This is shown by correlating test scores with important relevant measures of job performance. Typically used measures, in addition to work proficiency, may include training time, supervisory ratings, regularity of attendance, and tenure on a job. When a statistically significant showing is made, an individual's test score can then be used to predict how that person would perform on the job for which he or she is being considered.

Criterion-Related Validity Case Study

In 1975, the Supreme Court for the first time looked at a validation study in *Albemarle Paper Co.* v. *Moody.* The Court objected to a number of aspects of the validity study that had been undertaken by the employer only after a trial date had been scheduled. First, it was noted that the tests were being used to select people for jobs for which the test had neither been validated nor been shown to resemble other jobs for which the test had been validated. The Court noted:

> The study in this case involved no analysis of the attributes of, or the particular skills needed in, the studied job groups. There is accordingly no basis for concluding that "no significant differences" exist among the lines of progression, or among distinct job groupings within the studied lines of progression.

> Albemarle's supervisors were asked to rank employees by a "standard" that was extremely vague and fatally open to divergent interpretations. . . . (T)here simply was no way to determine whether the criteria actually considered were sufficiently related to the Company's legitimate interest in job-specific ability to justify a testing system with a racially discriminatory impact.

> The fact that the best of those employees working near the top of a line of progression score well on a test does not necessarily mean that that test, or some particular cut-off score on the test, is a permissible measure of the minimal qualifications of new workers entering lower level jobs.

> Albemarle's validation study dealt only with job-experienced white workers; but the tests themselves are given to new job applicants who are younger, largely inexperienced, and in many instances nonwhite.

The Court concluded that the employer's validation study was "materially defective in several respects" and remanded the case to the District Court for "precise fashioning of the necessary relief" rather than issuing an injunction against the use of testing at the plant as the Court of Appeals had ordered.

The Supreme Court in *Moody* also discussed the concept of differential validation—validation of a test for whites and blacks. Where tests are valid for both whites and blacks, which tends to be the rule rather than the exception, the test can be used for making selection decisions for both of these groups, since performance on the test has been shown to be related to performance on the job. In *Moody,* the company's failure even to attempt to investigate the possibility of single-group validity was one of the critical deficiencies noted by the Supreme Court.

A second approach to validity is the sampling strategy identified as content validity. As the *Uniform Guidelines* note in this regard: "A selection procedure can be supported by a content validity strategy to the extent that it is a representative sample of the content of the job." The key to content validation is in recognizing that, since it is a sampling strategy, it always requires, as a first step, that the job be analyzed. Without the information developed from a job analysis, there is no way to judge whether a job's frequent or critical behaviors are being sampled by the selection procedure. The adequacy of a claim of content validity cannot be judged by the eye of the beholder alone.

Probably the most frequent abuse of testing by those not familiar with the rigors of test validation is the misuse of content validation. All too frequently, justification for the use of a test is based on a well-intended selection of a test because it appears to be related to a certain job. Such appearances, known by the term *face validity,* are hunches without documentation of the operations performed (such as job analysis leading to the selection or construction of a test). Such hunches do not provide the information needed to substantiate the claim of the test's validity. And without a thorough job analysis to define the knowledges, skills, and behaviors required on the job, and a description of how the test samples these critical and/or frequent components of a job, a claim of content validity cannot be substantiated. Obviously, the closer a test comes to replicating the frequent and/or critical components of a job, the stronger would be the evidence of that test's content validity.

Job-skills tests, which are miniature work samples, such as typing and shorthand, replicate the job and are among the tests most readily recognized as content valid. For simple jobs, in which performance can be readily observed, the operational sampling is rather straightforward. As job performance becomes more cognitive and less directly observable, however, claims of content validity require ever more rigorous attention to sampling methods. Abuses of content validation are typically found where inferences are made that some verbal and/or quantitative ability is required to perform a job. On such incomplete analysis, a test of verbal aptitude or even of abstract reasoning might be claimed to be content valid.

This is what the Supreme Court had in mind when it said that "Any test used must measure the person for the job and not the person in the abstract" (*Griggs* v. *Duke Power,* 1971). Herein lies a major pitfall for content validity users. All too often, inferences as to underlying abilities are made which, pursued to their logical conclusion, would simply require that performance on an intelligence test be rationalized under the guise of content validity. Such inferences about underlying abilities may well be hypotheses to be tested in a criterion-related study. A properly conducted content validity study, because of the operations performed in sampling job knowledge, skills, and behaviors, all but eliminates such inferences. Simply stated, a content valid test should sample the job for the applicant and give that person a fair chance to demonstrate his or her competence.

Efforts to develop the *Uniform Guidelines* were entangled for years by the public sector's use of tests that were claimed to be content valid. Tests such as the former Federal Service Entrance Exam (FSEE) required a high-level verbal comprehension, much like a Graduate Record Exam, to do well. Users of general ability tests claiming content validity have two strikes against them. First of all, because of the high verbal difficulty of such an exam, there would be a corresponding substantial adverse impact. Second, it would be difficult to meet the sampling requirements of content validity for general ability measures. A recent court decision involving a public employer's claim of content validity is a case in point.

Content Validity Case Study

In September, 1979, the Federal District Court in the Northern District of New York rejected the claim of content validity for the exam used by the state for selection of recruits to the New York State Police (NYSP) Academy (*United States* v. *State of New York*). The case had been brought by nine white males who had challenged the hiring of minorities, without regard to strict numerical order of eligibility, after an earlier court decision held that the New York State Constitution required merit appointments to be made in numerical order. The Court observed that less than 1 percent of the NYSP was black, Hispanic, or females combined, although these groups were 11 percent, 3 percent, and 39 percent, respectively, of the labor market.

Over one and one-quarter million dollars had been spent on the development and administration of the 1975 exam, which had been built with technical assistance provided to the state by the then U.S. Civil Service Commission. A number of federal officials involved in writing the *Uniform Guidelines* were involved in the litigation for both the plaintiffs and the state.

In this case, a "job element/*j*-coefficient" validation effort had been undertaken under Civil Service Commission direction where an "element" was defined as "a worker characteristic which influences success in a job including combinations of abilities, skills, knowledges or personal characteristics." A panel of 155 so-called "subject matter experts" from the NYSP had generated 1,400 + job elements which were consolidated into the following 15 elements to which 223 "subelements" were assigned, suggesting what activities/situations could be used to measure the job elements as defined by the subelements:

> Possess good judgment
> Thoroughness
> Ability to function while in physical danger
> Ability to assume responsibility
> Ability to make decisions
> Ability to work without supervision
> Possess dependability
> Have common sense
> Ability to take orders
> Ability to combine personal resources: mental and physical
> Enthusiasm toward the job
> Ability to act under pressure
> Ability to communicate well with others
> Possess motivation for the job
> Ability to make decisions under pressure/Ability to act under pressure

Of 32,000 applicants, 22,000 took the exam and 4,000 passed it. The exam had two parts:

1. A *written* "situation test" of hypothetical/simulated police situations/activities represented 65 percent of the exam. Some 21 percent of the whites, 10 percent of the Hispanics, and 8 percent of the blacks passed this part.
2. A *physical* "performance test" represented the remaining 35 percent of the exam. This part was passed by 98 percent of the males and 67 percent of the females.

Of the males, 22 percent got veterans' preference; 0 percent of the females got it. Some 1,100 offers were made. Of the 545 subsequent appointments, 2.6 percent of them were to blacks, 1.5 percent to Hispanics, and 0 percent to females.

The District Court threw out the validity evidence and awarded a remedy in which 40 percent of each new class of recruits was to be black and Hispanic and 10 percent female. The following verbatim excerpts are from the Court's opinion:

Jobs may be placed on a continuum. One end of the continuum are jobs involving processes that are directly observable. At the other end of the continuum are jobs involving processes that are abstract or unobservable. In a worker-oriented job analysis, the workers are making inferences about the individual differences of characteristics that are associated with superior performance. The lower the job on the continuum, i.e., a job consisting primarily of observables, the less of an inference is made between what is done on the job and the personal characteristics necessary to do the job. For instance, in a typing job the task is typing and the inference about individual characteristics, the ability to type, is not speculative. Likewise, in a task-oriented analysis, the closer one is to the abstract or unobservable end of the continuum, the inference as to what psychomotor activities are associated with performance of the job becomes highly speculative. The more speculative the inference is from observable, the greater is the "inferential leap." Therefore *content validity alone is an appropriate strategy to follow only at or near the observation end of the continuum such as trade and craft jobs, where the inferential leap is small* (emphasis added).

The 1975 trooper examination developed by the NYSP constituted an effort to test for good judgment, common sense, ability to size up a situation, thoroughness, reliability, dependability, and a host of other intangible characteristics and mental processes. While it is certainly true that a trooper must possess good judgment, it is questionable whether the utilization of a content validity strategy alone was appropriate for such an examination.

. . . The job element method of job analysis as followed by the NYSP in development of the 1975 trooper examination does not focus on what troopers actually do on the job, but only on the underlying traits or characteristics that troopers believe characterize successful job performance.

In the NYSP development of the 1975 trooper examination, a definition of job tasks and responsibilities is not documented. A study of job tasks or duties was not conducted in the course of development of the trooper examination. In addition, relative frequency, importance, and skill level of job tasks or duties were not identified. Furthermore, there was no study of the relative criticality of the subelements and the relative importance of the different subelements was not established. To the extent that the job analysis for the position of trooper did not study the tasks and duties for the position of trooper and did not study the frequency, importance, and skill level of such tasks and duties, it was not and could not have been brought before members of the psychological profession or the Court for scrutiny and consideration.

The 1975 written examination for the position of trooper was a situations test which, in essence, sought "will do" responses to situations that normally do not occur behind a desk. The fact that someone selects a particular course of action as appropriate on such an examination does not mean that the same course of action would be followed by that individual under different circumstances in a real life situation. . . . Sitting at a desk selecting the best alternative and the worst alternative in response to a written situation, I find, is quite different from being in a real life situation deciding what to do and doing it effectively. Essentially, the situations test developed by the NYSP represents a sampling of a portion of the job content universe for the position of New York State Trooper that had been gathered under the rubric of judgment along with thoroughness ar.d common sense. No one, however, is able to determine which subelements under these job elements are actually measured by the measuring instruments. A review of the documentation of the job analysis and test development does not show what the examination measures. Members of the job analysis detail and various evaluation and rating panels, collectively, are the only ones who know what subelements are sampled by the situations test. This information, however, was not and could not have been presented to members of the psychological profession or the Court for scrutiny. Furthermore, there are no written operational definitions of the 223 subelements upon which the 1975 trooper examination was based, although a few are self-explanatory behaviors such as "Ability to take accurate measurements such as using a 50-foot tape measure at an accident scene." To this extent, there has been no showing that the subelements identified through the job analysis are critical or important job behaviors and represent a departure from professional standards and federal guidelines.

A task-oriented analysis was not done during the development of the 1975 trooper examination. There is no documented linkage between the content domain of the examination and the actual tasks, duties, and activities of the position of New York State Trooper. To the extent that this was not done, the development of the 1975 trooper examination based on a content validity strategy was not in accordance with professional standards or in compliance with federal guidelines.

Insofar as the NYSP appointed a class of . . . troopers . . . on the basis of a selection procedure that excluded females, this was a violation of Title VII. The preexistence of an eligible list cannot be used to escape the obligation of prevailing law.

The generally accepted procedures adopted by the psychological profession reflect the present inability of the science of psychology to set forth definitively proper standards or principles to follow in the validation of employee selection procedures under all circumstances.

Inasmuch as the legal principle to be applied with regard to the job-relatedness of an employee selection procedure is one of generally accepted standards of the psychological profession, a court cannot be expected to draw solely upon its own resources in fashioning such standards. Of necessity, therefore, a court must rely in its search for the proper interpretation of applicable law on the various federal agencies whose responsibilities include enforcement of this legislation and the psychological profession itself for guidance. To this end, the salutory purpose behind the new *Uniform Guidelines on Employee Selection Procedures* is to be greeted with weary relief. Indeed, a lack of coordination of policy and independence of counseling, I am sure, has led to ramifications that Congress could not have envisioned. Nonetheless, it must be recognized that the *Uniform Guidelines,* as well as previously issued federal guidelines, the APA Standards, and the Division 14 Principles, all of which are written in a style that would make the works of Shakespeare appear to be written for children, merely represent the evolving standards of the psychological profession and are not set in cement. Although the

Uniform Guidelines were not finally adopted until after the trial of this action was completed, I do not believe it is improper for the court to give them consideration along with all other writing, published before, during and after 1975, representing the thinking of members of the psychological profession. Moreover, in my judgement, the *Uniform Guidelines* do not represent a radical departure from previous thinking in the psychological profession as some would contend. Furthermore, while great deference should be accorded to guidelines interpretive of Title VII, this deference should not blind a court to new and generally accepted methodologies as they are developed by members of the psychological profession.

. . . The evidence also supports the conclusion that certain parts of the Physical Performance Test portion of the 1975 trooper exam could have been scored differently thereby reducing adverse impact on females and at the same time serve the New York State Police's legitimate and creditable interest in obtaining a highly qualified applicant pool from which to make appointments to the position of trooper. In my judgment, as administered, the 1975 Physical Performance Test was nothing more than a speed and agility test and to the extent indicated above was an independent violation of Title VII.

The unfortunate, although I am sure, ultimately salutory clash between civil service and equal employment opportunity laws must not be used to put an end to the underlying principles that precipitated either's enactment, but rather to bring about a synthesis beneficial to our society.

Why Bother with Testing?

Probably the most important question to be asked in meeting the objectives of fair employment, then, is why bother using tests at all if their validation is so demanding and subjected to such demanding review by the courts? An even more salient question might be why bother with tests when the casual interview continues to be the most frequently used of all personnel decision-making procedures? (For a detailed discussion of the interview, see Chapter 6.)

In terms of hiring the person who can do the job, use of the typical unstructured interview for decision-making purposes is far less likely to result in decisions with demonstrable validity than are more objective sources of information, such as patterned interviews, job simulations found in assessment centers, and pencil and paper tests. The answer lies in the relationship between reliability and validity. Reliability is a necessary, but not necessarily sufficient, prerequisite to validity. Simply stated, reliable information *may* be demonstrated to be valid, but unreliable information is virtually impossible to validate. For this reason, the most valuable aspect of pencil and paper testing is that it is the most reliable of all assessment procedures and, as such, provides the greatest likelihood of demonstrating validity.

It is well documented in industrial psychology that the casual interview of the ''I know one when I see one'' variety is notoriously unreliable. In practice, this unreliability means that independent raters are unlikely to agree, and/or the same rater on a separate occasion is unlikely to come to the same conclusion about the interviewee. Under such circumstances of unreliable information, it is virtually impossible to determine the validity of such decision making. Reliability is typically enhanced by adding structure to the assessment procedure. For this reason, patterned interviews are likely to result in at least some reliability compared to the unreliable casual interview. Even greater reliability can be attained through well-developed assessment centers, particularly where attention is given to rater training. The fact remains, however, that the pencil and paper test has been and continues to be the most reliable of all personnel assessment techniques. Hence, the odds-on favorite assessment procedure for the empiricist developing valid selection procedures will continue to be pencil and paper testing because of the resulting reliability of information, which, by its nature, has the greatest likelihood of validity. Reliability, of course, is a prerequisite to, but by itself is insufficient for, addressing the question of validity. This is where professional standards and federal guidelines come into play. The most controversial set of guidelines is the *Uniform Guidelines on Employee Selection Procedures.*

UNIFORM GUIDELINES: COMPETENCE OR "NUMBERS"?

With the adoption of the *Uniform Guidelines on Employee Selection Procedures* in 1978, the EEO enforcement agencies were finally able, after a six-year effort, to articulate federal standards of fair employment. While the *Uniform Guidelines* are ostensibly a set of standards for determining whether employment practices are job-related, they in effect give, if literally applied, employers little choice but to adopt "numbers-oriented" race- and sex-conscious employment procedures. According to the *Uniform Guidelines,* such preferential treatment is the way to avoid adverse impact and, accordingly, the way not to have to meet the *Uniform Guidelines'* rigorous technical validation standards and copious documentation requirements.

In the *Uniform Guidelines,* as noted by Sharf (1978), the enforcement agencies have given themselves a *pro forma* job of establishing a *prima facie* presumption of discrimination, compared to the increasingly heavy burden given to the employer in rebuttal in establishing the job-relatedness of employment standards adversely impacting classes covered by Title VII.

The "Numbers Game" of the Enforcement Agencies

Equal employment parity (i.e., equality of results) is what the enforcement agencies are advocating. Under this advocacy, the *Uniform Guidelines,* if literally applied, become but a subterfuge under the guise of equal employment opportunity. The enforcement agencies have construed the law to their own egalitarian agenda of redistributing jobs for those classes for whom the agencies advocate. The agenda of the agencies is nothing less than redistribution of jobs for these classes in proportion to their representation in the general population. The very effective way in which this agenda is being accomplished is by appearing to give a set of fair employment guidelines. If literally applied, however, the *Uniform Guidelines* offer unattainable standards for even the largest employer and the most expert professionals. Hence, the practical choice for most employers may be to remove the adverse impact by hiring and promoting equal proportions of the various classes of individuals for whom the enforcement agencies advocate, rather than struggle with the substantive technical standards and copious documentation requirements. In order to eliminate adverse impact, the employer necessarily has to give preferential consideration on grounds of race or sex so as to hire equal proportions (quotas) of classes afforded preferential status by the enforcement agencies.

"Systemic Discrimination"

The *Uniform Guidelines* are but one of the roadmaps to litigation being used in the enforcement agencies' advocacy of employment parity. Prior to the September, 1978, adoption of the *Uniform Guidelines,* the EEOC had announced its "Criteria for Selecting Companies for Major Pattern and Practice Cases." This set of criteria provided the framework of what has yet to become the Commission's focus on so-called "systemic discrimination."

According to the list of criteria, the EEOC (1978) can bring systemic discrimination charges against "Employers or other persons subject to Title VII who employ available minorities and women at a substantially lower rate than other employers in the same labor market who employ persons with the same general level of skills." In other words, for any given job a *presumption* of discrimination could be made by the EEOC by comparing EEO-1 data for all employers in a given labor market to the EEO-1 data of the employer with the best "utilization" rate, who may have achieved top utilization in a labor market by voluntarily adopting preferential treatment. In effect, one employer's program of preferential treatment could likely be construed by the EEOC as another employer's potential liability, because of the latter's apparent underutilization. This is currently the heart of the EEOC's targeting of employers against whom the Commissioner's charges of systemic and/or pattern and practice charges may be brought.

In addition to the EEO-1 recordkeeping obligation imposed by the EEOC, the *Uniform Guidelines* require employers to keep personnel records as follows:

> Each user should maintain and have available for inspection records or other information which will disclose the impact which its tests and other selection procedures have upon employment opportunities. . . (on the basis of) sex and the following races and ethnic groups: Blacks (Negroes), American Indians (including Alaskan Natives), Asians (including Pacific Islanders), Hispanic (including persons of Mexican, Puerto Rican, Cuban Central or South American, or other Spanish origin or culture regardless of race), Whites (Caucasians) other than Hispanic, and totals.

A *Question and Answer* (*Q&A*) supplement to the *Uniform Guidelines* issued in March, 1979, required these personnel records to be kept for each and every employment decision for each and every job (EEOC, 1979): "The *Guidelines* call for records to be kept and determination of adverse impact to be made of the overall selection process on a job by job basis. Thus, if there is adverse impact in the assignment or selection procedures for a job even though there is no adverse impact from the test, the user should eliminate the adverse impact from the assignment procedures or justify the assignment procedures."

Having announced an adverse impact recordkeeping requirement with which virtually no employer is able to comply, the agencies then gave themselves the discretion to presume a *prima facie* case based on the failure of the employer to keep such records:

"Where the user has not maintained data on adverse impact as required by the documentation section of applicable guidelines, the Federal enforcement agencies may draw an inference of adverse impact of the selection process from the failure of the user to maintain such data, if the user has an underutilization. . . ."

Finally, in addition to various threshold comparisons, such as the "four-fifths" rule of thumb for comparing selection rates of various applicant groups, the agencies gave themselves license to administratively conclude that an employer is presumed to have a *prima facie* case: ". . . (1) where the selection procedure is a significant factor in the continuation of patterns of assignments of incumbent employees caused by prior discriminatory employment practices, or (2) where the weight of court decisions or *administrative interpretations hold that a specific procedure* (such as height or weight requirements or no arrest records) *is not job related in the same or similar circumstances*" (emphasis added).

Having given themselves the "administrative and prosecutorial discretion" to presume that a given employment selection procedure might have an adverse impact, based on their experience elsewhere with the same selection procedure, the EEO enforcement agencies again have given themselves a *pro forma* job of arguing in effect that certain selection procedures are now *per se* violations because they say so.

In other words, the agencies have announced that they intend to generalize adverse impact findings from one employer to another. The obverse argument by the employer who wants to transport validity evidence, however, finds seven paragraphs of restrictive conditions "encouraged" by the following:

> If there are variables in the other studies which are likely to affect validity significantly, the user may not rely upon such studies, but will be expected either to conduct an internal validity study or . . . choose to utilize alternative selection procedures in order to eliminate adverse impact. Such alternative procedures should eliminate adverse impact in the total selection process, should be lawful, and should be as job-related as possible.

In addition to the advocacy of equal employment in *Uniform Guidelines,* the "numbers game" of the EEOC can be seen elsewhere. First is the policy statement on affirmative action found in Section 17 of the *Uniform Guidelines:*

> Voluntary affirmative action to assure equal employment opportunity is appropriate at any stage of the employment process. The first step in the construction of any affirmative action plan should be an analysis of the employer's workforce to determine whether percentages of sex, race, or ethnic groups in individual job classifications are substantially similar to the percentages of those groups available in the relevant job market who possess the basic job-related skills.

The second place the "numbers game" is revealed is in the EEOC's *Affirmative Action Guidelines* of 1979:

> The objective of self analysis is to determine whether employment practices do, or tend to, exclude, disadvantage, restrict, or result in adverse impact or disparate treatment of previously excluded or restricted groups or leave uncorrected the effects of prior discrimination. . . .

If the self analysis shows that one or more employment practices: (1) have or tend to have an adverse effect on employment opportunities of members of previously excluded groups, or groups whose employment or promotional opportunities have been artificially limited; (2) leave uncorrected the effects of prior discrimination; or (3) result in disparate treatment, the person making the self analysis has a reasonable basis for concluding that action is appropriate. . . . Such reasonable action may include goals and timetables or other appropriate employment tools which recognize the race, sex, or national origin of applicants or employees.

A third source of the "numbers game" can be seen in the criteria for systemic discrimination noted before (EEOC, 1978), by which the EEOC can institute systemic proceedings against: "Employers or other persons subject to Title VII who continue in effect policies and practices which result in low utilization of available minorities and women despite the clear obligation in Title VII to fairly recruit, hire and promote such persons."

The reason that the "numbers game" of the EEOC is particularly contentious is that the advocacy of the rights of the *class* is extralegal in going beyond both Congressional intent and the precedent of Supreme Court case law. As noted previously, the language of Title VII expressed Congress' intent in prohibiting employment discrimination against the *individual*: "It shall be an unlawful employment practice for an employer: (1) to fail or refuse to hire or to discharge any *individual*, or otherwise to discriminate against any *individual* . . ." (emphasis added).

The rights of the individual under Title VII, as opposed to the rights of the class, was emphasized by the Supreme Court in a 1978 decision, *Los Angeles Dept. of Water & Power* v. *Manhart:*

The question of fairness to various classes affected by the statute is essentially a matter of policy for the legislature to address. Congress has decided that classifications based on sex, like those based on national origin or race, are unlawful . . . *the basic policy of the statute requires that we focus on fairness to individuals rather than fairness to classes.* Practices which classify employees in terms of religion, race or sex tend to preserve traditional assumptions about groups rather than thoughtful scrutiny of individuals (emphasis added).

Technical Assistance from Enforcement Agencies

Not only is literal compliance with *Uniform Guidelines* unattainable for most employers, the EEOC and the OFCCP have seen to it that technical assistance in complying is nonexistent. The EEOC is required by statute (Title VII of the Civil Rights Act of 1964): ". . . to furnish to persons subject to this title such technical assistance as they may request to further their compliance with this title or an order issued thereunder . . . (and) to make such technical studies as are appropriate to effectuate the purposes and policies of this title and to make the results of such studies available to the public."

If an employer were to seek such technical assistance on the *Uniform Guidelines* today, that employer would find all of two persons having any relevant training between the EEOC, the Department of Justice, and the OFCCP combined! The absence of technical assistance has obviously helped keep the employment community in the dark as to its prerogatives, given by both the statute and the precedent of case law, in making job-related standards of competence the cornerstone of the means of equal employment opportunity.

Even if an employer were to meet the rigorous technical validation standards of the *Uniform Guidelines*, it is inconceivable that the staff of two professionals between the EEOC and OFCCP could give more than a cursory review of the copious documentation required for all of the jobs for any given employer. The employment community is being held accountable to the most rigorous of technical standards and required to meet copious documentation requirements for each and every job, when the government by its own priorities appears disinterested. With over 300 attorneys at the EEOC alone, the *Uniform Guidelines* appear to be more a tool of litigation than of guiding employers in developing and administering fair employment practices.

In addition, the field investigators from EEOC and the compliance staff from OFCCP have never been given more than an acquaintance with job-relatedness issues. As a result, field reviews are "numbers" oriented with the objective of identifying a possible affected class with attendant back-pay liabilities, rather than the more central question of whether employment decisions are meritorious.

Documentation Requirements

In the absence of training on substantive issues of job-relatedness, agency field staff are given documentation requirements which lead to a "checklist mentality," where the compliance officer is able to go down the documentation checklist and, upon finding a requirement that cannot be checked, presumes that the employer is out of compliance and discriminating. In effect, the compliance officer becomes the trier of fact rather than the court of law—especially given the OFCCP's implicit threat of passover, set-aside, and disbarment proceedings.

Not only are the documentation requirements themselves of questionable legality, the administrative discretion of the enforcement agencies can clearly be seen in hundreds of documentation reporting requirements identified as *essential* which "should" be reported where "The term 'should' as used in these guidelines is intended to connote action which is necessary to achieve compliance with the guidelines, while recognizing that there are circumstances where alternative courses of action are open to users" (Huffman, 1979). The EEOC's advocacy is particularly noteworthy in light of the legislative history of the Act which specifically withheld substantive rule-making authority from the EEOC and limited its authority "to issue . . . *procedural* regulations. . ." such as required for the EEO-1 recordkeeping.

Role of Professional Standards

Whereas the potential for abuse of administrative discretion is created by the *essential* requirements in the Documentation section, the likelihood of abuse is guaranteed by *Q&A#40* (EEOC, 1979):

Q: What is the relationship between the validation provisions of the *Guidelines* and other statements of psychological principles, such as the *Standards for Educational and Psychological Tests,* published by the American Psychological Association . . . ?

A: The validation provisions of the *Guidelines* are designed to be consistent with the generally accepted standards of the psychological profession. These *Guidelines* also interpret Federal equal employment opportunity law, and embody some policy determinations of an administrative nature. *To the extent that there may be differences between particular provisions of the Guidelines and expressions of validation principles found elsewhere, the Guidelines will be given precedence by the enforcement agencies* (emphasis added).

This administrative advocacy of an absolute checklist of validation requirements necessarily has to be contrasted with the position of the psychological profession articulated in both the APA Standards and the Division of Industrial/Organizational Psychology of the APA's *Principles for the Validation and Use of Personnel Selection Procedures* (1975):

A final caveat is necessary in view of the prominence of testing issues in litigation. This document is prepared as a technical guide for those within the sponsoring professions; it is not written as law. What is intended is a set of standards to be used in part for self-evaluation by test developers and test users. *An evaluation of their competence does not rest on the literal satisfaction of every relevant provision of this document.* The individual standards are statements of ideals or goals, some having priority over others. Instead, an evaluation of competence depends on the degree to which the intent of this document has been satisfied by the test developer or user (emphasis added).

Clearly, the administrative agencies have constructed the standards of the profession in a manner suggesting a checklist of *essential* requirements which clearly contradicts professional opinion in this regard.

In April, 1976, the Deputy Attorney General at the Department of Justice received a memorandum from David L. Rose (*Daily Labor Report,* 1976), the Chief of the Employment Section of the Civil Rights Division at Justice. In the memo, Rose commented as follows on the 1970 EEOC *Guidelines on Employee Selection Procedures,* which were in effect until replaced by the *Uniform Guidelines:*

Under the present EEOC *Guidelines,* few employers are able to show the validity of any of their selection procedures, and the risk of their being held unlawful is high. Since not only tests, but all other procedures must be validated, the thrust of the present guidelines is to place almost all test users in a posture of noncompliance; to give great discretion to enforcement personnel to determine who would be prosecuted; and to set aside objective selection procedures in favor of numerical hiring.

That comment by Rose was written about the former EEOC *Guidelines* that did not have a documentation requirement. While the *Uniform Guidelines* offer at least a choice between validation strategies that the 1970 EEOC *Guidelines* did not, the documentation requirements now add considerably to the likelihood that a field compliance review will find an employer to be in noncompliance and give impetus to the compliance officer's suggestion that the employer's option is to remove the adverse impact (by adopting quota-based hiring).

Use of "Alternative" Selection Procedures to Eliminate Adverse Impact

The *Uniform Guidelines* call for comparisons of selection rates for various classes covered by Title VII as the basis for determining whether or not there is a *prima facie* presumption of discrimination: "A selection rate for any race, sex or ethnic group which is less than four-fifths (or eighty percent) of the rate for the group with the highest rate will generally be regarded by the Federal enforcement agencies as evidence of adverse impact, while a greater than four-fifths rate will generally not be regarded by Federal enforcement agencies as evidence of adverse impact."

If adverse impact is shown, the burden then falls on the employer to show "job-relatedness" through a validation study: "The use of any selection procedure which has an adverse impact on the hiring, promotion, or other employment or membership opportunities of members of any race, sex, or ethnic group will be considered to be discriminatory and inconsistent with these guidelines, unless the procedure has been validated in accordance with these guidelines. . . ." It is suggested that the employer need not be concerned with considerations of competence provided that the adverse impact of the selection procedure is eliminated. In other words, if the employer hires or promotes equal proportions of each class covered by Title VII, there will be no presumption of discrimination by the enforcement agencies.

In effect, the employer is encouraged to adopt the *end of equal employment* rather than the more burdensome job of validating and documenting the "job-relatedness" of one's employment decision-making process: "A user may choose to utilize *alternative selection procedures* in order to eliminate adverse impact or as part of an affirmative action program. Such alternative procedures should eliminate the adverse impact in the total selection process, should be lawful and *should be as job-related as possible*" (emphasis added).

This language is the enforcement agencies' way of saying in effect they don't care whether or not the organization considers competence as long as the numbers look good by hiring/promoting equal proportions of classes for whom the enforcement agencies advocate.

Advocacy of "Alternative Uses"

Contrary to the holdings of the Supreme Court, the *Uniform Guidelines* have construed the law in its advocacy of equal employment so as to place the burden on the employer of eliminating adverse impact through the newly-imposed obligations to "search for alternatives" and to search for "alternative uses." The EEOC's advocacy was well articulated by Eleanor Holmes Norton, former head of the Commission, in 1977:

> There is not any way in which black people tomorrow as a group are going to, no matter what kind of test you give them, score the same way that white people score. . . . I can't live with that. I think employers can. And I think test validation gives them an A-1 out. Because if you validate your tests you don't have to worry about exclusion of minorities and women any longer, you have done what it seems to me is increasingly a fairly minimal thing to do . . . unless somebody pushes employers to find other ways other than tests to find qualified people. . . . But I sincerely believe that tests do not tell very much about who is qualified to do the job. If I wanted really to find out whether or not

you could do the job for me, I wouldn't give you the test. I'd call around and find out about you. The employer community has now caught on to a nice new thing, and if they continue to rely as heavily on validation they could actually undercut the purposes of Title VII. Thus, I think that by giving alternatives, we relieve especially minorities of the frustration they find inevitably in taking validated tests.

In keeping with this suggestion that it is the employer's obligation to come up with alternatives and alternative uses, the *Uniform Guidelines* note that: *"Federal equal employment opportunity law has added a requirement to the process of validation.* In conducting a validation study, the employer should consider available alternatives which will achieve its legitimate business purpose with lesser adverse impact. *The employer cannot concentrate solely on establishing the validity of the instrument or procedure which it has been using in the past"* (emphasis added).

This requirement conveniently ignores the teaching of the Supreme Court in 1975 in *Albemarle Paper Co.* v. *Moody,* which clearly places the burden of alternatives with a lesser adverse impact on the plaintiff: "If an employer does then meet the burden of proving that its tests are 'job-related,' it remains open to the complaining party to show that other tests or selection devices, without a similarly undesirable racial effect, would also serve the employer's legitimate interest in 'efficient and trustworthy workmanship.' "

Not only has the enforcement agencies' advocacy of equal employment miscon-strued the teachings of the Supreme Court, it has similarly confounded the intent of Congress to give the employer the right to select the most competent candidate. The *Uniform Guidelines* press mightily for "alternative uses" with minimum cutoff scores of valid selection procedures, so as to minimize adverse impact:

> The setting of a "cutoff score" to determine who will be screened out may have an adverse impact. If so, an employer is required to justify the initial cutoff score by refer-ence to its need for a trustworthy and efficient workforce. Similarly, use of results for grouping or for rank ordering is likely to have a greater adverse effect than use of scores solely to screen out unqualified candidates. If the employer chooses to use a rank order method, the evidence of validity must be sufficient to justify that method of use.

> The evidence of both the validity and utility of a selection procedure should support the method the user chooses for operational use of the procedure, if that method of use has a greater adverse impact than another method of use. Evidence which may be sufficient to support the use of a selection procedure on a pass/fail (screening) basis may be insuf-ficient to support the use of the same procedure on a ranking basis under these guide-lines. Thus, if a user decides to use a selection procedure on a ranking basis, and that method of use has a greater adverse impact than use of an appropriate pass/fail basis, the user should have sufficient evidence of validity and utility to support the use on a ranking basis.

This pressure to use a valid selection procedure so as to minimize adverse impact clearly contradicts the legislative history of the statute. Specifically, the requirement to-tally ignores Congressional intent as articulated in the "Clark-Case" memorandum of understanding cited with favor by the Supreme Court in its unanimous opinion in *Griggs* v. *Duke Power Co.*:

There is no requirement in Title VII that employers abandon *bona fide* qualifications tests where, because of differences in background and education, members of some groups are able to perform better on these tests than members of other groups. *An employer may set his qualifications as high as he likes, he may test to determine which applicants have these qualifications, and he may hire, assign, and promote on the basis of test performance* (emphasis added).

The teachings of the Supreme Court in *Teamsters* have similarly been disregarded. In this case the Supreme Court recognized:

. . . The two most common legitimate reasons on which an employer might rely to reject a job applicant: an absolute or relative lack of qualifications or the absence of a vacancy in the job sought.

(In rejecting an applicant) the employer might show that there were other, more qualified persons who would have been chosen for a particular vacancy, or that the nonapplicant's stated qualifications were insufficient.

Finally, the issue of both "search for" and "alternative uses" which minimize adverse impact was squarely addressed by the Supreme Court only months before the *Uniform Guidelines* were issued. Again, the teachings of the Supreme Court in *Furnco Construction Corp.* v. *Waters* (1978) were ignored:

The Court of Appeals, as we read its opinion, thought Furnco's hiring procedures not only must be reasonably related to the achievement of some legitimate purpose, but also must be the method which allows the employer to consider the qualifications of the largest number of minority applicants. We think the imposition of that second requirement simply finds no support whether in the nature of the *prima facie* case or the purpose of Title VII.

. . . (T)he burden which shifts to the employer is merely that of proving that he based his employment decision on a legitimate consideration, and not an illegitimate one such as race. To prove that, he need not prove that he pursued the course which would both enable him to achieve his own business goal and allow him to consider the most employment applications. *Title VII* forbids him from having as a goal a workforce selected by any proscribed discriminatory practice, but it *does not impose a duty to adopt a hiring procedure that maximizes hiring of minority employees* (emphasis added).

Court Deference to Professional Opinion

Having given themselves total discretion to pull the *prima facie* "trigger," the enforcement agencies have placed virtually every employer in the position of either having to attempt to meet a set of validation standards and documentation requirements which, if literally applied, are unattainable as a rebuttal to the plaintiff's *prima facie* case, or to remove the adverse impact by adopting employment practices built on preferential race and sex-conscious treatment. The agencies' "numbers game" is so blatant that the employer is now told via a *Q&A* (EEOC, 1979) that: "Even apart from affirmative action programs, a user may be race, sex or ethnic conscious in taking 'appropriate and lawful' measures to eliminate adverse impact from selection procedures."

The professional communities of industrial and organizational psychologists and employee and industrial relations managers have been frustrated by the *Uniform Guidelines'* development process to the point where it no longer is realistic to expect any accommodation from any of the federal enforcement agencies. The advocacy to the end of employment parity, instead of employment opportunity in the *Uniform Guidelines,* leaves little choice to employers but to meet this advocacy by asking the courts to clarify the employer's statutory right to place competence at the heart of the employment decision-making process and not preferential treatment based on the candidate's race, color, religion, sex, or national origin.

Experience during the past several years has clearly demonstrated that the civil rights enforcement agencies have not the least intention of responding to the concerns of either the professional or employment communities. While the overview of the *Uniform Guidelines* mentions that 1,200 pages of comments were received, and professional input had been received in public hearing from the Division of Industrial and Organizational Psychology of the American Psychological Association, the International Personnel Management Association, and the American Society for Personnel Administration, what the casual reader would not learn from reading this self-serving overview is that each of these professional groups has gone on public record with telegrams to the White House withdrawing public support of the *Uniform Guidelines.*

Since Congress and the White House are hostage to the civil rights enforcement agencies and special interest groups, and cannot be expected to exercise any meaningful oversight, the enforcement agencies can be expected to continue their advocacy of the "numbers game," accountable to no one but the courts. If recent experience is any indication, the enforcement agencies may in fact be construing themselves as the court of last resort. Ultimately the "court of public opinion" may be the only means of getting the laws prohibiting discrimination in employment enforced!

One alternative for the employment community under these circumstances is to recognize the benefits of cooperative validation research for jobs they have in common across organizational lines (Smith, 1979). An increasing number of trade and industry groups are now providing the focus for consortium efforts aimed at developing job-related standards of competence, which will provide the weight of evidence if challenged to rebut the contentious, numbers-oriented advocacy of the federal enforcement agencies. Such weight of evidence will obviously be of assistance in overcoming the "numbers game," but it appears that the best answer can be found in footnote 20 of *United States* v. *South Carolina* (1977), where the Supreme Court affirmed a lower court's approval of a validation study and noted that: "To the extent that the EEOC Guidelines conflict with well-grounded expert opinion and accepted professional standards, they need not be controlling."

Discussion Questions

1. What is meant by the term *adverse impact?*

2. Explain two ways a *prima facie* presumption of employment discrimination might be argued by a plaintiff.

3. Who has the burden of demonstrating "alternative selection procedures" having less adverse impact, according to the Uniform Guidelines? According to the Supreme Court?

4. Compare and contrast content validation with criterion-related validation strategies.

5. What does the term *business necessity* mean as defined by the Supreme Court in *Griggs?*

PART FOUR

EVALUATION AND REINFORCEMENT OF WORK PERFORMANCE

"People problems" loom large in organizations today. Perhaps from the organization's point of view, however, the most salient problem is declining productivity. Organizational responses to declining productivity can and do vary, but three of these are evaluation, reinforcement, and motivation of work performance.

Performance evaluation, as an important personnel activity, directly addresses the productivity issue and can be an effective means for controlling and improving work performance. When we consider internal control systems in organizations, performance evaluation stands as one of the most fundamental and effective.

The topic of performance evaluation, however, lacks adequate theory. For many years, the emphasis here, as with a number of other topics in personnel management, was on method. Only recently have attempts been made to better understand the performance evaluation *process*. In Chapter 8, Kavanagh presents a comprehensive review of performance evaluation and the results of behavioral science research. Additionally, he discusses the shift in focus from method to process and highlights future critical issues and potential areas of inquiry.

Another important personnel activity that affects worker productivity is the structuring and administration of pay and compensation. As an extrinsic motivator, pay satisfies basic physiological needs. For others, pay satisfies recognition and/or status needs. The proper structuring and administration of pay and compensation is of direct importance to organizations, as well, since programs in these areas can represent an ongoing demand of up to 50 percent on cash flow.

Pay and compensation administration in recent years has become more complex because of changing economic conditions and the influences of unions and the federal government. Today, with the nation's economy experiencing a relatively high and often uncertain rate of inflation, cost of living adjustments (COLAs) have become a major burden for many organizations to plan for and bear. In addition, sizeable increases in pay often tend not to be reinforcing since they are something employees have come to *expect*. In Chapter 9, Mahoney examines issues related to the structuring and administration of pay and compensation, including a timely concern with job evaluation and the enforcement of the Equal Pay Act of 1963.

A third way to address the issue of declining productivity in organizations is to focus on ways of motivating employees toward increased work performance. The emphasis then is not only on understanding motivation as a psychological phenomenon, but formulating motivational strategies for encouraging higher productivity. While the personnel function seeks to identify and attract people who have the requisite abilities and skills (the *can do* factors) to perform the job, motivational strategies attempt to structure the work situation so that employees also have the interest and desire (the *will do* factors) to perform well. The age-old question of whether employers can motivate employees may, in the final analysis, necessarily be answered *No*. At best, perhaps, employers can only structure the job and work environment to enable employees to motivate themselves. In Chapter 10, Mitchell discusses the fundamental bases of some motivational strategies and their implications for work behavior.

CHAPTER EIGHT

EVALUATING PERFORMANCE

Michael J. Kavanagh

Michael Kavanagh is Professor of Psychology and Director of the Ph.D. Program in Industrial and Organizational Psychology at Old Dominion University. He received his Ph.D in Industrial/Social Psychology from Iowa State University. Professor Kavanagh has established a reputation for his research and consulting in the area of performance appraisal. He has authored and co-authored numerous papers, publications, and professional association presentations. Professor Kavanagh is also the author and coauthor of several textbooks, including *Performance Measurement*. Professor Kavanagh has consulted with many organizations, including IBM and the Center for Creative Leadership.

This chapter will discuss the evaluation of employees in terms of how well they perform their jobs. The growing emphasis on worker productivity, the passage of the Civil Service Reform Act, and an increasing activism on the part of employees all combine to make the performance appraisal function central to the management of human resources in organizations. From a scientific perspective, this topic has been extensively researched and labeled "the criterion problem" (Wallace, 1964). The focus here will be on current issues in the field of performance appraisal, with emphasis on their expected impact in the 1980s. Background material will be presented where necessary for understanding. However, there is no way this single chapter can comprehensively cover the entire field. The interested reader seeking more depth will be referred to other literature. Prior to beginning the more substantive sections of this chapter, two general perspectives on the performance appraisal function will be discussed.

JOB PERFORMANCE MEASUREMENT: A FUZZY PROCESS

The measurement of human performance in work roles is, at best, fuzzy. Decades of research and practical experience have not, as yet, resulted in a measurement and appraisal program without some problems. The source of this fuzziness can be traced to at least three different groups: managers, personnel specialists, and employees. Among other factors, managers balk at doing job performance appraisals ("too much paperwork"), and even more so at telling their employees how well (or poorly) they are doing. DeVries and McCall (1976) cogently observed that managers painfully ask the question "Is it tax time again?" when annual performance appraisals are due. Furthermore, managers often complain that the appraisal form in use does not reflect their employees' "real" job performance. This perception of the weakness of the form affects the manager's *confidence* in the system.

Professional practitioners are also at fault for the fuzzy nature of the measurement of human performance. Existing performance appraisal programs in many organizations are a result of what Guion (1961) has called "residual judgment"—the job performance measure was chosen because it was readily available and cheap. Choosing a measure based on its scientific (e.g., valid) or practical merits (e.g., cost-effectiveness) was not expedient for the development of a program that management needed *yesterday*.

Another influence on the choice of a performance appraisal program has been the tendency to choose whatever is currently in vogue. Thus, graphic rating scales rode the wave of popularity until behaviorally anchored rating scales (BARS) stole the show. Rather than choosing a program based on a diagnosis of their organization's needs and its scientific and practical merits, many personnel specialists have blindly "jumped on the bandwagon" of the current fad.

Finally, employees themselves have helped to muddy the waters. Sometimes they "work to rule," performing at minimally acceptable levels. Other times, group norms have a powerful influence on the performance levels of employees. Further, employees often engage in gaming behavior to "beat the system"—knowing when to perform at high levels (immediately before an annual appraisal) and when to relax.

Certainly there are other ways these three groups affect the quality of the performance appraisal process, and there are other factors (e.g., legal considerations) that influence the performance appraisal system. The important point is that all of these considerations in real-world organizations lead to problems in the measurement of human job performance. These problems suggest several important points for the reader. First, it makes it very difficult, if not impossible, to prescribe or endorse any specific, correct performance system for *all* organizations. A specific process and a set of evaluative criteria will be given, but there will be no attempt to crown one type of performance appraisal the "very best." Another implication, if one follows the guidelines presented here, is that developing and implementing a performance appraisal system will still be a complex and difficult task.

For those who are itchy about the use of the word *fuzzy,* job performance measurement may be viewed as varying on a continuum of *certainty of information.* Efforts to increase the certainty of information about employees' job performance beyond a given level are not cost-effective. However, a great deal of uncertainty in job performance information will doom a program to disuse and, most likely, abuse. The scientist and practitioner alike must choose a compromise between cost-effectiveness and certainty/accuracy.

THE SCIENTIST-PRACTITIONER MODEL

In approaching the study of performance appraisal, another useful perspective is that offered by the scientist-practitioner model. This model has been primarily promulgated by industrial psychologists, but it is a valuable viewpoint for all professional practitioners. Underlying the model is the notion that there is continuous interaction between the findings of basic research and applications of that research in organizations. The results of this interaction provide prescriptive advice to professionals working directly with performance appraisal programs in organizations and, in the other direction, new research issues for the scientist.

Persons working in the field of performance appraisal must constantly try to straddle both worlds. They must be sensitive to the requirements of good theory and good practice, even though they may bring different perspectives to the field. For example, the scientist typically would be much more concerned about reducing the systematic error in performance measures than the practitioner. Conversely, the practitioner would be more concerned with cost-benefit analysis to demonstrate the cost-effectiveness of a performance appraisal system. These differences in orientations will be considered as the research and practical concerns in performance appraisal are discussed.

WHY PERFORMANCE MEASUREMENT AND APPRAISAL

One way to understand the need and the role of performance appraisal in organizations is to imagine the situation when there is no performance measurement program present. Does this mean that the organization will stop functioning? Not likely. Pay raise, promotion, and termination decisions will still be made. However, the information upon which those decisions are being made is likely to be low in certainty, or fuzzy. Information on job performance will be gathered through the informal grapevine, usually accurate in terms of the extremes (excellent to poor performers), but most likely not reflective of each individual's performance with respect to job duties and responsibilities. Thus, the information on the effectiveness of human resources is ambiguous and generally distorted. The question is: "How can management operate the enterprise and make operating decisions when information on one of their most costly resources is highly questionable?" Would the enterprise operate if this same state of affairs existed with respect to its fiscal or capital resources?

Given the undesirable situation when no performance appraisal program exists, there are, thus, several practical and scientific reasons for the considerable concern about the evaluation of individual efforts on the job. First, and most important, human performance is of vital interest to the behavioral scientist. I would agree with Ronan and Prien that "the criterion, as an evaluative index of performance behavior, is really a sub-problem in the field of understanding human performance'' (1971, p. v), as well as Wallace (1964), who emphasized that ''the answer to the question 'Criteria for What?' must always include _____ for understanding.'' Finally, Brayfield (1965) underscored the need for the study of human effectiveness by stating:

> My primary and limited purpose . . . has been to suggest an orientation which is con-genial and relevant to the interests of diverse psychologists and *responsive to the per-ceived needs of our culture and the members of our society.* We are, in my view, a science and a profession uniquely concerned with human effectiveness—with the estab-lishment and maintenance of the effective performance of the members of society in all their required tasks, their social roles, and their human relationships. This is our chal-lenge—and our opportunity (p. 651).

Second, individual effectiveness in organizational roles remains of primary impor-tance to the management of that organization. The economic basis for the more effec-tive utilization of human resources is still as strong today as it was when Munsterberg re-sponded to a management request and designed a situation test for the selection of train operators in Boston (Munsterberg, 1913). The definition and measurement of job per-formance remains a central parameter in this economic utilization process. As Barrett (1966) rather cogently stated, ''Management has no choice as to whether it will have a program of performance evaluation. It has a program . . . and the results of the evalua-tions are continuously used . . . employees are transferred, promoted, demoted and fired on the basis of the opinions of management'' (p. 1).

Finally, the need for the accurate description and measurement of employee job effectiveness flows from the needs of employees to best use their capabilities. A well-designed performance appraisal program will result in the proper (maybe optimal) use of employees' abilities, developed and directed through selection, promotion, transfer, training, and retraining. Performance appraisal is at the heart of the personal manage-ment process.

This argument is based on the assumption that human beings desire to maximize the use of their personal capabilities in performing significant tasks. This also means that employees would be more highly motivated in those jobs which they felt better used their abilities. This assumption differs from the traditional view, in that it empha-sizes that employees are ''proacting'' as well as ''reacting'' to the environment. Tradi-tional views of human behavior in organizations, such as Scientific Management, stressed control of the employees' performance by organizational policies; thus, the em-ployee was considered to be passive and only ''reacted'' to the environment. The current view argues that employees also ''proact,'' in that they attempt to influence and struc-ture their working environment.

Realizing that employees can influence their organizational environment, it is a log-ical step to argue that they attempt to obtain an optimal match between their capabili-ties and the requirements of the job. This argument is similar to the transactional view of Jahoda (1961), who argued that a ''match'' or ''best-fit'' of individual to environ-ment results in positive benefits, whereas a ''lack of fit'' leads to negative ones. It also bears a relationship to the underlying assumption of many motivational theories applied to human job performance (e.g., Maslow, 1943, 1965; Herzberg, 1959), which is that people seek growth and fulfillment of their potentialities in their jobs. Finally, it agrees with theory regarding human performance (Astin, 1964; Ronan and Prien, 1971).

In this connection, it should be noted that current prescriptive techniques (organization interventions) to improve employee motivation, quality of work life, or both, all appear to include an improvement in the quantity and/or quality of the feedback the individual employee receives concerning job performance.

Several examples are readily apparent. The implementation of a behavioral modification plan (see Hamner, 1975) in Emery Air Freight involved, as a critical element, that employees keep records of their own performance for comparison against established standards or goals. In the Volvo experiment (*Organizational Dynamics,* 1973), which involved the use of autonomous work groups, the quality of feedback was enhanced so that the workers could see the finished product rather than a single piece. A key element in job enrichment programs (Lawler, 1969) is that employees exercise greater control over more elements of their individual jobs. This would improve both the quantity and clarity of feedback. Management by objectives (MBO) and other goal-setting programs have, as part of their design, the identification and development of organizational data against which performance goals can be evaluated. In general, it would seem that the desired end state of these motivational programs, if one extends the logic, would be *self-regulation of individual performance* through improvements in the quantity, quality, and clarity of performance feedback data. These developments, together with the increasing employee activism expected in the 1980s, underscore the need for a performance appraisal program that provides accurate and timely feedback for the growth and development of the individual employee.

While examining the reasons for appraisal, the three generally accepted purposes of performance appraisal—administrative, employee growth and development, and research—have been covered. In addition, it is becoming apparent that a performance appraisal program will be necessary for legal reasons. There is no doubt that performance appraisal, as an employment procedure, falls under Title VII of the Civil Rights Act of 1964. Recent discussions (Cascio, 1980; Edwards, 1976; Holley and Feild, 1975; Lazer, 1976) have documented, with reference to court cases, that performance appraisal programs are being examined in Equal Employment Opportunity (EEO) cases. There is evidence that this trend will intensify during the 1980s as protected minorities, who were selected into organizations in large numbers during the 1970s, are being considered for promotion, transfer, or demotion. Because of the importance of this trend, a later section of this chapter will be devoted to performance appraisal and the law. For now, it is enough to recognize that performance appraisal programs need to exist and be in compliance with fair employment laws.

All of this discussion has a purpose. When designing a new program or changing the present program of performance appraisal, the first and most *critical* determination is what purpose or purposes will it serve. It must meet legal requirements, so the question really involves which other three major purposes will it serve. This determination *must* be made by top management, and *must be made prior* to any further work on developing the program. As will be seen later, this decision will have major implications for the design features of a program of performance appraisal. Before moving on, however, it is necessary to examine what the program is being built for.

WHAT IS PERFORMANCE APPRAISAL?

Trying to define performance appraisal is, like most definitional tasks, quite difficult. A complete definition, with all the ramifications of dimensionality, dynamism, and systems orientation, would result in something akin to an inkblot; that is, each person will see it in terms of what he or she wants. It seems reasonable to begin with a more simple and understandable definition, and discuss the implications in detail. Thus, for this chapter, *performance appraisal is the process, for a defined purpose, that involves the systematic measurement of individual differences in employees' performance on their jobs.*

Process Orientation

The first part of the definition emphasizes that performance appraisal is a process of identifying good and poor employees. Actually, performance appraisal involves several processes to fulfill this primary one. First, there is the *judgmental process* of the professional practitioner who must choose specific criteria and the way to measure them. This *should* involve decisions based on the best criteria and methods to measure them, but, unfortunately, as Guion (1961) has noted, it frequently involves a ''residual judgment'' on the best *available* criterion. This is not a desirable strategy, and this issue will be returned to later.

A second process that occurs, particularly when performance ratings are used, is also judgmental. In completing a rating form, the rater goes through a judgment process that is based on the following types of information: (1) perceptual—observations of the ratee's work behavior; (2) affective—personal feelings about the ratee; and (3) cognitive—knowledge and evaluation of the ratee's job performance. These three are interrelated, and the judgmental process involved in performance appraisal must consider these components.

The final process involved in performance appraisal is interpersonal. This process occurs during the performance review between supervisor and subordinate. In communicating the results of a job performance appraisal to an employee, the supervisor is in a highly sensitive, emotionally-charged situation that calls for extremely good interpersonal skills. This process will be discussed in detail later. Suffice it to say at this point that this is a most critical part of a performance appraisal program in terms of maintaining and/or increasing employee job motivation, as well as promoting employee development.

Defined Purpose

These three processes should be related in a total performance appraisal program. One cannot expect performance appraisal to succeed if these are not coordinated in relation to the overall defined purpose(s). For example, if the primary purpose of the performance appraisal system is administrative (i.e., to determine promotions and merit increases), it would be incongruous to urge supervisors to focus on personal growth of the employee during the performance review interview. The interview should be used to explain to the employee why a merit increase was not granted. The determination of a merit increase may be the result, in part, of individual performance, but other organizational factors (e.g., amount of available merit pay) affect individual employee merit increase decisions. Furthermore, the content of a performance review interview aimed at employee growth and development is *ipsative,* based on the strengths and weaknesses within the person's job performance. By contrast, a performance review interview session concerned with explaining the reasons for an administrative decision will be based on *normative* information; i.e., strengths and weaknesses of the person's job performance in comparison with that of *other employees.* The important point is that the processes involved in performance appraisal should be congruent with management's purpose for the program.

The importance of a process orientation in performance appraisal has been recently underscored by Landy and Farr (1980). Based on a review of the literature, they derive a process model of performance rating. The most important aspect of their model is the identification of two subsystems in the rating process: (1) the cognitive process of the rater involving observation, storage, retrieval, and judgment; and (2) the administrative rating subsystem of the organization involving such things as purpose and rating format. Their model is likely to strongly influence research and practice in this field during the next decade.

Systematic Nature

A critical feature of any performance appraisal effort is that it be systematic or orderly. Reliance on informal, "grapevine" information, as noted earlier, has many difficulties. Because of its unsystematic nature, this type of informal evaluation provides information primarily on the extremes; that is, the manager is likely to hear about the very best and the very worst employees, but nothing about the many others. The systematic features of a well-designed performance appraisal program insures that information on the job effectiveness of all employees is available to the manager to aid in personnel decisions.

Measurement Orientation

The third emphasis in the definition is perhaps the most important part. No matter how smooth the three processes work, and no matter how systematic the collection of information on employees' job performance, if the evaluation program does not meet the criteria established for valid measurement, it is all quite useless (APA, 1973).

The application of measurement theory to the evaluation of employee performance has several distinct advantages. As Nunnally (1967) has noted, in order to discuss the advantages of measurement, one must compare them to what is left without measurement. In the case of performance evaluation, one would have subjective, intuitive estimates of employee performance mixed with informal "gossip" that would be difficult for the manager to use in personnel decisions. Nunnally (1967) discusses the following four advantages of measurement: (1) objectivity, (2) quantification, (3) communication, and (4) economy. The interested reader may wish to consult Nunnally for further details.

Individual Differences

The fourth part of the definition of appraisal is its emphasis on individual differences. A performance appraisal program should provide information on both inter- and intra-individual differences in job performance. Interindividual differences or *normative performance information* forms the basis for comparisons *between* employees and subsequent administrative actions like promotion. This has been the major goal of most employee appraisal programs. However, intraindividual differences or *ipsative performance information* is of growing importance. Differences in job skills and abilities within a given employee should be considered in either transfer or retraining. As noted earlier, the purpose(s) of the performance appraisal program, as determined by management, will dictate the type of performance information to be collected.

The growing change in management philosophy that emphasizes better placement and transfer as alternatives to dismissal and/or voluntary turnover underscores the importance of the measurement of intraindividual differences in job performance—a profile of the strengths and weaknesses of the employee's abilities. I am in agreement with Toops (1959), who stated that "the profile is basic, because only it, of all proposals to date (in industrial psychology), comes close to *representing as a scientific scheme the whole functioning individual*" (emphasis added).

Job Relatedness

The final part of the definition implies that the measured job performance be job-related. In a sense, this argues for the elimination of error (nonjob-related elements) from the appraisal. These error elements are numerous. They include, for example, the biases in measurement that could arise from employee differences in sex, race, religion, physical characteristics, or national origin—in short, any factor that *may be irrelevant* to job performance.

It is critical to determine the degree to which a job performance appraisal is error-free; that is, if it *really measures* what is intended. In fact, this problem of determining whether the measurement of job performance truly represents job performance—technically called establishing construct validity—is the "bottom line" in designing and implementing a performance appraisal program.

WHAT IS JOB PERFORMANCE?

Now that performance appraisal has been defined, the construct (job performance) one is attempting to measure must be defined. Of course, these two definitions will be related. More important, the other issues and problems in performance appraisal will be discussed in relation to these definitions. These definitions provide the basic conceptual material for the development of a program of performance appraisal. The definition of job performance will not be all-inclusive; rather, it will cover the major themes in the literature.

Job performance is a dynamic, multidimensional construct, assumed to indicate an employee's behavior in executing the requirements of a given organizational role.

Dynamic Nature

The *enduring notion* that human performance, particularly on the job, is a *stable phenomenon* has been evidenced in most of the theory, research, and practice surrounding the criterion field. Most predictors of employee performance used for selection of employees (tests, interviews, physical examinations) have been validated against measures of job performance collected at one time. In practical settings, the same production record or rating form has been used for years with few modifications. This is based on the assumption that job performance is stable over time, an assumption that is severely challenged. The important question is, "How valid are these practices if job performance changes over time?"

In a classic article, Ghiselli (1956) identified a property of performance criteria he named "dynamic dimensionality." By this he meant that "the performance of workers does change as they learn and develop on the job" (Ghiselli, 1956, p. 3). MacKinney (1967), in summarizing the relevant empirical literature on the dynamic nature of job performance, arrived at the following inductive generalization: "The nature of performance is changing over time" (p. 64). Regardless of whether these changes are attributable to job procedure changes, organizational changes, individual changes, or some interaction among them, the critical point is that human performance on the job must be considered to be changing over time.

One implication of this idea is that an additional term must be added to the regression equations in predicting job performance. This term would best be described as a "time" element and would reflect changes in *performance by individual* over time. Of course, this would be based not only on the assumption that job performance changes, but that it changes in a predictable fashion. Research on the development of techniques for the measurement of these change components by jobs, as well as modification of the present paradigms in industrial-differential psychology, seems an important avenue for the future. Using the mathematical and statistical techniques for time series data introduced by Box and Jenkins (1976), Kavanagh and Vaught (1978) have proposed a method to investigate this dynamic component in performance appraisal.

The process of change in the performance of individuals is further complicated by the fact that what might be considered "good" behavior or performance by the organization changes over time.[1] Thus, employees are changing in terms of their perceptions of what is "good" job performance, and the company's perception of what is "good" job performance is also changing. This is the strongest argument for building a dynamic component into performance appraisal programs.

---

[1]The writer is indebted to Terry Mitchell for this insight.

Multidimensional Nature

Some of the earlier difficulty in defining and measuring job performance had resulted from treating it as a unitary construct, or as a single dimension. Trying to define and measure job performance as a single dimension (e.g., quantity of production) had led to difficulties in both research and practice, as well as ignoring the complexity of human behavior. It seems illogical to develop a job description that contains a number of different dimensions and then design a performance appraisal program around a single dimension of overall performance. Job performance is multidimensional and this must be considered when attempting to measure it.

Ghiselli also has discussed this property of job performance as "static dimensionality. . . . There is no way to combine the independent scores of an individual into a single value that will describe him uniquely. Rather it will be necessary to locate his position in the multidimensional criterion space" (Ghiselli, 1956, p. 1).

This measurement problem places the researcher/practitioner in a dilemma situation; that is, a composite measure is often demanded by organizational policies to fulfill an administrative purpose (e.g., merit pay). Organizations often must have employees ranked on job performance in order to make decisions about rewards. Multidimensionality makes this decision difficult. Suffice it to say, a reasonable resolution of this problem has been offered by Schmidt and Kaplan (1971), and the interested reader should check their recommendations.

Job Performance as a Construct

Labeling job performance a construct means that it belongs in the domain of theory. One assumes a certain phenomenon (which has been called job performance) exists and is represented by the behavior of employees on their jobs. Although this may appear a moot point to some readers, there are several important implications of considering job performance a construct.

First, since job performance is a construct, it is not directly observable. What one does observe is the individual's behavior on the job, and one assumes this corresponds to job performance. Thus, there is a set of observable phenomena (job behaviors) that one hypothesizes do, in fact, represent job performance, an abstract conception.

Understanding this first point helps one understand why there is a multiplicity of criteria that have been used for performance appraisal. Since job performance is an abstract construct, there can be many ways to define and measure it. One can legitimately use production records, wages, achievement tests, and supervisory ratings to measure job performance. The actual choice of one measure over the others represents a judgment or hypothesis that the chosen measure will best define job performance in the given situation—best represent the construct.

This leads to the choice of what constitutes "best." It is important to note that since job performance is a construct, the quality of its measurement by a particular organizational index must be judged in part by its "construct validity." Construct validity addresses the question "Does the chosen measure *really* measure what it is supposed to measure?'' This double-talk can best be summarized by defining construct validity as an attempt to understand the ''meaning of the measure.'' This issue, as well as the other standards to evaluate a performance appraisal program, will be discussed later.

PERFORMANCE APPRAISAL—CAPSTONE OF THE PERSONNEL FUNCTION

The personnel function of any organization involves the optimal utilization of human resources of the organization. There are several major interrelated activities associated with this function: recruiting, selecting/placing, training, evaluating performance, and the feedback of performance information. Their relationships are shown diagrammatically in Figure 8–1.

As a simplistic systems model for the utilization of human resources, the personnel function includes inputs, conversion programs, and outputs. The inputs are the people available for employment within the organization. The conversion programs involve all four of the traditional personnel functions, which are aimed at eliciting job behaviors (outputs) from employees that will maximize organizational performance without alienating the individual members. If the four functions are considered in this manner, their interrelatedness becomes apparent. The operation of one function has direct consequences on the others. Hypothetically, if recruiting resulted in obtaining employees who were *perfectly* matched in terms of organizational requirements and personnel expectations, there would be no need for the other functions. Realistically, each function operates in a partially imperfect fashion—thus, the need to socialize, train, direct, and elicit satisfactory employee performance.

Examination of the place of performance appraisal in Figure 8–1 is very revealing. It is the function that serves as a monitor on the other personnel activities and programs. The effectiveness of the individual employee on the job is really the best measure of the effectiveness of the personnel system that put them there, as well as a measure of management's ability to best use the human resources of that organization. Figure 8–1 is meant to convey the concerns of both personnel and management over the effective utilization of their human resources. As such, performance appraisal can be seen as the *capstone* of the personnel function, as well as helping to define other stages in this human resource utilization process.

EVALUATION OF PERFORMANCE APPRAISAL TECHNIQUES

The previous section should have provided a brief picture of the performance appraisal function as an intergral part of the larger personnel management system. As such, it interacts with the other subsystem programs such as selection and wage and salary administration. It must be seen as distinct from the many techniques or formats for evaluating employee job performance. As noted, the choice of performance appraisal technology by organizations has often been characterized by ''following the Zeitgeist,'' or going with the latest fad.

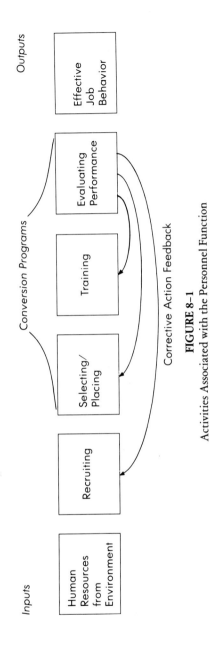

Inputs

Outputs

Conversion Programs

Corrective Action Feedback

Human Resources from Environment

Recruiting

Selecting/ Placing

Training

Evaluating Performance

Effective Job Behavior

FIGURE 8-1
Activities Associated with the Personnel Function

This faddish nature of the field is not meant to be critical of the techniques themselves. All of the various performance appraisal formats available can be effective means of evaluating human effectiveness on the job. Rather, the criticism is aimed at the practice of selecting a performance appraisal format *because it is currently popular without a proper diagnosis of the organization's requirements* for evaluating employee performance. A common mistake, when developing or changing a performance appraisal program, is to first choose the technique rather than diagnose the needs of the organization. The purpose of this section is to discuss a logical and systematic way to select from the many performance appraisal techniques currently available in the literature.

Several writers (Glueck, 1978; Porter, Lawler, and Hackman, 1975) have noted that the various performance techniques have strengths and weaknesses, but the most comprehensible approach has been completed by McAfee and Green (1977). In Table 8–1, which is taken from McAfee and Green (1977), judgmental comparisons among ten techniques on a number of criteria were made for the job of nurse. The table entries are based on a seven-point scale from + 3, highly effective, to – 3, highly ineffective. The "U" entries mean the authors could not make a judgment. Using this matrix, the authors could decide, weighing positive and negative values, which technique was best for this job in this organization.

There are several important considerations to keep in mind when examining Table 8–1. First, the table entries represent the personal judgments of the writers. Second, the rating judgments on the methods were made for the evaluation of job performance of nurses. Thus, these judgments would likely differ for different jobs, and might also differ if other persons made the ratings. Finally, it should be noted that the table entries are not based on empirical investigations comparing these methods, but rather, personal judgments. In spite of these drawbacks, the judgmental matrix developed by McAffee and Green (1977) would be quite useful as a diagnostic tool for an organization in the process of developing a performance appraisal program. Use of the matrix in Table 8–1 would be vastly superior to jumping on the bandwagon of the latest fad.

The previous discussion should underline the need for empirical investigations comparing the various techniques. Kavanagh (1976) examined the empirical literature contrasting rating methods, and compiled a table, presented as Table 8–2, summarizing the review. There are several points worth noting with respect to Table 8–2. First, the number of comparative studies done is rather small, although the recent flurry of studies comparing BARS (Landy and Farr, 1980) has increased the total number. Second, many of the techniques enumerated in Table 8–2 have not been empirically examined. Third, most of the studies in Table 8–2 use graphic rating scales as their "straw man" for empirical comparisons. Close examination of these studies, as well as the literature since 1975, indicates that the graphic rating scales used are normally poorly developed in contrast to the other technique(s) in the study, a somewhat unfair comparison. Finally, with the exception of the Mahler (1948) study, which used rater acceptability, all of the other studies have used only psychometric criteria to judge the value of the techniques. Examination of McAfee and Green's list of criteria in Table 8–1 indicates that there are many other criteria that can be used for this purpose. Research in this field is *totally inconclusive.*

TABLE 8–1

Criteria for Evaluating Performance Appraisal Methods

Methods / Criteria	Employee Comparison	Management by Objectives	Direct Indexes	Weighted Check-list	Forced Choice Check-list	Essay	Rating Scale-Single Word Anchor	Rating Scale-Short Phrase Anchor	Rating Scale-Paragraph Anchor	Rating Scale-Behaviorally Anchored
Counseling Criteria										
1. Provide feedback	2	3	2	2	2	1	1	1	+3	+3
2. Set objectives-convey stds.	−3	+3	+2	+2	−2	+1	−1	+1	+3	+3
Administrative Criteria										
3. Promotion	−1	+2	+1	+2	+2	0	+2	+1	+2	+2
4. Discharge	−2	+2	+1	+2	+2	+1	+2	+2	+3	+3
5. Transfer	−1	+2	+1	+2	+1	+1	+2	+2	+2	+2
6. Training	−2	+1	+1	+2	+1	0	+1	+2	+3	+3
7. Discipline	−2	+2	+1	+2	+1	+1	+2	+2	+2	+2
8. Pay	+1	+1	+1	+2	+2	+1	+2	+2	+3	+3

Personnel Criteria									
9. Test validation	-1	+2	+2	+2	-2	+2	+3	+3	+3
10. Personnel Research	-2	+2	+2	+2	-2	+2	+3	+3	+3
11. References	+1	+1	+2	+1	+1	+2	+2	+3	+3
Economic Criteria									
12. Cost of development	+3	-3	-1	-3	+3	+3	+1	-2	-2
13. Speed & ease in filling out	+2	-2	+2	-1	+1	+3	+3	0	+2
Other Criteria									
14. Comparison of employees between departments									
15. Reliability	-3	+2	+2	+1	-2	+1	+2	+3	+3
16. Freedom from Halo & leniency errors & errors of central tendency	+1	+3	+2	+1	U	+1	+1	+2	+2
	+2	+3	+1	+2	-2	-1	+1	+1	+1

Source: B. McAfee and B. Green. "Selecting a Performance Appraisal Method." *The Personnel Administrator* 76 (1977): 61–64. Reprinted from the June, 1977, issue of *Personnel Administrator*, 30 Park Drive, Berea, Ohio 44017, $26 per year.

TABLE 8–2

Studies Comparing Rating Methods

Study	Rating Methods Used	Results	Evaluation Standards
Bayroff, Haggerty, and Rundquist (1954)	Graphic scale Forced-Choice	No difference	Predictive validity (class standing and efficiency report)
Mahler (1948)	Graphic scale Weighted Checklist	Slightly in favor of graphic scale	Bias, concurrent validity (sales), rater acceptability
Stoltz (1958)	Overall rating (graphic) Forced-Choice	Graphic better	Reliability
Sharon (1968)	Graphic scale Forced Choice	Forced-Choice better	Leniency error
Obradovic (1970)	Graphic Scale Forced-Choice Modified Forced-Choice	Modified Forced-Choice better	Concurrent validity (forced distribution ratings), less skewness
Bell, Hoff, and Hoyt (1963)	Critical Incidents Weighted Checklist Graphic Scale	Critical Incidents and Graphic better than Weighted Checklist	Concurrent validity (GATB aptitudes)

Study	Scales compared	Findings	Criteria
Burnaska and Hollman (1974)	BARS—anchored BARS—unanchored Trait Graphic Scale	BARS scales better for reducing leniency; no difference for halo, reliability	Leniency error, halo error, reliability
Maas (1965)	BARS Trait Graphic Scale	BARS better	Interrrater reliability
Campbell, Dunnette, Arvey, and Hellervik (1973)	BARS Summated Rating Scale	BARS better on all three standards	Leniency error, halo error, method variance
Keaveny and McGann (1975)	BARS Trait Graphic Scale	BARS less halo and better discriminant validity; no difference in leniency or factor solution.	Halo error, leniency error, factor analysis, discriminant validity
Borman and Vallon (1974)	BARS—anchored BARS—nonanchored	No differences	Interrater reliability, halo, restriction of range, leniency
Borman and Dunnette (1975)	BARS—anchored BARS—nonanchored Trait graphic scale	BARS better on three of four standards, but differences are small	Leniency, halo, interrater reliability, degree of differentiation among rates

This indicates that a choice of a performance appraisal technique should be based on a thorough diagnosis of the organization's needs, starting first with an assessment of the purpose or purposes that management wants the system to serve. This diagnosis could be based on the criteria developed by McAfee and Green (1977). One should also be concerned with system-level criteria—a point which will be returned to later in this chapter. Thus, the choice of a technique should be guided by a careful analysis of the personnel management system and organizational needs.

ISSUES IN PERFORMANCE APPRAISAL[2]

The topic of job performance measurement is dominated by ratings, usually made by supervisors, and it seems apparent that ratings of job performance will continue to be the dominant type of performance measure used. The reason for this is twofold. First, other, so-called objective, measures have many of the same theoretical and empirical problems as ratings. They are judgmentally defined, plagued by measurement error, and usually not seen as acceptable by employees. A second reason for the continued use of ratings is the feeling that human job performance cannot really be reduced to a set of numbers on objective indices, and the boss is *usually* in the best position to truly evaluate his or her employees' job performance.

Given that ratings are the most frequent form of performance appraisal, this section will examine six issues related to performance ratings and, where possible, indicate the resolution of the issue. An issue, in this case, is best seen as a question that needs to be answered while designing the program. It is part of the diagnostic information that *should always* be collected and examined *prior to* developing or redesigning a performance appraisal program. These six issues are:

1. *Should* rating be done at all?
2. Is there an *unavoidable conflict* of interest inherent in the rating process?
3. What should the *purpose* of the rating be?
4. *Who* should do the rating?
5. *What* should be rated?
6. *How* should the rating be made?

Should Ratings Be Done?

The first issue, whether ratings should be done at all, is partially an ethical question. Is it ethical for one person to make judgments about another when these judgments will have a significant effect on that person's future? McGregor (1957) came very close to saying that supervisors do not have the right to rate their employees since the supervisors

---

[2]These issues in performance appraisal were identified by Arthur MacKinney and communicated to the author.

are, in a sense, playing God. McGregor suggested participative goal-setting and *shared* evaluation of employees' performance as alternatives to the boss' making these important judgments alone. Although this may work in some situations (Lowin, 1968), supervisors generally still maintain a margin of power in the evaluative process of rating employees; and, as Lowin (1968) argues, participation may be inappropriate in certain situations.

Is there a resolution to this issue? Judgments about other people, including those in the work place, are an inherent part of everyday life. In fact, it can be argued that these judgments are necessary for the orderly flow of everyday events. If judgments about employee performance are going to be made anyway (as argued earlier), why not attempt to do them in as orderly and as systematic a way as possible through the use of supervisory ratings. The degree of participation in goal-setting should be a function of situational variables (Lowin, 1968), and not be prescribed across all situations. But to argue that somehow *formal* appraisals should not be done means the organization will operate on information about employee job performance derived from informal communication channels. Not only does this create measurement problems, as discussed earlier, but, as shall be seen, an informal, nondocumented performance appraisal program is quite difficult to defend in litigation involving fair employment issues.

Conflict of Interest

This issue strikes at the heart of the supervisor's role. The supervisor must respond to demands from above his or her level for *accurate information* on employee performance. On the other hand, the supervisor must maintain a *trusting relationship* with employees. The supervisor must play the dual role of being responsible to both the organization and the employees. Thus, what is seen as rating of performance by the organization is often seen as "rat-ing" by employees.

There are two further considerations in relation to this issue. First, it is parallel to the conflict between the two major purposes of performance appraisal—namely, administrative and employee development. Organizations are more frequently concerned with performance information for administrative uses, whereas the supervisor is more frequently concerned with employee utilization. The second consideration relative to this issue involves the often observed operational problems in appraisal programs caused primarily by the supervisor. Failure to complete the form, inflation in the ratings, and poor performance feedback interviews can all be traced, in part, to this conflict of interest felt by the supervisor.

There does not really appear to be any easy resolution to this issue. What, then, can be done? First, and most important, this issue should be included in supervisory training programs. Open discussion may not eliminate the problem, but it should sensitize the supervisor to it; thus enabling the supervisor to more effectively handle it. Second, top management also should be sensitized to this issue, and, where necessary, remedial action should be taken to correct any problems in the current program that might exaggerate this conflict. An example of this would be a situation in which the current appraisal forms are outdated, and therefore are not adequate to appraise all employees' performance. Finally, separate forms can be created within the appraisal program. One form can be used for administrative purposes and the other for employee growth. This is similar to the program Michael Beer and his associates developed at Corning Glass (Beer et al., 1978), and is also a partial solution to the next general issue.

Purposes Issue

This is the most critical of all the issues. To what use should the performance appraisal information be put? If the information is to be used for research purposes *only,* then little controversy is generated. The major conflict is between administrative and employee growth purposes. Before examining this conflict in detail, the following general axiom needs to be stated: A decision on purpose(s) acceptable to top management *must be the first step* in the design (or redesign) of the performance appraisal program. There are two important corollaries of this axiom. First, it should be obvious that a performance appraisal can be used for multiple purposes within the same organization. This is difficult and more costly to accomplish, and management should be informed of this fact. Second, the purpose(s) of the appraisal program should guide its total development. The choice of a form or technique, the type of rater training, the computerization of the system, and the technical personnel needed, will all depend on the purpose(s) of the program.

The major conflict with most appraisal programs is between the administrative and employee growth purposes. There are several reasons why these purposes conflict. The first, of course, is the uncomfortable role of the supervisor providing honest information to the organization, while protecting the interests of employees. The second involves the type of information relevant for the two purposes. Systems designed for administrative purposes demand performance information about *differences between individuals* (normative data), while systems designed for employee growth demand information about *differences within individuals* (ipsative data). It should be obvious that these two different types of information are not interchangeable in terms of purposes. This is why a program designed to meet both purposes is more complex and costly—two different types of information must be gathered.

To examine the more practical side of this issue, what normally happens in an organization? Typically, only one type of performance appraisal information is collected, and usually it will be used for some administrative purpose. However, supervisors are being urged to help their employees grow and develop on the job, and to use the appraisal program as a tool in this effort. Therefore, if a naive supervisor completes honest appraisals, none of the employees may receive a merit increase. Not only does this create a morale problem for the supervisor, but it can destroy the future use of performance feedback for employee growth. If the employee realizes the supervisor's evaluation is to be used for administrative purposes, he or she will be defensive and reluctant to accept negative information during a feedback interview. Unfortunately, for the performance feedback to be effective, there must be an open and trusting relationship. Although this has been known for some time (Meyer, Kay, and French, 1965), there are few organizations that have modified their practices to deal with this issue.

What is the resolution to this issue? There really is not a completely satisfactory one. Most managers want a program that fulfills both purposes. However, the costs involved usually prevent an effective program from being developed. Management must be offered the choices, and the alternative costs and consequences must be explained. Most important, however, a decision by management must be made. The personnel scientist/practitioner who attempts to design or redesign a performance appraisal program without this decision will find the task nearly impossible.

Who Should Rate?

The "who" issue, in terms of performance ratings, refers to the four major sources of ratings: the supervisor, the self, peers, and subordinates. In a broader context, this issue raises the question as to the appropriate source for performance appraisal information. Should the information be based entirely on sources inside the organization? Or are some jobs such that outside sources should be used? Should production records be the sole source of performance appraisal? Or should ratings also be used to evaluate employee performance?

This issue, like the others, has advocates on all sides. Ideally, it would be desirable to have instruments that record employee job behavior, and automatically and accurately translate it into numerical indices of effectiveness. There are some people who still believe this is possible, but the overwhelming feeling is that this degree of precision is neither technically feasible, nor would it be cost-effective. What then can be done from a practical standpoint? What are the best sources of information on employee job performation?

To answer the last question, one must ask "best for what?" On what basis will a judgment be made as to the value of the source information for the performance appraisal task? If one is concerned with increasing accuracy in ratings, then it appears that more than one source should be used (Kavanagh, MacKinney, and Wolins, 1971; Whitla and Tirrell, 1953). However, as Borman (1980) has noted, accuracy (or relevance) of the ratings may not be increased by using multiple raters. Borman correctly argues that different raters (supervisors, peers, subordinates, and self) all have different perspectives on the ratee's job behavior. Thus, although one gains more information from multiple raters, the accuracy may not increase.

Increasing accuracy does not mean simply adding sources of performance information, but rather, *selectively* adding sources that can make a *relevant* contribution to the measurement task. For example, it would be foolish to use only supervisory ratings for salespersons who travel from the home office to industrial customers. Objective indices like sales volume and number of new contracts would help improve the measurement of job performance; and, if possible, evaluations by sales customers would improve the measurement more. In each case, more information *relevant* to the appraisal of the salespersons would be added.

To return to the question, "Best for what?"—what if one were concerned with insuring that the performance measurement program did not lead to personnel decisions that had an adverse impact on protected minorities? Although this legal issue will be covered later in this chapter, at this point it is important to realize that some sources of performance appraisal information may be more open to charges of unfair discrimination than others.

Content Rating

The content issue in performance ratings centers on the controversy of traits versus behaviors as dimensions on the form. In spite of the fact that there is no strong empirical evidence supporting the superiority of one type of content over the other (Borman and Dunnette, 1975; Kavanagh, 1971; Kavanagh, MacKinney, and Wolins, 1971; Massey, Mullins, and Earles, 1978), there is a strong bias to avoid "traits only" formats. In fact, this may be the real heart of the matter. Researchers and practitioners alike should avoid a "traits only" rating scale on which the dimensions are described with only a single word, e.g., cooperation; and the rater is expected to evaluate the ratee along a continuum of effectiveness. More generally, any rating scale format with only a single word or term to define the job performance dimension, for example, quantity of production, without any verbal description or scale anchors, should be avoided.

As the previous paragraph indicates, the central problem in this issue seems to be poorly developed rating scales, rather than the specific content of the scale itself. However, if traits are included, they need to be clearly defined in terms of observable job behaviors, and these descriptions included on the rating form.

Rating Format

This last issue concerns the specific techniques or format one uses for the rating of employee performance. Research and practice in the field of performance appraisal has seen many formats developed, used, and then discarded. The previous discussion on choosing a format based on a diagnosis of the organization's needs seems logical, but it is likely that choices on formats will be based in part on the popularity of current formats. The literature on formats has shown no marked superiority of one over another. Perhaps most telling is that Landy and Farr (1980), in an extensive review of different formats, could find no superiorities for one over the others in terms of psychometric qualities.

The main danger in this issue of rating scale format is that formats are often chosen haphazardly. Proper diagnosis of the needs of the organization should guide the choice of the format to be used. Then, as has been demonstrated by research (Bernardin et al., 1976; Borman and Dunnette, 1975), *careful development* of the rating scale format will result in performance measurement adequate for the organization. Of course, these recommendations are consistent with the earlier discussion of Tables 8–1 and 8–2.

RATER TRAINING

It is axiomatic in organizational life that the quality of performance ratings is higher if the person doing the rating has been trained. Training seems to be the antidote that management often uses to help resolve personnel problems, and problems with performance appraisal and feedback plague most organizations. However, one of the common errors associated with rater training is that it will somehow overcome and compensate for a poorly designed or outdated performance appraisal program. For example, if the performance dimensions being used are not reflective of actual job duties, no amount of rater training can resolve this problem. The performance appraisal program must be analyzed for problems, and if the problem is one that rater training can help to resolve, then it should be used.

What then can rater training accomplish? To answer that question, one must examine the scientific literature. Even though it was generally assumed that rater training improved the rating process, and most organizations included it in supervisory training, there was no solid research on the effectiveness of rater training until 1975 (Borman, 1975; Latham, Wexley, and Pursell, 1975). These researchers were able to demonstrate that training raters resulted in reduced psychometric errors, such as halo effect and leniency. Subsequent research (Bernardin and Walter, 1977, 1978; Ivancevich, 1979) supports this reduction in psychometric error.

This research seems to demonstrate the value of rater training in improving the quality of the ratings. However, Bernardin (1980) and Bernardin and Pence (1980) have argued that although rater training may reduce psychometric error, it does not improve the accuracy of the ratings. In the two studies examining the effects of rater training on accuracy (Borman, 1975, 1979), rating accuracy was not improved by training. More devastating are Bernardin's (1980) results that indicate rater training can decrease accuracy. Raters trained in a typical rating error program (RET) had less psychometric error than raters in rating accuracy training (RAT) and raters receiving no training. However, significantly less accuracy was found for the RET group of raters than for the other two groups.

Where does this leave us? Bernardin (1980) and Bernardin and Pence (1980) suggested that the typical approach to training raters to avoid the classic rating errors be abandoned. Instead, emphasis in rater training should be placed on *observing* more accurately, rather than rating errors. Thus, the content and emphasis of the rater training program changes from entering the proper numbers on the form, the *rating* process, to the daily observing and recording of employee job behaviors, the *observing* process. Future training programs concerned with improving the skills of the raters need to incorporate these suggestions.

Although training programs can improve the *skills* of raters, another use of rater training is to change the *attitudes* of the raters. Frequently, a performance appraisal program is used improperly (or not at all) simply because of poor rater motivation. Raters may not understand the system, may not be able to see the results of their ratings, may perceive the rating as another piece of paperwork, or may want to be told what is to be done. Whatever the reason, the poor quality of the ratings may not be a result of poor observing or judgment skills, but rather an attitude that the ratings are unimportant. Rater training concerned with changing these attitudes should improve the rating process. Attitude training *alone* may not resolve the problem of improving the quality of ratings, but its exclusion, and emphasis on rating skills *only,* will never resolve the quality problem.

Training aimed at improving the attitudes of the raters is primarily focused on the acceptability criterion for appraisal systems. The importance of this criterion has been underscored (Beer et al., 1978), particularly in implementing a new system of performance appraisal. In fact, this is the most frequently overlooked, and perhaps most important, use of rater training. If one moves from a limited perspective of concern with the *format* of the rating to a concern with the *program* of performance appraisal, then the acceptability criterion becomes clear. Training on rating *skills* (judging and observing) is aimed at improving the quality of the format, while training aimed at improving the attitudes of the raters, and thus, acceptability, plays a crucial role in the implementation of any new or changed performance appraisal program. The reason for rater training, using this perspective, becomes increased acceptance of the appraisal system rather than increased accuracy or reduction of psychometric error. The content and process orientation of the training program becomes more one of attitudinal change than changes in skills. In fact, it may be that changes in attitudes, and concomitantly, motivation, could impact on both accuracy and psychometric error.

Before leaving rater training, one final issue needs to be covered. It may well be that rater training should focus its efforts in part on legal issues in the performance appraisal process. Considering the potential for legal suits that can arise between supervisors and subordinates based on violation of either the Civil Rights Act or the Equal Pay Act in relation to performance appraisal, it seems only reasonable to use rater training to help supervisors avoid these problems. Many discrimination investigations and legal suits arise from the actions of a single supervisor and a single employee (Cascio, 1980). Perhaps one of the roles rater training should play is to address these issues, and, hopefully, provide proper information to guide supervisory actions in the area of performance appraisal.

GOAL-SETTING IN PERFORMANCE APPRAISAL

Goal-setting works! A variety of studies has consistently shown that specific goals lead to better performance than general goals and that difficult goals, if accepted, lead to better performance than easy goals (Latham and Yukl, 1975a; Locke, 1968). In terms of performance appraisal, this means that, during the appraisal interview, specific and difficult goals should be accepted by the employee for the next performance period.

The exact manner in which specific and difficult goals are made acceptable to employees is not yet clear. The supervisor could assign them, or the goals could be arrived at by mutual agreement in a participative manner. Various research (Latham, Mitchell, and Dossett, 1978; Latham and Saari, 1979; Latham and Yukl, 1975a; Latham and Yukl, 1976) has led to inconclusive results on this issue. In an attempt to explain these conflicting results, Latham and Saari (1979) suggested that the major role of participation in the goal-setting process may be in helping employees understand better how to achieve high goals. They further suggested that when goals are set low, participation may have little, if any, effect. From a practitioner's viewpoint, it would appear that setting of specific goals for employees is the first step. If, in the supervisor's opinion, the performance goals to be set are high, then participation should be used in the process.

The practice of goal-setting in the performance appraisal process is usually associated with management by objectives (MBO). Even though goal-setting has been mostly associated with MBO, it can occur within most appraisal programs. In some cases, e.g., Corning Glass (Beer et al., 1978), it is formally required as part of the appraisal interview process. However, managers frequently use goal-setting in the performance appraisal interview, even though it is not required. The bottom line is that goal-setting should be used in a well-designed performance appraisal program, whether the goals are formally recorded or not. Supervisors should be trained on the goal-setting process, and the best way to use it both in the appraisal interview and in daily interaction with their employees. Finally, and most important, goal-setting should not be the entire appraisal program. As is being argued here, performance appraisal is a program with many components. Goal-setting is one of these.

LEGAL ISSUES IN PERFORMANCE APPRAISAL

If performance appraisals are used for personnel decisions or to validate a selection procedure, they will fall under the provisions of Title VII of the Civil Rights Act of 1964 and, in some cases, the Equal Pay Act of 1963. Although the provisions of the Equal Pay Act could have impact on the design and use of performance appraisal, there has not been much litigation under this act in regard to appraisal programs. Most litigation with implications for performance appraisal has been filed under the Civil Rights Act. Furthermore, it appears that a performance appraisal system that meets the guidelines established by the Equal Employment Opportunity Commission (EEOC) for compliance with Title VII would also be in compliance with the Equal Pay Act. Therefore, the relationship between performance appraisal and EEOC guidelines will be the focus of this section.

There have been several articles and reviews on performance appraisal and fair employment guidelines (Edwards, 1976; Holley and Feild, 1975; Lazer, 1976; Lubben, Thompson, and Klasson, 1980). However, the most comprehensive review of the implications of recent legal rulings on performance appraisal is presented by Cascio (1980). Examining court cases that reached the Appeals or Supreme Court level, Cascio noted that eight prescriptions for good practice in performance appraisal were violated. These eight prescriptions are:

1. Appraisal of job performance must be based upon an analysis of job requirements as reflected in performance standards. Graphically:

$$\text{Job Analysis} \qquad \text{Performance Appraisal}$$
$$\searchrow \qquad \nearrow$$
$$\text{Performance Standards}$$

2. Appraisal of job performance only becomes reasonable when performance standards have been communicated and understood by employees.
3. Performance dimensions should be factorially pure (only homogeneous clusters of activities should be grouped together).
4. Performance dimensions should be behaviorally based, so that all ratings can be supported by objective, observable evidence.
5. Avoid abstract trait names (e.g., loyalty, honesty) unless they can be defined in terms of observable behaviors.
6. Keep anchors brief and logically consistent.
7. As with anything else used as a basis for employment decisions, appraisal systems must be validated, as well as the ratings given by individual raters.
8. Provide a mechanism for appeal if the employee disagrees with a supervisor's appraisal (Cascio, 1980, pp. 1–2).

These eight prescriptions appear to be so well engrained in good personnel practice that one wonders how they could be violated and form the basis for legal action. Certainly inattention to the appraisal program and bad advice could have caused some of these problems. But the key objective for professional practitioners and managers alike, of course, is to avoid adverse legal rulings in the future. Cascio (1980) made the following recommendations: (1) encourage internal review of appraisal systems, (2) be sure performance appraisal systems meet the EEOC *Guidelines,* (3) be sure the use of the appraisals matches their original purpose, and (4) expand research on rater training and rater accuracy.

Cascio's last point is similar to the one made earlier in regard to rater training. It may be necessary to modify rater training programs to sensitize raters to legal issues regarding the use of their ratings. Cascio's third point reemphasizes the axiom that the stated purpose of a performance appraisal system will dictate its use. Using an appraisal system for a purpose other than that for which it was designed could lead to serious personnel, managerial, and legal problems. Cascio's first two points are self-evident, but bear repeating. Perhaps the most common problem in fair employment litigation is the poor condition of personnel records resulting from inattention.

Two final points need mentioning. First, because of the technical complexity of the legal issues surrounding performance appraisal, it is wise to have expert advice on designing or modifying a program. If this expert advice is not available within the organization, outside help should be obtained. The final point involves the avoidance of fair employment practice suits. No set of prescriptions or expert guidance will guarantee that an organization will avoid all fair employment complaints or litigation. Often, discrimination occurs on a one-to-one basis between a supervisor and employee, regardless of the safeguards the management of the organization has established. The prescriptive advice in this section, if followed, should help the organization minimize fair employment complaints and enable it to better defend its personnel practices in regard to performance appraisal.

PERFORMANCE FEEDBACK

As indicated earlier, performance feedback is one of the most important reasons for the existence of a performance appraisal program. In fact, if the performance appraisal program is to monitor effective job performance, and change behavior where appropriate, performance feedback may be the central concern of the entire system. It is argued that all other parts of the program (e.g., the type of format used, the stimuli evaluated, and the purpose(s) of the system) either directly or indirectly impact on the quantity and quality of the feedback employees receive. What is it that makes performance feedback so important?

First, current prescriptive techniques (organizational interventions) to improve employee motivation, quality of work life, or both, all appear to include an improvement (often a reduction in noise) in either the quantity or quality of the feedback the individual employee can obtain concerning his or her performance. In most cases, this is achieved by making the feedback loop shortened in time and by improving visibility, or objectivity, of the performance feedback information.

Another trend in current years that emphasizes the role of the feedback function has been the emergence of Behaviorally Anchored Rating Scales (BARS) to improve the assessment of human performance. Although the evidence on their assumed psychometric superiority has been mixed, and serious questions remain regarding their cost-effectiveness, one thing seems clear: Employees (raters and ratees) like BARS more and are more likely to use them as compared to traditional, trait-only ratings. One cannot help but wonder if this increased attractiveness is not a function of the fact that BARS performance dimensions provide clear (unambiguous) feedback of employee performance.

Another reason for emphasizing the importance of the feedback function is theory-based. Following Maslow (1965), among others, one could argue that people want to effectively utilize their personal abilities in fulfilling their job requirements. In addition, as Festinger (1954) noted, not only do people want to use and evaluate their abilities, they also want to find that they are good. This ''goodness'' in their use of their abilities can occur only via the feedback function. Although the previous statement appears to be almost a ''truism'' in terms of individual psychology, it is also a ''truism'' that not all employees can become the Chief Executive Officer; and that most appraisal programs in organizations emphasize ''improvements needed'' or force the feedback of negative information under the guise of ''growth and development.''

As a final thought on the importance of performance feedback, I will draw on some personal, anecdotal evidence. In various relationships with organizations either for research or consulting purposes, I make it a point to interact with employees at various levels in the organization. Two questions that are most revealing involve performance feedback: ''How do you know when you are doing a good job?'' and ''How do you know when you are doing a bad job?'' Most people cannot answer the first question—they simply do not get that kind of feedback. On the other hand, most can answer the second question, and the most typical answer is ''When my boss yells at me.'' Such is the nature of feedback in organizations.

A description of a model that involves the important linkages in a performance appraisal and feedback program is shown in Figure 8–2. The model includes two categories of characteristics, direct and indirect, so named because of their effect on the type, quality, and quantity of feedback. The aspects that would have direct effects on individual performance feedback are: (1) rater training; (2) a goal-setting or MBO program; (3) whether performance evaluation data is based on objective and/or subjective standards; (4) for rating scale data, the descriptive clarity (e.g. BARS) versus purely numerical data (e.g., simple trait rating graphic scales); (5) the degree of correspondence between the performance appraisal program and the reward program in the organization; (6) for ratings, the source of the appraisal data used, that is, superior, peer, self, subordinates; and (7) the comparison standard for individual data, that is, normative versus ipsative. These are in the first circle around the center in Figure 8–2.

Somewhat more indirect in terms of their impact on performance feedback are: (1) the traditional psychometric properties of reliability, validity, and freedom from bias; (2) the ''practicality'' standard, but only in terms of time requirements to evaluate employee performance and the time requirement for the feedback interview; (3) the major purpose of the performance assessment, whether administrative or employee growth; (4) the general managerial philosophy in the organization; (5) the presence of a

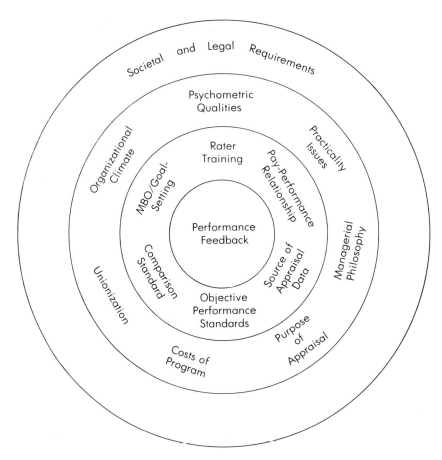

FIGURE 8-2
Generalized Feedback Model

union; (6) the organizational climate; and (7) the costs of the appraisal program. These are in the second circle in Figure 8–2.

The reader should realize that the preceding lists do not exhaust all the factors that will affect the performance feedback function, but they certainly represent some major ones. The final circle in Figure 8–2 indicates that the appraisal program and the feedback given are also influenced by societal and legal requirements. Furthermore, in order to place these aspects of the organization in perspective as they affect the performance assessment system, one should envision a flow diagram with the indirect effect factors flowing into the more direct effect factors. These, in turn, affect the quantity, quality, and type of individual job performance feedback. Continuing with this model, there would be a direct effect on changes in job behaviors from the feedback, and, in turn, effects on job attitudes flowing from the changes in job behaviors.

It should be apparent, from considering feedback in this flow model, that when there are incongruities in the system, the quality of feedback will suffer and this will affect the remainder of the model. For example, an organization with an "autocratic" managerial philosophy that emphasizes employee growth through the use of ipsative performance profiles and goal-setting interviews will probably cause a personal conflict for supervisors, who then will be forced to "beat the system." This discussion indicates that a given managerial philosophy and stated purpose for the performance assessment system will greatly affect the quality of the performance feedback. It should finally be emphasized that, in designing a new performance assessment system (or revising a current one), an initial step should be the diagnosis of those direct and indirect aspects that will affect the feedback function.

EVALUATION OF PERFORMANCE APPRAISAL PROGRAMS

Earlier in this chapter, when evaluating various techniques for appraising performance, a distinction between performance appraisal programs and the various techniques or formats was made. As has been emphasized throughout, one needs to use a system-level perspective when designing or modifying performance appraisal programs. This section will examine some general issues and specific criteria implied by this perspective.

There has been a limited view of the evaluation of the "goodness" of performance appraisal in the field. It has been characterized by: (1) a concern with formats (as seen in Tables 8–1 and 8–2); (2) basing evaluative information and decisions on developmental evidence *only*, to the exclusion of implementation evidence; and (3) reliance on psychometric criteria. This limited perspective in the evaluation of performance appraisal programs is not a "straw man," as many practitioners can personally attest. This limited view of evaluation has been caused in part by a preoccupation with refining performance appraisal forms or techniques, while ignoring the organizational context in which the measurement operates.

Another, and perhaps more important, factor causing this limited view of evaluation to dominate in the field is a confusion between validating a performance appraisal form or technique and a performance appraisal program. Since validity addresses the inferences made from the measurement process, doesn't it seem foolish to argue that the instrument effect (in this case, the superiority of one over the other) is *the* major factor in explaining the variance in employee performance—employee performance that is intimately tied to the organizational context? Landy and Farr's (1980) graphic representation of the performance rating process should convince most critics that the instrument used is only one of many sources of variance in employee job performance. Consideration of performance appraisal, as a program in interaction with other programs in the organization, implies a variety of evaluative considerations that go well beyond those necessary for determining the effectiveness of appraisal techniques only.

Evaluation Criteria: General Considerations

Recognizing the distinction between techniques and programs to appraise job performance implies that evaluative criteria must be developed separately for techniques and programs. A start on techniques was presented in Table 8–1. Although there may be some overlap, it is apparent that the standards used to evaluate and compare different appraisal techniques cannot be directly applied to the evaluation of a performance measurement program. It appears that the opposite has been occurring in the *professional* literature.

Using this broader view for the evaluation of performance appraisal implies a second general consideration: one must draw from a more extensive literature to develop a comprehensive set of standards. It is simply not adequate to use the classic psychometric considerations, originally developed by Thorndike (1949), and add a general criterion like program acceptability. These criteria must be drawn from the following topical literature: (1) measurement or psychometrics; (2) organization theory and development; (3) program evaluation, specifically cost-effectiveness; and (4) general management.

In addition to expanding one's scope when developing a set of evaluative criteria for performance appraisal programs, another general consideration is that it will not be possible to maximize a program for performance measurement on all criteria. For example, a program that meets predictive accuracy in administrative decisions, like promotions and merit increases, may not meet EEO requirements. Likewise, a program that is accurate and meets EEO requirements may not be either cost-effective or acceptable to employees. What this suggests is that a trade-off analysis be done, recognizing that any program that is developed will have strengths and weaknesses. Simple consideration of the *many* evaluative criteria that *can be used* for judging the program's effectiveness makes it rather obvious, from a practical (and perhaps scientific) perspective, that one cannot maximize on all standards. One needs to carefully diagnose what is needed in a given organization, and then attempt to develop a performance appraisal program whose strengths match the diagnostic information.

This discussion of a "satisficing" trade-off analysis in the evaluation of performance appraisal programs leads to the fourth and final general consideration—the concept of alternative programs. The management-staff relationship is analogous to the client-consultant relationship in many ways. The staff consultant function requires the use of expert, professional knowledge to help resolve an often loosely and ambiguously defined management problem. The role of the staff consultant is to bring in a professional problem-solving process, grounded in scientific methodology, to develop a recommended course of action to resolve the management problem. The recommended course of action, at this point, has been judged "best" on a set of criteria from the professional scientist's perspective. Typically, these criteria are similar, but not completely congruent, with those of a professional manager. This fact often confuses the communications and the shared priorities between the staff consultant and the manager. Further exaggerating this confusion is the previously mentioned ambiguity that typically characterizes the definition of the management problem.

As a result, the *"one best"* solution inherent in the professional scientist model is inappropriate as an outcome in the staff-consultant-management relationship. Instead, the staff consultant is required to generate, with supporting arguments and evidence, several "best" alternative solutions. This requires that solution quality be assessed on a set of predefined evaluative criteria, encompassing both managerial and scientific perspectives. This multiple criteria approach emphasizes that, in a realistic setting, one cannot maximize on all criteria within a given situation. The classic example is the dilemma faced by management in trying to maximize on both cost-effectiveness and EEO requirements. One alternative may be better at meeting EEO requirements, but terribly costly, whereas another alternative may be the opposite.

With these four general considerations in mind—separate evaluative criteria for programs and techniques, numerous evaluative standards from various literature sources, satisficing through trade-off analysis, and comparison of alternative systems—the development of specific criteria for evaluating programs of performance appraisal should be considered.

Evaluative Criteria for Appraisal Programs

In an attempt to employ the techniques in the preceding paragraphs, a matrix of personal judgments has been constructed (see Table 8–3). The rows represent the general criteria to evaluate performance appraisal programs, and the columns represent different (alternative) appraisal programs. Several considerations must be kept in mind when examining the matrix in Table 8–3. First, the set of criteria listed is based on considering a variety of sources in both the behavioral and managerial literature, and thus serves as a set of *predefined* evaluative criteria against which future assessment of performance appraisal program alternatives can be made. Second, the entries in the cells of the table are being made on the basis of the author's *personal judgment* and an understanding of the programs and the criteria. These judgments must be seen as a starting point for subsequent discussion and refinement, rather than an end point.

The programs were chosen for comparison for several reasons. First, they had to be programs of performance appraisal, not methods. Methods such as BARS, mixed standard scales, and critical behavior scales were excluded unless they were part of a total integrated management program of performance appraisal. Second, it was desirable to have performance appraisal programs from both the public and private sectors.

With these thoughts in mind, the following performance appraisal programs were chosen for comparison:

1. The program implemented in the state of Arkansas for civilian employees (Jones, 1980)
2. The program implemented in Corning Glass for managerial employees

In addition to these "real" programs, three general programs were created to reflect current practice in regard to performance appraisal. These three have been labeled "autocratic," "human relations," and "mixed" (or "human resource"), to represent current prevailing managerial philosophies that define these general programs.

Table 8–3 contains judgments of the five programs *against* the standards or criteria listed. The pluses, minuses, and question marks indicate where the system ranks on the criteria. Two points should be noted. The cell entries are absolute, not relative, judgments; however, the programs can be compared against each other. The second point is that no one program is "perfect" on all criteria. Rather, it is better described as a set of trade-offs between the various criteria.

TABLE 8–3
Comparison of Performance Appraisal Systems

CRITERIA	PUBLIC SECTOR		Autocratic Model	PRIVATE SECTOR	
	State of Arkansas	Corning Glass		Human Relations Model	Mixed Model
1. Meets EEO guidelines	?	+	?	+	+
2. Pretested before implementation	+	+ +	–	+	+
3. Psychometric quality	+	+	–	?	+
4. User acceptance	–	+ +	–	+	+
5. Ease of use for employees	+	–	+	+	+
6. Equitable for merit pay	?	+	+	+	+
7. Susceptible to inflation of ratings	– –	+	–	–	–
8. Development costs	–	– –	+	–	–

9. Maintenance costs	+	+	+	−	+
10. Rater training	++	+	−	+	+
11. Supervisor-employee interaction	?	++	−	++	++
12. Administrative interfaces	+	+	+	+	+
13. Amount of management control	+	−	+	−	−
14. Appeals	+	+	−	+	+
15. Periodic review/feedback	−	−	−	+	−
16. Measure of potential	−	+	−	+	−
17. Susceptible to gaming	−	−	−	−	−
18. Employee motivation	−	+	−	++	+
19. Cost effectiveness	?	+	−	−	+

The criteria in Table 8–3 represent a search of the literature (and some common sense) on the evaluation of personnel systems. Each criterion will be discussed as well as the reasons for the ratings.

Criterion 1: Meets EEO Guidelines.   As can be seen in Table 8–3, no program receives a "double plus" mark, since meeting EEO is a legal, not a research, question. The private sector models typically are designed around, and sensitive to, EEO *Guidelines.* Since the Arkansas program was developed intuitively, it remains questionable on this criterion.

Criterion 2: Pretested.   In order to successfully implement a new performance appraisal program, both in terms of administrative ease and employee acceptance, it is generally accepted that a pretest should be conducted. As can be seen, some programs excel on this criterion while others fail.

Criterion 3: Psychometric Quality.   This criterion involves the reliability, validity, accuracy, and freedom from bias characterizing each program. Since the question of validity or accuracy is always difficult to demonstrate, no program receives a "double plus." Since the autocratic model is generally implemented without a pretest or validity data, it receives negative marks on this criterion.

Criterion 4: User Acceptance.   User acceptance and confidence in the program are critical to its effect on employee motivation and management control. As can be seen, private sector programs generally fare better than public sector programs because their programs are generally not mandated (except the autocratic model). The Arkansas program is somewhat negative because it was mandated, developed, and implemented with little employee input. The Corning program scores best since it had extensive employee input during both development and implementation. However, its development and implementation costs were quite high.

Criterion 5: Ease of Use, Computerized.   The Arkansas program is easy to use and is already computerized. With a few exceptions, most of the programs in the private sector are not computerized. The Corning program is also complex to use, whereas most other programs in the private sector are easier to use. This criterion requires that the program generate performance data that will discriminate between satisfactory and unsatisfactory employees. The central issue is whether it can be used to help make decisions on pay, promotion, reassignment, demotion, and termination. The Arkansas program is most acceptable on this criterion. In the private sector, most programs, with the exception of the Corning program, are not strong on this criterion. The other major exception is the autocratic program, but, as noted, it suffers in terms of user acceptance.

Criterion 6: Merit Pay Equity.   The private sector programs can be "open" in terms of merit pay; that is, there is not a fixed amount of merit pay, but rather, it is tied to profitability. Public sector programs will suffer most on this criterion because of the often "closed" nature of the total merit pay available. This criterion refers to the *perceived* equity by the employees, not objective equity.

Criterion 7: Inflation. As can be seen, all programs are susceptible to inflation with the exception of the Corning program because of its ipsative measurement scheme. However, the overall ratings in the Corning program are also susceptible to inflation. One way to control inflation is through standardized, well-developed training programs. As can be seen in Criterion 10, the Corning program scores high on this criterion, which helps to partly resolve inflation. The Arkansas program has only brief training, and may suffer because of this.

Criterion 8: Development Costs. The development costs are high for most quality programs. Note the high cost of the Corning program.

Criterion 9: Maintenance Costs. Since the Arkansas and Corning programs were pretested and are computerized, they should have fewer maintenance costs over time. Other programs have to "shakedown" in the field, and may require major modifications, thus increasing maintenance costs.

Criterion 10: Rater Training. Already discussed.

Criterion 11: Supervisor-Employee Interaction. With the exception of the autocratic model, all programs fare well on this criterion.

Criterion 12: Administrative Interfaces. All of the private sector programs interface well with wage structures, employee selection, and career progression. The administrative interfaces are a question mark for the Arkansas program.

Criterion 13: Amount of Management Control. This criterion is most clearly found in programs being used only for administrative purposes, thus the higher marks for the Arkansas and the Autocratic programs.

Criterion 14: Appeals. The marks are self-explanatory.

Criterion 15: Periodic Review/Feedback. In the private sector, with the exception of the human relations model, periodic review is not formalized within these programs. The need for feedback is often "mouthed" in the private sector, but infrequently built into the system. The Arkansas program does not include periodic reviews *within* a rating period.

Criterion 16: Measure of Potential. In order to make more effective promotion decisions, a measure of potential, in addition to current job performance, would be quite desirable. As can be seen, very few programs have this feature. Perhaps a better way to handle this is through assessment centers.

Criterion 17: Susceptible to Gaming.   All programs have problems on this criterion, particularly when the merit pay decision rests with the immediate supervisor.

Criterion 18: Employee Motivation.   This really is a summary criterion, but is heavily influenced by the mandated nature of a program. It would appear that the more carefully developed and pretested programs, with rater training and emphasis on openness in the employee-supervisor interaction, will have more positive long-term effects on employee motivation.

Criterion 19: Cost Effectiveness.   This is also a summary criterion, and it involves a judgment of costs and benefits of each program. Programs that are not pretested and carefully developed "cost" less, but have negative benefits in terms of both employee acceptance and ease of use.

In closing this section, it should be emphasized that *these criteria can be used as diagnostic categories* to judge what type of program will best "satisfice" the needs of the organization. It is only with this comprehensive diagnosis that effective programs can be developed and implemented successfully. It should also be noted that this section only briefly evaluated the programs on the evaluative criteria, without an in-depth analysis of any one. The purpose of this section, however, was to *illustrate* this approach to the evaluation of performance appraisal programs, not to provide a "best one" for all organizations.

DIRECTIONS FOR THE FUTURE

Over the next decade, performance appraisal, as a part of the personnel function, will become increasingly more important. With increasing attention on performance appraisal in fair employment litigation, more and more organizations will be under pressure to review and revise their current programs. In addition to court cases, another major influence in the next decade will be the implementation of the various performance appraisal and merit programs in federal agencies as required by the Civil Service Reform Act of 1978 (CSRA). The specific requirements of CSRA in regard to performance standards, dominant and critical job elements, and relating job performance directly to rewards, will certainly influence research and practice on performance appraisal during the 1980s. Court tests and union challenges of performance appraisal programs developed under the provisions of the CSRA are certain to provide guidelines for both public and private sector organizations. Given this expected importance of performance appraisal, consideration should now be given to specific future directions in basic research, applied research, and practice.

Basic Research

With the appearance of the Landy and Farr (1980) review, it seems likely that the *processes* in performance ratings will receive attention during the next decade. In particular, this research will focus primarily on how raters make judgments about their employees' job behaviors in relation to effective job performance. As Landy and Farr stated, "We must learn much more about the way in which potential raters observe, encode, store, retrieve, and record performance information, if we hope to increase the validity of the ratings" (1980, p. 100).

This concern with processes in performance appraisal should mean greater attention to the attribution process involved in supervisory evaluations of employee performance. Recent work on how supervisors judge the causes of subordinate performance through an attributional analysis (Ilgen and Knowlton, 1980; Knowlton and Mitchell, 1980) based on a theoretical model of this process (Green and Mitchell, 1979) indicate this will be an important theme in basic research in the 1980s. More attention will be paid to the *processes* involved, rather than a search for better forms to evaluate employee performance.

Closely allied to research on how raters make judgments will be research on training raters to become better observers. Bernardin's (1979, 1980) argument that rater training programs have only altered the response set of the trainees, but not affected rating accuracy, will be tested. More important, Bernardin's (1980) call for training raters to be better observers of behavior will spawn considerable research on how best to do this. It will be interesting to see whether this new approach to rater training will significantly affect rating accuracy.

The final major direction for basic research during the next decade will be a continuation of research on accuracy in performance measures. Borman (1980) has chronicled the search for accuracy in performance ratings. His summarization indicates that research has demonstrated that accepted approaches to improving rating quality (e.g., rater training, different formats) have little effect on accuracy. Rather than discouraging research on rating accuracy, these findings mean scientists must move diligently and creatively to examine what does affect rating accuracy. Borman's (1980) work on individual differences in personal characteristics of raters as they relate to accuracy of ratings is one exciting new avenue. Concentrating on observing skills, as both Bernardin (1980) and Landy and Farr (1980) have suggested, seems another way to approach the accuracy problem. Another possible, but not yet explored, approach would be the development of time series data and dynamic models of the rating process. Rating accuracy has to be based, at least in part, on the frequency and length of interaction between rater and ratee. This observation indicates that longitudinal studies of the rating process be initiated to examine the developmental processes of performance observation and recording by raters. Finally, there have been several alternate approaches offered, in terms of measurement systems (Cone, 1980) and altering organizational factors (Kane, 1980) to affect accuracy, that merit serious research efforts.

Applied Research

Although there are a number of future directions in applied research, these will all have the overriding concern of meeting legal guidelines. Just as the accuracy criterion will dominate basic research, compliance with employment laws for minorities, women, veterans, and the elderly will be the ever-constant criterion in applied research. This is not to indicate that all applied research must include legal guidelines as research variables, but rather, applied research must be sensitive to the legal implications of the findings. With every applied research finding will come the question: "How does this fit with legal guidelines?"

A second major theme in the next decade will be research on performance standards. Since this concept has been given publicity and emphasis through the provisions of the CSRA, it can be expected that considerable research will be conducted in this area. Questions as to how best to set standards, the number of performance levels within a standard, and how to combine standards are examples of some of the research issues.

Coincidental with basic research on rater training, one can also expect considerable applied research on this issue. If Bernardin's (1980) argument is correct, almost all current rater training programs will need to be modified, but modified in what way will be the applied research issue. One can expect to receive some guidance from basic research, but the application and implementation issues must be answered in real organizational contexts. If training is to be used to improve the acceptability of performance appraisal systems, as has been argued in this chapter, one can expect a growing body of research on how best to design rater training to affect user acceptability.

Another trend in applied research will lie in assessing the utility of performance appraisal programs. This will involve primary cost-benefit analyses and will involve all aspects of the program. Training programs, different formats, and multiple sources of performance information will all be evaluated in terms of their costs and benefits. In addition, as has been discussed in this chapter, total programs will be evaluated on cost-effectiveness. For an example of excellent work in this area, the reader should check the cost analysis of the Arkansas program (Jones, 1980).

The concept of evaluating performance appraisal programs on multiple criteria, as reviewed in this chapter, will also be a dominant theme in applied research during the 1980s. Utilizing and researching the concept of a "satisficing trade-off analysis" in terms of the best performance appraisal program for a given organization will help guide the development and redesign of programs. It seems likely that some analytic schemes will have to be borrowed from other disciplines (e.g., economics) to assist in this research.

It seems clear that applied work on performance feedback and the appraisal interview will continue in the 1980s. As has been emphasized in this chapter, performance feedback is the heart of the total performance appraisal program. Research on how to provide the clearest, and correct amount of, feedback to affect changes in job behavior will be important issues. In terms of the feedback interview, research on factors that help or hinder the process will serve as guides for training supervisors. Ilgen, Martin, and Peterson (1980) have already begun work in this direction. Finally, research tying specific interview behaviors to changes in employee job behavior and satisfaction needs to be done.

A final area of applied research, closely allied to performance feedback, will be the evaluation of alternate sources of performance information. These alternate sources (in some cases, outside the organization) must be evaluated on their accuracy, their cost-effectiveness, their use in appraisal interviews, and their use within legal guidelines. The end of a decade may find that these alternate sources are no better than a well-developed supervisory rating program. If so, that will be an important lesson for applied researchers and managers.

Performance Appraisal Practice

As a result of both the recent legal decisions (Cascio, 1980) and the passage of the CSRA, performance appraisal will play a more important role and receive greater attention in the personnel management function. Just as many organizations revised and updated their recruiting and selection procedures as a result of early fair employment court cases, the same will occur with performance appraisal programs. This means companies will be auditing their performance appraisal program, and correcting where necessary. In practice, this means a tremendous amount of paperwork for organizations. In larger organizations, computerization of the performance appraisal program will become a necessity. Compliance with the various fair employment laws will require accurate information that needs to be readily accessed on classes of employees.

In addition to this major concern with meeting legal guidelines, there will be considerable work on developing standards of job performance tied to job descriptions. In some cases, this will involve converting current appraisal formats (for example, a BARS), to performance standards on each job dimension. Performance standards imply, at the minimum, that fully satisfactory and unsatisfactory performance can be defined *a priori* on each performance dimension or job duty. As currently used, few rating formats take this approach; thus, modifications will be necessary. In many organizations, this process will involve revising job descriptions. In organizations without a currently effective performance appraisal program, the whole process will have to begin with the notion of developing performance standards.

The final major practical concern for the next decade will be the increasing emphasis on the justification of performance appraisal programs (and all personnel management functions) in terms of cost-effectiveness. Primarily through legal decisions, management has learned that faulty personnel policies or programs can cost dearly. Management's reaction has been to focus more of the organization's fiscal resources to improve the functions of personnel. With these added resources, management demands to see benefits. Although applied researchers can help provide some answers, the practitioners are "on the line" *now* to demonstrate cost effectiveness. This pressure in terms of the development and redesign of performance appraisal programs will continue through the 1980s.

In sum, developments in the 1980s should help remove some of the "fuzziness" from the measurement of individual employee job performance. However, as indicated at the beginning of this chapter, performance information with absolute clarity (no fuzziness) is an ideal that will never be realized—it may be socially embarrassing!

Discussion Questions

1. Discuss how the problem of accurately measuring employee performance (the fuzziness problem) affects the researcher and the personnel practitioner. Give specific examples in terms of your own experience.

2. Job performance is dynamic in several ways. How would you start to develop an appraisal form for a given job (e.g., nurse) that would reflect this dynamic nature of job performance?

3. Briefly discuss the six major issues in performance appraisal. Why is it important to collect diagnostic information on these issues prior to designing or changing a performance appraisal program?

4. Discuss how various characteristics of the organization and the performance appraisal program can either positively or negatively affect performance feedback. Give at least one practical example of each case.

5. What is meant by a "satisficing trade-off analysis" in evaluating a performance appraisal program? How can it be used in designing or changing performance appraisal programs?

CHAPTER NINE
COMPENSATING FOR WORK

Thomas A. Mahoney[1]

Thomas A. Mahoney is Professor of Industrial Relations at the University of Minnesota. He received his Ph.D. in Economics from the University of Minnesota. Professor Mahoney has conducted research in several areas and is the author of numerous journal articles. He has authored and coauthored eight monographs and books, including his recent book *Compensation and Reward Perspectives.* Professor Mahoney is active in the profession, serving as President of the Personnel/Human Resources Division of the Academy of Management in 1976, and as editor of the *Academy of Management Journal,* 1982–1985. Professor Mahoney has been a consultant to business, industry, and a number of governmental agencies, and has conducted numerous management and executive development seminars.

Compensation, work, and employment are concepts that are so closely intertwined that one rarely questions their meaning or the accepted linkages among them. Most people accept implicitly that work and compensation are exchanged for each other in an employment relationship. One commonly does not think of someone accepting a job without a promise of wage or salary compensation. This assumed linkage between work, employment, and compensation constitutes what is known as the employment relationship or the employment contract.

One can better understand the implicit assumptions of the employment contract if some exceptions to it are examined. Consider the concept of work, for example. Most people think of work as something performed in an employment relationship in exchange for pay, yet refinishing one's basement may be just as challenging, tiring, and gratifying as the work one performs in an office or factory. Activities such as housekeeping, home repair, and even tennis are usually excluded from the concept of work, unless

[1]Comments and suggestions from Donald Schwab and Sara Rynes are gratefully acknowledged.

they are performed for pay. Similarly, one excludes volunteer activities such as supervising the school lunchroom, stuffing envelopes for a political campaign, or soliciting donations for a charitable organization from the concept of work, unless these activities are performed for pay. Thus, the definition of the concept of work appears to turn upon whether or not activities are performed in exchange for pay or compensation, rather than upon the nature of the activity itself.

A further distinction may be made between what one author, Elliott Jaques, called "entrepreneurial" and "employment" work (Jaques, 1961). He would include as entrepreneurial work that of a farmer who operates a farm hoping to realize a profit after all costs have been covered, of a free-lance writer who produces and sells stories to magazines, and of the owner-manager of a restaurant. The entrepreneur may realize a profit or loss from operations, while an employee fully expects a regular payment in exchange for work. Another difference between entrepreneurial and employment work relates to differences in authority to determine one's actions at work; the entrepreneur enjoys wide discretion, while the employee operates within a circumscribed sphere of discretionary opportunities.

Most people think of work as employment-work activities performed in return for the promise of wage or salary compensation. While other benefits such as pride, sense of accomplishment, and social status also may accrue from employment work, they are not unique to employment work and may be realized in other ways as well. It is this implicit association between work and pay that characterizes employment work, and the assumption of an exchange of work and pay constitutes what is considered as the employment contract. Wage and salary payments are a primary, defining characteristic of the employment contract and are critical to shaping the employment relationship between an individual and the employing organization.

THE EMPLOYMENT CONTRACT

What has been termed the *employment contract* constitutes, like most contracts, an agreement for an exchange between two parties. Most people have encountered contracts when securing a loan from a bank, purchasing a car, or renting an apartment, and may find it difficult to see the analogy with an employment contract. This is because contracts often are implicit in the employment relationship and often are not as explicit or formalized as the contracting for a bank loan. In fact, employment contracts take many forms and may be quite formal or relatively informal.

Employment contracts tend to be most explicit for short-term, specific work assignments and for relatively specialized work assignments. For example, a performer hired for a musical or theatrical production, an accountant employed to perform a specific audit, or a typist employed to produce a document often will be hired with an explicit employment contract that specifies the exact work to be performed and the conditions for compensation. Explicit employment contracts tend to be employed only where details of the work to be performed can be anticipated and specified in advance. Persons employed under explicit employment contracts may even be termed *independent contractors* to distinguish their relationship from the more common status of an employee working under an implicit employment contract.

More commonly, individuals accept employment with an organization with an expectation of indefinite tenure, varying or changing job assignments, relatively unspecified output expectations, and variable compensation over time. Detailed specification of output expectations by an employer in advance of hiring is difficult and expensive in the case of a continuing relationship, particularly because of the probabilistic nature of future anticipations. Rather, these expectations of work to be performed are developed and communicated over time through the process of supervision, and the employee in the typical employment relationship accepts an authority relationship. The employment contract in these instances may take the form of a collectively bargained agreement with a union or, more commonly, the work expectations expressed in job descriptions, disciplinary codes and supervisory directives, and the payment expectations expressed in wage or salary schedules and compensation administration policies. In this sense, wage and salary administration is the heart of the employment contract for most organizations and employees.

Economists note that the demand for labor is a "derived demand"; employers seek labor for the output to be realized through employment and not for the mere presence of labor. In an abstract sense, the employment contract ought to specify an exchange of labor's output for pay such as illustrated by commission payments or straight piece-rate payments of compensation. Employment contracts would be explicit and employees would contract independently to exchange their outputs for compensation. Such a contracting process is quite expensive, however, and relatively uncommon. Rather, the typical employment relationship calls for the exchange of compensation for individual skills, time, effort, and submission to an authority relationship in the direction of effort. Difficulties encountered in attempting to specify precise outputs or behaviors desired are illustrated often in tales of employees "working to the book," following explicit rules, and thus disrupting the flow of production that is normal under a cooperative relationship in the exercise of authority.

Typically, individuals, not outputs, are employed. An employer seeks to realize desired output objectives through the supervisory process and employee acceptance of an authority relationship. Wage and salary compensation is provided to the employee in exchange for the skills, time, and effort expended in the employment (authority) relationship. The compensation provided usually varies with the job, personal characteristics, and performance of the individual employee as the amount of work output implicit in the skills, time, and effort varies. It should also be noted that an implicit employment contract requires considerable trust. The compensation policies and the process of supervision in the employment organization must induce trust of employees if the employment contract is to remain relatively implicit rather than explicit; explicit contracts will be sought by employees to the extent that trust is lacking.

Every contract involves exchange between two parties, and both parties must judge the exchange to be desirable. In the employment exchange, individual workers provide contributions or inputs and the employer provides inducements or outcomes. Exchange is possible because the parties assign different values to these inputs and outputs. For example, an employee values the monetary and nonmonetary returns from employment more than the time and effort required at work, while the economic value of labor services to the employer exceeds the cost of compensation and other payments to labor. These differing valuations derive in part from different utility functions applied by individual employees. One rationale for providing a variety of forms of compensation (wage or salary, vacation, pension, insurance) is that this variety provides greater opportunity to appeal to different individuals. Since utility functions are personal, it is difficult to specify compensation principles that are equally applicable to all potential employees. Monetary compensation is the one inducement for which most employees will agree that "more is always better," and thus serves as the example of compensation most commonly employed in discussion throughout this chapter. Manipulation of other rewards to induce employment behaviors requires considerably more knowledge about employee utility functions. Limited research into employee preferences suggests that preferences vary with demographic characteristics, but more study is required before compensation packages can be designed with confidence to fit different employee populations (Mahoney, 1964; Nealey, 1963; Dunn, 1979).

Employment contracts are of obvious social concern in a society in which about 60 percent of the adult population is employed and in which wage and salary compensation constitutes about 76 percent of national income. These social concerns are expressed in the form of both state and federal legislation, which establish various constraints upon employment contracts and which indirectly influence employment contracts through tax treatment of compensation. Minimum wage legislation, both federal and state, specify minimal rates of compensation applicable to various industries and locations of employment. Related legislation regulates working hours, premium rates of compensation for overtime work, minimal hiring ages, and related conditions of employment. Still other legislation concerns compensation for occupational injury and for retired persons. Wage controls imposed during periods of inflation also regulate compensation provisions of the employment contract, and still other legislation prohibits differential compensation based upon sex, race, and related personal characteristics. Finally, provisions of the Internal Revenue Code specify the tax treatment of alternative forms of compensation. Discussion of these various social and legislative constraints upon compensation is beyond the scope of this chapter and the reader is referred to other sources (e.g., Bureau of National Affairs). Knowledge of these constraints is vital, however, in the design and administration of compensation systems.

COMPENSATION AND MOTIVATION

The topic of motivation is the subject of another chapter in this book. However, compensation administration is an application of motivation theory and it is difficult to discuss compensation without consideration of motivational concepts and theories. Set forth in this section is the motivational framework that underlies the analysis of compensation; Chapter 10 provides a more extensive analysis.

Most behavior is in some sense motivated; it can be explained or rationalized in terms of human wants or desires exercised within a specific setting. Whether conceptualized as net advantage, marginal utility, or expected valence, one assumes that people make behavioral choices in such a manner as to best realize their objectives, given perceptions of reality. Choices are assumed to be rational, and different choices made by different people in similar circumstances are attributed to different objectives and/or different perceptions of outcome linkages.

While all behavior can be cast in terms of a choice model, it is more realistic to distinguish between conscious choice behavior and other behavior that appears habitual in nature (Mahoney, 1979a). Certain behaviors such as acceptance or termination of employment are relatively easily conceptualized as resulting from choice among alternative behaviors. (See Chapter 5 in this book.) Other behaviors such as particular task performances and pace of task performance are not as apparently a consequence of conscious choice. These more habitual behaviors may be repetitive of some previous choice now maintained without questioning, but viewing such behavior as a series of repetitive choices would be unrealistic and unproductive.

Concepts of choice behavior connote awareness of alternative behaviors and a conscious evaluation of, and choice among, these alternative behaviors. This arousal to, and awareness of, choice situations is assumed in models of choice behavior but need not be descriptive of all behavior. Awareness of choice alternatives may occur in several ways. This awareness may develop from a chance encounter not often experienced; for example, receipt of an unexpected job offer. Alternatively, an awareness of other choices may develop through conscious search for alternatives; for example, an unemployed person searches advertisements for job opportunities. Search behavior, a common precedent to awareness of choice alternatives, is itself motivated behavior—behavior motivated, presumably, by dissatisfaction currently experienced by the individual (March and Simon, 1958). This general model of behavior is illustrated in Figure 9-1, which distinguishes between choice and habit behaviors. Experienced dissatisfaction in this model stimulates a person to seek alternative behaviors judged to be more satisfying. Lacking dissatisfaction, a person will likely continue habit patterns of behavior unless externally aroused and made aware of alternatives that might be undertaken.

Behavioral choice models, whether based in economics or psychology, are basically similar; all propose some means for evaluation of alternatives and some decision rule for choice. Adam Smith (1937) proposed that individuals consider the "whole of the advantages and disadvantages" of different employments and choose that employment that offers greatest net advantage. While he identified various job characteristics that are

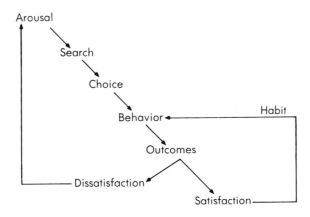

FIGURE 9-1
A Model of Habit and Choice Behaviors

considered in the calculation of net advantage, both the definition and weighting of job characteristics in this calculation were admitted to vary among individuals. Expectancy theory from psychology proceeds similarly to suggest that individuals characterize alternatives in terms of outcomes that are assigned valence or value based upon attractiveness to the individual (Vroom, 1964). Attractiveness of an alternative in the expectancy model is roughly analogous to net advantage as conceptualized in economics.

The expectancy model of choice makes a clear distinction, however, between attraction and choice—a distinction not made as clearly in other models. Individuals consider both the attractiveness of an alternative and the likelihood (expectancy) of realizing the alternative when making decisions. Attractiveness and expectancy are subjectively combined in a concept of expected valence employed in the choice process. Thus an attractive alternative with little likelihood of realization may be discarded in favor of a less attractive alternative with a high probability of realization. (A person attracted to the occupation of physician may opt for the occupation of teaching biology because of different expectancies of attaining the two occupations.) Choice is a function of behavior-outcome contingencies (expectancies) as well as outcome attractiveness (valence).

Habit patterns of behavior in Figure 9-1 are reflective of behavior patterns described in stimulus-response or reinforcement models of motivation (Hamner, 1974). Whatever the initiating reason for a specific behavior, a person has experienced reinforcement as a consequence of the behavior and continues to repeat the behavior when in the presence of associated stimuli. Thus, for example, a sales clerk smiles to a customer approaching the counter, or a machine operator presses an appropriate switch when material is positioned in the machine. These behaviors have been learned in the past and are engaged in without conscious choice considerations. They have been shaped by reinforcement contingencies experienced in the past and, presumably, will be continued until the person becomes aware of both the need and opportunity to change behavior and achieve more satisfying outcomes. While experienced satisfaction is one condition, it is not the only condition for continuing a particular pattern of behavior. A person experiencing dissatisfaction presumably will search for alternative choices, but may choose to continue the past behavior if it appears as the relatively most satisfying alternative available. Dissatisfaction appears to be a necessary, but not sufficient, condition for behavioral change. A person may be dissatisfied with current employment, yet unable to find more attractive feasible alternatives, and so continues a dissatisfying job. Turnover rates, which vary inversely with unemployment rates, indicate the role of expectancy in choices to terminate employment.

The concept of satisfaction employed here refers to some emotional response to a comparison of one's experiences with some set of valued standards (Locke, 1976). Job satisfaction, for example, is a response to experienced job characteristics relative to a criterion set of job characteristics. This criterion set is derived from various sources. The criterion set implicit in Adam Smith's formulation of net advantage is derived from the range of alternatives available to a person; that is, other jobs in the market. Equity models from social psychology propose that the criterion set is derived from what is experienced by some "relevant other" with whom an individual chooses to make comparisons (Adams, 1965). This relevant other may be the second party to an exchange, as in a husband-wife relationship, a co-worker also in exchange with an employer, or a more distant comparator, such as employees in another company perceived as relevant in making judgments about the equity of one's employment exchange. Job characteristics in the equity model are viewed as outcomes (such as fatigue, compensation, and pride) and inputs (such as skill, experience, and effort), and the outcome/input ratio observed for a relevant other provides the criterion for judgment of the equity of one's job or employment exchange. Perceived inequity is disturbing and dissatisfying, and stimulates search to identify actions that might restore equity; equity is satisfying and provides no stimulus for change.

Other sources of job characteristics criteria in the determination of job satisfaction would include past experiences and aspirations (Locke, 1976). Past adaptations to specific levels of job characteristics, such as pace of work, compensation and closeness of supervision, are carried forward as expectations or felt needs that serve as criteria in the evaluation of current experiences. Similarly, aspiration levels for skill utilization, compensation, and recognition provide another set of criteria. Dissatisfaction, which stimulates search for alternatives, thus may proceed from perceived inequity, needs or expectations which are unmet, and from aspirations not yet realized.

Programs of employee compensation are designed and administered with the intention of influencing specific employee behaviors sought by the employing organization. These behaviors can be differentiated in terms of the model presented in Figure 9–1 and related to different elements of a total compensation program. The behavioral outcomes typically sought through employee compensation are attraction of persons to join the organization as employees, retention of employees, and various types of job behaviors, such as minimal role performance as prescribed in the job description, and innovative behavior beyond minimal role performance.

Individuals joining an organization as employees exhibit a rather clear form of choice behavior. Acceptance of employment for most persons is not a common, repetitive form of behavior; rather, it is a relatively conscious choice among alternatives. The relevant alternatives considered vary among individuals, however, particularly as illustrated by different employee sources. The relevant alternatives for unemployed persons are organizations seeking employees, and the obvious alternative of whatever unemployment benefits are available. For persons newly entering the labor force, such as people graduating from school, the relevant alternatives are those organizations recruiting new employees, particularly those organizations recruiting at the school. The same alternatives, as well as the alternative of continued employment in the present job, are relevant to employees who are dissatisfied and seeking a change of employment. Relevant alternatives are more restricted for persons not in the labor force or satisfactorily employed elsewhere; these persons are not engaged in search activities and probably consider their current situation as the most relevant alternative for comparison with an offer of employment.

While a choice to seek and/or accept employment with an organization is a function of judgments about all characteristics of the employment contract, hiring wage is one characteristic to which all react in the same manner—the higher the hiring wage, the more attractive the employment. One central element of compensation policy, the determination of hiring rates, can be related directly to models of choice behavior in the attraction of a labor force.

Typically a person accepts employment with an implicit expectation of continuing in that employment role, and is prepared to develop habit patterns of working behaviors. Habit patterns of reporting to work at specific times, pace of work, and specific task performances are developed over time through the administration of behavior-reward contingencies such as discipline, withholding compensation for tardiness and absence, and the granting of increases for completion of probationary periods. Maintenance of these patterns of behavior is sought through contingency relationships that penalize performance below some minimal standard, and continued employment is maintained through membership rewards contingent on employment.

Once attained, changes in patterns of minimal role performance would, according to the model of Figure 9–1, typically result from experienced dissatisfaction and a choice of alternative behavior. Termination of employment, for example, is the consequence of a choice to change an established relationship and the associated behavior. Employee termination thus reflects experienced dissatisfaction and the expectation of realizing more desired outcomes in other employment or in not working. Efforts to retain employees through compensation proceed in two directions: (1) attempts to prevent dissatisfaction with the current employment, and (2) attempts to make continued employment appear more desirable than other alternatives. The maintenance of perceived equity to prevent dissatisfaction is sought through determination of wage structure and the pricing relationships of this structure with market rates of compensation. Job evaluation, whatever form it takes, is applied in the development and maintenance of a structure of wage differentials associated with different jobs, and is perceived as a primary element in maintaining a stable, cooperative workforce.

Another focus of employee compensation concerns differentially rewarding individuals on the basis of performance or output (e.g., incentives), behavior presumed to be related to performance (e.g., attendance bonus, seniority increment), or personal qualifications (e.g., skill differentials). These individual variations in compensation are intended to motivate specific performances and behaviors sought by the employer, and to reward equitably differentials of individual inputs to a job.

Compensation administration thus typically distinguishes among three different rationales for compensation and three different bases for compensation: (1) "membership pay," contingent upon maintaining the employment relationship and intended to attract employees and maintain commitment; (2) "job pay," which varies with the job or position performed; and (3) "individual pay," which varies with personal characteristics and individual performance. The compensation received by an individual is a function of all three bases, each focusing upon a different criterion.

INTERNAL LABOR MARKET STRUCTURE

The distinction between explicit and implicit employment contracts implies a distinction between contracting for a specific job or work output and contracting for an individual performing within an authority relationship. This distinction also appears in characterizations of what is called the "internal labor market" (Doeringer, 1967). Traditional economic analyses of the employment relationship view workers as competing for employment in specific jobs. Prospective employees compete for employment in specific jobs through wage competition, that is, their willingness to accept employment at wages lower than another prospective employee. Employers, in this model, are perceived as recruiting to fill each position from a labor market. Wages for individual jobs are determined through competitive action of employers and workers in the market. The employment contract in this model can be relatively explicit, the employer hiring for the performance of relatively specific jobs and/or tasks.

Alternatively, organizations may hire into relatively few jobs and fill other jobs in the organization through promotion of individuals who qualify through training and experience. At the extreme, all employees may enter through a single job, all other jobs being staffed through promotion and transfer. The relevant market for most jobs in this illustration is an "internal labor market" comprising all current employees of the organization. Employers in this model employ individuals for careers, not jobs, and the employment contract is relatively implicit in the policies and practices of the organization. Wage rates for most jobs are determined administratively and not through competitive action in the external labor market.

Practice in employing organizations varies between the two extremes of an "open" internal labor market, where each job is staffed through external recruiting, and a "closed" internal labor market, where most jobs are staffed through promotion and transfer. Choice of the degree of openness of the internal labor market is influenced by the tradition of the industry, degree of standardization of jobs among companies, degree to which an employer can rely upon training obtained external to the organization, anticipated tenure of employment, and employer philosophy. The construction industry, for example, typically is characterized by a relatively open internal labor market. Apprentice training in the crafts is standardized for the industry and is not unique to each organization; job or occupational requirements are relatively common to all employers, and employment tenure often is relatively short term as the need for different crafts varies considerably among projects. A relatively closed internal labor market would be characteristic of an organization such as the U.S. Foreign Service, or the managerial workforce of many corporations. Jobs are relatively specific to the employing organization and, particularly at advanced levels, require considerable knowledge about the organization that can be acquired only through experience. In such organizations, individuals qualify externally for entry jobs and qualify through experience in the organization for other jobs.

The degree to which an organization's internal labor market is open or closed influences considerably the role and function of wage and salary compensation in the employment contract. The employment contract in an organization with an open internal labor market focuses on the individual job to be performed and each job is characterized by a separate contract. The employment contract in an organization with a relatively closed internal labor market must be focused more upon the individual and the individual's career. Compensation for the immediate job into which an individual is hired will characterize the employment contract in an open internal labor market, while compensation anticipated over an individual's tenure in the organization will be more characteristic of the employment contract in a closed internal labor market.

COMPENSATION FUNCTIONS

Wage and salary compensation in the context of the employment contract is the primary means by which an employing organization secures labor services. The labor services obtained are a function of the number of persons who accept employment, the hours they work, and the skills and effort expended at work. Wage and salary compensation is intended to influence all of these dimensions of labor supply. Typically, these functions are identified as: (1) attraction of persons to seek and accept employment in the organization, (2) retention of employees as members of the organization, and (3) motivation of the behavior or performance desired—acceptance of job assignments, hours worked, and the level of effort expended on the job.

Attraction of Employees

People are attracted to employing organizations for many reasons (see Chapter 5 of this volume). In general, they have decided that working offers advantages relative to not working, that one occupation offers advantages relative to others, and that a specific employer offers advantages not offered by others. The earlier discussion suggested that the supply of applicants for employment varies with the perceived relative attractiveness of employment in an organization and the expectancy of employment. The perceived relative attractiveness of employment varies with the anticipated compensation and with nonpecuniary employment characteristics, such as nature of the job, ease of commuting, and stability of employment. Decisions to make application for employment are influenced also by expectancies of employment; companies that are known to be employing receive more applications for employment than companies known to be not hiring, other things being equal. The role of expectancy in employee job search is illustrated in research findings that indicate that unemployed workers conduct a relatively extensive job search (visit employment agencies, search want ads, and make application at many companies) during periods of high unemployment, and conduct a relatively intensive job search (rely upon friends and relatives for information) during periods of relatively low unemployment (Sheppard and Belitsky, 1966). Extensive job search can be viewed as a search for jobs, an attempt to increase the expectancy of employment, and intensive job search can be viewed as an investigation of specific job characteristics, on the assumption that opportunities for employment are already high. Both expectancy of employment and the attractiveness of employment can be manipulated in the attraction of applicants. When the expectancy of employment with other organizations is low (e.g., during periods of high unemployment), individual employers will be less concerned with making employment attractive through wage comparisons; the relative attractiveness of hiring wage rates is of most concern during periods of relative scarcity of labor supplies. The focus here is upon the compensation aspects of attracting candidates for employment rather than the recruiting aspects.

Potential candidates for employment must perceive the opportunity presented by the employer as preferable to alternative opportunities available. Other things being equal, an employer will seek to offer a hiring wage rate equal to or somewhat higher than the wage alternatives available to potential employees. The jobs into which people are hired vary with the degree of openness of the internal labor market. The wage rates of only those jobs into which people are hired are of primary concern in the attraction of candidates. Thus, in the extreme case of a perfectly open internal labor market where people are hired into all jobs, the wage rate for every job is compared with wage rates of comparable jobs with other employers. For employers hiring into only a relatively few entry jobs, only the wage rates for those jobs are of particular concern in the attraction of employees. The wage rates of nonentry jobs in a closed internal labor market may contribute to the impression that the employer is a high- or low-wage employer, but the wage rate of the entry job(s) is of most importance in the attraction of labor supplies.

Establishment of wage rates for entry or hiring jobs requires some comparative standard, but this standard varies with the traditional or intended source of applicants for employment. Often labor market and/or industry wage surveys are cited as the source for these comparative data, but the relevance of these standards may vary from employer to employer, depending upon traditional sources of employees. Candidates for employment compare an employer's wage rates with those of known alternatives, not necessarily the full range of employers in a labor market. Graduating MBA students, for example, tend to compare wage offers with those of other companies recruiting at the school, typically a select sample from a regional or national population of employers. Unemployed, unskilled workers more likely compare wage offers with the alternative of continued unemployment and/or with other wage offers encountered in the local labor market. Secondary and/or part-time workers compare employment offers with attractive alternatives such as retirement, school, or housekeeping, and with a select sample of alternative employers offering easily available employment that also fits their primary schedules.

Except in instances of employers seeking to hire scarce, high-talent individuals, most candidates for employment are seeking jobs; they are not being pirated from other employers. The pool of relevant employers to consider for comparison in the establishment of hiring wage rates thus will vary with the occupation and the traditional source of employees and may be unique to each employer. Relevant labor market comparisons may be identified empirically through inquiry of employment candidates about alternatives being considered, or may be designed by the employer through structuring of recruiting activities to tap specific sources of candidates.

Wage Level Determination. Wage surveys of relevant labor market competitors provide a base for determination of wages an employer ought to offer in order to attract candidates. The establishment of wage rates also is constrained by cost considerations. To remain competitive, every employer seeks to control per unit labor costs to the level of labor costs among competitors in the industry or product market (Mahoney, 1979b). For this reason, there are pressures to standardize wage rates among employers in a single industry, and one finds industry and/or association bargaining between employers and unions in the auto, steel, coal mining, construction, and other industries. Given comparable wage rates among product competitors, any labor cost advantage is achieved only through the occupational mix of employees, technology employed, and productivity achieved through supervision. The average wage per employee probably is a better indicator of labor cost constraints than is the full array of wage rates for different jobs; an employer seeks to control the average wage to the level of average wages paid by product market competitors with similar technology and capital investments.

Using average wage of product competitors as a maximum constraint and hiring wage of relevant competitors in the labor market as a minimum constraint, an employer has various options available to satisfy both. An employer with a relatively open internal labor market encounters wage rate minima for every job. The average wage rate paid can be controlled, within the limits of the technology employed, by substituting lower paid jobs and occupations for higher paid jobs. Alternatively, an employer may seek out labor markets with relatively lower wages than the labor markets in which product competitors operate; industry development in the southern sun-belt and along the Mexican border illustrates this strategy. Employers with relatively closed internal labor markets have somewhat greater opportunity to control average wages since they hire into relatively few jobs. Wage rates for entry jobs may be set relative to the relevant labor market alternatives, while wages for nonentry jobs are not as rigorously constrained. Employees in nonentry jobs are relatively less mobile, since they have greater tenure with the employer and typically have developed more company-specific skills and knowledges than employees in entry jobs. The average wage within the organization can be manipulated through control of nonentry wages to compensate for any disadvantages incurred through payment of relatively high entry rates (Bronfenbrenner, 1956). The resulting tendency to raise entry rates while controlling nonentry rates has, in some instances, resulted in wage compression where newly hired employees may receive as much as or more than more tenured employees, a problem which will be considered later.

The rigor of the constraint of product market competitor wages varies considerably, depending upon the degree of competition in the product market. Highly competitive industries, such as soft-goods manufacturing and hosiery and garment manufacturing, seek to pay only the wage rate required to attract employees and change rates in response to changing conditions in the labor market. Less competitive industries, such as hard-goods manufacturing and steel and auto manufacturing, typically pay somewhat more than the minimum required by the labor market and change wages in response to changes in the cost of living more often than in response to labor market conditions (Ross, 1957; Wachter, 1970).

Given the tendencies toward standardization of wage rates among product competitors, competitive advantage must be sought through differentials in employee productivity. To the extent that wage and salary administration succeeds in attracting high potential candidates, encourages long tenure in the organization, and motivates personal development and high performance, it contributes to this competitive advantage. Other elements of the personnel function, such as selection, recruitment, training, and development, also are directed toward achievement of productivity.

Labor-Force Retention

Labor-force retention, or the absence of turnover, usually is viewed as a desirable goal for personnel management. Turnover occasions costs of replacement, recruitment, and training, which may in certain instances be considerable. Typically, turnover is viewed as causing a temporary drop in productivity as new, less capable employees are recruited and trained to the level of performance of the terminated employee. While that view is adopted in this section, an important exception to it should be noted. The costs occasioned by employee turnover obviously vary with the ease of replacing terminated employees, the availability of candidates for employment, the complexity of the jobs involved, and the amount of training required for new employees. Turnover in a relatively open internal labor market often is less costly than turnover in a relatively closed internal labor market, since jobs are standardized among employers and most training occurs prior to employment. Given an adequate labor supply, employers with open internal labor markets will be relatively less concerned about employee turnover and, in fact, many craft employees change employers quite often. Concern for employee retention, then, is more prevalent among employers with a closed internal labor market, and among all employers during periods of relative labor shortages.

Employee terminations of employment are rejections of an employment contract previously accepted. For one reason or another, the employment contract is viewed less favorably than previously, and the employee chooses to leave the organization for another specific alternative (job, school, unemployment), or to search for a preferred alternative. Numerous studies of employee turnover suggest that terminations are a direct function of prior intentions to leave, dissatisfaction experienced in current employment, and the availability of attractive alternatives (low unemployment rates) (Ross and Zander, 1957). As in the attraction of individuals to employment, both the attractiveness of outcomes and the expectancy of those outcomes appear to influence decisions to terminate employment.

Labor market research suggests that most people accept employment with the intention of staying, and that once employed in a job do not actively seek out alternative employment opportunities, unless dissatisfied with something in the current employment (Parnes, 1954). There are instances in which people with particularly scarce qualifications are pirated away from what had been a satisfying job, but most terminations probably proceed from a prior dissatisfaction and consequent search for attractive alternatives. Top management recruiters often are employed to seek out particularly qualified individuals and to bring to their attention attractive job alternatives; many of those recruited through this process were not actively seeking alternative employment.

Employees experience dissatisfaction in an employment situation for many reasons, pecuniary and nonpecuniary. Theories of employee satisfaction (dissatisfaction) suggest that satisfaction is an emotional response to the congruence between what one experiences and what one values (expects, desires, or seeks). Dissatisfaction, viewed as the converse of satisfaction, reflects experienced incongruity. Various dimensions or factors of job satisfaction have been proposed by different theories, such as compensation, promotion, nature of work or tasks, recognition, benefits, working conditions, supervision, coworkers, company policy, and management (Locke, 1976).

Compensation figures in one form or another as a dimension of job satisfaction, and, viewed in terms of the overall model of satisfaction, compensation can serve to balance or compensate for dissatisfaction experienced in other dimensions. Wage and salary administration is by no means the only element influencing employee satisfaction, but it clearly can be a major element. Compensation elements typically considered in job satisfaction and in the design of compensation programs are: (1) wage level paid by one's employer relative to wage levels paid by other employers, (2) wages for one's job relative to wages for other jobs, and (3) wages paid one relative to wages paid others in the same job. These three dimensions of satisfaction with compensation, although derived empirically in many models of job satisfaction, correspond to what one might expect from consideration of equity comparisons and the attraction, retention, and performance dimensions of labor supply.

Judgments of equity and compensation require comparisons with some "other" compensation referent, and the behavioral relevance of other referents varies with the type of behavior considered. Decisions regarding applications for employment involve comparisons between different employers, and the compensation offered by feasible alternative employers provides a relevant standard. Decisions to seek or reject an alternative job assignment involve comparisons of the compensation and requirements of alternative jobs. And choices among alternative behaviors within a job (exert more effort, work overtime) involve comparisons of the compensation received by people performing differently in the same job. Wage comparisons with other employers, other jobs in the same organization, and other persons in the same job are relevant both in determining the equity of one's own payment and in influencing choices of alternative behaviors.

Not surprisingly, employers address these three concerns in the compensation issues of determining wage level, the structure of wages within the organization, and the establishment of schedules of individual compensation. Wage level determination is of most relevance in the attraction of employees and was discussed in the previous section; determination of the structure of wage differentials among jobs probably is most relevant in preventing dissatisfaction, and in maintaining and eliciting the cooperation of the organizational labor force; and individual schedules of payment are most relevant in influencing individual performance on the job.

Wage Structure.   Equal pay for equal work is an accepted principle for achieving equity of compensation. Consistent with this principle and with the concept of an employment exchange, people expect to be paid differentially for work in different jobs. A major task in wage and salary administration is the determination of a structure of compensation differentials that both employer and employees can accept as being reflective of differences in the work associated with these jobs. The process of determining the structure of compensation rates typically is termed *job evaluation*.

Determination of the relative worth or value of different jobs requires some standard for comparison. Adam Smith struggled with the concept of worth and identified two somewhat different standards: the market value and the use value of an item (Smith, 1937). *Use value* refers to the value an individual buyer or seller anticipates through use or employment of the item, and it varies among individuals and over time. Thus, a bushel of corn typically has higher use value for the hog farmer than for the auto mechanic, and the use value of corn to a hog farmer is greater during periods of high pork prices than during a period of low pork prices. The use value of labor services varies with the intended employment and estimated productivity of those services in the production of goods and services. The use value of a physician's services will be greater to a medical hospital than to a bicycle repair shop.

Market value refers to the price an item fetches in a free market of buyers and sellers. A market price in the context of a competitive market model is that price at which use value of an item for all who possess the item equals or exceeds market price, and market price is greater than the use value for all without the item. Market price in a free market reflects that use value at which demand and supply are equal.

Employer approaches to the structuring of wage differentials among jobs in an organization vary in terms of reliance upon the market criterion of value, the degree of reliance upon market wages varying with the degree of openness of the internal labor market. A perfectly open internal labor market is one in which the employer hires directly into each job. In order to do so, the jobs must be standardized among employers and educational and training qualifications must be obtainable prior to employment. For example, apprentice training for craft jobs provides standardized training to qualify workers for almost identical jobs with a wide variety of employers. Through prior occupational choices, artisans have already committed to a type of job, and choice of employer remains the primary decision regarding employment. Similarly, employers are competing with each other in the attraction of workers from a single pool, hence wage offers must be competitively attractive. Market surveys of wages offered for each job provide the basis for valuing each job, and differentials among jobs within the organization reflect directly those observed in the labor market. Since the perfectly open internal labor market does not rely upon internal training and development and promotion to staff vacancies, the internal structure of wages is not particularly relevant in the motivation of employees. While individuals might perceive inequities in the compensation provided two different occupations and experience dissatisfaction, there is no opportunity to change occupations without terminating employment and seeking training qualifications for the preferred occupation in the labor market. Employment alternatives immediately available to an individual are identical jobs with alternative employers—jobs offering the same rate of compensation. Dissatisfaction with the equity of compensation comparisons between occupations is less likely to create change in labor supply behavior than if inequity were perceived between equally feasible alternatives.

Reliance upon a market criterion of value is somewhat less feasible in the determination of wage structure for a relatively closed internal labor market, and the concept of use value is invoked as an alternative criterion. First, jobs in a relatively closed internal labor market tend to be less standardized among employers, since job performance is a function of both external training and internal training unique to the organization. The identification of similar jobs among different employers for purposes of wage surveys is more difficult. Also, employees in a relatively closed internal labor market are more likely to identify careers with employers than with jobs, progressing among jobs with a single employer rather than moving among employers within a single job. Job comparisons most relevant for equity considerations and career choices are other jobs within the same organization, not similar jobs in other organizations. Finally, the strategy of a closed internal labor market relies upon considerable employee cooperation in the training of less experienced employees (Thurow, 1975). Maintenance of satisfaction with the employing organization is critical in eliciting this cooperation, as well as in controlling turnover. The maintenance of perceived equity in the comparison of wages paid by other employers is important to employees in a closed internal labor market, but would appear to be less critical than in an open internal labor market and less critical than maintenance of equity within the internal labor market.

Job Evaluation.   Job evaluation is an administrative technique typically employed in the determination of wage rates and wage differentials among jobs within a single organization. Job evaluation performs the pricing function in organizations which, for one reason or another, do not rely solely upon wage surveys in the determination of wage rates for all jobs. Job evaluation typically is related to labor market wage surveys, although the degree of relationship varies considerably from one job and organization to another. It is an approach to the determination of equitable pay differentials within a single organization, not the overall labor market, although reference to labor market rates may be considered in the definition of equitable wage rates. Nevertheless, the major focus of job evaluation is upon job and compensation comparisons within the organization rather than upon comparisons between organizations. As an administrative technique for job pricing, it is most relevant for jobs for which no immediate market comparison is available (unique jobs), or jobs for which market comparisons are less relevant than comparisons within the organization (closed internal labor market).

Specific approaches to job evaluation vary from organization to organization, yet all reflect a common model for job pricing. Common steps in the development and application of job evaluation are the following:

1. *Sampling key jobs for development of system.*   Job evaluation systems are developed and validated on a sample of jobs and then generalized in application to a larger population of jobs within the organization. A sample of jobs is used in order to reduce the number of different jobs considered at the developmental stage and to make easier the development of an acceptable criterion of validity. This sample of jobs, called *key jobs,* reflects several considerations (Livernash, 1957). Job clusters reflective of social comparison norms can be identified in any organization, that is, clusters of jobs that typically are compared by incumbents in making comparisons of equity of payment. Job clusters are empirical phenomena and may reflect similarities of location, administrative grouping, skills, stage of production process, or anything that makes the jobs visible to one another, and provides a bond suggestive of comparable compensation treatment. Examples of job clusters might include maintenance jobs regardless of skill classification, different jobs within an occupation such as secretary, or all jobs in an oil well drilling team. Each cluster typically has several jobs that serve as benchmarks against which all other jobs are compared, and that serve to make comparisons between job clusters (see Figure 9–2). These benchmarks or key jobs are representative of other jobs in their respective job clusters, tend to be highly visible both within the cluster and to employees in other job clusters, and tend to be comparable with similar jobs in other organizations. Many of these jobs also will be key in the sense that they represent a relatively large proportion of total wage costs of the organization, since jobs with large numbers of incumbents will more likely meet the criteria for key jobs than will jobs with relatively few incumbents.

Job clusters that commonly are compared with one another often will be grouped into a single population for job evaluation purposes. Production jobs may constitute one such population, office technical and clerical jobs another population, managerial and administrative jobs another population, and engineering and scientific jobs still another population. The assumption underlying this identification of different populations of job clusters is that jobs in one population are rarely compared with jobs in another

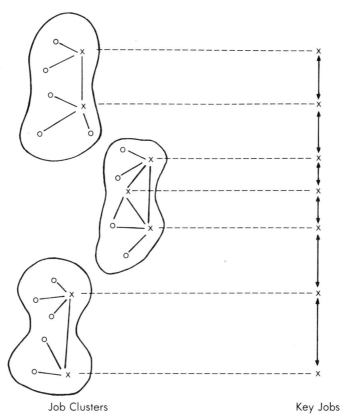

Job Clusters   Key Jobs

FIGURE 9–2
Job Clusters and Key Job Relationships

population in making judgments of equity of compensation. Job evaluation systems designed for more homogeneous populations are assumed to more validly capture critical dimensions of job variation than a general system designed to cover a wider range of jobs. The different populations of job clusters, in a sense, represent differentiated internal labor markets—employees are recruited from different sources, and careers are constrained within a single population with relatively little movement from one population of job clusters to another. Job evaluation systems designed for, and applied to, different populations of job clusters do, in fact, differ considerably in terms of criteria for differentiation of wages and the degree of compensation differentiation among jobs.

2. *Determination of criterion of equitable relationships.* Since key jobs serve as the benchmarks for evaluation of all other jobs, the criterion for validation of a job evaluation system is a set of compensation relationships among key jobs that can be accepted as equitable. There are various alternative bases for this criterion that may be employed singly or, more commonly, as a joint basis for the criterion. Labor market wage surveys provide one such criterion. Rates of compensation for key jobs ought to be competitive with the labor market if employees are to be recruited into and retained in

the organization. Industry wage surveys of key job rates also provide a criterion in the control of wages and labor costs for competitive purposes. Finally, employee attitudes and reactions provide another basis for the criterion of key job relationships. Employees in the workforce must accept these relationships as equitable before they are generalized to other jobs in the organization. Also, criterion rates for key jobs may be negotiated between a union and management. Not uncommonly, existing wage relationships among key jobs will provide the operational criterion, so long as these are accepted by all parties as generally equitable.

　　3. *Development of measurement and rating system.*　Four basic types of systems are traditionally identified in the discussion of job evaluation rating systems (Lytle, 1954). These four types are variants of two underlying dimensions: (1) whether the job is viewed in a holistic fashion or considered as the sum of separate components, and (2) whether jobs are compared directly one with another or compared with some prescribed standard of measurement. These dimensions and the four variants are represented in Figure 9–3. The simplest approach is the Ranking method, which involves consideration of all jobs and establishing a rank hierarchy among them. All components of each job are considered at once in determining this hierarchy. While specific job components may be identified in structuring job descriptions, the combination of these components in reaching an overall judgment about relative job worth is subjective. Key jobs, once ranked, provide a structure within which other jobs may be ranked on the basis of comparison with the key job ranks. Application of the ranking approach is limited to situations in which there are relatively few jobs, such that rankers can be reasonably familiar with all and make comparisons. This, however, would not be feasible within a large organization with hundreds of different jobs.

　　The Classification approach involves development of a standard of comparison in the form of differentiated job categories, with definitions of job elements necessary for classification in each category, and then a sorting of jobs into different categories, with the categories ranked in terms of job worth. The Classification approach can be viewed as an extension of the Ranking approach. Key jobs are ranked and then differentiated into groups judged to be significantly different in terms of worth. Job characteristics descriptive of each category are determined from the descriptions of key jobs and used in the specification of requirements for classification into each category. Nonkey jobs are then evaluated by assignment to categories on the basis of job descriptions and the cate-

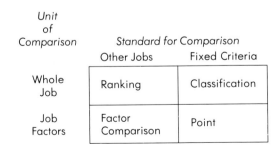

FIGURE 9–3
Approaches to Job Evaluation

gory classification requirements. The Classification approach was commonly used in governmental organizations with a wide range of jobs to be covered, but jobs that tended to be relatively stable in terms of content. It has given way in many instances to the Point approach, which is somewhat more flexible and appears to be less arbitrary than the Classification approach.

The Point approach to job evaluation requires specification of a number of factors or dimensions of job content to be evaluated, design of measurement and weighting scales for each factor, application of the scales to job descriptions, and summing of the points assigned the different scales for each job. Jobs are evaluated, factor by factor, through comparison of job content with the different factor scales. Overall evaluation reflects the sum of the factor evaluations. The Point approach highlights the different dimensions of factors responsible for the relative worth of jobs and thus provides a clear rationale for evaluation. The approach employed can be easily evaluated independently of the results of application. The approach is somewhat more limited in application than the Ranking or Classification approaches, however, since the factors employed must be common to most of the jobs being evaluated; job cluster populations that are significantly different in job content call for different sets of factors and weights for evaluation. The Point system is the most commonly used approach to job evaluation and is used here to illustrate other stages in job evaluation.

The Factor Comparison approach also focuses upon job factors one at a time, but involves direct comparison among jobs rather than with a standard set of degrees and weights as in the Point system. Factor Comparison involves a reasonably sophisticated and complex system of determining relative job worth and is not as commonly employed. Because of its complexity, it is more difficult to develop and to explain to employees.

The development of measurement and rating systems, whatever the specific approach taken, involves a process analogous to multiple regression analysis. Measures of job characteristics are sought which, when weighted appropriately, will reproduce the criterion measures of relative worth. Validation of the approach is demonstrated when the approach, applied to key jobs, reproduces the criterion of relative worth previously discussed. In a purely statistical sense, it is immaterial what job factors are employed and how they are weighted so long as the criterion is reproduced. However, acceptability of an approach also involves questions of face validity. An acceptable approach must consider and weigh job characteristics in a manner that appears reasonable to those affected. The job factors considered in the evaluation system, the scales for measurement of each, and the weights assigned different degrees of each must appear relevant to the determination of job worth. Examples of commonly employed job factors include responsibility, skill, working conditions, physical demands, and required education and training. Since the factors relevant to differentiation among jobs in one population of job clusters may be different from those relevant in another population of job clusters, quite different systems of job evaluation often result for the different populations. Factors such as responsibility and decision making would appear in evaluation systems for managerial jobs, physical demands and skill might appear in systems for factory jobs, and accuracy and amount of supervision received might appear as factors in clerical and technical evaluation systems. As noted later, difficulties in describing and evaluating engineering and scientific jobs have led to the development of maturity curves based upon discipline and years since graduation as the characteristics accepted as relevant in those populations of job clusters.

Job evaluation dimensions or factors in the Point system are operationalized into measurement scales, which identify different degrees or levels of each dimension, and weights are assigned to the different degrees of the various dimensions. Weights often are prescribed initially on the basis of subjective judgments of relative worth. Key jobs are described and evaluated using the weighted scales, and a total score is developed for each job. The validity of the system is then assessed through comparison of the evaluation measures assigned the jobs and the criterion of relative worth specified earlier. The weights assigned factor degrees are adjusted until the system produces a set of job evaluations reasonably aligned with the criterion. It should be noted that empirical analysis employing multiple regression or linear programming is an alternative to subjective judgments in development of job evaluation factors and weights, and has been employed in selected situations. Recently developed approaches that rely increasingly upon statistical analysis and policy capturing analysis may be employed in combination with subjective judgment (Robinson, Wahlstrom, and Mecham, 1974). More commonly, subjective judgment is employed, probably because the process is more easily understood and thus accepted as equitable by the employer and employees concerned. Analogous approaches are applied in the development of the Classification and Factor Comparison systems.

4. *Implementation.* Once a system is judged valid, several steps are required in implementation. The first step, conceptually simple but often costly and involved, requires generalization of the system to all nonkey jobs. This involves development of job descriptions for all other jobs and evaluation of the jobs using the system developed and validated on key jobs (see Chapter 4 of this book).

Another element in implementation involves specification of a structuring of compensation reflective of job evaluations, the determination of pay grades or groupings of jobs to be paid comparably, and the structuring of rate ranges for these pay grades. Jobs are automatically structured into pay grades in the Classification system, all jobs in a class being paid comparably. But the Point and Factor Comparison approaches produce evaluation points unique to each job; 1,000 different jobs might be assigned 1,000 different point evaluations. Pay grade structuring breaks the total range of evaluation points into some smaller number of classes, and all jobs with evaluation points in a single pay grade are compensated in comparable manner. Various considerations enter into the structuring of pay grades; one of these relates to hierarchical authority and promotional relationships among jobs. Two jobs related by a hierarchical reporting relationship, one job reporting to the other, should not be classed in the same pay grade. The same principle would apply to two jobs linked in a promotional career sequence. A noticeable difference between jobs in a career or authority relationship must be confirmed by a noticeable difference in compensation. At the same time, pay grades should be broad enough to permit some change in job duties without requiring reevaluation and assignment to a new pay grade. Tradition also influences pay grade structuring, some organizations recognizing relatively few pay grades with wide ranges of job differences, and other organizations recognizing many pay grades with narrow ranges of job differences. The former permits greater administrative flexibility, but may not satisfy traditional equity considerations within the affected workforce. Typically, something like ten to sixteen pay grades may be recognized for a population of job clusters, but more would be required as the range of job clusters covered increases.

While promotion from one job to another calls for movement from one pay grade to another, jobs within a single pay grade may be linked in the sense of learning and advancement. Learner, operator, and senior operator positions relative to a single job often are distinguished within the same pay grade. These distinctions among performance expectations within a single job call for some equitable distinctions in compensation, which are accommodated through structuring of compensation ranges for the different pay grades. A range of compensation for a single pay grade permits distinction between different positions in the grade, as well as the distinction between performance of different employees in the same job (considered in the next section). A common rule of thumb for establishing rate ranges suggests that the range be ±5 to ±20 percent of the range midpoint, but the appropriate range will vary with several considerations (Henderson, 1979). The pay range probably will vary with the breadth of the pay grade, possible differentiation among rates of compensation varying directly with the variability among jobs in the grade. In similar fashion, the rate range will vary directly with the variability of performance recognized within a job in the pay grade, relatively little variation in compensation being necessary if a job is so standardized that there is little opportunity for variation in performance. Finally, it is common to structure overlap in the rate ranges for adjacent pay grades in recognition of the fact that top performers in a job in one pay grade ought at times to be compensated more than low performers in a job in the next higher pay grade.

Pay grade and compensation range structuring typically is illustrated, as in Figure 9–4, in charts. Relationships between pay grades and compensated worth may be linear or, as in Figure 9–4, curvilinear, depending upon the rationale employed. Many argue for a curvilinear relationship, particularly among managerial pay grades. There is evi-

Job Evaluation Pay Grades

FIGURE 9–4
Relating Compensation to Pay Grades

dence to suggest that compensation differentials of about 33 percent are necessary between adjacent levels in a managerial authority relationship to be judged equitable (Mahoney, 1979c). Assuming that jobs in adjacent ranks are classified in adjacent pay grades, this would imply a curvilinear relationship with compensation. The exact nature of the relationship will vary, however, depending upon the fineness of distinction between pay grades and empirical observations of relationships accepted as equitable.

A final aspect of implementation involves pricing the structure, assigning exact rates of compensation to the preceding rate structure. Pricing typically is accomplished through consultation of wage survey information, which also provides another test of validity of the evaluation system. The general structure of job evaluations should correspond generally with the structure of compensation observed in the relevant labor market(s) if employees are to be recruited and retained in the organization. Assuming correspondence between job evaluations and surveys of compensation paid in the labor market, particularly for the key job structure, the entire job structure is priced by anchoring key jobs to these market data. Anomalies between job evaluations and market survey data may reflect significant differences between the job evaluated and that job in other organizations, temporary market imbalances distorting traditional compensation differentials, or lack of validity in the job evaluation system. The latter explanation calls for revision of the evaluation system, while the other explanations can be accommodated through assignment of temporary rates within the appropriate wage ranges. The pricing element of job evaluation is repeated periodically, usually annually, as a continuing check on the validity of the system and as a guide to necessary compensation adjustments.

Maturity Curves. Job evaluation is most feasible as a means of establishing a compensation structure where jobs are relatively standardized over time and across relatively large numbers of job incumbents. It is less feasible where job content changes frequently or where jobs are unique to individual incumbents. Where the number of people in unique jobs is small, compensation can be negotiated on an individual basis, as in the case of a chief executive, or the sole physician employed in a large firm. Individual negotiation is not feasible where relatively large numbers of people are involved, as in the case of research scientists in a pharmaceutical firm, and an alternative to traditional job evaluation is sought. The maturity curve approach to compensation illustrates one such alternative often employed for engineers and scientists. Engineers and scientists, particularly in research organizations, often perform varying and nonroutine assignments that are difficult to describe in traditional job evaluation factor descriptions. Two dimensions that seem to capture common perceptions of relevant inputs for equity comparisons and to reflect market variations in compensation are: (1) discipline of degree, and (2) years since graduation (see Figure 9–5). Market rates for hiring engineers and science graduates vary by discipline. Similarly, judgments of worth of engineers and scientists tend to vary with experience, presumably reflecting the worth of development and training acquired through experience. Discipline and years of experience (years since graduation) can be rationalized as proxies for more direct measures of job content and worth of job content. Discipline and years since graduation are also more reliable survey classification measures than the nebulous job titles assigned engineers and scientists.

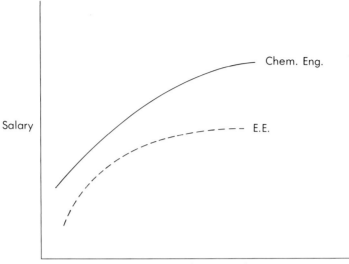

Salary

Chem. Eng.

E.E.

Years Since Graduation and Degree

FIGURE 9-5
Illustrative Maturity Curves

The inherent face validity of maturity curves, the ease of operational application, and the acceptance by engineers, scientists, and employers as an equitable basis for compensation meet the criteria for a job evaluation system, although maturity curves appear to be quite different from more traditional forms of job evaluation.

Job evaluation has evolved over the years into a reasonably well-accepted approach to the determination of a structure of relative compensation within organizations. In a sense, it combines concepts of market value and use value in the determination of equitable compensation for jobs. Market value is easily determined only for those jobs that are standardized among employers and thus easily surveyed, and market value is most relevant as a criterion of equity for jobs into which people are hired from the external labor market. Market value is less relevant and less easily determined for jobs that are filled by promotion from within the organization, and thus likely to differ from jobs with similar titles in other organizations. A job evaluation system that captures employee judgments of relative worth is an operationalization of the concept of use value. Tying this structure of judgments to market rates for key jobs operationalizes the concept of market value in determining rates of compensation. A job evaluation system with rationally defensible factors and weights provides a framework for the judgment of equity of compensation differentials, a framework that can channel employee perceptions and judgments of equity. Such a framework, over time, develops traditions supportive of the equity of the established differentials. Job evaluation does face challenges as a method of determining equitable compensation differentials, however. This issue will be discussed in a later section.

Performance Motivation

An overall compensation program is viewed as having three general objectives: (1) to attract candidates for employment, (2) to retain individuals in the organization working in a succession of jobs, and (3) to motivate specific job performances. Viewed from a behavioral or decision-making standpoint, these objectives are somewhat different and require different compensation influences. The behaviors sought in job performance are much more specific and related to output than are the behaviors sought in the attraction of employees. Similarly, the acceptance of initial employment is more easily conceived as a result of choice and decision making than is hour-to-hour variation in effort expended on the job. This section will consider the motivation of specific job performances and the characteristics of a compensation program most likely to elicit those performances.

One should first distinguish between job performance and behavior. Performance is usually conceptualizd in terms of output-related dimensions such as quantity and quality of production, level of productivity, scrap and wastage measures, and the meeting of deadlines and schedules. However, behavior relates to the actions of individuals on the job, actions such as computing estimates of costs, typing manuscripts, negotiating a sale, and operating a machine. Output types of performance are a function of behavior, but they also are a function of the machines used, the nature and quality of raw materials, and the skill level of the individual in the job. What is termed *motivation to perform* refers to the behavior of the individual on the job and, while important in achieving output, it is only a partial determinant of output.

Compensation programs attempt to direct performance behavior by providing rewards that are contingent upon achievement of specific behavior outcomes. Contingent compensation is intended to direct individual choices of behavior and to reinforce desired behavioral patterns. Certain relevant behaviors can be viewed clearly as choices (e.g., decision to skip a day of work for deer hunting), while others are less conscious and reflect habits or patterns of behavior developed over time (e.g., cleaning up the work station or taking a coffee break). Contingency compensation is designed to influence choices in the first instance and to reinforce desired habitual behaviors in the second.

Contingency compensation can be viewed either in terms of incentives to behavior or as rewards for behavior. An incentive is something that is anticipated, a potential reward, whereas a reward is experienced. An incentive is intended to influence choice, while a reward is intended to reinforce past behavior. Insofar as experienced rewards are associated with past patterns of behavior, anticipations of behavior-reward associations are established and serve as incentives. Incentives are not restricted to experienced rewards, however. Behavior-reward contingencies may be inferred from observations of others' experiences or from policy statements, and thus serve as incentives prior to the experiencing of specific reward contingencies. Contingency compensation programs are designed to provide incentives through the announcement of behavior-reward contingencies and to provide reinforcement of behavior through experience of behavior-reward associations.

The distinction between incentive and reward is particularly relevant if one distinguishes between behaviors that are a clear function of choice, and behaviors that are more obviously a function of an established habit pattern. Decisions to accept or terminate employment, to accept or refuse transfer, or to be absent from work on the opening day of deer hunting season illustrate choice behaviors. Work pace maintained throughout the day, cooperation with co-workers, and responsiveness to supervisory requests are more illustrative of habit behaviors. What is here called *choice behaviors* would appear to result from conscious decision making in which the individual weighs the consequences of alternative actions and selects the most attractive action. Expectancy theory and the concept of incentive as anticipated reward would appear most relevant in understanding this behavior. What is here called *habit behaviors* are less clearly the result of conscious decision making and more clearly resemble habitual responses to some stimuli. Reinforcement theory and the concept of reward would appear most relevant in understanding these behaviors. While the implications of expectancy theory and reinforcement theory for the design of performance contingent compensation are often congruent, they occasionally differ in relevant ways and the distinction between choice and habit behaviors can be important.

Compensation contingencies should satisfy several conditions if they are to affect choice, and the establishment and maintenance of habit behaviors. The first and most obvious condition is that the compensation reward associated with behavior ought to be perceived as desirable or as possessing positive valence. In hedonistic terms, individuals seek outcomes that are perceived as pleasurable and avoid outcomes that are perceived as painful. Monetary compensation is one outcome for which most people would agree that "more is better" and thus figures importantly in most contingency reward systems. Other elements of compensation, such as time off, dental insurance, pension rights, and sick leave, hold differing appeal for different individuals. One cannot as confidently assume that all employees will value these forms of compensation in a similar manner. What is termed a "cafeteria" approach to compensation has been proposed as a means of capitalizing upon differing utility assessments of nonmonetary compensation; employees are permitted at least limited choice among amount and form of nonmonetary compensation. The cafeteria approach is considered in more detail later in the chapter.

A second, closely related condition concerns the amount of compensation extended as an incentive. While monetary compensation is viewed as generally appealing to most people, it is not clear how much appeal is associated with a given amount of money. Economists assume that money has diminishing marginal utility, that equal increments of money are less appealing as the base for the increment increases. Similarly, psychologists often refer to Weber-Fechner relationships in determination of "just noticeable differences" of stimuli including money; a barely noticeable difference in money might require a constant ratio of the increment to the base of comparison. Relatively little is known about the utilitarian appeal of additional compensation, although, in practice, it often is assumed that equal percentage increments possess equal valence or utility. Clearly, however, the incentive effect of contingent compensation will vary with the amount of the incentive offered (Krefting and Mahoney, 1977). The incentive effects of differing contingency relationships clearly require more study, however, before one can specify the motivational power of different relationships.

A third condition for an effective contingency compensation program is that the employee must be aware of contingency associations, the outcomes associated with different behaviors and the expectancy of these outcomes, given a behavioral choice. Knowledge about these associations may be gained through experience (as assumed in the reinforcement model), through observed experience of others, or through probabilistic analysis of information obtained in other ways (as permitted in the expectancy model). Contingency compensation programs designed to serve as incentives to direct choices are clearly dependent upon prior knowledge of the association between behavior and reward. Piece-rate and commission formulas are designed for communication in advance of performance in order to direct behavior, and performance contracting through some form of management by objectives also is intended to communicate in advance this association between specific performances and reward levels. Performance-reward associations learned through experience, such as learning that a supervisor is more responsive to time off requests for medical reasons, are no less effective in the direction of behavior, but time is often required before the individual learns and responds to the association.

A fourth characteristic of contingency compensation relates to the degree of association between behavior and consequences, or the schedule of reinforcement. Behaviorist learning experiments indicate that behavior is patterned most quickly under conditions of constant reinforcement, yet maintained longer under conditions of variable reinforcement (Hamner, 1974). Expectancy theory hypothesizes that attraction to an action varies directly with the product of the valence of consequences and the probability of those consequences, implying that constant reinforcement schedules are most powerful in directing behavior. Both reinforcement theory and expectancy theory would agree that behavior patterns are most easily established under conditions of constant reinforcement where the relationship between performance and consequences is certain. Conditions for constant reinforcement, such as commission payments, can be designed into a contingency compensation program. However, these require close supervision and administration of the program in order to maintain the desired relationship between performance and consequences. Changes in technology and production methods and changes in raw materials often alter the relationship between production performance and rewards. These, in turn, require a change in the incentive formulas to maintain a desired relationship between performance and consequences.

Contrary to the implications of expectancy theory, reinforcement theory indicates that behavior learned under variable reinforcement conditions (expectancy less than 1.00) is maintained longer than behavior learned under conditions of constant reinforcement (expectancy of 1.00). Similarly, observations of gambling behavior suggest that receipt of an unexpected reward is often more valent than receipt of an expected reward; i.e., behaviors with lower expected value of reward are selected over behaviors with higher certain reward. In a related manner, results of research by Edwin Locke and his associates indicate that performance varies directly with goal difficulty, or lower probability of achievement (Locke, 1968). Expectancy theory is consistent with these observations only if one assumes that valence of an outcome varies inversely with expectation of achievement of the outcome, or if one assumes that sense of achievement or accomplishment is itself a related outcome of performance. Expectancy theory, in contrast to reinforcement theory, distinguishes between at least two contingencies—the expectation that an action will result in some specified performance, and the expectation that that specified performance will be accompanied with specific outcomes. Contrary to Locke's observations, expectancy theorists would argue that the expectation of achievement of performance positively influences the attractiveness of an act. Compatibility can be achieved only through an admission of the sense of achievement as a desired outcome, and recognition that the valence of this outcome varies inversely with the expectation of achievement. Lacking any more specific theory or research, it is suggested that the expected monetary reward and the sense of achievement from performance be considered in the design of any contingency reward system to motivate performance levels.

While contingency compensation calls to mind most quickly piece-rates and commissions, it should be noted that there are many forms of contingency compensation. Compensation contingencies are designed to elicit various specific behaviors. These relatively more specific forms of contingent compensation include production bonuses, awards for suggestions, attendance bonuses, and tuition refunds for successful completion of educational courses. Considerations applicable to contingency compensation programs in general also apply to the design of these relatively specific programs as well. Many such contingency compensation programs appear to have at least short-run impacts upon behavior and performance, although the long-range impact is questionable (Hamner and Hamner, 1976). Novelty of a program appears to influence its impact, just as unexpected rewards appear to have greater potency than fully anticipated rewards. Thus there appears to be a rationale for periodic change in contingency compensation programs, change that may appear to be merely faddism.

No discussion of contingency compensation can neglect to call out the many contingencies present in a work situation in addition to those designed into a compensation program. Just as the potentially potent outcome of the sense of achievement has been noted, there are other critical outcomes that may result from job performance. Numerous studies of industrial piece-rate systems, for example, have noted the frequent negative consequences of high production levels that may counterbalance the positive consequences of monetary compensation (Whyte, 1955). High rates of individual performance may be expected to result in increased pressure for production from low producers, social sanctions against the high producer, or recalculation of the incentive formula to reduce the effort-payoff relationship or reduce staffing, all such expectations based upon past experiences. Contingent outcomes in this instance are contained in social responses and managerial responses to performance in addition to the intended compensation outcomes. These unintended consequences may, as in the reported illustrations, outweigh the intended consequences and negate the intended influence. Approaches such as group incentives, commission compensation only for relatively independent and self-contained production (sales) positions, and the linking of bonuses to individually-established performance objectives, represent attempts to integrate contingent compensation with the social setting of the job and to avoid the development of counter-productive reward systems. Group incentives seek to enlist social support for the performance sought through incentive compensation, while restricting incentive usage to isolated positions or relating incentives to individually established objectives are intended to reduce the influence of social comparison.

Behavioral outcomes leading to a sense of achievement and social approval can be inferred as motivating behaviors to "beat the system"; behaviors which have been observed in various employment settings, including those with performance under incentive compensation systems. Employees devise ingenious methods of earning rewards without achieving the specified prior conditions for rewards, for example, falsifying production records and expense accounts or discovering and employing easier ways to meet prior conditions for reward. Every performance-reward contingency system invites unintended innovative behavior and requires careful design and administration to ensure that the intended consequences are achieved.

Performance incentives are effectively limited to those behaviors on the job that can be specified in advance as desirable. They are not easily designed for the unusual, innovative, and unexpected behavior that cannot be specified in advance but only recognized later as desirable. Successful performance incentives might effectively channel behavior in specified directions, but would not provide for recognition of the unexpected, yet important, performance. Rather, some means of providing rewards in ways other than incentives must be sought as well (Katz, 1964). This is possibly the most striking gap in most compensation programs, and one worthy of more attention in the future.

ADMINISTERING COMPENSATION

Compensation policy commonly is analyzed in terms of anticipated effects upon employee behavior and satisfaction. There is an implicit assumption that policy dictates the compensation treatment of individuals. Like other policies, however, compensation policy is administered by managers and supervisors, and the effects of policy are determined by policy administration, not intent. A policy of differentially rewarding for performance may be frustrated through administration of equal rewards for all. While there is considerable anecdotal and experiential information concerning compensation administration, relatively little is available in the way of research findings, and the discussion here ought to be viewed as setting forth hypotheses worthy of investigation.

Experiential reports suggest that managers and supervisors often administer compensation in ways contrary to policy intent for a variety of reasons. The administration of discretionary increases provides illustrations of managerial practice seemingly inconsistent with policy intent. Discretionary compensation increases are intended to provide the opportunity to differentially reward employees, and commonly are to be based upon some form of performance appraisal. Differential rewarding of employees on the basis of subjective assessments of performance is open to challenge, and many supervisors appear to try to avoid challenge by recommending increases with relatively little variance. Such practice avoids challenge from a majority of employees and, interestingly, from compensation administrators who require justification for discretionary increases that differ from some norm. The policy intent of differential rewards thus is frustrated in practice, and high-performing individuals are denied recognition through compensation.

Experience with subjective appraisals as the basis for compensation increases also suggests that performance appraisals often are written to justify some particular compensation treatment determined on other grounds. This distortion of appraisals to justify desired compensation treatment has led many organizations to require independent appraisals for development and compensation (see Chapter 8 in this volume).

Policies of secrecy concerning compensation have been examined in terms of effects upon motivation. Several observers recommend open communication of compensation information as a means of communicating contingencies and expectancies (Lawler, 1972). Interestingly, recent research suggests that dissemination of information about compensation influences supervisory reward allocations and may frustrate the translation of policy intent into administrative practice. There is evidence to suggest that less variance in reward allocations is realized under conditions of full information and knowledge than under conditions of secrecy (Peters and Atkin, 1980).

The administration of compensation is in many ways more critical than compensation policy. Actions taken and/or received, rather than policy intent, are rewarding and punishing, and provide the basis for contingency expectations. Yet relatively little is known about how managers and supervisors administer compensation and what the influences of their decisions are. Compensation policy designed in ignorance of supervisory administration processes often is ineffectual, and considerably more research into these processes is justified.

UNRESOLVED ISSUES AND CHALLENGES

Compensation administration faces a number of very real practical issues and challenges. Solutions for certain of these issues are by no means obvious, and the issues are presented here without recommended solutions.

Cost of Supplementary Benefits

The compensation cost of supplementary benefits is a very pressing issue of compensation administration and one that is growing annually. Monetary compensation has been referred to throughout this chapter to illustrate various principles and hypotheses, yet, 40 percent of total compensation paid to employees is in the form of supplementary compensation. What was once termed a fringe benefit is now a significant component of the total compensation package. These supplementary benefits take many forms: social insurances (unemployment compensation and OASDI), vacations, medical, hospital, dental and disability insurances, holidays, pensions, overtime and shift premiums, tuition refunds for education, and subsidization of employee social clubs and eating facilities. Some organizations now provide paid holidays for employee birthdays, the first day of deer hunting season, and "go to hell" days when an employee may arbitrarily be absent from work.

While limited supplementary benefits were provided prior to the 1940s, the real growth in benefits can be traced to the negotiation of pensions during World War II. Pensions were negotiated then as alternatives to wage increases that were limited by wage controls. Since that time, fringe benefits have evolved to the point where their provision is at times regarded as a right of employees and not as a supplement to wages.

Any cost-benefit analysis of supplementary benefits is difficult; each benefit must be analyzed individually and it is difficult to generalize findings. Costs, for example, vary with corporate and individual tax codes, and the size and demographic characteristics of the employee group covered. Costs also vary over time as tax codes and employee demographic characteristics change. Long-run costs of various benefits are particularly difficult to estimate in advance. Often, what appears to be relatively inexpensive in the short run develops into significant long-run obligations.

The benefit of supplementary benefits is also difficult to measure in any form other than current employee preferences. While supplementary benefits are presumed to reduce employee turnover or to discourage absenteeism, research evidence concerning performance and behavioral effects is very meager. Despite the few studies concerning employee perceptions of benefits, relatively little is known about employee assessments of supplementary benefits or perceptions of contingency relationships with behavior.

Meanwhile, the cost of supplementary benefits continues to grow both absolutely and relative to direct wage payments. In fact, since certain benefit levels are related directly to wage payments, the cost implications of a wage increase often are underestimated. Benefit relationships to wage rates often multiply the cost implications of wage changes, rather than serving as alternatives to direct wage payments.

Both the economic and social implications of an increasing portion of the compensation bill being paid in the form of supplementary benefits, as well as the implications of alternative benefits for employee mobility, retirement, and performance, are relatively unknown. Considerable imaginative research into these issues is warranted for both individual employers as well as society.

Cafeteria Compensation

Evidence concerning the obvious has been collecting for some years—evidence that people differ in the assignment of value to various forms of nonmonetary compensation and that the values assigned often differ from the monetary cost of compensation. Various authors have proposed that employees be permitted at least limited choice in the forms of compensation received, thus, presumably, maximizing the individual utility of a fixed sum of monetary expenditures (Lawler, 1971). Objections raised to the cafeteria plan relate largely to administrative problems—effects of a changing population base on charges, tax treatment of different forms of compensation, and coping with preferences that change over time. However, these administrative problems obviously can be overcome, if desired.

Perhaps more important than the administrative issues is understanding the potential benefits of a cafeteria plan for compensation and the likely effects upon employee behavior. Put more simply, a cafeteria plan for compensation permits achievement of greater individual utility from a fixed sum expended for nonmonetary compensation. Opportunity to participate in a cafeteria plan would truly be a "fringe" benefit and might, other things being equal, affect the attraction of candidates. Since other considerations are not often equal, it is unlikely to impact noticeably upon the attraction of candidates. Since most nonmonetary forms of compensation are contingent solely upon membership and are not related to performance, a cafeteria plan cannot be expected to significantly influence employee job performance. Being contingent upon continued membership, a cafeteria plan might influence decisions to remain with the organization, and in the same fashion increase satisfaction of employees. Main effects of a cafeteria form of compensation are likely to be observed in turnover/retention rates rather than in other forms of employee behavior. Even so, it is difficult to assess the likely relationship between cafeteria compensation and turnover rates. Despite the simple logic of a forms of cafeteria compensation plan, the anticipated benefits of such a plan relative to costs of implementation are problematic. They likely will vary considerably from one organization to another. One potential benefit of cafeteria approaches might be the control of benefit costs while permitting realization of individual desires for different benefits. These cost-control implications are worthy of serious study.

Validity of Job Evaluation

Although the process of job evaluation has become reasonably well accepted within employing organizations as a method of developing wage structures, the validity of the approach is challenged by social pressures external to the organization. One such concern relates to inflation and wage spirals as employers rely upon wage surveys to price job evaluation structures. Surveys of wage rates paid by other employers are only that and need not reflect rates dictated by supply and demand considerations. The findings of wage surveys, particularly during periods of high unemployment, ought not to be interpreted as economic market rates, it is argued. Wage increases may be initiated by firms protected from product market competition for reasons other than difficulties in the recruitment of labor; reasons such as maintaining real wages or employee satisfaction. Yet these increases are incorporated into wage survey results and trigger adjustments by other employers. Thus wage rates may increase during periods of high unemployment in response to collective bargaining or social comparison and not because of any need in the attraction of labor supplies.

Job evaluation also is challenged as being biased toward predominantly male jobs and as perpetuating male-female wage differentials (Smith, 1978a, 1978b; Thompsen, 1978). It is noted that different systems of job evaluation typically are employed for managerial jobs (predominantly male) and for clerical jobs (predominantly female) and that these jobs are rarely compared directly in terms of job factors or relative worth. It also is noted that factors more common in traditionally male jobs (physical effort) often are weighted more heavily than factors more common in traditionally female jobs (dexterity), resulting in higher evaluations for the traditionally male jobs. More equitable systems of job evaluation, it can be argued, would employ a common set of factors for the evaluation of all jobs and would avoid assignment of higher evaluations based solely upon characteristics of traditionally male jobs. Current job evaluation systems merely perpetuate past traditions of wage discrimination for women (National Academy of Sciences, 1979).

These criticisms of job evaluation argue, in effect, that while job evaluation ensures "equal pay for identical work," it fails to achieve a goal of "equal pay for work of equal worth,'' and they challenge the market criterion of worth used in the validation of job evaluation. Market rates, it is argued, reflect past discrimination in the form of channeling occupational choices of women, education, and selection, job assignment, and promotion within organizations. A socially justifiable norm of worth is sought to replace the more traditional norm of market rate as measured in wage surveys. An alternative criterion of acceptability already is employed in certain organizations. Thus, for example, many breweries often pay a single rate to all plant jobs, while manufacturing firms more often differentiate among jobs with small, but apparently meaningful, differentials in wages. Where applied, these practices have become traditional and are accepted as just and equitable by the affected employees, although it could be difficult to find validating measures in the surrounding labor markets. Whether or not acceptance of analogous social norms can be achieved within a national society remains to be seen. (SeeOettinger, 1964, for an account of national job evaluation in the Netherlands.)

Wage Compression

Wage compression, in simple terms, relates to the compression of some previously established differential in wages that may have been based upon tenure, skill level, or performance. Any erosion of wage differentials reduces the relative reward associated with the higher paid status, with consequent perceptions of inequity by persons in that higher paid status, and of reduced incentive associated with movement into the higher paid status. One form of compression that has been experienced periodically is occasioned by an escalation of hiring rates in particular occupations, without comparable adjustments of wages for experienced employees in those occupations. Hiring rates for engineers, for example, may escalate by 15 percent in a single year because of competition for engineering graduates, while the compensation for employed engineers increases by a smaller proportion. Wage compression of this form has its most serious equity implications for occupations without clearly differentiable jobs in a promotional or career sequence. Salary progression and not job progression is the only clear reward associated with experience and performance in these occupations. The obvious solution to compression, advancement of all related salaries proportional to increases in hiring rates, often is not feasible. Further, hiring rates often vary in response to short-run market influences and should not be the criterion for overall adjustment of the entire salary structure. Some means for recognizing the worth of experience, other than proportional adjustment of salaries as recruiting rates vary, must be sought in order to maintain perceptions of equity of treatment.

A related form of wage compression is occasioned by inflationary price increases and wage level increases associated with cost of living changes. Whether so-called cost of living adjustments are occasioned by a collective bargaining agreement, employer policy, or adaptation to other employers' wage increases observed in wage surveys, across-the-board increases erode any wage differentials associated with employee performance levels. Wage differentiation according to performance level is common in many organizations, particularly for clerical, technical, and managerial employees. Periodic performance reviews serve as the basis for recommending appropriate wage and salary adjustments within the salary grade for the job. Performance or merit increases lose meaning, however, they significantly exceed cost of living increases. A wage increase of 15 percent provides little recognition for performance if cost of living increases average 12 to 13 percent for the same period. Maintenance of a performance increase and recognition policy becomes difficult with inflationary rates and cost of living increases above 10 percent annually. A merit increase program combined with cost of living adjustments also becomes quite expensive to maintain if, as is common, a merit increase for one year is factored into the base from which increases are determined for the following year. One proposal that has been advanced, but is not yet widely practiced except for executives, is to view performance rewards as bonuses or revertible increases. Increases are granted for a year, but are not factored into any base pay and need not be renewed the following year. This proposal would permit annual recognition of performance at less cost over a period of time. Other innovative proposals are necessary if performance differentials are to be maintained as meaningful during periods of rapid price inflation.

Executive Compensation

Issues in the motivation and compensation of executives, while similar in concept to issues in motivating and compensating other employees, appear in somewhat exaggerated form and attract considerable interest. Executive salaries and other compensation are published annually for public information. Forms of executive compensation and contingency relationships to performance vary considerably over time, giving the impression of fads that come into and go out of style. Performance shares, stock options, performance bonuses, deferred compensation, and perquisites such as automobiles, club memberships, and personal services are among the forms of compensation often provided executives. One might well question the rationale for these various forms of compensation and their changing contingency relationships with performance.

While the amount spent for executive compensation in any organization is relatively small compared with total employee compensation, the performance of executive functions may be critical to organizational performance. The supply of individuals capable of performing executive jobs is relatively limited, and organizations face somewhat more competition in the attraction and retention of executives than is associated with other jobs. Executive jobs also are relatively free of constraints of technology and procedures, thus allowing greater scope for variation in individual performance. Finally, executives' incomes are subject to relatively higher rates of taxation than the incomes of other employees. Executive compensation provisions differ from other employee compensation provisions in terms of a performance contingency relationship and a concern for finding forms of compensation that maximize the after-tax compensation. Because of the potential for variation in individual performance, contingency forms of compensation are common for executives and may amount at times to more than the individual's base salary. Also, because of tax implications, such compensation may take the form of deferred compensation bonuses or capital gains associated with stock options. Nontaxable perquisites, where available, also are utilized more extensively in compensating executives than in compensating other employees.

What may appear as faddism in changing styles of executive compensation may be explained by the ever-changing provisions in the Internal Revenue Code and the inventing of new forms of compensation as older forms are subjected to income taxation. These changing styles also may be explained in terms of the diminishing motivational impact of contingency compensation over time and the need for constant renewal of contingency compensation with alternative rewards. Given the relatively limited market for executives, it is likely that social comparison is a major factor in the attribution of valence to different forms of compensation, and that compensation in the form of relatively new compensation provisions possesses more valence than warranted solely by monetary value. Since executives perform a key role in an organization, it is likely that experimentation with alternative forms and contingency schedules of compensation will continue and that each successive change will elicit positive responses from the affected individuals.

Compensation for Changing Organizational Forms

Traditional compensation programs and practices such as job evaluation and wage surveys were designed for organizations with a reasonably stable technology and structure of jobs. Traditional practices are based upon job descriptions that assume a relatively fixed structuring of tasks and operations in individual jobs. Rates of compensation are based first upon the job and second upon the individual within the job. The assumption that jobs rather than individuals provide the more stable and enduring framework for compensation is being challenged by new forms of work organization. The concept of jobs performed by individuals is giving way to a concept of jobs performed by teams, individual assignments within teams varying considerably among individuals and over time. Matrix and project organizations also challenge the traditional assumptions about jobs insofar as matrix and project assignments are shared among individuals. It was noted earlier how maturity curve compensation was developed for engineers and scientists to replace traditional job-oriented compensation. Similarly, alternative approaches to compensation must be developed for team, matrix, and project organizations.

Compensation criteria for matrix and project organizations tend to reflect both functional competence of the individual and assignment performance measures. An engineer in a project organization, for example, might be compensated on the basis of maturity curve relationships and on the results of specific project assignments. Conceivably some analogous approaches to compensation might be developed for other occupations in a matrix organization, with accountants, personnel representatives, computer programmers, and draftsmen being compensated on some combination of professional and performance criteria. In a sense, people, and not jobs, would be assigned to pay grades, and performance would be compensated within the grade structure. Somewhat similar shifts have been proposed for the compensation of workers on team assignments, teams being compensated on the basis of team performance and individuals on the basis of flexibility within the full range of team assignments.

Perhaps the greatest challenge occasioned by newer developing forms of organizations is the challenge to the concept of the job as the primary basis for compensation. This chapter began with an examination of the relationships between work and compensation, noting that employing organizations seek the outcome of work behavior, not the work behavior itself. For reasons developed earlier, the tendency is to compensate work behavior specified in the form of a job description. As it becomes more difficult to specify work behavior with stable job descriptions, compensation will likely increasingly reflect worker inputs in work behavior, that is, the competencies and skills brought to the employing organization by the worker. The employment contract will refer to worker characteristics, and the behavioral implications of the contract will develop only through employment experience in the organization. As the formal employment contract becomes still more general, greater reliance will be placed upon the process of supervision and management to elicit the specific work behaviors desired over time. Employee compensation will continue as a significant element in the employment contract, but it will serve increasingly to reinforce the overall management process and ought not to be viewed as the primary or dominant element of the employment contract. The wage nexus, while important in an employment relationship, will not be sufficient to attain the desired labor outputs in developing organizations.

CONCLUDING NOTE

Employee compensation is a definitive characteristic of work; among other things, work is behavior performed in anticipation of compensation. Compensation form and amount vary appropriately with variations in the work performed. Viewed either as an incentive or a reward, the variations in compensation are presumed to motivate the related work behavior. Compensation is not the only nor, perhaps, the primary motivational influence on work performance. Other significant influences include nature of the work itself, supervisory style, and social influences of the work group. Given the many motivational influences present in any work setting, it would be unrealistic to expect that compensation might motivate performance in directions contrary to other motivational influences at work. Employee compensation serves best when reinforcing work is consistent with other significant motivational influences on work.

Employee compensation is perhaps best understood when viewed as a significant component in the employment contract, rather than as an independent motivational factor. Variation in the amount and form of compensation is appropriate as other elements of the contract vary. Thus employee compensation will change as occupational and job demands, supervisory style, employee attitudes and values, and organizational norms change in future years. Variations in employee compensation are best viewed as symbolic of a changing employment contract, not as evidence of fad and fashion.

Discussion Questions

1. What are the advantages and disadvantages of each of the following criteria of job worth?
   a. Wage rates paid by other employers
   b. Profit directly attributable to job performance
   c. Length of experience of job incumbents
   d. Level of education of job incumbents

2. How can one rationalize increases in wage rates over time for an occupation which exceed any apparent increases in productivity, e.g., wage increases for teachers while class size remains constant and instructional time decreases?

3. What changes in employee compensation would you recommend to accompany each of the following?
   a. Change from functional to matrix organization
   b. Greater employment of part-time labor force
   c. Change from individual to team assignments
   d. Annual inflation rate of 20 percent

4. What arguments can be made for basing compensation upon: (1) characteristics of the individual, and (2) characteristics of the job performed?

5. What would be the consequences of wage controls that freeze existing differentials among occupations and employers, all being permitted the same annual proportional increase?

CHAPTER TEN

MOTIVATIONAL STRATEGIES

Terence R. Mitchell

Terence R. Mitchell is Professor of Management and Organization and of Psychology at the University of Washington. He received his Ph.D. in Psychology from the University of Illinois at Urbana-Champaign. Professor Mitchell has been an active researcher, and is the author of over fifty journal articles and author or coauthor of three books. He serves as an editorial review consultant to several journals. His research has been funded by such organizations as the Office of Naval Research and the National Science Foundation. In addition to building an excellent research reputation, Professor Mitchell has served as a consultant to numerous organizations on such topics as leadership, motivation, and program evaluation.

The topic of motivation is frequently discussed at both very broad and very specific levels. The more general inquiry includes questions such as "Why is she like that?" or "What motivates him?" The responses to these questions are often put forth in terms of general perspectives about human nature.

At the more specific level are questions about specific behaviors: "What will motivate her to go to work?" or "How can we motivate him to work harder?" The responses to these questions are frequently couched in terms of a more specific analysis—both person-specific and situation-specific. This chapter will discuss both of these levels of inquiry. It will begin with a discussion of general perspectives about human nature. Both organization theory and psychology views will be presented. A description of some of the more specific theories of motivation, including need-based, cognitive, job characteristics, and operant theories, will be reviewed. The chapter concludes with a section that summarizes what has been learned and suggests directions for future research.

PERSPECTIVES ON HUMAN NATURE

Much of the literature from management and psychology that is less technical and more general in nature makes numerous assumptions about human nature. These assumptions may cover the kinds of things people want (e.g., money), the degree to which they want freedom on the job, or the extent to which people are able to change. Over the years, fairly well-articulated positions on these issues have evolved and the debates still go on. The following sections describe some of these positions in more detail.

Management Theory Positions

One can find in the management literature three basic positions on the human nature question (Scott and Hart, 1971). At one extreme is the negative or pessimistic view. Authors holding this position see humans as basically lazy, motivated by money and fear, and needing close supervision. Such assumptions can be found in the fields of political science, the natural and social sciences, as well as economics and management. Hobbes, for example, saw people as motivated by prestige, material goods, and power. People are predisposed toward evil and their life in the natural state is "solitary, poor, nasty, brutish and short." Machiavilli argued that it was better for leaders to be feared than loved and that humans are generally covetous of gain. From natural science, Darwin's view of survival of the fittest suggested a highly competitive, aggressive nature for human beings, and the recent work of many ethologists, such as Robert Ardrey or Desmond Morris, also see the human species as governed by somewhat unflattering drives. Ardrey, for example, describes human beings as predators with an instinct to kill and a genetic affinity for weapons. Freud also saw human beings as driven by internal negative forces: "The primitive, savage and evil impulses of mankind have not vanished in any individual."

In business, these views were readily translated into theories of economics and management. Adam Smith spoke of human beings motivated by self-love and Frederick Taylor saw employees as naturally lazy with a major concern being self-interest expressed in economic terms. Management's charge was to direct and control.

Some authors staked out a more neutral position. In political science, John Locke spoke of the Tabula Rasa and the role of experience in shaping behavior. Some natural scientists, such as Allee, saw cooperation as necessary for survival and many of the neo-Freudians, such as Sullivan and Fromm, emphasized the importance of interpersonal experiences.

In the organizational setting, Elton Mayo argued that human beings have a great potential for change and development. The keys to motivating employees were education, positive social norms, and satisfactory interpersonal relationships. The advocate of the neutral position who has received the most attention is, of course, B. F. Skinner. His early work (e.g., *Walden II*) and his recent writings (e.g., *Beyond Freedom and Dignity*) have suggested a theory of social engineering. People are controlled by their environment. To change behavior one must simply change the contingencies upon which the behavior is dependent. People are neither inherently good nor inherently bad.

The logical extention of this environmental position has been the proliferation of contingency views. These theories argue that one must match people with environments, and that some people and some settings might function best with a controlling managerial philosophy, while other people and settings would be more motivated by participative democracy.

Finally, there are those who suggest a positive perspective. From Cicero to Rousseau, authors have argued that human beings are simple, good, naive, and trusting. They behave badly when they have been externally corrupted.

The organizational proponents of the positive position are numerous. People like McGregor see human beings as good and work as natural. Control stifles development. Chris Argyris is probably the best-known speaker for this position (Argyris, 1962). For years he has written about employees being in a constant state of development toward self-fulfillment. Human beings are seen as needing creativity, a chance for growth and expression, and stimulating jobs.

These three positions vary in at least two major dimensions. First, there is their obvious affective nature. One manages people quite differently, depending upon which of these orientations one believes. And, it might be added, most employees can readily tell which approach pervades the organization. Each of these orientations can often be viewed as an organizational climate.

The second dimension upon which they differ is the degree to which people are seen as preprogrammed. Both the positive and negative positions see an inherent nature for human beings, while the neutral position tends to focus more on the role of the environment. Whether people are regulated by the environment or by something about their basic nature has been debated for a long time in the field of psychology, and it is that literature which will now be surveyed.

Psychology Positions

A closer inspection of the positive-neutral-negative trichotomy seems to raise more questions than answers. The terms *positive* and *negative* are obviously value-laden. Other issues that relate to human nature seem to be less emotionally charged and more relevant for decisions about organizational design. For example, one would like to know how flexible or changeable people actually are. Is their nature fixed or maleable? To what extent can training be used to modify one's behavior? Can people really be changed once they join the organization? An equally important topic that is frequently debated by social scientists is whether the causes of behavior are internal or external events. Those who argue for external events tend to see the environment and immediate situational variables as causes of behavior. Those who believe in internal causes use instincts and personality traits as their explanations. To the degree that internal explanations are true, the organizational processes of selection and placement are crucial. It would be very important to initially select the right type of person and place him or her in the right type of job, since there would be little chance of changing the individual later. If external events are the major cause of behavior, then the proper organizational environment could produce those behaviors deemed to be appropriate.

A related issue deals with the uniqueness of human beings. Are people clearly different from their animal ancestors, or are they guided by and subject to the same urges as animals? Also important is the question of uniqueness among human beings. Exactly how different are individuals from each other? If they are all very different, and if much of their behavior cannot be predicted from simple observations of animal behavior, then an organization must build in flexibility to handle complex, unique human characteristics. However, if they are all the same basically, then everyone can be treated alike (a boon for designers of any system).

The debates over these questions are far from over. They raise some profound philosophical and practical issues. There is, however, some consensus among most social scientists on these topics, and the evidence that led to these positions will be briefly reviewed. The following questions will be addressed:

1. Are human beings unique?
2. How much and what kind of change can occur in people?
3. Are individuals controlled by internal or external processes?

Uniqueness. For most of recorded history, human beings have been seen as unique, as holding a set of characteristics above and apart from those held by animals. Religious thought helped to support this interpretation. Human beings had souls and had a special relationship to God. Darwin, however, changed all of that. Darwin's revolutionary works (*The Origin of the Species,* 1859, and *The Descent of Man,* 1871) argued that human beings were like other animals and that similar laws of selection, evolution, and even higher mental processes were the same for human beings and animals. This position argues against uniqueness and it has been recently reasserted by writers such as Ardrey, Morris, and others. In most cases, as mentioned, these authors present a generally negative view of human nature. This view suggests that the human race will continue to have wars, injustice, greed, and aggression because of basic urges. Humans are not unique; they are highly evolved apes.

There are numerous critics of this position. They point out the simple fact that because certain behaviors seem to be similar across species does not necessarily mean that the motivation for that behavior or its consequences are also similar across species. The simple fact that similar words or labels are used to describe the behavior (e.g., aggression) does not mean that the explanations are the same. Additional information is needed to show that the behaviors have the same underlying cause and biological function.

There are also some areas of human behavior that seem to be unique to the species. First, and most obvious, is language development. People's ability to use linguistic symbols is not found elsewhere. While it is probably true that many animals communicate with one another, there is little evidence that they can make known anything more than very simple emotional reactions.

Recently, there has been some research that has shown that chimpanzees can learn a rudimentary form of sign language. These chimps, if continuously trained from an early age, can learn about one hundred different signs and can string them together in sentence-like sequences. However, the sort of language sophistication reached by the best of these apes is little beyond what is expected from a three-year-old child. One can conclude that while language development may not be completely unique, it is many magnitudes more sophisticated than that illustrated by the best of animals.

There are also some differences in the way that people adjust to their environment. Human beings clearly control and manipulate their environments in ways that facilitate adaptation. For most species, an inhospitable environment meant a change in the species or death. Human beings, on the other hand, will change the environment to suit their needs. This is a basic difference, which in many respects can be seen as the reason humans have survived and prospered as a species. Again, while there is evidence that some animals can use rudimentary tools (e.g., chimpanzees), the difference between human beings and animals on this dimension is great.

Where does this lead with respect to the uniqueness of the human race? As usual, a position somewhere between the two extremes seems to be most widely held. While it is true that animal ancestry may have more to do with current behavior than previously believed, it is also true that there are certain dimensions that clearly differentiate the human species from others. It is these dimensions of language, control, and adaptability that compound human complexity. An understanding of animal behavior will not be sufficient to understand human behavior.

Possibilities for Change. One often hears the saying, "You can't teach an old dog new tricks" with reference to human beings. The essence of this statement is that with age, people become more rigid and more fixed in their behavior patterns and habits. It becomes increasingly difficult to learn new skills and behaviors.

The implications for organizations are obvious. Most organizations need and desire some degree of flexibility, especially in the current complex, rapidly changing environment. Yet, there is some reason to believe that older, more senior, people (who probably hold more responsible positions) are less flexible than other younger employees. If this is true, organizations may be placing the people with the least flexibility in those positions where flexibility is needed most. The homily about old dogs and new tricks needs to be thoroughly examined.

Evidence from a number of sources suggests that people do, in fact, become more rigid with age. Personality traits, if firmly imbedded and learned at an early age, would limit change, as would also be suggested by much of the literature on cognitive consistency. These consistency approaches argue that people build up elaborate value, belief, and attitude systems that are internally consistent, and hard to change. Finally, people tend to have the same friends and family, over time, who are usually similar in many ways and supportive of their behavior. One also selectively exposes himself or herself to information and other people who reinforce one's point of view. Thus, there are many forces limiting change.

The evidence may seem to suggest that it is, in fact, hard to teach an old dog new tricks. There are both personal and environmental pressures that reduce change and increase constancy. But before closing the debate, one should examine these issues further. What, in fact, can the organization do? It is unlikely that most organizations will be able to change the basic personality structure of their employees. On the other hand, management does have some control over the organizational environment. Rules, regulations, policies, rewards, chains of command, and other formal aspects of the organization's structure can be modified. Communication lines can be influenced, as well as the type of people who are selected to join the organization. Some social aspects of the situation can be controlled.

The crucial question then becomes ''Which is the most important determinant of behavior—the internal personal characteristics of the individual or the outside environment?'' If the answer is personal characteristics, then there probably is little that can be done in organizations, where people do not even enter the situation until their late teens or early twenties. If the answer is the environment, however, there is much that can be done. The next section examines this debate in more detail.

Internal vs. External Determinants of Behavior.   As pointed out earlier, both the positive and negative positions described in the management literature see human beings as having a basic nature, while the neutral position sees learning and experience as the causes of behavior. In psychology, the argument has been between what might be described as internal causes of behavior (e.g., instincts, personality traits) and external causes (the environment). Over the years, the shift of opinion has generally been away from the internal position to the external position, but not completely. The debate goes as follows.

First, early in the century, instincts were seen as the predominant cause of behavior. Further research, however, suggested that very few behaviors are somehow preprogrammed. Most people see some broad developmental patterns as part of the human condition, but specific actions and behaviors are mostly learned. A second, somewhat less extreme, internal position was that personality traits cause behavior. It is argued that patterns of behavior are learned at an early age and are persistent across time and situations. Therefore, a person who is shy in one situation should be shy in all situations. The environmentalist says, on the other hand, that someone can be shy in one setting and extroverted in another; it all depends on the demands of the situation.

Recently, there have been some summaries of studies that examine both positions. These papers review research where both personality variables and situational variables are simultaneously measured and observed as determinants of behavior (e.g., Sarason, Smith, and Diener, 1975). The results support both positions, but are more supportive of the environmentalist point of view. While personality traits do seem to be useful for predicting behavior across settings, the situational variables do about twice as well. The obvious conclusion is that both personality and situational variables must be taken into account in order to explain an individual's behavior.

The third and final internal versus external argument is between behaviorist and cognitive points of view. The strict behaviorist believes in environmental determinism: Almost all behavior is caused by past and present environmental events. To understand one's behavior, all one has to know is the individual's past responses to similar stimulus situations and the rewards or punishments that followed that response. There is no reference to internal cognitive events such as attitudes, beliefs, or values as causes of behavior.

The cognitive viewpoint says that, yes, the environment is important as are past rewards and punishments, but it is cognitive interpretations (e.g., evaluations, memories, expectations) that actually cause one's behavior. The behaviorist model might best be represented as a stimulus-response model (S-R model), and the cogntive model, by a stimulus-organism-response model (S-O-R model). Both approaches see learning and the environment as having a major impact on behavior. However, the cognitive position says that there is an intermediate step between the external environmental stimulus and the response. This intermediate step is the cognitive processing and evaluation of the environment. While both approaches might make similar predictions about how an individual would behave, their explanation for the behavior would be very different.

Again, one finds that the position held by most social scientists is not the extreme point of view. Most of them would reject the idea that behavior can be completely explained by external environmental events and contingencies. There is ample evidence that in some cases cognitive events are better predictors of behavior.

An examination of all of these questions shows that certain positions seem to cluster together. Some people believe that behavior is mostly caused by instincts and personality traits that are formed at an early age. They think that change is very difficult for the individual and that one's capacity is severely limited. Some schools of thought still hold these views today. The opposite position is that behavior is mostly learned through interactions with the environment, that current events rather than past events are important, and that, even though there are some limitations on capacities, people are capable of great amounts of change (see Crawford, 1979, for a discussion of these issues).

While these issues are far from settled, one thing is clear. There is an overwhelming consensus that the environment has a much greater effect on behavior than was once believed. The implications for organizations are important. It means that large areas of human behavior are modifiable. Organizational design, training, and development can have a profound impact on the behavior of the members of an organization. Thus, it becomes imperative that one understands the specific processes of motivation in organizational settings.

BASIC MOTIVATIONAL QUESTIONS

The review of motivation, as described in a general sense, has drawn an interesting picture. Human beings are probably influenced fairly extensively by their environment. They are unique in some ways, but generally governed by some common psychological and physiological processes, and they are capable of great but not infinite change. These points suggest a somewhat neutral perspective on the question of underlying predispositions. And they are encouraging in that, to the degree that organizations can change environments and rewards, people's behavior can be influenced and changed. This summary leads to an attempt to define motivation in a more specific sense within an organizational context.

Motivation in Organizations

Upon observing people at work, one is frequently struck by their different styles or work habits. Some people are always on time, put in a good day's work, and stay late. Others are less punctual and tend to get through the day with a minimal amount of effort.

Some investigators have estimated that the best employee may be two to three times as productive as the worst employee. Part of this difference may stem from styles, some from skills, and some from attitudes the employee brings to the task. The tendency, however, is to attribute some of the differences between these two extremes to skill. That is, one says that the employee with poor performance simply does not have the ability. But there is something more than that. There also seems to be a willfulness about the difference. The employee with excellent performance seems to want to do well, while performance may seem irrelevant to the marginal employee. In this instance, one usually refers to motivation. It is suggested that one individual is more motivated or driven than the other person (Lawler, 1973).

Thus, motivation is partly inferred from performance. In behavioral terms, it is often seen as the effort one exerts. In psychological terms, it is frequently described as wanting or intending to do well. One of the first questions that needed to be solved was to ascertain to what extent performance was in fact influenced by effort or by ability.

Motivation and Performance

Knowing that numerous factors, including motivation, were important for predicting performance led a number of writers to postulate what these factors were and how they combined. Vroom (1964), for example, suggested the following formula:

Performance = f(Ability × Motivation)

The postulated relationship is multiplicative, which implies that both ability and motivation must be high for good performance. If either component is low or zero, performance will be low. According to Vroom, one must exert a great deal of effort and be able to do it correctly in order for performance to be high.

A book by Porter and Lawler (1968) added a third factor to the equation. They argue that performance is a joint function of effort, ability, and role perceptions. This latter variable is concerned with the norms and specifications of what one was supposed to do. Not only does one have to work hard and be skillful to perform well, but one has to know what to do.

An evaluation of the research on these various factors suggests that the assessment of skill or ability factors has outdistanced the understanding of the motivational factor. In a paper entitled ''Performance Equals Ability and What,'' Marvin Dunnette concluded, ''ability differences still are empirically the most important determiners of differences in job performance'' (Dunnette, 1973, p. 22). There is still little idea about how and in exactly what way motivation combines with other variables to contribute to performance.

It should be pointed out that, while the preceding analysis has not led to a complete understanding of exactly how motivation was related to performance, it did increase the recognition of two important points. First, motivation is only one of a set of factors that contributes to good performance. It is necessary but not sufficient. The reason that it seems to be such a major focus of attention is that most writers feel that somehow motivation is easier to influence than abilities or traits. Motivation is somehow under the control of the individual and can be strongly influenced by the environment. Thus, changing motivation is seen as an easier route to good performance than changing traits or abilities.

A second point, which is less widely recognized, is that *the contribution made by motivation to task performance varies over tasks, settings, and people.* Some tasks have a high ability component (e.g., computer programmer), while others are more dependent upon effort (e.g., delivering mail). The crucial point here is that, for some tasks and some people, influencing effort will make little difference in performance. This point will be returned to later in the chapter.

Areas of Study

Given the more limited view of the role of motivation in understanding task performance, one can now turn to a discussion of what is known about motivation in organizations. But, before reviewing the specific theories and their empirical support, some preliminary distinctions are necessary. The focus of most motivational research is to understand two psychological processes: arousal and choice. When speaking of arousal, one is dealing with the question of why one does anything at all. What gets one going? Why does one initiate action? The second process, choice, occurs after one is aroused. Given that people are active and seeking some goal, why do they attempt to do one thing rather than another? What are the determinants of one's choice of action? So, the concern is with what activates people, and after they are active why they choose the particular behaviors that they do.

The earliest ideas about what motivates people dealt with choice behavior. The writings of Greek philosophers, and later the work of the British philosophers John Stuart Mill and Jeremy Bentham, were focused on this issue. The underlying idea, called hedonism, was that people behave in a fashion that will maximize their pleasure. They do what they do because they believe that what they do will give them more pleasure than anything else they might do. However, since these authors never attempted to assess just what people anticipated to be the consequences of their acts, the theory was of little use empirically. That is, it did little to further an understanding of how these choices came to be more or less favorable.

Further developments in the choice area began to shed some light on the answers to this question. First, it was argued that of several responses an individual makes to a situation, those that result in satisfying or pleasurable consequences are strengthened. Those that lead to uncomfortable or unpleasant outcomes are weakened. Those that are strengthened become more probable, and those that are weakened become less probable in response to the same situation. Present choices were explained in terms of past consequences. People choose a given alternative today because in the past this alternative led to more favorable consequences than any other alternative. However, this "law of effect," as it was called, still did little to explain why the consequences were pleasurable or not pleasurable.

The explanation of why the individual behaves at all (arousal), and consequently why responses are more or less pleasurable, was tied to the idea of physiological needs. The individual was seen as having hunger, thirst, and other drives, and pleasure resulted from reduction of these drives. At this point, the law of effect or reinforcement would become important.

A simple example might help. A child is aroused by the drive of hunger. There are physiological cues and internal cues that trigger the arousal (such as a rumbling stomach). At first, perhaps, the child reacted to these cues by randomly moving around, crying, and generally trying out a whole set of behaviors. Magically, after one set of these actions, some food appears. Those activities that immediately preceded the presentation of the food (and the reduction of the need) would become strengthened. That is, they would be more likely to occur the next time the child was hungry, since they have been positively reinforced. Over time, rather strong links between behavior and anticipated outcomes are created and what are called "habits" are established. The following list shows a simple representation of these relationships:

Basic Motivational Questions

1. Question of arousal. Physiological or social needs and drives cause arousal.
2. Question of choice. Behavior likely to lead to most positive outcomes is chosen.

In an analysis of most organizational theories of motivation, one finds that they can be easily categorized into two approaches. Those theories that attempt to specify and codify the drives that motivate people are concerned with arousal. Those that try to describe people's choice behavior will be designated as choice theories. Although this distinction is not clear for every theory, it points out quite nicely the differences stressed here so far.

There are, however, rather major differences in opinion within each of these camps. There are arguments over which needs are most important, and there are some writers who have attempted to generate comprehensive classifications of needs. These latter approaches attempt to specify when and under what circumstances certain needs will be motivating.

Within the choice arena, there are people who argue that there are very different types of underlying processes governing the relationship of outcomes to behavior. Some writers suggest that obtaining a goal is most important or that being treated fairly is the key, while others advance theories based more directly on rewards and the value of these rewards.

There is also controversy and disagreement across these two broad categories. Some writers have argued that need-based approaches are mostly irrelevant for understanding motivation (Salancik and Pfeffer, 1977, 1978) and that information processing or social interaction models hold more promise. Some of these issues will be discussed at the end of the chapter. But first, the different approaches and the extent of their support should be reviewed.

THEORIES OF MOTIVATION: AROUSAL

This section describes those theories that have attempted to explain the arousal process. Theories of individual needs are discussed first. Classification systems of needs are then reviewed, and finally some new directions in this area are presented.

Individual Needs

There are at least four individual needs that have received extensive research attention and recognition: competence and curiosity, achievement, affiliation, and power.

Competence and Curiosity. A now classic paper by Robert W. White (1959) stated the evidence for what he called a need for competence. Animals and human beings show a desire to master their environment and this mastery is pleasurable and independent of outside rewards. White argues that all organisms must learn to interact successfully with their environment, and that this behavior is a combination of both instinctual and learned drives. This motive is supposedly aroused when individuals are faced by new challenging situations and dissipates after repeated mastery of the task. The obvious implications for job design are that challenging jobs are motivating in themselves, and that if enough variability is present the competence motive may be maintained.

A highly related set of motives is described as curiosity, or activity motives. Early animal research discovered that organisms seemed to enjoy activity and exploration for their own sake. Rats will prefer places filled with objects to an empty box, and monkeys will persist in solving puzzles for many days without any contingent rewards. Children, when given control of what can be shown on a television, will choose complex stimuli over simple ones (Smock and Holt, 1962; Miles, 1958).

Research on adults shows similar findings. One well-known study had college students placed in a darkened room that was partially sound-deadened. They wore opaque goggles and gloves to reduce other sensations. They were provided with a cot and food. Almost none of the subjects could endure the lack of stimulation more than two days, and numerous examples of hallucinations were reported (Bexton, Heron, and Scott, 1954).

In studies in organizational settings, similar findings are available. People develop negative attitudes toward highly repetitive tasks and report experiencing fatigue and boredom. They increase their work breaks and attempt to vary their environment (Scott, 1969).

Theoretical explanations are available for these kinds of motives. Berlyne (1967) has argued that people become adapted to certain levels of stimulation. Slight discrepancies from this level appear to be pleasurable, but large deviations are noxious and prompt a person to reduce the discrepancy. Given this type of rationale, one would expect people to differ in terms of their adaptation levels and, therefore, in the attractiveness of stimulus variability on the job. In fact, research by Bills (1923) many years ago suggested that this may be the case. Highly complex jobs were pleasant for bright people, but caused high rates of turnover for people who were less intelligent. The reverse was true for highly repetitive jobs. If one believes that intelligence is partly related to one's preference for complex stimuli, then Bill's evidence is supportive of the adaptation idea.

The Achievement Motive. Perhaps the most thoroughly researched individual motive is the achievement motive. David McClelland (1961) is most closely connected with this work and has developed a rather comprehensive theory around the need for achievement (nAch). He suggests, first of all, that people differ in their need for achievement and that this need is illustrated in their writing and behavior. His technique for assessing nAch is the Thematic Apperception Test (TAT), which presents the subject with an ambiguous picture and asks for his or her interpretation of what is happening in the picture. Achievement-related themes are counted and the subject's score supposedly reflects the individual's desire for high achievement.

The behavioral characteristics of high achievers have also been investigated. First of all, they tend to prefer moderate risks to situations where there is no risk or where the risk is very high. Situations where outcomes are left to chance, such as gambling, are avoided. A second major characteristic of high achievers is that they like immediate feedback. They desire to know how they are doing, and will tend to gravitate to jobs where there is frequent assessment on fairly specific performance criteria (e.g., sales or certain management positions). Finally, high achievers seem to enjoy doing a task simply for the sake of accomplishment. Task completion provides intrinsic rewards and money is desired only as a measure of excellence, not as a provider of material wealth. Because of this interest in accomplishment, the high achiever is frequently involved with the task and may be seen as "task oriented." Hall (1976) has presented data showing that high-need achievement managers are characterized by candor, openness, sensitivity, and receptivity. They tend to use a participative leadership style and find meaning in their work. Low-need achievement managers, on the other hand, see work as less central and are more secretive and insensitive than those with high need for achievement.

How does one become a high achiever? McClelland suggests that child-rearing practices are most important. Children who are fairly independent, but have parents who provide clear expectations and feedback (preferably physical rewards such as hugging), develop into high achievers. But McClelland also believes that adults are changeable and can acquire greater nAch. He has developed a comprehensive training program designed to increase achievement motivation and has tested it in numerous settings.

The theory has been developed on a broader scope than individual behavior. McClelland feels that the productivity of whole cultures and societies can be predicted from the degree to which the population illustrates a need for achievement. He cites historical examples of analyzing the major written works of a culture for nAch. He reports that societies that exhibit high nAch will later experience economic growth and prosperity. Countries low on nAch will face economic decline.

Thus, there are two major propositions: first, that the productivity of a firm or country can be tied to the nAch of its members and second, that people can increase their nAch through training. Some empirical support for these hypotheses has also been presented. Warner and Rubin (1969) reported that company growth rates of a number of technically based firms in the Boston area were predictable from nAch scores and similar findings were reported for small firms in India.

In a series of studies, McClelland and his colleagues attempted to increase nAch through various training procedures. They report that, in a number of cases, those who were trained experienced subsequent entrepreneurial success and were more active in stimulating business growth and in new economic ventures. A recent paper reviews this research and its implications (McClelland, 1978).

Affiliation Motive.   In contrast to nAch, not much research has been conducted on the motive to affiliate with others. Harlow's (1958) research with monkeys suggested that people have some sort of innate need for contact. He provided two surrogate mothers, one of wire and the other of cloth. Even though half of the monkeys were fed from the wire mother (by means of a bottle inserted in the wire), almost all of the monkeys preferred to cling to the terry-cloth mother. If one believes in physiological drive reduction as the explanation of behavior, then either mother should have been equally attractive. However, it appears from Harlow's research that monkeys develop an attachment to their mothers based partly on contact comfort.

Another series of studies by Schachter (1959) showed that people who were anticipating some stressful situations (e.g., an experiment where they might be shocked) preferred to wait with others, especially if the other person was facing the same stress. There is some sociological literature about how people tend to congregate together during a crisis. Reports from combat situations indicate that soldiers frequently bunch up during a battle, which may be exactly what the enemy wants. There are also a number of organizational case studies that discuss similar problems. The classic example is the systems expert who rearranges all the desks in the office in such a way that productivity should be greatly increased. However, in the process, the employees' ability to communicate with each other is also severely restricted. And rather than increases, productivity decreases are observed.

To date, however, very little research has been specifically conducted on this motive. McClelland has a measure of need for affiliation, but the nAch results are far more substantial. Part of the problem is that affiliation is so complex, and it is hard to separate out the factors. One cannot be sure whether someone seeks out the comfort of another for stimulation, status, love, or simply to be with someone else. Thus, while this motive may be important, it is hard to isolate.

Power.   The research on the need for power has had a recent revival. This reappearance has come from a number of sources. First, there has been a number of popular books advocating the use of power to get ahead in organizations. This literature argues that one needs to be assertive and "go for it" to be successful in organizations. While these prescriptions are definitely not scientifically based, they do have some descriptive information suggesting that people who aspire to power frequently get it and are successful because of it.

There has been an extensive research program conducted by Kipnis (1976) which describes what sort of power is used most frequently in organizations and what the effects of power use are (Kipnis and Cosentino, 1969; Wilkinson and Kipnis, 1978). The discussion of power as a need has been most prominently presented by McClelland. In one paper, McClelland (McClelland and Burnham, 1976) reviewed this work and suggested that effective managers frequently have a high need for power. These managers are characterized by a preference for influencing others over being liked, but this need is tempered by social norms of restraint and goal commitment. That is, people with high need for power are successful only if that need is accompanied by a commitment to organizational goals.

In summary, a number of individual motives seem to affect people's behaviors. In general, it is presumed that these motives are dispositional characteristics—they are similar to traits in that they are seen as consistent over time and settings, fairly hard to change, and learned at an early age. The problem has been that different people seem to have different degrees of these needs at different times in their lives, as well as differences when comparing one another at any given time. A part of the response to this problem was the development of motive classification systems.

Motive Classification Systems

There have been a number of major approaches to classifying needs and they are described below.

Maslow's Hierarchy of Needs.   The first major attempt to classify needs relevant to organizational behavior was produced by Abraham Maslow (1954). His formulation suggested that people have a prepotency of needs: some needs were more important than others, and those that were initially most important had to be satisfied before the other needs could serve as motivators. He postulated that there were five need categories, and they are ordered below in terms of their prepotency or importance.

1. Physiological needs. Fulfillment of thirst, hunger, and sex drives.
2. Safety needs. The freedom from fear of external harm, climatic extremes, or criminal activity.
3. Belonging needs. The desire for affection and caring relationships; personal liking and support from others.
4. Esteem needs. The respect and positive evaluation of one's peers and associates. Status and recognition are major factors.
5. Self-actualization. The opportunity to fulfill one's basic potential—to become more like one's natural self.

There are a number of specific elements of this theory that need elaboration. First, Maslow argues that this category system holds for most normal, healthy people. It is not necessarily applicable to everyone. Second, while the idea of prepotency is important, it is not entirely rigid. More specifically, while Maslow would have argued that love needs must be fulfilled before esteem needs begin to operate as motivators, he would probably not have argued that the love needs had to be 100 percent fulfilled. The general idea is that the greater the fulfillment of a particular need, the less it serves as a motivator.

A final point is that in American society the physiological and safety needs play a relatively minor role for most people. Only the severely deprived and handicapped are dominated by these lower-order needs. The obvious implication for organization theorists is that higher-order needs should be better motivators than lower-order ones. This fact seems to be supported by surveys that ask employees about what motivates them on the job (Porter, 1964).

Unfortunately, the empirical research that specifically tests Maslow's theory has shown only limited support for some aspects of his theory (Alderfer, 1969; Wahba and

Bridwell, 1973). The ordering suggested by Maslow is perhaps more flexible and less specific than he originally suggested. Employees seem to be able to readily distinguish between rather broad categories of higher- and lower-order needs. Managers, for example, seem to prefer self-actualization and esteem motivators to love and safety rewards. But there is very little evidence to support the specific five-category system.

The prepotency idea has also been criticized (Alderfer, 1969; Wahba and Bridwell, 1973). It is not clear that fulfillment of one need automatically means that the next higher-order need is activated as a motivator. Also, it has not been shown that deficient needs are necessarily important ones. Thus, some of the specific dynamics of the theory have received minimal support.

But the impact of this approach should not be dismissed. Maslow's hierarchy was the first clear statement that management should recognize the importance of higher-order needs. The emphasis began to shift the attention of organization theorists from the more traditional lower-order motivators (pay, promotion, hours of work) to higher-order motivators (autonomy, responsibility, challenge). This was an important contribution to management thought.

A second implication is that people will be at different levels of the hierarchy at different times. Managers must be aware of individual differences in reward preferences. What will motivate one subordinate may not motivate another. Different people want different things, and managers must be sensitive to these needs if they want to motivate their subordinates.

Alderfer's ERG Theory. One recent modification of Maslow's ideas has been presented by Alderfer (1972). He postulates that there are three main categories of needs: existence, relatedness, and growth. The parallel with Maslow's theory is shown in Table 10–1. Alderfer's approach, while keeping the basic higher-order and lower-order need distinction, does not include any reference to prepotency of needs or to the idea that deprivation leads to activation. Both higher-order and lower-order needs can serve as motivators. In some cases, once a higher-order need is satisfied, people may be motivated by lower-order needs. Also, all the needs may be active to given degrees at any specific time. A need may never cease to be a motivator, and, in fact, Alderfer suggests that growth needs may increase in intensity the more they are satisfied.

While the empirical data seem to fit Alderfer's ideas a little more closely than Maslow's, there has been little research designed to specifically test it. However, the basic higher-order and lower-order need classification is still apparent, and it is this idea which should be emphasized.

TABLE 10–1
Maslow and Alderfer Need Classification Systems

	Lower-Level Needs		*Higher-Level Needs*		
Maslow	Physiological	Safety	Love	Esteem	Actualization
Alderfer	Existence		Relatedness		Growth

Related Approaches. While not specifically designed as need classification approaches, there are two other major motivational theories that fit nicely with the higher- and lower-order-needs idea. An early statement on the topic of management was made by McGregor (1960). His argument is that there seem to be two distinct and different approaches to management and motivation. The first, called Theory X, assumes that people are motivated by lower-order needs, while the second, Theory Y, advocates the use of higher-order needs. Table 10–2 summarizes some of McGregor's points.

It is easy to see the similarities between Maslow's hierarchy and McGregor's analysis. Both researchers place a strong emphasis on the higher-order needs and argue that organizational scientists have been remiss in their frequent dependence upon Theory X or lower-order need incentives.

The last approach that can be seen partly as a need classification system was developed by Herzberg (1966). The emphasis of this approach is on those rewards in the organization that are related to job satisfaction and job dissatisfaction. Herzberg suggests that organizational rewards can be broken down into two categories, the motivators and the hygienes, which are listed below:

Hygienes

1. Monetary rewards
2. Competent supervision
3. Policy and administration
4. Working conditions
5. Security

Motivators

1. Achievement
2. Recognition
3. Responsibility
4. Advancement

Herzberg argues that the hygienes are related to job dissatisfaction, while the motivators are related to satisfaction. More specifically, the theory suggests that having all the hygienes present at an acceptable level will produce a neutral feeling about the job—it is almost as if they were expected. Of course, if hygienes are at an unacceptable level, dissatisfaction will occur. On the other hand, if management really wants moti-

TABLE 10–2
McGregor's Approach

	Theory X	*Theory Y*
Management's role	Organizing, directing.	Organizing, directing.
	Emphasis on control, coercion, and punishment.	Emphasis on growth, autonomy, and reward.
View of human nature	People are lazy, lack ambition, like to be led, and are motivated strictly by personal economic concerns.	People by nature enjoy work, want to do well, and are motivated by self-control and self-development.

vated and turned-on employees, they should use the motivators. It is this factor that will produce high job satisfaction. The relationships are shown below.

Dissatisfied $\xrightarrow{\text{hygienes}}$ Neutral $\xrightarrow{\text{motivators}}$ Satisfied

Since much of the job satisfaction research defines satisfaction as the extent to which job-related needs are fulfilled, the inference is that hygiene rewards or outcomes satisfy what would be called lower-order needs. The motivators, on the other hand, satisfy higher-order needs. It is these latter types of needs that Herzberg argues are frequently unfulfilled in today's organizations.

The controversy over the support for Herzberg's ideas has been intense. The theory has been extensively tested and reviews of the research are available (House and Wigdor, 1967). In general, the evidence against the theory seems to be greater than the evidence for it. The theory suffers, first of all, from its assumptions that the motivator and hygiene factors operate in the same fashion for everyone. This statement is simply not true. The second area of skepticism is about the methods used to gather the data. Herzberg originally used the "critical incident" technique to generate his theory. This technique requires employees to indicate specific incidents that they felt were related to their satisfaction or dissatisfaction with their job. Validation studies using this technique have generally supported the theory, while other techniques have not (Schneider and Locke, 1971). The theory, therefore, appears somewhat method bound.

In spite of these criticisms, Herzberg's theory was responsible for some major contributions to the understanding of motivation. First, the theory took some of Maslow's ideas and attempted to apply them to the work setting. His emphasis on the role of job content factors had been neglected by other theorists. His applications of job enrichment principles are perhaps too simplistic, but they have had a major impact on managerial practices. Overall, then, his additional refinements have considerably improved the knowledge of the conditions most likely to lead to job satisfaction.

In summary, the hierarchical concept has played an important role in theory and practice. Its appeal is obvious. If true, it would suggest what sorts of organizational rewards will be the most efficient motivators for employees at different levels and how this will change throughout one's professional career. While it came up short of providing all that was originally suggested, it has helped to clarify why different people are motivated by different rewards and what is the content of these rewards.

New Directions

In a recent *Annual Review of Psychology* chapter, this writer had the opportunity to review the motivation research from 1975 to 1978 (Mitchell, 1979). One of the most striking conclusions reached in that review was that need-based approaches to motivation have been declining in importance, as indicated by the very few articles that have been published on this topic. This diminished interest has come from two sources. First, the empirical work on individual needs or on categories of needs has not been very impressive. The amount of variance controlled in performance by factors such as need for achievement is fairly low. This fact has led many researchers to include needs as a contingency factor or moderator variable in motivational theories. Needs have assumed a secondary role.

The second set of criticisms is more basic. Authors like Salancik and Pfeffer (1977, 1978) have questioned the utility of the concept of need. Their argument is that social processes and current information cues are much better predictors of behavior. Both of these viewpoints have led to the development of some new ways of looking at the question of arousal.

Needs Combined with Other Factors.   One of the most prominent new approaches to motivation, which still includes some reference to needs, is the job characteristics model developed by Hackman and Oldham (1975, 1976). These authors argue that characteristics of the job cause various psychological states and that these states are the causes of motivation and performance. Figure 10-1 presents their model. It should be noted that individual needs for growth (called "growth need strength") moderates the posited relationships. Growth needs are seen as causing arousal and the job inputs supposedly will have an impact on the psychological states, and hence performance, if this arousal is high. Thus, enriched jobs (jobs with much variety, identity, significance,

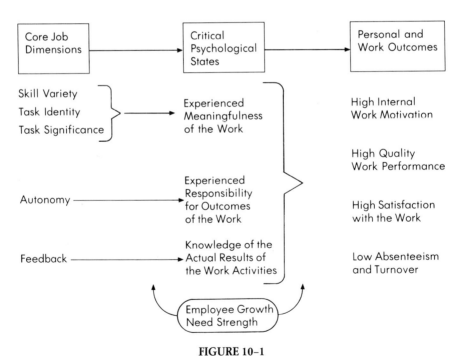

FIGURE 10-1
The Hackman and G. R. Oldham Job Characteristics Model

Source: J. R. Hackman and G. R. Oldham. "The Job Diagnostic Survey: An Instrument for the Diagnosis of Jobs and the Evaluation of Job Redesign Projects." *Journal of Applied Psychology* 60 (1975): 161. Copyright 1975 by the American Psychological Association. Reprinted by permission.

autonomy, and feedback) will have a motivating effect only on people with high growth needs.

The research using this model has provided mixed support (e.g., Hackman, Pearce, and Wolfe, 1978; Evans, Kiggunda, and House, 1979; Umstot, Bell, and Mitchell, 1976). In general, the findings seem to suggest that job enrichment has a more powerful impact on satisfaction than performance and on quality of work rather than quantity. The moderating effect of growth needs is stronger for the satisfaction criterion than for performance, and generally weak when apparent at all. A fair conclusion would probably be that the major contribution of the model is its emphasis on the task characteristics of enrichment and the intervening psychological states that enhance motivation, rather than the emphasis on growth needs.

Other Explanations of Arousal.   Two other recent approaches to arousal have been suggested. The first is based on the concept of consistency. Based on earlier work in the area of consistency, Korman (1976) has suggested that arousal is a function of the inconsistency of beliefs about oneself and one's job and self-esteem.

Korman argues that people choose an occupation, effort levels, friends, and interpersonal behaviors based upon the consistency between their perceptions of their self-esteem and the demands of a job or the expectations of their friends. For example, for people with high self-esteem, there should be consistency between (1) the characteristics of the person and his or her chosen occupation, (2) task success and satisfaction, (3) perceived similarity of others and liking for others, and (4) measured abilities and job performance. For example, Inkson (1978) has recently shown that intrinsic satisfaction is correlated with performance for people with high self-esteem, but unrelated for people with low self-esteem. Self-esteem, it should be added, is only partially defined as a personality variable; Korman also sees immediate situational factors, such as task success or others' expectations, as part of the definition of self-esteem. Korman's 1976 paper presents a good review of the theory and its empirical support, and Dipboye (1977) and Korman (1977) have presented a debate on some criticisms of the theory.

The important point to note about Korman's approach is that arousal is caused by inconsistency and that the main factors causing arousal are current perceptions of the job, one's success, and so on. This approach can be easily contrasted with earlier need-based approaches that suggested needs were developed early in life and that people were locked into a progression of needs.

The second, new explanation of arousal has been based on social cues and, more specifically, the idea of social facilitation (Ferris, Beehr, and Gilmore, 1978). The early work on social facilitation simply argued that the presence of others caused arousal, which prompted the use of dominant responses (Zajonc, 1965). Cottrell (1972) modified this explanation by suggesting that the arousal was caused partly by evaluation apprehension. That is, people are aroused by the presence of others because they feel they are being evaluated by them.

Research on this idea has gone in a variety of directions. First, White, Mitchell, and Bell (1977) were able to demonstrate that evaluation apprehension did indeed result in higher performance than when there was no evaluation apprehension, and that this effect was *independent* of goals (set or not set) and social cues given off by co-workers (positive versus negative). The second direction of research has focused on the social cues given off by others.

The White, Mitchell, and Bell (1977) study also showed that a supportive co-worker could stimulate higher performance from a subject than a negative co-worker. Tying this to social facilitation and evaluation apprehension suggests that the employee (1) is aroused by the presence of others, (2) wishes to be evaluated favorably by others, and (3) is therefore influenced by and conforms to the wishes or opinions of salient co-workers. Recently, there have been three studies that were specifically designed to test whether social cues about the pleasantness of a job were better predictors of a worker's evaluation of that job than the actual characteristics of the job itself (Weiss and Shaw, 1979; O'Reilly and Caldwell, 1979; White and Mitchell, 1979). The designs were similar in that all three studies had enriched/unenriched conditions and positive/negative cues given off by co-workers. The job evaluations in all three studies were significantly affected by social cues, and, in some cases, the social cues controlled more variance in these evaluations than did the enrichment conditions. Social cues are salient and have powerful effects on attitudes and behavior.

Summary and Implications

The research on need-based approaches has generally been deemphasized in current motivational work. The use of single motives, like need for achievement or growth-need strength, has not generated wide support, either as a major predictor of performance or as a moderator (White, 1978). Motive classification systems helped to recognize important organizational rewards that had been deemphasized, and led to an emphasis on job enlargement and job enrichment. But the specific prescriptions of these classification systems are seen today as being of mainly historical importance.

Instead, the study of arousal has shifted to a more present, cognitive-based approach. For example, instead of assessing some general "growth need," Cherrington and England (1980) have shown that simply asking employees "Do you want an enriched job?" is a better predictor of employees' responses to enrichment. The research on social cues based on social facilitation and evaluation apprehension has reached similar conclusions. Arousal is perhaps better understood by looking at current informational cues and social conditions than by assessing deep-seated, enduring dispositional characteristics. The implications of this shift are that the motivational models focusing on behavioral choice have become more important. These choice models by and large focus on current rewards, goals, evaluations, and expectations as causes of behavior.

THEORIES OF MOTIVATION: CHOICE OF BEHAVIOR

Given the shift from deep-seated dispositional characteristics to social and informational cues as causes of arousal, it is not surprising that most of the action in motivation research has taken place in the area of choice theories. These theories tend to focus on the current situational or informational factors that influence an individual to choose one action rather than another. In the last five years, probably 80 percent of the motivation research has focused on these approaches as opposed to need-based theories.

There is one major distinction among the choice theories that should be pointed out. Three of the approaches see behavior as caused by some cognitive process such as expectations, intentions to reach a goal, or perceptions of equity. One of the approaches sees behavior as caused by environmental contingencies (operant approaches) rather than any internal psychological mechanism. While in practice the operant approach may be similar to goal-setting or expectancy theory, it has a very different underlying theoretical rationale. For that reason, it will be treated separately in the present review.

Cognitive Approaches

The major cognitive approaches are expectancy theory, goal-setting, and equity theory. All three of them focus to some extent on the individual's perceptions of outcomes that result from one's behavior. In terms of quantity of work, expectancy theory and goal-setting have been studied more frequently and they will be reviewed first.

Expectancy Theory.   One approach to the motivational process suggests simply that people try to maximize their payoffs. More specifically, expectancy theory states that people look at their various alternatives (e.g., coming to work versus not coming to work) and choose that alternative they believe will most likely lead to those rewards they want most. If they believe that staying home is likely to lead to more good things than going to work, they are likely to stay home.

There are a number of important elements in this type of analysis. First, it is the anticipation (expectation) of what will occur that influences choice. It is the estimate of the future that is important. A second point is that the theory includes two major factors: the expectation that some outcome will occur, and the value (anticipated satisfaction) of that outcome. These two factors are formally called *expectancies* and *valences*.

The earliest statement of this approach was made by Victor Vroom (1964). He presented two models: one to predict certain choices such as what occupation an individual will choose or how much effort the person will exert on the job, and the second to predict an employee's attitudes about the job. Figure 10–2 presents an example of the choice model.

The researcher can assess the expectancies and valences shown in the figure with questionnaires or an interview. Each expectancy score is multiplied by its valence score, and these products are summed for a particular behavioral alternative. This process provides a sum of the expectancies times valences for each alternative, ΣEV. This ΣEV roughly represents an ''expected value'' or an expected return. The theory predicts that the individual will choose the alternative that has the highest payoff or expected return.

In the situation described in Figure 10–2, one individual might value a pay raise and advancement more highly than socializing or reading, and if the person thinks that working hard is likely to lead to the attainment of those outcomes, he or she will probably choose to exert a great deal of effort on the job. If, on the other hand, socializing and reading are more highly valued than a raise or a promotion and the individual is more likely to attain those outcomes by simply getting by, the person will probably choose not to work very hard.

It should be noted that it is a combination of both expectancy and value that determines what one will choose. If a choice leads to something a person values highly,

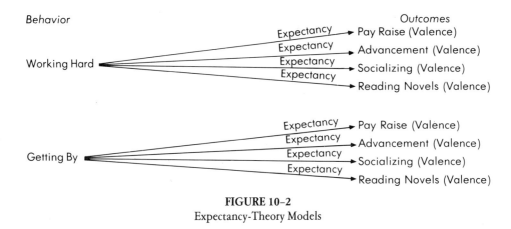

FIGURE 10-2
Expectancy-Theory Models

but is very unlikely (a long shot), or something he or she does not care about, but is very likely (a sure thing), the person probably will not choose it if it is compared to an alternative that is likely to lead to something he or she values highly.

The research on this model is fairly extensive. Over seventy studies have been done and a number of comprehensive reviews are available (Mitchell and Biglan, 1971; Heneman and Schwab, 1972; Mitchell, 1974, 1979, 1980; Wahba and House, 1974; Connolly, 1976; Schwab, Olian-Gottlieb, and Heneman, 1979). The results of these empirical investigations have been fairly encouraging. It appears as if expectancy models can do an excellent job of predicting occupational choice and job satisfaction and a moderately good job for predicting job effort. For example, a review article on occupational choice reported on sixteen different studies using expectancy or expected-value-like models (Mitchell and Beach, 1976). Every single study provided strong, significant support for the theory. In some cases, the model was able to predict actual job choice with 80 to 90 percent accuracy.

The implications for management practice are threefold. First, it is the anticipation of reward that is important. People make choices based upon what they think they will get, not what they got in the past. Second, rewards need to be closely and clearly tied to those behaviors that are seen as desirable by the organization. If attendance, punctuality, or working hard are important, then they should be rewarded explicitly, publicly, and frequently. Finally, since different people value different rewards, there should be some attempt at matching organizational outcomes or rewards with the particular desires of the individual employee. These techniques should increase the degree to which employees are described as highly motivated.

In summary, expectancy theory has generated considerable research, and most of the results have been supportive. In general, people work hard when they think that working hard is likely to lead to desirable organizational rewards. However, one final point should be made. Expectancy theory is based on a normative model. Expected-value approaches argue that if people (1) knew all the alternatives, (2) knew all the outcomes, (3) knew all the action → outcome relationships, and (4) knew how they felt about these outcomes, they would use a rather complex formula to come up with an estimate of the best choice of action. It is obvious that people don't have all of the above information, nor do they use a complex formula in determining their actions (see Behling, Schreisheim, and Tolliver, 1975 for a discussion of these issues). Rather, expected value should be seen as a general approximation of people's behavior. It points out the factors of importance (i.e., expectancies and valences) and it suggests ways in which these variables alone and in combination influence behavior. In that perspective, it has made a valuable contribution to the field.

Goal-Setting.   Another major contribution to our understanding of motivation has been made by Edwin Locke (1968). He argues that employees have certain goals they set for themselves and that an organization can have a strong influence on work behavior by influencing the employees' goals. Figure 10–3 is a graphic representation of the theory.

The major concepts in this theory are intentions, goals, acceptance, and commitment since they are described as the motivators. Their definitions are as follows:

Intentions or conscious goals. The target the individual reports he or she is shooting for.
Task goals. Some sort of performance standard. The conscious goal and task goal may or may not be the same.
Goal acceptance. The degree to which the task goal becomes the conscious goal or intention.
Goal commitment. The amount of effort expended to achieve the goal.
Incentive. An outcome that has positive or negative properties.

The theoretical generalizations have suggested that hard goals are better than easy ones, as long as they are accepted. One would also expect that participation in the goal-setting process would be more effective than assigning goals. Participation should increase commitment and acceptance. It appears that individual goal-setting is more powerful than group goals. It is the impact of the goals on individual intentions that is important. Finally, the more specific and well defined the goal, the greater the impact on motivation. Supposedly, a general goal such as "do your best" is ineffective.

Locke's argument is somewhat different from expectancy and equity notions. While incentives or rewards may affect goal acceptance and commitment, they are not the crucial factor; the goal is. Locke argues that people are constantly engaged in the goal-setting process and that the major antecedent to task-relevant behavior is the intention to

FIGURE 10–3
Goal-Setting Theory

reach some goal. Comparisons with others and the expectations of rewards are important only insofar as they affect the goals. It is the goal that causes motivation, not the reward.

There are now a number of reviews available on the empirical work on goal-setting (Latham and Yukl, 1975a; Steers and Porter, 1974; Yukl and Latham, 1978; Locke, 1978; Mitchell, 1979) and the findings are very clear on some issues. First, almost every study that has tested the question has shown that goals lead to higher performance than situations without goals. Second, most of the research has clearly supported the idea that difficult goals lead to better performance than easy goals. For example, Latham and his colleagues have carried out a number of field applications of goal-setting with Weyerhaeuser employees. One report shows that a group of pulpwood producers and their logging crews, who engaged in a training program on goal setting, produced significantly more cords of wood than a control group. Another study found that logging truck drivers increased their productivity 50 percent (resulting in a savings of hundreds of thousands of dollars) when specific hard goals were set and accepted (Latham and Baldes, 1975; Latham and Kinne, 1974).

However, there are still some areas of goal-setting research that are surrounded by controversy. For example, it is still not entirely clear what the effects of participation in the goal-setting process are. A number of studies have shown that participative goal-setting leads to higher satisfaction, but the effects on performance are more ambiguous. Latham and Yukl (1975b), in a study of uneducated loggers, found that participation led to higher goals and higher performance than for a group with assigned goals. This finding was not replicated for educated loggers. Other studies (e.g., Latham and Yukl, 1976; Latham, Mitchell, and Dossett, 1978) report no difference in performance between assigned and participative goal-setting.

The question seems to be, "What, if anything, besides increasing satisfaction, does participation do?" The only finding that seems to have some support is that participation may increase the difficulty of the set goals, and if this occurs, then performance might also be higher because of a goal difficulty effect. Some support for this proposition is available. The Latham and Yukl (1976) study with loggers may be interpreted this way, and the study by Latham, Mitchell, and Dossett (1978) clearly shows that participation leads to more difficult goals when goal difficulty is assessed in numerical terms. However, in studies where goal difficulty is measured by questionnaires (rather than the assessment of a specific numerical goal), this finding does not appear (e.g., Carroll and Tosi, 1970). In studies where goal difficulty level was held constant (e.g., Dossett, Latham, and Mitchell, 1979), there were either no differences in performance between the assigned and participative group or performance was better in the assigned group. These findings suggest that assigned goal-setting can serve an important motivational function, especially if the assigned goals are difficult but attainable.

Another set of studies has questioned the proposition that other factors, such as rewards, knowledge of results (KOR), or social pressures, influence motivation only insofar as they influence goals. A number of studies have shown that rewards (e.g., bonuses) have an independent motivating effect on behavior, as does social pressure (e.g., Latham, Mitchell, and Dossett, 1978; White, Mitchell, and Bell, 1977). Also, goals combined with feedback seem to be more effective than goals alone (Strang, Lawrence, and Fowler, 1978; Becker, 1978). Combining these studies with Ivancevich's

(1976, 1977) findings that the effects of goal-setting may diminish over time suggests that perhaps goal-setting combined with incentive systems, appraisals, and feedback is the best way to increase and maintain high levels of performance.

In summary, it appears rather convincingly that goals are a major source of work motivation. Goal-setting is one of the most frequently tested theories in the field of organizational behavior, and the recent paper by Locke (1978) suggests that most of the other major theories of motivation (e.g., expectancy theory, behavior modification) include goals in their formulation. The recent research is both large in number and frequent in its support. Two areas of research need to be pursued. First, there is a need to know more about the psychological processes underlying goal-setting. Little is known about the role of commitment and acceptance, and their relationship to goal difficulty or goal specificity. Second, more research is needed on how external factors—such as financial rewards, social pressure, and evaluation apprehension—complement, enhance, or act independently of the goal-setting process.

In terms of practice, the implications are clear. Hard (but accepted) specific goals combined with feedback and rewards for goal attainment should result in highly motivated employees.

Equity Theory. There is a large body of literature that suggests a more exchange-like relationship as the underlying dynamic of motivated behavior. Somehow individuals have an internal balance sheet that they use to figure out what to do. The theory predicts that the individual will choose that alternative for which a fair exchange exists. The major components of this exchange theory are somewhat different from expectancy theory. A description of these components and the way they combine is presented here:

Reward. Any outcome that contributes to need gratification.
Cost. Activity as part of process required to attain the outcome (e.g., fatigue, anxiety).
Outcome. The result in reference to rewards minus costs. One has a profit if it is positive and a loss if it is negative.
Comparison level. A comparison of outcomes across alternatives and the choice of the outcome that represents a "fair" exchange.

The idea of rewards and comparison levels is similar to expectancy theory. However, the idea of subjective probability is not included in the exchange analysis, while the idea of cost or input invested is made more explicit than in the expectancy approach.

The interesting application of this theory to the organizational setting is called "equity theory" (Adams, 1965). The comparison-level component is, in many cases, defined as one's co-workers. The idea is that people look at how hard they are working and the payoff received, and they compare that to what they think other people doing a similar job are getting, or to what they got when they worked on similar jobs at some other time. If a state of equity exists—that is, if there is little difference between these comparisons—then people are comfortable with the situation and no change is predicted to occur.

However, when inputs are seen as too great relative to outcomes when compared to others, then a state of underreward inequity is experienced. Obviously, employees can:

(1) reduce their inputs, (2) increase their outcomes, or (3) change their internal standard. If outcomes are too great when compared to inputs, a state of overreward inequity exists, and to relieve this tension employees can: (1) increase their inputs (e.g., work harder), (2) decrease their outcomes (e.g., accept less pay), or (3) change their internal standard.

The research on equity theory has been reviewed a number of times (Campbell et al., 1970; Goodman, 1977; Carrell and Dittrich, 1978; Mitchell, 1979). The findings about underreward and overreward have produced some interesting results under salaried conditions. When people experience underreward, they generally decrease their effort. When they experience overreward (they are getting paid more than others for doing the same job), they increase their effort. On a straight incentive plan (piece-rate), the results are somewhat different. People experiencing underreward are likely to decrease the quality of the output, and if they perceive overreward they attempt to increase the quality. Obviously, to increase or decrease the quantity of output under a piece-rate system would simply increase or decrease the inequity. Thus, both changes in quality and quantity of output can be predicted from the equity theory approach.

Other research-related topics should be mentioned as well. For example, one study found that feelings of inequity were positively related to turnover in a large aerospace firm (Telly, French, and Scott, 1971), and another more recent study showed perceptions of inequity of clerical employees to be related to both absenteeism and turnover (Dittrich and Carrell, 1979). Also, a couple of studies show that people with lower compensation for the same job have feelings of inequity and, in some cases, reduced performance (Carrell, 1978; Lord and Hohenfeld, 1979).

It should be pointed out that, relative to expectancy theory and goal-setting, very little research on equity theory has appeared the last few years. Goodman's (1977) comprehensive literature review points out very well what some of the problems are. First, very little is known about how people select a "comparison other." Second, it is very hard to define inputs and outcomes. Third, there is little known about how combinations of inputs and outcomes are accomplished, and, finally, it is hard to know when and how these factors change over time.

Most of the recent empirical work seems either to modify slightly or to challenge the basic equity notion. Middlemist and Peterson (1976), for example, found that people were a little more comfortable with a condition in which they had a slight competitive edge over their comparison co-worker than they were with a condition of complete equity. In a similar vein, Kopelman (1977) showed that a return on investment (ROI) measure of motivation was related to performance. This ROI measure reflected the difference between expected outcomes under different conditions of input, and suggested that people will choose that level of effort that leads to the highest payoff for the lowest investment of effort.

Finally, research by Larwood and her colleagues (Larwood et al., 1979; Larwood, Kavanagh, and Levine, 1978) showed that under certain conditions employees prefer reward distribution systems that are different from equity. Larwood and Blackmore (1977), for example, showed that salaried employees prefer equality (everyone gets the same), while those under an hourly rate prefer equity. In some cases, people choose a winner-take-all strategy. Finally, some work by Weick, Bougon, and Maruyama (1976) showed that equity ratios and resolution strategies are influenced by a number of contextual factors related to culture, family orientation, and personal values (e.g., value of independence).

In summary, the emphasis of equity theory is different from that of goal-setting or expectancy theory. Equity theory suggests that people choose a level of effort on the job that they somehow think is fair or equitable. There is not the same emphasis on maximizing rewards as there is for the expectancy theorist. Thus, an expectancy model might predict that an individual will choose that work level that brings the highest payoff, while an equity theorist would predict the choice of that level of effort that produced the fairest level of reward.

Two major implications seem important. First, organizations must strive to reward people equitably. When people feel they are not getting a fair shake, they may be dissatisfied, reduce their effort, and/or leave the job. But an equally important implication is that employees see rewards in a relative, rather than an absolute, fashion. It is not how much one is getting that is important; it is how much one is getting compared to other people who have the same type of job. It is the social or interpersonal comparison that is important, not the absolute amount. An employee may be getting $25,000 a year for driving a delivery truck, but if the person down the street gets $26,000 for the same type of work for another company, unhappiness, dissatisfaction, and reduced performance may be the result.

Noncognitive Approaches: Operant Conditioning

One of the dominant influences in the field of psychology has been the work of B. F. Skinner on behaviorism. His contribution to an understanding of human behavior is immense. Recently, he has applied his ideas to the field of organizational behavior, and his approach is quickly becoming one of the more controversial topics in this field (Skinner, 1971).

The two major components of the theory are the ideas of reinforcement and environmental determinism. To define these concepts, one must understand that the two types of behavior attributed to humans are operant and respondent. Respondents are controlled by instincts and direct stimulation, such as sneezes. Operants, on the other hand, are emitted in the absence of any apparent external stimulation and are the major focus of analysis.

Whenever an operant behavior is followed by an environmental event (consequence) that changes the likelihood that the behavior will occur again, that event or consequence is called a reinforcer. If the consequence increases the frequency of behavior, it is called a *positive reinforcer*. If it decreases the frequency of the behavior, it is a *negative reinforcer*. Skinner's argument is that once a person discovers what consequences serve as positive or negative reinforcers for a particular behavior (e.g., coming to work), he or she can manipulate the frequency of the behavior by manipulating the reinforcers.

It should be noted that there are no references to any internal cognitive processes. Reinforcers do not feel good or bad; they simply change the frequency of the behavior. The true behaviorist believes that operant behavior is caused by environmental events.

This philosophy is called *environmental determinism*. It is the past history of reinforcement that causes current behavior.

Besides these underlying ideas, there are some practical principles that have been developed and are relevant for this discussion. One major research emphasis has been to develop schedules of reinforcement that describe the optimal frequency with which rewards should be administered. Rewards could be given every time a certain behavior occurred (continuous rewards), or they could be given on some sort of intermittent or variable schedule.

A study by Latham with tree planters illustrates the technique (Latham, 1974). The individuals in one group received a $2.00 bonus for each bag of trees planted (continuous schedule); in a second group, they received a $4.00 bonus for planting a bag of trees and correctly guessing the toss of a coin (called variable-ratio-2 schedule); in a third group, they received $8.00 for planting a bag of trees and correctly guessing two coin tosses (a variable-ratio-4 schedule); and a fourth group, which continued receiving their regular wage, served as a control group. The three experimental groups in the long run will theoretically receive the same amount of money; $2.00 every time, or $4.00 half of the time, or $8.00 a fourth of the time. The results were interesting. The three experimental groups showed an average increase in productivity of around 14 percent, while there was no change for the control group. From both a cost-benefit analysis and a productivity-increase perspective, the continuous schedule did best (a 33-percent increase in productivity and a savings of $4.14 per bag of trees). Reinforcement in this case seemed to be very beneficial.

Reviews of the empirical research using this approach are available (Mitchell, 1979; Locke, 1977; Babb and Kopp, 1978; Arvey and Ivancevich, 1980). In general, two types of studies have been done. The first simply introduces some sort of procedure described as reinforcing and compares people's behavior under those conditions with that of people who are not reinforced. Studies by Adam (1975), Komaki, Waddell, and Pearce (1977), and Stephens and Burroughs (1978) use this type of methodology, and all three studies provide support for their hypothesis that reinforcement increases performance.

The second type of study compares different types of reinforcement schedules; that is, the frequency with which a reinforcer is made contingent upon a specific response. The three types of schedules most frequently studied are the continuous (where a reinforcer is made contingent upon every incidence of the desired behavior), fixed ratio (where a reinforcer is provided, for example, every second or third incidence of the desired behavior), and variable ratio (where a reinforcer is provided on the average for every second or third incidence of the behavior). The results from this type of research are highly confusing. Yukl and Latham (1975) and Yukl, Latham, and Purcell (1976) described results with tree planters where a continuous schedule did better than a variable ratio, but Deslauriers and Everett (1977) suggested that a variable schedule did better for inducing people to ride the bus. Studies by Yukl, Wexley, and Seymore (1972), Berger, Cummings, and Heneman (1975), Pritchard et al. (1976), and Latham and Dossett (1978) compared variable ratio to fixed ratio or continuous schedules. The data are difficult to summarize since all four studies have somewhat different findings. However, it is safe to conclude from these studies that (1) there is little difference in performance between the types of schedules, and (2) there is a big difference in performance between using a schedule and not using one.

To implement such a system in an ongoing organization requires a number of steps. The behavior to be changed must be clearly measurable, observable, and countable. One must initially have some idea of its frequency (called a base rate). One can then administer various outcomes contingent upon the behavior and observe changes in frequency. Eventually one should be able to determine what works best in terms of the type of reward and the particular type of schedule (Luthans, 1974).

There are a number of similarities between operant and expectancy techniques. Both theories argue that the contingency between the behavior and the reward is important. Both of them include the positive or negative aspects of the reward itself. However, the major contribution of the operant technique is the emphasis on schedules of reinforcement. Knowing when, how frequently, and how much to reward is an important addition to an understanding of organizational behavior.

A number of criticisms have also been leveled at the operant technique (Mitchell, 1976). The problems are partially definitional and partially methodological. In many cases, the definitions of schedules and reinforcement are inconsistent across studies, and with the original definitions provided by Skinner. Mawhinney's (1975) paper discussed in detail some of these problems, but they do not seem to have been resolved in current studies.

The second issue is methodological. In many cases, the use of reinforcement introduces other factors that are equal, if not more plausible, explanations of the findings. For example, the study by Adam (1975) used feedback and the study by Komaki, Waddell and Pearce (1977) used goals as part of its reinforcement procedures. Perhaps the best review of these methodological problems is presented by Locke (1977). In an examination of most of the studies using an operant procedure, Locke points out how numerous other confounding factors could cause these results. He argues quite convincingly that reinforcement most probably affects action through goals, expectations, and other cognitive processes. The response by Gray (1979), Locke's rebuttal (1979), and a further note by Parmerlee and Schwenk (1979) all discuss these problems in more detail.

From both a theoretical and applied perspective, these problems are crucial. If one believes in operant conditioning and its philosophical foundation of environmental determinism, then reference to internal cognitive events is irrelevant for the prediction of behavior. With this belief, it is easy to omit consent, participation, and the joint setting of goals in applications of operant conditioning. The operant research may demonstrate increases in organizational effectiveness, but it does little to increase the understanding of how and why the increases occur. More operant studies that gather empirical data and rule out alternative interpretations are sorely needed, as well as investigations that examine how operant procedures and cognitive events jointly result in increased motivation.

New Directions

The preceding four theories represent the major theoretical approaches to motivation that have dominated the field for the last ten years. Except for a few articles on specific motivational issues, most of the work has focused on these topics. One major new development has been the controversy surrounding the motivating effects of intrinsic and extrinsic rewards. Intrinsic rewards are those outcomes that supposedly come from simply doing the task (e.g., feelings of accomplishment), while extrinsic rewards come from external sources (e.g., pay).

There are at least two major issues that are being discussed in the literature on this topic. The first is simply a descriptive question: "What do we mean by intrinsic and extrinsic and how are these terms being used in the research literature?" A recent paper by Broedling (1977) discussed this issue in detail. She pointed out the conceptual distinctions between such terms as *psychological states, traits,* and *consequences or outcomes of action.* While there is some agreement that extrinsic rewards (e.g., pay) are somehow external to the person (and perhaps controlled by others), and intrinsic rewards (e.g., an interesting task) are more internal and controllable by one's self, there is still little agreement on the specific meaning and use of the terms (Guzzo, 1979). However, it is clear that people have different preferences for these types of outcomes as a function of age, class, and job, and that they influence work behavior.

The second question, and the one around which most of the controversy revolves, is whether the effects of these two types of rewards are compatible or conflicting. The argument is as follows: People work at certain levels of effort and they observe these effort levels. In order to explain their behavior, they make attributions (causal explanations) about why they are doing what they are doing. These attributions then change people's work-related attitudes and behavior.

In some cases, people are faced with a task for which there are few intrinsic and extrinsic rewards. This situation is described as the *insufficient justification condition.* If a person is induced to do the task, then it is predicted that he or she will change one's initial evaluation of its intrinsic properties—"I must find this task interesting; otherwise, why am I doing it?" Numerous studies have supported this hypothesis (Staw, 1977).

The controversy arises in a situation in which there is oversufficient justification. Deci (1975) has shown that, if an external reward (e.g., a financial bonus) is added when people are engaged in an intrinsically interesting task, motivation will decrease rather than increase. In this case, intrinsic and extrinsic rewards are seen as competing or conflicting rather than additive. This type of finding is seemingly in direct contradiction to an operant analysis, which would argue that positive reinforcers are additive.

A number of reviews and critiques of Deci's work have appeared (Calder and Staw, 1975; Mitchell, 1979; Notz, 1975; Scott, 1976; Pate, 1978; Mawhinney, 1979), and the empirical work has left the issue unresolved. Some studies have failed to support the overjustification effect, while others have reported support for the hypothesis. One study by Pritchard, Campbell, and Campbell (1977) was explicitly designed to account for earlier methodological problems in this type of research, and it generated strong support for the nonadditive effects of these types of rewards.

On the theoretical level, a paper by Scott and Erskine (1977) suggested some ways in which the overjustification hypothesis and an operant approach can be seen as compatible. They argued that reinforcements could produce the "Deci" effect. Thus, with certain assumptions being agreed upon, certain parts in the controversy can be resolved.

The important development that has come from the debate on the intrinsic/extrinsic issue has been the emphasis on understanding the individual's psychological interpretation of events in the work place. There are now a number of studies which suggest that it is not merely the reward or punishment that produces motivation (i.e., whether one objectively succeeds, fails, is given a bonus, is docked) but the interpretation of that event by the individual. For example, a study by Kovenklioglu and Greenhaus (1978) showed that one's attributions about his or her past success and failure on a task can influence future success or failure. When the subjects thought that their past success was the result of their ability, they did much better on subsequent tasks than when they thought their past good performance was caused by luck. This type of analysis is likely to increase in the future.

Summary and Implications

Important materials have been reviewed in this chapter, and there are some principles that should be emphasized.

1. Performance can be seen as a combination of both ability and motivation. Both aspects are probably necessary for good performance to occur.
2. Motivation is important in terms of two major questions: ''What gets one started or aroused?'' ''What process determines the direction in which one chooses to go?''
3. Theories of individual needs and classification systems of needs focus on the question of arousal. One major conclusion is that different people want different rewards from their job.
4. The need classification systems brought recognition of the importance of higher-level needs. Most employees today are more concerned with belonging, esteem, and actualizing needs than physiological or safety needs.
5. The process theories of motivation are attempts to explain the choice of behavior. Most of them suggest some sort of underlying rational system that determines what people will do.
6. Both expectancy theory and operant conditioning place their emphasis on contingency relationships. The most important factors for motivation are the direct link between appropriate behavior and rewards and the value of the reward itself. Operant techniques can be used to suggest when, how much, and how frequently rewards should be administered.
7. Equity theory calls attention to the fairness of the reward system. People are often motivated by comparison with their co-workers. One must conclude that fair, equitable rewards are a necessity.
8. Finally, goals are an important motivator. Having clear, specific, agreed-upon objectives increases effort on the job.

Underlying these principles are some fairly simple ideas. First, that performance is a joint function of ability and motivation must be reemphasized. Since the organization can select and change abilities, and since it can motivate people through the type of organizational environment that it presents, motivation should be seen as a central concern and responsibility of management. All too frequently, attempts at increasing motivation are seen as being softheaded or impossible to do ("if they don't have it, they just don't have it"). What is suggested is that selection procedures, training programs, performance appraisal, and reward systems can have a powerful impact on performance.

A second point is that people have different needs and different desires. A reward system that is flexible and provides people with some choice of rewards will probably be more effective than one that is more rigid in nature. Both hierarchical need approaches and expectancy approaches would support such a prediction. People will work harder for something they value.

Another important principle is that contingencies should be made explicit and open. People are more likely to feel they are being equitably treated if they have a good idea of why people receive the rewards or punishments that they do. People may not like it, but at least they will understand it, which is better than what currently happens all too frequently. But besides the equity function of making contingencies known, there is the feedback function as well. Almost all of the models described include feedback (see Nadler, 1979; Ilgen, Fisher, and Taylor, 1979, for reviews) as part of the motivational process. People need to know what they are doing well, and where they need help. Again, expectancy theory would also make similar predictions. The higher the perceived relationship between a particular behavior (e.g., working hard) and a desired reward (e.g., a bonus), the greater the chance the behavior will be performed. The message is clear: be explicit and open about what leads to what.

Finally, some targets should be laid out. People like to have something to shoot for. Any job is routine and boring some of the time. Goals provide incentives. They can give a sense of accomplishment. They can be used as a reliable, agreed-upon system of evaluation. Motivation increases when task goals are present.

One last point regarding these generalities: rewards, feedback, goals, and equity all assume one fundamental point—that management knows what constitutes good performance in the first place. At the heart of any good motivation program is a good performance appraisal system. Almost everyone agrees with the principles previously described. In many respects they reflect simple common sense. What they fail to recognize is that implementing such ideas requires an excellent appraisal system, concerned and dedicated management, and the willingness to use resources to increase motivation. These are the areas in which failure is most likely to occur.

EVALUATION AND DISCUSSION

In general, the conclusions drawn at the end of the last section represent the current state-of-the-art. Much has been learned about motivation. However, recent reviews of this literature are hardly complacent (Steers and Mowday, 1977; Mitchell, 1979). While some important motivational principles have been recognized, there is also a stronger awareness of where knowledge is inadequate. This final section addresses this issue.

One of the major points to be emphasized is that to some extent all of the approaches are viable and important. For many years, the research has proceeded with each study attempting to prove or disprove only one approach. Thus, there were studies on two-factor theory, need achievement, goal-setting, expectancy theory, and so on. Each research effort was designed to demonstrate the effectiveness of one approach.

Recognition of the fact that all of the different theories may have a piece of the truth leads one to a slightly different strategy. Rather than asking whether goal-setting works or not, one should be asking, "How important is goal setting relative to social cues?" or "In what types of settings or with what types of people is goal setting most effective?" There are two types of questions being asked here. The first simply asks about the additive or interactive effects of various approaches. Are goals with rewards better than either one by itself? The second set of questions deals with contingency notions. Are some people more responsive to goal-setting? Are there situations where goal-setting is more likely to work? The next two sections address these questions.

Interactive and Additive Approaches

The following sections are not meant to be comprehensive reviews of all of the studies that have taken these two approaches. Rather, it is meant to be illustrative of the strategies involved. More comprehensive reviews are available elsewhere (Campbell et al., 1970; Dunnette, 1976; Mitchell, 1979).

One can find a new interactive or additive studies that are fairly old. For example, Schachter et al. (1951) manipulated the social cues of a co-worker (confederate) and the cohesiveness (interpersonal attraction) of the group (dyad). The co-worker either gave highly motivating messages (e.g., let's work hard on this task) or the reverse (let's take it easy). The results showed a strong interaction effect on productivity. The groups that were cohesive and had positive social cues were the most productive. The groups that were cohesive and had negative social cues were *least* productive. Thus, having a highly cohesive group (positive attitudes toward the task or co-workers) can help or hurt motivation for good performance, depending on the social support for working hard.

Similar types of studies with social cues have been done recently. For example, the studies mentioned earlier by White and Mitchell (1979), Weiss and Shaw (1979), and O'Reilly and Caldwell (1979) all showed that perceptions of satisfaction with a particular task was jointly determined by the task itself and the social cues about the task. The most positive attitudes about the task (and supposedly the greatest motivation) occurred when the task was enriched *and* the co-workers liked the task.

Similarly, the work by Hackman and Oldham (1976) suggested that growth-need strengths and need for achievement moderates the enrichment-performance/satisfaction relationship. People who have high growth needs or need for achievement respond more positively to enriched jobs.

A number of similar studies have appeared in the goal-setting area. For example, three recent studies have demonstrated that goal-setting combined with feedback results in higher performance than either feedback or goals alone (Nemeroff and Cosentino, 1979, Strang, Lawrence, and Fowler, 1978; Becker, 1978). A study by Umstot, Bell, and Mitchell (1976) showed that goal-setting combined with enrichment was likely to lead to high performance and high satisfaction, and a paper by Bassett (1979) showed that a difficult goal combined with a compressed work schedule leads to higher productivity than either one alone. Finally, a study by White, Mitchell, and Bell (1977) showed that goals, evaluation apprehension, and social cues all had significant effects on performance and that the individuals who had goals thought they were being evaluated and had a supportive co-worker produced the most. Similarly, Latham, Mitchell, and Dossett (1978) showed that individuals with goals and financial rewards for goal attainment were the most productive.

All of these studies come to fairly similar conclusions: rewards, goals, social pressure, evaluation apprehension, enrichment, and feedback can influence performance independently of the other. When combined, they result in strong motivational effects. The obvious implication is for managers and practitioners not to get locked into merely one approach. The implication for the theoretician is to better ascertain what combinations are best, when they work, and why.

Contingency Notions

The second new development is far less well researched or articulated than the additive or interactive position. Except for a very few examples, few people have attempted any sort of contingency type approach to motivation. Yet it seems obvious that this is the direction in which research must proceed. There is now massive evidence that motivation is jointly a function of something about the person (e.g., attitudes, needs, values) and something about the setting (e.g., rewards, social pressure). The critical point is that there are differences across and within people and there are differences across and within settings. More specifically, people change over time and are different from one another. Tasks change over time and are different from one another.

The implication of these points is that different motivational strategies will be more effective in some settings with some people than other motivational strategies. Sometimes goal-setting will be most effective, sometimes enrichment, and sometimes need-achievement training. In order to pursue some specific contingencies, one needs to review what is known about differences in people and differences in settings.

People Differences. There is a good deal of evidence that people value different things and have preferences for different types of rewards. If one sees motivation as partially determined by these preferences (as would be predicted by operant, expectancy, and equity approaches), then some understanding of how these differences develop and change is important. Obviously, if one wants rewards to be maximally motivating, he or she must know what is desired and valued by the person to be motivated.

One can, of course, slice the individual difference pie many ways. For example, personality differences seem to be related to reward preferences (Andrisani and Miljus, 1977). People with high need for achievement are likely to value recognition, people with an internal locus of control value autonomy, and so on. Also, as Porter (1964) showed, there are some differences in reward preferences at organizational levels. Higher-level managers rate higher the importance of opportunities for personal growth, independent thought and action, and participation in goal-setting than lower-level employees. Related work by Cherrington, Condie, and England (1979) showed that older workers are more inclined to believe in the moral importance of work, have pride in craftsmanship, and value money and friends less heavily than younger workers.

A third, and perhaps most important, focus has been the work of a variety of authors emphasizing a developmental approach (e.g., Gould and Hawkins, 1978; Hall, 1976; Katz, 1980). The work of both Hall and Katz is noteworthy in that they have presented comprehensive theories of job or career development and change. The argument is that people go through distinct job or career stages and that they value different things during these stages. Katz, who is concerned with longevity on a particular job, sees stages of socialization followed by innovation and then adaptation. In the socialization stage, there is greater emphasis on getting feedback and the significance of the job, while the innovation stage brings in needs for achievement, recognition, and good performance. In the adaptation stage, enrichment factors become less important and more extrinsic factors like money are salient.

Hall's work (Hall and Nougaim, 1968; Hall, 1976) suggests stages over one's career rather than simply one job (see Chapter 13 in this volume for a detailed discussion of careers). The employee is seen as going through stages of establishment, advancement, and maintenance. In the establishment stage, one values the work itself, pay, and good peer relationships. In the establishment stage, interest and challenge are also important. In the advancement stage, the individual becomes concerned with achievement and promotion. Finally, in the maintenance stage, there is reduced competitiveness and self-indulgence and a greater acceptance of one's role.

The importance of the work of these authors cannot be underemphasized. They have clearly attempted to describe what factors are most likely to be valued at different stages of tenure within a job and across one's career. Any success with motivational techniques will require an understanding of these changes in preferences and values.

Situational Differences. What the preceding research shows is that people who differ in their background, job longevity, career stage, and personality are likely to value different rewards. This knowledge would suggest that different types of motivational systems will be appropriate for different types of people.

A second line of research that reaches the same conclusion has focused on situational parameters. Factors related to group structure, task type, and reward systems all are important for understanding this perspective.

One point that must be recognized initially is that the task type itself determines to some extent the degree to which any motivational system will work. It is recalled that individual performance can be seen as a joint function of ability, motivation, and the clarity of expectations. In some circumstances, performance on a task may be far more related to skill than effort.

Hackman and Oldham (1980) have recently elaborated on a model that discusses this issue explicitly for groups. They argue that the performance of any organizational unit can be seen as a joint function of norms, the ability mix, and motivation or effort. On those tasks where motivation is of minor importance for either individuals or groups, it is unlikely that any motivational program will be effective. What may be more important are factors like training to work on ability, or team building to work on communication.

Besides the point that performance on some tasks is simply not strongly related to motivation, there is also the recognition that many tasks are carried out in a group context. The variable of critical importance with respect to motivational implications is the degree of interdependence of group members. Some tasks require that everybody work together to accomplish a goal (e.g., a basketball team) and some require independent effort (e.g., a golfer). On tasks where interdependence is required, the use of motivational strategies becomes far more complex and difficult to determine.

The difficulty of determination occurs partly because it is more difficult to specify at an individual level what constitutes good performance. If a research proposal is truly a joint effort, it is hard to tease out individual contributions. The issues raised here not only question what type of motivational system should be used, but whether feedback, goals, and rewards should be implemented at an individual or group level (Lawler, 1971). While it is fairly clear that independent efforts require individual motivational systems and completely interdependent groups require group motivational strategies, it is hard to specify what to do for the vast array of tasks in between. Unfortunately, there is little guidance in this area.

There are also some differences in tasks that are unrelated to interdependence. For example, some tasks are more ambiguous than others. That is, some tasks are fairly well structured while others are not. There is extensive literature that illustrates this point, using the concepts of role ambiguity and conflict. It appears that the higher up one is in the organization, the greater the ambiguity (House and Rizzo, 1972; Miles, 1976). Ambiguity means that expectancies are unclear and unclear expectancies mean low motivation. It may, for example, be easier to set goals, but harder to tie rewards specifically to behavior in these ambiguous settings.

Another specific factor about the task has to do with its work structure. Besides the degree of interdependence, there are different degrees and types of cooperation (e.g., see Kabanoff and O'Brien, 1979) and different norms about how rewards should be distributed. Larwood and her colleagues (e.g., Larwood and Blackmore, 1977) have shown, for example, that salaried employees prefer equal distributions, while hourly folks prefer an equity-like formula for compensation.

Conclusions

Little of this research specifies exactly that goal-setting ought to be used in certain places, while operant approaches may be more effective in other settings. However, some general principles about what seems to work where can probably be inferred. It should be emphasized, however, that these inferences are mainly speculation—there is little in the way of specific data to support them.

First, one could probably argue that specific need-based approaches will be most helpful in those tasks in which individual differences (ability, personality) are most important. The more that performance is determined by motivational and situational properties, the less that individual differences will be important (as long as some valued rewards are part of the motivational program).

The operant and expectancy type approaches focus on the explicit link between rewards and behavior. Lower-level employees working on tasks for which performance can easily be monitored and attributed to individuals are most likely to benefit from such approaches. Ambiguous tasks, in which it is hard to know who contributed what, cause major problems for these approaches.

Equity theory emphasizes a fairness norm. While fairness is always important (as are rewards), it is probably relatively more important as one goes higher up the organizational ladder. At some point, the relative amount of pay increase may become as important as, or more important than, the absolute amount.

Goal-setting and feedback, while always important, probably are most suitable when it is easy to clarify and specify goals. Some settings with higher ambiguity and interdependence may present difficulties for goal-setting approaches.

What evolves out of such reasoning is a sort of diagnostic approach to motivation. What one needs to teach managers is the correct questions to ask about a particular setting in order to determine what sort of motivational system will be most effective. Similar type models have been developed for the areas of decision making (e.g., Herold, 1978) and leadership (Vroom and Yetton, 1973), but are still unavailable for the topic of motivation. Such a model is beyond the scope of this chapter, but some of the important issues might be ordered as follows:

1. Determine the extent to which performance is determined by motivation or other factors (e.g., ability or norms). If motivation is important, proceed in the analysis.
2. Ascertain the degree to which desirable behaviors can be specified. If they can be precisely described and assessed, develop a validated appraisal procedure to do so. If there is too much ambiguity, lack of specificity, or interdependence, one may need to proceed to group rewards, making rewards dependent on goal attainment (not behavior), or use some sort of social team building that enhances commitment.
3. Given a good appraisal instrument, find out what the people prefer as outcomes of their performance. This step includes an understanding of individual differences, values, longevity in the job, and career stage.
4. Implement a system that ties rewards to behavior, introduce goals with rewards for goal attainment, give frequent and consistent feedback, and make sure people are treated fairly and equitably. Have a flexible enough reward system that people may receive rewards they value highly.
5. Through the process of participation and group communication, attempt to gain group acceptance and commitment to the program. Social support for any motivational system is important.

Obviously, things are easier where people work independently on tasks where good performance is easy to describe and measure. Unfortunately, there are more and more groups, committees, and interdependencies being established in most organizations and increasing problems of ambiguity about what needs to be done. It is precisely these areas where the least is known about successful motivation. It is also the type of setting over which the organization has the least control.

Thus, the task for the future is a formidable one. Researchers must develop more complex models that describe these complex contingencies. And in some settings, there may be limited capabilities to do anything. Perhaps, from the investigation of such settings, some new ideas will emerge to help cope with these problems and complexities. One certainly hopes so, because the problem of motivation at work promises to be around for a long time.

Discussion Questions

1. Many organizations have bonus plans. If you were asked to design such a plan, how would you go about it? What would you want to know? How frequently and for what would bonuses be given? What motivational principles would be operating?

2. Should the amount of pay one receives be made public? Discuss the pros and cons of such a proposal with an emphasis on motivational issues.

3. With which motivational position are you most comfortable? How would you rank the ideas of equity, maximization, need fulfillment, and goal attainment as producers of motivation?

4. Do you believe that people's behavior is regulated by internal or external forces? Discuss each of these positions and the reasons for your own opinion.

5. To what extent do you think people work hard because of social pressure? Describe some ways that an organization could influence that pressure in a positive direction.

PART FIVE

PERSONNEL TRAINING AND DEVELOPMENT

Personnel training and development activities are of growing importance to organizations. When the costs of replacing an employee are considered, programs of training and development often represent major savings to organizations. It was estimated in the early 1980s, for example, that the costs of replacing a typical middle manager, including the costs of recruitment and selection, exceeded $45,000.

Other factors also attest to the growing importance of these activities. As suggested in Chapter 1, a shift in emphasis from selecting to training employees may be occurring as a result of fair employment practices legislation during the past two decades. Earlier, most organizations were more concerned with selecting employees; that is, keeping the "false positive" and "false negative" decisions to a minimum and maximizing the job-person match, than training and developing them. A wide range of well-designed training programs are often necessary to prepare new employees for their current responsibilities. In addition, with continuing technological advances in the office as well as the plant, training programs are required to update employees' skills in the use of these advances and in the management of the organizations created for them.

Informational inputs from a variety of personnel activities, including human resource planning and the employment interview, impact on training and development activities. A principal informational input or determinant of who needs what kind of training when is the performance evaluation process, where weaknesses in an individual's work performance may be attributed to lack of training or formal preparation for the job. It is primarily for this reason that the next two chapters of this book follow the discussion of the performance evaluation process in Chapter 8.

In Chapter 11, Lacey, Lee, and Wallace provide an overview of personnel training techniques and present a general conceptual model of human resource development. Rather than confining their discussion to training at a specific organizational level, they propose their conceptual model as a framework through which the training and development process can be applied at all levels and to all learning situations.

In Chapter 12, Boehm gives special emphasis to training and development at the managerial level and provides a detailed presentation of a specific technique that has enjoyed a considerable degree of attention and success—the assessment center. After providing a historical overview, Boehm analyzes the different uses of the assessment center in organizations. While she acknowledges that its principle use to date has been in selection, she projects more extensive developmental uses for the assessment center in the future.

CHAPTER ELEVEN

TRAINING AND DEVELOPMENT

David W. Lacey, Robert J. Lee, and Lawrence J. Wallace

David W. Lacey is Corporate Director of Management Development and Training at INA Corporation. He received his Ph.D. in Counseling/Industrial Psychology from the Ohio State University. Previous to his current position, Dr. Lacey held positions as both Director of Human Resources Development and Manager of Organization and Management Development at Celanese Corporation. Dr. Lacey has served also as Director of Corporate Personnel and Psychological Services for American Home Products Corporation and as Senior Behavioral Scientist for Western Electric Company. In addition to his professional experience, Dr. Lacey has conducted research and published in the areas of career counseling and development and management development and training.

Robert J. Lee is President of Lee-Hecht Associates in New York City. His firm offers training, organization development, management counseling, and human resource services. He has sixteen years of experience as a consultant to organizations, including six years of major corporate experience with W. R. Grace and Union Carbide. Dr. Lee received his Ph.D. in Industrial/Organizational Psychology from Case Western Reserve University.

Lawrence J. Wallace is a candidate for the Doctor of Education degree at Harvard University with a specialization in Organizational Behavior. While at Harvard, he has been a summer intern at INA Corporation and served as a teaching assistant to Dr. Harry Levinson. Mr. Wallace holds both the master's and bachelor's degrees from Pennsylvania State University. He has done consulting work in the area of training program design.

This chapter examines some of the issues concerning how personnel training and development occur and should occur within organizations. The discussion begins with the characteristics of adult learners, concentrating on adult managers. An Adult/Manager as Learner (A/ML) model is proposed to describe five ways managers are unique students. A basic andragogical approach to the design of personnel training for managers and other employees is then offered. Finally, special attention is paid to the career progress of managers. The Management Development Matrix attempts to address the problem of how training activities can best support a manager's career development.

Any discussion of training—whether it be in the large business organization, or in settings ranging from the military to human services agencies—begins with a discussion of how people learn. The personnel professional responsible for training is, above all else, an educator. For this reason, his or her work must be solidly grounded in a theory of adult learning.

All trainers operate either implicitly or explicitly with a theory of learning. For many people, the theory is based on their earliest educational experiences. As students, most individuals were passive participants in an educational process that centered around an all-powerful teacher. This structure, and its underlying learning theory, gave the teacher almost complete authority to determine the substance and form of classroom instruction. It assumed that learners could best benefit from a prescribed curriculum, rather than one that was designed to address individual needs. It also assumed that learners were motivated mostly by rewards inherent in the curriculum or the way it was taught. For this reason, grades and reinforcements from the teacher became extremely important. With this as the model, people carry into their adult lives expectations of what teaching and learning should be. Even though the subjects and settings have varied throughout formal education, all of this experience has taught individuals much about how to be a student: to be dependent and deferential in the classroom and to expect the teacher to be responsible for the planning, design, implementation, and evaluation of the learning.

Malcolm Knowles, a leading theorist of adult education, points out that these assumptions based on childhood experiences are not a valid basis for designing training for adults. He uses the word *andragogy* to describe the unique ways adults learn. The word *pedagogy* has come to be used as a synonym for education. In fact, the root, *peda-*, stems from the Greek *pais,* meaning child, and pedagogy literally means youth learning. Andragogy, from the Greek *andros,* for man, more appropriately describes adult education and is needed if one is to consider the important ways in which adults differ from children as learners. Knowles summarizes these differences:

> Adults see themselves as self-directed and independent; children are dependent on parents, teachers and others.

> Because they simply have not acquired much of it, experience may be of little value to children in the classroom. With adults, experience is an important resource for learning. In training, we must recognize that adults have significant experience. Indeed, they often define themselves as the sum of their experiences. Good training draws from this experience and builds on it.

> Children must postpone the application of much of their formal learning. Adults need to see immediate application of the learning if it is to be meaningful.

Children's readiness to learn is determined by biological development and social pressure. For adults, readiness is based on the developmental tasks that result from social roles.

Children's orientation to learning is subject-centered; adults' orientation to learning is problem-centered (Knowles, 1978, p. 110).

All of these differences impact on the trainer's work. Knowles points out that the andragogical learning climate needs to be informal, collaborative, and mutually respectful, as opposed to the formal, authority-oriented, and competitive pedagogical climate. In a pedagogical model, planning, diagnosis of needs, the formulation of objectives, and evaluation are all the responsibility of the teacher. The andragogical approach involves learners in mutual planning, self-diagnosis, negotiation, and, as far as evaluation is concerned, mutual rediagnosis of needs. Teaching techniques become more experiential and move away from the pedagogue's transmittal techniques that rely on an all-knowing teacher and a passive learner. (Knowles, 1978)

THE ADULT MANAGER AS LEARNER

With Knowles's theory providing a context for how adults learn, one can turn to the special case of how managers learn. In discussing leadership, Harry Levinson, the noted organizational psychologist, says, "By and large, executives are a serious lot, as much concerned as professionals in medicine or teaching with learning how to do their jobs better." (Levinson, 1970, p. 127). In as much as this motivation to learn stems from a need to foster organizational productivity, the manager's learning dilemma is at least twofold: he or she needs to keep abreast of technological innovations in one's field, but the manager also needs to learn how to deal with the complex "people problems" that arise in the organization. Management development and training programs become an essential tool for managers who seek to upgrade their skills in both these areas. The extent to which a manager can learn, through these programs and other means, to solve unanticipated people and technological problems is often directly linked to the productivity and profitability of his or her unit of the organization.

Experience suggests that managers have particularly unique qualities as learners. An Adult/Manager as Learner (A/ML) model is proposed because it relates directly to how the present authors feel personnel development should occur, and because it helps explain why some management training and development efforts have traditionally encountered problems.

It is useful to look first at the implicit model underlying many organizations' training programs. The model includes the following elements:

The trainer (and training program) has the right answers and will give them to the trainees.
Optimum success is achieved when all of the trainees learn the same points (ideas) and the same materials.
The trainees do the same prework and participate equally in the same exercises.
Learning is intended to happen in the classroom, while on-the-job time is for application.

Implied in this model are important pedagogical principles. The prediction is that such goals and methods will not be effective for adult learners generally, and for managers particularly. The A/ML model attempts to deal with the reality that students are in fact adult people, not children. It is an andragogical model. Breaking away from the assumptions that equate student with ''child'' and trainer with ''teacher'' is difficult, but it must be done if training efforts are to have meaning for adults.

Managers are not typical of all adults. Managers have greater responsibilities, control, demands, and resources than many other adults. In most cases, they have received a string of recent rewards for being successful and competent. They are important people—or at least they're told they are.

The Adult/Manager model builds on these features and integrates them with what is known about learning in general. It is consistent with the assumptions underlying a successful personnel development effort. The A/ML model has five key elements:

1. Style
2. Needs
3. Authority
4. Self-Image
5. Studying

The model is illustrated in Figure 11-1.

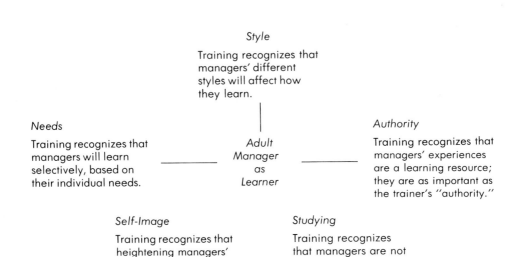

FIGURE 11-1
The Adult Manager as Learner: An Andragogical Model

Source: Adapted from M. Knowles. *The Adult Learner: A Neglected Species.* 2nd ed. Copyright © 1978 by Gulf Publishing Co., Houston, Texas. Used with permission. All rights reserved.

Style

The A/ML model suggests that managers have different styles of living and working, and that these styles are reflected in how they learn from personnel development programs. A training program that does not allow for this diversity is less likely to succeed. The most obvious differences have to do with varying communication styles and preferences. There are those who prefer to learn by reading and there are those who do not. Some have an "action" style, while others absorb more from observing. There are talkers and there are listeners.

One version of stylistic preferences has been codified by organizational psychologist David A. Kolb in his "Learning Styles Inventory." He describes four modes of learning: concrete experience, reflective observation, abstract conceptualization, and active experimentation. According to Kolb (1971), each individual has a dominant learning mode that is determined by his or her goals and needs.

> A mathematician may come to place great emphasis on abstract concepts, whereas a poet may value concrete experience more highly. A manager may be primarily concerned with active application of concepts, whereas a naturalist may develop his observational skills highly. Each of us in a more personal way develops a learning style that has some weak points and strong points (p. 28).

Another version, also based on Jungian theory, is the Lee-Hecht "Workstyles Survey." Again, four styles are proposed with the expectation that each manager combines elements of all four, yet has one that is dominant.

An example of how these style differences affect training designs occurred when the Workstyles Survey was used at a meeting of tax directors from about forty large corporations. Most of the participants scored highest on "systemizer," a data-oriented, very logical style. However, a 25-percent minority were dominant on the "forecaster" dimension, a creative, big-picture style. These ten or so participants turned out to be primarily engaged in tax planning, whereas most of the group were in their jobs because they were good at tax compliance work, a systemizer kind of task. At the coffee break, several people suggested to the trainer that the program would have been better if there had been more emphasis on theory and alternative uses for the material—and these people were all forecasters! The program, of course, had been designed with systemizers in mind, and what they wanted was more discussion about how the materials were validated and used in actual situations.

Needs

As with styles, adult managers have a way of imposing their needs onto learning programs. Many will learn selectively, taking what they want as if from a Swedish smorgasbord. In the same program, two apparently similar people will learn very different things. Sometimes they learn material quite unrelated to what was on the trainer's agenda. All of these "impositions" are seen as inevitable; in fact, they are valuable and desirable in the A/ML model.

A frequent question from managers is "How does this relate to my job?" They want and deserve relevance to the tasks they are working on back home. This is what makes the learning meaningful. A central issue, then, is for the trainer to be aware of the participants' current assignments and of their somewhat longer-range personal development tasks. A program that is not related to those tasks is likely to be rejected or rated poorly.

Authority

In describing the conflict that employees experience in authority relationships, Harry Levinson (1970) has said:

> The roots of a man's relationship to his boss lie largely in his own personality development. From his most helpless infantile experiences through childhood, adolescence and into maturity, each person has always had to deal with others who were more powerful than he and who exercised authority over him. As everyone knows from his own experience, and has learned again from whatever experiences he has had with adolescents, coming to terms with authority is a path fraught with conflict (pp. 117–118).

This conflict is often played out on the job. People have learned to respect authority in organizations, yet they rebel against it. They require the structure that authority brings, yet in the wish to maintain control over their lives, they seek independence. There is tension between needs to be dependent on the one hand and independent on the other.

Authority relationships have particular relevance in any discussion of training for managers. Successful managers have had to come to terms with many of the more conflict-laden aspects of these relationships. They are able to strike a balance of interdependence in relationships with others. Therefore, they are less likely to *automatically* invest power and authority in the trainer. Trainers need to earn that status from adult managers.

As a trainer, one begins to do this by recognizing that adults place great value on their experiences. In the training setting, adult managers have an opportunity to make meaning out of their current and past experiences. When training is designed to draw on an individual's experience, the person is more likely to be introspective about his or her past and, consequently, becomes more aware of behaviors that inhibit effective problem solving. Latent conflicts over authority are less likely to arise during training sessions that use the participant's experience as a resource for learning.

Similarly, in as much as adult managers have learned to develop interdependent relationships, they are able to learn quite effectively from their peers. They can also learn by serving as a "trainer" or helper to their peers.

Self-Image

Simply put, a self-image is what one thinks of himself or herself. Each person has a conception of oneself as a certain kind of individual. For everybody, there is additionally an "ideal" image, which in psychological terms is called the *ego ideal*. One's actual accomplishments in life usually do not measure up to the ego ideal; nevertheless, it is held out as a standard. The closer one's achievements come to the ego ideal, the greater the self-esteem tends to be. If one perceives himself or herself as falling short of the ideal standards, one's self-esteem is diminished. The ego ideal puts great demands on an individual, and one becomes angry and feels guilty when he or she is not living up to those demands. Conversely, one likes oneself when he or she approximates these demands. Striving toward our ego ideal is a powerful motivator (Levinson, 1976).

Even successful, mentally healthy managers do not escape the pressures that are exerted by the ego ideal. These pressures are at times heightened by the demands their own bosses and organizations place on them. Managers as trainees tend to put a great deal of energy into protecting their self-image. For managers, failures are potentially quite embarrassing. At times, people in power positions over the managers observe the training. Here, the observed manager's ignorance may appear as a weakness and is less likely to be disclosed. There may be great hesitance toward experimenting in discussion or role playing.

This is not to suggest that training should avoid these areas. Rather, it says that greater care and effort should be given to creating a supportive, safe climate, and that expecting too much, too soon in terms of disclosure or even involvement can be very risky. It is important for trainers to realize that managers may experience intense internal or external pressure to live up to their ego ideal, and that they bring these pressures with them to training sessions. Effective training heightens self-esteem by recognizing that people wish to see themselves in terms of their ego ideals, and are greatly motivated when they are helped to do so. In fact, training programs that are built on a skills competency model rather than a performance deficit model are perceived by managers as more useful; and are offered on a continuing basis in the organization.

Studying

Perhaps because of age or the passing of time since the formal school years, many adult managers don't "study" well. For example, reading assignments are notorious for never being read. As students, managers have worse study habits than their own school-age children. Paradoxically, they often overestimate how quickly they can learn—"Just give me the executive summary, please." This seems very consistent with their lives on their jobs: never enough time, so "learn it and do it fast."

TRAINING PROGRAM DESIGN

Organizations are frequently more concerned about the training and development of managers than of other employees. This is understandable. Questions of "What makes a good manager?" are harder to answer than "What makes a good drillpress operator?" or "What makes a good bookkeeper?" Although training professionals may at times concern themselves with all of these questions, their most complicated task is to develop effective managers. These are the people who are empowered to make the key decisions and to solve the complex problems that determine how productive an organization is and will be. A good manager is an invaluable resource for an organization, and it is the training department's job to assist with or, in the case of high potentials, accelerate the development of managerial talent.

The A/ML model begins to describe how training that is more likely to fit the manager's unique characteristics and responsibilities can be designed. Next, a framework that translates these points into a step-by-step process will be provided for putting a training program together. While this process is faithful to the principles of the A/ML model, it is much broader. It is essentially an andragogical system that can be applied to the training of any adult.

Two comprehensive reviews of the training literature have appeared in recent years. Both Goldstein (1980) and Hinrichs (1976) presented analyses of topics related to individual learning and the impact of the training intervention on the organization as a whole. The attempt here is to give the reader a less ambitious overview of the training process, yet one that will provide both a fundamental structure for training and a sampling of real issues that surround the problem of implementing such a structure.

Many discussions of training use a systems model as a context for explaining the training process. This is valuable in as much as it relates the instructional system to other organizational systems that interact with training in a variety of complex ways. Most of the work in this area includes the following: (1) setting instructional goals and objectives based on a needs analysis, (2) determining suitable learning experiences to achieve those goals and objectives, and (3) designing an evaluation of the learning that measures the trainee's improved performance. This suggests a basic, four-step process for the training program design presented in Figure 11–2.

1. *Needs analysis.*   A determination of the skills, knowledge, and attitudes an employee must learn in order to better perform a job-related task.
2. *Training objectives.*   Based on the needs analysis, a series of statements describing the outcomes of training; that is, what is to be learned—usually written in behavioral terms.
3. *Training methodology.*   Learning activities that will produce the desired outcomes as stated in the training objectives.
4. *Evaluation.*   A measurement of how well the training methods actually improved the employee's ability to perform the prescribed task.

Needs Analysis

Needs analysis is a process through which skills required of employees for successful job performance are uncovered. Today, it is axiomatic to say that any training within an organization should be based on the assessed needs of individuals or groups. For an organization to function at a required level, workers need to perform at a given standard. When they fall short of that standard, they *may* need training, which, if effective, will enhance their performance. In turn, this increased individual or group productivity results in desired organizational outcomes. Comprehensive diagnosis is more likely to reveal the *range* of factors that inhibit effective employee performance. If discrepancies (differences between actual and desired performance) exist because of skill deficiency,

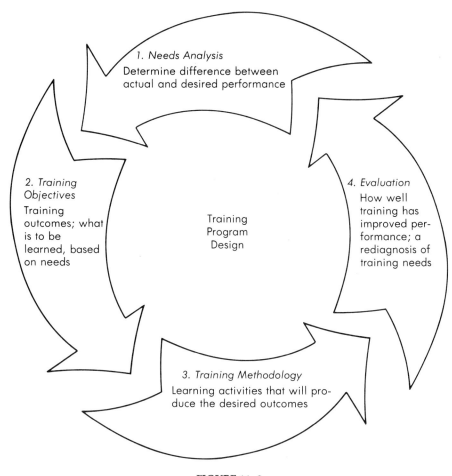

FIGURE 11-2
Four-Step Process for Training Program Design

then training is an appropriate intervention (Moore and Dutton, 1978). However, the discrepancy may be rooted in a different problem, that of worker motivation, for instance. Training cannot be expected to address such a problem. A thorough needs analysis should, above all, determine whether the problem is a "training problem."

Training units compete with other organizational units for limited resources. In order to justify their function, they must supply an answer to the question, "Why train?" Showing a relationship between their efforts and improved employee performance is a way to do so. An important element in this relationship is the assurance that training is based on real needs.

Methods of needs assessment vary. McGehee and Thayer's (1961) important work on the subject presents organizational analysis, operational analysis, and individual analysis as the three essential aspects of training needs analysis. Organizational analysis is a procedure that shows where training can be utilized within an organization; operational analysis attempts to break down a given job into a series of specific tasks and standards of performance for each task; individual analysis determines how satisfactorily an individual is performing the tasks required to do his or her job, and, subsequently, areas where one's performances needs to be improved.

In their review of the needs analysis literature, Moore and Dutton (1978) outlined several methods of collecting data in each of these three areas. Using organizational analysis as a means of determining needs, one can look at organizational goals; manpower inventories, which pinpoint areas where training can cover losses caused by retirement, turnover, and age; skills inventories, which look at number of employees in various skill groups and the scope of particular training needs; organizational climate indices, such as labor-management data, grievances, turnover, absenteeism, suggestions, accidents, attitude surveys, customer complaints, quality of products, costs of distribution, waste, down time, and late deliveries; repairs, changes in systems or subsystems; management requests (one of the most frequent determinants of needs), exit interviews; and MBO systems.

Operation analysis relies on the following techniques: job descriptions; job specification or task analysis (more specific and detailed than job descriptions); performance standards; review of literature concerning the job, including research in other industries, professional journals, government sources, and Ph.D. theses; asking questions about the job of the jobholder, the supervisor, or of management; and training committees or task forces.

Personal or individual analysis includes performance appraisals, observation, interviews, questionnaires, tests, devised situations such as role plays or case studies, assessment centers, and coaching.

Despite these extensive lists of methods for determining training needs, Moore and Dutton (1978) concluded that needs analyses are conducted as relatively isolated activities within organizations. They are either geared to single programs, used as a means to avert a crisis, or conducted in some mechanical fashion on a periodic basis. Instead, needs analysis should be able to generate a continuous source of information and should be interrelated with all other aspects of the organization's functioning.

Experience tends to confirm this view of how organizations use needs assessments. If it can be described as a "top down" process—one in which training or personnel administrators call for formal needs assessment to support a particular program or to achieve some other perfunctory purpose—then a more "bottom up" approach would be advocated.

Each individual is ultimately responsible for meeting his or her own personal and competency needs, however those are understood. Each immediate supervisor is responsible for influencing the individual subordinate's definition of his or her needs so that they are clear, realistic, and integrated with foreseeable organizational needs. It is this partnership between supervisor and employee that is the key element in establishing an ongoing needs assessment process. The professional training staff is responsible for helping all employees implement their developmental strategies effectively. Training's efforts are wisely placed in fostering the individual supervisor-employee relationship by offering courses in performance appraisal, counseling, coaching, and career planning.

Through this process, employees are more likely to take the initiative to inform training departments of their real needs. As this happens, organizations will find alternatives to general training programs aimed at nonspecific needs.

Training Objectives

Training objectives are the link between needs analysis and the actual content of an instructional program. If needs analysis describes a discrepancy in performance, then the training objective is the statement of posttraining behavior that the employee will display to indicate that the discrepancy either no longer exists or has been decreased. Training objectives tell what the *outcome* of a training program will be, and should specify predicted change in the trainee's skill-level, knowledge, or attitudes. As such, objectives suggest the selection of appropriate training techniques and resources for learning.

Although most trainers agree that objectives are a necessary programmatic component, controversy exists over the proper form objectives should take to be most useful to those who design training and to those who participate in it. Knowles (1978) distinguished between terminal-behavior-oriented procedures and inquiry-process-oriented procedures. The former are precise, measurable, observable statements. Terminal behaviors refer to the observable actions ("describing," "identifying," and "performing," as opposed to nonobservables like "knowing," "understanding," and "realizing") that the trainee is expected to demonstrate at the end of training. The latter sees learning as a much more fluid, less predictable, process. Goals emerge out of the learning process, changing often and varying in degree of clarity. An inquiry-oriented approach leaves no room for prescribed objectives.

Gagne (1972) sees an important function of behavioral objectives to be their role in communicating the expected outcomes of a program to its various organizational constituencies. Instructional designers must communicate clearly to course planners if planners are to choose the proper materials to achieve desired outcomes. The trainer's notion of outcomes needs to be consistent with planners, so that proper instruction and assessment occur. Objectives are a key communication tool between trainer and trainee. They can reassure trainees that the training is geared to their needs, or serve as a basis of negotiation if disputes arise in this area. Finally, objectives help participants' supervisors, top management, and others to form realistic expectations of training.

Some authors, however, feel behavioral objectives used by themselves have little purpose. Kneller (1972) noted that "the use of behavioral objectives is characteristic of a culture which sets a high value on efficiency and productivity, [one that] seeks to measure accomplishment in standard units" (p. 397). He is critical of a strict, behavioral approach to learning. Learning that is thought of as a series of measurable responses to prearranged stimuli leaves little room for individual differences or idiosyncratic learning. He supports an educational process in which objectives play a less controlling role. Scandura (1977), on the other hand, believes that behavioral objectives do not go far enough. In stating only what the learner will be able to do after training, they ignore the underlying competence required to perform the task. Nor do behavioral objectives tell what the teacher must teach. Used by themselves, behavioral objectives do not get at these fundamental aspects of the learning process.

The present view is that the importance of behavioral objectives should not be ignored. Not only do they serve the communications functions that Gagne speaks of, but they are key to the process of training program evaluation. Although evaluation will be dealt with later in this chapter, it is necessary to point out here that the essence of evaluation is measuring the extent to which a person's behavior was changed during training, and determining the impact of that change once the person has returned to his or her job. Measuring the relationship between training and behavior change is a fairly straightforward activity when behavioral objectives have been used as a basis for the design and implementation of training. When they have not, determining whether this relationship exists is an exercise in guess work and inference.

If behavioral objectives are useful, they must remain practical. Training departments ordinarily do not have resources to fine-tune the objective-setting process to the point where objectives reflect all possible learnings from a program, or all the varied learning needs of the participants. Although strict behavioralists might say this is possible and desirable, it is impractical. We are convinced that such compulsive attention to objectives tends to overshadow other important aspects of the training process. Behavioral objectives are best used as a guide for designing learning activities and a mechanism for ensuring that people's expectations of training are adequately met.

Training Techniques

The choice of an appropriate training technique to accomplish certain training objectives is perhaps more of an art than a science. The literature in this area is limited (Carroll, Paine, and Ivancevich, 1972). Much of it is nonempirical and nontheoretical, and it has not convincingly demonstrated the usefulness of particular kinds of techniques to accomplish given objectives in respective knowledge, skill, or attitude domains (Goldstein, 1980). Indeed, a trainer's ability to select effective techniques is sometimes more a function of one's intuition and experience than of one's reliance on sound, scientific writing.

Noting the inadequacies of the literature, Carroll, Paine, and Ivancevich (1972) surveyed 200 training directors from *Fortune* 500 companies in order to identify the relative effectiveness of training techniques. Training directors were asked to rate the methods of case study, conference/discussion, lecture, business games, movies, programmed instruction, role playing, sensitivity training, and television lecture according to their effectiveness in achieving objectives in the following six areas: (1) knowledge acquisition, (2) changing attitudes, (3) problem-solving skills, (4) interpersonal skills, (5) participant acceptance, and (6) knowledge retention. Their ratings are shown in Table 11–1.

The authors suggest that the current popularity of experiential learning may account for the negative reactions to the lecture technique. Also, the lecture is the most adaptable technique for the nonprofessional and this may have biased the training directors against it. For whatever the reason, this survey confirms the widespread feeling that lecture-type training is the most primitive and the least likely to produce lasting behavior change. Andragogists point to the need to involve adults by asking them to

TABLE 11–1
Ratings of Training Directors on the Most and Least Effective Training Techniques for
Various Training Objectives

Objective	Most Effective Technique	Least Effective Technique
Acquisition of knowledge	Programmed instruction	Lecture
Changing of attitudes	Sensitivity training	Television lecture
Problem-solving	Case study method	Lecture
Interpersonal skills	Sensitivity training	Television lecture
Participant acceptance	Conference/discussion	Television lecture
Knowledge retention	Programmed instruction	Television lecture

Source: Adapted from S. J. Carroll, Jr., F. T. Paine, and J. J. Ivancevich. "The Relative Effectiveness of Training Methods—Expert Opinion and Research." *Personnel Psychology* 25 (1972): 498.

assume responsibility for their learning, helping them to become self-directed, and recognizing and building on their experience. A didactic technique that allows for little interaction between trainer and trainee makes this difficult.

Keys (1977) categorized alternatives to the lecture in his "Management of Learning Grid." He considers both the trainer's style and his or her choice of technique to be the most important elements influencing the accomplishment of objectives. Included in the styles he describes are the "Experiential Teacher," who advocates learning-by-doing; the "Socratic Teacher," who uses questions and feedback; and the "Academician," who relies on content and testing. The synthesis of these different styles is one called "Manager of Learning," who simultaneously focuses on content, experience, and feedback, thereby integrating features of all the styles. The purpose of this is to demonstrate the suitability of experiential techniques to accomplish cognitive objectives. Traditionally, experiential techniques have been used to address objectives in the attitudinal domain; Key's work provides a provocative argument that their use can be more far reaching.

In recent years, computer-assisted and programmed instruction methods have been seen as devices for training departments to cut costs, individualize learning, and generally streamline the work they do. Nash, Muczyk, and Vettori (1971) concluded that although programmed instruction techniques nearly always reduced training time, they do not necessarily improve retention. Seltzer (1971) talked of the unique contribution computer-assisted instruction has made in the areas of simulations, gaming, and problem solving. Even though computer-assisted instruction cannot automatically be expected to reduce costs, Seltzer argues that costs should be a secondary consideration in those cases in which computers offer more creative and efficient solutions to instructional problems.

Aside from choosing training techniques based on their ability to foster particular types of learning, McGehee and Thayer (1961) suggested additional considerations: number of employees to be trained, their skill level, their individual differences, and the relative costs.

Evaluation

Conducting meaningful evaluations is probably the most difficult aspect of a training professional's job. Although writing on the topic has proliferated in recent years, researchers have yet to propose models that can be easily or efficiently integrated into existing organizational systems. Extensive evaluations, though infrequently conducted, depend almost always on the use of outside consultants. Most evaluation of training done within organizations consists only of trainees reporting their level of satisfaction with a particular training program at its conclusion. Such evaluations are called "smile sheets" because of their obvious positive bias.

As has been suggested, precise, measurable training objectives can be a basis for evaluating the extent to which training has had an impact on an employee's ability to perform one's job. Because objectives focus on outcomes, they force planners of training to think about evaluation from the initial phases of a program's design.

Measuring objectives are only one component of the evaluation process, however. Donaldson and Scannell (1978) proposed a four-step procedure for comprehensive evaluation: (1) reaction, (2) learning, (3) behavior, and (4) results. The first step, reaction, involves using a questionnaire or other device to solicit the trainee's feedback about the program. To find out what was actually learned (step two), it is necessary to conduct pretests and posttests. The authors suggest written tests, demonstrations, problem discussions, and role play as techniques to test learning. The third step involves asking the trainee's supervisors and peers to report posttraining behavior change on the job. Finally, results can be evaluated by looking at direct cost reduction, grievance reductions, improved work quality, lowered absenteeism, increased sales volume, greater worker efficiency, and fewer customer complaints.

Blumenfeld and Holland (1971) advocated an empirical approach to training evaluation. According to them, criterion measurement is the single-most important facet of any serious evaluation study. A criterion is a *pre*specified goal of training; it needs to be relevant, reliable, free from bias, and acceptable to management. A basic model is proposed as the minimally acceptable design to generate evidence of behavior change that is caused by training. The design involves pre- and posttests and the use of control groups. Experimental and control groups are tested on the criterion variables prior to training and again following the experimental group's exposure to training. Statistical measures of the training effect are derived.

Perhaps only an empirical process such as Blumenfeld and Holland's (1971) can be called a true evaluation. Pre- and posttests measure behavior change and the use of control groups determines whether the change has been caused by training. Anything less cannot make these claims. This, however, is a much more sophisticated approach to evaluation than most organizations take or, for that matter, would consider taking. Many practitioners feel that such exhaustive evaluation is not necessary to prove that training is making a difference in their organization.

Practitioners recognize a need to do more thorough evaluation. Most training professionals do some evaluation of their programs, but few progress beyond the reaction phase previously mentioned. This probably indicates that not enough attention is being paid to evaluation.

A missing element for many organizations is the close relationship between managers and training departments that can support a more extensive evaluation of training impact. In order to fully assess training outcomes, managers must first make an effort to help a subordinate integrate his or her learning into the day-to-day operation of a department, and then evaluate how effectively this has been done. Baumgartel and Jeanpierre (1972) have done some interesting work in illustrating the importance of the back-home organizational climate for facilitating the application of new knowledge. They found that such factors as the degree higher management is considerate of the feelings of lower management, the degree the organization stimulates and approves innovation, and the degree of free and open communication contribute significantly to how well new knowledge and concepts from training were applied.

Knowles (1978) sees an important part of the evaluation process to be the rediagnosis of needs. Having completed a learning program, the employee first assesses how well he or she has acquired the competencies he or she set out to learn, and then looks for what remains to be done. Perhaps the employee's projection for future learning will not be immediate, but, rather, will anticipate needs that might arise once new skills have been tested on the job. This process is meant to lead to the employee's ongoing self-assessment of learning needs.

The A/ML model began with needs assessments, and, in as much as the evaluation process can inform training departments of new or unmet learning needs, returns to that starting point. There is something of a cyclical nature to the model. Training units are involved at all points. To be most effective, however, they also need to involve their clients at all points. Much, if not most, of training's impact is determined by how receptive the work setting is to new learning. Supervisors and managers need to be responsible for creating climates in which employees' learning and development is not only supported, but stimulated.

Personnel development is an intrinsic, ongoing aspect of everyday organizational life, not an event "put on" by the training staff. The appropriate measure of the training staff's effectiveness is how much value they add to this ongoing process in terms of

Helping others identify the "people" issues likely to affect the company

Helping others to recognize their proper roles and responsibilities in dealing with these issues

Helping others to implement their responsibilities by giving them tools and supports

Delivering certain programs of instruction to augment the learning that is happening every day in each job

The ultimate goal is to help the company achieve its business strategy. Some of the factors affecting this goal have little to do with the human side of the business. On the other hand, it seems fair to ask that the personnel development function be evaluated for its contribution to the company's overall ability to have enough of the right people at the right time and place, and adequately trained to do their jobs—all at a reasonable cost.

THE MANAGEMENT DEVELOPMENT MATRIX: A LEARNING MODEL[1]

Often, training by itself is not the issue; rather, the personnel professional is concerned with the overall career development of employees, especially managers. An organization contains people at differing stages of their own development. The Management Development Matrix described here has proved to be a useful way to understand the progress of professional managers and to guide efforts to assist them. It not only identifies the specific stages of managerial career development, but it also pairs these stages with appropriate career interventions. The Matrix, as shown in Table 11–2, delineates specific roles for the employee, the boss, and the training activity.

The Management Development Matrix is built on an organizing principle: the pairing of four stages of managerial career development with four types of career interventions. The four stages of managerial career development have been defined as:

1. *Apprenticeship.* Learning about the organization and completing job assignments under supervisory direction.
2. *Craftsmanship.* Choosing a specialty and performing competently and independently in the organization.
3. *Mentorship.* Heading an operation/staff department and assuming responsibility for the work of others.
4. *Spokesmanship.* Setting the tone and making policy for the internal organization and articulating for external constituencies the business direction of the enterprise.

Whether the career stage is apprenticeship, craftsmanship, mentorship, or spokesmanship, four types of career interventions are common to these stages, but vary in content and impact. These career interventions are identified as:

1. *Dominant job elements.* The "make or break" tasks that will partially determine a person's success in/impact on his or her organization.
2. *People relationships.* The key individuals a person interacts with to accomplish his or her job assignments.
3. *Organizational adjustments.* The major accommodations an individual makes from the initial role of apprentice to the final role of spokesman.
4. *Management development activities.* A range of supportive programs for educating and developing a manager.

The initiator of, or the driver behind, these career interventions can be the training department, the new professional, his or her boss, his or her mentor, or any combination of these with other members of the organization. This statement makes explicit the need for a partnership of resources to successfully implement a managerial career path.

Although these stages are typically thought of as separate and sequential (and often are), an individual may pass through these stages more than once. For example, in mak-

[1]The Management Development Matrix was developed by the senior author.

TABLE 11–2

Management Development Matrix

Stages	Dominant Job Elements	People Relationships	Organizational Adjustments	Mgmt. Dev. Activities
Apprenticeship	–apply and enhance technical expertise –build performance record –look at business enterprise & work w/formal organization –test creative ideas	–establish mentor, supervisory, and peer relationships	–accept job tasks, but reach out for challenges –tolerate low visibility while building influence –get confirmation from supervisor	–orientation and skill building programs –task force participation –assume responsibility of completing a major assignment
Craftmanship	–choose technical specialty and establish visibility –solve job-related problems and assume more managerial responsibility	–maintain peer relationships in other offices –accept responsibility for others word –become less dependent on supervisor	–anticipate transitional problems –evaluate what is needed in the technical area –get feedback on performance	–career assessment and planning –identification of managerial skills
Mentorship	–assume leadership role in organizational unit and make business decisions –relate objectives to company objectives –contribute to policy statements	–become a mentor –extend interpersonal relationships to include external constituencies –provide feedback to subordinates	–mediate organization's and individuals' demands –balance giving freedom to and controlling subordinates	–acquire managerial skills of planning, organizing, and leading –acquire "people" skills of career appraisal, coaching, and counseling
Spokesmanship	–lead business management team –implement corporate objects –perpetuate business enterprise through strategic planning	–frequent contact w/other executives and also "grassroots" –increased visibility to large community	–make more complex decisions –manage demands of multiple constituencies –balance career with outside demands	–university-sponsored executive programs –executive sabbaticals and individual counseling –manage organizational change

ing a job change a person may move from mentorship to apprenticeship. Quite obviously, the transition from apprenticeship to mentorship in the new position occurs at a faster rate and, indeed, an individual may skip over the craftsmanship stage. Furthermore, these four stages of managerial career development can be viewed as open systems. As such, an individual may enter and leave a stage at different points, depending on an individual's competencies and the business needs of an organization. For example, in a sales management structure a person may be refining one's skills as a skillful negotiator—a dominant job element in the craftsmanship state—and simultaneously be interviewing candidates and making selection recommendations to his or her boss for openings in the territory—a dominant job element in the mentorship stage.

The next sections cite examples of interventions under each type that distinguish one stage from another.

Apprenticeship

The Management Development Matrix applied to the apprenticeship stage for someone in an industrial organization would result in the career interventions and behaviors described below. For this initial stage, the dominant job element interventions include competently applying (technical) skills to job assignments and enhancing technical expertise. In the apprenticeship stage, the prospective manager completes routine and detailed job assignments, identifies and works with the formal organizational structure, and completes work tasks, while supervisors observe both his or her present level of competence and future potential. A consistent performance record is built. Through all of this, the employee takes a critical look at the business enterprise and undertakes job experiences that require an application of creativity and innovative ideas.

The second career intervention at the apprenticeship stage—people relationships—requires the establishment of a strong relationship with the immediate supervisor, developing crucial mentor relationships, and forming solid peer relationships within the organization.

Organizational adjustments, the third career intervention, include at this stage an ability to balance realistic acceptance of initial job tasks with an aggressive reaching out for new challenges or opportunities. The apprentice must also build visibility and influence in the organization through task accomplishment, while at the same time tolerating initial low visibility and detailed work assignments. The supervisor needs to provide confirmation and approval especially in relation to ratings of performance and potential.

Management development activities include new employee orientation programs that give a person a realistic perspective on an organization's history, mission, goals, policies, major products or services, and overall competitive position in its industry. The apprentice should participate in key-issue task forces and assume singular responsibility for a major project assignment. Skill programs in interviewing, oral/written communication, and technical fields should be completed. Finally, the process of identifying the skills required of a managerial position is begun.

In the apprenticeship stage, as with the succeeding stages, the new professional's boss provides an environment for professional growth, but relies on a person's initiative to ask for what is specifically needed. As evidenced in the preceding list, a boss has at this point at least twenty options. A boss can emphasize and mix the interventions to meet the appropriate developmental needs.

Throughout the apprenticeship stage, a boss is developing human resource talent by using the career interventions to: (1) facilitate a new professional's taking hold in the organization, (2) develop and acquire the skills that represent the foundation of a managerial career, (3) build and maintain effective interpersonal relationships with his or her immediate supervisor and organizational peers, and (4) relate performance on the current job to probabilities of future success in the organization. Overall, the boss' primary roles are to select promising professionals, assign them to appropriate job assignments, and then follow-up with coaching and counseling as required. In short, the new professional in the apprenticeship stage is attempting to answer the developmental question "How do I take hold in an organizational world of work?" Or, how can I shape a career dream that fully utilizes my abilities, captures my interests and, finally, demands a significant personal investment of energy, enthusiasm, and effort with a realistic hope of success?

Craftsmanship

If the developmental task of the apprenticeship stage can be described as "How do I take hold in an organizational world of work?" then in the craftsmanship stage, the task can be defined as "How can I become a competent technical professional who works independently to achieve significant business results?" In short, the interventions of the craftsmanship stage are built on the foundation blocks of apprenticeship. Success at mastering the tasks of entry is presumed before a boss can direct one's subordinate to the interventions of the craftsmanship stage. The employee chooses a technical specialty; as such, he or she becomes recognized as an independent leader in a chosen specialty and maintains "state of the art" knowledge. The craftsman becomes increasingly visible and is called upon to solve job-related problems and perform job assignments with minimal supervision. More managerial responsibility is assumed through the coordination of special projects or in a variety of project management roles. The expectation is for the craftsman to contribute to the success and productivity of the organization by creating an impact on a significant business problem.

People relationships at that stage build on already established peer relationships within the organization and spread across functional departments. The supervisor's or mentor's directions are less important as the craftsman becomes more confident in business decision making and less dependent on others. The acceptance of responsibility for others' work on a team project is a key developmental step. Professional relationships are broadened through professional associations and peers in other organizations.

In the craftsmanship stage, the organizational context in which the dominant job elements are accomplished and the people relationships built is a very crucial variable, especially since more visibility brings with it potentially more vulnerability and certainly more assessment by crucial superiors. Therefore, the interventions of organizational adjustments include balancing the current satisfactions of specialization with the anticipated transitional problems of moving into a management position. One begins to evaluate what is needed by the organization from a technical point of view and to assess the risks associated with the choice of one's specialty and the perceived organizational value of that specialty.

Increased visibility enables the employee to feel more confident when making presentations to, and handling questions of, department heads, company staff, and corporate executives. Critical feedback is sought from one's boss and other critical supervisors on strengths and areas for improvement.

In support of these interventions, the management development activities for this career stage are career development and career planning and counseling. Motives for remaining a technical specialist, as opposed to choosing a managerial career, are assessed. A supervisor, together with other significant resources, provides data about career opportunities. The supervisor frequently acts as an interpretor of organizational data. In this stage, a new professional expects his or her supervisor to be a data provider and interpreter. However, if a supervisor elects to restrict a person's access to data and/or acts as a career caretaker—''trust in me for career growth''—his or her position and influence will fall sharply.

The craftsman begins to differentiate between skills of a technical expert and those of a manager, and to develop managerial skills. The self-management process accelerates—time, priority setting, and individual goals.

In the craftsmanship stage, an individual professional becomes more competent in accomplishing the tasks of one's specialty and more visible. As a result, the career interventions of this stage are intended to: (1) solidify the professional's position of technical leadership in the organization, (2) extend his or her network of interpersonal relationships internally and externally, (3) access realistically and manage the risks of increased visibility, and (4) evaluate his or her true interests in a managerial role. Successful mastery of these tasks, defined in the four kinds of career interventions, is an important developmental step prior to the transition into a managerial role during the career development stage of mentorship.

Mentorship

In the mentorship stage, a technical professional uses his or her performance record as an individual contributor to launch one's managerial career. As a result, the individual is preoccupied with those developmental tasks that differentiate a managerial position from a technical, individual-contributor role. Also, mastery of these tasks will assist a person in making a smoother transition into a managerial position. In short, the interventions of the mentorship stage focus on managerial skills, especially the skills associated with a functional management position.

During the mentorship stage, the interventions grouped under dominant job elements include assuming a leadership role in an organizational unit and providing a focus for its business growth. The appraisal, coaching, counseling, role selection, and development of subordinates is undertaken. The objectives and work plans of one's business unit are related to the company's objectives. Responsibility is assumed for the work others do.

The mentor contributes to policy statements for multiple external constituencies: government, community, consumer, and trade professional association. Increasingly, more business decisions are made and the organization is informed of the need for more freedom of action and autonomy.

In accomplishing these dominant job elements, an individual is viewed as a manager of doers and not simply as a doer with a manager's title. At this state of managerial career development, people relationships consist of identifying and influencing the key formal and informal decision makers in the organization. As the name of this phrase implies, the employee becomes a mentor and learns to influence, guide, direct, and be responsible for subordinates' work. Interpersonal relationships are broadened to include planned contact with government, community, and consumer and trade professional associations. Peer relationships are established and maintained. Subordinates receive timely, concrete, and specific performance-potential feedback.

In accomplishing these job/interpersonal tasks, an individual confronts a more demanding organizational environment and becomes more visible in it. As a result, the mediation of demands—often competing—of individuals and the organization is an important organizational adjustment intervention.

The mentor balances personal standards of work performance with acceptable and "stretch" standards that motivate—but do not intimidate—subordinates. One must balance the coaching/guiding role of the mentor who emphasizes freedom to act with the need to maintain control and dictate "how-to's." Oganizational conformity and the expectations for creativity and initiative among subordinates are frequently at odds, and the mentor must build confidence and encourage successful performance of subordinates without being personally threatened.

In support of these on-the-job interventions, management development activities during the mentorship stage include managerial skills of planning, organizing, controling, budgeting, and leading. Part of this process is to identify objectives, specify performance standards, and provide feedback on results as compared to objectives. Skills are developed in areas of appraisal and career planning, and coaching, counseling, and consultation. Additionally, small group skills—building an effective management team by integrating interpersonal competencies with business results—are important. The mentor continually updates business knowledge and managerial skills.

In the mentorship stage, an individual assumes significant managerial responsibility for the performance/career success of individual contributors. Therefore, the career interventions of this stage are intended to: (1) strengthen the individual's position as a functional business leader, (2) enhance the person's effectiveness as a people manager, (3) expand his or her internal and external interfaces, and (4) solidify his or her managerial acumen. In addition to these career-related outcomes, a manager confronts the relative trade-offs of, as well as one's investment in, four career/life anchors: career, family, community, and self. These four anchors will take on even greater importance as a manager moves into the spokesmanship stage of his or her career.

Spokesmanship

If the mentorship stage can be perceived as launching a managerial career, then the spokesmanship stage can be defined as an orbit of influence, typically as a plant manager, general manager, or corporate executive. Quite often, influence is equated with being a spokesman—within the organization as a climate/tone-setter and externally as the corporate presence within a community or the voice to external constituencies. As a spokesman, an executive focuses on the perpetuation of a business enterprise and is concerned about the allocation of resources (human, financial, and capital) for profitable business performance and future growth. In executing this mandate, the career interventions are more varied and complex. First, there are interventions that are grouped under *dominant job elements.*

The spokesman becomes the leader of a business management team through innovative policy development. He or she specifies and monitors the implementation of corporate/company objectives in the areas of human resources, product/services development and delivery, and financial return. Relationships with key constituencies—corporate officers, members of the board of directors, and stockholders—are built and maintained. The business is perpetuated through systematic strategic planning, coupled with rigorous tactical planning and execution, as well as systematic development of key human resources as part of an overall succession plan. Through it all, the spokesman must combat personal obsolescence.

To accomplish these six critical job elements, an executive enhances one's people relationships through frequent and substantive contact with other key executives to select and develop key human resources. Visits are regularly scheduled at the "grass-roots" of the organization. There is increased interface with the board of directors and stockholders, plus increased visibility with members of the financial community: banking and investment, as well as governmental policy makers. The spokesman acts as a mentor for new, young professionals in the organization. Key relationships outside the organization, as well, are developed on company boards, in industry associations, and on boards of community education or fine arts organizations.

If pulled together, these task and interpersonal interventions represent a more strategic, total perspective on the executive role in an organization. Furthermore, an executive, in attempting to integrate these varied task and interpersonal needs, is affected by, and must adjust to, the pulling away from daily operations versus the need for strategic planning: it is not simply a question of time management, but perhaps more a question of interest management. As more complex decisions with greater degrees of risk are made, the spokesman adjusts to the role of policy maker. There is the need to accustom oneself to being alone at times as an executive and yet develop a tightly knit group of advisors. Also, key elements of the organization/work environment are: (1) responding to and managing the demands of multiple and varied constituencies, (2) handling high levels of responsibility and power without evidence of emotional stress, (3) confronting discrepancies between an ideal career goal and actual achievement, and (4) learning how to balance career demands with personal, nonwork demands.

Finally, within an executive orbit the recommended management development activities are university-sponsored executive development programs. These act as a refresher, reduce parochial thinking, and help build an informal network of friendships with concerned executive decision makers in other industries. Also, strategic business planning and policy development, executive sabbaticals for renewal and recreation, and individual counseling are important interventions. All of this aims to minimize executive stress.

In the spokesmanship stage of career development, an executive is responsible for all the operations of a total business unit. As such, his or her specialist background and related work experience equip the individual with an in-depth knowledge of one function within a multifunctional organization. Therefore, one's success in the spokesmanship stage is not dependent on developing a task familiarity with all functions, but rather to use one's specialist strength as a primary route to understanding the business enterprise and, in fact, relating other specialties to this function. In short, a person's technical specialty provides a ladder to climb the organization. However, once an individual becomes a spokesman, he or she must throw away the ladder or else it will become a crutch and slow one's growth in this stage.

Furthermore, an executive's development of a broad business perspective results from understanding the interrelationships across functions, asking probing questions to further explore these relationships and, finally, from developing policies that integrate the short-term tactical planning and strategic planning of all key elements of a business enterprise. Therefore, in the spokesmanship stage, the career interventions are intended to: (1) strengthen one's position as a business leader and integrative policy maker, (2) increase one's visibility/contact with key employee groups and external constituencies, (3) help one balance the multiple demands of an executive position, and (4) enhance one's strategic skills in planning for the business enterprise.

SUMMARY

The Management Development Matrix removes the mystique or magical quality from developing managerial talent within an organization. This matrix describes the four stages of managerial career development and pairs them with appropriate career interventions. These interventions, as shown in Table 11–2, have been defined as

1. Dominant job elements
2. People relationships
3. Organizational adjustments
4. Management development activities

A manager and/or training staff can choose from these four groups the appropriate interventions for aspiring managerial candidates, depending on the person's mix of strengths, weaknesses, interests, and ambitions. Furthermore, a manager can more precisely direct the development of a managerial candidate and prioritize those interventions that are more leveraged in the organization and, therefore, presumably more related to managerial success.

The Management Development Matrix not only benefits the "directing" manager, but also the aspiring manager. To be specific, the aspiring manager understands the type and range of skills to be developed at each stage, and, furthermore, that mastery of these developmental tasks at each stage of managerial development better positions him or her for future stages of managerial succession. An aspiring managerial candidate can use this matrix to plan and take responsibility for one's own development. Also, a manager and a managerial candidate can use it as an assessment tool—evaluating a person's skills repertoire against what is needed for success at a particular stage of management development.

We have looked from several perspectives at how management development and training occurs and should occur within an organization. As a departmental function, there may be temptations to act in ways that appear to protect the department, but these ways reduce the ability to successfully assist with the organization's larger, longer-term needs for on-the-job, day-to-day learning.

The Management Development Matrix and the Adult/Manager as Learner models are offered as ways to define managers' developmental stages and their special characteristics as learners. They provide the training and development specialist with information that should help him or her to define goals and programs for the training department. It will be useful to validate these models by following an andragogical process of needs assessment, setting specific objectives based on needs, choosing training and development techniques where employees can assume responsibility for their learning, and evaluating programs by rediagnosing needs.

Discussion Questions

1. What are the differences between the traditional learning model and the Adult/Manager Learning (A/ML) model?

2. What are the principal components of a training and development process?

3. What are three approaches to needs analysis? Compare the advantages/disadvantages of each approach.

4. What are the approaches to training evaluation? Compare and contrast these approaches.

5. What are the four stages of the Management Development Matrix? What are the implications of each stage for the design and delivery of management development programs?

CHAPTER TWELVE

ASSESSMENT CENTERS AND MANAGEMENT DEVELOPMENT

Virginia R. Boehm

Virginia R. Boehm is Manager of Psychological Services at the Standard Oil Company of Ohio. She received her Ph.D. in Social Psychology from Columbia University. Before joining SOHIO, Dr. Boehm held the positions of Personnel Supervisor and later of Project Manager for American Telephone and Telegraph Company. In these positions, she was actively involved in the development and validation of systems for management selection and staffing. She served also as Employment Consultant for the New York State Department of Labor in which capacity she developed and validated aptitude and interest tests for employee selection and counseling. Dr. Boehm has published numerous articles on employee selection issues and on the assessment center. She is a licensed psychologist in the state of Ohio and a diplomat of the American Board of Professional Psychology.

One of several tools available for use by the personnel practitioner is the assessment center. This chapter is designed to aid the student or practitioner in understanding what an assessment center is and how it works, determining whether this tool is a suitable one to bring to bear on specific problems, and, if so, how it might most effectively be used.

No single topic related to assessment centers is covered in depth in this chapter and this chapter should not be viewed as a substitute for a textbook or "how to" manual. References are provided for the reader who desires to explore the topic in more depth.

While a variety of uses of assessment centers in business and industry will be mentioned, a primary focus of the discussion will be on the use of assessment centers for purposes that might broadly be termed management development.

Several definitions of the term *assessment center* appear in the literature. For example:

An assessment center consists of a standardized evaluation of behavior based on multiple inputs. Multiple trained observers and techniques are used. Judgments about behavior are made, in part, from specially developed assessment simulations (Task Force on Assessment Center Standards, 1979, p. 4).

. . . An assessment center can be thought of as both a place and a process. It is a place where individuals participate in a variety of measurement techniques. It is also a process designed to provide standardized and objective conditions of evaluation (Moses, 1977, p. 4).

It is a process in which individuals have an opportunity to participate in a series of situations which resemble what they might be called upon to do in the real world (Jaffee and Sefcik, 1980, p. 40).

Each of these definitions focuses on different elements of what constitutes an assessment center. An assessment center might be viewed as consisting of six key elements: (1) a measuring process, (2) using multiple measurement techniques, (3) focusing on the measurement of behavior relevant to ''real world'' situations, (4) conducted by multiple assessors, (5) who are specifically trained to observe and evaluate behavior, and (6) where the processes of observing and evaluating behavior are separated.

Three perspectives (some might consider them biases) have markedly influenced this chapter's content:

1. The primary purpose of an assessment center is to produce results useful for the personnel management process in organizations. Considerations of assessment center validity cannot be separated from considerations of organizational utility.
2. While assessment centers do not come close to matching other measurement devices in terms of low cost and rapidity of administration, this author views the gain, in terms of better behavioral description, higher validity, and better representation of organizational reality, as more than offsetting the additional cost and time required.
3. Because of the complex nature of the assessment center, theoretical, technical, and practical aspects of assessment centers are so closely interwoven as to make discussion of any of these aspects in isolation from the others virtually meaningless. Assessment centers can be meaningfully discussed only as a total system.

BRIEF HISTORY OF THE ASSESSMENT CENTER METHOD

Assessment centers represent a meeting ground of three theoretical approaches to the study of individual differences: (1) psychometric theory, (2) behavioral observation, and (3) clinical assessment.

Psychometric theory grows out of an experimental tradition which maintains that human behavior can be divided into more or less independent categories, and that behavior in these categories can be measured in such a way as to permit comparison between individuals. Pure psychometric theory is exactly what the name implies—it makes the assumption that psychological differences between people are potentially as precisely measurable as physical differences such as height and weight. Psychometrics focuses on improving measurement tools and techniques in order to improve the accuracy of measurement.

The psychology of behavioral observation is more characteristic of the approach of social psychology, sociology, and anthropology. Inferences regarding individual differences are based on observation of an individual within a particular social or cultural context.

The third approach, clinical assessment, investigates individual differences by comparing the observed behavior of the individual to what the clinician regards as optimal behavior for that particular person. The aim of clinical psychology is consequently to maximize the effectiveness of an individual's functioning.

While all three of these approaches focus on individual differences, both the means and interpretation of measurement differ: psychometric measurement compares the individual to a predetermined standard; behavioral measurement compares the individual to other individuals in the same environment; clinical measurement compares the individual's current performance level to his or her own judged potential. The possibilities for conflict among these three historical approaches are manifold and conflicts have, in fact, been common. The issues involved are philosophic as well as scientific.

Assessment centers represent a meeting ground of these three traditional approaches for the study of individual differences. The success of an assessment center depends to a considerable extent on the degree to which these three approaches are successfully amalgamated in the design and implementation of the assessment center.

Early Uses

During World War II, the British War Office Selection Boards began the attempt to combine these approaches in order to improve the selection of officers. This combined approach was taken up and expanded upon by the U.S. Office of Strategy Services (OSS).

A group of psychologists, led by Henry Murray, was asked to aid the OSS in the selection of operatives who could sucessfully operate as behind-the-lines intelligence officers (the more common term would be "spy"). The story of their endeavors is recorded in a book, *Assessment of Men* (OSS Assessment Staff, 1948), and is summarized by Donald Mackinnon (1977), who was one of the psychologists on the staff.

Within a very brief time, an elaborate assessment center was devised and exercises were developed aimed at assessing the participants on nine dimensions: motivation, practical intelligence, emotional stability, social relations, leadership, physical ability, observation and reporting, propaganda skills, and maintenance of cover. This last was assessed by the interesting means of having each candidate during his stay at the assessment center "build up and maintain as completely as possible a cover story for himself claiming to have been born where he wasn't, to have been educated in institutions other than those he had attended, to have been engaged in work or profession not his own, and to live now in a place that was not his true residence" (Mackinnon, 1977, p. 18).

Aside from these such novel features, the process and procedures followed by the OSS assessment center are very similar to those used in assessment centers today. The basic steps in designing an assessment process, as given in *Assessment of Men,* still are basic to the technique:

Step 1: Make a preparatory analysis of all the jobs for which candidates are to be assessed. . . .
Step 2: On the basis of this analysis, describe those personality traits required for success in each job and select those which the program will assess. . . .
Step 3: Design a rating scale for each of the selected variables.
Step 4: Design an assessment program which will reveal the strength of the selected variables. These procedures are to be set up with a social matrix consisting of staff and other candidates and are to vary in type in order to afford ample opportunity for observation. . . .
Step 5: Express another basic principle. It is that one must see the personality as a whole before making specific ratings. . . . (OSS Assessment Staff, 1948, p. 28).

After the conclusion of World War II, a few sporadic attempts were made to utilize a similar method for industrial selection. For example, one such attempt (Taft, 1948) utilized a primitive form of the approach to select executive trainees for an Australian shoe factory.

But it was not until 1956 that the first full-scale trial was given to the use of the assessment center method in American industry. The Management Progress Study, conducted under the leadership of Douglas Bray of AT&T, began in 1956. It is still an active research project and was designed as, and still is, a pure research effort, with no operational use made of the results. Many publications have resulted from this study including Bray (1969), Bray and Grant (1966), and Bray, Campbell, and Grant (1974). The role of this research in the subsequent development of the assessment center method has been a key one.

Although the Management Progress Study was purely a research effort, the assessment center approach to the measurement of management skills was sufficiently impressive that Michigan Bell, an AT&T subsidiary, established an operational assessment center in 1958. During the early 1960s, a number of other organizations followed suit—The Standard Oil Company of Ohio (SOHIO), followed by General Electric, IBM, J. C. Penney, Sears, and others. By 1969, twelve American corporations operated assessment centers (Byham, 1977), and research other than that conducted by AT&T began to appear (see, for example, Bentz, 1967—the Sear's program; Donaldson, 1969—SOHIO; Greenwood and McNamara, 1967—IBM). The pioneering days were over for the assessment center method and the mass usage ones had begun.

Utilization of Assessment Centers Today

The exact number of organizations that are currently making use of the assessment center method is difficult to estimate. Byham (1977) stated the number at that time as being 1,000 or more, and Parker (1980), more recently, stated the number to be in excess of 2,000. The 1970s obviously represented a period of explosive growth for assessment center utilization.

Byham (1977) listed several reasons why this growth occurred: publicity in general management publications, as well as professional journals; the emergence of consulting firms with expertise in the method; the development of off-the-shelf assessment exercises, allowing smaller organizations to utilize the techniques; the beginnings of systematic vehicles for interorganizational communication of their experiences with assessment centers; and pressure for equal employment opportunity.

During the last few years, other developments have reinforced this explosive growth. In 1978, the *Journal of Assessment Center Technology* was founded, providing a professional journal devoted solely to the dissemination of research concerning assessment centers. The publication of *Applying the Assessment Center Method* in 1977 gathered much of the data available at the time into one place for more ready usage.

Consequently, the focus of assessment center utilization today has moved from "Should my organization use assessment centers?" to "How can my organization make better use of assessment centers?" The question of the purpose of an assessment center is discussed below.

FUNCTIONS OF ASSESSMENT CENTERS

There are three primary reasons why an organization might elect to utilize assessment centers as a part of its personnel system:

1. The selection of people for a specific job or job level
2. The identification of people with long-range potential for organizational advancement
3. The diagnosis of training and development needs

The intended function of the assessment center plays a major role in determining how it will be designed and administered, and how the results will be disseminated.

The three primary functions previously listed are ordered in terms of the complexity required for the design and administration of the program. In general, an assessment center process designed purely for selection purposes is easier to design, administer, utilize, and evaluate than one designed for identification purposes. An assessment center process designed to serve an identification function is in turn less complex than one designed for diagnosis.

Selection of People for a Specific Job or Job Level—The Selection Center

The assessment center established by the OSS (1948) was purely a selection center. It was designed to select, from among the assessees, those who should be chosen as behind-the-lines operatives during World War II. The exercises, while sophisticated, were designed solely to contribute data to the selection decision. The dimensions evaluated were based on a "job analysis" (admittedly and under the circumstances, unavoidably, an informal one), the final reports were brief and quickly prepared, and no feedback was given the assessees. These characteristics are still common ones for selection centers to possess. The OSS assessment center made recommendations concerning what type of assignment would be most suitable for an assessee, in addition to evaluating the assessee's overall suitability for selection. These recommendations were purely of the selection variety, and placement was not viewed as in any way intended to be "developmental" for the assessee.

Beginning with the first operational use of assessment centers in American industry, selection has been the predominant purpose of assessment centers established by organizations (Standing, 1977).

While selection may be targeted at a specific job, as it was in the case of the OSS center, or at a particular job level (first-level supervision in the early AT&T application), the focus is on direct input to organizational staffing decisions either immediate or of a relatively short range. Benefit to the individual assessee comes primarily from being presented with the opportunity to be considered for the position. If feedback is given to the assessee in a selection center, it is descriptive rather than prescriptive, focusing on what the assessee did, rather than on what might be done to remedy identified weaknesses.

In contrast, both identification centers and diagnostic ones are designed to serve developmental purposes and to directly benefit individual assessees, as well as organizations.

Identification of Long-Range Potential—The Identification Center

If properly designed, the assessment center can yield information that goes beyond that relevant to an immediate selection decision. Because the traits measured by an assessment center tend toward stability over time (Bray, Campbell, and Grant, 1974), the measurement of an individual's attributes can have long-term organizational utility. The AT&T Management Progress Study represented the first assessment center designed to make a judgment of long-term potential. Young men, who had recently assumed positions at the lowest level of management, were assessed for their suitability for middle-management positions (positions they would not be expected to reach for eight to ten years). Since the study was conducted solely for research purposes and the results not fed back either to assessees or their management, the finding that assessment outcome did in fact predict management progress (Bray and Grant, 1966) indicated clearly that assessment judgments could be used for long-range decision making.

The results of the Management Progress Study also clearly indicated that the types of assignments and opportunities made available to these young managers also played an important role in the extent to which high potential people were able to utilize the abilities they possessed (Bray, Campbell, and Grant, 1974). Consequently, the use of assessment centers as a means for identifying high-potential people for subsequent development and utilization is an increasingly prevalent use for assessment center information.

While the specific details of such programs vary widely, they commonly involve the use of some type of career pathing or system of assignments for people with identified high potential, substantial organizational monitoring and/or control over the movement of these individuals, and have as their goal the upward organizational movement of individuals identified as having high potential (see Chapter 13 in this volume for a more detailed discussion of careers). Feedback of assessment results may be separate from, or combined with, a career planning discussion aimed at capitalizing on strengths the individual has exhibited at the assessment center. Action taken as a result of potential identification may be individualized, or may involve the placement of an individual in an established training or job progression program. Regardless of the details, development programs following an identification center are aimed at maximizing the organization's utilization of high potential people and normally include only such high potential individuals.

Diagnosis of Training and Development Needs— The Diagnostic Center

While development programs arising out of identification centers are intended to capitalize on the utilization of identified strengths, developmental programs based on diagnostic centers are more or less remedial.

At an assessment center conducted primarily for diagnostic purposes, the principal emphasis is not on making a decision regarding the individual's present qualifications for a specific job or job level (the mission of the selection center), or on determining long-range potential (as is the case in an identification center), but rather on deriving a profile of the strengths and weaknesses of an individual. Since the profile is regarded as the most important product of the assessment center, an overall assessment rating may not be given as a product of the assessment center.

Ideally, the weaknesses identified are keyed to specific training and development suggestions given to the individual. Feedback tends to be detailed and focused on specific areas. In most cases, subsequent attempts at the reduction or removal of weaknesses thus identified are viewed primarily as the responsibility of individual assessees, with perhaps some involvement of immediate supervision. The goal of developmental activities is viewed as being both increased individual satisfaction and improved job performance. While organizational benefit is seen as forthcoming from a diagnostic center, benefits to the individual assessee are viewed as equally important, or more so, in most instances. In a few programs, a diagnostic center is more heavily weighted toward organizational outcomes and is used as a vehicle for training needs analysis. Table 12–1 from Boehm and Hoyle (1977) summarizes the key differences between programs aimed at identification and diagnosis.

While not all assessment center applications with developmental objectives are pure examples of one of these two strategies, the differences between them should be kept in mind. More detailed descriptions of specific development-oriented assessment center programs designed to serve both identification and diagnostic purposes will be presented later.

TABLE 12–1
Identification and Diagnosis—Two Major Development Strategies

Differences	*Identification Strategy*	*Diagnostic Strategy*
Population	Primarily high-potential people	All interested assessees
Focal point of feedback	Overall rating with some attention to individual variables	Individual variables; overall rating perhaps not given
Developmental concentration	Technical and job administration skills	Weaknesses in management skill areas
Organizational involvement	High; centralized monitoring and control functions	Low; reliance on self-development and possible immediate supervisory involvement
Goal of development	Upward advancement within organization based on systematic career plan	Individual's increased satisfaction and improved job performance

Source: V. R. Boehm and D. F. Hoyle. "Assessment and Management Development." In J. L. Moses and W. C. Byham (eds.), *Applying the Assessment Center Method* (Elmsford, N.Y.: Pergamon, 1977).

PRINCIPAL COMPONENTS OF ASSESSMENT CENTERS

Regardless of the function a particular assessment center is designed to serve, the core of the assessment center is its exercises. This section outlines some of the major types of exercises and the purpose they commonly serve in an assessment center.

Group Simulation Exercises

Simulation exercises where assessees interact as a group are probably the most nearly universal component of assessment centers. Group exercises were included in the OSS assessment process (OSS, 1948), in the assessment center used in the Management Progress Study (Bray, Campbell, and Grant, 1966), and in virtually every early application of the assessment center method in industry. While it has recently been pointed out (Byham, 1980) that the types of group exercises commonly used may not be good task representations of management and supervisory positions, group simulations are a part of assessment center tradition and will probably remain so for reasons of administrative practicality, as well as maintenance of a tradition.

A typical group problem, where assessees interact with one another while assessors observe behavior, represents an efficient use of both assessee and assessor time. A substantial amount of data is generated, and such an exercise provides an opportunity to observe behavior relevant to a substantial number of assessment dimensions. Although group situations may not represent a large proportion of most managers' on-the-job time, a simulated meeting does have substantial face validity for both assessees and assessors.

Group exercises are of three primary types: assigned role, unassigned role, and team exercises. In the usual assigned role exercise, each assessee is asked to accomplish two not particularly compatible objectives—successful advocacy of a given position, and the facilitation of a solution that can be agreed upon by the group. Two common scenarios for assigned role exercises are civic organizations, in which each member has a proposal and the decision must be made as to how to allocate dollars among the proposals, and personnel committees, where each assessee has a candidate for selection or promotion and the group must come to a decision as to how to rank the candidates.

An assigned role exercise provides an opportunity to observe a wide range of inter-personal behaviors related to negotiating skills, persuasiveness, and ability to compromise. But because roles are assigned to an individual and preparation time is provided, such exercises provide little opportunity to observe behaviors related to stress and tolerance of uncertainty, ability to provide one's own structure, and ability to adjust to rapidly changing circumstances.

The second type of group exercise—the unassigned role exercise—allows better observation of behaviors of this type. In the traditional unassigned role exercise—a business game scenario—the members of the group are partners in a business (small manufacturing companies and mutual funds are favorites) who must buy and sell stocks or products in a situation in which market conditions change every few minutes. Initial instructions are intentionally complex and ambiguous and the group is given inadequate or no preparation and organization time before the game begins. The group plays against a changing market and an administrator who role-plays a buyer-seller or banker role.

Both assigned role exercises and business games are extremely common components of traditional assessment centers. The other type of group exercise, the team exercise, is considerably less common. In a team exercise, half the group selects or is assigned one position to advocate and the other half an opposing one. The group must negotiate and reach an agreed upon position. Common scenarios are that the group members are partners in a management consulting firm or appointees to a civic advisory panel who must agree on a recommendation to be made to a client or the appointing official. As well as providing an opportunity to observe behavior in a situation where teamwork and negotiation are both required, team problems frequently provide complex data as input, and provide an opportunity to observe behaviors related to analytic skill and problem-solving ability.

Individual Simulation Exercises

When individual simulations in assessment centers come to mind, one type of exercise is clearly the most pervasive—the in-basket. With the possible exception of an assigned role group exercise, no other exercise comes as close to being a universal component of assessment centers.

An in-basket exercise is exactly what its name implies—a simulation of the task of going through a pile of paper that accumulates in a manager's in-basket, determining what should be handled on a priority basis and what can be deferred, making decisions regarding actions that need to be taken, planning approaches for dealing with problems, scheduling meetings, and so forth.

In an assessment center, a "scenario" of some sort is provided for the exercise, and the assessee role-plays within the context of the scenario. The content of the in-basket represents, in nearly all instances, material the assessee found waiting upon the assumption of a new position. Some rationale is provided concerning why the assessee has come in on a weekend or evening to get a head-start on the job, the assessee's secretary is absent and the files are locked, and so on.

Within the confines of the assigned role and the constraints of the scenario, the assessee must deal with the accumulated paperwork within a time limit (the rationale for which is also part of the scenario). The work product the assessee generates consists of notes on or about the in-basket items, meetings scheduled, outlines drawn up, memos and letters written, and so forth. In addition, most in-basket exercises also include an assessee questionnaire or a follow-up interview to provide the assessee with an opportunity to explain the way the task was approached, the way items were prioritized, the rationale behind decisions, and the assessee's general perceptions of the organization and of his or her predecessor's approach to the job.

The dimensions evaluated on the basis of an in-basket relate to administrative ability—planning, organizing, quality of decisions, decisiveness, management control, and delegation.

While the in-basket is by far the most common type of individual simulation, there are two others that should be mentioned: the irate customer and the sales presentation. In an irate customer simulation, the assessee receives a visit or a phone call from a client/customer who is unhappy about the goods or services received from the assessee. The customer/client is role-played by an assessor. Usually, the assessee is provided with some information regarding the case, the company's prior dealings with the client or customer, and is given some time to prepare for the contact. As is the case with an in-basket, a scenario is provided. The assessee's task is to determine the facts of the matter and deal with the problems presented. The dimensions evaluated are both analytic ones (fact finding, interpreting information, etc.) and the administrative dimensions commonly found in in-baskets. A variation of the irate customer problem is the irate employee situation in which the assessee must deal with a subordinate with a grievance. In this type of simulation, behaviors relating to interpersonal skill dimensions are also evaluated.

In the sales presentation simulation, the assessee is called upon to convince a customer/client to purchase a product or service. The customer/client is role-played by an assessor who is instructed to be challenging, skeptical, not sure the service/product is necessary, and so forth. The assessee is given information concerning both the product/service and the client/customer's circumstances and is given time to prepare a persuasive sales pitch. The dimensions evaluated are primarily interpersonal—persuasiveness, oral presentation and defense, flexibility—but some measurement of analytical skills may also be incorporated.

These latter two exercises with role-playing by assessors require substantial assessor skill and considerable training. For these reasons, they are not as common in assessment centers as in-basket exercises.

Paper-and-Pencil Tests

While assessment centers focus on behavioral simulations, it is not uncommon for an assessment center to also include more traditional paper-and-pencil tests of either aptitude or personality. These are aimed at obtaining information relevant to motivational and intellectual traits.

Personality tests were included in the OSS assessment center (OSS Assessment Staff, 1948), and in the assessment center used in the Management Progress Study, as were traditional paper-and-pencil aptitude tests (Bray, Campbell, and Grant, 1974). Projective personality measures and aptitude tests were also components of SOHIO's assessment program (Finkle and Jones, 1970) and have been included in some, but not all, assessment centers developed more recently.

The assessment center conducted by the Canadian Public Service Commission includes paper-and-pencil tests, but does not present the results of them to the assessors, thus permitting an evaluation of their contributions to prediction that is separate from that of simulation exercises. A study by Slivinski, McCloskey, and Bourgeois (1979) indicated that the addition of paper-and-pencil tests to an assessment process significantly improves the accuracy of prediction. Two longitudinal studies of AT&T assessment results (Moses, 1973; Moses and Boehm, 1975) indicated that paper-and-pencil aptitude measures are significantly related to subsequent management progress, although the correlation is lower than that of behavioral dimensions. A recent SOHIO study (King and Boehm, 1980) showed that paper-and-pencil aptitude tests contributed significantly to the prediction of long-range managerial potential, although these results entered the regression equation after a dimension evaluated by means of behavioral simulations. These findings appear to indicate that paper-and-pencil tests make a significant contribution to an assessment center, but that their contribution tends to be less substantial than those of group and individual simulation exercises. Consequently, the bias that assessment centers exhibit in favor of assessment based on direct behavioral observation and evaluation appears to be justified, but the fact that more traditional paper-and-pencil tests can play a significant role in assessment center evaluations should not be overlooked. It is not inappropriate to include more traditional measuring instruments as part of an assessment center where their use is supported by job analysis.

BASICS OF ASSESSMENT CENTER TECHNOLOGY

The construction and conduct of an assessment center is a complex undertaking and one that can best be viewed as a sequence of processes that begins with a determination of the purpose of the assessment center and ends with the dissemination of the information gathered by means of the assessment center.

Establishing the Framework

When a decision is made that an organization will establish an assessment center, this decision is based on two underlying assumptions: (1) there exists or will exist an organizational problem, and (2) an assessment center will contribute to the solution of this problem.

The statement "we need an assessment center" is not a statement of a problem, but rather a statement of a proposed solution. To hastily develop or purchase a group of exercises "off the shelf" and link these together is a shortsighted and usually nonproductive approach to assessment center design. If the problem is not defined, the odds that a hastily established assessment center will appropriately address it are very small.

Once the problem is defined—"We don't know who we should be promoting to the foreman's job," "We seem to have a shortage of potential higher-level management talent," or whatever—the purpose of assessment is implied. The type of assessment should address the problem. For example, a diagnostic assessment center won't solve an immediate selection problem.

Determining the problem should also aid in the determination of the target job or job level. Even when a diagnostic assessment center is planned, a target job or job level needs to be specified.

Once the type of assessment and target job or job level has been determined, it is then necessary to answer some basic organizational policy issues, since the answers will have an influence on the subsequent development of the assessment center. Some illustrative examples of these questions are:

How many assessees will be assessed over what time period?
How will eligibility for assessment be determined?
Who should serve as an assessor?
How often should assessors serve in that capacity?
Who will have access to assessment reports?
How will the assessment center's effectiveness be evaluated?
What will the policy be on reassessment?
How will the assessment center interface with other personnel systems?
Who will administer the assessment center?

While the content is diverse, questions such as these have two points in common: they are matters of policy rather than strictly technical and the way they are answered can affect subsequent stages of assessment center design and administration. A more detailed explanation of some of these policy issues and their impact on assessment center design and administration can be found in Jeswald (1977).

Failure to address policy considerations early in the process of assessment center design can result in a situation in which assumptions have been made about these issues that prove to be incorrect, and the assessment center fails as a consequence of this initial oversight.

An assessment center is not an economical measurement procedure when compared with more traditional paper-and-pencil tests. It also cannot equal such devices in its ability to handle a large volume of people in a short period of time.

The impetus to establish an assessment center in an organization frequently comes from the personnel department, but operating divisions of organizations are unlikely to willingly undertake a program simply because the personnel department thinks it is a good idea! This is especially true when the program is likely to require a substantial investment of time and resources. Usually, assessment centers have to be "sold" as being worth the investment. This ordinarily involves the active participation of the client organization in every phase of the center's design, beginning with the problem diagnosis. Most particularly, the policy decisions related to the center's operation must be made by, or agreed to by, the client organization.

Without organizational commitment to the assessment center, there is very little hope of program success. Even if the technical aspects of assessment center design and administration are carried out optimally, lack of before-the-fact organizational commitment will operate to undermine the success of the undertaking.

Identifying the Appropriate Dimensions

Whether an assessment center is to be used for selection, or the developmental purposes of identification and/or diagnosis, the central principle around which it must be constructed is the same—it must provide a means whereby the abilities and skills of assessees can be measured against the requirements of the target job or job level. The common sense rationale for job analysis is obvious. Professional principles and standards also point out the necessity for job analysis (Division of Industrial/Organizational Psychology, 1975). In addition, governmental requirement regarding for selection procedures specifically require job analysis (Equal Employment Opportunity Commission, 1978).

A variety of methodologies are available for the conduct of job analysis (McCormick, 1979) and some of these methodologies are specifically aimed at analysis of managerial positions (e.g., Hemphill, 1960; Tornow and Pinto, 1976). One recent application of job analysis technology (Byham, 1980) is specifically aimed at the utilization of job analysis results for the development of assessment centers and the demonstration of their job relatedness. (See also the discussion of job analysis in Chapter 4.)

A number of techniques are frequently utilized in order to obtain job analysis information. These include interviews with job incumbents and/or their supervisors, questionnaires, observation, activity logs or diaries, analysis of critical incidents, and comparison of various positions. Each of these techniques is potentially useful in designing, and establishing the validity of, an assessment center. The specific technique(s) utilized should depend on the type of validation study planned, the use to be made of assessment results, and organizational factors (Boehm, 1981).

In the job analysis literature, a traditional distinction is made between task-oriented and worker-oriented approaches. In broad terms, the task-oriented approach focuses on "the distinct activities that constitute the logical and necessary steps in the performance of work by the worker" (U.S. Department of Labor, 1972, p. 3). "The worker-oriented approach tends to characterize, or strongly imply, the human behaviors that are involved in jobs. . ." (McCormick, 1979, pp. 4–75). In broad terms, task-oriented approaches focus on *what* is accomplished (outcomes) and worker-oriented ones on *how* it is accomplished (process).

When complex positions are considered, these two approaches do not represent a dichotomy. Unlike the situation on an assembly line, the process utilized by a manager is not obviously observable. Similarly, the manager's "product" may be less concrete than that of the assembly-line worker.

Nonetheless, the fact that such a dichotomy exists in theory (if not in fact) leads to a key issue in the application of job analysis results to assessment center technology and its utilization. How is the "inferential leap" made between the tasks performed by a manager or supervisor and the worker-related characteristics required to perform these tasks? This "inferential leap" is the process used to move from the job analysis results to the identification of the assessment dimensions that are to be measured in the assessment center.

Once job analysis has identified behaviors relevant to job performance, these behaviors are grouped into dimensions. This grouping can be done by judgmental or statistical procedures. Ideally, a direct relationship can be shown between those behaviors that are grouped together and a dimension. A dimension can be defined "as a description under which behavior can be reliably classified" (Byham, 1980).

The number of dimensions that should be measured in an assessment center depends, of course, on the nature and complexity of the target job or job level, and on the length of the assessment center. When only a brief period of time is available for assessment, it may be necessary to focus on only those dimensions most critical to job performance and exclude some relevant but less critical ones. One example of how selection of the most critical dimensions might be made is provided by Moses (1973), who selected eight dimensions for measurement in a one-day assessment process from among eighteen used in a two-day process.

Another consideration that should influence the number of dimensions is the purpose of the center. An assessment center aimed solely at selection for a specific job can usually be targeted on a relatively small number of highly critical dimensions, while an identification center that seeks to identify long-range potential for a target level, rather than a specific job, may need to assess a larger number of dimensions. A center designed for diagnostic purposes may include still more dimensions, because dimensions may be less broad and include small groupings of behavior. (For example, a diagnostic center might examine organizing behaviors separately from planning ones.)

There is no fixed number of dimensions that is considered correct. Various listings of the dimensions used by organizations in assessment centers (see, for example, Standing, 1977) show a range from as few as six to as many as twenty-five. There is also no generally accepted nomenclature and behaviors of the same variety that might be grouped under different labels in different organizations.

What a dimension is called is not as important as how well it is understood. Do assessors agree on the dimension under which a given behavior should be classified? Are differences among dimensions, particularly subtle ones, understood and agreed on by those who will be serving as assessors? Having good descriptive labels for dimensions, as well as clear definitions, is helpful, of course, but to assure that the accurate categorization of behavior occurs and that subtle differences among dimensions are recognized, there is no adequate substitute for thorough assessor training. Job analysis is a valuable tool for assuring that an assessment center includes the correct dimensions, but making proper use of the dimensions depends heavily on the skill of the assessors.

Developing Means of Measurement

Once the assessment dimensions have been determined and defined, the next decision concerns how these dimensions will be measured in the assessment center. As was indicated earlier, and is discussed in more detail elsewhere (Crooks, 1977), certain types of assessment exercises are designed to allow assessees to exhibit behaviors relevant to specific dimensions. The relationships between assessment dimensions and exercise type are intuitively reasonable for the most part—exercises that permit assessees to interact with one another or with assessors are best for the observation of interpersonal behaviors; administrative dimensions can best be observed through exercises involving paper handling, and so forth.

The product of this matching of dimensions to exercises is a "dimension × exercise" grid, specifying for each dimension, the type of exercise(s) to be considered in rating the dimension, and, for each exercise, the dimensions that can be rated using the exercise as an information source.

Ideally, such a grid should show that information for evaluating each dimension is available from at least two exercises and no two exercises should elicit behavior on exactly the same set of dimensions. If sufficient time can be allocated to the assessment process, it is strongly advisable to have more than two sources of input for each dimension, especially for dimensions that are less easily observable and consequently more difficult to rate. The "dimension × exercise" grid indicates the type of exercises that will be needed in the assessment center, and also is a key document for use in assessor training.

Once it has been determined what type of exercises are needed, exercises are either designed or selected from those already developed elsewhere and available for purchase. While the simplest solution to the problem of exercise design is to purchase or develop exercises solely on the basis of the dimensions they are to measure, Byham (1980) has pointed out that exercises, as well as measuring the correct dimensions, should ideally represent tasks similar to those identified in the job analysis and should be comparable in complexity and difficulty level to the target job or job level.

In addition to exercise content, other considerations such as the time taken to administer the exercise, the type of materials needed for exercise administration, and the way the exercise fits into the design and schedule of the assessment center as a whole must be taken into consideration.

With the selection of exercises and the scheduling of them into an assessment center, the focus of assessment center technology shifts from design considerations to those related to administration.

Assuring Proper Administration

One of the keys to the success of an assessment center is proper administration. Once the design issues have been dealt with satisfactorily, the success of the center depends heavily on the details of proper administration. There are four administrative issues that can provide "make or break" decision points for an assessment center:

1. Assessor selection and training
2. Standardization of assessment procedures
3. Development of "paper flow" procedures
4. Establishment of procedures for the dissemination and use of assessment information

Assessor Selection and Training. The Standards and Ethical Considerations for Assessment Center Operations (Task Force on Assessment Center Standards, 1979) specify six areas in which assessors' expertise is required:

1. Knowledge of assessment techniques and the kinds of behaviors they are designed to elicit
2. Knowledge of assessment dimensions and examples of behaviors related to them
3. Skill in behavioral observation and recording
4. Knowledge of evaluation and rating procedures
5. Knowledge of organizational assessment policies and practices
6. Where appropriate, knowledge of feedback procedures

None of these is likely to be transmitted to assessors without formal training. While there may be analogies in the day-to-day requirements of a manager's position, being an assessor involves the development and utilization of a specialized body of knowledge and skills. Slighting assessor training is one of the most certain ways to assure the failure (or less than maximal utilization) of an assessment center.

In addition to the cognitive issues key to assessor training, there are attitudinal ones. The task of an assessor requires a high degree of discipline and a willingness to defer judgment. An assessor must be able to separate the process of observing behavior from the process of evaluating it. The step-by-step process of observing and evaluating behavior that is required of an assessor is sometimes analogized as a "funnel." Figure 12–1 represents the judgmental "funnel" involved in making assessment judgments.

The ability to structure and evaluate observations in this manner, i.e., appropriately deferring judgment, is not a universal one. Even if good assessment training is provided, not all managers can or should serve as assessors. The task is one that is uncomfortable to some managers even with training. Careful consideration needs to be given to assessor selection, as well as assessor training, if assessment center administration is to be properly conducted.

Standardization of Assessment Procedures. The relationship between assessment center administration and the validity of assessment center outcomes is the same as that between the reliability and the validity of a more traditional paper-and-pencil test; that is, the one establishes the limit of the other.

The primary function of the administrator of an assessment center is to serve as the guardian of the integrity of the process in order to insure its reliability. While reliability does not guarantee the existence of validity, the absense of reliability virtually assures that validity will be absent.

FIGURE 12-1
Assessor Judgments—A Behavioral Funnel

While perfect standardization is not an achievable goal, certain basic precautions should be taken to assure reasonably standard conditions of assessment center administration. These include uniform adherence to time limits, uniform physical conditions (e.g., space, light), preassessment checks of materials to be used, and other similar basics of good test administration. While such seemingly simple matters would appear to be so obvious as to not require restatement, overlooking them can lead to organizational difficulties with assessment center acceptance and results utility.

In addition, there are some standardization issues more specific to assessment centers. These include differences in prior knowledge that assessees have of the process, unscheduled contacts between assessees and assessors, and assessor fatigue. These matters can create problems in the absense of good control and preplanning. To avoid or minimize these problems, organizations commonly provide brochures to assessees describing the program, permit assessors to "sign off" on observing or evaluating assessees they know, and adopt other controls on the process to assure standardization. The best single assurance of a standardized process is adequate assessor training. The more thoroughly the assessors understand their role in the assessment process, the more likely they are to carry it out in a standardized, as well as high quality, fashion.

Development of "Paper-Flow" Procedures. An assessment center generates an enormous amount of paper during the assessment process. Even if the final product is only a two-page report on an assessee (not uncommon), the process behind that product can easily result in the generation of eighty to one hundred pieces of paper per assessee, including schedules, inventory sheets, assessor's written work, paper related to the exercises themselves (such as in-basket items), exercise rating forms, exercise reports, and rating booklets. Simply keeping track of this intermediate paper and keeping the assessment center from getting bogged down in a paper jam presents a complex administrative task, and one in which assessment centers frequently encounter difficulties.

Many of these paper-flow problems can be dealt with by better design and workflow planning. Is the only purpose of a given form to summarize what is on two other forms? If so, is it really necessary? Are there forms filled out by the assessors that are not of direct input into the evaluation session? If there are, do they serve any useful purpose? Are there instances in which information gathered on one form is simply copied or recoded onto another for long-term retention? If so, why not code it in the form needed initially?

Extraneous paper not only slows down the assessment process, it increases the opportunity for errors to take place. In some respects, an assessment center is a production operation. As such, the information flow should be examined as carefully as the flow of processes in a manufacturing situation.

Establishment of Procedures for the Dissemination and Use of Assessment Information.   Once the assessment center has been conducted and the report of assessment results prepared, there still remains the most difficult administrative problem —making sure that assessment results reach their intended audience, do not reach audiences they should not reach, and are properly utilized for their intended purposes.

Given the universal availability of copy machines, there is simply no way to guarantee that an assessment report, once prepared, will not be duplicated and used for purposes other than the intended ones. Numbering copies, logging them in and out of files, stamping a report "Confidential—Do Not Reproduce" and similar procedures are helpful. But ultimately, the control of assessment information rests in the hands of the users. If the users have been involved in the development of the assessment process, and are aware of the role that assessment information is designed to play in the personnel system, proper use is likely and misuse will probably be rare. Without some form of systematic "user education," an administrative control system is likely to be ineffective.

In addition to educating users concerning how the information should be utilized, good administration also involves ongoing monitoring of information usage. This is easiest when the assessment center is one conducted for selection purposes, since actual post-assessment movement can be tracked via payroll changes and other personnel actions. Identification centers or those conducted for diagnostic purposes require more inventive approaches to monitoring and tracking.

RESEARCH ON ASSESSMENT CENTERS

Research on assessment centers has developed rapidly, keeping pace with the growth of assessment center use. The body of research knowledge is currently large enough to have produced three reviews of the research literature (Cohen, Moses, and Byham, 1974; Howard, 1974; Huck, 1977). New research on assessment centers appears regularly in the professional literature. Summarizing the research basis of assessment centers in a comprehensive fashion is, therefore, beyond the scope of this paper. Consequently, highlights of research in only four areas will be summarized:

1.   Reliability and stability of assessment results
2.   Predictive validity

3. Acceptability to participants and organizations
4. Fairness and impact on protected groups

Omission of other research types is not intended to indicate lack of importance, but rather lack of space.

Reliability and Stability of Results

When the reliability of a measurement process depends on the degree to which different observers agree on their observations of an individual's behavior, the investigation of the reliability of these observations is called for.

At least three studies have compared the ratings given participants by different assessors and demonstrated satisfactory, although not outstanding, reliabilities (Greenwood and McNamara, 1967; Hinrichs and Haanpera, 1976; Schmitt, 1977). In general, it appears that the more directly observable the dimension, the higher the reliability. Strictly behavioral dimensions, such as energy or leadership, tend to be more reliably observed than ones such as creativity or organizational sensitivity, where assessors are required to make an inference concerning an internal state based on observed behavior.

Two studies have compared the ratings given by psychologists and managers when serving as assessors (Greenwood and McNamara, 1967; Thomson, 1970) and have concluded that there was no difference in the way the two performed the rating task. Apparently, the assessment center provides sufficient structure so that these two groups, when abiding by the same rules, obtain the same results.

A study by Moses (1973) looked at another aspect of reliability. The same group of assessees attended two different assessment centers and were evaluated by different staffs on the basis of their performance on different exercises. Substantial and highly significant correlations were obtained between the overall ratings received by the participants in the two assessment centers. In addition, the ratings on all of the dimensions common to both assessment centers were significantly correlated.

Assessment center rating stability is another issue that has been investigated. The extent to which an assessment center yields stable results across assessor teams and across time is clearly important, when assessees who were assessed by different people at different times are to be compared. Two recent studies have focused on this issue. Sackett and Hakel (1979) examined the ratings given by successive assessor teams who served as assessors in the same established assessment center and found that different teams formed overall assessment judgments using similar decision-making strategies. King and Boehm (1980) compared assessment ratings over assessees during three time periods in a program in which assessors normally serve only once, and obtained high degrees of similarity over time periods in both the factor structure of assessment ratings and the order in which dimensions entered a multiple regression equation to predict the final assessment rating.

In general, the research that has been conducted indicates that the behavioral dimensions rated in assessment centers can be reliably rated and that the rating process is carried out in a highly similar fashion by different assessors at different points in time.

Predictive Validity

The evidence pertaining to assessment center validity utilizes indices of organizational movement and advancement as a criterion measure more frequently than any other index. Assessment center predictions have frequently been compared to such indices of organizational advancement as salary increase, promotion, and job level with almost uniformly positive results. There are over twenty studies indicating that assessment center performance predicts criteria of this type (see reviews of this literature by Cohen, Moses, and Byham, 1974; Howard, 1974; Huck, 1977). When measured against a criterion of organizational advancement and movement, the validity evidence underlying assessment centers is both convincing and compelling, even though not technically flawless because of criterion contamination. In most situations in which assessment center results were compared to subsequent movement, the managers making promotional decisions had access to the assessment results and hence might have used them in making decisions.

Some evidence is available indicating that this predictability occurs in the absence of criterion contamination. In the Management Progress Study (Bray and Grant, 1966; Bray, Campbell, and Grant, 1974), assessment results were not made available to the organization or to the participant. Consequently, the finding of substantial validity for the assessment process should be given considerable weight. Two other studies (Moses, 1972; Moses and Boehm, 1975) have used organizational advancement to a position above that for which the assessment process was designed as a criterion measure. These studies, examining the predictability of movement above the target level of the assessment process, have also demonstrated the validity of assessment centers in situations in which there was some control for criterion contamination.

Because assessment centers have now been in operation long enough to establish a generalizable "track record" for the validity of the assessment center method as a predictor of subsequent organizational advancement, scientific and professional concerns have shifted to other areas.

Questions have been raised concerning the suitability of an advancement criterion (Klimoski and Strickland, 1977) and regarding the contribution of an assessment integration session over and above an actuarial combination of assessment results (Hinrichs, 1978; Slivinski, McCloskey, and Bourgeois, 1979). The question "Do assessment center results significantly predict future organizational advancement?" has been quite definitively answered in the affirmative. The jury is still out, however, on the issue of whether this is the most appropriate question to ask. This matter is considered further in a later section.

While most empirical studies of assessment center validity have focused on organizational movement criteria, such as salary growth and promotions, a few studies have examined post-assessment job performance. In general, the results have been positive. Thomson (1970) compared assessment performance to supervisory reports of job performance and obtained results that indicated significant congruency, although the supervisory rating criterion was not of the best psychometric quality. Huck and Bray (1976) related the assessment center performance of black and white women who had been promoted to the target position following assessment, and found significant relationships. Parker (1980) reported positive and significant correlations between assessment center results and subsequent job performance for an assessment center used by many organizations.

Slivinski et al. (1978) conducted a longitudinal study of assessees in the Canadian Federal Government and found that supervisors' rating of overall job performance was significantly correlated with overall assessment evaluations two years after assessment, but not three and one-half years later. For the same individuals, organizational progress criteria—salary increase and job level increase—not only were significant at both time periods, but actually showed higher correlations when the elapsed time increased. A similar result of increasing validity over time when an organizational criterion was used was also reported by Mitchel (1975).

It would appear that assessment center evaluations are related to subsequent evaluations of performance in the target job, at least in the short run. But problems of range restriction, criterion contamination, and other difficulties that organizational appraisal systems are heir to may result in outcomes not as striking as when assessment centers utilize long-term organizational outcome criteria, such as salary increases or promotions. It could perhaps be the case (although this has not been investigated as such) that assessment centers (themselves behavioral measures of individuals) are more predictive of organizational outcomes (such as raises and promotions) because these criteria represent "behavior" on the part of organizations, whereas supervisory performance measures are more attitudinal. This area might present a fruitful topic for future research.

Acceptability to Participants and Organization

While the focus in assessment center research has been primarily on questions related to validity, research investigating the attitudes of participants, assessors, and users of assessment information has been given some emphasis.

Dodd (1977) summarized attitude studies conducted in a number of organizations and concluded that assessees were, in general, quite positive toward most aspects of their attendance at an assessment center. Assessment centers received particularly positive reactions in terms of their face validity, the perceived accuracy of feedback, and the usefulness of the feedback information as perceived by the individual. Less positive attitudes were held regarding the extent to which participants viewed their behavior while at the assessment center as typical of their behavior in general.

Slivinski, McDonald, and Bourgeois (1979) surveyed the attitudes of a large group of assessees at three points in time: immediately after attending, after receiving feedback, and a year and a half to three years after attendance. They found highly positive attitudes at all three time periods, even from the majority of those who had obtained a negative rating. As well as responding positively to the center itself, participants felt that attendance had had a positive influence on their self-development and career development.

Nirtaut (1978) conducted a survey of organizations currently conducting assessment centers and found that the companies reported positive participant reactions toward assessment centers. Kraut (1973) found favorable attitudes toward assessment on the part of assessees in seven countries where a multinational corporation conducted assessment centers.

It would appear, then, that studies of participant attitudes toward assessment centers show generally positive results. What little information is available concerning the attitudes of assessors, managers, and others in the organization seems to indicate a similar pattern. Dodd (1977) compared the attitudes of managers who had served as assessors and those who had not. While both groups reported positive attitudes toward the assessment center, those who had served as assessors held somewhat more positive attitudes than those who had not done so. The attitudes of others in the organization toward assessment centers have not been surveyed as systematically as those of the assessees themselves, perhaps because a more behavioral measure is available—the organization's adaptation and continued use of the assessment center. While there is insufficient evidence to conclude that organizational attitudes toward assessment centers are positive, the widespread and rapidly growing use of this technique by organizations would seem to indicate a substantial degree of management acceptance.

Fairness and Impact

The consideration of fairness and impact as research issues is still quite new in personnel research. Research of this sort crosses the boundary between scientific psychology and social policy. Because the period of rapid growth of assessment centers occurred concomitantly with the evolution of equal employment legislation, research regarding the fairness and impact of assessment centers has been more or less integrated into the mainstream of assessment center research.

Employment selection procedures are regulated by the *Uniform Guidelines for Employee Selection Procedures* (EEOC, 1978). These guidelines specify that a selection procedure that has adverse impact against a "protected" group must either be demonstrably valid or else used in a way that does not result in adverse impact. The definition of "selection procedure" used in the *Uniform Guidelines* leaves no doubt but that assessment centers are included in the definition (Boehm, 1981). Consequently, when a selection process of which an assessment center is a part has adverse impact, the impact of the assessment center on race/sex groups must be examined.

The *Uniform Guidelines* define "adverse impact" in terms of the "80 percent rule" (EEOC, 1978). This standard specifies that a selection procedure that results in a selection ratio for minority group candidates that is less than 80 percent of the selection ratio for majority group candidates will ordinarily be interpreted as indicating unfair discrimination unless evidence of job-relatedness is documented. This calculation of impact usually depends on the "bottom-line" ratio—the proportion of applicants from various groups compared to the proportion of hires (EEOC, 1978).

A number of components might be involved in the overall selection process, the results of which are indicated by the "bottom line." The overall finding of adverse impact indicates that the impact of specific components should be calculated and validity evidence presented for those components in which there is "adverse impact."

One component of a selection process might be an assessment center. Other components might be such items as prescreening of applications, an interview, or a medical examination.

The *Uniform Guidelines* require that the validity of those specific components with an impact ratio of less than 80 percent must be demonstrable. What is the usual impact of this requirement on assessment centers?

Two published studies have directly addressed this issue. Moses and Boehm (1975) compared the assessment center performance of large numbers of men and women who attended the same assessment program. They found that the distribution of overall assessment ratings for men and women was virtually identical and that assessment ratings were equally predictive of men's and women's subsequent organizational progress. They also examined the relationship between individual assessment dimensions and subsequent management progress and found the dimensions most highly predictive for one sex to be most highly predictive for the other. In this instance, the assessment center did not have adverse impact, so that its use would have been substantiated from a regulatory standpoint, even if the highly positive validity results had not been obtained.

Another study (Huck and Bray, 1976) compared the job performance of black and white women who were promoted to supervisory positions subsequent to assessment. While there were significant differences in assessment results for some of the dimensions, assessment results significantly predicted job performance for both blacks and whites, and an examination of the factor structure of assessment dimensions showed very similar patterns. While this study did indicate possible adverse impact, the use of the assessment center was supported by validity evidence.

Given the overall positive results of assessment center validity studies, assessment centers are unlikely to be unfair to women or to minorities. The question as to whether they might have adverse impact in a particular instance is one to be investigated as circumstances dictate.

Assessment Centers and Management Development

Management development is one of the most used and least well-defined terms in the personnel professional's vocabulary. Boehm and Hoyle (1977) identified five common uses of the term. Each of these implies a type of development program or strategy:

1. The informal process of on-the-job learning
2. Formal training and course work
3. Moving through an established sequence of positions
4. Individualized career planning and career pathing
5. Self-development and self-improvement

These uses of the term *management development* are not mutually exclusive, of course, and various management development programs that include assessment centers as a component use different combinations of these strategies.

These strategies represent assumptions about the nature of learning, change, and adult development that are largely philosophical; the development literature being more rhetoric than research at present.

The "on-the-job learning" assumptions are that adults usually learn best through informal processes of trial-and-error, observation, and receiving feedback primarily from work outcomes and from a supervisor who provides a good observational model. The kind of management development visualized by this strategy is a very informal one that heavily depends on learning by "osmosis."

Underlying the "training and course work" strategy is the assumption that learning most effectively takes place in an environment (classroom or laboratory) specifically designed to serve an educational purpose, and is free from the ordinary work environment distractions. The strategy is essentially that of conventional education.

The philosophy underlying "position sequencing" as a developmental strategy is that the lines of job progression that are established and survive in an organization are ones that have proved to be organizationally workable.

The "individual career planning" strategy is based on the assumption that development within an organizational setting is optimal when the "best fit" is sought between the interests and abilities of the individual and the goals of the organization. Development occurs when the individual and organization jointly agree on outcomes and work on devising a strategy to bring about this "best fit."

"Self-development" strategies imply that the individual is responsible for development within an organization and that organizations do not develop people and should not be expected to. Rather, people develop themselves. The role of the organization is to provide a climate in which individuals have sufficient freedom for "self-development."

In this section, four assessment and management programs will be described and compared and contrasted in terms of content and mix of these five strategies.

Uses of Assessment Center Information in Management Development

As indicated, assessment center information may be utilized in the management development process in a number of ways. In this section, four ways of utilizing this information will be presented and their similarities and differences discussed.

The AT&T Management Assessment Program. In January 1973, AT&T and agencies of the U.S. government entered into a consent agreement, one portion of which dealt with a class of college graduate women employees hired into exempt positions between July 1965 and December 1971. Under the terms of the agreement, these women were to be given the opportunity to attend an assessment center and those identified as having middle-management potential were to be developed for these positions. The strategy was thus clearly the identification variety. Feedback was to be given to the individual participant in all cases, but a written report was sent to management only in those cases in which the woman was identified as having middle-management potential.

Individual career plans were to be developed for all women identified as having middle-management potential. These career plans were drawn up by a team consisting of the identified woman, her boss, and a career planning coordinator. Development plans were to include specification of a target position or positions, intermediate assignments that might lead to this position, training needed, and some estimate of time frames (Boehm, 1974). To assure that the career plans would not be lost over time, as the women and their bosses changed assignments, the coordinator was to monitor development plans and report progress on a regular basis. Also, this program was coordinated with internal corporate affirmative action efforts (Hoyle, 1975; Boehm and Hoyle, 1977).

Over 700 women were identified as having middle-management potential as a result of this program (Hoyle, 1975) and their progress was tracked and evaluated over the six years covered by the consent decree. One basis of evaluation was the comparison of their utilization at middle management with that of male college graduates hired into a "fast-track program" during the same period.

In January 1979, 37 percent of the identified women who were still with the company had reached middle management as compared to 41 percent of the males in the equivalent group, a utilization ratio of 90 percent when the women and men were compared (Hoyle, 1979). This clearly meets government guidelines concerning utilization and exceeds the "80 percent rule" (EEOC, 1978). The program demonstrates that an identification-type development program based on assessment center results can yield measurable outcomes when administrative and control procedures are instituted and results are systematically monitored.

The FBI Management Aptitude Program. The FBI Management Aptitude Program (Quigley, 1976) is an example of an assessment program that uses assessment results for purposes of identification and diagnosis.

During the first three days of a ten-day program, participants undertake a series of assessment exercises in which they are observed by managers at least two organizational levels above their present position. Immediately after this, participants begin a five-day training program, covering a variety of general management topics. While the participants attend the training program, the management assessors meet to review the participant's behavior during the assessment phase as it relates to each of the assessment dimensions and to prepare a summary report. The final two days of the program consist of feedback of two varieties. There is a feedback interview with the program administrator, which focuses on the participant's strengths and weaknesses. Suggestions for development are discussed and are intended to be used as the basis for a development program devised by the individual. There is also feedback by means of a play-back of a videotape of a group exercise and the opportunity for peer discussion.

The information gained from the assessment center is intended to be used both by the individual as a basis for devising an individual development plan and by the organization as one source of input into promotional decision making. An established job progression exists for moving individuals with advancement potential into supervisory positions following one or two post-assessment developmental assignments. As such, the program has elements of both identification-oriented and diagnosis-oriented approaches to the use of assessment center information.

Xerox's Pre-Field Executive Development Program. Xerox's Pre-Field Executive Development Program (Cohen et al., 1979) is a diagnostic use of assessment center results aimed almost totally at individual development. It also combines self-assessment components with assessment center elements in order to broaden the scope of information available to the individual.

The participants attend the program for five days, two days of which involve participation in an assessment center designed to evaluate the participant's skills on dimensions related to successful performance of the branch manager's position. As well as attendance at the assessment center, participants complete a job knowledge inventory designed to provide a measure of the individual's technical competence. This is self-scored and discussed with other participants to determine areas in which individuals need to develop further technical expertise.

Additional opportunities are also provided for self-assessment. A case study is utilized wherein the participants evaluate the branch manager in the case study on the same set of dimensions that are being used to evaluate the participants themselves in the assessment center. This provides an opportunity for participants to develop a better understanding of the branch manager's position and indicates the relevance of the assessment dimensions to the target job (that of branch manager). In addition, participants are given an opportunity to view videotapes of three of the assessment exercises.

On the fifth day of the session, participants receive feedback of their assessment center results and develop a detailed action plan, which they subsequently discuss with their supervisors. The written report of the assessment center results is sent *only* to the participant.

Follow-up contacts occur at ninety-day intervals to determine whether problems exist in the implementation of the action plans and attempts are made to remedy problems that arise.

Kaiser's Maintenance Management Development Program. Kaiser Aluminum & Chemical Corporation's Maintenance Management Development Program (Albright, 1980) represents another approach to the diagnostic use of assessment center information. The assessment center is a part of an organizational change effort aimed at upgrading and restructuring the management of the maintenance function. The focus of the management development effort is on both organizational and individual change.

All present incumbents of foremen positions are participating in an assessment center based on dimensions drawn from an analysis of maintenance management positions. Rather than being based entirely on the present job, however, the dimensions chosen are those that are expected to be required in the future as a result of changes in the organization and in technology. Technical skills are also assessed by means of job knowledge and performance tests.

While results are fed back to the participant, there is no feedback of individual results to management, and the main purpose for which results are used is to determine training needs and to design the training and development programs that will be required to enable foremen to perform their jobs following the restructuring of the maintenance management organization.

Some individualization of training programs is planned, as well as the development of group training aimed at widespread skills deficiencies. It is estimated that up to three years will be required for the full implementation of planned changes in job content and organizational structure.

The Relationship between Assessment Center Information and Development Strategies

While these four programs are all examples of the developmental use of assessment centers, it is clear that they differ from each other in many respects. Table 12–2 compares some key content features of the programs.

All four programs are development-oriented rather than selection-oriented, utilize standard assessment center techniques, and provide feedback to participants. But beyond those commonalities, they are very different. The four differ in the type of development being sought and subsequently differ in how (and if) feedback is provided to the organization. The development of individual plans and the monitoring of individual progress subsequent to assessment occurs in some of them, not in others. Two aim assessment at a specific target position, the other two at a target level.

All, however, represent approaches used by organizations to deal with specific management development concerns utilizing assessment centers as part of the solution. In aggregate, these programs represent a cross-section of such approaches and, by their diversity, serve to illustrate the flexibility of the assessment center as a management development tool.

The diverse content of these four programs reflects varying mixes of the five developmental strategies mentioned earlier. Table 12–3 compares the underlying strategies of the four programs.

The differences in program content are reflected in the diversity of program strategy. But two common elements are evident: (1) none of the four developmental programs is based on the use of only one strategy, and (2) all four allow some degree of consideration of individual interests (as indicated by the use of "sometimes"), and consequently have some degree of flexibility.

Another common feature of these programs, not evident in Table 12–3, should be pointed out—they are all relative newcomers to their organizations. The AT&T program that began in 1973 is the "old timer" of the four, and consequently the only one that has been formally evaluated up to this point. The FBI and Xerox programs began later in the 1970s, and the Kaiser one is currently in the early stages of implementation. The use of assessment centers in management development programs is still a new and exciting area and one currently characterized by diversity in program content, strategy, and practice. This diversity in existing programs is rapidly creating a variety of interesting possibilities for future research and program development.

TABLE 12–2

A Comparison of the Content of Four Developmental Programs that Include Assessment

Program Feature	AT&T	FBI	Xerox	Kaiser
1. Program purpose	Identification	Identification & diagnosis	Diagnosis— Individual	Diagnosis— Organizational & individual
2. Target job	Middle management	Administrative management	Branch manager	Maintenance foreman— Restructured
3. Feedback given to individual	Yes	Yes	Yes	Yes
4. Feedback given to organization	In some cases	Yes	No	Aggregate only
5. Individual development plans	Yes	At individual's discretion	Yes	No
6. Post-assessment progress of individuals monitored	Yes	No	Yes	Undetermined as yet

TABLE 12–3
A Comparison of the Strategies Underlying Four Developmental Programs that Include
Assessment

Strategy Used	AT&T	FBI	Xerox	Kaiser
1. On-the-job learning	Yes	Yes	Yes	Sometimes
2. Training and course work	Sometimes	No	Sometimes	Yes
3. Position sequencing	No	Yes	No	No
4. Individual career planning	Yes	Sometimes	Yes	No
5. Self-development	Yes	No	Yes	Sometimes

ASSESSMENT CENTERS IN THE 1980s

The 1970s were a time of coming of age for assessment centers. As was indicated in the review of the history of assessment centers, the number of organizations in the United States using assessment centers went from about a dozen to perhaps two thousand during the 1970s.

Along with this exponential growth came the first systematic uses of assessment centers for management development purposes. Four such programs were outlined in the previous section, and serve to illustrate the versatility of the methodology and its future promise. Along with the growth and expansion came the questions. As the decade drew to a close, there were indications that some fundamental issues underlying assessment center use were being examined. Boche (1977) examined, along with technical issues, the morality of assessment centers, their long-term impact on careers, and the degree to which they place stress on participants. Klimoski and Strickland (1977) raised the issue of what assessment centers should accomplish and how their success should be evaluated, questioning the appropriateness of organizational advancement as a criterion. Thornton (1979) raised a number of concerns, including the possibility that validity evidence pertaining to the assessment centers might have been oversold.

These concerns, and others, are likely to be addressed in the 1980s along with administrative and technical matters that have become more important as the assessment center method has grown and matured.

This section will look at five issues considered to be key issues of the 1980s:

1. The costs and benefits of assessment centers
2. The linkages between assessment programs and other personnel systems
3. The role of assessment in changing organizations
4. New directions in assessment center research
5. Ethical considerations related to assessment centers.

The Costs and Benefits of Assessment Centers

As indicated elsewhere in this chapter, there is very little question but that a well-designed and administered assessment center can yield data that predict both the capacity of an individual to perform successfully in a managerial/supervisory position and his or her likelihood of attaining such a position.

The question "Should we use an assessment center?" is consequently one that focuses on utility rather than validity. Given the facts that assessment centers are more expensive than most other selection devices for the positions for which they are commonly used, and that they also provide more valid predictive data, the question becomes a cost-benefit one. Is the expenditure required to conduct an assessment center a worthwhile use of an organization's resources and of the time of the managers who serve as assessors?

The evaluation of assessment centers using this hard, data-dollars approach is a very new undertaking, but preliminary results are positive. Cascio and Silbey (1979) indicated that positive gains in utility can be achieved with validity coefficients as low as .10 when assessment center results, rather than random selection, are used. A survey of organizational experience with assessment centers that attempts to look at both cost and benefit (Cohen et al., 1979) indicates that the average Return on Investment (ROI) for an assessment center exceeds 300 percent, even though the average cost of evaluating a candidate is substantially higher when an assessment center procedure, rather than a briefer evaluative procedure, is used.

Part of a cost-benefit analysis is an investigation of the effect of additional information on the accuracy of predictions made on the basis of available data. A study by Slivinski, McCloskey, and Bourgeois (1979) indicated that the behavioral simulation data obtained as part of an assessment center leads to significant predictability over and above that gathered from biographical data and the results of paper-and-pencil tests.

There are some preliminary data to indicate that biographical data might be an effective way of determining who should attend an assessment center and that using this data should increase the cost-benefit ratio per assessee (Ritchie and Boehm, 1979; Ritchie, 1980).

While "hard" evidence regarding utility and the costs and benefits of assessment centers is still in short supply and the technology of determining the dollar worth of assessment centers consequently not fully developed, the information that is available strongly suggests that the question of whether assessment centers are worth what they cost will be eventually answered in the affirmative. Investigation of this issue will play an important role in the assessment center literature of the 1980s.

Linkages between Assessment Centers and Other Personnel Programs

As assessment centers move beyond use primarily for selection purposes and become increasingly called on to serve purposes of management development and organizational diagnosis, the question of the interface between the assessment center and related personnel systems becomes increasingly important. The development programs identified earlier that used assessment centers as a component indicate ways an organization might begin to deal with some aspects of the interface issue. Each of these programs (and others of their type) deal with the issues of who gets feedback, what sort of follow-up development plans are devised, and whether or not there is organizational post-assessment monitoring of the activity that actually occurs.

But other aspects of the linkage between assessment centers have not been dealt with systematically to date. Some of these essentially unanswered linkage questions are:

1. What is the optimal organizational relationship between an assessment center and an internal placement organization in order to maximize the benefit of development plans to individuals and the organization?
2. How should assessment center information be input into an organization's training organization in order to assure that the right kind of training is made available to the people who can benefit from it?
3. How should assessment information be integrated with other information (appraisals, education, experience, etc.) in making promotion decisions?
4. How should long-range corporate plans, staffing forecasts, and changes in business direction be input into assessment center operations so that the content of the assessment center can remain organizationally responsive?

These questions are crucial ones to answer if an assessment center is to serve as an effective organizational selection and/or development device over time. If assessment centers are not integrated into the personnel systems of the organizations that conduct them, their long-term organizational survival is doubtful and less than maximal utility is virtually assured.

With the exception of Question 3, these linkage questions are not vital matters when assessment centers are used primarily for selection purposes. But when assessment is used for developmental purposes, they become very important.

The indications strongly point in the direction of increased use of assessment centers for developmental purposes. Consequently, developing answers to questions such as these will be a major challenge of the 1980s.

The Role of Assessment in Changing Organizations

One of the compelling criticisms that has been leveled against the assessment center method is that it is an essentially static technique that tends to perpetuate organizational status quo (Klimoski and Strickland, 1977; Thornton, 1979). Since assessment centers are based on job analysis and assessors are managers in the organization who evaluate behavior based on their concept of an organizational norm, the tendency would be to select assessees for promotion who resemble those already in the position. The predictive validity evidence indicating that individuals who do well in assessment in fact show superior future performance in terms of salary growth and organizational advancement is seen as supporting the argument. The counterargument is that an assessment center will lead to the identification of those who have skills equal to those of the best of the incumbents and thus result in an improvement of managerial quality rather than a perpetuation of the status quo. Since both sides of this controversy use the same data to support their arguments, its resolution is problematic. In the case of a relatively static organization, it is basically academic since continuation of the status quo may be the desired outcome.

However, if assessment centers were in fact to operate in a manner that perpetuated the current mode of organizational functioning, adverse consequences could result during periods when organizational change is necessary.

Adaptations of traditional assessment center technology are probably required if a major change in the target job or job level is anticipated. One such adaptation is to design the assessment center on the basis of a future-oriented job analysis (Albright, 1980). This approach requires an organization to actively plan the change process and define the future job.

Organizational change, however, is frequently less well preplanned and is often the result of social and economic changes outside the corporation itself. Different types of adaptations of assessment center technology and practices are called for under these circumstances. One externally triggered change that has markedly affected organizations is the legal and social mandate for equal employment opportunities for women and members of ethnic minorities. Here, assessment centers have demonstrated a capacity to serve as a useful tool for identifying talent in previously overlooked populations. The AT&T program was one effort to utilize assessment centers as a vehicle for bringing about organizational change.

Another possible adaptation of assessment center technology to a changing organization would be the inclusion of dimensions in the assessment center aimed at the measurement of an individual's adaptability to change. Some dimensions that would appear to be related to adaptability to change are currently included in some assessment processes. Dimensions such as tolerance of ambiguity, behavior flexibility, and need for structure would appear to be related to adaptability to change and are relevant to some jobs and job levels. An argument could be made that adaptability to change could be considered job-related even when this is not indicated by a current job analysis, if it is certain or likely that the job or its organizational context is likely to change in the near future. This would seem to be especially defensible when the assessment center is aimed at identification, rather than immediate selection.

Another use of assessment centers in changing organizations is assessment for alternative placement. As organizations shift emphasis and business focus, it is not infrequent to have current or projected staffing surpluses in one area of the business at the same time that current or projected staffing shortages exist in another. Assessing employees, who are likely to be surplus in their present areas for potential to perform in positions in areas where shortages are anticipated, would seem to operate for the mutual benefit of both the employees and the organization.

It is not unlikely that future uses of assessment centers will be increasingly focused on meeting the needs of changing organizations. Given the flexibility of the assessment center and the fact that it is already used for a variety of purposes, the view that assessment centers are a static selection device seems an overly narrow analysis of their utility.

New Directions in Assessment Center Research

Assessment center research during most of the 1970s focused primarily on the predictive validity of the assessment center, although this focus was not so single-minded as had been the case during the 1960s. Huck (1977) reported published validity studies by organizations that had published more than one such study and counted seven studies from AT&T, five each from IBM and Sohio, and two each from General Electric and Sears. While a number of other organizations have conducted validity studies and a number have published them, these five early users of the assessment center method with twenty-one validity studies among them have made traditional validity studies of assessment centers something of a drug on the market. While organizations need to continue to conduct such studies in order to comply with government regulations (EEOC, 1978) and professional standards (Division of Industrial/Organizational Psychology, 1975), assessment center predictive validity studies can now be considered as more of a maintenance item than as a new direction for research. There are, however, at least three areas where further research regarding the assessment center and its use are innovative, interesting, and badly needed.

Content Validity. While the predictive validity of the assessment center has been extensively (perhaps exhaustively) investigated, assessment center validity based on a content validation strategy has been frequently alleged, but seldom researched. Figure 12–2 (Byham, 1980) illustrates the relationships that must be shown in order to establish content validity.

Since a content validity strategy is the only practical alternative available to most small- and medium-sized organizations for establishing the validity of their assessment centers, reports of content validity research are badly needed, and the Byham model shown in Figure 12–2 may provide a valuable model for this research.

The evaluation of development programs that include assessment. With the exception of the AT&T identification-type program (Hoyle, 1979), evaluation of assessment center programs aimed at serving developmental purposes is virtually nonexistent. Evaluation research, especially of diagnostic programs, is badly needed. The author agrees with the statement of Thornton (1979) on this topic: ''What evidence exists that

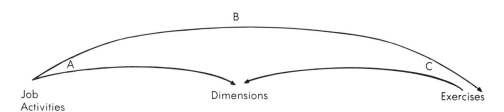

A. Dimensions must be shown to be job-related and to describe all common and important parts of the job.

B. Exercises must be shown to be job-related and to represent the most common and significant job activities. They also must be shown to be comparable in complexity and difficulty level to that required on the job.

C. The dimensions must be shown to be observable in the exercises.

FIGURE 12–2

Relationships That Must Be Established to Show the Content Validity of an Assessment Center

Source: W. C. Byham. ''Starting an Assessment Center the Correct Way.'' *Personnel Administrator* 25 (1980): 27–32. Reprinted from the December 29, 1980, issue of *Personnel Administrator.* 30 Park Drive, Berea, Ohio 44017.

assessment centers lead to growth and development as a result of the experience itself? As far as this author knows, no such research evidence has been reported. Some programs emphasize that individual self-insight leads to development. Has this been tested? Again, to my knowledge it has not" (Thornton, 1979, p. 4).

As the developmental use of assessment centers becomes more common, this gap in the research literature becomes increasingly obvious. A new and virtually untouched area of research awaits the investigator, and it is almost certain that this will become a major thrust of assessment center research in the 1980s.

"Second generation" research on assessment center technology.   As assessment center technology has become better established and consensus has emerged regarding the "state-of-the-art" on many basic issues (Task Force on Assessment Center Standards, 1979), operational focus has shifted to methodological and administrative issues as opposed to theoretical ones. For example, Cohen and Sands (1978) examined the influence that order of assessment center exercise presentation had on assessment results. Schmitt and Hill (1977) investigated the impact on assessment center results of various race/sex group membership combinations. Denning and Grant (1979) examined the question of whether prior knowledge of the assessment center process on the part of assessees impacted their performance. Thornton and Zorich (1980) investigated the impact of various types of group exercise observation training on the accuracy of assessor observations.

All four of these studies represent a "second generation" of assessment center research that operates from a basis of generally accepted validity for the method in general, and uses this foundation for further research.

These studies also address themselves to issues directly related to the "how-to's" of assessment center administration. Assessment center research in general has been both applied and theoretical. Those studies aimed at aiding assessment center administrators in answering procedural questions—"Is it o.k. to have only one woman in a group?" "Can I vary the schedule without undermining the process?" "What happens if someone who has already been assessed tells his or her friends about the process?" "How can I best use training time to maximize report accuracy?"—are almost totally applied, rather than theoretical.

The growth in the use of assessment centers in organizations is almost certain to result in an increasing amount of such second-generation assessment center research in the 1980s as the emphasis moves from external assessment center validity to internal process concerns, such as those reflected in the studies previously mentioned.

Ethical Considerations

To some extent, the ethical considerations surrounding the obtaining and utilization of assessment center information are similar to those surrounding psychological tests. Problems can arise concerning informed consent on the part of the assessee, prevention of improper information disclosure, misuse of information, and so forth.

However, assessment centers have the potential to create other, less familiar and more serious types of ethical problems. These are dealt with to some extent in the Standards and Ethical Considerations for Assessment Centers (Task Force on Assessment

Center Standards, 1979). The potential for sticky ethical issues to arise is especially strong when an attempt is made to utilize the information diagnostically for development purposes.

The ethical issue that must be dealt with here is the extent to which those who develop or administer the assessment center are, or should be, responsible for post-assessment activities and the use of assessment center information. Does a "diagnostic" assessment center include recommendations for treatment and an evaluation of the treatment's effectiveness? From an ethical standpoint, it probably is permissible to answer this query "yes," "no," or "maybe." The real problem comes when different people (the assessors, assessees, line management, trainers, and so forth) do not discuss it and agree on an answer, so that someone is misinformed or misled as to what will happen as a result of assessment.

A second hazard is related to the first. Suppose the assessment center developer or administrator does attempt to recommend treatment, but does so on the basis of inadequate knowledge of likely success. This is highly likely, given the current state-of-the-art. There simply is not much information available concerning the extent to which weaknesses identified in assessment can be overcome. Some evidence (Bray, Grant, and Campbell, 1974) indicates that, in the absense of systematic intervention, little change in individual behavior is likely. But systematic attempts to produce changes in specific assessment-related behaviors, and then measure the effectiveness of the intervention, are lacking. It appears probable that the recommendation of procedures to overcome weaknesses identified in assessment may result in raising false expectations on the part of assessees or their managers. Professionals simply do not know enough about the extent to which traits that are measured in assessment are able to be developed. Nor is enough known about the effectiveness of various change strategies. Substantial research is required in this area, and its conduct should be given high priority for ethical as well as scientific reasons.

Another type of potential ethical problem is a direct outgrowth of the general success and organizational acceptability of assessment centers, whether used for selection, development, or both. The high "face validity" of assessment centers can create an ethical problem. The risk of overuse of assessment center results is stronger than is the case with paper-and-pencil tests, and the weight given to the results may be greater than the validity evidence justifies. No measurement device is perfect, and the developer or administrator of an assessment center must walk a fine line between underselling and overselling the utility of the product. Where this line should be drawn is somewhat foggy since investigation of assessment center utility is still a new undertaking (Casico and Silbey, 1979; *Journal of Assessment Center Technology,* 1979). Both under- and overutilization of assessment results can have ethically undesirable consequences.

The development of assessment center theory and technology has consistently been user-oriented and aimed at the achievement of organizational objectives. From the OSS experience (1948) to the present, assessment centers have been an example of "applied" (rather than purely "scientific") psychology. Because of this "applied" orientation, ethical considerations must be viewed as an integral rather than ancillary concern.

The scientific value of assessment centers as a selection tool has been adequately demonstrated and their worth as a developmental tool is currently being explored. Initial indications are positive. But regardless of their scientific value, the long-range future of the assessment center method may well depend as much on the extent to which they are viewed as "right" in an ethical sense as the extent to which they are regarded as "accurate" in a scientific sense. Coming to terms with these ethical issues may well prove to be the real challenge of the 1980s.

Discussion Questions

1. Describe the three major functions of assessment centers. How would you evaluate their relative success?

2. How would you define management development? How is assessment center information utilized in management development?

3. Numerous studies have suggested that assessment center results significantly predict future organizational advancement. Is this an appropriate criterion measure? Would the results be the same without the use of an assessment center?

4. Discuss the relationship between performance appraisals and assessment centers in personnel management.

5. "Assessment centers have the potential to create other, less familiar and more serious types of ethical problems." Discuss these problems and their management.

PART SIX

CAREER OPPORTUNITIES AND THE WORK ENVIRONMENT

Efforts to improve opportunities for individual growth and development and the general work environment pervade the Quality of Work Life philosophy. Important factors, which interact with each other and significantly contribute to desirable or undesirable attitudes and behavior at work, are career planning and development, stresses in the job and the organization, and union-management relations.

Considerable attention is being given in organizations today to creating a meaningful flow in the sequences of jobs held by employees. Career planning and development can be a mutually beneficial process by which employers and employees simultaneously attempt to maximize their own self-interests without sacrificing the potential gains of the other. In Chapter 13, Milkovich and Anderson review some of the contemporary concerns with career planning and development systems. They also discuss future issues of importance to this personnel activity.

The negative effects of work-related stresses are readily apparent when one examines, for example, the increased incidence of alcoholism, drug abuse, psychosomatic disorders, and suicide among executives, office employees, and factory workers. In addition, some retaliatory behaviors (e.g., sabotage and fighting) and withdrawal behaviors (e.g., absenteeism and turnover) can be attributed to excessive amounts of stress at the workplace. Beehr and Schuler, in Chapter 14, review different theoretical approaches to stress and then discuss several issues bearing on the antecedents and consequences of stress in the work environment.

Historically, the champions of improved working conditions for employees have been the labor unions. The influence of unions on the management of human resources in organizations cannot be underestimated. In Chapter 15, Fossum begins with a discussion of the structure of labor organizations and the laws that define and regulate union-management relations. He then gives primary attention to the collective bargaining process and several related matters, including contract negotiations, contract administration, and their impact on personnel practice.

CHAPTER THIRTEEN

CAREER PLANNING AND DEVELOPMENT SYSTEMS

George T. Milkovich and John C. Anderson

George T. Milkovich is Professor in the New York State School of Industrial and Labor Relations at Cornell University. He received his Ph.D. in Industrial Relations from the University of Minnesota. Professor Milkovich formerly served as Professor in the School of Management at the State University of New York at Buffalo and Professor of Business and Industrial Relations at the University of Minnesota. Professor Milkovich has conducted research in the areas of organizational careers and human resource planning and is the author of numerous publications. He has also served as a consultant on a wide range of human resource issues to such organizations as AT&T, General Motors, Sears, and General Electric.

John C. Anderson is Associate Professor in the Graduate School of Business at Columbia University. He received his Ph.D. in Industrial and Labor Relations at Cornell University. Professor Anderson formerly was Assistant Professor of Business at Queen's University and also served as Assistant Professor in the Graduate School of Management at the University of California, Los Angeles. Professor Anderson has been an active researcher in a number of areas, including labor relations and career planning. He has been the recipient of several research grants and is the author and coauthor of numerous publications. Additionally, Professor Anderson has served as a consultant to several organizations in both Canada and the United States.

The notion of careers may have as many definitions as there are people talking about it. The educational system offers assistance in "career counseling." "Career days" provide information on "career options." Self-help books exhort readers to manage their own careers. Recruiters discuss their organization's ability to offer a "rewarding career" to a prospective employee. Specialty shops even sell "career clothes." But there exists little consensus on defining a career.

PERSPECTIVES ON CAREERS

The research literature also contains many definitions of careers. Hall (1976) identified four prominent meanings attached to careers: (1) advancement in the status hierarchy of the world of work; (2) a profession—doctor, lawyer, Indian chief; (3) a lifelong sequence of jobs, regardless of the occupation or level in the organizational hierarchy; and (4) a lifelong sequence of role-related experiences. However, it is also possible to take an organizational rather than individual perspective and look at a career as a sequence of positions that an organization has defined as a career path or ladder. Others have argued that there is no such thing as a career; there is only random mobility (March and March, 1977). What is clear is that careers mean different things to different people. Such differences in interpretation inevitably result in differences in the way that careers are studied. Four dominant perspectives are outlined here.

The Individual Perspective

Much of the current research takes the career of the individual as the major focus. Psychological theories of career development, the analysis of the stages of an individual's career, the developmental tasks that individuals face at each stage, and the effect of these tasks on the individual's attitudes and behaviors are the central issues addressed by this perspective (Hall, 1976; Super and Hall, 1978). As a consequence, how and why people choose careers, how their attitudes, behaviors, and lives change as they move through the stages of a career, how they adapt to mid-career change and retirement, and how they manage their own careers are the questions the research addresses. This perspective assumes that people have some degree of control over their destiny and can manipulate opportunities in order to maximize career success and satisfaction. It further implies that employers' human resource activities should recognize career stages and assist employees with the developmental tasks faced at each stage. Planning is important because the consequences of career success or failure are closely linked with the individual's self-concept and identity as well as with career and life satisfaction.

The Organizational Perspective

In contrast to the individual perspective, others have identified careers not only as characteristics of individuals, but also as attributes of organizations (Anderson, Milkovich, and Tsui, 1981; Milkovich, Anderson, and Greenhalgh, 1976). Careers are defined as a sequence of roles or positions, usually related in work content, through which employees move, pulled by opportunities within an organization. From this perspective, the career is something that is not simply left to employees; instead, it may be managed by the organization in order to ensure the efficient allocation of human and capital resources. Major issues of interest to researchers in this group include the causes of differences in rates of mobility across departments or organizations; the way in which mobility can be planned to simultaneously fulfill organizational requirements and individual needs; and the role of change in environmental conditions, organizational structure, and workforce composition on the career system. The starting point for this perspective is the determination of what career sequences and rates of mobility are present in an organization (e.g., Vroom and MacCrimmon, 1968).

The Sociological and Economic Perspectives

Another perspective on careers focuses on the role of mobility within the social structure. Sociologists in this tradition study such issues as what factors lead to higher status attainment, to movement up the occupational hierarchy, and to intergenerational mobility (Blau and Duncan, 1967; Miller and Form, 1951). Economists interested in the status attainment of individuals have examined the human capital and institutional factors that promote or inhibit social mobility. The main purpose of research in these streams is to identify the causes of socioeconomic mobility in order to ensure the efficient and equitable allocation of resources in society (Thurow, 1975, 1980). For example, the role of civil rights legislation and affirmative action policies in influencing the allocation of minorities and women out of "overcrowded occupations" into traditional "white male-dominated occupations" is becoming an increasingly important issue (Bergman, 1974; England, 1981).

Purpose and Perspective of This Chapter

Since a complete understanding of career planning and development in organizations cannot be accomplished by adopting only one of the four perspectives mentioned, the focus of this chapter will be on the individual and organizational perspectives and the ways in which they may be integrated to provide a basis for the design and establishment of effective career systems in organizations. The state of knowledge and practice in each of these areas is reviewed as a basis for suggesting future directions. First, research on the individual perspective is discussed, followed by research on the organizational perspective. Finally, a third section addresses the organizational policies, procedures, and techniques available to influence the development of organizational career systems.

This chapter explicitly assumes that careers, or at a minimum patterned mobility, exist within organizations and that the development of an effective career system is vital to the efficient allocation of human resources; moreover, it is believed that the future of the notion of organizational careers is in its utility as a research construct. It is time to call a moratorium on "Practical Guides to Your Career," "Organizational Survival Kits," and books on how to get ahead in various fields. Much more knowledge about the concept and its organizational determinants and consequences is needed before any prescriptions are handed down.

CAREERS: THE INDIVIDUAL PERSPECTIVE

Careers are typically seen as attributes of individuals—something individuals experience and/or pursue. However, even with the individual as the focus, an agreed-upon definition does not seem to exist. Super and Hall (1978), in a review of career research, identified an objective and a subjective definition of individuals' careers. Super and associates (1957) stressed the objective view: "A career is a sequence of positions occupied by a person during the course of a lifetime (p. 58)." Hall (1976), however, defined a career more broadly to include "the individually perceived sequence of attitudes and behaviors associated with work related experiences and activities over the span of the person's life (p. 4)."

While both authors see careers as an individual experience, the latter view seems to incorporate all the behaviors, attitudes, and experiences associated with work. While such a definition may serve to integrate, it also suffers from being too broad to provide any useful understanding of the linkage between careers and work behaviors.

Regardless of the specific definition adopted, the individual perspective emphasizes a developmental concept of individuals at work over a life span. Workers are viewed as facing tasks related to growth, exploration, establishment, maintenance, and decline as they cycle through career stages. The developmental tasks associated with each career stage are seen as the major determinants of employee attitudes and behaviors.

Career Stages

Researchers have attempted to identify the major developmental tasks that employees face during their work lives and to organize these into career stages. As might be expected, several theoretical alternatives have emerged, with certain consistencies and inconsistencies among them. At one level of abstraction, the sequencing of stages is consistent across researchers, resembling biological growth and decay cycles—trial and growth, exploration, establishment, maintenance, decline, and withdrawal. Differences between perspectives include the number of distinct stages an individual may pass through, the overlapping tasks and issues faced in each stage, the role of transition periods between stages, and the degree to which career stages are seen as age-linked. A few examples of career stages are examined, followed by a consideration of some relevant research and its implications.

Much of the current speculation about career stages derives from developmental and vocational psychology (Hall, 1976; Rush and Peacock, 1980). Erickson (1950), for example, asserted that each life stage is characterized by unique developmental tasks that must be mastered in order to advance to the next stage. Major tasks in the "Later Adolescence Stage" (ages 18–22) include achieving autonomy from parents, establishing a role identity, and making vocational choices. Levinson et al. (1978), on the other hand, posited that stages tend to overlap. In their "Early Adult Transition Stage" (ages 17–22) the major issues include reshaping attitudes, values, and behaviors for adulthood and differentiation from parents, and beginning professional commitments to new work and life roles.

A composite of the earlier developmental work is shown in Figure 13-1 (Hall, 1976). The teens and early twenties are a period of trial jobs; the mid-twenties to mid-thirties are a period of getting established, forming commitments, and settling down; entering the forties, individuals cut relationships with mentors and enter mid-career. Mid-career is a period of tumultuous struggles; every aspect of life is questioned, goals are reexamined, life's accomplishments are compared to initial goals and dreams, and a

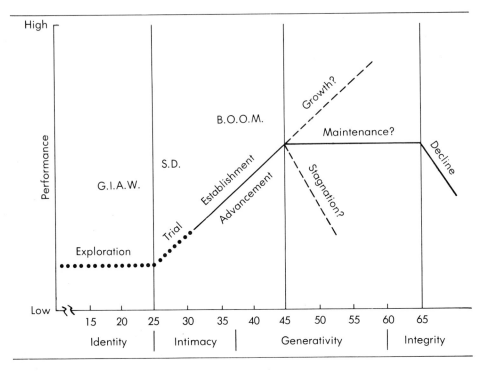

FIGURE 13-1
Stages in Career Development

Source: D. T. Hall. *Careers in Organizations* (Palo Alto, Calif.: Goodyear, 1976), p. 57.

sense of aging, and of physical and psychological limits, prevails. It is a time for reflecting on what a person is producing of lasting value. This stage may be characterized by growth, maintenance, or decline, depending on situational and personal factors. The later period (age 60 on) of work life is presented as a time in which withdrawal from work begins. Anticipating retirement, a person faces and must come to terms with his or her work life cycle.

More recently, several students of careers have identified in greater detail the tasks and issues that characterize each stage. Two of these lists are briefly considered here (Dalton, Thompson, and Price, 1977; Schein, 1978). Dalton, Thompson, and Price developed an empirical model of four distinct stages in a work career. Each stage differs in the tasks expected to be performed, in the types of relationships to be engaged in, and in the psychological adjustments to be made (see Table 13-1).

The first stage starts when an individual joins the organization and is confronted with several challenges or tasks. The person must learn to competently perform some of the organization's tasks and to discover which elements of work are critical and which activities require the greatest attention. In this stage, the individual must be a subordinate and work with a mentor to learn organizational competence, or the politics of the

TABLE 13-1

Activities, Roles, and Psychological Issues in the Four Career Stages

	Stage I	*Stage II*	*Stage III*	*Stage IV*
Central Activity	Helping Learning Following directions	Independent contributor	Training Interfacing	Shaping the direction of the organization
Primary Relationship	Apprentice	Colleague	Mentor	Sponsor
Major Psychological Issues	Dependence	Independence	Assuming responsibility for others	Exercising power

Source: Reprinted, by permission of the publisher, from "The Four Stages of Professional Careers: A New Look at Performance by Professionals," G. W. Dalton, P. H. Thompson, and R. L. Price, *Organizational Dynamics*, Summer 1977, p. 23 © 1977 by AMACOM, a division of American Management Associations. All rights reserved.

organization. The basic dilemma of the Apprentice Stage is adjusting to the dependence inherent in the role of a subordinate at a time when the individual expects independence.

The major psychological task of the Colleague Stage is to move from dependence to independence. The individual must develop ideas on what is needed in a given situation and develop judgment. Activities within this stage involve having one's own project or area of responsibility, honing professional skills to a high level, and developing an area of specialization. These activities enhance a sense of competence and self-esteem, and serve to increase individual visibility in the organization. Peer relationships take on importance as the individual relies less on the mentor for direction.

Stage Three is called the Mentor Stage because of the increased responsibility for influencing, guiding, directing, and developing other people. There are three roles played in the Mentor Stage: informal mentor, idea generator, and manager, the latter being the most common. During this stage, the individual must develop a sense of confidence in his or her ability to produce results, help others do the same, build the confidence of junior people, and be psychologically willing and able to take responsibility for someone else's output. At the same time, however, a person in this stage must learn to derive satisfaction from seeing apprentices become independent and perhaps even pass him or her on the organizational ladder.

Finally, a person may (or may not) reach the Sponsor Stage; the sponsor is responsible for directing the organization or some major segment of it. For example, such roles as negotiating and interfacing with key parts of the environment, developing new ideas, products, markets, or services, or directing the resources of the organization toward specific goals may be within the sponsor's domain. This individual is concerned with the selection and development of key people and becomes heavily involved with pivotal relationships outside the organization, such as external boards, committees, and associations.

Perhaps the most detailed pinpointing of tasks associated with various stages is developed by Schein (1978). His list is presented in Table 13–2. While the number of stages Schein identifies is greater than in Dalton's model (nine versus four), the specific tasks that individuals must face over their work lives are similar.

Evaluating Career Stages and Their Organizational Consequences

There has been little research to date to test these or any other total work life models of career stages. Dalton, Thompson, and Price's (1977) model is based on professional and technically trained individuals; it remains an open question as to whether or not the model is generalizable to other occupational groups. Levinson et al. (1978) model is based upon intensive, in-depth analyses of forty males (ten biologists, ten managers, ten laborers, and ten writers). Hall's (1976) model, drawing upon the earlier work of Erickson, Levinson, and Super, is untested. Schein's (1978) model is "the pulling together of strands of work which have been going on for the last fifteen years" (p. vi), drawing upon forty-four alumni who were studied over their careers.

Two recent studies attempt to provide tests of theories of career stages. The major problem in studying career stages is in determining how to measure them. Gould and

TABLE 13–2
Stages and Tasks of the Career Cycle

Stages	General Issues to Be Confronted
1. Growth, fantasy, exploration (age 0–21) (Roles: student, aspirant, applicant)	1. Developing a basis for making realistic vocational choices 2. Turning early occupational fantasies into workable realities 3. Assessing the realistic constraints based on socioeconomic level and other family circumstances 4. Obtaining the appropriate education or training 5. Developing the basic habits and skills needed in the world of work

Passages into an Organization or Occupation

2. Entry into world of work (age 16–25) (Roles: recruit, entrant)	1. Entering the labor market—getting a first job that can be the basis for a career 2. Negotiating a viable formal and psychological contract to ensure that own needs and those of employer will be met 3. Becoming a member of an organization or occupation—passage through first major inclusion boundary
3. Basic training (age 16–25) (Roles: trainee, novice)	1. Dealing with the reality shock of what work and membership are really like 2. Becoming an effective member as quickly as possible 3. Adjusting to the daily routines of work 4. Achieving acceptance as regular contributing member—passing the next inclusion boundary
4. Full membership in early career (age 17–30) (Roles: new but full member)	1. Accepting the responsibility and successfully discharging with duties associated with first formal assignment 2. Developing and displaying special skills and expertise to lay the groundwork for promotion or lateral career growth into other areas 3. Balancing own needs for independence with organizational restrictions and requirements for a period of subordination and dependence 4. Deciding whether to remain in the organization or the occupation or to seek a better match between own needs and organizational constraints and opportunities
5. Full membership, mid-career (age 25+) (Roles: full member, tenured member, life	1. Choosing a speciality and deciding how committed to become to it vs. moving toward being a generalist and/or toward management 2. Remaining technically competent and continuing to learn in one's chosen area of specialization (or management)

Source: E. G. Schein. *Career Dynamics: Matching Individual and Organizational Needs*, © 1978 (Reading, Mass.: Addison-Wesley, 1978).

TABLE 13–2 (Cont.)

Stages	*General Issues to Be Confronted*
member, super- visor, manager) (person may re- main in this stage)	3. Establishing a clear identity in the organization, becoming visible 4. Accepting higher levels of responsibility, including work of others as well as one's own 5. Becoming a productive person in the occupation 6. Developing one's long-range career plan in terms of ambitions, type of progress sought, targets against which to measure progress, etc.
6. Mid-career crisis (age 35–45)	1. Major reassessment of one's progress relative to one's ambitions—forcing decisions to level off, change careers, or forge ahead to new and higher challenges 2. Assessing one's career ambitions against more general aspects of mid-life transition—one's dreams and hopes vs. realities 3. Deciding how important work and one's career are to be in one's total life 4. Meeting one's own needs to become a mentor to others
7(A). Late career in nonleadership role (age 40 to retirement) (Roles: key member, individual contributor or member of management, good contributor or deadwood) (many people stay in this stage)	1. Becoming a mentor, learning to influence, guide, direct, and be responsible for others 2. Broadening of interests and skills based on experience 3. Deepening of skills if decision is to pursue a technical or functional career 4. Taking on more areas of responsibility if decision is to pursue general-management role 5. Accepting reduced influence and challenge if decision is to level off and seek growth outside of career or work

Passage through Inclusion and Hierarchical Boundary

7(B). Late career in leadership role (may be achieved at early age, but would still be thought of as "late" in career) (Roles: general man-	1. Using one's skills and talents for the long-range welfare of the organization 2. Learning to integrate the efforts of others and to influence broadly rather than making day-to-day decisions or supervising closely 3. Selecting and developing key subordinates 4. Developing broad perspective, long-range time horizons, and realistic appraisal of the role of the organization in society

TABLE 13-2 (Cont.)

Stages	General Issues to Be Confronted
ager, officer, senior partner, internal entre- preneur, senior staff)	5. Learning how to sell ideas if in individual contributor or internal entrepreneur role
8. Decline and disen- gagement (age 40 until retirement; different people start decline at dif- ferent ages)	1. Learning to accept reduced levels of power, responsibility, and centrality 2. Learning to accept and develop new roles based on declining competence and motivation 3. Learning to manage a life that is less dominated by work

Passage out of the Organization or Occupation

9. Retirement	1. Adjusting to more drastic changes in life style, role, standard of living 2. Using one's accumulated experience and wisdom on behalf of others in various senior roles

Hawkins (1978), who examined the moderating influence of career stage on the relationship between satisfaction and performance, selected seniority in the organization to assess career stage. Specifically, three career stages were defined: establishment (tenure < two years), advancement (two years ≤ tenure ≤ ten years), and maintenance (> ten years), based on research by Katz and Van Maanen (1976). Very little difference was found in the relationship under investigation as a result of the career stage of the individual.

Rush, Peacock, and Milkovich (1980) attempted a test of Levinson's (1978) theory by measuring career stages through the use of vignettes based on the tasks or issues faced by the individual at each stage. In addition to examining whether or not people pass through the stages in the expected sequence, they investigated the linkage of age ranges to each stage and hypothesized changes in the commitment, satisfaction, and performance of the individual in each stage. Little or no support was found for any aspect of the theory. Only a small proportion of the respondents followed the hypothesized sequence of stages, and wide overlaps in ages across stages were discovered.

A number of other studies have been done that examine the behavior of individuals within one career stage (Berlew and Hall, 1966) or within specific age ranges (Hall and Mansfield, 1975). However, given that there is little empirical support for the existence of the hypothesized career stages, it is unclear that career concepts can or should be used to explain these results. In fact, there is very little, if any, agreement as to whether career stages are age-linked or not. Most of the theorists give age ranges for each stage, but these vary widely. Gould (1978), for example, indicated that the stages are time-dominated, but that there are wide individual differences across people. On the other hand, Dalton, Thompson, and Price (1977) did not present age ranges for their model of organizational career stages, but indicated that progression involves successful attainment and completion of the tasks, roles, activities, and adjustments necessary in each stage.

It may be more appropriate to think in terms of a "time-linked" relationship, for this would permit a "career clock" to begin at different points for different individuals, based on their background and experiences. For example, a teenager with working parents who discuss their jobs and who held summer and/or part-time jobs may be ready for "getting into the adult world" much earlier and pass through it much faster than another teenager whose parents were unemployed and who never held part-time jobs. In this way individual differences are taken into account in determining the start of the first stage and the rates of progression through other stages.

In summary, there is reason to believe that there are stages in individual careers and that understanding these stages may help one understand workers' behaviors and attitudes. However, the theoretical frameworks of career stages and their associated characteristics and tasks need to be more fully developed; operational definitions and hypotheses need to be complete enough to allow an understanding of a process that spans entire work lives. Finally, several methodological issues must be addressed before worthwhile data may be collected to test these theories.

Career Outcomes

A vast majority of research on careers from the individual perspective has not adopted a career-stages approach. Rather, the emphasis has been on the attitudinal and behavioral outcomes of career experience (Hall, 1976). A variety of operational definitions of career experience have been used, including level in the organizational hierarchy; amount of mobility within the organization; number of promotions, demotions, or transfers; and preferences for promotion. Measures of career experience are then generally correlated with commitment, satisfaction, performance, and turnover. A brief review of this literature is presented.

Several studies discovered a positive relationship between mobility and job satisfaction (Grusky, 1966; Lehman, 1966; Pruden, 1973), commitment, attitudes toward administrators (Grusky, 1966), intrinsic versus extrinsic values (Pennings, 1970), upward career anchorage, local orientation, and a negative relationship with alienation (Pruden, 1973). Kipnis (1964) found that naval petty officers with lower expectations about promotion had less favorable attitudes toward personnel management and technological change, the comparability of their work with that of their peers and their officers, pressure, the speed with which time passes, and their naval careers in general. In addition, Hall and Schneider (1972) found that organizational identification was greater for people with single organization careers than for those with multiorganization careers. Thus, in general, upward mobility within a single organization is related to favorable job attitudes, although the amount of evidence is limited.

Mobility, as one indicator of career experience, is also likely to have an influence on work behavior. The research provides some support for the hypothesis that unrealized expectations for upward mobility lead to a higher incidence of absenteeism (Murrel,

Griew, and Tucker, 1957) and turnover (Anderson and Milkovich, 1980; Friedlander and Walter, 1964; Hulin, 1968; Knowles, 1964; Porter and Steers, 1973; Ronan, 1967; Saleh, Lee, and Prien, 1965). No literature was found that examined the relationship of mobility expectations or mobility experiences and performance. It appears that where individual expectations for mobility are unfulfilled, negative consequences to the organization may result; and conversely, where expectations are met, individuals are likely to exhibit attitudes and behaviors more favorable to the organization.

A substantial amount of research has also been conducted that investigates the intercorrelation of mobility expectations and other job-related attitudes. These studies suggest that perceived autonomy, desire for responsibility, perceived job success, and positive labor relations attitudes are directly related to interest in promotion (White, 1974); a commitment to work as a central life interest increases upward orientation (Goldman, 1973); and job satisfaction is related to a preference for promotion (Harlow, 1973). Organizational commitment and job satisfaction were found in another sample to be associated with a preference for promotion (O'Reilly, Bretton, and Roberts, 1974), and Vardi and Hammer (1977) found positive correlations between career interest, career effort, career satisfaction, and job satisfaction. Thus, attitudes toward mobility within the organization are clearly related to other job-related attitudes.

Finally, career expectations have been discovered to be associated with individual characteristics. Expectations about mobility were found to decrease with age (Bowin, 1971; Harlow, 1973; Kipnis, 1964; O'Reilly, Bretton, and Roberts, 1974; Pennings, 1970; Tausky and Dubin, 1965; White, 1974); to increase with education (Moore, Miller, and Fossum, 1974; O'Reilly, Bretton, and Roberts, 1974; Tausky and Dubin, 1965); and to be lower for females than males (Livingstone, 1953). Moreover, Harlow (1973) found tolerance for ambiguity and need for dominance associated with preference for promotion. While no empirical studies were found, it has been suggested that blacks are less optimistic about career success (Gurin, 1974).

Although the results of these studies would suggest that career experiences are important determinants of work-related attitudes and behaviors, problems with the measurement and conceptualization of careers make generalizations very difficult. Moreover, few of these studies controlled other job, organizational, or individual characteristics that may have explained the variance in career outcomes. Furthermore, only one study was found that explicitly examined whether or not individual career planning, or just random experience, explained career outcomes (Gould, 1975), and that study indicated that individuals with more positive career experiences and attitudes were more likely to plan. Thus, while a substantial number of correlational studies of career outcomes exist, they are not generally tied into a broader theoretical framework.

CAREER SYSTEMS: AN ORGANIZATIONAL PERSPECTIVE

In the previous section, the notion of an individual career was discussed; that is, the major tasks and issues people face during various career stages. Organizations also may be conceived as offering careers to their employees (Wilensky, 1960). From this perspective, an organization can develop a career system within its structure that is made up of a

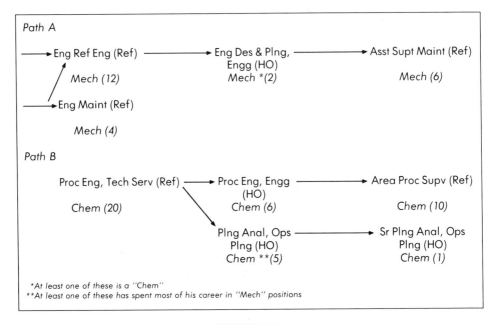

FIGURE 13–2

Engineering Positions Analysis: Traditional Career Paths among Positions

Source: J. Walker. ''Let's Get Realistic about Career Paths.'' *Human Resources Management* (1976): 2–7.

number of career paths or ladders for different occupations and individuals at different hierarchical levels (Bartlett, 1977; Walker, 1976; Pinto, Gutteridge and Tsui, 1975). Walker, for example, reported a traditional career path within a group of engineering positions in a major oil company. Figure 13–2 illustrates the path. ''In this example, mechanical engineers normally progress through Path A; chemical engineers progress through Path B. This created an impression among engineers in the refineries that career opportunities were quite restricted. There has been resulting turnover and expressed dissatisfaction among the younger engineers'' (Walker, p. 309).

From the organizational perspective, the planning and development of career systems becomes an integral part of the human resource management function. It is one strategy that aids the efficient allocation of employees by planning the orderly and efficient movement of individuals through the organization.

The purpose of this section of the chapter is to identify the characteristics of organizational careers and discuss the factors that may shape its development.

Career Systems: Toward a Definition

The concept of a career structure within the organization is not new; it is one that has been used by many theorists in several disciplines. For example, it was an important part of Weber's ideal bureaucracy. ''The (office) . . . constitutes a career. There is a system of 'promotion' according to seniority, or to achievement, or to both. Promotion is dependent on the judgment of superiors'' (Merton, 1957, p. 22). Weber's concept has its basis in the structure of the organization.

Dunlop (1966) conceived of an organization in terms of internal labor markets: administrative units within which the movement of human resources is governed by sets of rules and procedures. Jobs within the administrative unit are structured in terms of channels of workforce mobility, and criteria for regulating this movement are developed. The ideal model of an internal labor market presents human resources being recruited through specific entry ports (usually lower-level positions), while all other jobs tend to be staffed via the internal allocations based upon rules and procedures, such as seniority, performance, and experience. Prescribed avenues of mobility link jobs in career channels or ladders (Doeringer and Piore, 1971). Thus, examining careers from the perspective of the organization rather than from the perspective of the individual has historical precedent in both sociology and economics.

Organizational careers, then, are an attribute of the organization, having the dual properties of (1) a patterned sequence of positions related in work content, and (2) an ordered movement of individuals among these positions. Each of these two characteristics of organizational careers—sequence of positions and movement of employees—also has several dimensions. Regarding the sequence, the first dimension is the length of the sequence, (i.e., the number of positions in a sequence among which patterned movement of individuals occurs). Earlier in this century, it was possible (and may still be in some organizations) for an individual to start with a firm as an office employee or production worker and after hard work, many years, and considerable luck, to reach the upper managerial ranks or even become company president. Experience and skills were gained on each job. On the other hand, for the typical production worker, the sequence of positions may involve only a single job, or a single promotion to group foreman. While these are extreme examples, they indicate the extent to which the length of a position sequence may vary. In fact, there are situations in which two individuals starting at the same point in the organizational hierarchy may hold a different number of positions to reach the same ultimate job. Prime examples of this phenomenon are ''fast track'' programs in some organizations for employees to move quickly to high-level positions by skipping several jobs along the way.

The second dimension of a position sequence is its ceiling; that is, the highest position normally reached within the job cluster (cf., Thompson and Carlson, 1962). Some sequences have ''early ceilings'' (e.g., research scientists and engineers), requiring the individual to change into another career sequence (e.g., dual ladder for administration) in order to progress further in the organizational hierarchy. Conversely, managerial career sequences may have a great number of positions before reaching their ceilings. For example, managerial employees in larger organizations may move from small to large branches, through different functional responsibilities in regional, national, or international headquarters.

The second characteristic of an organizational career, the movement of employees, also has two dimensions. First is the rate at which individuals move from position to position. This has been examined as the proportion of people moving between positions within the career sequence per unit of time (Vroom and MacCrimmon, 1968), the time it typically takes to get from the start to the ceiling of a career sequence (Jennings,

1967), or the amount of time an individual is expected to remain in each job in the sequence (Roth, 1968). The rate of mobility may be of most interest to new entrants, who may want to know where they are likely to be within five years.

Mobility also has another dimension: direction. The direction of movement reveals how closely tied the sequence and the movement of employees are in defining organizational careers. The extent to which employees move upward, downward, or laterally may be designed into the career sequence. For example, in some organizations, to move to higher levels within the personnel department, the individual is required to gain experience in several specialized areas (e.g., compensation, recruiting, training), or in a line management position. Lateral movement is built into the sequence.

In summary, an organizational career may be conceived as a sequence of positions usually related in work content having both length and a ceiling, with the movement through that sequence at a certain rate and direction.

Determinants of Organizational Careers

Although it is possible to identify the components of an organizational career, it is clear that not all organizations have explicitly developed career paths or ladders. In many cases, patterns of mobility occur over time without any planning on the organization's part, but rather as a result of ad hoc policies, rules, regulations, and decisions made by individuals. Why do some firms have planned career paths while others do not? Why do mobility rates vary across organizations and even among different units within an organization? Under what conditions are career sequences likely to vary in length as well as direction? The purpose of this section is to explore the major factors that are likely to shape the nature of careers within an organization.

Figure 13–3 presents a rudimentary conceptual framework of organizational careers. The properties of the organizational careers are explained by three major sets of factors: environmental, organizational, and workforce characteristics. Each of these sets of variables influences the sequence of positions and rates of mobility that describe an organizational career. Moreover, to some extent, the influence of these dimensions is regulated by the policies, procedures, and mobility criteria that are established to govern mobility. Finally, the relationship between effectively managed organizational careers and satisfied and productive employees, or an optimally allocated workforce, or a more effective organization, needs to be considered (Anderson, Milkovich, and Tsui, 1981).

Environmental Conditions.   The nature of the economic, legal, and social environment in which the organization exists is likely to have a profound influence on organizational careers, as well as other aspects of organizational functioning. The rate at which individuals move through the relevant career sequences within the organization is largely dependent upon prevailing economic conditions. The demand for organizational products is likely to increase the demand for labor within the organization, which in turn will increase vacancies and the rate of movement within the career sequence. Not only does the nature of the organization's product market have an influence, but the labor market may also have a strong impact. When a large number of jobs are available in the economy (i.e., unemployment is low), people are more likely to consider quitting

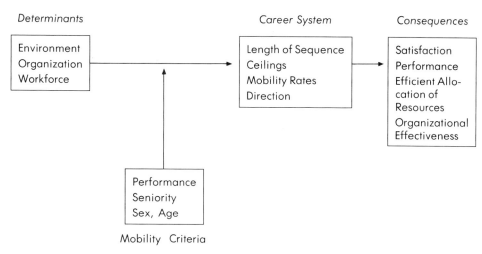

FIGURE 13-3
The Organization Career System—A Conceptual Framework

their present job (Anderson and Milkovich, 1980; Stoikov and Raimon, 1968), which creates opportunities within the system, increasing the overall rate of mobility. For example, one study (Gitelman, 1966) found that under progressively tight labor market conditions, mobility rates within the organization tended to increase. Conversely, under loose conditions, mobility rates tended to be stable or decline. Thus, it appears that the economic environment may play a significant role in determining the rates of mobility within an organization.

Recently, however, the legal environment may have taken on equal importance. With the enactment of equal opportunity legislation, not only the criteria governing promotions within the organization but also rates of movement and career sequences have been influenced (cf., Consent Decrees for AT&T and General Electric in Bureau of National Affairs *Fair Employment Practices Manual*). Although the majority of the literature on equal employment opportunity has focused on eliminating discrimination in initial hiring decisions, there has also been attention directed toward ensuring similar promotion rates and hierarchical distribution of minority and nonminority employees (*MOE* v. *General Motors,* 1980; Milkovich and Dyer, 1979). As a consequence, affirmative action plans have often called for increased rates of promotion of minority employees, the elimination of discriminatory career ceilings, and special career sequences to rectify past injustices.

In order to increase the proportion of females in the managerial ranks, AT&T (Bureau of National Affairs *Fair Employment Practices Manual*) established a fast-track career path to assist the movement of women into higher levels of management. General Electric in a consent decree (Bureau of National Affairs *Fair Employment Practices Manual*) agreed to offer bonuses to attract women and minority employees from office and clerical jobs into manufacturing and supervisory jobs. The basic steel industry (Moore,

1977) agreed to restructure its promotion and seniority rules to enhance promotion rates for blacks.

A further result of external regulatory pressures on organizations has been to require them to explicitly identify the normal "lines of progression" (career paths for different occupations) in order to determine the existence of career ceilings and dead-end jobs. Moreover, it required them to carefully examine the rate and direction of movement of employees within the organization. Therefore, where organizational careers may have been implicit or ad hoc in many organizations, compliance agency interpretations of legislation are pressuring employers to establish and articulate career paths and career development programs.

Unfortunately, very little evidence is available that either theoretically or empirically links the nature of the social environment to organizational career systems.

Organizational Characteristics.   It is well documented that different organizations offer different career paths to their employees (Allan, 1972; Elliott, 1966; Mahoney and Milkovich, 1972). But the role of organizational characteristics in shaping mobility patterns is less clear. Some researchers have investigated the relationship between the size, shape, and technology of the organization and careers. Wilensky (1960) asserted that organizations with tall hierarchies and more divisions and geographic locations provide greater opportunities for movement, primarily by increasing the degree of horizontal movement. Comparing a national with a multinational company, it is likely that, because of a larger number of geographic locations, a typical career sequence in the multinational organization will include a larger number of horizontal moves in order to ensure broad managerial experience within the organization. An increase in the number of separate divisions is likely to increase both the number of separate career sequences and the amount of vertical as opposed to horizontal movement (Martin and Strauss, 1956). Thus, it would seem that divisionalization increases the probability that individuals will pursue careers within their particular segment of the organization, rather than moving back and forth between divisions.

In addition to organizational structure, the size of the firm has also been related to organizational careers (Starbuck, 1965). The number of employees has been related to the frequency of succession of top management officials (Grusky, 1961; Kriesberg, 1962; Parker, 1965). Since succession is likely to cause a chain reaction in the organization as vacancies along the career sequence are filled, it increases both amount and rate of movement of employees through the sequence (Levinson, 1961). Size is also likely to have an indirect effect on the career system by increasing the complexity of the organizational structure and thus the number and types of positions available.

Finally, the technology of the organization is likely to play a role in shaping the characteristics of the career system. Stone's (1953) research revealed that career paths that include mobility from production to managerial work are more likely to exist in "mixed types" of technology (skilled and unskilled employees) than in a "modern" technology, which reduces the production process to semi-skilled or unskilled work. Using Thompson's (1967) technological types, another study (Vardi and Hammer, 1977) found that movement was primarily lateral in long-linked technologies and that it was more likely to be upward as the technology became mediating and intensive. Both of these studies suggest that the direction and length of a career sequence are partially determined by technology. Technology determines the manner in which tasks are clustered into jobs, as well as the relationship between jobs. Thus, it defines the most probable lines of job progression.

Workforce Characteristics. The demographics of the current labor supply within the organization are the third set of variables that influence organizational careers. As Holt and David (1966) pointed out, quits, retirements, and terminations are the main source of vacancies and these are partially influenced by employee composition. Given younger workers' higher quit rates, vacancies are likely to be greater when the proportion of employees in the older (near retirement) and younger segments of the workforce is higher. Moreover, vacancies will be greater as the proportion of female, minority, and low-tenure workers increases (Stoikov and Raimon, 1968). The composition of the workforce may, therefore, influence the organization by changing mobility rates through the rates of retirements, quits, and terminations.

The composition of the workforce may have other effects as well. Research suggests that expectations regarding mobility change with age, education, and sex (O'Reilly, Bretton, and Roberts, 1974; White, 1974). Therefore, as the proportion of employees in each of these groups changes, so may the career system. As discussed in the previous section of this chapter, the issues and tasks that individuals face during their work lives vary as they move through the various career stages. Therefore, the demands for mobility may be substantially greater when a greater number of people in the organization are in early career stages.

The Role of Criteria Governing Mobility

In designing career systems, organizations develop administrative rules, regulations, and procedures to govern the internal allocation of human resources (Doeringer and Piore, 1971). Despite the central role that these policies play in regulating the flow of employees through career sequences, they have been almost totally ignored in the research on organizational careers. Three characteristics of these rules and regulations can be identified as important to the mobility process: (1) the types of criteria used, (2) the level of criteria, and (3) the universalism or particularism with which they are applied. One of the most important criteria in a career system is a policy of "promotion from within" (Torpey, 1952). Obviously, no career sequence is operable if people are not moving through it. The extent to which experience is established as a criterion will heavily influence the rate, direction, and pattern of mobility in the organization (Roth, 1968). Thus, the nature of criteria chosen to regulate mobility is likely to play an important intervening role between determinants and characteristics of the career system.

The required level of the criteria is also an important moderator. That is, experience, education, or performance requirements for movement may vary from minimal to very stringent for a given position. Greater rates of mobility are likely when the criteria level is low. Rates of promotion to associate and full professorships in universities would be higher if research requirements were lower. Where the established criteria for movement are universally applied to all employees, mobility patterns are likely to be well developed and articulated.

Finally, it is important to point out that the criteria within an organization are likely to change as environmental and organizational conditions change. Equal opportunity legislation has made some criteria previously used illegal: age, race, and sex. The longer a vacancy exists, the more likely the criteria applied will be lowered (Wachter, 1974). Research on the employment interview (Wright, 1969) has revealed that the further the interviewer is from the established quota, the lower the standards a candidate must meet in order to obtain a favorable evaluation. Halaby (1978) and Maniha (1975) found that as bureaucratization of the organization increased, the use of universal as opposed to particular criteria also increased.

Consequences of the Career System

Why should an organization be concerned with managing the overall career system? The underlying theoretical argument is that management of career systems will result in the efficient allocation of human resources, which will lead to increased organizational effectiveness. Further, career systems must be adapted to changing environmental and organizational demands in order for the organization to maintain effectiveness. Unfortunately, no research was found that empirically evaluates the impact of career systems on organizational performance. Thus, the actual consequences of organizational careers are still only a topic of speculation.

Translated to the individual level of analysis, this perspective suggests that the appropriate design of the career system leads to individual behaviors consistent with organizational goals—good performance, positive attitudes, and low turnover and absenteeism. While some research has examined these relationships (see the Career Outcomes section in this chapter), the results are scant and often contradictory.

CAREER PLANNING AND MANAGEMENT

Career planning and management have become ''big business'' over the past few years. Several reasons may account for this:

1. Rising national concerns for quality of work life in America for all levels of workers among all economic, racial, and sexual groups
2. A chronic need for capable, talented personnel, particularly among individuals with technical and managerial skills
3. Continuing pressures from equal opportunity and affirmative action agencies to upgrade and promote minorities and women into managerial and ''nontraditional'' jobs
4. Rising aspirations and expectations of new workers coupled with a diminished rate of economic growth and advancement opportunities

This section of the chapter explores the techniques that are available to manage individual careers and organizational career systems. In so doing, it is assumed that the management and planning of careers is an important component of the human resource system.

Managing Individual Careers

The current practices within the career planning and management field can be divided into two approaches: those pertaining to organizational assistance to individuals at various career stages and those pertaining to managing one's own career. The first perspective suggests that the issues and dilemmas faced by employees over the stages of a career should drive the strategies developed by the employer for managing human resources.

One of the best developed frameworks for tailoring the personnel management system to career stages is shown in Figure 13–4 (Schein, 1978). The three components of the model should be noted:

Individual needs. The major developmental tasks faced by employees at various stages of their work lives

Organizational Needs. Human resource planning activities such as planning for staffing, growth, and replacement

Matching Process. The techniques common to most employers including job analysis, recruiting, training, and so forth.

The model illustrates how one may rethink an employer's human resource activities in light of the proposition that every employee goes through career stages. But organizational "needs" may include efficiency, productivity, cost control, performance, EEO, and control of turnover and absenteeism. Similarly, individual "needs" may include achievement, self-determination, a sense of self-worth, security—the list is long. While Schein recognizes the importance of these needs, their linkage to individual and organizational outcomes is not well developed.

The diagram in Figure 13–5 focuses on the consequences of matching career stages with the available personnel programs. What are the individual and organizational consequences of developing personnel programs that "match" the developmental tasks hypothesized to be inherent in an employee's work life? How will an employee's job satisfaction and work behaviors be affected, and how will these attitudes and behaviors affect organizational outcomes? The linkage between the matching process and outcomes remains to be investigated. Indeed, it is not at all clear that the major developmental issues have been adequately examined.

The second perspective focuses on programs designed for individual self-career exploration and planning. Essentially, planning one's own career is similar to any other planning process:

1. Develop a self-inventory.
2. Establish personal occupational objectives.
3. Obtain occupational, organizational information.
4. Design actions to achieve objectives.
5. Evaluate progress.

An enormous pool of references, self-help guides, and "organizational survival kits" directed toward individual and career planning exist (cf., Irish, 1973; Mardon and Hopkins, 1969; Simon and Kirschenbaum, 1972; Fitzroy, 1973; Bolles, 1972; Jennings, 1967; Hall, 1976). These approaches provide such commandments as "be an outstand-

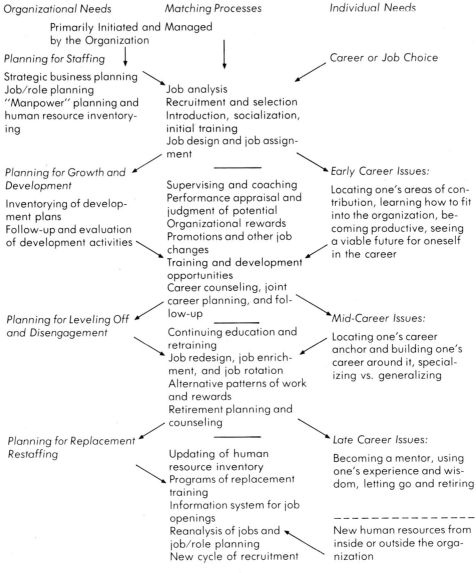

FIGURE 13–4
Human Resource Planning and Career Stages

Source: E. G. Schein. *Career Dynamics: Matching Individual and Organizational Needs.* © 1978 (Reading, Mass.: Addison-Wesley, 1978), p. 201.

ing performer; don't be blocked by an immobile superior; always favor increased exposure and visibility; (and) practice self-nomination.'' These programs seem to imply that all individuals have a uniform set of aspirations and values, an assumption that is generally not supported by research.

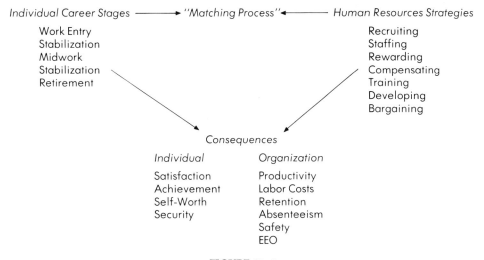

FIGURE 13-5
Organization Careers: What Are the Consequences?

Several unique approaches to career planning exist. General Electric, for example, publishes four volumes entitled *Career Action Planning* (Storey, 1976). The six basic issues addressed in these volumes, along with an example project, are shown in Table 13-3. By contrast, the portion of General Motors' *Career Development Guide* (1977), shown in Table 13-4, is more tailored to careers within General Motors. Both approaches have one thing in common: they are intended to get the individual to do the assessment and planning. However, they do not promise a career, regardless of how the plan turns out.

Many organizations, through a variety of human resource programs, offer a process within which an employee may plan his or her own career. They may provide such information as career options available, forecasts of employment trends, or sources of career counseling. However, career planning is usually tailored to the individual's self-interests; while some employers may assist in that process, contracts to offer the "career" that evolves from the planning are seldom offered or implied.

Managing Career Systems

Although a substantial body of literature has developed concerning the nature of individual careers and career stages as well as organizational practices to deal with individual career issues, the opposite is true for careers from an organizational perspective. Further, little is known regarding the consequences of career planning and management from either the individual or the organizational perspective (Gutteridge, 1976). Thus, researchers and managers of human resources face several challenges in the future:

1. *Investigate the consequences of designing human resource systems to assist individuals through the developmental tasks.* The influence of career plan-

TABLE 13–3

An Approach to Help You Think and Plan Realistically for Your Future, Your Growth and Your Career

1. Where are you now? How did you get there?
2. Where are you going?
   • Personal life
   • Career
3. Will it work for you? What's out there?
   • Career realities
4. How do you get there?
5. How do you tell how you're doing?
6. What do you do if . . . ?

Source: Adapted from W. D. Storey. *Career Action Planning* (Croton, N.Y.: General Electric Company, 1976).

TABLE 13–4

Employer-Assisted Career Planning

Where have you been?

1. Draw a horizontal line in the space below.

2. Put a circle at each end of the line.
3. In the circle on the left, write the year you joined GM.
4. Now, estimate the year you think your career with GM will end. That's a tough question, but think about it. Then write that year in the circle on the right.
5. Place an "X" on the line at the point in your career where you are now.
6. Look at the "career line" you have drawn and think about it. How do you feel about the time you've already spent with GM? Are you satisfied with what you've accomplished? What about the years ahead? Are there some important things you'd like to accomplish in the future portion of your career?

Where are you now?

Based on your own evaluation of your career to date, decide to what extent you agree with the following statements by putting a check mark in the appropriate boxes.

TABLE 13–4 (Cont.)

	To a very small extent				To a very great extent
1. I'm satisfied with what I've accomplished so far in my career.	1	2	3	4	5
2. There are some important things I want to accomplish in the time I have remaining.					
3. I have well-defined career goals.					
4. I am satisfied with my plan for accomplishing my career goals.					

Take a look at how you've responded to these four statements.

What do your answers tell you about yourself and your career?

BASED ON THE THINKING YOU'VE DONE . . .

DO YOU FEEL A NEED TO BETTER DEFINE YOUR CAREER GOALS AND SELF-DEVELOPMENT PLANS? Then Section I is the best place to start. It lays out a thought process for you to follow and provides useful tips and guidance in using the process. You'll find that it's an approach which has questions similar to the ones you've just considered—not necessarily easy questions, but provocative ones.

ARE YOU INTERESTED IN LEARNING ABOUT OTHER CAREERS IN YOUR DIVISION, STAFF, OR IN THE CORPORATION? Then Section II of this guide is a good place to start. It gives a bird's-eye view of career areas in GM. It does not, of course, tell the whole story, but it is a good sampler of what's available. To learn even more about a particular career area, talk to your supervisor or personnel representative, who will supply you with further information or the names of people you can contact to get information.

DO YOU WANT TO MAKE USE OF GM RESOURCES AVAILABLE TO HELP YOU ACCOMPLISH YOUR CAREER GOALS? Then turn to Section III. It will outline the major resources available to you and fill you in on what your supervisor and others can do to help.

We hope you've found this Guide interesting so far. Whether you read further is, of course, up to you, and maybe this introduction has helped you to decide. Whatever your decision, keep the Guide in a handy place. We think you'll find that planning your growth and development is not a one-time thing and that what's in this Guide will be useful even if you decide not to go further into it right now.

Source: A Career Development Guide. General Motors Corporation, 1977.

ning and management on productivity, employee attitudes, labor costs, concepts of self-worth, attendance, safety, EEO, and so forth, are not well researched.

2. *Identify existing career sequences.* Most organizations are not even aware of the career paths that are present in their structures. How many career lines exist? Do they have early or late ceilings? Are there dead-end jobs? What is the

typical time required to traverse the career? A discussion of some of the techniques available for examining these issues are presented by Dyer in Chapter 3 of this volume.

3. *Identify discrimination in the career system.* Current affirmative action legislation goes far beyond hiring procedures to include promotion and transfer policies. Do minorities have the same opportunities to enter and progress through all career sequences in the organization? Are minority and nonminority employees moving at the same rate? Are similar criteria applied to all employee groups?

4. *Describe and analyze organizational, workforce, and environmental factors.* It is clear that the design of career systems is tightly coupled with the structure and technology of the organization as a whole. However, the relationships are still not well investigated. How will new forms of organization structure change the nature of career systems? How do worker participation plans impact career sequences? How does transition to a no-growth economy affect career planning and development? How does the aging and professionalization of the workforce change the expectations (or requirements) for career structures and mobility rates? What is the relative impact of each of these factors on the components of the career system?

5. *Integrate career planning and management with human resource and strategic planning in the organization.* In general, career planning and development has been considered separately from other aspects of the planning function. However, it is obvious that all are concerned with the same goal—efficient allocation of resources. Career paths and projected mobility rates cannot be developed in isolation from estimates of product demand, diversification, and organizational growth, or without estimates of internal labor supply, turnover, and retirement.

6. *Consider innovative and alternate career systems.* Changes in the workforce and expectations of work require that more attention be paid to alternate career systems in the future. Will fast tracks and rotational programs successfully fill the needs of new professional employees? How does the career system take into consideration not only dual-career families, but also work-sharing arrangements between spouses? With slowed economic growth, how can career expectations be met or modified?

SUMMARY

The clarion call for more research is standard fare in the human resources field. Yet careers as a concept has the potential to play an unique role in the management of human resources and in understanding individual work attitudes and behaviors. There is a need for more empirical inquiry into careers, its usefulness as a concept, its determinants, and its consequences for both individuals and organizations. Careers are unique because the concept cuts across individual and organizational levels of analysis and may prove to be a useful notion for understanding the complex interaction that occurs between individuals and work organizations.

Discussion Questions

1. Career planning assumes that it is possible to plan and prepare for future job opportunities. Yet another perspective implies that a plan with detailed actions overlooks unexpected influences, such as economic conditions, personal health, or luck. In summary, one approach suggests, "I'm the captain of my fate," while the other suggests, "Toil in your garden and be prepared." What are the strengths and limitations of these perspectives?

2. From both the individual and organizational perspective, what are the equal employment opportunity and affirmative action implications of career planning? Consider not only race and sex, but also age and physical handicap issues.

3. Only minimal research regarding the consequences of career planning for individuals or organizations has been undertaken. Speculate about the consequences of career planning. What, if any, are possible negative results for an individual and for an organization?

4. Career stages, an important concept in the individual perspective of careers, are defined in terms of basic tasks or issues that individuals must face. Consider your own situation.
   a. What are the basic tasks or issues you currently face?
   b. What actions or programs have you undertaken to resolve these issues?
   c. How will you evaluate the "effectiveness" of these actions?
   d. What "career stage" are you in?

5. Considering the state of knowledge regarding careers and career planning, list five research propositions that, if answered, would greatly advance the state of knowledge.

CHAPTER FOURTEEN

STRESS IN ORGANIZATIONS

Terry A. Beehr and Randall S. Schuler

Terry A. Beehr is Associate Professor of Psychology at Central Michigan University. He received his Ph.D. in Psychology from the University of Michigan. Prior to assuming his present position, Professor Beehr was a faculty member in the Department of Psychology at Illinois State University and served as Research Investigator and Consultant at the Institute for Social Research, University of Michigan. Professor Beehr has been active in research and has published over twenty journal articles and papers. More recently, his research interests have focused on the area of job stress.

Randall S. Schuler is Associate Professor of Organizational Behavior at the University of Maryland. He received his Ph.D. in Organizational Behavior from Michigan State University. Professor Schuler has written articles in the areas of task design, employee satisfaction, and job stress. He has done consulting and research for several organizations and, in addition, has conducted numerous workshops and continuing education programs for managers in both public and private organizations. Professor Schuler has served also on the faculties of Ohio State University, Pennsylvania State University, and Cleveland State University.

John R. is a 38-year-old middle-level sales manager in a large corporation. He is considered hard-working, dependable, loyal, and productive by his superiors, who nevertheless feel that he does not have executive suite potential. This belief was formalized eight months ago when a key promotion was given to one of John's subordinates, instead of John. Since then his on-the-job behavior has gradually changed. His attention to detail has slipped. He has become withdrawn and seems to have lost enthusiasm for his superiors, who view his changed behavior as confirmation of their decision not to promote him. (From B. Blau, *Management Review,* August 1978, p. 57).

Although what happened to John R. was unfortunate, it is even more unfortunate knowing that in organizations there are many John R.'s who suffer from mid-career stress. But there are many more people who are exposed to several other types of stressors every day, sometimes with even more severe symptoms of stress than John R.'s. Fortunately, however, there is a growing concern about the existence of stress in organizations and ways that individuals and organizations can manage and even reduce it. This concern is based on several reasons, only one of which is what happens to employees like John R. and others who are exposed to stress in organizations. In this chapter, we will review these reasons and the ways to deal with stress.

In order that individuals and organizations can begin to manage and perhaps reduce stress, it is important to know what stress is and how it occurs in organizations. Thus, after a discussion of the reasons for being concerned with stress in organizations, stress will be defined and a conceptualization of individual stress in organizations offered. Based upon this definition and conceptualization, the existing stress research will be presented and evaluated. Then, current ways that organizations and individuals can deal with stress will be examined. Because concern for and research in stress in organizations is relatively recent and somewhat limited, the second major section of this chapter will consider and recommend future research and practice in the area of organizational stress for both organizations in general and the professional practitioner and the organizational stress researcher in particular.

Importance of Stress in Organizations

There are four major reasons why stress in organizations is becoming such a prominent topic of discussion.

Health.   The World Health Organization defines *health* as the presence of physical and psychological well-being. With this definition of health, a review of the research on stress plainly indicates that "stress may be hazardous to one's health." Some of the *major* ill-health indicators associated with stress in organizations are neuroses, coronary heart disease (CHD), alimentary conditions such as dyspepsia and ulcers, cancer, asthma, high blood pressure, backaches, and the related use of alcohol and drugs. In addition to the increased susceptibility of these ill-health indicators to those working in stressful conditions, is the increased likelihood of incurring accidents on the job when under stress.

Financial Impact.   It is estimated that the economic cost of peptic ulcers and cardiovascular disease alone in the United States is about $45 billion annually (Putt, 1970; Moser, 1977). The cost to society and organizations of the stress-related symptom of backaches is also high. Based on a survey conducted by the National Center for Health Statistics in 1977, backache was the fifth most common reason for visits to office-based physicians in 1975. In 1976, 14.2 percent of the disability claims filed by companies for individuals and 17.7 percent of the benefits paid involved back disorders (Warshaw,

TABLE 14–1
Costs of Executive Stress

	Conservative Estimate	Ultraconservative Estimate
Cost of executive work loss days (salary)	$2,861,775,800	$1,430,887,850
Cost of executive hospitalization	248,316,864	124,158,432
Cost of executive outpatient care	131,058,235	65,529,117
Cost of executive mortality	16,470,977,439	8,235,488,720
	$19,712,128,238	$9,856,064,119

Adapted from J. W. Greenwood. "Management Stressors." In *Reducing Occupational Stress* (Cincinnati, Ohio: NIOSH Research Report, 1978).

1979). In addition to these data, the estimated costs of stress that executives undergo are shown in Table 14–1.

Although these figures are only estimates of the financial impact, they do offer reasons for the concern over stress in organizations. Nonetheless, these data do not necessarily provide a convincing case for immediate action by organizations to reduce or even manage employee stress. Furthermore, employee stress may not be a result of organization conditions, but rather conditions outside the work place.

This being the case, should organizations do anything more than regard the effects of stress as merely "a part of doing business"? It appears that many organizations have already answered this question affirmatively, with the development and implementation of strategies to deal with stress. Their resolution to confront the issue of stress is based in part on the view that stress is a financial threat and a threat to the effectiveness of the entire organization.

Organizational Effectiveness. The increasing concern shown by some organizations about stress reflects an expanded definition of the basis on which to evaluate organizational effectiveness. Although many organizations still utilize profit or productivity as the main criterion on which to evaluate how well the organization is doing, other organizations and observers of organizations are recognizing the need for several criteria on which to evaluate organizations. This need is evident from viewing organizations as open systems rather than closed, self-sufficient systems (see Chapter 1 in this book). With this description of organizations as open systems are the assumptions that: (1) some means have to be devoted to such nongoal functions as service and custodial activities, including means employed for the maintenance of the organization itself, and (2) employees and society have as much of a stake in what the organization is and does as its owners and managers (see Etzioni, 1971; Steers, 1977; Katz and Kahn, 1978; Brief, Schuler, and Van Sell, 1980).

With an open systems view of organizations, it is necessary and legitimate to evaluate organizations on the basis of employee satisfaction, health, accidents, turnover, absenteeism, as well as efficiency, profitability, productivity, and return on investment.

Since stress in organizations is related to many of these factors, stress itself becomes a necessary and legitimate concern for organizations. But even if organizations do select the open systems view of evaluation, they are still confronted with two particularly important trade-offs. The first, as an example, is how much profit or productivity has to be given up to get increased employee health? And the second is, should short-run benefits be allowed to outweigh long-run costs? An illustration of these two trade-offs is provided in an example where workers were switched from a nonincentive-based pay system to an incentive system. On the basis of the incentive system, production rose an average of 113 percent without any corresponding increase in mistakes. However, nearly all the workers complained of head and back pains and were generally physically and mentally exhausted. Furthermore, the production of the stress hormones, adrenaline and non-adrenaline, increased 27 and 40 percent, respectively. And these effects were manifested after only two days! The researcher in charge of this experiment highlighted the short-versus long-run trade-off with this concluding statement:

> One can reasonably suppose that, if this condition of stress had been allowed to continue, it would have broken *out* in the form of nervous complaints, increase muscular pains, low morale, a higher incidence of sick leave, and an increased turnover of personnel. The resultant losses would no doubt have been reserved for a separate ledger, far away from the immaculate statistics of hourly production. But the ultimate cost, in terms of company profits, national expenditure and human values would not (Levi, 1972, p. 83).

Legal Compliance and Worker Compensation. Worker compensation laws now make an employer legally liable for an employee's mental illness as well as physical illness, whatever its cause, if it is aggravated, accelerated, precipitated, or triggered to the point of disability or need for medical care by any condition of employment (McLean, 1979). Furthermore, fault or absence of fault on the part of the employee or employer has no bearing on the determination of liability of the employer for payment of worker compensation benefits (Lesser, 1967). Thus, it is necessary only for an employee to show that an illness was precipitated by an organization to claim compensation, regardless of other nonorganizational events to which the individual may have been exposed. This suggests, then, that organizations should become concerned with the effects of stress regardless of whether the individual comes to work already stressed or not.

Organizations also need to be concerned with stress because they are legally responsible for the presence of stressful conditions, according to the Occupational Safety and Health Act (OSHA) of 1970. According to the act, the employer is liable for both physical conditions causing employee physical harm (e.g., chemical poisons and physical obstructions) and sociopsychological conditions causing employee mental or psychological harm (OSHA regulations, 1970). Although the impact of OSHA may have been somewhat diminished by the ruling forbidding unannounced entry to organizations, it is still a potent force and one whose influence is likely to remain. The research arm of the agency that administers OSHA, the National Institute of Occupational Safety and Health (NIOSH), continues to fund extensive research programs regarding stress in organizations.

NIOSH's primary goals are to identify conditions associated with stress, or at least the symptoms of stress, and to develop strategies for dealing with stress. But crucial to the attainment of these goals is an understanding of what stress is. On the basis of such an understanding, a conceptualization of stress in organizations can be developed.

DEFINITION AND CONCEPTUALIZATION

The definition and conceptualization of stress in organizations address themselves to several important questions:

1. What is stress?
2. How is stress in organizations conceptualized?
3. What are the consequences of stress?
4. What are the events or conditions in organizations associated with individual qualities that result in these stress events or conditions being "one person's meat and another person's poison?"

What is Stress in Organizations?

Stress has been defined in numerous ways. A review of four of these definitions will provide the basis for the definition of stress to be used here. Selye (1956) defined stress as the nonspecific response to any demand. Stress, according to French, Rogers, and Cobb (1974), is a misfit between a person's skills and abilities and demands of the job, and a misfit in terms of a person's needs supplied by the environment. Beehr and Newman (1978) defined (job) stress as a condition wherein job-related factors interact with the worker to change (disrupt or enhance) his or her psychological or physiological condition, such that the person (mind and/or body) is forced to deviate from normal functioning. And lastly, McGrath (1976) defined stress in terms of a set of conditions having stress in it: "Stress involves an interaction of person and environment. Something happens 'out there' which presents a person with a demand, or a constraint or an opportunity for behavior."

Based on these definitions and others not presented here, the following definition of stress in organizations is used here (Schuler, 1980):
It is a dynamic condition in which an individual is faced with

An *opportunity* to do/be/have what he or she really desires, and/or
A *constraint* on doing/being/having what he or she really desires, and/or
A *demand* on being able to do/be/have what he or she really desires, for which the resolution is uncertain, and, upon resolution, may result in a less than favorable outcome.

This definition incorporates several important aspects of stress:

1. Stress can be positive (an opportunity) or negative (a constraint or demand). For example, a promotion can be perceived as a positive stress if the employee thinks

that the promotion will lead to valued outcomes, but is unsure about whether he or she can succeed or not. An example of negative stress is where an individual perceives he or she is on a really meaningless job and wants to get out of it (because it cannot satisfy any important desires), but is not sure how.

2. Stress results from the interaction of the person and the environment. The environment presents dynamic conditions (potential stressors) that can be perceived as opportunities, constraints, or demands, and that have perceived levels of uncertainty of resolution, as well as important outcomes. But what is important to one person may not be important to another, because each person has different needs and values. The needs and values on which individuals can differ (at least in degree) are certainty/predictability, achievement, recognition/acceptance, meaningfulness, responsibility, knowledge of results, fairness, variety/stimulation, safety/security, self-esteem, and physiological needs, such as food, water, physical safety, warmth, and physical stimulation (see Locke, 1976; Cox, 1978; Schuler, 1980 for a more extensive review and discussion).

3. Stress can be associated with physical conditions as well as sociopsychological conditions. The stress associated with the physical conditions, however, is less perceptual than that associated with the sociopsychological conditions. Thus, the dynamic state of demand is used to refer to physical conditions associated with stress, such as heat, light, and noise, and the dynamic state of opportunity and constraint refers to sociopsychological conditions. In essence, therefore, there are three types of stress: opportunity, constraint, and demand.

4. Stress is an additive concept across situations and over time. The more events in the organization perceived as stressful, the more stress that is experienced (Theorell, 1978). Holmes and Rahe (1967) found that individuals with more severe illnesses had experienced more stressful events in the months preceding their illnesses than individuals with fewer severe illnesses. Their study, in addition to indicating the importance of the accumulation of stressful events over time, supported the notion that both positive (e.g., getting a new job), as well as negative events (e.g., losing one's job), can be associated with stress.

5. Stress and the desire for resolution are precipitated by events that cause a disruption of homeostasis, either physiological or psychological. To demand conditions in the environment that disrupt physiological homeostasis, the body involuntarily seeks to restore homeostasis. A classical explanation of stress, for example, is that under conditions of physical threat the body produces increased blood sugar, adrenaline, and nonadrenaline to help the individual in removing the physical threat (by providing the energy for either a "flight or fight response"; Cannon, 1929). The physical activity of the flight or fight response then utilizes the stress-produced physiological responses and the body is restored to homeostasis. Unfortunately, with the opportunity or constraint stress associated with sociophysiological stress conditions, the body also responds involuntarily, as with the physical stress conditions, with similar physiological reactions. In this case, however, it is less likely that the increased blood sugar, adrenaline, and nonadrenaline will be utilized through any physical exertion to restore the sociopsychological disequilibrium caused by the situation of opportunity or constraint. If other strategies for dealing with the stress are not utilized, long-run wear and tear on the body will occur as the body fights to restore physiological homeostasis, resulting in diseases of adaptation

(Selye, 1956). Thus, while the resolution of the dynamic state of opportunity may result in a situation that is very positive (e.g., the promotion and attendent increases in income), it may result in a situation that is very negative. (Especially over the long run with continued exposure to stress, extreme physiological diseases of adaptation, such as severe illness or even death, may occur.)

Conceptualization of Stress in Organizations

A conceptualization of stress in organizations is important, not only because it provides an understanding of what stresssors exist in an organization and how they work, but also because it shows what the outcomes of stress are, what and where qualities of individuals influence its existence in organizations, and what possible strategies can be developed and used by individuals and/or organizations to deal with it.

Each of these aspects of a conceptualization of stress in organizations, as shown in Figure 14–1, is discussed. Although research evidence will be presented and evaluated in the next section, it is important to note that many of the relationships shown in Figure 14–1 should be regarded as tentative until further research is concluded.

Organizational Stressors.   There are seven major categories of potential stressors in organizations. Within each of these categories are several specific conditions or aspects of organizations that have been or can be related to stress as defined in this chapter (see Cooper and Marshall, 1976; Brief, Schuler, and Van Sell, 1980, for a more complete description of these stressors). As such, they are referred to as stressors. Although all of these stressors are crucial in understanding stress in organizations, space limitations permit a discussion of only a few. Additional reference is made to them in reviewing the existing stress research. The reader, however, is urged to examine Table 14–2 and trace through how each stressor could be perceived by an individual as stressful.

As shown in Table 14–2, the stressors include physical conditions. The primary stressors, however, are the sociophychological conditions. As noted earlier, the impact of the physical conditions such as heat, light, and noise, although significant for an individual's stress (Cox, 1978; Shostak, 1980), is probably less subject to an individual's subjective perception and interpretation than are the sociopsychological conditions. Thus, in the case of the sociopsychological conditions, the individual perceives the condition, then interprets and evaluates (Lazarus, 1966) it vis-à-vis his or her desires (which are a reflection of his or her needs and values). To the extent it is perceived as creating a lack of fit and disrupting a sociopsychological homeostasis, the condition becomes a stressor (McGrath, 1976). Between the stressors and the individual perceptions relationship and between the individual perceptions and the stress relationship, as shown in Figure 14–1, are the potential effects of several individual characteristics.

Individual Characteristics I.   The individaul characteristics shown in Figure 14–1 are needs and values, Type A/B behaviors, experience, ability, life stages, and locus of control. Although an individual's needs and values may influence what one perceives, the major influences of needs and values is on the individual's evaluation of the organi-

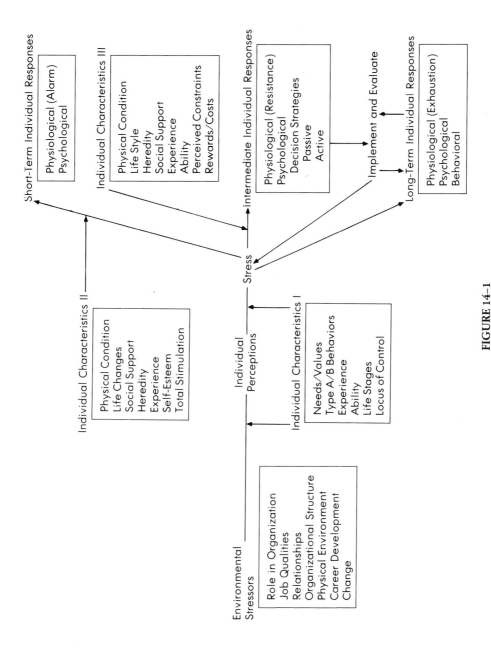

FIGURE 14-1
Conceptualization of Stress in Organizations

397

TABLE 14–2
Organizational Stressors

Roles in the Organization	*Job Qualities*
Role ambiguity	Quantitative overload/underload
Role conflict	Qualitative overload/underload
Too little management support	Time pressures
Holding a middle management position	Responsibility for things/people
	Work pace
Relationships	*Organizational Structure*
With supervisors	Lack of participation
With subordinates	No sense of belonging
With colleagues	Poor communications
Inability to delegate	Restrictions on behavior
Inability to delegate	Lack of opportunity
	Inequity in pay and performance evaluation
	Hours of work
Physical Environment	*Career Development*
Temperature, noise, lights	Status incongruity
Spatial arrangements	Underpromotion
Crowding	Overpromotion
Privacy	Mid-career
	Obsolescence

Change

Organizational
Individual

Source: Adapted from C. L. Cooper and J. Marshall. "Occupational Sources of Stress: A Review of the Literature Relating to Coronary Heart Disease and Mental Ill Health." *Journal of Occupational Psychology* 49 (1976): 11–28.

zation's conditions as causing a lack of fit between what the environment supplies and the individual's needs and values.

Also influencing how an individual perceives the environment are the qualities of an individual's behavior or personality as being either Type A or Type B (Friedman and Rosenman, 1959, 1974). According to Cox (1978), the qualities of a Type A person are:

1. An intense sustained drive to achieve self-selected, but usually poorly defined, goals
2. A profound inclination and eagerness to compete
3. A persistent desire for recognition and advancement
4. A continuous involvement in multiple and diverse functions constantly subject to time restrictions
5. An habitual propensity to accelerate the rate of execution of many physical and mental functions
6. An extraordinary mental and physical alertness

The qualities of a Type B person are held to be the opposite of a Type A person. As a result of Type A qualities, the individual may be more likely to perceive more stressors in the same environment than a Type B, as well as experience more situations with potential stressors.

Individual characteristics also enter the conceptualization of stress between the stress and the individual's short-term responses to that stress. These will be examined after discussing the short-term individual responses to stress.

Individual Responses: Short Term. The short-term individual responses are of two types: Those physiological effects that occur immediately after the individual's perception of stress and those psychological responses that also occur immediately after stress is perceived. The physiological effects that occur at this point (corresponding to Selye's alarm stage) are increased blood and urine catecholamines (adrenaline and nonadrenaline) and corticosteroids, increased blood glucose levels, and increased heart rate and blood pressure (Selye, 1956). Whereas the short-term physiological effects occur regardless of the type of stress (i.e., opportunity, constraint, or demand), the short-term psychological effects depend on the type of stress. Associated with the stress from situations of opportunity are psychological symptoms such as excitement, joy, and high self-esteem, and irritability from the stress associated with constraint and, to a lesser extent, demand stiuations. Regardless of the type of stress, however, there is the tendency to become forgetful, disorganized, and impatient, and to block out information.

Individual Characterisitics II. The degree of severity of the short-term physiological responses is moderated by all seven characteristics shown in the Individual Characteristics II box in Figure 14–1. Individuals respond physiologically with less severity (that is, less increased blood and urine catecholamines) to a stress situation when they are in good physical condition, have fewer life changes, have socially supportive relationships, are hereditarily strong, have had many experiences with stress (and therefore developed what amounts to immunity), have high self-esteem, and have a moderate level of total stimulation than individuals with the opposite characteristics. Individuals who have socially supportive relationships are more physiologically capable of dealing with stress because of the acceptance shown by others and the awareness of those who can and will help if and when needed (Klein, 1971; House, 1980).

Individual Responses: Intermediate Term. If the short-term physiological responses to stress are not utilized, for example, in a flight of fight response, the body will seek to restore equilibrium. The body in Selye's term enters a stage of resistance or adaptation, seeking to diminish or resist the initial physiological responses of the alarm stage. But, as a consequence of this process, the body suffers from "diseases of adaptation." During this stage, the body's immune system becomes less effective. These diseases include asthma, chest and back pains, faintness and dizziness, migraines, neuroses, insomnia, nightmares, psychoses, and skin rash (Selye, 1956; Cox, 1978).

At this intermediate stage (which also can be conceived of as a coping stage), the individual's primary psychological response is deciding what to do. Although laden with the short-term psychological responses, which may include tendencies to be disorganized and forgetful, as well as to block out potentially useful information from the environment, the individual will decide to be either passive or active vis-à-vis the stressor and stress situation (Gal and Lazarus, 1975, present a fuller description of these strategies).

The passive response includes an individual's decision to ignore the stressor and the situation, to deny or create illusions about the stressor and the situation (Lazarus, 1979), to change the level of importance of the outcomes related to the stress situation, or finally to resign oneself to the situation. In the choice of the active response, on the other hand, the individual makes the decision to take an action such to remove the stressor, to increase one's ability, or to leave the situation.

Individual Characteristics III.   The severity and the type of the intermediate physiological responses of stress are influenced by the individual's physical condition, life style, heredity, social support network, and experiences. These characteristics, as shown in Figure 14–1, also influence an individual's long-term physiological responses. Life style qualities, which aid in reducing an individual's likelihood of incurring severe disease at this stage, include: (1) a diet of low fat and low cholesterol, (2) no smoking, (3) moderate drinking, and (4) regular exercise two or three times a week. Again, an individual's heredity, social support networks, and experiences have the same moderating effects here as they do with short-term responses.

An individual's experiences, abilities, and perceptions of environmental constraints play a role in the selection of a strategy and its effectiveness in dealing with the stressor and the stress situation. A passive strategy may be selected by an individual with minimal experience with the stressor, low ability to deal with the stressor and/or when he or she perceives that the condition cannot be changed. An individual possessing the opposite characteristics may be more likely to select an active strategy.

Individual Responses: Long Term.   To this set of responses is added the behavioral category. Although there are behaviors associated with the implementation of the active strategies, those behaviors are more a function of the individual's intermediate-term psychological reaction than they are of stress. As shown in Figure 14–1, however, the implementation of a strategy influences the long-term behavioral responses, as well as the psychological and physiological responses of the individual. But this influence occurs regardless of whether the strategy used is passive or active (and involving more behavior activity). Consequently, the long-term behavior responses presented here are associated with stress in organizations.

Individual behavioral responses have immediate implications for organizational effectiveness. The direction of the responses, however, depends on the type of stress. Negatively associated with opportunity stress are employee turnover and absenteeism, and positively associated with it is the quantity of performance, especially on tasks the employee knows how to perform. The relationship between opportunity stress and quality of performance is curvilinear, with quality being higher at moderate levels of stress (see McGrath, 1976; Schuler, 1980, for a more extensive discussion). Stress associated with constraint and demand situations, on the other hand, appears to be negatively related to both aspects of performance, and positively related to employee turnover and absenteeism.

The long-term psychological responses of an individual are also dependent on the type of stress. With increased opportunity stress are associated higher levels of employee satisfaction, involvement, sense of responsibility, self-esteem, and sense of challenge and accomplishment. But with increased constraint or demand stress are associated lower levels of these same psychological responses, as well as feelings of tension and anxiety. To the extent, however, that the individual can implement an effective strategy to cope with constraint or demand stress, these essentially negative psychological responses can be minimized. The same is true for physiological responses.

Although the individual's psychological and behavioral responses are influenced by the type of stress, physiological responses are the same regardless of the type of stress. This stage of long-term physiological responses could be depicted as Selye's (1956) exhaustion stage. In this stage (particularly after long and continuous exposure to stress or intermittent periods of intensive stress), common physiological responses include hypertension, coronary heart disease, bronchial asthma, diabetes, Mellitus, ulcers, and even cancer (Cox, 1978; Beehr and Newman, 1978).

Some of the current research on stress will now be reviewed in relation to our conceptualization. A review of the strategies currently being used by organizations and individuals will also provide a basis for suggesting future approaches for dealing with stress.

RESEARCH ON STRESS IN ORGANIZATIONS

Review of the Research

Because several excellent reviews and compilations of the research on stress in organizations currently exist (Cooper and Marshall, 1976; Cox, 1978; Beehr and Newman, 1978; McLean, 1979; Schuler, 1980; Brief, Schuler, and Van Sell, 1980), this section will review a limited body of research only to highlight what has been done, particularly in relationship to the definition and conceptualization of stress in organizations. Research focusing on organizational conditions associated with stress will be reviewed first, followed by a review of the research on individual characteristics. Stress research uniquely related to occupational groups will also be highlighted, since it identifies important research strategies.

Organizational Stressors. The organizational conditions most frequently identified and researched as stressors are job qualities, roles in the organization, and relationships at work. The job qualities commonly associated with stress are *work pace or control* and *work underload and overload* (both qualitative and quantitative), although only limited research exists regarding underload. French and Caplan (1973) indicated that at least nine different psychological and physiological responses have been found to be associated with qualitative and quantitative overload: job dissatisfaction, job tension, lower self-esteem, threat, embarrassment, high cholesterol levels, increased heart rate, and increased smoking. Qualitative overload is a condition where the individual has job duties to perform that appear to exceed his or her abilities. This, of course, is compatible with the definition of stress, as is qualitative underload, which is a condition that may not supply enough needs to the individual. Quantitative overload is a condition of having too many job demands. With either overload condition, it is likely that the individual becomes uncertain about whether or not he or she can meet all job demands. In either case of underload, the individual may desire to have more needs satisfied, but is uncertain about how to change the current situation. There appear to be several needs not satisfied by either underload or overload conditions, particularly challenge, meaningfulness, and self-control.

Work pace, particularly who or what controls the pace of the work, is another important potential stressor in organizations. Machine pacing is a work condition in which the speed or pace of the operation and the work output are controlled to some extent by a source other than the operator. Employee pacing is a work condition in which the individual has control of the operations. The effects of machine pacing are severe. Frankenhaeuser and Gardell (1976) reported that workers on machine-paced jobs felt exhaustion at the end of the shift and were unable to relax soon after work because of the increased adrenaline secretion during work. Caplan, et al. (1975) reported that assembly line workers reported the highest level of severity of stress responses out of the twenty-three white- and blue-collar occupations studied.

The two qualities of roles in an organization that have been widely researched are *role conflict* and *role ambiguity* (Brief, Schuler, and Van Sell, 1980). Role conflict is a potential stressor because it may prohibit an individual from doing well in all roles, or at least cause uncertainty about whether that is possible. Similarly, role ambiguity may also prohibit an individual from experiencing a sense of accomplishment, because the individual is *unclear* about what to accomplish.

Relationships with supervisors are often stressors for individuals in organizations. "Two major subjective stresses that blue-collarites associate with supervision involve the enervating pettiness of various work rules and the enervating nature of relentless pressure for more and more production" (Shostak, 1980). In either case, however, the individual is denied the fulfillment of a need to control, as well as the needs for recognition and acceptance as an individual. As a result, individuals try to bend or violate rules—in essence regain some control of their work situation.

Relationships with co-workers have also been found to be a stressor, at least when poor relations exist such as "those which include low trust, low supportiveness, low interest in listening to and trying to deal with problems that confront the organizational member" (French and Caplan, 1973). Mistrust of co-workers has been found to be positively related to role ambiguity and inadequate communications, resulting in low job satisfaction and feelings of job-related threat to one's well being (Kahn et al., 1964; French and Caplan, 1972; Buck, 1972). In addition, Kahn et al. (1964) indicated that poor relations with one's subordinates are highly related to feelings of threat with colleagues and superiors.

Individual Characteristics.   Stressors and stress in organizations evoke different reactions from different people. "Some people are better able to cope with these stressors than others, they adapt their behavior in a way that meets the environmental challenge. On the other hand, some people are more characterologically predisposed to stress, that is, they are unable to cope or adapt to the stress-provoking situation" (Cooper and Marshall, 1976, pp. 22–23).

Two major characteristics that have been extensively investigated in the past twenty years are life changes and Type A/B behavior and personality (Holmes and Rahe, 1967; Rahe, 1974; Friedman and Rosenman, 1974). Generally, the findings have indicated that the more life changes an individual experiences, the greater the likelihood of his or her having severe stress responses. These results are consistent with the definition and conceptualization of stress, since change conditions for many often give rise to uncertainty and a desire to bring resolution to those conditions. Thus, when using life changes as a moderator, the group with many life changes (therefore already at high stress levels) has stronger relationships between other stressor conditions and stress responses than the group with few life changes.

Type A personality characteristics of individuals have been shown to increase the likelihood of coronary heart disease (Friedman and Rosenman, 1974). Consistent again with the conceptualization of stress is the finding by Caplan and Jones (1975) that Type A behavior moderated the relationship between workload and anxiety. That is, Type A's reported a stronger relationship between their perception of workload and anxiety than Type B's; although this could be accounted for by the fact that the Type A may have perceived the level of workload as higher than Type B. It could as well be explained by the fact that the Type A interpreted the condition as more stressful. Since Type A's desire to get many things done and generally be in control, a high workload may be perceived as reducing one's probability (or increasing one's uncertainty) of getting those things done.

Individual Characteristics III have been described in part as being related to the development of *individual strategies* to deal with stress. The two categories of strategies were identified as active and passive. Active strategies have been shown to be effective in reducing the relationship between organizational stressors and individual responses.

Passive strategies (similar to Kahn et al.'s Class II, 1964) can also be effective in moderating the influence of stress. Two strategies shown to be effective are relaxation techniques (Beary and Benson, 1977; Benson, Beary, and Carol, 1974), and social support groups (House and Wells, 1978). Relaxation techniques have been shown to reduce chronic sympathetic nervous system overactivity, including blood pressure, heart rate, and adrenaline and nonadrenaline levels. In addition, it has been shown "that relaxation through the regular practice of meditation is associated with a significant reduction in fasting serum cholesterol levels" (Cooper and Aygen, 1979).

House and Wells (1978) concluded that under maximum levels of social support, symptoms of ill health increase only slightly, if at all, as stressors increase. Yet when social support is low, with increasing stress, symptoms of ill health are high (McLean, 1979). Social support groups appear to aid individuals in dealing with stress by conditioning or buffering the individuals to the effects of stress. Social support groups can also aid individuals in a much more active way as well, for example, by helping to reduce role conflict or role ambiguity.

Although much of the stress research has been done with a primary focus on the relationships between specific stressors (e.g., role conflict or role ambiguity and individual responses, such as job satisfaction), some of the research has also been done using occupational groups as the primary focus. Because occupational groups differ greatly in reported stress, they often serve as the basis for epidemiological studies of stress. Identifying groups of individuals by specific work sites or organizations, as well as occupations

with high levels of stress, can serve as an efficient means of studying stress, and of bene-
fiting more individuals if strategies for effectively dealing with stress are developed
(Colligan and Smith, 1978; Smith, Colligan, and Harrell, 1978; and Murphy and Colligan, 1979).

Occupations and Stress

> HELP WANTED: World's busiest airport seeks radar jockies for unusually stimulating,
> high-intensity environment. Must be able to direct at least 12 aircraft at one time and
> make instant decisions affecting the safety of thousands. No degree required, but prior
> experience as traffic cop, seeing-eye dog, or God helpful. Severe stress will jeopardize
> sanity and result in early termination from job, but employer will absorb cost of medical
> and psychiatric care (*Psychology Today,* February, 1977, p. 71).

Although this ad never appeared, it does illustrate one of the most stressful occupations—an air traffic controller. The stressors of this occupation are a grueling pace (not
controlled by the controller), split-second decisions (time pressure), and the constant
threat of mid-air collisions. In addition, there are numerous conflicts between their employers and the Federal Aviation Administration (FAA). The results are predictable:
ulcers, high blood pressure, arthritis, colitis, headaches, allergies, upset stomachs, alcoholism, depression, and acute anxiety (Martindale, 1977).

"Stress in the work lives of America's 35 million workers (blue-collar) appears to
have three major sources: anxiety over joblessness, anxiety over workplace accidents or
work-linked illnesses, and anxiety over workrole insults to one's adulthood" (Shostak,
1980). And there is also the stress from wanting to do a job one way, but being told to
do it another way. "For years and years, it was most important to the company that we
give excellent service. But it's more important now to get it finished than to get it right,
and the guy who considers himself a real craftsman can no longer be a craftsman" (*Business Week,* June 25, 1979, p. 96).

Stress for white-collar workers (especially managers) has been associated with decision making and its consequences, responsibility for people, heavy demands for cooperation with superiors and subordinates, time pressures, fear of failure, fear of poor
performance, mid-career crises over lack of promotion (as in John R.'s case), and managing a workforce with rapidly changing values (McLean, 1979; Warshaw, 1980;
Cooper, 1979).

Although the research done on occupational groups indicates that different stressors
are more important in the stress of one group than another, perhaps one of the most important conclusions is that blue-collar workers do not necessarily suffer from fewer stress
responses than white-collar workers. If anything, some white-collar workers probably
suffer from less stress, or at least enjoy it more than some blue-collar workers.

This overview of the research on stress in organizations indicates that several aspects
of the present definition and conceptualization of stress are consistent with the work
done thus far. Many aspects of the definition and conceptualization, however, remain
unexamined. In addition, based on the research methodology used in most of the studies, their results and support should be interpreted conservatively. Since these comments have implications for future research, each will be examined here in more detail.

Evaluation of the Research on Stress in Organizations

The methodological evaluation of the existing research is based in large part on evaluations already done (c.f., McGrath, 1976; Cooper and Marshall, 1976; Beehr and Newman, 1978; Jenkins, 1979), although this chapter will also evaluate that research in light of the definition and conceptualization of stress presented earlier. Then there will be a brief evaluation of the practicality of the research and predictions on future research.

> A major weakness of most stress research has been its limitation to a two-variable research design, i.e., a noxious stimulus is introduced and then a response of discomfort or disease is observed. In the most common study design, participants are defined in terms of the presence of a physical or psychiatric illness and then antecedent stress inputs are sought through patient's recall of recent life history (Jenkins, 1979, p. 3).

Another common design for organizational stress research is to select an organization or an occupational group and administer questionnaires to gather the individuals' perceptions of both organizational conditions and individual responses. Occasionally, objective measures of each are also gathered (e.g., Sales, 1969; Frankenhaeuser and Gardell, 1976). Then a two-variable research design is used, generally determining the relationship (by correlational analysis) between the two variables (generally called the stressor and the stress response). Correlational analysis, however, precludes making inferences about causality and the two-variable design fails to point out the role of intervening variables. In addition, measurement of the two variables is generally made at the same time, further adding to the inability to determine cause-effect relationships. But even when the variables have been measured at two different time points (as illustrated in Jenkin's quote), one has been measured retrospectively. As stated by Jenkins (1979):

> Such studies have illuminated the relation of stressors of physical and mental disorders, but I submit that these simplistic retrospective studies have also generated inconsistences across different study groups and are unlikely to guide health scientists to more advanced levels of understanding (p. 3).

When more than two-variable designs have been used, they have often included a third variable as a moderator. Most frequently, this moderator has been an individual characteristic such as Type A behavior, age, physical condition, or social support. Results from these three-variable moderator studies generally support the presence of a moderating effect; however, the number of variables used as moderators has been limited. Although many other issues remain regarding the methodology used in stress research, such as method-variance, response patterns, and objective versus subjective measures (see McGrath, 1976), the question remains "What is being measured?"

The majority of these studies measure the stressor by the individual's perception of a job condition, for example, a task design characteristic or role conflict and role ambiguity. In the same studies, the stress response is generally the individual's subjective feelings (e.g., job satisfaction, tension, or job involvement). As noted, however, some studies have included objective measures of stress responses, such as blood pressure and catecholamine levels. Nevertheless, it is implied that what has been measured is "stress," or a variable "causing stress," and the fact that there is an association between this stress surrogate and the stress response supports this implication. Thus, either stress is not actually measured, or the term stress is defined, not as a state or condition, but rather as a process which includes the stressor and the stress response.

Earlier, a tentative definition and conceptualization of stress in organizations was presented so that several of these conceptual issues could be addressed. Still remaining, however, is how to best address some of the methodological issues that have been raised. Since these are particularly important in understanding stress in organizations, they will be dealt with in the remainder of the chapter, after briefly discussing current organizational strategies for dealing with stress in organizations.

ORGANIZATIONAL STRESS STRATEGIES

There are numerous ways in which stress can be dealt with in organizations. It should be noted, parenthetically, that the concern about stress in organizations and strategies to deal with it are not and should not be limited to the organizations themselves or the individuals within them. For example, in the United States, the Occupational Safety and Health Administration (OSHA), the National Institute of Occupational Safety and Health (NIOSH), and the Center for Occupational Mental Health (COMH) at Cornell University represent two federal organizations and one private organization also concerned with stress. Furthermore, concern for stress in organizations is not limited to this country. In fact, in many other nations the concern about stress is legislated to a much greater degree than in the United States. "In the Scandinavian countries, for instance, employers are required in some instances to provide meaningful work and appropriate job satisfaction with a minimum of occupational stress"(McLean, 1978). In addition, there are two world associations, the International Committee on Occupational Mental Health (ICOMH) and the Permanent Commission and International Association on Occupational Health, established to promote interdisciplinary communication and understanding of stress.

Specific programs that may be implemented on the basis of the information gathered are in large part related to each of the organizational stressors identified in Table 14-1. Thus, specific programs could be those designed to change aspects of the organization, the physical environment, job qualities, and offer career development opportunities to employees. While it is unlikely that an organization would use all of these programs, many are using at least a few of them.

At TRW, several steps to stress management and reduction were implemented, such as: (1) crisis-counseling training sessions with the industrial relations staff, (2) increasing the employees' general awareness of stress and what they can do about it, (3) adding stress discussions to the supervisory training program, (4) adding a module on stress to the middle-management programs, and (5) offering after-hours programs, such as workshops in the use of biofeedback, meditation exercises, and other relaxation techniques (Shirley, 1978). Also based on the nature of the situation (e.g., reorganization in this instance), Pennsylvania Bell adopted special seminars in which executives could discuss their life changes (that in turn cause personal and job problems), identify their own strengths and weaknesses in adapting to the changes, and then develop methods for adopting. "So far, it seems to be working," one manager commented. Before the seminar, it was a policy to not bring personal problems to the job; now "the words out, so to speak—it's O.K. to feel frustrated, its O.K. to feel stress" (*Business Week,* May 28, 1979, p. 106).

With this greater willingness on the part of some organizations and individuals to be more open about stress, and, based upon the understanding of stress presented here, the major question that remains is: What *will* and *should* researchers and organizations be doing about stress in organizations in the future?

FUTURE RESEARCH AND PRACTICE: PREDICTIONS AND RECOMMENDATIONS

There are two major types of statements that one can make about the future: predictions and recommendations. This section of the chapter bravely ventures some of each. Predictions are statements regarding the probable next activities of both researchers and practitioners in job stress, and they are to be based on two assumptions: (1) that current trends will continue into the future (an extrapolation principle), and (2) that there is a sequence of events common to many topics in personnel research and practice, with each specific topic differing in content but imitating the same sequence of processes of previous topics (an imitation principle). Recommendations are assertions regarding what is desirable for the future, and they need not be the same as predictions. They are based on needs and ideals. There are often activities that have been neglected and seem logically to be necessary to provide more complete knowledge or to lessen negative effects of stress in organizations.

Recommendations can also be idealistic, since they need not be bounded by the practical constraints of many researchers and practitioners. For example, some researchers, for the sake of their careers, may need to work on *quantities* of publications or grants; this constraint would encourage, if not dictate, that the researcher conduct many small studies, using familiar techniques that require little commitment from participating organizations. It may be the case, however, that fewer large studies utilizing novel methods and requiring more commitment from participating organizations would be more beneficial. Fortunately, some researchers (e.g., Caplan, et al., 1975) seem able to conduct this type of research; therefore, the ideal can be realized, at least for some investigators.

Similarly, many practitioners may also have constraints preventing them from performing some of the ideal activities in their profession. Some typical constraints are lack of money (from company budgets for the personnel department or from private income for independent consultants) or lack of expertise (very common in job stress, since so many different types of expertise are important). Again, fortunately, some people are able to overcome such constraints and to attempt at least some service in the stress area. An example is the Douglas McGregor Memorial award-winning effort of Taber, Walsh, and Cooke (1979), who were able to put together a multidisciplinary team composed mostly of volunteers in an attempt to alleviate adverse effects of the loss of jobs during a plant closing.

This section of the chapter presents predictions first and then recommendations, because the recommendations are at times aimed at filling in the gaps that would be apparent if the predictions were to come true. The recommendations are an attempt to *influence* the future.

Until now, it appears that most people interested in stress are either research- or practice-oriented, but not both. A recommendation offered later in this chapter is that research and practice in stress be merged and be made more complementary. Based on the extrapolation principle, however, it is predicted that this will not happen in the near future.

Predictions for Research

Simply extrapolating from the recent past, it is likely that the quantity of research on stress will increase rapidly in the near future. Occupational stress first appeared as a key word in *Psychological Abstracts* in 1973, indicating that there was not enough published research in the area prior to that year to warrant the use of a key word (Newman and Beehr, 1979). Quantity of published research in the area has been consistently increasing ever since, however. Indeed, there are some signs that job and organizational stress are taking their place alongside more established topics in both organizational behavior and personnel, as some of the newer books are including sections devoted to stress (e.g., Organ, 1978; Rowland, et al., 1980). Beyond the overall quantity of research, however, some specific predictions can be made regarding the types of research likely to be conducted in the future.

Replication.   A great deal of the research will replicate prior studies, making only small innovations. Replication often comprises a part of most studies. For example, the *Handbook of Leadership* (Stogdill, 1974) indicated that the relationships of leader consideration and initiating structure with subordinate behaviors and attitudes have been investigated many times. What has happened in the traditional topics, such as leadership, is also likely to happen with newer topics such as job stress (imitation principle).

Because of the difficulty of conducting research in this area, it is necessary to replicate previous findings in order to be confident of the results. Only after several replications of the relationship between role ambiguity and employee absenteeism (e.g., Gupta and Beehr, 1979) in several different types of organizations, for example, can it be stated with certainty that this relationship constitutes a general principle.

Small-Scale Studies.   The second prediction is that there will continue to be many small-scale studies; that is, studies with (1) limited samples, (2) few of the elements of the stress domain included, or (3) very few types or only one type of data collection method. This has been true of other topic areas, and it is the easiest and often the most inexpensive way to do research. The alternative for many researchers might be to do very little research at all. This especially applies to many college and university faculty who have relatively large teaching loads and limited amounts of time to devote to research.

Combined Emphasis on Individual and Organizational Consequences. Much of the early research on stress focused on the relationship between stressors and consequences to the individual (e.g., Cobb and Rose, 1973; Kahn et al., 1964; Selye, 1956). This has been especially true of researchers with medical backgrounds. More recently, however, some researchers are investigating the consequences of stress for the organization (e.g., absenteeism, turnover, and job performance), as well as the consequences for the individual (e.g., Beehr, Walsh, and Taber, 1976; Schuler, 1975; French and Caplan, 1973). This probably results in part from the entry of organizational researchers into this topic area. These people are typically more interested than medical researchers in organizational outcomes.

Studies of Coronary Heart Disease. One individual consequence, coronary heart disease (CHD), will continue to receive a great deal of attention. Cooper and Marshall (1976) have noted that over the past ten to fifteen years, CHD and mental ill health (MIH) have been the focus of many of the studies of occupationally related diseases. CHD is a focus because of the relative severity of this consequence to the individual. Although recent review articles in organizational journals have given special attention to CHD (e.g., Matteson and Ivancevich, 1979; Cooper and Marshall, 1976), medical researchers are most likely to dominate this focus in the future, as they have in the past.

Mental Ill Health Studies. MIH will also continue to receive attention from future researchers. There are two reasons for this prediction besides simple extrapolation: (1) there is a group of researchers especially interested and skilled in MIH (those in clinical psychology), and (2) many of the instruments that are available to measure at least some of the mild psychological problems are easier to administer than the measures of physiological symptoms. This area is likely to continue to receive attention from psychologists of many specialties (clinical, organizational, social, etc.).

Epidemiological Studies. Research utilizing epidemiological approaches, i.e., searching for diseases that are common to certain occupations or certain organizations, are likely to continue also. These will be conducted especially by researchers with training in areas such as sociology and public health.

Innovative, Interdisciplinary Studies. A few researchers will make pioneering forays beyond merely extending present techniques to replicate past studies. Although it is difficult to know where innovation will come from, a likely event is that it will occur at some of the places where past pioneering efforts were conducted. One obvious example is the Institute for Social Research, which has rendered one of the most frequently cited early stress studies focusing on jobs (Kahn et al., 1964), interdisciplinary research teams (e.g., Caplan et al., 1975), and novel studies such as the investigation of the effects of a plant closing on worker health (Cobb, 1974). Another is the National Institute for Occupational Safety and Health, which supported the Caplan, et al. study. Some other researchers will undoubtedly help to shape the future of stress research, but it is likely to come especially from the larger, more experienced, and better funded research institutes.

Predictions for Practice

It also seems likely, based on extrapolation, that efforts aimed at treating or preventing stress in organizations will increase rapidly in the near future. Indeed, a recent review of the literature discloses that there are many strategies recommended for solving stress-related problems at work (Newman and Beehr, 1979). The predictions here are arranged according to the primary target of the treatment strategy, the individual or the organization. The individual is the target when the strategy's immediate aim is to treat the individual consequences of stress (e.g., CHD, or mental ill health), or to create in the individual an ability to alter his or her own environment in a way that will make it less stressful. The organization is the primary target when the strategy's immediate aim is to alter the organization in a way that is expected to make it a less stressful environment for employees.

Individually Oriented Strategies. The first prediction is that many of the individually oriented strategies in the near future will be descendents of programs that are already in existence and have been created for purposes other than treating job stress. Some techniques already exist that are believed to be effective for problems similar to job stress (e.g., for other types of stress or for CHD and mental ill health, whether caused by stress or not). Although job stress is a recently popularized concept, CHD, mental ill health, and the other consequences of job stress have been around for a long time and already have fairly standardized treatments among medical and psychological practitioners. Thus, diet, drug treatments, and psychotherapy of all sorts will continue to be recommended treatment programs. Newman and Beehr's (1979) review noted relaxation techniques, human relations training, meditation, and education as also among the recommended strategies. Thus, if the future continues to follow this trend, one would expect to see other strategies such as t-groups, transactional analysis, and assertiveness training used for treating job stress. The fact that these strategies were not developed for the problem currently at hand makes them neither more nor less effective; the principle is simply that practitioners, like researchers, will primarily continue to do what they know how to do and are used to doing. This principle applies to medical doctors, psychologists, and nearly all other professionals.

The second prediction is that there will be a strong movement aimed at treating executive stress in particular. This would be a continuation of some current work (e.g., Rice, 1979; Rummel and Rader, 1978) that is usually justified on the grounds that: (1) executives' jobs are more stressful than most other jobs (although this is questionable; Caplan, et al., 1975), and (2) executives' work effectiveness has an extremely strong influence on the effectiveness of an organization and therefore on the lives of all others who work for the organization. It is believed, therefore, that the organization will get the most benefit per dollar if it is spent on executives. This prediction is most likely to be true where money is an especially important consideration, viz., in programs that are paid for by profit-making organizations.

It is also predicted that the use of outside consultants will expand in the near future. Professionals traditionally seen as health service providers (medical and psychological) are already entering the field of job stress, offering advice, giving workshops, and so forth. As noted earlier, the first inclination will be for such people to follow a "familiarity principle," i.e., to use techniques they have been using in the past for other types of problems. The move toward the use of outside consultants will occur partly because most organizations do not believe they already employ people who have the expertise to deal with job stress.

Organizationally-Oriented Strategies. Although the implementation of organizationally oriented strategies will increase, they will probably not increase at as fast a pace as the use of individually oriented strategies. There are three reasons for this. First, it is recognized that the stress-producing characteristics of organizations often exist in their present forms explicitly for the purpose of enhancing organizational effectiveness. As recognized in most versions of systems theory (e.g., Katz and Kahn, 1978), altering parts of the organization for one purpose (e.g., alleviating negative effects of stress) may have consequences for criteria other than the intended one. Realizing this, managers will be wisely inclined to move slowly in implementing any organizationally oriented strategies for dealing with stress. Second, organizational strategies will begin more slowly than the individual strategies because it is more difficult to see the organizational cause than the individual consequence in observing stress. Physiological, behavioral, and even some psychological problems of individual employees are easier to recognize than are their potential organizational causes. Therefore, it is easier to conceive of ways to attack these consequences than to work on the causes. The third reason why organizational programs will occur slowly is that there often tends to be some inertia that prevents organizational change. This "resistance to change" probably has many causes, but it is partly caused by the belief of some organizational members that their own personal interests will be threatened by the change. The present organization and its workings usually have some benefits, perceived or real, for the organization, or at least some parts of it. Because of this likelihood, there will be resistance to organizationally oriented stress programs in many organizations.

One prediction regarding organizationally oriented strategies is that, similar to the prediction for individually oriented strategies, many of these will be programs that were originally designed for some purpose other than treating stress in organizations. Thus, one should not be surprised to see management by objectives, participative management, and so forth, proposed as techniques for alleviating stress, even though these have long been favored for other purposes, such as increasing productivity and satisfaction. The principle is that people will attempt to solve any problem, old or new, with familiar methods.

Another prediction regarding organizational strategies is that some of the most inexpensive types of programs will be among the first tried, because it is expected that organizations will fund such strategies. For these strategies, the organization itself (i.e., its representatives) is directing, or at least agreeing to, the change(s). Thus, it is expected that most such changes will occur with organizational sanctioning (and funding). As noted previously, free enterprise organizations usually attempt to obtain a favorable cost-benefit ratio from their activities. Since it is difficult to be sure of reaping great benefits from programs in a relatively new and unknown area, many companies may attempt to obtain a favorable ratio by keeping costs low.

Finally, it is predicted that claims for the effectiveness of some organizationally ori-ented strategies will quickly go beyond what is known about them; consequently, some techniques will be in danger of becoming passing fads before their effectiveness can be adequately evaluated. It has been suggested elsewhere that this process may be happen-ing with programs designed to treat other organizational problems (e.g., job enrich-ment; Hackman, 1977). When this occurs, the unwarranted claims will usually be in regard to programs provided by outside consultants in a position to gain economically from the programs' popularity.

Some of the following recommendations, if heeded, would alter or add to these predictions. As with the predictions, the recommendations are offered separately for research and for practice.

Recommendations for Research

It is probably impossible for anyone to incorporate into one study all of the elements shown in Figure 14–1. Therefore, recommendations in this section will be made regard-ing several subtopic areas that are especially in need of study and that are reasonable-sized chunks of the domain to investigate. Specific methodologies will also be recom-mended.

Topic Areas Recommended for Research.   First, a few comments are appropriate regarding whether the events predicted would also be recommended. The prediction has been made that there will be many small-scale studies and that, in part, they will be rep-lications of previous work. This may have some positive value, since a new topic area needs replication. Therefore, this trend is not only predicted; it is also recommended. An increased emphasis on combining individual and organizational consequences within the same study design has also been predicted and it is highly recommended. In addition, the prediction has been made that there will be a continued emphasis on epi-demiological studies; that is, attempts to determine whether stress is more prevalent in some jobs, organizations, or organizational locations than in others. This is especially recommended in the beginning phases of studying a topic such as stress, because it helps to: (1) pinpoint areas in need of further study, (2) pinpoint areas in which practitioners are most likely to be needed, and (3) increase the confidence that the phenomena collec-tively labeled stress are real. Over time, both the replications and the epidemiological studies will become less useful, however.

It has also been predicted that there will be a continued emphasis on CHD and MIH as individual consequences of stress. While these are indeed important, it is recom-mended that other potential individual consequences be studied (e.g., gastrointestinal disorders, respiratory system effects, headaches, etc.). The same comment is applicable to many potential organizational consequences of stress (e.g., absenteeism, turnover, performance, and various measures of organizational effectiveness); relatively few inves-tigations (e.g., Gupta and Beehr, 1979; Lyons, 1971; Sales, 1970) have included these consequences, although that may be changing with the entry of organizational research-ers into the stress domain.

Second, and related to the idea of broadening the types of consequences under investigation in stress research, special efforts should be made to include measures of potentially beneficial effects of stress. Broadening the list of dependent variables or potential individual consequences will allow for the possibility that some beneficial effects of stress will be found. The recommended research could have implications for managers and consultants who are concerned about application. It would be more difficult to decide how to deal with the "problem," for example, if it were determined that some stressors result in both positive and negative consequences.

Third, it is recommended that more interdisciplinary research be undertaken on stress in organizations (Beehr and Newman, 1978; Cooper and Marshall, 1976; Schuler, 1980). Without interdisciplinary teams of researchers (including, for example, people from business, medicine, and psychology), it will be difficult to implement some of the other recommendations offered here, such as the recommendation to broaden the types of consequences studied. It has also been predicted that there will be a few innovative, interdisciplinary studies, mostly from the large, well-established research institutions. Ideally, there should be more innovative studies, however, since they hold the greatest promise and will have the greatest influence on the future thinking in the area.

A fourth recommended research topic is the effect of combinations of different stressors in or out of the workplace. It is easy to assume that employees with two stressors experience greater consequences than employees with only one stressor. It may be, however, that the effects of stressors are not additive, and that someone with many types of stressors is not in a much worse position than somebody with only one stressor. This possibility is very seldom addressed.

At an extreme, some combinations of stressors may be additive and others may not; each individual stressor would need to be investigated in combinations with each of the other stressors in order to come to an overall conclusion regarding stressor additivity. This would be an enormous task. Since such research would be informative, however, it is recommended that the task be begun. It is further recommended that the task proceed initially by investigating the additivity of relatively diverse types of stressors: psycho-social stressors in the organization, physical stressors in the organization, and nonorganizational stressors. The psycho-social stressors are primarily the role, task, and interrelationship characteristics of an employee's job; the physical stressors are characteristics of the physical work environment, such as heat and noise; and the nonorganizational stressors refer to any stressful event that occurs in the employee's life that is not directly attributable to his or her employment. House, et al. (1979) have begun work in this area by investigating combinations of psycho-social stressors with physical health hazards among blue-collar workers in the rubber industry. They have found that there are interactive effects of some psycho-social stressors and some physical stressors. The relationships between the psycho-social stressors and the individual consequences, for example, were strongest for workers who were exposed to noxious physical stressors. More research investigating the effects of combinations of stressors is recommended.

Research into the whole area of work and nonwork stressor relationships is recommended. The popular life-stress scales (e.g., Holmes and Holmes, 1970) contain both work and nonwork events. Stressors are thus thought to exist either at work, or in one's nonwork life, or in both places. In addition, the consequences of stress can become evident at work (e.g., absenteeism) or in other areas of one's life (e.g., divorce). Finally, adaptive responses to stress may occur in either work or nonwork parts of one's life (e.g., seeking social support at work or elsewhere). These possibilities are all in need of research. It is therefore recommended that research be conducted to determine the relationships between the work and nonwork locations of (1) stressors, (2) consequences, and (3) adaptive responses. There are many variations on this theme of work-nonwork stress relationships, and nearly all of them are relatively unexamined.

Fifth, it is recommended that potential sex differences in stressors, consequences, or adaptive responses be investigated. Some of the early studies (e.g., Kahn et al., 1964) were of male workers only; other studies (e.g., Beehr, 1976; Schuler, 1977) have employed samples including both sexes, but have not analyzed the data with employee gender as a variable. It is still relatively unknown, therefore, whether and how employee sex might be an important factor in the phenomena included in the domain of stress. In many studies of stress, there are enough males and females included to perform meaningful analyses; therefore, specific studies aimed primarily at this topic may not always be necessary. Researchers should be aware that this approach is desired so that they will perform the analyses, however. Sex could be investigated as a potential predictor of stressors, of consequences, or of adaptive responses, or it may be studied as a potential moderator of relationships among these variables.

Finally, a sixth stress topic recommended for research is the effectiveness of adaptive responses to stress at the workplace. There is very little rigorous research evaluating most of the recommended techniques (Newman and Beehr, 1979). Accurate knowledge about stress should lead to logical and effective techniques for its treatment, but the ultimate decisions to recommend specific types of treatments should be based on evaluation research. This research has yet to be done.

Methodologies Recommended for Research.   Chapter 2 provides an account of research methods that would be helpful in uncovering useful information about stress, as well as about the other topic areas covered in this book. Methods that would be especially useful for stress will be listed here without providing the details of those methods. For more information, therefore, the reader is referred to Chapter 2 of this book or to other standard methods sources (e.g., Cook and Campbell, 1976).

Most organizational researchers are becoming aware of the problems inherent in overreliance on surveys for measurement. Since much of the stress research is weak because of other problems (for example, inability to make strong inferences regarding causality because of heavy reliance upon nonexperimental methods), the measures need to be as accurate as possible. Thus, the first recommendation is that future research utilize multiple methods of measurement, including the use of some measures that are objective. In stress research, variables that are amenable to measurement by nonsurvey methods include some characteristics of the employee's work environment (e.g., physical conditions, location of the job in relation to organizational boundaries, frequency of work interruptions), some individual and organizational consequences (e.g., medical record, absenteeism, and turnover), and some potentially adaptive responses (e.g., frequency of physical exercise, use of vacation, medication). Total reliance upon the survey in the area of stress is seldom necessary.

The second recommendation regarding research design is the use of longitudinal studies. Studies that take measurements at more than one point in time are likely to produce the greatest increase in the understanding of the phenomena. We do not mean to discourage the use of cross-sectional designs; instead, the wish is to promote the use of longitudinal designs whenever feasible. Cook and Campbell (1976) have recommended several designs that can be used with longitudinal data in organizational research. The specific techniques that are particularly useful for the study of job and organizational stress will be reviewed briefly here. Interested readers should refer to Cook and Campbell (1976), Campbell and Stanley (1966), and Chapter 2 for more details on these and other designs. The primary interest in this chapter is to indicate how stress variables can fit into some of the designs.

The first longitudinal design is *cross-lagged panel correlation,* in which no independent variables are manipulated. Measures of relevant variables are taken at several points in time, however, and correlations are computed between all variables measured at all points in time. In order to infer causality, the researcher assumes, among other things, that there is a causal relationship among the variables measured and that causation is not instantaneous. It might be concluded, for example, that a stressor causes an individual consequence if the correlation between the stressor measured at an earlier time and the consequence measured at a later time is stronger than the correlation between any other combination of the two variables (especially the correlation between the consequence measured at the earlier time, and the stressor measured at the later time). This is especially useful in the study of job stress because it is a "passive" design (i.e., it does not require manipulation of variables). Although researchers have traditionally considered passivity to be characteristic of weak designs, it is actually helpful or often necessary in job stress research for ethical reasons. Manipulation of variables that the researcher has reason to believe may cause people to become ill or to quit their jobs, for example, is irresponsible research. Parts of the model proposed earlier in this chapter could be tested by measuring (ideally with multiple measurement techniques) key variables at several points in time and utilizing cross-lagged panel correlations.

The rest of the recommended methodologies include the manipulation of one category of variable—what has been called an *adaptive response* (Newman and Beehr, 1979). These are experimental and quasi-experimental designs (Cook and Campbell, 1976). The ethics problem with manipulating variables related to job stress is smaller here because the variable being manipulated is an attempt to help employees and their organizations. Presumably, there is less inherent evil in manipulating a variable that is expected to result in benefits, than there is in manipulating a variable that is expected to result in aversive consequences. In addition, many organizations are likely to attempt programs on their own that are aimed at improving a stressful situation. In these cases, the researcher can take advantage of naturally occurring events to study the phenomena involved in stress.

The first of these methodologies involving manipulation of some independent variable is the *true experiment.* It is common to assume that true experimental designs (i.e., those including randomization of people to experimental treatments, manipulation of independent variables, and subsequent measurement of a dependent variable) are impossible in real-world organizational investigations. Researchers occasionally overlook an opportunity to conduct experimental research, however, simply because this assumption is so ingrained.

The other recommended methodologies involving manipulation of an independent variable are *quasi-experiments*. For the investigation of the stress domain, three of Cook and Campbell's (1976) quasi-experimental designs are especially recommended: (1) nonequivalent control group, (2) regression-discontinuity, and (3) interrupted time series.

It is clear that most of these recommendations are not the norm in this field; that is, one does not see them used very often in the major journals in personnel and related fields. It is suggested that this is the result of each researcher's habits and typical modes of thinking. Even when only beginning to think about a research project, most researchers will already have become committed to thinking in terms of their own past research designs. Kaplan (1964) has stated the problem aptly, writing, ''Give a small boy a hammer, and he will find that everything he encounters needs pounding. It comes as no particular surprise to discover that a scientist formulates problems in a way which requires for their solution just those techniques in which he himself is especially skilled'' (p. 28). In order to follow the prescriptions of this chapter, most researchers will need to avoid this tendency.

Recommendations for Practice

Recommending specific treatment strategies for stress that draw on the current state of knowledge would be irresponsible. Most treatment programs for stress are virtually untested in any meaningful manner (Newman and Beehr, 1979). This does not mean that no strategy should be used, however. The potential usefulness of many of the strategies is based on logic, and in the absence of more convincing evidence, that is the next best reason for directing practice in this field. Since the problem does appear to exist for many organizations and their employees, it is recommended that attempts be made to alleviate it.

The primary recommendation in this section is that such attempts proceed in an orderly, systematic manner so that future attempts to deal with stress at the workplace can benefit from knowledge gained by previous attempts. Since it is presently unknown what treatment programs are best, the use of many different types of programs can be very beneficial if each is evaluated as it is applied.

Also recommended is the use of more strategies in which the organization is the primary target. These organizational strategies are likely to be less frequently utilized than the individually oriented strategies, simply because there are more people practicing the individual strategies: medical doctors, psychiatrists, and clinical and counseling psychologists. The most skilled people to promote and direct the organizational strategies are managers, personnel and human resource specialists, organizational development specialists, and others with backgrounds and training in industrial/organizational psychology and organizational behavior. Organizationally oriented strategies potentially are among the most useful in the long run, since they are more likely to attack some of the causes of stress than are some of the traditional individually oriented strategies.

Individually oriented strategies such as medication and psychotherapy, for example, are likely to be implemented only after the stress has included some damaging consequences for the individual; that is they often treat the effects instead of the causes.

Four major practices in the area of stress are recommended: (1) diagnosis of stress by personnel and human resource departments, (2) use of human resource accounting to measure the cost of stress to the organization, (3) search for ways to help alleviate harmful stress if it is found to exist in a given organization, and (4) evaluation of treatment techniques to whatever extent possible.

Diagnosis by Personnel Departments. Periodic monitoring of stressors and their consequences and the development of measuring instruments with reliable norms are recommended, and personnel departments are logical units in most organizations to perform this monitoring function (Beehr, 1980). The implementation of stress treatment programs logically is preceded by the observation that some stress exists in the organization. For the most effective use of treatment, it is necessary to know: (1) whether stress does exist in the organization, (2) what parts of the organization are experiencing the stress, and (3) what types of stressors and/or consequences are present.

Some of the stressors can be monitored through the use of periodic company surveys (some are published in references cited in this chapter). The individual consequences would include dispensary visits, sick leave use, and physical, psychological, and behavioral problems. The organizational consequences include absenteeism, turnover rates, grievances, and poor performance. Stressors, individual consequences, and organizational consequences all need to be monitored periodically; the best rule of thumb at present is that stress is indicated when there are problems in all three of these areas simultaneously.

As the personnel or human resources department accumulates a record of these periodic measures, it can begin to determine what absolute levels on the measures indicate excessive stress in the organization. Rapid increases in these measures for certain subunits of the organization above their past norms would indicate the need for implementation of a treatment strategy.

Human Resources Accounting of the Costs of Stress. It is recommended that human resource accounting (e.g., Likert, 1967; Paperman and Martin, 1980) be applied to the organizational consequences of stress. Computations would need to be made of the current costs of stress to the organization, the costs of a proposed treatment program, and (once the relative effectiveness of a training program is known in terms of reducing the costly organizational consequences) the savings to the organization of any given training program. Since business organizations, in classical theories at least, operate on a profit maximization principle, this is a logical extension of such thinking.

In practice, many organizations seem to operate in terms of other principles as well, however, such as the popular concept of corporate social responsibility. In reference to work-related stress, this notion takes into account costs that are not directly borne by the organization, e.g., individual's costs of health and life expectancy, and the nation's costs in terms of scarce medical resources and lost Gross National Product when its citizens are less productive during their lifetimes than they could be. Thus, whether organizations ought to undertake stress treatment programs based only on their own costs is a value question, but until some sort of accounting procedures are developed to assess costs and benefits to the organization (as well as to various other parties), decisions are made or not made in a vacuum of information.

Search for Treatments.   Some of the traditional personnel functions may be useful in alleviating job stress. Once the personnel department has monitored stress and determined what types, if any, are prevalent in the organization, it could devise some stress treatment strategies of its own by altering some of the selection and placement procedures (e.g., keep stress-prone employees out of particular jobs), training programs (e.g., develop training aimed at helping employees alleviate their own stress), performance appraisal techniques (e.g., include appraisal of employee's success at dealing with stress and of manager's success in alleviating subordinate's stress), and career planning activities (e.g., mapping out, with the individual, a career plan that takes into account his or her desire for, and ability to handle, specific kinds of stress).

The second major approach recommended for personnel specialists is to contact and use the skills and knowledge of experts from other specialty areas (e.g., counseling and clinical psychology and psychiatry, medicine, and various organizational practitioners). Since many different specialty areas all have some skill in this domain, their combined efforts are likely to lead to innovative new programs for both monitoring and treating stress in organizations.

Evaluation of Treatments.   The final recommendation for practitioners in the stress domain is that all treatment techniques be evaluated. This cannot be emphasized enough in this newly developing area. Whether the professionals administering the treatment programs are full-time employees of the organization or external consultants, and regardless of the strategy used, assessment of program effectiveness is the only way advancement will occur in the ability to deal with stress. When the organization is paying for all or part of the program, its representatives are in a position to insist on sensible evaluation of its effectiveness. Often, external consultants will not consider this necessary, will not have the interest in evaluation, or will not have the expertise in evaluation. In such cases, the consumer-organization should broach the subject and urge an evaluation. An overall recommendation, consistent with many of the specific recommendations made in this chapter for both research and practice, is that research and practice should be merged. The most obvious area where this can be done is in the evaluation of intervention practices.

Discussion Questions

1. What are the most important reasons for organizations to be concerned about the stress their employees experience?

2. Should stress always be regarded as bad or something to avoid? If not, why not? Would you even be willing to recommend that under certain circumstances stress should be increased?

3. What are some strategies that can be used by individuals and organizations to manage or reduce stress?

4. What is the most important topic for research on job stress in the near future? Why? What would be the best way to research this area?

5. What is the *best* way to reduce harmful job stress? Describe it in detail. Why do you think it is the best way? What evidence is there to support your choice of this technique for stress reduction?

CHAPTER FIFTEEN

UNION-MANAGEMENT RELATIONS

John A. Fossum[1]

John A. Fossum is Associate Professor of Organizational Behavior and Industrial Relations at the University of Michigan. He received his Ph.D. in Labor and Industrial Relations from Michigan State University. Professor Fossum has conducted research on such topics as job satisfaction and compensation systems, and has authored numerous journal articles. In addition, he is the author of *Labor Relations: Development, Structure, Process* and a co-author of *Personnel/Human Resource Management*. Professor Fossum has had management experience in both military and industrial organizations. He has worked in the general personnel area for Honeywell, Inc., and in personnel research for the Corporate Staff Division of Control Data Corporation.

Union management relations is not simply a separate activity in the organization's personnel management system. It is inextricably tied into many of the processes examined previously. It also has been the catalyst for the development and elaboration of several personnel management activities that are now generic to both organized and nonunion employers. As an example, many aspects of compensation systems have evolved because a coherent white-collar pay plan became necessary after a union had negotiated one for blue-collar employees. Nonunion organizations modified their systems to meet the competition of more attractive reward systems offered elsewhere. Given that unions are interested in a wide variety of employee-oriented bargaining issues, the negotiation and administration of the collective bargaining agreement may determine how several of the personnel management functions are practiced, for example, wage and salary administration, personnel testing, personnel training, career planning, and organizational exit.

Personnel management and union management relations have been commonly thought of as separate fields. Actually, the two are closely intertwined. The major differ-

[1]This chapter was written while Professor Fossum was on leave as Visiting Associate Professor of Industrial Relations in the Graduate School of Management, University of California, Los Angeles.

420

ence between personnel management and union-management relations is that the personnel practices applied to the affected employees are collectively bargained and fixed in the short-run, rather than unilaterally determined and subject to change without notice.

Another divergence that has created a gulf in understanding between practitioners of personnel management and union-management relations is the divergent backgrounds sometimes found in the preparation of each. Personnel management scholars have generally developed from backgrounds in industrial/organizational psychology and industrial engineering, while union management relations owes its primary debts to economics and sociology. The former tend to focus on individuals, the latter on organizations. Recently, students schooled in both areas and a variety of behavioral disciplines have begun to introduce a distinctly behavioral perspective into the study of union-management relations (Strauss, 1979). Some take a distinctly social-psychological perspective and focus on bargaining behavior (Rubin and Brown, 1975; Stephenson and Brotherton, 1979). Other theories and research have examined attitudes toward unions and the process by which individuals make choices about union membership (Brett, 1980; Getman, Goldberg, and Herman, 1976; Kochan, 1979). Texts are also beginning to reflect an increasingly behavioral perspective in examining the processes of union-management relations (cf., Fossum, 1979; Kochan, 1980a; Holley and Jennings, 1980). Finally, proposals to synthesize new levels of understanding in union-management relations by wedding economic, institutional, and behavioral research have been made (Kochan, 1980b, 1980c).

This chapter has several objectives. First, organizational structure of the labor movement must be understood. Second, the impact of laws and regulations on the practice of collective bargaining must be appreciated. Third, the processes involved in organizing employees will be explored. Fourth, the issues and tactics involved in collective bargaining will be detailed. Fifth, the impact of unions on personnel management functions and outcomes will be analyzed.

THE BASIC STRUCTURE OF THE LABOR MOVEMENT

In the United States, most employees are not represented by labor unions. Many employers have no organized employees and most do not bargain with unions representing white-collar or professional employees. In these situations, employers are free to devise and implement employment policies including wages, hours of work, fringe benefits, promotion structures, job security provisions, and the like, without employee input. Employees are also individually free to negotiate any of these and other areas with their employers, but there is no obligation on either party to respond to the other. While union representation is the exception rather than the rule in the United States, in western European countries union membership is much greater.

The Structure of Labor Organizations

There has been a variety of organizational structures during the development of the American labor movement. The structure that exists in the present American labor movement is similar to the model originally established by the trade unions that formed the American Federation of Labor (AFL) in 1886. The labor movement has three primary components in its structure: the labor federation (AFL-CIO), the national unions, and the local unions. Figure 15–1 represents the structure of the labor movement.

The diagram in Figure 15–1 shows that the power in the labor movement resides in the national unions. (These are frequently referred to as international unions because of significant Canadian membership.) The AFL-CIO is a creature of its affiliated nationals. While it can expel nationals that fail to comply with its rules, it cannot stop them from engaging in union activities or strip their membership. This lack of power has been made obvious by the success in organizing experienced by the dissident unions that formed the Congress of Industrial Organizations in 1935, the failure of the expulsion of the Teamsters in 1959 to blunt their organizing success, and the withdrawal of the United Auto Workers in 1968.

Except for independent local unions or those directly affiliated with the AFL-CIO, local organizations are chartered by, and subordinate to, their parent nationals. A portion of each member's dues, usually about 50 percent, is sent to the national to support its activities. Local unions are required to have national approval before striking and before signing an agreement. The national supplies locals and their members with technical assistance and information for negotiating contracts, administering grievance procedures, and organizing nonunion employees. Subject to statutory constraints, locals that ignore national rules can have their officers removed and be operated under trusteeships by the national.

Most of the individual members' contacts are with the local union's officials. Besides the executive officers, the most important committees or officers for rank and file members are the negotiating committee and the stewards. The negotiating committee is responsible for bargaining contracts and for deciding the merit and importance of pursuing member grievances that have been denied by management. The steward is the individual member's representative in the work area. Contract clauses are interpreted for members by the steward, and the steward acts as an initial advocate for the member in pursuing grievances under the contract.

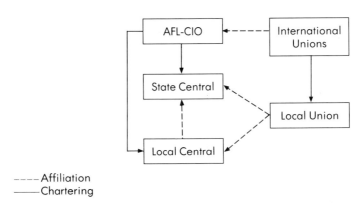

---- Affiliation

———— Chartering

FIGURE 15–1

Structure of the Labor Movement

Source: Adapted from J. G. Kilpatrick and M. C. Stanley. *Handbook on Central Labor Bodies: Functions and Activities.* West Virginia University Bulletin, Series 64, No. 4–6, October 1963, p. 5.

The Union Member

It may seem paradoxical, but union members seem notoriously uninterested in local union government, particularly if contracts appear adequate. Membership attendance at union meetings seldom exceeds 10 percent (Anderson, 1979; Sayles and Strauss, 1967). In his study, Anderson (1979) found participation at meetings was related to involvement in union political affairs, but not to filing grievances under the contract. Electoral participation through elections of officers, strike votes, and contract ratifications is usually quite high—in fact, higher than public participation in national elections.

A recent national survey (Kochan, 1979) also found that not only the general public but rank and file union members were not positively impressed by the images of national union leaders. On the other hand, the same survey found that members and nonmembers believed that unions were effective in obtaining important outcomes for their members.

It is likely that most union members see their unions as agents in the employment relationship. In return for dues, the union is responsible for advocating grievances, negotiating contracts, and eliminating the individual effort that might be necessary to advance one's employment conditions. The members frequently make their individual and collective wishes known, but, except for those who prefer organizational activism, the others have signaled by their noninvolvement that the union is accomplishing its purpose and needs no intervention on their part.

The practice of collective bargaining includes both union rules and statutory requirements. These laws and their impacts on union management relations are discussed next.

PUBLIC POLICY AND STATUTORY LAW

Union-management relations in the United States have been subject to increasing statutory control since World War I. Prior to that time, there was no legislation regulating the activities of either management or labor. There was, however, a rather extensive body of common law limiting union activities and making available injunctive relief to employers involved in union-sponsored activities (cf., Dulles, 1966; Rayback, 1966; Taft, 1974). Public opinion in the nineteenth century was generally opposed to unions and union activity.

Union-managment relations began to be regulated through the War Labor Disputes Act passed in 1918 to reduce the possibility of strikes that might cripple the allied war effort. However, it was not until the 1930s that labor legislation covering major portions of the private sector was passed.

There are four major statutes that regulate union-management relations in the United States. The basic thrust of these laws has been to legitimize collective bargaining as the method to be used for resolving industrial conflict, to legitimize the union as an institution for representing groups of employees, to limit the conduct of both parties toward their members and toward each other, and to establish governmental agencies to oversee and assist in the relationship. Table 15–1 provides a summary overview of current federal legislation and applicable executive orders.

TABLE 15-1
Federal Union-Management Relations Laws and Regulations

Law	Coverage	Major Provisions	Federal Agencies
Railway Labor Act	Nonmanagerial rail and airline employees and employers in private sector.	Employees may choose bargaining representative for collective bargaining, no yellow-dog contracts, dispute settlement procedures including mediation, arbitration, and emergency boards.	National Mediation Board, National Board of Adjustment.
Norris-LaGuardia Act	All private sector employers and labor organizations.	Outlaws injunctions for nonviolent union activities. Outlaws yellow-dog contracts.	
Labor-Management Relations Act (originally passed as Wagner Act, amended by Taft-Hartley Act and Landrum-Griffin Act)	Nonmanagerial employees in nonagricultural private sector not covered by Railway Labor Act, postal workers.	Employees may choose bargaining representative for collective bargaining. Both labor and management must bargain in good faith. Unfair labor practices indicated in-	National Labor Relations Board, Federal Mediation and Conciliation Service.

Act	Coverage	Provisions	Administering Agency
Landrum-Griffin Act	All private sector employers and labor organizations.	cluding discrimination for union activities, secondary boycotts, refusal to bargain. National emergency dispute procedures. Specification and guarantee of individual rights of union members. Prohibits certain management and union conduct. Requires union financial disclosures.	U.S. Department of Labor.
Executive Order 10988 (as amended) and Civil Service Reform Act, Title VII	All nonuniformed, nonmanagerial federal service employees and agencies.	Employees may choose bargaining representative for collective bargaining. Bargaining rights on noneconomic and nonstaffing issues. Requires arbitration of unresolved grievances.	Federal Labor Relations Authority.

Source: H. G. Heneman, III, D. P. Schwab, J. A. Fossum, and L. D. Dyer. *Personnel/Human Resource Management* (Homewood, Ill.: Irwin, 1980), p. 46, as adapted and expanded from J. A. Fossum, *Labor Relations: Development, Structure, Process* (Dallas: Business Publications, 1979) p. 62.

Statutory Definition of Collective Bargaining

The labor acts specify the meaning of collective bargaining succinctly if somewhat indefinitely: "to meet at reasonable times and places and to confer in good faith with respect to wages, hours, and other terms and conditions of employment" (National Labor Relations Act, Section 8d). Basically, good faith means that the parties will respond to the initiatives of the other to discuss issues during contract negotiations or *any other time* during which the union is the representative of the employees, and that information being used by a party to support a position is available for evaluation to an opponent (*NLRB* v. *Truitt Mfg. Co.,* 351 U.S. 149 (1956)). While concessions are not required to be bargaining in good faith, an adamant refusal to respond to information or to give the opportunity to provide alternative approaches is not (*NLRB* v. *General Electric Co.,* 418 F. 2d 766 (U.S. 2d Circuit Court of Appeals, 1969)). Both parties incur the duty to bargain as soon as and as long as a labor organization has been lawfully shown to represent a majority of employees in a bargaining unit.

A number of statutorily determined aspects are of primary importance in union-management relationships in the United States. Four are of particular importance in understanding the basic required relationships between and within union and management organizations. These are the concept of *exclusive representation,* the defintion of the scope of the *bargaining unit,* the scope of *mandatory bargaining issues,* and the required *duty to bargain.*

Exclusive Representation

In unorganized establishments, management has unilateral rights in personnel decision making (subject to constraints included in EEO, Health and Safety, and Wage and Hours laws). It is not required to attend to individual or collective employee complaints or suggestions. Subject to the provisions of other laws, it can decide what criteria will be used for hiring, promotion, firing, rewarding, job assignment, and so forth. However, when a majority of employees designates a labor organization as its bargaining agent, the employer is prohibited from engaging in unilateral actions with any or all of its employees if that area is covered by the contract. This prohibition applies not only to those favoring the union, but also to those opposed. The union has the exclusive right to represent all employees in the unit in collective bargaining. It has become the employees' agent.

Bargaining Units

The bargaining unit is the group of employees represented by the labor organization in collective bargaining. The employees to be included in a bargaining unit are either agreed to by the employer and the union or defined by the National Labor Relations Board (NLRB) during a representation election processes (to be discussed later). There is a variety of criteria used for deciding inclusion (Abodeely, 1971), but management employees cannot become members of any unit and professional employees (as a group) cannot be included in a broader unit against their will. Frequently, unions only seek to represent certain occupational groups or certain units of a multiunit organization. Both unions and managements have a voice in the scope of the unit, either through negotiated agreements (consent elections) or through NLRB determinations. Bargaining unit scope may be increased by the mutual agreement of the parties at times following its initial designation. This is most frequently done for effectiveness in negotiating.

Mandatory Bargaining Issues

Unions and managements are not obligated to discuss and bargain over all issues its opposite may raise. But each is required to respond to any issue related to wages, hours of work, and terms and conditions of employment (aspects affecting the work environment and job security). Management usually reserves, and in fact need not discuss, the rights to decide product and marketing strategy, pricing, and the like. Table 15–2 lists many of the issues that NLRB and court decisions have defined as mandatory.

Duty to Bargain

When one of the parties to the agreement raises a mandatory issue, the other must be willing to discuss it. This requirement relates not only to contract negotiations, but also to disagreements or new initiatives during the contract (if they have not been ruled out by contract language). Disagreements and grievances require a response from the other party; otherwise an unfair labor practice would exist.

Other Major Employment Laws

Besides statutes defining and regulating the scope and conduct of collective bargaining, a number of other laws constrain employment practices and may limit the contents of a collective bargaining agreement. Wage and hour laws establish floors for the future negotiations of wage levels and entitlements to overtime. The provisions of these and other laws may not be waived by unions as concessions during negotiations. Health and Safety legislation reduces the amount of effort unions must place on bargaining over working conditions. While unions would generally prefer bargained outcomes to legislation, laws may be more readily achieved than contracts. The law then serves as a floor for bargaining positions or may allow unions to concentrate more efforts in other areas since trade-offs in these would be unnecessary.

Equal employment opportunity laws and regulations, particularly Title VII of the 1964 Civil Rights Act and Executive Order 11246 (as both have been amended), forbid employer and union involvement in job discrimination based on race, sex, religion, color, or national origin. The Executive Order also requires federal contractors to take affirmative steps to overcome the effects of past or apparent present differential impacts related to group membership. To the degree that contract clauses, particularly seniority clauses governing job progression, lead to contradictory results, collective bargaining and equal employment opportunities may be at odds. However, the Supreme Court has

TABLE 15-2
Mandatory Bargaining Issues

Wages
Hours
Discharge
Arbitration
Holidays—paid
Vacations—paid
Duration of agreement
Grievance procedure
Layoff plan
Reinstatement of economic strikers
Change of payment from hourly base to salary base
Union security and checkoff
Work rules
Merit wage increase
Work schedule
Lunch periods
Rest periods
Pension plan
Retirement age
Bonus payments
Price of meals provided by company
Group insurance—health, accident, life
Promotions
Seniority
Layoffs
Transfers
Work assignments and transfers
No-strike clause
Piece rates
Stock purchase plan
Workloads
Change of employee status to independent contractors
Motor carrier—union agreement providing that carriers use own equipment before leasing outside equipment
Overtime pay
Agency shop
Sick leave
Employers insistence on clause giving arbitrator right to enforce award
Management rights clause

Cancellation of seniority upon relocation of plant
Discounts on company products
Shift differentials
Contract clause providing for supervisors keeping seniority in unit
Procedures for income tax withholding
Severance pay
Nondiscriminatory hiring hall
Plant rules
Safety
Prohibition against supervisor doing unit work
Superseniority for union stewards
Checkoff
Partial plant closing
Hunting on employer forest reserve where previously granted
Plant closedown and relocation
Change in operations resulting in reclassifying workers from incentive to straight time, or cut work force, or installation of cost-saving machine
Plant closing
Job posting procedures
Plant reopening
Employee physical examination
Union security
Bargaining over ''bar list''
Truck rentals—minimum rental to be paid by carriers to employee-owned vehicles
Musician price lists
Arrangement for negotiation
Change in insurance carrier and benefits
Profit-sharing plan
Company houses
Subcontracting
Discriminatory racial policies
Production ceiling imposed by union
Most favored nation clause

Source: R. C. Richardson. ''Positive Collective Bargaining.'' In D. Yoder and H. G. Heneman, Jr. (eds.). *ASPA Handbook of Personnel and Industrial Relations* (Washington: Bureau of National Affairs, 1979), 7–128. By permission of the Bureau of National Affairs, Inc.

held that even in situations where seniority provisions have had a negative impact on minorities, if their inclusion in a contract was not intended to discriminate, they are not unlawful (*International Brotherhood of Teamsters* v. *U.S.*, 431 U.S. 324 (1977)).

UNION ORGANIZING

Recent reports indicate that about 20 percent of U.S. employees are members of labor unions. This represents a decline from the post-World War II peak of about 26 percent (U.S. Department of Labor, Bureau of Labor Statistics, 1976). The proportion of organized employees varies widely by industry and occupational group. Outside of federal, state, and local government, the proportion of white-collar and professional employees who are organized is minimal. Table 15–3 details the present percentages organized by industry.

Why do these differences exist? What leads to employee organizing activities? What activities are permitted to unions and managements during organizing campaigns?

TABLE 15–3
Union Membership Proportions by Industry

75% or More	*25% to 50%*
Transportation	Printing, publishing
Contract construction	Leather
Ordinance	Furniture
Paper	Electric, gas utilities
Electrical machinery	Machinery
Transportation equipment	Chemicals
	Lumber
50% to 75%	*Less than 25%*
Primary metals	Nonmanufacturing
Food and kindred products	Textile-mill products
Mining	Government
Apparel	Instruments
Tobacco manufacturers	Service
Petroleum	Local government
Manufacturing	State government
Fabricated metals	Trade
Telephone and telegraph	Agriculture and fishing
Stone, clay, and glass products	Finance
Federal government	
Rubber	

Source: Adapted from U.S. Department of Labor, Bureau of Labor Statistics. *Directory of National Unions and Employee Associations 1973* (Washington: Government Printing Office, 1974), p. 81.

The Motives for Employee Organizing

Much of the early theory and research on union formation dealt with collective outcomes and not individual choices. For example, analyses of the earliest labor organizations find that they were formed to resist employer powers to arbitrarily set wage (Commons, 1973). The introduction of psychological approaches to the study of organizing focuses more on the reasons an individaul decides to join or not join a labor organization. By understanding individual choice processes, one can better understand the differences in organized proportions by occupation and industry.

Individual Choice

In a perceptive explanation to practitioners why individuals join unions, Bakke (1945) stated:

> The worker reacts favorably to union membership in proportion to the strength of his belief that this step will reduce his frustrations and anxieties and will further his opportunities relevant to the achievement of his standards of successful living. He reacts unfavorably in proportion to the strength of his belief that this step will increase his frustrations and anxieties and will reduce his opportunities relevant to the attainment of such standards (p. 37).

Earlier in this volume, Mitchell has elaborated on expectancy theory as an explanation of human motivation. Expectancy theory is a powerful heuristic model that helps sharpen insights into human behavior (Campbell and Pritchard, 1976) and can easily be applied to choices about joining unions. In a recent review, Brett (1980) established several propositions related to union organizing which she feels are supported by substantial research evidence. First, employees will be more likely to seek organization if an employer is perceived to have demanded different behavior than was expected, or if an employer failed to provide rewards expected. Second, an individual must believe that there is little likelihood of changing conditions except through collective action. Third, some critical mass of like-minded activists is necessary to begin the organizing attempt. Fourth, organizing by this activist coalition depends on their understanding of how collective bargaining works and their belief that the likely benefits of organizing outweigh the losses. From an individual's standpoint, Fossum (1979) showed how two individuals in the same organization may make different choices about engaging in organizing activity given their perception of the consequences of organizing. The results become increasingly unpredictable if the group to be organized comes from heterogeneous outcome preference groups. Figure 15–2 portrays two hypothetical individuals.

There is further evidence to support the contention that choice processes in organizing involve a considerable time lag between intention and action. In a study of several union representation elections, Getman, Goldberg, and Herman (1976) found that employee dissatisfaction predicted organizing activity and willingness to support and ultimately vote for union representation. Dissatisfaction levels measured during the earlier periods were found to be related to the subsequent intensity of union-organizing activity in units of a large organization (Hamner and Smith, 1978). In terms of the facets of dissatisfaction most often associated with organizing, working conditions and eco-

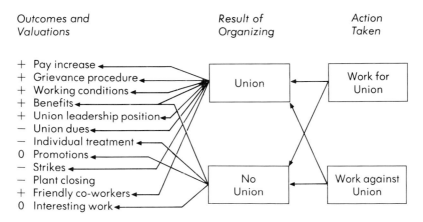

Individual A

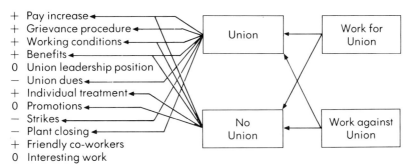

Individual B

FIGURE 15–2

Hypothetical Beliefs about Organizing Outcomes

Source: J. A. Fossum. *Labor Relations: Development, Structure, Process* (Dallas: Business Publications, 1979), p. 120.

nomic issues outweigh job content issues (Kochan, 1979; Schreisheim, 1978). This is consistent with beliefs about issues on which unions are effective (Kochan, 1979) and the issues union members rank as most important to them (Olson, 1979).

Organizing Campaigns

The union-organizing campaign is one of the most bitter and volatile situations in union-management relations. Employers face a situation in which they have the potential to lose substantial amounts of discretion in their management activities. Coupled with this loss is the realization that substantial proportions of their employees are expressing the belief that they would be better off represented by an outside organization in the formulation of personnel policies and practices. Within the employee group in which union representation is sought, substantial proportions of fellow employees may oppose organization. Because of these difficulties, substantial bodies of rules for organizing campaigns have emerged from statutory law and court and NLRB interpretations.

The right to organize or to refrain from union activity is guaranteed by law in Section 7 of the Labor Management Relations Act, which delineates these guarantees as follows:

> Employees shall have the right to self-organization, to form, join, or assist labor organizations, to bargain collectively through representatives of their own choosing, and to engage in other concerted activities for the purpose of collective bargaining or their mutual aid or protection, and shall also have the right to refrain from any or all of such activities except to the extent that such right may be affected by an agreement requiring membership in a labor organization as a condition of employment as authorized in Section 8 (a) (3).

The organizing campaign can begin within the organization through the efforts of present employees or as the result of a union deciding it would like to organize a group of employees. If it is an internal organizing campaign, the leaders usually try to obtain outside assistance from a union experienced in organizing similar employees. Union-sponsored organizing campaigns seek employees favoring unions since a majority must ultimately favor the union for recognition to be gained. Further, substantial efficiencies of access to employees accrue for employee organizers as compared to union organizers. Union organizers can be barred from the target organization's property (*NLRB* v. *Babcock and Wilcox, Inc.,* 351 U.S. 105 (1956)), while employee organizers can solicit workers in nonwork areas during nonworking time (*Republic Aviation Corp.* v. *NLRB,* 324 U.S. 793 (1945)).

Normally, it is to the union's advantage to conceal organizing activity until a majority of employees desire representation. This blunts management's attempts to convince employees to remain nonunion. However, it may, in some instances, be to the union's advantage to make the company aware of organizing, particularly if it is likely the company would take action against employees based on their membership. This would help to establish the employer's conduct as motivated by an anti-union animus. While laws do protect individuals in their Section 7 rights, the length of time necessary and the small penalties associated with a NLRB unfair labor practice finding are such that they might inspire rather than inhibit unfair practices (Greer and Martin, 1978).

The union will more likely be successful in organizing where the employees have relatively similar goals and perceive management behavior somewhat similarly. There should also be a relatively stable workforce so that employees have a likelihood of sharing common experiences and the organizing of newly hired workers does not become a continual overhead burden to the union. A number of procedural issues are important to the union and to the management in the course of organizing. Many of these involve the NLRB. A schematic diagram of the process is contained in Figure 15–3.

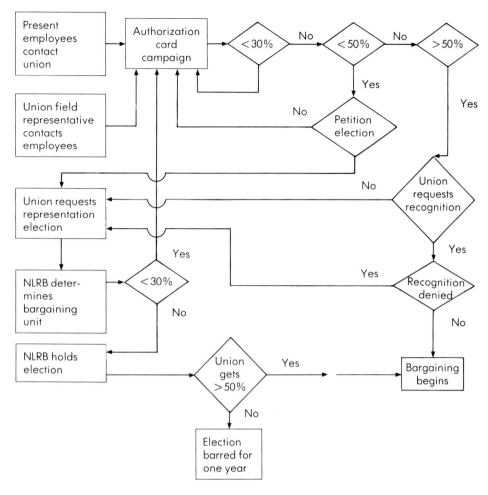

FIGURE 15–3
Sequence of Organizing Events

Source: J. A. Fossum, *Labor Relations: Development, Structure, Process* (Dallas: Business Publications, 1979), p. 130.

Authorization Card Campaign. As employees are contacted about union organizing, they are asked to sign cards authorizing the union to act as their collective bargaining representative. The union collects these to make a later recognition demand on the employer or to show sufficient interest to obtain a NLRB representation election. If the union fails to collect at least 30 percent of those it desires to bargain for, the NLRB will not order an election. When the union collects more than 50 percent it can directly demand recognition by showing proof to the organization. Most employers refuse, arguing that employees were coerced to sign or may have changed their minds, so an election is demanded.

Election Petitions.   If an employer denies recognition and if more than 30 percent have signed cards, the NLRB will order an election to determine whether or not the employees in the defined unit desire representation. If a majority does, the union is certified as the representative of all employees (whether or not they favored the union individually). This certification bars a further representation election for a one-year period to allow the winner to implement its position and/or negotiate for a collective bargaining agreement.

Bargaining Units.   The bargaining unit is initially the group of employees the union seeks to represent. It could consist of all nonmanagerial employees in a single establishment, or a group of employees in a single occupation in one or more establishments of the same organization, or a variety of combinations within these boundaries as long as it is within a single corporate entity. If the employer agrees with the union that this is the appropriate unit for a bargaining election and there are not statutory roadblocks to that unit, the NLRB holds a consent election.

The company might disagree that the union's proposed unit is appropriate. It may recommend a smaller or larger unit. Both desire units where chances of an election victory are greater or where the consequences of the election will be least aversive. For example, a company may urge the NLRB to find a plant-wide unit appropriate where the union has organized in only one occupational area. The union may seek to represent a unit containing employees critical to continued operation to gain more leverage in bargaining. There are a variety of criteria the NLRB uses to determine an appropriate unit (Abodeely, 1971) with the employees' community of interests being a prime criterion. Once the NLRB decides the unit, an election is ordered.

Campaign Strategy and Tactics.   One immediate benefit to the union resulting from an order for an election is that the company must furnish it with a list of employees in the proposed bargaining unit and their addresses (*Excelsior Underwear, Inc.*, 156 NLRB 1236 (1966)). The union can then contact employees directly during nonworking hours, where previously it may have had little knowledge about how to reach them. Union campaigns generally stress that the union will establish grievance systems to prevent employer unfairness, improve wage levels, and create an employee voice in wage and working conditions issues; that it is an organization of the employees, not of outsiders; that dues and requirements are reasonable; and that its record for obtaining gains elsewhere is proven (Getman, Goldberg, and Herman, 1976).

Management may attempt to counter union positions by holding meetings on company time to explain its position. Themes stressed by management include the position that improvements do not depend on unionization, present wages are as good as or better than union contracts, union dues are costly, the union is an outsider in the organization, costly strikes may follow if the union wins, and that the employer has treated employees fairly in the past (Getman, Goldberg, and Herman, 1976).

While both sides devote considerable energy to the post-petition campaign, there is little evidence that the voters are markedly swayed. Getman, Goldberg, and Herman (1976) found that pre-petition intentions predicted voting with a high degree of accuracy. The usual erosion of union strength as the result of a campaign seldom exceeded 5 percent.

The NLRB has imposed several rules and general policy statements for the conduct of representation elections. Elections are to take place under "laboratory conditions" to allow the employee to make a considered, uncoerced choice. To insure this, the employer is forbidden to interrogate employees about their preferences for or against a union and the employer can make no promise of benefit to take place if the union loses. Both unions and employers are forbidden to direct campaign statements to employees within twenty-four hours of the election since the opponent may not have time for a rebuttal (*Peerless Plywood Co.*, 197 NLRB 427 (1953)). Finally, neither the union nor management may make a statement containing a substantial untruth (*Hollywood Ceramics Co.*, 140 NLRB 221 (1962), reversed by *Shopping Kart Food Market, Inc.* 228 NLRB 190 (1977), which was reversed by *General Knit of California, Inc.*, 239 NLRB No. 101 (1978); Truesdale, 1979).

The Getman, Golberg, and Herman (1976) study raised substantial evidence questioning the necessity of the Hollywood Ceramics rule. They found that voters in representation elections did not pay much attention to the campaign. On the average, about fifty-five issues were raised by contending unions and managements, but electors could remember only about five. Threats involving possible losses of jobs if the union won seemed to have a counter effect since those who remembered this most clearly as an issue were those most often voting for the union. Attendance at campaign meetings increased issue familiarity but had little impact on voting.

Types of Representation Elections.   There is a variety of types of NLRB representation elections. A group of employees may seek a representation election (RC), an employer may seek a vote to force an end to union efforts to win recognition by picketing (RM), a group of employees may seek to oust or decertify a presently representing union (RD), or a group of employees may desire to deauthorize a contractual union shop clause (UD). (Union shop clauses are a form of union security to be discussed later.)

Outcomes from Representation Elections.   Recent results have generally shown that unions win slightly less than half of representation elections, and generally the larger the unit, the lower the likelihood of a union victory (NLRB, 1980). Besides the fact that many available larger units have already been organized, the sophistication and preparation of larger employees, the innate heterogeneity of employees in larger units, and the number of contacts that must be made to successfully organize inhibits union efforts in large establishments.

In an examination of all NLRB certification elections conducted during the six years beginning in 1973 and ending 1978, Sandver (1980) found that union election success was generally related to smaller unit sizes, consented rather than contested bargaining unit definitions, and less than establishment-sized bargaining units. North-south regional differences in election outcomes were minimal.

While decertification elections are far less common than RC and RM cases, the reasons for decertification have been closely scrutinized recently. A variety of union characteristics has been shown to be related to decertification. The size of the local was inversely related to probability of decertification (Dworkin and Extejt, 1979; Chafetz and Fraser, 1979), and internal local characteristics, such as a lack of leadership, low member involvement, and a change in the member composition within the unit, were related to decertification (Anderson, Busman, and O'Reilly, 1979; Anderson, O'Reilly, and Busman, 1980). The larger the size of the chartering national union, the more likely decertification occurred (Dworkin and Extejt, 1979). This may mean that large nationals are not perceived as adequately servicing small locals. Many craft unions have permanent local union business agents who handle internal servicing, while large industrials more often rely on traveling representatives. The results also suggest a strong interest among members in the union fulfilling its agency function.

Some decertification elections are begun to replace an existing union with another. Anderson, Busman, and O'Reilly (1979) found that this is frequently successful. In very few situations are both contending unions rejected with employees opting for no representation. Overall, the characteristics of unions and their internal affairs appear to be much more important to the outcomes of decertification elections than do the campaign tactics themselves.

Post-Election Aspects. If the company or union has objections to the fairness of the conduct of the campaign, each might file unfair labor practice charges with the NLRB. If the NLRB finds that the conduct disturbed the employees' free choice, then a new election would be ordered. In extreme cases where the NLRB finds that the company's conduct has permanently undermined a union's previously demonstrated authorization card majority, it may order the company to bargain with the union, as if it had won the election (*NLRB* v. *Gissel Packing Co.,* 395 U.S. 575 (1969)).

Where no objections are filed with the NLRB, considerable problems may still be encountered. Both parties have recently completed what is usually an acrimonious campaign. Management has lost its unilateral personnel decision-making power. It has implied to its employees that the union would not gain large concession and that a strike was likely. The union has made several campaign promises and has suggested that bold, militant action will gain its ends. Neither party has negotiating experience at the local level and may easily misread the other's position.

For organized establishments, either after elections or when existing contracts are expiring, new collective bargaining agreements must be negotiated. The next section covers the bargaining issues, structures, and strategies and tactics used in contract negotiations and their impacts on contract terms.

BARGAINING ISSUES

The issues involving the parties in collective bargaining can be examined at a general or a specific level. Some issues are of primary concern to one of the parties. Union security arrangements (discussed later) would be one example in which the impact is much greater for one side than the other. Other issues, such as economics, affect both heavily.

Union Goals in Bargaining

The union's goals must be examined from two standpoints. First, there is a variety of work-related outcomes important to union members as individuals. Second, as an organization, certain issues are important to the growth and security of the union as an institution. Economists have argued (Cartter, 1959) that there are two predominant union goals: wages and membership. Membership is usually seen as subordinate to wages, since unions negotiate layoff provisions rather than accepting wage cuts. Actually, breaking union goals into only two areas is simplistic, particularly because neither of the two is closely related to due process. A more complete and descriptive set of goals would include the following: wages, job security, income security, working conditions and rules, internal mobility, industrial due process, and union security.

Wages. Wages cover payments from the employer to and on behalf of employees in cash or kind for membership, length of service, and effort. Included in this definition would be fringe benefits (see Chapter 9), bonuses, discounts, recreation program contributions, company stores, and the like.

There are a number of implicit criteria unions use in formulating pay demands. *Equity* is an important criterion. Unions want their members' pay to be at least comparable to that of other reference groups. Some settlements are pattern setters, e.g., the auto or steel workers. Other unions bargain toward these achieved levels. Within the employing organization, unions desire to insure that their members' benefits are equivalent to or better than those of nonunion employees. Within the bargaining unit, historical differentials may be preserved or restored to satisfy an important internal faction such as craft workers.

Ability to pay is also an important criterion. By this, the union expects to share in the firm's prosperity. Large demands can be expected during periods of rising profits (although unions are reluctant to tie wages or bonuses to profit-sharing plans). While equity between firms is usually a more important consideration than ability to pay, since a union is likely to represent employees of several organizations in the same industry, each with differing levels of profitability, unions are not interested in driving employers from business. Employers can exist without unions, but the opposite, if possible, is trivial. As an example of the ability to pay criterion in operation, the 1979 United Auto Workers-Chrysler Corporation negotiations saw the UAW make substantial concessions to Chrysler in comparison to the 1979 Ford and General Motors pacts.

Standard of living is a third criterion. This criterion refers to the preservation of the employees' real income level. Most cost-of-living clauses would be aimed to at least partially protect negotiated real wage bases. Many wage demands during an inflationary period will be labeled as ''catch-up'' demands.

Job Security. Union members are concerned with the procedures that management will use to ration jobs. Union leaders and others have argued that employees establish property rights to jobs through continued tenure (Gomberg, 1960). Unions want rules to govern layoffs, usually by seniority, the ability to move to other jobs within the bargaining unit by senior employees facing lay off and where junior employees remain on the job, and the establishment of rights if substantial changes in production technology occur. Management frequently blunts job security gains associated with seniority by using short-term plant closings to handle production downturns, rather than selective workforce cutbacks.

Income Security.   Where layoffs or permanent shutdowns of operations are unavoidable, unions desire to have negotiated provisions to protect the income of members. Supplemental unemployment insurance plans typically allow a worker to receive as much as 90 percent of regular straight time take-home pay when added to state unemployment insurance entitlements. Income security may also be included in guaranteed wage levels offered to induce unions to alter work rules.

Work Conditions and Rules.   These issues are related to the work environment. While hours of work could be classified as a separate issue, it would be included here. These issues include such items as crew sizes, safety provisions, entitlements to or requirements for working overtime, breaks, prohibition against supervisors doing work that is assigned to the bargaining unit, and so forth.

Internal Mobility.   Most contracts specify the rules to be used in assigning promotions and transfers. Unions are concerned that management will treat workers equally and that more desirable jobs will be awarded as the result of easily understandable criteria. Promotion opportunities are usually viewed as rewards. Unions feel that since an individual builds job property rights with prolonged tenure, then tenure should be used as the basis for promotion.

Industrial Due Process.   In the absence of unions, managers can dispose of employee complaints as they choose. Unions demand a grievance procedure as one of the major results of collective bargaining. Grievance procedures are negotiated to detail the steps each party will follow when there is a disagreement as to contractual meaning and obligation. Usually the union will also insist that contract interpretation differences that cannot be resolved by the parties be handled by an independent third party who will arbitrate the dispute.

Union Security.   The leaders of the union are interested in ensuring its permanency as an institution in the work organization. Several provisions have the effect of reducing administrative effort in dues collection and enrolling new employees as members. Various basic negotiated forms of union security are as follows: *closed shop*, individuals must be union members to obtain employment (illegal); *union shop*, all employees must become union members after completing their initial probationary employment; *agency shop*, all employees must pay dues or a service fee to the union regardless of membership; *maintenance-of-membership*, all union members agree to remain members during the term of the contract; and *checkoff*, union dues will be deducted from pay by the employers for delivery to the union.

Some of these may be used in combination, e.g., an agency shop with maintenance-of-membership clause and provisions for a checkoff. There is usually little, if any, economic cost to the employer related to any of these alternatives.

Management Goals

Obviously, the management is concerned with the magnitude of the union's economic demands. Its greatest concern in this area is that it not be placed in a vulnerable cost position relative to its competition. This is one of the reasons why a group of employers in the same industry will generally have contracts with similar provisions. Employers expecting to encounter difficulties in passing wage-cost increases through to consumers via price increases will also be more concerned with economic demands.

Certainty. Employers desire to operate in an environment in which many of the possible variables affecting the accomplishment of organizational goals can be held constant. Thus, employers desire long contracts with terms stated as specifically as possible. They favor straight wage increases over fringe payments since insurance premium rates for fringes are outside their control. They avoid cost-of-living clauses if possible, or attempt to negotiate a "cap" on the total additions that are possible during the contract.

Management Rights. Managers also negotiate contracts to preserve their rights to direct and discipline the workforce. They desire to retain as wide latitudes as possible in scheduling, subcontracting, introducing new production processes, and the like.

The joint consideration of management and union goals has a direct impact on forms of bargaining behavior (to be discussed later). Obviously, some issues are of greater importance to one party than the other, and these frequently form the basis for the horse trading that achieves positive ends for both.

BARGAINING STRUCTURES

The bargaining structure consists of the set of organization and union units involved in negotiating labor agreements. From a very simple standpoint, the initial bargaining structure in a collective bargaining relationship is the union-represented bargaining unit and the involved employer establishment. More elaborate bargaining structures frequently evolve to meet the joint needs of the parties (cf., Weber, 1961).

Bargaining power is an important determinant of bargaining structure. Chamberlain and Cullen (1971) defined bargaining power as "my cost of disagreeing on your terms relative to my cost of agreeing on your terms" (p. 227). For example, if the lost profits resulting from granting a wage increase demanded by the union were less than the anticipated profit loss associated with a shutdown, bargaining power would be low, particularly if the union was aware of this assessment. It is apparent, however, that the assessment of costs is not isolated to this single negotiation. Both unions and managements might take a strike in a situation in which their costs exceeded their gains in order to build credibility of future bargaining threats. Mitchell (1980) suggests that periodic strikes, in which wages lost are not recouped by wage increases gained in that negotiation, may have investment value to the union in establishing the credibility of its threats.

It is also important to note that unions, in particular, may acquiesce to employer-instigated bargaining structures that tend to increase management power vis-à-vis the unions. An underlying explanation for this seemingly irrational behavior is that the acquiescence most often occurs where employers are in some jeopardy of going out of business if their individual costs increase and that unions reduce internal divisiveness if members' settlements are roughly equivalent.

There is a variety of establishment attributes that have an impact on management's bargaining power. Many organizations have distinctly seasonal operations. A few years ago, California vegetable packers were struck just as the tomato crops matured. Canneries depended on the short harvest period to generate most of their plants' yearly revenue. The costs of failing to agree to labor's terms would have been exceedingly high. It is also no accident that the United Auto Workers contract expires every third year close to the introduction of new models (Walton and McKersie, 1965). Thus, the company cannot build up an inventory to ride out the strike, since all would be last year's models and subject to heavy discounts in the market.

The establishment's production technology affects its bargaining power. Generally the more automated or capital-intensive the organization, the greater is the ability to take a strike. These organizations generally have larger proportions of technicians and shorter spans of control than many assembly operations. They are often found in continuous flow processing organizations (Woodward, 1965). If a strike such as that between the oil refiners and the Oil, Chemical, and Atomic Workers (OCAW) in 1980 occurs, nonunion and supervisory employees can operate the plants as long as significant maintenance is unnecessary.

In more labor-intensive organizations, the availability of strike replacements increases management's bargaining power. Unemployment rates and the skill level required by the jobs and available in the labor market are necessary considerations.

Finally, competition is important. The more competitive the firm's product market, the less is management's bargaining power, since customers will use more reliable supplies. A monopolist, on the other hand, simply postpones sales and may ultimately recoup most of the lost revenue. (Parenthetically, so will striking workers recoup wages through subsequent overtime schedules.) In this regard, public school strikes are relatively costless to both labor and management if they are not excessively long. The school initially loses state aid because of strike-caused student absences. Teachers lose their paychecks. But after settlement, the school year is simply extended to make up the lost days, which later yield state aid when students attend and paychecks for teachers holding make-up day classes.

Bargaining Structure Variants

The most simple type of bargaining structure is the single union-single establishment model. Within its type, the simplest form is one in which the organization has a single establishment and the employees who are unionized are represented by a single union. If the employer is in a competitive industry, given the type of establishment, and the union represents employees among several employers, its bargaining power is quite high. This situation leads to a bargaining variant called the multiemployer bargaining unit.

Multiemployer Bargaining. In this situation, several employers in the same industry bargain with a single union for an overall contract. The union must agree to the multiemployer unit, and once a contract is negotiated and remains in effect, an employer may not drop out of the unit. If a multiemployer unit has been established, employers can engage in strong concerted actions to preserve it, including locking out employees if the union decides to engage in selective strikes.

Industry-Wide Bargaining. Industry-wide bargaining is the multiemployer analog at the national level. Here, industry groups negotiate with a single union. Typical examples of industry-wide (or at least major portions of industries) involved with unions in collective bargaining include the Bituminous Coal Operators Association (BCOA) and the United Mine Workers (UMW), the major freight haulers and the Teamsters (IBT) culminating in the National Master Freight Agreement, and the big steel producers and the United Steelworkers (USW). These groups have generally been much more difficult to hold together than local multiemployer units.

National-Local Bargaining. In many large organizations, the national union and the employer have agreed to negotiate economic issues on a national level. This makes sense to the union since competing locals are not able to stir up local member political unrest through a patchwork of wage levels. It is also reasonable since the national union ultimately must approve local contracts anyway, and the economic concerns are relatively common or would lead to intraunion competition. On the other hand, work rules are negotiated at the plant level. Thus, a national agreement on economics could be followed by several local plant strikes if agreement cannot be reached on noneconomics.

Coalition or Coordinated Bargaining. This is the union analog (usually at the national level) of multiemployer bargaining. Where several unions represent similar employee groups, they coordinate demands, sit in on each other's negotiations to present a united front, and bargain for contract terms to increase their bargaining power, such as common contract expiration dates. Without this approach, the employer's bargaining power is very great since production at struck plants can be shifted elsewhere (cf., Hildebrand, 1968).

Multinationals and Conglomerates. The multinational corporation (MNC) is a single entity with facilities, branches, or subsidiaries in several countries. As previously noted, U.S. national unions have not extended their jurisdiction beyond North America. Thus, a corporation operating on at least two continents is dealing with multiple labor organizations (cf., Flanagan and Weber, 1974). Bargaining power for unions is decreased markedly because they negotiate separately for only a portion of employees at only a few facilities. A MNC could hold out for long periods of losses in a small subsidiary operation in a single country. Some international union cooperation has occurred, but it seldom extends past policy statements or moral support.

Conglomerates pose a similar domestic problem to unions. Conglomerates are made up of a variety of establishments in diverse industries. The rationale behind the conglomerate is that at least some of the industries will be performing well in any economic situation. The mix might change, but insulation through diversity continues to exist. Also, the conglomerate continually examines its holdings and other firms to determine which should be pruned and which companies are attractive for acquisition bids.

Diversity in industry and frequent sales and acquisitions means that representing unions are likely to be diverse. It further means that a recalcitrant bargaining unit might become a candidate for sale, and it means that bargaining power is low (as in the MNC), because each contributing unit is small and the company may expect adverse conditions in some at any time (Craypo, 1975).

Synthesis.   On balance, with the exception of coalition bargaining, most structural adaptations have been to the benefit of management. Taking wages out of competition may improve the internal union climate in the multiemployer unit, but it is more important to the survival of the firms through their ability to avoid whipsawing strikes. Most adaptations have increased certainty for one or both parties and may have increased management's bargaining power. Besides structural bargaining relationships, the issues and methods of negotiation strongly affect the outcomes of the contracting processes.

CONTRACT NEGOTIATIONS

Contract negotiations typically take up a small proportion of time in the collective bargaining relationships. Even in a major organization such as General Motors, the parties seldom meet to negotiate a new contract until about two months before the existing contract expires. Even then, serious bargaining (that leading to movement) seldom begins before about ten days preceding expiration. This is not to say that either party begins from scratch as they sit down. Both have researched and prepared for bargaining. Each has established priorities among issues, expected concessions it will have to grant for an agreement, and limits on its willingness to concede or amounts it must gain to agree (Richardson, 1979; Ryder, Rehmus, and Cohen, 1966). In this section, the types of bargaining the parties encounter will be discussed, the tactics and strategies used, and the individual and organizational characteristics associated with outcomes.

Contract Negotiation Processes

In their classic work on collective bargaining negotiations, Walton and McKersie (1965) defined four bargaining processes: distributive bargaining, integrative bargaining, attitudinal structuring, and intraorganizational bargaining.

Distributive Bargaining.   Simply stated, distributive bargaining determines how the pie will be sliced. If labor gets a big slice, by definition management receives a small slice. One's gain is the other's loss. Most economic issues fall within the distributive area.

Distributive bargaining issues are those that lead to the possibility of bargaining impasses and subsequent strikes or lockouts. Each party has a desired settlement position and each probably has determined a position beyond which it will not go. Assume that an expiring contract has a wage level of $8 per hour for bargaining unit employees.

Settlements in other firms and industries have varied from about 50¢ per hour to $1.50. The employer, in the absence of compelling reasons, such as a severe economic reversal, probably does not expect to give up less than 50¢. The union can hardly hope for much more than $1.50, unless there are strong equity or standard-of-living issues recently arising. Both know the settlement will likely occur within this range, but the actual outcome is unknown.

Some bargaining theorists argue (Zeuthen, 1930) that the settlement will be jointly determined by the demand and the probability that action will be taken to enforce it. For example, if the company offers 60¢ on a ''take it or leave it'' basis and the union counters with $1.00, the question of who will concede depends on the belief of each about the firmness of the position. If the union believes management is adamant, while management does not feel the union's position is unmodifiable, the union will be the first to concede. It may not concede to 60¢; however, it will be seen in the section on attitudinal structuring that it is to the advantage of a party in distributive bargaining to get its offer on the table first, particularly if it can establish firmness in its position.

In the example here, if management is willing to concede as much as $1 and the union is willing to accept as little as 80¢, a bargain should be successfully concluded within that range. Peterson and Tracy (1977) found that early commitment to a firm position and clarity and specificity of one's position was perceived as being associated with success in distributive bargaining.

Integrative Bargaining. In situations in which both parties stand to gain from a particular settlement, integrative bargaining is said to exist. Most issues associated with integrative bargaining include increased management flexibility in return for guarantees of job security to the union, or increased production efficiency coupled with labor savings sharing with union members as in the Scanlon Plan (LeSieur, 1958).

One example of an integrative bargaining outcome that is included in most contracts is the grievance procedure. In these, management agrees to give up its right to solely interpret the contract; instead, it leaves an unresolved disagreement to the interpretation of a third party in return for the union's agreement not to strike over these disputes during the agreement.

A landmark integrative bargaining success resulted in the Experimental Negotiating Agreement between the United Steelworkers and the basic steel producers (Maloney, 1974). For several previous contract negotiations, either a prolonged strike or the threat of a strike had caused steel users to stockpile in advance or switch to imports as substitutes. This action meant that steel companies had to operate and ship at inefficiently high levels prior to contract expiration and then shut down because of a lack of orders if a settlement was reached. These shutdowns resulted in large numbers of furloughed steel workers.

An agreement to submit issues unresolved after bargaining to arbitration lessens customers' beliefs that a stoppage will occur. For its part, basic steel could operate more smoothly and profitably while the USW members were less frequently laid off and shared in the estimated $80 million in cost savings associated with foregoing a strike.

Most of the examples used to demonstrate integrative bargaining involve crisis situations in which unions and managements perceive themselves to be in deep mutual trouble. To accomplish integrative goals, Peterson and Tracy (1977) see the following conditions necessary for success: clarity and specificity in stating issues, withholding positions and commitment while exploring solutions, freedom of negotiations from pre-imposed constraints, farsightedness on issues, and the availability of necessary information.

One area in which problems exist, but in which both teams have negotiated projects of an integrative nature, is in Quality of Work Life (QWL) programs (Davis and Cherns, 1975; Davis and Taylor, 1979; Ephlin, 1974; Lawler, 1976; Locke, 1976; Maccoby, 1975; Macy and Mirvis, 1976, Mills, 1976; Seashore, et al., 1980). While there are usually problems for each party, the solution to these problems is through mutual action. For example, production quantity and quality have been simultaneously increased while union members gained more direction over their work time (Maccoby, 1975). Most QWL programs are not spelled out in the contract. In fact, several agree to suspend the contract in some areas or simply create an extra-conceptual mechanism for joint cooperation (Dyer, Lipsky, and Kochan, 1977).

Attitudinal Structuring.   Attitudinal structuring involves the activities and behaviors of the parties designed to affect the beliefs of the other party. Walton and McKersie (1965) suggested that four attitudinal dimensions—motivational orientation and action tendencies toward others, belief about other's legitimacy, level of trust, and friendliness—affect the relationship ranging over conflict, containment-aggression, accommodation, cooperation, and collusion patterns. The attitudinal configurations are shown in Figure 15–4.

Peterson and Tracy (1977) found that recognition given to the other team and farsightedness in work relationships contributed toward cooperation. This, in turn, positively impacts integrative bargaining.

It is likely that initial bargaining takes place in a conflict or containment-aggression mode as a result of the antagonism of the organizing campaign, the distrust associated with the pro-union vote, and management's usual denial of legitimacy. It is also reasonable to assume the parties are in an initially conflict-oriented situation since the union may block management's attainment of its goals in several areas (Schmidt and Kochan, 1972). While Walton and McKersie (1965) pointed out that a range of interdependence exists for labor and management, because going below the range workers would go elsewhere and above the range employers would go out of business, for all practical purposes, the initial onus for accommodation is on the union. Except in situations in which other employment opportunities are unavailable (e.g., a severe recession), employees are probably above the minimum level necessary for retention. Otherwise, a critical majority large enough to gain a representation election might never exist. Also, it is necessary for employers to exist before unions are possible. Unless there is an initial recognition and accommodation to at least the top end of the settlement range, the union will fail. While an attitudinal structure may retreat later to containment-aggression on a longer-run basis, initially it must move toward accommodation.

There is a variety of behaviors that intentionally or unintentionally structure attitudes and subsequent behavior between the parties. In preparing for bargaining,

Attitudinal Dimensions	Pattern of Relationship				
	Conflict	Containment-Aggression	Accommodation	Cooperation	Collusion
Motivational orientation and action tendencies toward other	Competitive tendencies to destroy or weaken		Individualistic policy of hands off	Cooperative tendencies to assist or preserve	
Beliefs about legitimacy of other	Denial of legitimacy	Grudging acknowledgment	Acceptance of status quo	Complete legitimacy	Not applicable
Level of trust in conducting affairs	Extreme distrust	Distrust	Limited trust	Extended trust	Trust based on mutual blackmail potential
Degree of friendliness	Hate	Antagonism	Neutralism-courteousness	Friendliness	Intimacy—"Sweetheart relationship"

FIGURE 15–4

Attitudinal Components of the Relationship Patterns

Source: From *A Behavioral Theory of Labor Negotiations*, by R. E. Walton and R. B. McKersie. Copyright © 1965, McGraw-Hill, 1965, p. 189. Used with the permission of McGraw-Hill Book Company.

unions, in particular, generate interest in and support for positions among their memberships. Bargaining conventions may be held in major industries. Rank-and-file members and delegates will formulate and endorse bargaining positions. Powerful political subgroups will become apparent. For example, in the 1979 UAW-GM negotiations, the union desired to renegotiate pension benefits for retirees, an issue the company considered closed. Bannering by retirees and demonstrations at the bargaining meeting, which were highly publicized, sought to signal to the company the importance of this issue.

Further, the campaign commitment of union leaders to the rank-and-file may so purposely erode their bargaining latitude that the bargainers cannot credibly come back with less than they have promised to deliver. In fact, the union leaders can say to the membership, ''We must have $1.00 per hour or we will strike.'' (followed by a thunderous ovation and a unanimous strike authorization vote), and the settlement range floor has just been raised to $1.00 if management can pay and the threat is perceived as credible (Schelling, 1956). From a strategic standpoint, the first party to put forth a credible position backed up with an ultimatum should achieve that position if it is within the range.

Attributes and tactics of the parties also provide opportunities for attitudinal structuring. One party's concession behavior will be reinforced if matched by a reciprocal concession. However, a history of nondeference in bargaining may create the attitude that concessions will not be forthcoming. Individual characteristics suggesting a high interpersonal orientation also predispose taking an integrative bargaining approach by facilitating a cooperative rather than a conflict-oriented approach (Rubin and Brown, 1975).

Interorganizational Bargaining. Within the parties, negotiating teams and/or powerful subgroups are not always in agreement regarding their sides' position. For example, among management negotiators, sales and production managers may oppose a position advocated by financial managers, because sales will be lost and a complicated restart will be necessary. Within the union, skilled employees may feel that the negotiating team is concentrating too strongly on the larger numbers of unskilled employees. There is also a fair amount of attitudinal structuring involved in intraorganizational bargaining.

A particular variant of intraorganizational bargaining is practiced in some public sector negotiations and has been labelled *multilateral bargaining* (Kochan, 1974). Multilateral bargaining is most likely to occur as the result of major conflicts within the management negotiating team, resulting from political pressures exerted on elected officials by bargaining unions in particular and the labor movement in general. In turn, the elected officials urge management negotiators to make greater concessions than they would prefer in the absence of outside pressure.

Intraorganizational bargaining failures leading to the rejection of negotiated contracts have been noted by Burke and Rubin (1972). Their research showed that failing to consider certain groups, such as younger or older employees, skilled employees, and racial subgroups, may endanger a negotiated agreement facing ratification.

Occasionally, one side (usually management) may propose an issue that leads to the necessity for intraorganizational bargaining within the opponent group. An example of this occurred early in 1980 when the major league baseball owners proposed new compensation terms that would reduce future maximum salaries for junior service players and allow some compensation to club owners for the loss of players in the free agent re-entry draft. There were immediate conflicts introduced between extremely high-talent players and others who would command less on the market since the compensation requirement devalues the worth of the former. Second, if the contract were accepted with the new maximum salary levels for new players, a rift in the association would have developed between the "grandfathered" haves and the have-nots entering under the new provisions.

Settlements

All of the evidence suggests that most contracts are settled without work stoppages. From 1969 through 1978 only .17 percent of total private sector work time available was lost to strikes (U.S. Department of Labor, 1979). Where the parties have reached a deadlock, either before or after the expiration of the contract, an *impasse* is said to exist. The impasse could occur because the union's minimum and management's maximum acceptable settlements failed to overlap. It could also occur when an overlap existed, but failures in the communication process during bargaining did not allow the parties to recognize it.

IMPASSE RESOLUTION

The methods of impasse resolution to be discussed are those that involve more than a simple continuation in bargaining. By definition, an impasse requires something more than bargaining to break it. A variety of procedures can be used. Some are designed to put pressure, such as strikes or lockouts, on one's opponent. Others interject outside assistance at the request of the parties, such as mediation. Still others allow or require third party interventions, such as arbitration to determine and impose a solution.

Laws also have a major impact on the methods of impasse resolution that may be used. In the public sector particularly, certain modes are required or outlawed depending on the jurisdiction or occupation involved. Table 15–4 gives a general summary of the types of impasse resolutions and their general availability by employment sector.

Mediation

Mediation occurs when an outside neutral attempts to aid the parties in reaching a solution of their own after an impasse has occurred. The mediator usually meets separately with each side to gain an understanding of its position, its settlement range, and its perception of the other side's position. Where the impasse is the result of a breakdown

TABLE 15–4
Impasse Resolution Procedures Available by Sector

Procedure	Employment Sector		
	Private	State & Local	Federal
Strike	Yes	No[a]	No
Lockout	Yes[b]	No	No
Mediation	Yes	Yes[c]	Yes[d]
Fact-finding	Yes[e]	Yes[e]	No
Arbitration			
No-constraints	Yes[f]	Yes[g]	No
Final offer	Yes[f]	Yes[g]	No
Closed offer	Yes[f]	No	No
Injunctions	Yes[i]	Yes[j]	Yes[j]

[a]Permitted by a few states for nonuniformed employees. Usually not available unless the employer refuses arbitration.
[b]Only when an impasse has been reached and the contract has expired.
[c]May be required by some states.
[d]Mandatory.
[e]If required by statute. In private sector only if a national emergency dispute has been determined under Taft-Hartley provisions.
[f]Only if mutually agreed to by parties in expiring contract or during negotiations.
[g]Depends on state law, usually for uniformed services.
[i]In national emergency disputes.
[j]Where strike is illegal.

© 1980, John A. Fossum, reprinted by permission.

in communications and a misassessment of the real settlement range, the mediator may suggest concession patterns. Where no overlapping settlement range exists, the mediator may inject information about other settlements or problems that will occur to one of the parties if the other insists on a position. Mediators intercede at the invitation of the parties (except in major cases where the President may summon the contenders to Washington for some "mediation"). As such, their roles last only so long as both perceive the activities as fair and effective (Wall, 1980).

Mediators are generally strong proponents of collective bargaining; many having been union or management advocates prior to their present roles (Simkin, 1971). Among mediators, effectiveness is seen as following from the establishment of friendliness and trust between the parties, with lesser emphases related to the apparent benefits of settlements or their own expertise (Berkowitz, Goldstein, and Indik, 1964). The parties ascribe success to the mediator's intellectual competence, the ability to structure the situation, and the abilities necessary to keep them at work (Landsberger, 1960).

Some evidence exists that mediation is more successful when the impasse is caused by a negotiation breakdown rather than an inability to meet demands, the impasse was not highly intense, the parties were motivated to settle, and the mediator was aggressive and experienced (Kochan and Jick, 1978).

From a performance standpoint, mediation is an interesting tripartite situation. Both union and management negotiators must satisfy the demands of their constituents. Mediated solutions may increase the credibility of settlements they had previously proposed, but were rejected by their constituents. For their part, mediators are judged by whether they are able to get the parties to agree on a new contract. These three forces, combined with the voluntarism of the process, enhance its utility for impasse resolution.

Federal Mediation and Conciliation Service. The Taft-Hartley Act requires that the FMCS be notified sixty days before contract expiration for those under its jurisdiction if they desire to modify the agreement, and again at thirty days if they have not reached a solution. Thus, the FMCS can keep abreast of potentially problem relationships.

In situations where problems continually recur, a new program has been devised to try to eliminate the cause of recurrent impasses—Relationships by Objectives. This is a program to bring the parties together after contract negotiations. Major parts of the process are to focus on and communicate organizational goals, and to explore methods for achieving consensus in bargaining (Hoyer, 1980; Richardson, 1977). There are components of attitudinal structuring involved both within and between parties. Integrative issues are frequently identified. The atmosphere of trust created in successful programs may stimulate bargaining attention to these issues. If trust is created, a movement from a conflict or containment-aggression mode to a cooperative mode should occur.

Arbitration

Except for the provisions of the Experimental Negotiating Agreement, there have been few uses of interest arbitration (decisions regarding what contract terms should be) in the private sector. In many public sector jurisdictions, particularly the uniformed service, arbitration of bargaining impasses is seen as a *quid pro quo* for agreeing not to strike. Prior to the expansion in interest arbitration, many jurisdictions used fact finding (cf., McKelvey, 1969). Here, an outside neutral examined the situation, cited various "facts" discovered about the dispute, and recommended a settlement. This tended to be helpful only prior to an impasse (Allen, 1968; Stern, 1966) and only where it assisted in intraorganizational bargaining.

The basis for arbitration is for the parties to agree on an outsider to hear their dispute, giving the arbitrator powers to decide the terms of a new contract. The terms decided by the arbitrator are frequently somewhere between those suggested by the bargaining process at impasse. It has been suggested that where parties have tried arbitration, its effect is narcotic (Wheeler, 1975). Several variants have been proposed and implemented to alleviate this situation.

Final-Offer Arbitration. Final-offer arbitration requires that both parties propose a settlement package at, or after, impasse. After hearing both sides, the arbitrator selects, without modification, the position of labor or management. Thus, arbitrators cannot split the differences between the two.

Some evidence exists to suggest that final-offer arbitration has reduced the reliance on third parties where it has been tried (Kochan, et al., 1979; Long and Feuille, 1974). Others have argued that the proposal submitted to the arbitrator after impasse may be a substantial modification of the impasse position in an attempt to get the arbitrator to see the reasonableness of that position (Stern, et al., 1975). Thus, the process is not "final offer" in the sense that it is a "mine or your" position as in impasse.

Some arbitrators also dislike final-offer selection as a method, particularly where the selection is on a package rather than an issue-by-issue basis. They feel the contract may contain a relatively poor settlement because one side's generally better proposal was rejected as a result of an extreme offer in one area that was considered unworkable. If arbitrators are allowed an issue-by-issue determination, final offer may essentially revert to a "split the difference" approach, by balancing numbers of issues rather than positions between issues.

To alleviate this problem, Wheeler (1977) has suggested a "closed-offer" approach, where arbitrators receive information only on what each party's original position was without any information on the bargaining progress to date. The parties thus run the risk that the arbitrator may give one party less than was previously offered, thereby increasing the motivation to bargain their own agreements.

Part of the problem in public sector negotiations relates to the fact that the bargainers are relatively inexperienced compared to the private sector, operate in situations where statutes and managements do not recognize strikes as legitimate bargaining tools regardless of the price of alternatives, and are open to all sorts of elected official intervention (Kochan, 1974).

In the private sector, the FMCS has reported a much higher proportional need for services during first negotiations as compared to subsequent contracts. As the party's bargaining expertise increases, and as legislatures gain increasing evidence that society has not collapsed as the result of *any* public sector strike to date, arbitration and other third party interventions should become less necessary. Unions also will probably use them less frequently, as the replacement of striking public employees is upheld by the courts (*Rockwell* v. *Board of Education,* Michigan Supreme Court, 89 LRRM 2017 (1975); *Certiorari* denied by U.S. Supreme Court, 92 LRRM 2818 (1976)) and their power to influence the public declines.

Regardless of how a contract is settled, there may be disputes during the contract that require resolution as well.

CONTRACT ADMINISTRATION AND RIGHTS ARBITRATION

During the duration of the agreement, disputes may arise regarding the interpretation or implementation of the contract. Virtually all contracts provide a mechanism for handling these disputes without the necessity of reverting to a strike. These grievance procedures usually have several steps available for resolving a problem. First, a union steward may present and negotiate a grievance with a supervisor. If unresolved, the steward or a negotiating committee member meets with an industrial relations department representative. The third step may be between the negotiating committee and the plant manager. A fourth step would involve a national union representative and a corporate industrial relations staff executive. And the fifth, if still unresolved, requires submission to an arbitrator who decides the parties' rights under the contract.

It should be noted that the Taft-Hartley Act also allows union members to directly present grievances to management, but individuals must allow the union to participate in their settlement since the outcome could be contrary to the union's interpretation of the contract or create an undesirable precedent from the union's standpoint.

Contract administration involves intraorganizational bargaining, as the requirements of operations may lead to granting a grievance other management personnel would prefer to avoid. Within the union, certain subgroups may have grievances handled more vigorously by the union because they are politically powerful (Kuhn, 1961).

There have been relatively few reported innovations in contract administration. Those that do exist usually aim to reduce the number of formal grievances filed, by attempting informal settlement at first step levels without writeup or the establishment of precedents (McKersie and Shropshire, 1962). It is difficult to determine whether this reduces the number of grievances, but it does restore the grievance procedure to its contractual base by allowing greater involvement of first-line supervision. It may also reduce the time necessary to process grievances by cutting to a fraction those that reach the formal level.

Expedited Arbitration

If a management denies a grievance at the final step, the union may either abandon it or demand arbitration. When the latter occurs, the parties agree on an arbitrator and set a date for a hearing. The arbitrator hears the case with the parties offering evidence, calling witnesses, and cross-examining the opposing party's witnesses. Counsel for both sides may or may not be attorneys. After the hearing, the parties may submit post-hearing briefs and the arbitrator considers these, the evidence, and the contract in arriving at an award. While the process is generally well accepted by the parties and is viewed as a final decision subject to only the most limited court review (cf., Smith and Jones, 1965), critics have argued that the elapsed time necessary to finally receive an award from the filing of the grievance is far too long and the costs are too great. Zalusky (1976) estimated time from filing a grievance to receiving the award averaged 223 days with an average cost, shared equally by company and union, of $4,400 (1976 dollars).

Many cases are routine and may not involve major implications in cost to management or job loss for employees. To reduce costs and time delays, a new variant called *expedited arbitration* has been introduced. Typical cases heard in expedited situations might include discipline amounting to less than discharge, small alleged entitlements to overtime, and so forth. Lawyers are usually not used by the parties and awards are rendered quickly. Table 15–5 summarizes several currently implemented processes.

Problems in Representation

Two issues of major importance to unions and managements relate to the union's representation of bargaining unit members: *fair representation* and *adequate representation.* Since the union exclusively represents bargaining unit employees, it must scrupulously judge each case on its merits, not on union membership, union activity, or other noncontractual issues. The union may make its own judgment about whether or not to concede the grievance and whether or not to take it to arbitration even if it has merit. But it must do so conscientiously and consistently (cf., *Vaca* v. *Sipes,* 386 U.S. 171 (1967); Summers, 1977).

It is clear that unions have a duty to speedily process and adequately investigate grievances brought by their members (*Hines* v. *Anchor Motor Freight,* 424 U.S. 554 (1976)). But it is not as clear what a union's obligations are where any possible outcome will place one or more of the bargaining unit's members at an advantage relative to others. There was a recent Appeals Court case (*Smith* v. *Hussman Refrigerator Co., & Local 13889, United Steelworkers of America* (1980)) in which the duty of fair representation went unfulfilled because a union took to arbitration a grievance in which senior workers were awarded jobs the company had given to those most qualified. The contract held seniority and ability would govern. The company opted for ability in its promotions, while the union championed rejected senior candidates. The court held that the union must provide advocacy for both groups since it was an exclusive agent for both.

What differences does fair representation make to an employer? It seems, essentially, an internal union problem. But the reason the employee grieved initially is that the management allegedly violated the contract. If the grievant is inadequately or unfairly represented, the relief from the allegedly violative action taken by management cannot be redressed. The employee may go to court and obtain relief against the company there (*Vaca* v. *Sipes,* supra). Thus, it is to the company's benefit to ensure that the union regularly discharge its representation obligations to bargaining unit members.

Perspective

Problems in contract administration and arbitration have received considerable attention in the previous sections. Arbitration, in particular, has been one of the most widely incorporated and mutually satisfactory processes in U.S. collective bargaining. Dispute

TABLE 15-5
Expedited Arbitration Procedures

	Steelworkers—Basic Steel Industry	American Arbitration Association Service	AIW Local 562 Rusco, Inc.	American Postal Workers—U.S. Postal Service	Mini-Arbitration Columbus, Ohio
Source of arbitrators	Recent law school graduates and other sources	Special panel from AAA roster	FMCS roster	AAA, FMCS rosters	Its own "Joint Selection and Orientation Committee" from FMCS roster
Method of selecting	Preselected regional panels Administrator notifies in rotation	Appointed by AAA regional administrators	Preselected panel by rotating FMCS contacts	Appointed by AAA regional administrators	FMCS regional representative by rotation
Lawyers	No limitation, but understanding that lawyers will not be used	No limitation	No lawyers	No limitation but normally not used	No limitation

Transcript	No	No	No	No	May be used
Briefs	No	Permitted	No	No	May be used
Written description of issue	Last step grievance report	Joint submission permitted	No	Position paper	Grievance record expected
Time from request to hearing date	10 days	Approximately 3 days depending on arbitrator availability	10 days	Approximately 7 days depending on arbitrator availability	Not specified
Time of hearing to award	Bench decision or 48 hours	5 days	48 hours	Bench decision written award 48 hours	48 hours
Fees (plus expenses)	$100/½ day $150/day	$100 filing fee Arbitrator's normal fee	$100/½ day $150/day	$100 filing fee $100 per case	$100/½ day, 1 or 2 cases; $150/full day, 1 or 2 cases; $200/day, 3 or 4 cases

Source: J. Zalusky. "Arbitration: Updating a Vital Process," November 1976 *AFL-CIO Federationist,* the official monthly magazine of the AFL-CIO.

453

resolution in the public sector has evolved toward the private sector model, with the Civil Service Reform Act, Title VII, making arbitration the statutorily required resolution process where a union represents federal employees.

COLLECTIVE BARGAINING EFFECTS ON PERSONNEL MANAGEMENT PRACTICES

Up to this point, the chapters of this book have explicitly dealt with personnel management practices. The following chapter will do the same. The collective bargaining process affects all of these practices. In some cases it leads to innovations, since the costs of inadequate practice may rise considerably when employees can grieve over violations or negotiate changes, rather than simply acquiesce to management blunders. In other situations, less latitude is available to management in the types of practices it may select or the way they are implemented.

While the impact of collective bargaining on personnel management practices in several generic areas will be examined here, it should be noted that these areas require a response on the part of both union and nonunion employers. Further, organizations have involved employees through worker councils, task forces, work teams, and other approaches in the search for solutions to personnel problems.

Manpower Analysis

While the practices of job analysis and manpower forecasting and planning are not altered by union representation, the results obtained from these analytic tools increase in importance. The structures of tasks that make up jobs in the bargaining unit are subject to negotiation. If redesign is contemplated, this must be bargained. If a proposed strategic change or capital improvement is contemplated, the impact on jobs (both in structure and number) must be carefully assessed. While a union is entitled to negotiate and make suggestions regarding alternatives that will have less effect on its members, economically justified employer changes that result in costs lower than the union proposals can be implemented. The analysis function develops much of the information necessary to justify a management position.

Organizational Entry

Except in contract construction, where union hiring halls serve as the basic conduit for organizational entry, union contracts exercise no control over entry. Unions also exercise little control, by most contracts, over very early employment since most employers negotiate a probationary period during which grievances for discharge or discipline cannot be filed. It does mean, however, that if probationary periods, in themselves, do not adequately screen out unproductive employees, then the validity of selection procedures increases in importance since discharges, even for cause, will likely be contested by the union.

Performance Appraisal

Measuring performance may become more or less important. If all promotion decisions are made on a seniority basis among bidders for jobs, performance appraisal is redundant. If a combination of seniority and ability is important, and if appraisals are measures of ability, then their job relatedness must be shown. The construction of the appraisal system may have to be negotiated with the union (Fossum, 1977). Appraisal techniques for organized employees would likely take a critical incidents approach aimed at specific criteria, such as attendance, scrap rates, and so forth. While they may be used to attempt to improve individual performance, they are more often used as documentation to support management assertions that its disciplinary actions have not been arbitrary.

Pay and Compensation

In an organized situation, the factors upon which pay is contingent will be jointly determined. While management may prefer its own criteria, such as performance, quantity of output, and the like, the union may prefer seniority and attendance. To the extent that individual behavior is responsive to compensation systems, and individuals have strong collective preferences among systems, collective bargaining introduces the likelihood that the recipients will attempt to structure the system in order to have the greatest control over how important rewards are distributed. It is also instructive to note that employees have typically been most interested in structuring monetary (extrinsic) reward systems as compared to so-called intrinsic rewards (Olson, 1979; Winpisinger, 1973).

Training and Development

Management development is unaffected by collective bargaining, except to the extent that managers require training in labor relations. Training of union members is affected primarily through criteria used for selection as participants. There are situations, however, primarily in contract construction, where unions administer training programs for apprentices with some cooperation from employers.

Career Planning and Development

Career planning among organized employers will relate to the negotiated paths contained in the labor agreement. Evidence exists that organized employees have lower turnover rates (Block, 1978) and higher internal mobility rates than similar nonunion employees (Olson, 1980). This increases the importance of career planning and the negotiation of internal promotion ladders within the bargaining unit.

Organizational Exit

Given the discussion regarding stability in the workforce necessary for organizing to be successful, and the evidence that employees in organized establishments leave less frequently, the organization may objectively assess the impact of unions for the organization. While the benefits of low turnover have been questioned (Dalton and Todor, 1979), there are relatively high costs associated with replacing employees who quit. A measurement of turnover rate differences and wage differentials among unionized and nonunion employees can help to assess the real costs and benefits associated with union organization.

PERSPECTIVES FOR THE 1980s

Forecasting the future seems to be an obligation periodically required by society. The obligation is generally willingly, if not eagerly, assumed. Luckily for forecasters, even academic readers are likely to hold seers to as little account as grocery store customers scanning the latest issue of the *National Enquirer* or *Midnite* as they anxiously await their triple-digit orders being rung up.

Elsewhere, I have made some predictions regarding the future of U.S. union-management relations (Fossum, 1979). Collectively and individually, others have done the same (Somers, 1973). Since I have not been buried in criticism for my earlier predictions, and since some things have happened to reinforce or modify my earlier judgments, I will capsulize my view of the future within the framework used in the material presented above.

Laws and Regulation

Labor initiated two major campaigns during the 1970s to amend existing labor laws or to nullify the effects of a Supreme Court decision. During Gerald Ford's presidency, the building trades unions sought legislation enabling them to picket an entire construction site, rather than their single reserved gate during a labor dispute. This would have nullified the Supreme Court's decision (*NLRB* v. *Denver Building Trades Council,* 341 U.S. 675 (1951)) outlawing common situs picketing in construction. The Ford administration offered to support the legislation if it were tied to a bill reorganizing bargaining structures in the construction industry toward regional and national contracts. The unions agreed to this proposal by Secretary of Labor John Dunlop. Congress passed the legislation, but after intense pressure from small contractors and right-to-work lobbyists, President Ford vetoed the very legislation he had pledged to sign.

After President Carter was inaugurated, a labor reform bill was introduced to penalize employers with double and triple damages for intentional interference with organizing campaigns. It also proposed debarring employers with repeated and flagrant violations from receiving federal contracts. It also focused on expediting NLRB elections after petitions were filed. The bill passed the House and had an apparent majority in the Senate where it died as the result of a filibuster.

Business has also sought to amend laws in the wage and hour area. They have unsuccessfully attacked minimum wage increases and the application of prevailing wage requirements (Davis-Bacon Act) to federal construction contracts.

In this author's opinion, it is unlikely that unions will win any legislation in the 1980s that will ease their organizing attempts or increase their bargaining power, particularly during an inflationary period. It is even less likely that management will benefit from legislative "takeaways."

Structure of the Labor Movement

At the highest levels, the structure of the labor movement has undergone periodic changes since the founding of the AFL in 1883. Some of these changes have occurred simultaneously with changes in leadership. Philip Murray and William Green, presidents of the CIO and AFL, respectively, both died before the two federations could be merged. With the retirement and death of George Meany, new changes could occur. Although Lane Kirkland, Meany's successor, was considered by many to be a carbon copy, he has already invited the Teamsters to reaffiliate, something Meany would never have considered. I find it improbable that reaffiliation will occur except on the Teamsters' terms, because their size and jurisdiction have expanded greatly since their expulsion in the late 1950s. There appear to be no more compelling reasons for federation in the future than there have been in the past.

At the national union level, there is an increasing number of mergers taking place (cf., Taft (1973) for a prediction that this would occur). Recently the Retail Workers and the Butcher Workers merged to form the United Food and Commercial Workers International Union. District 1199 of the Retail Workers (a generally unskilled and semi-skilled hospital employee group) separated to join the Service Employees International Union, one which has a closer community of interests. Mergers will tend to increase where several unions represent employees within the same industry. As merging has become a practice in industry, to enhance profits or smooth profit cycles, mergers among unions will continue in an attempt to recapture or create bargaining power.

Union Organizing

Earlier, it was noted that the proportion of the workforce that was organized has declined since the end of World War II. Employment in heavily unionized industries has declined, new organizing attempts in large establishments are frequently unsuccessful, and an occupational shift from blue- to white-collar employment has occurred. The age distribution of the labor force has also seen a greater proportion of younger, high-turn-over employees than in the past. Kochan's (1979) finding that about one-third of a sample of U.S. employees would vote for union representation, coupled with Sandver's (1980) evidence that there is little real North-South difference in election results, and the changing age composition of the labor force, could signal an upswing in the proportions of employees unionized.

Ironically, some of labor's political advocacies contain the possible seeds of its ultimate demise. Since the 1930s, protection legislation has been passed for regulating wages, hours, safety and health, discrimination in employment, discrimination in wages, retirement benefits, disability and retirement income, and unemployment insurance. Many of these are issues previously involved in collective bargaining. With many employer activities constrained, and with federal and state agencies created to assume advocacy roles for employees, perceived needs for unions to counter capricious employer practices may decrease.

On balance, if the labor movement is to grow, it must successfully organize in occupations where its success has, in the past, been low. It must also demonstrate to the rapidly increasing numbers of women and younger workers its interest in achieving their goals.

Bargaining Issues

As long as inflation continues at a relatively high rate, one can expect economic issues to retain their continuing preeminence. In industries facing a secular decline in union employment (for example, autos and steel), more demands for pay for time not worked can be expected, such as twenty-five or thirty years of service and out for retirement, shorter work days, paid personal leaves, sabbaticals, and so forth.

Companies may be able to bargain for changing work rules to enhance productivity, but these will not likely occur unless the company has no relocation options. Examples of industries in which these bargains may occur would include mining, forestry, agriculture (if heavily unionized), and contract construction.

Contract Administration

The evolutionary shift that is occurring here and will continue to occur results from the industrial equivalent of the impact of medical malpractice suits. The courts have begun to make individual rights in the representation process an issue. Persons who may not have been part of the original organizing, but who become union members through union shop agreements, may feel little reason to defer to the union's disposition of their grievances. More elaborate justifications of decisions at each level and more forum shopping by grievants will decrease the efficiency of the procedure to the advantage of some individuals, but not necessarily to the collective group.

SUMMARY

In this summary, rather than rehash what has been said in detail, several pervasive issues will be reiterated. First, public policy in the United States is presently fairly neutral in its stance toward collective bargaining. It duplicates the basic American two-party approach to political issues and it binds all parties for a specific time period to a majority-favored outcome. Where employees prefer it, the union assumes exclusive representation rights and responsibilities. Obligations of members of the bargaining unit are essentially those of citizens. They can do as little as pay taxes and obey the union constitution and the collective bargaining agreement, or as much as direct activities as an elected official or participate as a negotiator.

Union and management goals involve both distributive and integrative bargaining. Generally, unions are concerned with economics, job security, and due process. Managements concentrate on costs and certainty of operations. Contracting helps to achieve this certainty. The goals are not completely compatible, but neither are they separate. To an extent, the union assumes some of management's obligations to deal with workers individually in a nonunion environment. It is difficult to conceive how a manager in a large-scale manufacturing operation could really wish to deal unilaterally and individually with each problem that came up in an atmosphere lacking the structure of a collective bargaining agreement.

Discussion Questions

1. Employee turnover has significant positive and negative effects on work organizations. What impacts would be expected on turnover as the result of the introduction of collective bargaining in an organization? What impacts would increasing turnover rates have on collective bargaining or union organizing?

2. Collective bargaining alters the operation of the organization's personnel management policies and practices. What major advantages and disadvantages might be expected for the employer with its introduction?

3. Exclusive representation eliminates individual bargaining by employees. Is this feature of labor law consistent with democracy in the work place?

4. As an advisor to labor organizations, what strategies would you recommend for dealing with the reduction in union bargaining power when negotiating with multinational or conglomerate organizations?

5. What advantages and disadvantages would follow from introducing arbitration into private sector negotiating impasse resolution procedures?

PART SEVEN
ORGANIZATIONAL EXIT

Organizational exit encompasses the processes by which individuals withdraw or depart from organizations and the circumstances under which these processes occur. In the overall sequence of topics associated with the activities of the personnel function, this topic logically represents the final one. While absenteeism and turnover, two aspects of exit, have been the focus of investigation for many years, these problems make up only the voluntary side of organizational exit. Recently, there has emerged a greater interest in involuntary exit; the withdrawal or departure of individuals from organizations due to circumstances beyond their direct control.

In regard to voluntary exit, attempts to understand why people do not come to work, or why they leave organizations, are perhaps among the most persistent and frustrating ones in personnel management. In the first part of Chapter 16, Steers discusses voluntary exit, focusing primarily on absenteeism and turnover. He suggests that a new conceptualization of these problems might assist personnel practitioners in dealing with them. The issue of commitment is raised by Steers as an integral component of voluntary exit.

Typically, the discussion of organizational exit ends at this point. Involuntary exit, however, has captured the attention of employers, since this area involves actions that could or should be taken by organizations relative to the rights of individuals within the employment relationship. In the context of the current Quality of Work Life philosophy, a concern with involuntary exit processes and the circumstances that cause them, may indicate a new level of social responsibility on the part of employers toward their employees. In the second part of Chapter 16, Stone reviews and discusses the contemporary issues involved in involuntary exit, including terminations due to injury, illness, plant closings, and retirement. He identifies programs that can be provided to prevent unnecessary involuntary exit, or, when necessary, to reduce the negative consequences. These programs include outplacement and retirement counseling.

CHAPTER SIXTEEN

ORGANIZATIONAL EXIT

Richard M. Steers and Thomas H. Stone

Richard M. Steers is Professor of Management at the Graduate School of Management, University of Oregon. He received his Ph.D. in Organizational Behavior from the University of California, Irvine. Professor Steers formerly served on the Corporate Industrial Relations Staff of Dow Chemical Company. He has been active in a number of professional associations, is a fellow of the American Psychological Association, and serves on the editorial boards of three organizational science journals. Professor Steers has published numerous articles and is the author and coauthor of six books on such topics as employee motivation and organizational effectiveness.

Thomas H. Stone is Associate Professor of Business Administration at the University of Iowa. He received his Ph.D. in Industrial/Organizational Psychology at the University of Minnesota. Professor Stone has served as Visiting Scholar in the Department of Accounting at the University of Texas at Austin, 1979, and as Visiting Associate Professor in the Faculty of Administrative Studies at York University, 1980–1981. Professor Stone has conducted research in the areas of performance appraisal and absenteeism and absence control. In addition to active professional association involvement, Professor Stone has served as a consultant to several organizations, including Collins Radio Division of Rockwell International and American College Testing.

The bulk of this book has examined the personnel functions directed toward acquiring, developing, motivating, and retaining an adequate supply of qualified employees. This chapter examines an equally important and inevitable phase of the employment relationship; namely, the termination of the relationship, or organizational exit. Organizational exit is defined here as a broad class of employee behaviors including temporary or permanent departure of an employee for voluntary or involuntary reasons. This broad class of behaviors may be classified into four basic categories. These four categories form a simple typology as shown in Figure 16–1. The typology presents different forms of organizational exit resulting from the duration of the exit (temporary or permanent) and the degree of employee choice (voluntary or involuntary) in the exit decision.

Temporary, voluntary exit (Type I) refers to *short-term* employee absences. These "illegitimate" absences are often caused by low employee commitment to their job and employer. Absences of this type occur when an employee is able to come to work, but decides not to do so. Temporary, involuntary exit (Type II) is distinct from Type I exit in that these are "legitimate" absences for reasons such as personal or family illness, jury duty, military leave, transportation or weather problems, or temporary layoff. Type II absences may range in duration from less than an hour, in cases of transportation or weather problems, to over a year for military or educational leave. In other words, Type II absences are "legitimate" absences (from the organization's standpoint) in which employees are motivated to attend, but unable to do so. The third type of exit (permanent, voluntary exit) is similar to Type I in that job commitment is often relatively low. However, in Type III exit the employee permanently leaves the organization. Examples of this type of exit are leaving one employer to take a better or higher paying job with another employer, electing to take early retirement, or dropping out of the labor force. The fourth type of organizational exit is permanent, involuntary turnover (Type IV). Examples of this type of exit include terminations caused by layoffs, poor job performance, plant closings, and mandatory retirement.

Managers, psychologists, and researchers have examined the first three types of organizational exit extensively. The first sections of this chapter review research and literature regarding these three types of exit. Until recently, interest in the fourth type of exit (permanent, involuntary exit) has been considerably less than in the first three. Involuntary exit, particularly permanent exit, will be discussed in the latter sections of this chapter.

First, the nature of employee commitment to organizations is considered, in regard to voluntary exit, including factors that facilitate organizational commitment. Next, major influences on employee absenteeism and what managers can do to minimize various forms of voluntary, temporary exit are examined. Third, major causes of voluntary,

	Voluntary	Involuntary
Temporary	I. Absences due to low job satisfaction, preference for nonwork activities, strikes and walkouts, leave of absence-education, etc.	II. Absences due to illness and accidents, family responsibilities, transportation problems, temporary layoff, employer lock-outs
Permanent	III. Turnover due to low job satisfaction, change of employer or quitting, preference for nonwork activities	IV. Turnover due to mandatory retirement, disabling illness, accident or death, permanent layoff, termination

FIGURE 16–1
A Typology of Organizational Exit

permanent exit or turnover, how turnover affects the organization, and what can be done about it are considered.

Following this discussion, attention will turn to an examination of involuntary exit. In particular, exit caused by illness and accidents, alcoholism and drug abuse, layoffs and terminations, and retirement will be examined.

EMPLOYEE COMMITMENT TO ORGANIZATIONS

When considering the nature of employee commitment to organizations, as well as various outcomes associated with high and low levels of commitment, it is possible to focus on two distinct aspects of the topic.

First, one can examine what is known as *behavioral* commitment; that is, one can consider how employees become ''locked in'' to an organization and find they cannot afford to leave for various reasons. Alternatively, one can look at *attitudinal* commitment, or the attitudes individuals form about their relationship with the organization. Both approaches shed light on the nature of the employment relationship, and both can help managers to better understand the motivational bases of employee participation.

Behavioral Commitment

Behavioral commitment refers to the process by which an individual makes a series of irrevocable decisions that serve to bind him or her to the organization on a relatively permanent basis (Salancik, 1977). These decisions are usually manifested through a series of behaviors, hence the term *behavioral commitment.* For instance, a blue-collar employee who undergoes an apprenticeship program to be a skilled machinist (and who accrues seniority in the process) may find that the sunk costs in time and seniority commit that person to the organization. He or she cannot afford to leave and go elsewhere.

The extent to which employees become behaviorally committed to an organization is largely influenced by the degree to which the behaviors are binding. Four characteristics of behavioral acts tend to make them binding. First, the acts must be explicit; they must be observed and unequivocal. The act of accepting a job in one firm and declining other offers represents such an explicit act. In addition, behavioral commitments are developed when the acts are irrevocable. Enlisting for four years in the U.S. Army is generally considered an irrevocable contract, although exceptions can be found. Third, behavioral commitments are enhanced if the individual was free to choose the particular behavior. (Did the individual join the Army out of choice or because he knew he was about to be drafted?) Finally, behavioral commitments are enhanced when the act is done publicly, when others know of the action. Hence, some companies run notices in the business sections of newspapers announcing that an individual has joined the company in a certain capacity.

As can be seen, behavioral commitment says little about an employee's agreement with organizational goals or a willingness to facilitate organizational goal attainment, only that the individual feels bound to the organization. When employees experience this ''locked in'' feeling, one would expect them to engage in some form of psychological bolstering. They may attempt to rationalize or self-justify their situation in an effort to demonstrate to themselves that they have indeed made the right choice by joining that particular organization. For instance, the individual may begin to accentuate the value of the company's fringe benefits or retirement program. In this way, he or she becomes convinced that a correct decision was made in joining and remaining with the organization.

Attitudinal Commitment

The second type of commitment to an organization focuses on the attitudes that employees develop toward their employer. From an attitudinal perspective, organizational commitment may be defined as the relative strength of an individual's identification with, and involvement in, a particular organization (Porter et al., 1974). It can be characterized by at least three factors: (1) a strong belief in, and acceptance of, the organization's goals and values; (2) a willingness to exert considerable effort on behalf of the organization; and (3) a strong desire to maintain membership in the organization.

Hence, commitment as defined here represents something beyond passive loyalty to an organization. Rather, it involves an active relationship with the organization, in which individuals are willing to give something of themselves in order to help the organization succeed and prosper. In exchange, the individual receives a variety of intrinsic and extrinsic rewards for service.

In general, people with high attitudinal commitment should exhibit several specific behaviors, including higher attendance, lower turnover, high job involvement, and increased job-related effort (March and Simon, 1958, Steers, 1977). Although highly committed employees would not always behave in this manner, one would expect them to tend in this direction far more than employees with low commitment.

In summary, then, it is possible to view commitment as an intermediate stage in the employee attachment process. As shown in Figure 16–2, three stages that employees

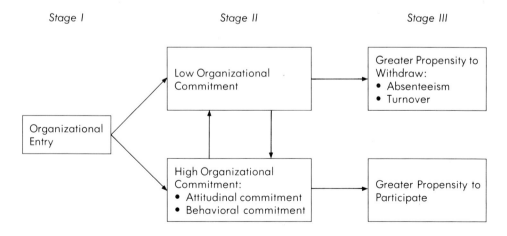

FIGURE 16–2
Stages in the Organizational Attachment Cycle
Source: Adapted from R. M. Steers and L. W. Porter. *Motivation and Work Behavior.* 2nd ed. (New York: McGraw-Hill, 1979), p. 303.

progress through during their tenure in an organization can be identified: entry, commitment, and withdrawal. Where employee commitment levels are low, one would expect greater incidences of absenteeism and turnover. On the other hand, where employee commitment levels are high, one would expect a greater propensity for employees to remain and actively participate in organizational activities. When viewed in this fashion, the importance of building a committed workforce is highlighted, and managers can better understand the necessity for accommodating employee interests, goals, and needs in order to help make them a part of the organization. In this way, the likelihood of facilitating organizational effectiveness is greatly enhanced.

MEASURING AND MANAGING EMPLOYEE ABSENTEEISM

There is a variety of ways to approach the study of employee absenteeism. Many managers approach the subject by using various rules of thumb derived from their years of experience and personal assessments concerning the major causes of absenteeism. For instance, one sometimes hears that ''When it is harder to stay off the job than it is to come to work, employees will have regular attendance.'' Such rules of thumb, while interesting, typically fail to get at the heart of the problem.

A second approach to understanding absenteeism is to consider various isolated facts that are made known about it. For example, one hears that females in general have higher absence rates than males. In a recent book on the subject (Yolles, Carone, and Krinsky, 1975), the following such (isolated) facts were presented:

1. Absenteeism is far more severe in major cities than in smaller towns and rural areas.
2. Absenteeism among females tends to decline during their career, while absenteeism among males tends to increase.
3. Cigarette smokers experience 45 percent more days lost because of illness and injury than nonsmokers.
4. In Belgium, which has very little absenteeism, the law requires that there be a bar in every factory where wine, beer, brandy, and vermouth are served.

Here again, the manager is faced with a problem of integrating these various pieces of information and determining the relative importance of each. A more useful approach than either of the first two is to view absence behavior systematically, and to attempt to gain a clear picture of the various major influences on such behavior and the way in which they are interrelated. Toward this end, a model of employee absenteeism aimed at highlighting many of the more important determinants will be presented. While no model can be all-inclusive, it is felt that such an effort can serve to provide a relatively clear portrait of the general process.

Before considering this model, however, it is useful to examine for a moment how serious a problem absenteeism can be for an organization. One way to answer this question is to look at nationwide absenteeism statistics. In the United States each year, approximately 400 million work days are lost as a result of absenteeism. This amounts to about 5.1 days lost per year per employee (Yolles, Carone, and Krinsky, 1975). In many industries, daily absence rates approach 15 to 20 percent per day! If one takes a commonly accepted estimate of the average daily cost per employee per absence of $66, including wages, fringe benefits, and so forth (Mirvis and Lawler, 1977), the estimated annual cost of absenteeism in the United States is about $26.4 billion. Using similar techniques, the estimated cost to industry in Canada would be about $10 billion. Clearly for managers, absenteeism represents a major problem that must be understood and dealt with.

In considering the costs associated with absenteeism, it is important to note that absenteeism does not always lead to reduced operating efficiency. For instance, Staw and Oldham (1978) have pointed out that some absenteeism may actually facilitate performance instead of inhibiting it. That is, absenteeism relieves dissatisfied workers of job-related stress and, in some cases, may allow them to be more productive when they return to work. Furthermore, Moch and Fitzgibbons (1980) have identified at least three conditions or stiuations that might serve to mitigate the effects of absenteeism on operating efficiency. These situations are the following:

1. Jobs that have been "people proofed" by automating production and reducing the role of employees to machine monitors.
2. Work environments that anticipate and adjust for expected ("legitimate") absenteeism. For instance, some companies use "floater pools" where people are employed primarily to replace absent employees throughout a plant.
3. Instances in which employees have little direct effect on plant-level efficiency.

Based on a study among blue-collar workers, Moch and Fitzgibbons (1980) found that absenteeism influences plant efficiency primarily in situations in which (1) production processes are not highly automated, and (2) the absences cannot be anticipated in advance. Hence, managers can have a significant impact on improving operating efficiency in certain types of work environments if they can succeed in reducing absenteeism.

A further way to understand the complexity of absenteeism problems in organizations is to consider how absence rates vary across time, industry, region, and organization. Figures 16–3 and 16–4 are illustrative in this regard. Figure 16–3 shows, among other things, that absenteeism increases around the holiday season, while Figure 16–4 shows that absence rates are higher in larger organizations and in nonbusiness enterprises.

Perhaps because of the lack of systematic attention concerning absenteeism, several misconceptions exist about the topic. To begin with, it is often assumed that the major cause of absenteeism is job dissatisfaction. As shall be seen, while job attitudes clearly play a part in determining absence behavior, many other factors are equally important. Second, it is often assumed that employees are generally free to choose whether or not to come to work. Again, such is not always the case. There are other events (e.g., illness, family problems, transportation problems) that at times inhibit actual attendance.

Finally, some people assume that absenteeism and turnover share common (if not identical) roots and, hence, can be treated with similar methods. Once again, such is not the case. Absenteeism as a category of behavior differs from turnover in several respects:

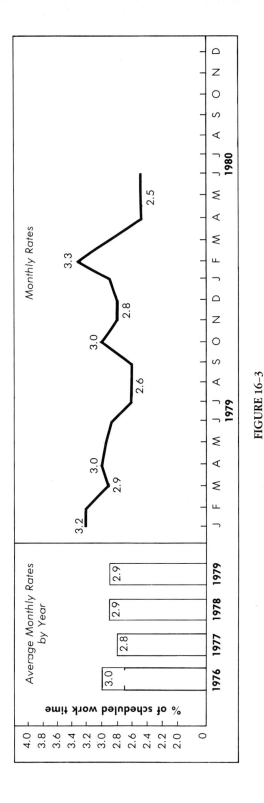

FIGURE 16-3

Median Job Absence Rates: All Companies

Source: *Bulletin to Management: BNA's Quarterly Report on Job Absence and Turnover.* Washington: Bureau of National Affairs, September 1980.

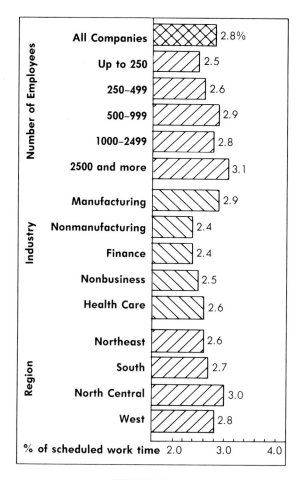

FIGURE 16-4
Average Monthly Absenteeism Rates: January–June 1980
Source: Bulletin to Management: BNA's Quarterly Report on Job Absence and Turnover. Washington:
Bureau of National Affairs, September 1980.

1. The negative consequences associated with absenteeism for the employee are typically much less than those associated with turnover.
2. Absenteeism is more likely to be a spontaneous and relatively easy decision, while termination is usually more carefully considered by the employee over time.
3. Absenteeism often represents a substitute for turnover when the employee is not in a position to quit (Porter and Steers, 1973).

Therefore, it would appear that sufficient reason exists to examine absenteeism in its own right as a separate behavior from turnover.

Measuring Absenteeism

Given the fact that absenteeism represents a serious problem for organizations, questions are logically raised concerning what can be done to reduce it. To begin with, in order to reduce absenteeism, managers must first know the extent of the problem in their own particular organization. Surprisingly, available evidence suggests that many organizations do not know the extent of their own problem. A survey of 500 U.S. firms found that fewer than 40 percent kept absenteeism records (Hedges, 1973). Moreover, a similar survey among 1,600 Canadian firms found that only 17 percent kept such records, despite the fact that 36 percent felt absenteeism ranked among their more severe problems (Robertson and Humphreys, 1978). Thus, it would appear that before one can solve a problem one must first understand its extent and severity.

In fact, there are several reasons why organizations should insist on keeping accurate records of attendance and absenteeism (Gandz and Mikalachki, 1979). Among these reasons are : (1) to more accurately and equitably administer the organization's payroll and benefits program, (2) to aid in manpower planning and production scheduling, (3) to identify absence problems, and (4) to measure and control personnel costs.

Once the decision has been made to keep such records, it is necessary to decide how to classify the various types of absences that are recorded. One such classification scheme is shown in Table 16–1 (Gandz and Mikalachki, 1979). This classification scheme differentiates between legitimate absences and illegitimate or questionable ones. Based on such information, it is possible to identify the extent of the absence problem, if one exists. That is, a manufacturing firm may experience a 15 percent absence rate, but closer examination may demonstrate that two-thirds of this rate is accounted for by job-related accidents (Type II exit in Figure 16–1). Such a finding would indicate that absenteeism may be more easily reduced through safety programs than through tightening the absence control policies.

TABLE 16–1
A Classification Scheme for Employee Absenteeism

A. Certified medical illness
B. Certified accident
    B-1. Work-related accident
    B-2. Domestic accident
C. Contractual absence
    C-1. Jury duty
    C-2. Bereavement
    C-3. Union activities
    C-4. Other
D. Disciplinary suspensions
E. Other absences
    E-1. No reports
    E-2. Personal or family reasons
    E-3. Uncertified medical illness or accident

Source: J. Gandz, and A. Mikalachki. *Measuring Absenteeism.* Working Paper No. 217, School of Business Administration, University of Western Ontario, 1979, p. 11.

In addition to identifying the reasons behind various absences, it is also useful to differentiate between the *frequency* of absences and the *severity* of absences. Frequency refers to the number of episodes of absence over a given period of time, while severity refers to the duration or length of each episode. Consider the following example: During the past three months (in which he was scheduled to work sixty-two days), an employee was absent nine days. Of these nine days, five were episodes of one-day duration, while the other four days were taken together and were the result of a job-related accident. Based on this information, a manager can calculate the following:

Frequency = 5 days in 3 months = 20 days per year

$$\text{Severity} = \frac{\text{No. of days absent}}{\text{No. of days scheduled}} \times 100\% = \frac{9}{62} \times 100 = 14.5\%$$

To go one step further, both of these measures can be broken down into categories based on the reasons behind the absences, as shown in Table 16-1. Hence, using the same example, this employee's absence record would read as follows:

Frequency = B-1 = 1 per 3 months = 4 days per year (because of accident)
Severity = B-1 = 6.5% (because of accident)
          E = 8.0% (unexplained)

These data highlight the fact that in terms of instances or frequency of absences, this employee is out more often for unexplained or unverified reasons than for certifiable reasons. Such an approach helps managers to track employee absenteeism and its various causes.

A Model of Employee Attendance

There are many ways one can attempt to model attendance behavior. The approach taken here is to divide the problem into two distinct parts. First, the major causes of attendance motivation (or one's desire or willingness to come to work) will be considered. Next, the major causes of actual attendance can be considered. Throughout this discussion, it is important to remember that the answers to these two questions are quite different.

Attendance Motivation. The absence model to be discussed is shown in Figure 16-5 (Steers and Rhodes, 1978). This model is based on a review of 104 empirical studies of absenteeism. As can be seen, *attendance motivation* is believed to be influenced by two primary factors: (1) satisfaction with the job situation, and (2) various "pressures" to attend. Hence, if an employee enjoys the work situation and the tasks associated with the job, one would expect him or her to be more likely to want to attend since the work experience would be a rewarding one. Moreover, even if the job is not pleasurable, employees may be motivated to come to work because of a series of external and internal influences that lead the employee to believe it is in his or her best interest to attend. Each of these motivational influences will be looked at separately.

In general, people tend to be more satisfied when the job situation and the surrounding work environment match up with their personal values and job expectations

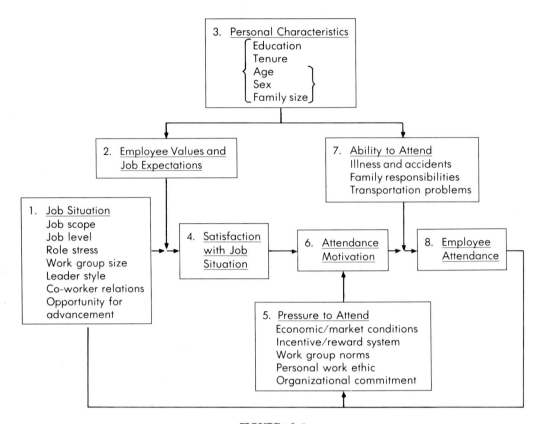

FIGURE 16-5

Major Influences on Employee Attendance

Source: R. M. Steers and S. R. Rhodes. ''Major Influences on Employee Attendance: A Process Model.''
Journal of Applied Psychology 63 (1978): 393. Copyright 1978 by the American Psychological Association. Reprinted by permission.

(Locke, 1976). This job situation, as shown in box 1 of Figure 16–5, can be characterized by many factors, including job scope, job level, role stress, and so forth. These factors are evaluated by employees and compared against their own values and job expectations (box 2) to determine the extent to which employees are satisfied or dissatisfied with work (box 4). These job expectations are, in turn, influenced by several personal characteristics, such as educational level, tenure, and so forth, as shown in box 3.

For example, in a situation in which an employee has considerable seniority (a personal characteristic) and, as a result, comes to expect certain perquisites because of his or her length of service, these expectations may include being first in line for promotion, receiving greater status, or working on higher-grade jobs. Where such expectations surrounding the work situation are met, one would expect the employee to be relatively satisfied and, as a result, increase his or her attendance motivation. Where such expectations are not met, the employee may be less satisfied and, consequently, less desirous of coming to work.

In addition to satisfaction, a second set of factors influencing attendance motivation may be categorized under the rubric of ''pressures to attend.'' Such pressures represent conditions, characteristics, and incentives that make attendance desirable from an employee's viewpoint, even if he or she finds the job dissatisfying. As shown in box 5 of Figure 16–5, these pressures can include: (1) economic and market conditions, including how easy it is to find an alternative job; (2) the incentive/reward systems of the organization, including the extent to which rewards are contingent upon good attendance; (3) work group norms favoring good attendance; (4) one's personal work ethic, reflecting the belief that one has a moral obligation to attend; and (5) one's level of commitment to helping the organization achieve its goals.

When taken together, these pressures can represent a potent force for attendance or nonattendance, particularly when combined with one's general satisfaction with the job situation. However, as noted, it is important to draw a clear distinction between attendance motivation and actual attendance. The relationship between these two variables can now be considered.

Determinants of Employee Attendance. As shown in Figure 16–5, actual attendance is jointly determined by attendance motivation and one's ability to attend. It is possible to identify at least three limitations on an individual's ability to attend (see box 7): (1) illness and accidents, (2) family responsibilities, and (3) transportation problems. Clearly the most significant problem here is illness and accidents. It has been estimated that about sixty percent of all absenteeism is health-related. In addition, approximately 40 million work days are lost each year as a result of work-related accidents (Hedges, 1973).

Beyond illness and accidents, family responsibilities can also take their toll. The importance of family responsibilities can be seen when one considers the fact that females, on average, are absent more often than males. When one looks behind such a statistic, it can be discovered, among other things, that some female absenteeism results from the traditional roles and responsibilities ascribed to women (that is, it is usually the wife or mother who remains at home with a sick child). Hence, as family size increases, so too does absenteeism among female employees.

The third ability to attend factor is problems in getting to work. Such problems can include distance from work, weather conditions, and the reliability of one's mode of transportation (e.g., auto, bus, etc.). These factors, while often overlooked, can represent a very real impediment to good attendance.

In essence, then, ability to attend serves a very important ''gatekeeper'' function in the attendance process. Assuming one has the ability to come to work, one would expect attendance motivation to predict actual attendance fairly accurately. The stronger the motivation, the more likely the person will come to work. On the other hand, when an employee is ill or has car problems, attendance motivation alone will probably not be sufficient to produce actual attendance. Hence, both factors must typically be present for one to expect high levels of attendance.

Finally, it should be noted that the model suggested in Figure 16–5 contains a feedback loop, highlighting the cyclical nature of the model. Thus, superior attendance is often viewed as an indicator of good performance and readiness for promotion, thereby possibly improving the work situation and the incentive for continued attendance. Poor attendance, on the other hand, may lead to a deteriorating relationship with one's supervisor and co-workers and could lead to a change in the various pressures to attend (e.g., the implementation of a stricter absence control policy). In any event, absenteeism or attendance should not be viewed as an end result. Rather, such behavior causes reactions (both positive and negative) that influence subsequent attendance behavior.

Reducing Absenteeism at Work

Now comes what is perhaps the most difficult part of the study of employee absenteeism. Reasons why absenteeism deserves managerial attention have been examined. A model that attempts to highlight several of the more common causes of absenteeism has been reviewed, and methods by which absenteeism can be measured and tracked over time have been reviewed. Based on this information, what can one tell the manager who hopes to reduce absenteeism in his or her particular department or organization?

Based on the materials presented, several specific methods for reducing absenteeism can be suggested. The first suggestion deals with the approach that managers take to analyzing the problem. Specifically, instead of using rules of thumb, managers can learn more about the causes of absenteeism in their own organization if they take a *systematic* approach to the problem. One can use the model outlined in Figure 16–5 as a diagnostic tool and work through the process, asking at each juncture whether this aspect of the model may be causing the problem. What is the nature of the job situation (box 1)? Are employees generally satisfied (box 4)? What about the various "pressures" to attend (box 5)? Do employees really have an ability to attend (box 7)? Answers to questions such as these can help managers to pinpoint where the problems are—and where they are not.

Second, if a diagnosis such as the one suggested reveals a problem with the satisfaction component of the model, efforts can be made to improve job attitudes. Several techniques may be employed here, including enriching employees' jobs, reducing job-related stress, building group cohesiveness and co-worker relations, clarifying job expectations, and providing career counseling for employees. Such techniques focus on the job situation and, if successful, should increase the likelihood that job expectations are met and positive attitudes developed.

Third, if the diagnosis suggests that the major problem lies in the area of "pressures" to attend, again several techniques are available for use by managers. These include clarifying rewards for good attendance, reviewing sick leave policies, encouraging an attendance-oriented work group norm, fostering a personal work ethic, and facilitating employee commitment to organizations.

Perhaps the most successful strategy here lies in the use of incentives for good attendance. For instance, in one experiment using operant conditioning, a sample of nurses were made eligible for cash prize drawings of $20 if they had no absenteeism for a three-week period. As a result of this simple attendance-reward contingency, absenteeism declined significantly (Stephens and Burroughs, 1978). In another study, it was shown that allowing employees to participate in the development of a bonus plan for perfect attendance also reduced absenteeism (Lawler and Hackman, 1969).

Fourth, if the diagnosis reveals that the major problems of absenteeism lie with employees' ability to attend, several additional strategies may be useful. For instance, organizations can encourage sound physical health (perhaps through company-sponsored exercise programs, physical examinations, etc.), institute employee counseling programs to foster sound mental health, be sensitive to problems of alcoholism and drug abuse and provide relevant programs where necessary, consider company-sponsored or -supported day care facilities for employees with young children, and consider using shuttle buses to clusters of employees living in outlying areas. All of these techniques have been used successfully by organizations concerned about insuring employees' physical health and ability to get to work.

By taking a diagnostic approach to solving problems of absenteeism, managers have a great opportunity to focus their solutions and their limited resources on the major causes of the problem, instead of applying more general solutions that may not get at the heart of the problem. In this way, greater progress should be made toward reducing avoidable absenteeism and facilitating a workforce more committed to the goals of the organization.

Reducing Absenteeism: An Example

As noted, there are several approaches that can be taken to managing employee absenteeism. Many organizations have found that when acute absenteeism is a problem (that is, when some individuals are *chronically* absent), the best approach focuses on some form of an absence control system. A typical example of such a control system in action can be seen in a recent experiment carried out among a sample of 336 production workers in a midwestern division of one of the automotive companies (Baum, 1978).

In this experiment, three departments of the company were used, one for the experiment and two as comparison groups. In the experimental group, a six-step procedure was instituted by management that was to be followed for all cases of unauthorized absences. These six steps were: (1) detailed attendance records were to be kept by the employee's supervisor, (2) written excuses from legitimate outside sources would be required for unauthorized absences, (3) questionable excuses would be independently investigated, (4) management would personally counsel all workers with unauthorized absences, (5) the existing progressive discipline system would be used to penalize excessive absenteeism, and (6) updated discipline and attendance records would be maintained on all employees.

These controls served several functions. First, employees became aware of the fact that management felt the problem was a serious one in need of change. Second, employees knew that unauthorized absences would be investigated. Third, by keeping updated records, supervisors were provided continual feedback and could track each employee's attendance record.

In the two comparison groups, existing attendance policies remained in effect. Under this policy, supervisors were given considerable latitude in dealing with absenteeism. Each supervisor made the initial decision as to what formal action to take, if any.

After the absence control procedures had been implemented, average annual days absent fell significantly among chronic absentees from forty-nine days absent per year to twenty-six days absent per year. This constituted about a 50-percent decline in the absence rate as a result of the implementation of controls. In the two comparison departments, absenteeism declined modestly, but not to the extent found in the experimental group. These findings led the researcher to conclude that "an attendance control policy based on legal compliance can lead to a significant reduction in absenteeism among workers who have a history of chronic absenteeism" (Baum, 1978, p. 78). Hence, for serious cases of high absenteeism, the use of absence control policies and/or incentive systems may prove more successful than other techniques in helping to find a solution to a costly problem.

New Directions for Research on Absenteeism

Clearly, a great deal has been learned in recent years concerning the causes—and possible solutions—associated with employee absenteeism. Even so, more remains to be learned. In particular, the following topics are suggested in need of further work in the area of employee absenteeism:

1. To begin with, it should be recognized that the conceptual model of absenteeism presented here rests largely on an integration of disparate research findings. Very few comprehensive multivariate studies of absenteeism are to be found. Hence, there is a need for further studies to test such models using longitudinal and experimental methods. Before this is done, the model suggested here must be considered more for its heuristic value than as a definitive statement on the topic.

2. Some potentially important influences on absenteeism have been omitted from the model because of a lack of information concerning their impact on such behavior. For instance, there is the problem of multiple commitments. What effect does a strong commitment to one's family or to a hobby (instead of the organization) have on attendance motivation? Moreover, what effect does psychosomatic illness (perhaps brought on by role pressures) have on actual attendance? Questions such as these are in need of answers before a more complete model of attendance can be suggested.

3. It would be helpful if further study could be done concerning the extent to which changes in absence rates do or do not have adverse consequences for organizational effectiveness. One such effort has been made by Moch and Fitzgibbons (described earlier). If reduced absenteeism is accomplished at the expense of product quality, accident rate, strike activity, or employee mental health, serious questions should be raised about the desirability of improving such attendance. Hence, some effort is needed to examine the potential trade-offs in rigorous as opposed to lax enforcement of attendance policies in organizations.

4. Finally, it should be noted that the vast bulk of research on absenteeism has focused on blue-collar workers. Ignored in these studies are managers, perhaps because researchers feel there is no problem with managerial absenteeism. However, in view of the increased autonomy that managers have (which makes short absences relatively easy), it may be useful to reexamine *de facto* absenteeism among such employees. This reexamination really suggests a need to consider the productivity of managers. That is, when an assembly-line worker is absent or present, but not actually working, it is quite noticeable. However, when a manager is "in conference" or "working privately," ques-

tions must be raised concerning the extent of actual work activity. Lenz has pointed out that one of the prerogatives of managers is the right to be absent. "It is the right to sit around the office and talk, the right to take a slightly longer lunch 'hour' than anyone else, the right to run personal errands during the day while blue-collar workers must wait until Saturday" (Lenz, as cited in Yolles et al., 1975, p. 17). In other words, it would be useful to consider more closely the active participation levels of managers as well as other employees, instead of simply determining whether or not they came to work.

MEASURING AND MANAGING EMPLOYEE TURNOVER

Interest in the study of employee turnover dates from the early 1900s when industrial engineers and industrial psychologists attempted to ascertain the major reasons behind employees' level of interest in various jobs. To date, well over 1,000 separate studies of turnover have been carried out (Steers and Mowday, 1981). Many of these studies attempted to determine the relative levels of employee turnover among various occupations. One way to do so is to examine the longevity or tenure rates of employees across industries. One example of this is shown in Table 16–2, where median years on the job of the employees in various areas are shown. As can be seen, longevity rates differ substantially across occupations and industries.

TABLE 16–2
Median Years on the Job for Male Workers in Selected Industries

Industry	Median Years on Job
Railroads and railway express	19.6
Agriculture	11.5
Postal service	10.3
Federal public administration	7.6
Automobile manufacturing	7.0
Chemical and allied products manufacturing	6.8
Mining	6.4
Electrical machinery manufacturing	5.7
Communications	5.2
Instrument manufacturing	5.1
Food and kindred products manufacturing	5.1
Finance, insurance, and real estate	4.0
Rubber and plastics manufacturing	4.0
Medical and other health services	2.8
Construction	2.7
Wholesale and retail trade	2.6
Entertainment and recreation services	1.9
All durable goods manufacturing	5.7
All nondurable goods manufacturing	5.3

Source: Bureau of Labor Statistics, 1975.

Other studies have attempted to calculate turnover rates for various organizations or types of work in percentage form. Such studies have found turnover rates ranging from almost zero to a high of 731 percent per year in one factory situation (Price, 1977). In this respect, Figures 16–6 and 16–7 show how (monthly) turnover rates can vary by month, organization size, industry, and region. Still other studies have attempted to look for primary factors that influence the turnover decision. Several reviews have pointed out that a multitude of factors have been found to be related to turnover (March and Simon, 1958; Mobley, Horner, and Hollingsworth 1978; Porter and Steers, 1973). These factors range from personal characteristics to job characteristics to economic factors. What is needed here is a conceptual framework to tie these various fragments of information together into a unified whole, so that managers can benefit from the information. Such a model is presented here. First, however, brief consideration will be given to how turnover is measured in organizations.

Measuring Turnover

There are many different ways in which employee turnover can be measured. The most common method is what is called "separation rate." It is calculated as follows:

$$\text{Separation rate} = \frac{\text{No. who left during time period}}{\text{Average no. of employees}}$$

Hence, if ten employees left during the past year and the average number of employees is 100, the organization experienced a 10-percent turnover rate.

For purposes of analysis, it is useful to calculate such rates for each department or subunit as a means of identifying potential trouble spots. If the accounts receivable department in Accounting has a 10-percent turnover rate and the accounts payable department (with similar kinds of jobs) has a 50-percent rate, attention is focused on other nonjob-related factors (e.g., supervisory style) that may account for the turnover. On the other hand, if Accounting in general has a 10-percent rate and the rate is 50 percent among the janitorial staff, perhaps the nature of the work is causing the attrition.

A final point needs to be made concerning the measurement of turnover. If effectiveness of operations is a chief goal of the enterprise, then one could argue that it may be desirable to minimize turnover among good or outstanding performers and *maximize* turnover among poor performers, particularly those poor performers who are incapable of change. Given this, it may be useful to calculate two sets of turnover rates based on performance level. (See Chapter 8 for a detailed discussion of performance evaluation.) Using this technique, one may discover something like the following:

Department	% Turnover Among All Employees	% Turnover Among Good Performers	% Turnover Among Poor Performers
Accounts receivable	10%	20%	5%
Accounts payable	50%	10%	80%

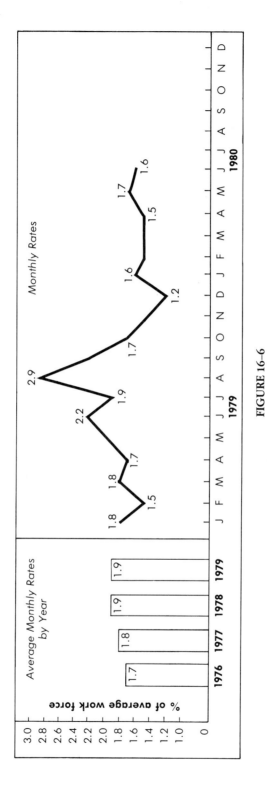

FIGURE 16-6

Median Turnover Rates: All Companies

Source: Bulletin to Management: BNA's Quarterly Report on Job Absence and Turnover. Washington: Bureau of National Affairs, September 1980.

479

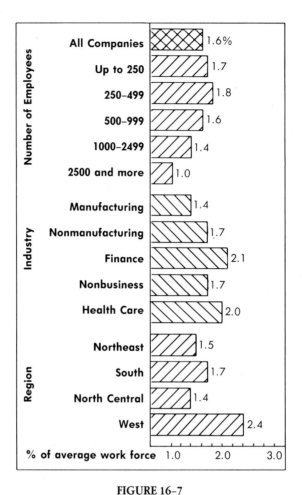

FIGURE 16-7
Average Monthly Turnover Rates: January–June 1980
Source: Bulletin to Management: BNA's Quarterly Report on Job Absence and Turnover. Washington:
Bureau of National Affairs, September 1980.

In such a situation, one may conclude that the high original turnover rate in the accounts payable department (originally 50 percent) was justified because only poor performers are leaving. In fact, one could further conclude that accounts receivable had the more serious problem since it was losing its better people. While decisions concerning the interpretation of turnover data are seldom so clear cut, this example does highlight many of the nuances of the problem.

A Model of Employee Turnover

As a result of the many studies of employee turnover, several useful efforts have been made to develop models of the processes leading up to the decision to stay or leave (March and Simon, 1958; Mobley, 1977; Price, 1977). While several models could be reviewed here, one of the most current efforts will be presented. This model, developed by William Mobley (1977), is based on a thorough review of existing studies and has been supported in several field tests.

Mobley's model represents a cognitive model of the withdrawal process. It assumes that employees typically make conscious decisions concerning job choices and tenure. It is also a process model in that it makes an effort to describe the processes leading up to actual attrition. The model itself is shown in Figure 16–8.

As can be seen, the model begins by considering an employee's evaluation of his or her existing job, shown in block A of the figure. This is the same starting point as was noted in the absenteeism model. That is, as employees begin to think about the positive and negative aspects of their jobs, they experience various levels of job satisfaction (block B). When an employee experiences a state of job dissatisfaction, two outcomes are likely to result. First, the employee may begin thinking about leaving (block C) and make alternate plans for employment. In addition, however, the employee may also initiate several alternative forms of withdrawal, including absenteeism, passive job behavior, and so forth (shown in arrow a).

As a result of the employee's thoughts of leaving, the utility and costs associated with searching for and possibly accepting a new job are then considered, as shown in block D. This expected utility of search could include such factors as the probability of finding a new job, the attractiveness of this new job, and the costs of search (e.g., travel costs, time away from the job). The employee's evaluation of the costs associated with quitting could include consideration of one's loss of seniority and status, loss of benefits in the retirement program, and so on. In sum, the employee at this phase asks whether the search for a possible new job is worth the effort.

If it is determined by the employee that the costs of search or the costs of leaving are too high, one would expect the employee to remain. Under such circumstances, the employee may proceed to reevaluate his or her job and begin to see it in a more positive light. The employee may come to believe that the job is actually better than was previously thought. If, on the other hand, the employee concludes that the costs of searching for a new position are reasonable and the expected utility of such a search is high, then one would expect that the employee would establish a behavioral intention to search for alternative jobs (block E). This intention to search could also be influenced by various nonwork factors such as a spouse's employment situation, geographic preferences, etc. (arrow b). Once decided, intention to search generally leads to actual search behavior (box F).

When search yields a suitable alternative job or jobs, or where a unique job opportunity suddenly presents itself (arrow c), the employee proceeds to evaluate the alternatives (block G). In this process, the alternatives are compared against one's current position (block H) to determine the relative merits of staying or leaving. As a result of this comparison, the employee makes a decision to stay or leave (box I), followed by actual behavior (box J). In this final process, it must be recognized that some individuals bypass the rational decision process just described and act more out of impulse (arrow e). That is, they simply decide to leave because of an argument with a co-worker, disagreement over a performance rating or pay raise, and so forth. Hence, whatever the reason, it is important to note that the turnover decision is not entirely a rational one. At times, impulsive behavior takes over and guides the employee very quickly to a decision to leave.

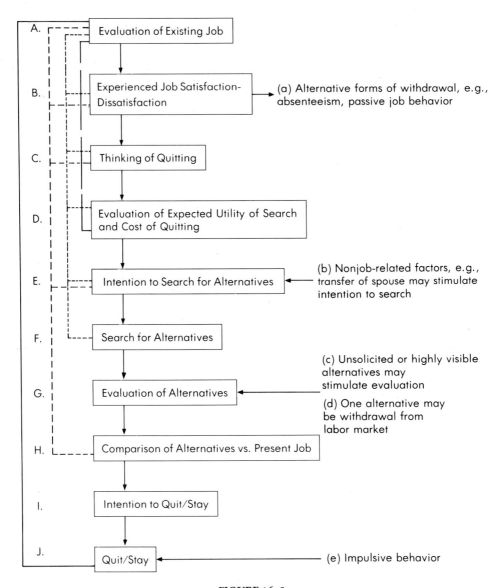

FIGURE 16–8

The Employee Turnover Decision Process

Source: W. H. Mobley. "Intermediate Linkages in the Relationship between Job Satisfaction and Employee Turnover." *Journal of Applied Psychology* 62 (1977): 238. Copyright 1977 by the American Psychological Association. Reprinted by permission.

While recognizing that this model does not describe every case of turnover, it is useful in providing a rather general description of the process that many employees go through in their decision to stay or leave. As such, the model can be quite useful for managers interested in learning more about managing employee turnover, as shall be seen next. First, however, a few words should be said about the effects of such turnover on individuals and organizations.

Consequences of Turnover

Research on employee turnover has been concerned almost exclusively with the factors leading up to the decision to stay or leave. Managers often assume that once this decision has been made, their concerns are over. Such is not the case, however. Managers have a responsibility to be concerned not only with the causes of turnover, but also with the *consequences* of turnover.

The consequences of turnover can be viewed from at least four perspectives (Steers and Mowday, 1981). First, the decision to stay or leave an organization clearly has important consequences for the person making the decision. The decision to leave carries with it a certain amount of disruption for the employee and his or her family. Existing work relationships are often broken, children are often relocated, and adjustments to a new job situation must be made. Hence, considerable adjustment is often required on the part of the leaver.

In addition, turnover by employees can have repercussions among other employees who choose to (or must) remain. Turnover can be interpreted by co-workers as a rejection of the job and a recognition that better job opportunities exist elsewhere. For those who remain, ways must be found to reconcile their decision to stay in the light of evidence from others that the job may not be good. As a result, those who remain may re-evaluate their present position in the organization and, as a result, may develop more negative job attitudes.

Third, employee turnover may also create problems for supervisors, since it is the supervisor who must initiate actions aimed at reducing such behavior. High turnover rates may reflect adversely on the effectiveness of the supervisor, particularly when the best performers are those who choose to leave. As a result, supervisors may attribute the causes of turnover to factors other than themselves in order to defend their own behavior. When this happens, top management fails to receive sufficient valid information with which to recommend strategies for change.

Finally, employee turnover can have fairly serious consequences for the organization as a whole. From the organization's standpoint, several negative consequences can be identified, including increased selection and recruitment costs, increased training and development costs, continued disruption of organizational processes, and the demoralization of the remaining members of the organization (Staw, 1980). Such factors represent real costs in terms of time, money, and effort. On the other hand, several positive consequences of turnover can also be noted for organizations. These include the possibility of increased performance brought about by recently trained and enthusiastic new employees, the possibility that long-running conflicts between people will be reduced or eliminated through attrition, increased chances for promotion and transfer for those who remain, and the possibility for increased innovation and adaptation brought about by the introduction of fresh ideas.

Hence, turnover appears to have both good and bad side effects for work organizations. As a result, it is not easy to categorically condemn high turnover rates in an organization. More information is first required concerning who is leaving, why they are leaving, and what will result from their departure. Only after this information has been secured can managers make reasoned decisions concerning the extent and nature of the turnover problem in their organizations.

Reducing Turnover at Work

An attempt has been made to suggest a general framework concerning how people decide whether or not to leave. As with the absenteeism model, this model clearly does not describe the process that every individual goes through. Rather, it attempts to identify a general process that many individuals go through, recognizing that there are exceptions to the process. Even so, if one uses the model for guidance, several recommendations for managing the turnover process come to mind:

1. It is important to clarify job expectations for new employees. One way to do so is to use "realistic job previews," where both the positive *and negative* aspects of a job are described to job applicants. In this way, people have a clear idea of the nature of the job and what is expected of them and can therefore make a more informed choice. Research has clearly shown that such realistic job previews clarify job expectations and, as a result, reduce subsequent employee turnover (Wanous, 1977).
2. Managers can attempt to insure that expected rewards or outcomes are closely tied to desired behaviors. In this way, the probability is increased that employees' expectations will be met following acceptable job performance.
3. As noted, it is often useful for managers to differentiate between good performers and poor performers when considering turnover rates. While most managers believe that reducing turnover among good performers is desirable, they may actually wish to increase it among poor performers. Hence, managers may want to pay particular attention to the reasons for termination among these good or superior employees.
4. It is important for managers to recognize the importance of job attitudes as one major factor capable of influencing subsequent behavior. While no direct relationship exists, turnover is at least moderately related to job dissatisfaction. Hence, efforts can be made to improve job attitudes at work through such techniques as job redesign.
5. Managers should recognize individual differences among employees and make an effort, where possible, to match employees to jobs. They should insure that employees have the necessary skills and abilities to successfully complete the required task assignments.

6. Managers should recognize that a series of nonwork factors can influence turnover. In many cases, employees do not leave by choice but because of outside factors (e.g., a lack of day care facilities, transfer of a spouse). Special attention by management may produce solutions to some of these problems, thereby enabling the valued employee to remain.

7. It is desirable in many cases to monitor employee job attitudes on a fairly regular basis (perhaps once a year or once every two years). If attitudes serve as an early warning system with respect to turnover, such monitoring through attitude surveys may tell managers in advance when a possible problem is developing. With this advance notice, managers can attempt to intervene and remove the problem in the hope of reducing subsequent turnover.

8. Managers should be sensitive to ''off-quadrant'' employees (that is, satisfied leavers and dissatisfied stayers). In many instances, actions can be taken to help such individuals accommodate their dilemma and find workable solutions to the problem.

In summary, it can be seen from this discussion that there are several specific actions that managers can take in an attempt to reduce employee turnover. While not perfect, such activities should help the organization in its attempt to maintain a stable and productive workforce.

Reducing Turnover: An Example

Employee turnover, like absenteeism, has been found to be influenced by many factors. Several strategies have been discussed that should facilitate a reduction in such withdrawal. The problem for management, then, is to translate these strategies into useful applications in real work environments. How can this be done? One example can be found in a recent experiment among bank tellers in a major West Coast bank (Krackhardt et al., 1978).

In this experiment, fifty separate branches of the bank were divided into a twenty-five-branch experimental group and a twenty-five-branch matched control group. Prior to intervention, interviews with various employees indicated that tellers were concerned with such issues as professional growth and development, working conditions, relationships with their supervisors, and communication to and from management.

In order to address these issues, branch managers in the twenty-five experimental branches attended a supervisor workshop where the general nature of the problem was discussed. Survey feedback indicated that the supervisor and his or her relations with subordinates were at the heart of many of the problems causing turnover. At the workshop, supervisors established goals for themselves that they intended to carry out upon their return to their respective branches. These goals included: (1) each supervisor would meet with each teller individually at least once in the next three months to discuss general work-related problems, as well as the personal needs and goals of the employee; (2) each supervisor would meet with the tellers as a group at least four times during the next three months to provide a forum for the exchange of information, to identify problems and possible solutions, and so forth; and (3) each supervisor would initiate a cross-training program for tellers who wanted to expand their job-related skills in preparation for advancement. In the twenty-five control branches, no such interventions were carried out.

Several interesting results emerged from this experiment. To begin with, some supervisors who went through the workshop and agreed to implement the changes returned to their branch and did nothing. This finding suggests to managers that it cannot always be assumed that all managers will carry out the tasks they agree to carry out. However, in those branches where the program was implemented, employee turnover was found to be significantly lower than in the matched control branches. In other words, it would appear that the intervention was successful in reducing turnover. By showing employees that management was sincerely interested in their wellbeing and in hearing their opinions and inputs, managers apparently strengthened the commitment of the employees to the organization, and they decided to remain to a greater extent than would have normally been the case.

New Directions in Research on Turnover

Despite the considerable amount of research carried out to date on turnover, several questions remain. Among the more important research questions outstanding are the following:

1. Little is known about the role of job performance in the turnover process. Specifically, do high performers leave for reasons different from those of poor performers? What is the effect of poor performance on subsequent job attitudes and desire to stay? Do high performers raise their level of job expectations, thereby making it more difficult for the organization to satisfy (and perhaps retain) them?
2. It was noted long ago that dissatisfied employees may make efforts to change the work situation or eliminate the more distasteful aspects of it (March and Simon, 1958). However, to date no systematic study of this phenomenon has taken place. If employees do undertake systematic efforts to change the work situation, what are some of the more common change mechanisms? Moreover, when such efforts are unsuccessful, are negative attitudes strengthened or do they remain unchanged?
3. Also ignored in most work on turnover is a host of nonwork factors that can influence staying or leaving. How, for example, do family considerations (e.g., a dual career family) affect turnover decisions?
4. Most turnover models, including the one described here, include the notion of search behaviors for more preferable job alternatives. However, surprisingly little is known about how people initiate search behavior, the quality of information they receive, or the way they process such information in arriving at a decision to stay or leave.

5. When an employee is unable to leave an undesirable job, how likely is he or she to find alternative modes of accommodation? What are these various accommodation mechanisms and which are used most often? Is there a generalizable sequencing of substitute behaviors, perhaps beginning with increased absenteeism and then proceeding to alcoholism and drug abuse, or do different employees simply select different accommodation mechanisms?

6. Finally, how do employees respond when their co-workers are seen as leaving on a fairly regular basis? How do they explain such "abandonment" to themselves and each other? In other words, how do employees interpret the causes of turnover by others and how do they cope with such interpretations? (see Steers and Mowday, 1981)

EXIT CAUSED BY ACCIDENTS AND ILLNESSES

To this point, voluntary exit of both a temporary and permanent nature has been discussed. While much of voluntary exit has been discussed and explained in terms of behavioral and attitudinal commitments, involuntary exit may not be explained so parsimoniously. Most forms of involuntary exit have received very little attention from researchers. Perhaps one reason for the relative lack of research on involuntary forms of exit is the inevitability of most forms of permanent exit and employers' inability to predict or control most forms of temporary, involuntary exit. Voluntary exit, on the other hand, is theoretically more susceptible to control by employers.

The remainder of this chapter will focus on the organizational and individual effects and implications of exit caused by illness, accidents, and injuries, as well as layoffs, termination, and retirement. In each part, the legal, economic, and psychological implications of exit will be examined.

Data from the National Safety Council show that in 1978 there were 13,000 work-related deaths and 2,200,000 disabling injuries. The total cost of these accidents was estimated at $20.7 billion (National Safety Council, 1979). Although this estimate includes wages lost, medical and insurance expenses, and indirect costs, it does not include the psychological costs of pain and grief of the accident victims and their families. Accidents represent losses not only in terms of money and human lives, but also in terms of productivity. Work injuries in 1978 cost employers $245 million in actual days lost, and another $200 million for nondisabling injuries and for persons dealing with accident victims (National Safety Council, 1979). Despite these grim and costly figures, work-related deaths have declined by over 70 percent since 1912. U.S. employers are taking steps to further improve job safety and health. The magnitude of their efforts are reflected by the fact that in 1979 U.S. industry planned to spend $4.9 billion (17 percent more than in 1978) on work-related safety and health (ASPA, 1979). Employers are making these expenditures for at least three different reasons. First, many safety- and health-related activities have been legally required since the passage of the Occupational Safety and Health Act in 1970. Second, from an economic perspective, work-related accidents, injuries, illnesses, and deaths are "bad business." Finally, from psychological, ethical, and public relations perspectives, safe and healthy work places are more desirable than unsafe and unhealthy ones. Each of these three reasons for employers' safety and health efforts will be discussed, beginning with OSHA.

Role of OSHA

OSHA requires employers to provide employees with a place to work free from recognized hazards that could cause death or serious injury to employees, and to comply with all standards of the act. Specific standards of the act include everything from compliance with detailed standards for equipment, buildings, and other aspects of the work environment to completing several types of safety records and forms. Enforcement of OSHA occurs under several conditions, including: (1) periodic inspections by OSHA Compliance and Safety Officers when there is a fatal or severe accident, or when an employee complains of dangerous working conditions; and (2) programs of inspecting targeted, high-injury rate industries. There are both civil and criminal penalties for violation of OSHA standards. To administer and enforce OSHA in 1981, $211.9 million was budgeted (ASPA, 1980). Additional millions were budgeted to the National Institute for Occupational Safety and Health (NIOSH), which conducts and supports research on hazardous materials, conditions, and safety and health-related methods. One of the most hazardous industries, mining, is covered under the Federal Coal Mine Health and Safety Act of 1969. In 1979, the Mine Safety and Health Administration's budget was $125.5 million (ASPA, 1978). This figure undoubtedly represents the largest per employee expenditure for safety and health since mining employs fewer than 1 percent of the labor force.

Despite the humane goals of OSHA and related safety and health legislation, OSHA has generally been unpopular with managers. There are several reasons for this, including arguments that many OSHA rules and regulations are "nit-picking" and unrelated to safety. OSHA agreed, in part, and in early 1978 dropped 1,100 job-safety standards believed to be a burden to employers while not contributing to job safety (Mossberg, 1977). A second reason is that since OSHA gives employees the right to monitor, complain about, and even walk off their jobs, the act has been used as a tool by both employees and unions to harass management. Foulkes (1973) has argued that OSHA has not been very effective since rules and standards are unclear and confusing, fines for violations are low, and the probability of inspection is low except in high-injury-rate industries. More recently, the probability of an inspection has increased since more inspectors have been hired and a high priority has been given to employee complaints of life-endangering hazards.

Have the costs of OSHA and employees' safety and health efforts resulted in fewer job-related accidents, injuries, and deaths? Death rate data from the National Safety Council show that the rate for all industries was 17 per 100,000 workers in 1970, compared with 14 per 100,000 in 1978. The bulk of this decline, however, was not in manufacturing, which has a comparatively low rate of 9 per 100,000. The nonmanufacturing work-related death rate declined from 20 per 100,000 in 1970 to 16 per 100,000 in 1977 (National Safety Council, 1979). While it appears as though OSHA contributed to the reduction in the death rate, one cannot make this conclusion with certainty, since equal or greater declines occurred over comparable periods of time prior to OSHA. Research evaluating the effectiveness of OSHA is rare since there are no control groups without OSHA. However, there are some studies that have examined safety programs from a cost-benefits standpoint. Research of this type may support economic benefits of legally mandated safety and health requirements.

One such study examined 140 Texas chemical, paper, and wood product manufacturing firms that had high rates of injuries. The study found that the costs of injuries and illnesses exceeded the costs of safety activities in the wood and paper companies, but not for chemicals. Of greater significance, however, was the recommended "mix" of safety activities to get the best results for the least cost. The recommended activities included safety rules, off-the-job safety, safety training and orientation, safety meetings, medical facilities and staff, and good top management support of safe work practices and conditions (Rinefort, 1977). A 1976 BNA survey of 124 companies examined the impact of OSHA. The most frequently mentioned changes attributed to OSHA were: (1) record keeping and reporting, (2) revised safety procedures, (3) new rules and regulations, (4) new safety equipment, and (5) safety training. Some 24 percent of the respondents to the survey reported that the company's safety record had been positively affected by OSHA. On the negative side, 20 percent reported instances of employees refusing to work because of unsafe conditions (Miner, 1977).

The future role of OSHA, as of this writing, is questionable. In 1980, a bill was introduced in the U.S. Senate that would exempt 90 percent of firms from OSHA inspections (ASPA, 1980). Passage of such a bill appears more likely since the 1980 elections resulted in a Republican majority in the Senate.

Economic Benefits of Health and Safety

There are several economic benefits to maintaining a safe and healthy workplace, as well as substantial financial costs associated with unsafe and unhealthy working conditions. A major benefit is avoidance of the costs of accidents resulting in property damage, injuries, death, and lost time, as mentioned earlier. Both individual employers and society must bear the costs of injuries, disability, and death. These costs are typically borne through two forms of insurance that all employers must provide. One type of insurance is Workers' Compensation. Workers' Compensation laws and programs are specific to each state, although they all share a common purpose of providing a continuing income to an injured worker or a deceased worker's survivors. Although discussion of Workers' Compensation laws is beyond the scope of this chapter, it is important to note that insurance premiums paid by employers depend upon both the accident rate of the particular industry and the individual employer's accident or loss experience. This, of course, can provide a substantial financial incentive to employers to reduce or eliminate accidents. A number of insurance companies providing workers' compensation policies offer "loss control" or safety and health programs to their clients.

Employers must also contribute to the federal OASDHI (Old Age, Survivors, Disability and Health Insurance) program, which is a part of Social Security. There is less economic incentive in this insurance program to reduce accidents and deaths than in Workers' Compensation since it is a nationwide system. Additionally, employees or their survivors frequently sue their employer for additional compensation for work-related accidents since accident compensation is often relatively small. Through Workers' Compensation and OASDHI, employers and the entire economy pay for work-related injuries, illnesses, and deaths.

Unsafe and/or unhealthy working conditions may have an indirect negative economic effect for both an employer and an industry. For example, the rash of accidents and problems with the DC-10 in the late 1970s hurt the business of companies flying these aircraft. The Three Mile Island nuclear plant accident has undoubtedly made recruiting employees into this industry difficult. Indeed, a serious accident in which one or more workers are severely injured or killed is likely to create anxiety among other employees. This may lead to reduced levels of job performance, increased absences, voluntary turnover, or labor unrest, including walk-outs and strikes.

Employee reactions to unsafe and/or unhealthy working conditions depend upon two major factors. The first major factor is expectations. Working conditions are usually known to employees even before they take a job. People become firefighters, police officers, aircraft fighter pilots, or underground miners knowing that there are substantial risks involved. Therefore, when injury or death occurs, the response to it by the victim, co-workers, management, and the community is more one of grief rather than anger toward the employer. Injury or death in these occupations is a socially tolerated, if not an accepted, consequence of the occupation. Societal tolerance for occupational illnesses and injuries has, however, declined as society has advanced. For example, lung cancer is no longer a tolerated occupational hazard of coal mining and asbestos workers.

The case of asbestos and the Johns-Manville (J-M) Company illustrates both the process of discovery of the hazardous effects of a substance and the economic consequences of the discovery. When Henry Ward Johns, founder of Johns-Manville Corporation, died in 1898 of a lung condition, the health hazards of inhaling asbestos fibers were unknown. Asbestos, which has excellent insulating and flame-retardant properties, was identified as a health hazard in the medical literature in 1932. It was not until 1964 that J-M began putting warning labels on their asbestos products. In 1979, the National Cancer Institute estimated that over two million people would die from asbestos-related cancer, but J-M claimed this estimate was high by at least a factor of ten (Solomon, 1979). Recently, the J-M Company has been experiencing hundreds of lawsuits from consumers, ex-employees, and others. Thus, the manufacture and use of a product has become unprofitable for the producer because of its health hazards. Since 1970, NIOSH (The National Institute for Safety and Health) has identified over 13,000 hazardous substances and materials.

The second major factor affecting reactions to unsafe or unhealthy working conditions is employee attributions of the causes of the conditions. For example, if a police officer is killed or injured by gunfire from an armed fugitive, no one is likely to blame the employer for the death or injury. However, if the death or injury of an officer results from a defective patrol car, especially when the defect is known, the reaction will be anger and perhaps legal action against the employer. Thus, the psychological response to an accident or injury victim may depend upon whether the cause of the accident or illness is attributed to the employee's own behavior or bad luck or, rather, to the employer's negligence. If the injury or illness is attributed to the employer, it is more likely that the employee will take some form of voluntary exit from the organization than if it is attributed to the employee's own behavior or bad luck. Future research should examine the relationship between occupational accidents and illnesses, attributions of their causes, and organizational exit. What effect, for example, does a severe accident have on productivity, absences, and turnover of employees close to the accident?

Reducing Accidents at Work

There are several avenues of preventing and reducing organizational exit brought about by physical causes. The first major approach is to take steps to provide a safe and healthy workplace. While some methods of doing so have been mentioned earlier, specific methods are beyond the scope of this chapter. The reader may wish to examine texts on safety management (i.e., Grimaldi and Simonds, 1975) and safety and health journals and publications such as the American Society for Personnel Administration's *Occupational Safety and Health Review* and the Commerce Clearing House's *Safety and Health Guide*.

A second avenue is to attempt to automate those jobs that are unsafe or unhealthy. There are many jobs, such as spray painting automobiles and trucks, moving heavy tires, and tending a blast furnace, that frequently cause injury or illness to the job occupants. Recently, Ford Motor Company, Sheller-Globe, and Goodyear have begun using robots to weld and paint cars and move large tires (Bylinsky, 1979). This appears to be a very promising approach to removing people from hazardous working situations.

A third approach to reducing organizational exit is to examine the effects of other organizational policies and programs upon safety and health. For example, recent accident statistics at a mine in Sudbury, Ontario, have led both union and management to seriously consider the possibility that the company's bonus system may contribute to hazardous job behavior (Lowe, 1980). In another example, AT&T found that accident rates of females hired into previously all-male jobs, such as linesman, was three times higher than for males with comparable job experience (Jason, 1978). This higher accident rate resulted despite extra training and equipment modification given to female employees. It is unfortunate that one of the costs of affirmative action programs may be higher accident and injury rates in some jobs.

EXIT RESULTING FROM ALCOHOLISM AND DRUG ABUSE

Although a large part of involuntary organizational exit is caused by work-related accidents and illnesses, alcoholism and drug abuse are responsible for some temporary and permanent absences from work, as well as contributing to accidents and illnesses. In 1974, the Harvard School of Public Health estimated that problem drinkers miss an average of twenty-two work days per year, have a two-to-four times greater probability of an accident than nondrinkers, and cost employers approximately $5 billion annually (Filipowicz, 1979). Although alcoholism and drug abuse may cause organizational exit problems, involuntary exit may lead to alcohol or drug abuse as a method of coping with job loss. Alcohol and drug abuse are similar in that both often create performance problems that may lead to some form of organizational exit. While reliable statistics are not available, drug abuse appears to be a much less common problem than alcohol. This results partially from the degree of social acceptance drinking has in society and the fact that drug use, except for medication, is illegal.

Employer response to alcoholism has generally changed from a strict disciplinary approach to one of treating alcoholism as a disease, to the most recent view—regarding alcoholics as "troubled employees" with job performance problems (Follman, 1976). Use of disciplinary layoffs or suspensions for alcohol-related work problems, especially as the only employer response, has been found to be an ineffective approach. Nevertheless, a 1974 survey found that 46 percent of employers dismissed alcoholic employees after one warning, while 53 percent attempted some helping response (Follman, 1976). There is evidence that there are economic as well as ethical benefits for employers who establish an alcohol abuse program. Kennecott Copper experienced a 52-percent improvement in attendance, a 75-percent drop in worker compensation costs, and over a 50-percent decline in health care costs through use of a counselor. A G.M. study found similar results (Witte and Cannon, 1979). One of the largest alcohol programs is a joint program between G.M. and the UAW. This program covers 600,000 employees and involves one hundred alcoholism committees in plants across the country. In two years, this program handled 9,000 alcoholic employees with a reported "cure rate" of 80 percent (Bureau of National Affairs Special Report, 1978). Finally, employers should examine other formal and informal policies and practices to see whether alcohol abuse is condoned or even encouraged. For example, one personnel officer threatened to stop the company bowling league if employees did not stop coming to work "hung over" the day after bowling.

Recent research suggests that use of the socially tolerated drug, tobacco, is associated with significantly higher rates of early retirement for health reasons by smokers than nonsmokers (Weis, 1981).

TERMINATIONS AND LAYOFFS

An older, experienced manager recently remarked that "as long as a company is making a profit, no one gets fired." Although this statement is not accurate for many firms, individual terminations and large layoffs have become common in many companies in 1979 and 1980, as the recession has reduced or eliminated profits of many employers. Employers are taking a hard look at any employee whose performance is marginal, as well as the profitability of entire units, plants, and divisions. The result is that individuals who may have been transferred or demoted are often being terminated instead, and aging plants are being closed earlier than they would have been in good economic times. While employers may use a recession to their financial advantage by eliminating "dead wood" from the payroll, and by closing and "writing off" aging plants during unprofitable years, there are still substantial human and economic costs to these terminations and layoffs. It is also clear that plant closings and large-scale layoffs are going to remain a common phenomenon through the decade of the 1980s.

Peter F. Drucker, well-known author and management consultant, argues that the U.S. economy has many industries such as steel, textiles, automobile, rubber, and shoe manufacturing that are no longer internationally competitive (Drucker, 1980). He further argues that this situation has created the need for "redundancy planning." Redundancy planning is defined as "anticipating structural and technological changes in the economy and preparing to retrain and find new jobs for workers who will have to be laid off" (Drucker, 1980). Redundant workers, Drucker argues, do not need economic security as much as they need psychological security. The need for redundancy planning means an additional heavy responsibility for human resource planners. It also means that employers must anticipate plant closings further in advance. One survey of 105 major corporations, however, found that over half said they could not give notice of a plant closing more than two to six months in advance (Greenberger, 1980).

Consequences for Employees

The consequences of termination for both employer and employee depend upon the causes of termination. There are two major causes. First, employees may be terminated for poor performance or violation of employer rules and regulations. For example, employees may be terminated for theft, excessive absenteeism, or for failing to reach a standard level of performance during a probationary period. Employers today, especially those subject to a labor agreement, are finding it increasingly difficult to terminate employees even for "just cause." The potential costs in time and money to an employer in terminating an employee, especially if the employee is a woman, minority group member, handicapped, or represented by a union, are so large that many employers do so very reluctantly and cautiously. The many labor relations and anti-discrimination laws protect employees' rights to a job to the extent that employee ownership of a job is nearly equivalent to ownership of property (McAdams, 1978). In cases in which terminating an employer-employee relationship results in legal action, an outplacement specialist is not likely to be used. However, proper handling of employee terminations and the availability of an outplacement service may well reduce litigation by terminated employees.

The second major type of termination is large layoffs or plant closings. This situation greatly increases the need for an outplacement service since many employees of varying ages, skills, and experience require assistance. Both employees and employer, in cases of plant closings, usually feel as if a death has occurred. In contrast, when an employee is fired, the situation is more like a divorce. The sadness of a plant closing undoubtedly makes searching for a new job more difficult. Unions, however, are seeking more influence in plant closing decisions, and recent court decisions suggest that employers may have to negotiate with union representatives before closing a plant (Lublin, 1980). In Canada, employees have occupied plants scheduled for closing in order to negotiate more severance pay and better pensions (McNenly, 1980), and legislation has been introduced in Ontario requiring employers to aid in relocating laid-off workers (*Toronto Star,* November 15, 1980).

No matter whether an employee is terminated individually or along with fellow employees, loss of one's job has a substantial psychological impact upon terminees. Work provides meaning and structure to the lives of most people. Job loss for many people means loss of identity and purpose in life. When faced with job loss, terminees must cope with the initial shock and anxiety. Job loss is rated as forty-seven points on a one hundred-point basis in the Holmes and Rahe (1967) social readjustment scale. This scale measures the degree of stress associated with various life events. (See Chapter 14 for further details.) Most studies of the impact of job loss on employees have been "after only" or "ex post" studies. One study by Cobb and Kasl (1977) obtained longitudinal data both before and after closings of two plants as well as data from four control companies. The terminees described their experience as very disturbing, requiring several months of adjustment, and as requiring as much life change as getting married. Cobb and Kasl also found increased frequency of peptic ulcers among the terminees and their wives, and hypertension and swollen joints. Financially, terminees lost a substantial portion of their pensions, and their remaining life earnings were somewhat reduced. On the positive side, some terminees discovered that their ex-employer did them a favor by forcing them to make a career change (Jackson, 1980) since many found as good or better jobs than they had previously (Driessnack, 1978).

Consequences for Employers

There are many consequences of terminations and layoffs for employers—some of them are positive, while others are negative. When an employer terminates or lays off employees, positive consequences of reduced labor costs or a more productive work force are expected. Staw (1980) discussed a number of positive benefits to employers in terminating redundant employees. In the case of large layoffs, the employer saves the costs of wages and benefits. Terminations of marginally performing employees serve as a model to other employees by demonstrating that poor performance and/or flagrant violations of company rules will not be tolerated. In this sense, *not* terminating poor performers can be very costly to the organization. This is especially true in a unionized setting in which tolerance of poor performance and rule violations set precedents that may define new levels of accepted employee performance and behavior.

Although there are a number of positive consequences resulting from terminations and layoffs, employers also encounter a number of costs. Among these costs are severance pay, pensions, unemployment insurance, and others.

First, many employers provide severance pay ranging from only one or two weeks' pay for low-level, short-tenure employees to one or two years' salary for long-tenure executives. While severance pay is not legally required, it has been traditionally provided by many employers and is a part of many labor agreements.

Second, prior to passage of the Employment Retirement Income Security Act (ERISA) in 1974, many employers saved money by denying or substantially reducing pensions to laid-off employees, and in some cases, employees did not even receive their own contributions to a pension. ERISA protects employees covered by employer- or union-operated pensions in several ways. One way is through the vesting requirements of the Act; employees are guaranteed of receiving 100 percent of their pension benefits after some specified length of service. The length of service required depends upon the vesting formula chosen by the employer, but fifteen years is the maximum service required for full vesting of an employee's pension rights. ERISA also set up the Pension Benefit Guarantee Corporation, which protects pensions against employer bankruptcy or closings. All employers or unions with private pensions must pay a premium to insure their pension. Thus, while ERISA provides greater income protection for employees covered by a private pension plan, this act increased pension costs to the employer.

Additional negative consequences include unemployment insurance, community relations, and other factors. When employers lay off employees, this also has an adverse effect on their unemployment insurance rates, as discussed earlier. Large layoffs will likely create poor community relations for the employer, since this leads to loss of business for local merchants and other community problems. There is also some evidence that layoffs of only a part of an employer's work force may lead to unexpected problems, including low morale and voluntary turnover by other employees (Fry, 1973; Greenhalgh and Jick, 1979). Layoffs may also cause unions to make stronger job security and income protection demands. Finally, one of the most serious consequences of a layoff is to discover within several months that the layoffs of good employees were unnecessary and, in fact, replacements for many laid-off employees must be recruited. Permanent layoffs of good employees should always be a "last resort" human resource planning alternative when labor surpluses occur.

Although there are some positive consequences of terminations and layoffs for both employers and ex-employees, these forms of involuntary organizational exit are generally regarded in very negative terms. Many employers have recognized that involuntary organizational exit requires a specialized personnel function. This function is called "outplacement."

Outplacement

Outplacement has been defined by Carl Dreissnack (1978) as "the removal from (the) payroll of redundant or marginal personnel with minimum disruption and cost to the company and with maximum benefit to the individuals involved" (p. 24). This new function has grown from virtually nothing in the 1960s, when a few companies worked with terminated executives to find them a new job, to a service provided by approximately one-third of major employers in 1979 (Walker and Gutteridge, 1979).

Although most outplacement services and agencies are directed toward managerial and professional employees, some employers have used outplacement consultants for laid-off blue-collar employees. Whether the client is an executive or a punch-press operator, outplacement involves the same basic activities, including: (1) building terminees' self-confidence and self-esteem and preparing them to work hard at landing a new job, (2) helping terminees prepare resumes and/or write letters, (3) teaching terminees how to best handle job interviews, and (4) providing a counselor to supply support and aid in the job search process. In some cases, terminees are encouraged to explore abilities and interests which were not used in their previous jobs. Programs such as this have been successfully used at Sears, American Can, and Goodyear (Bailey, 1980).

The availability of an employer-funded outplacement service with a good record of helping terminees should be useful in reducing some of the negative consequences of involuntary exit for both employer and employee. There are substantial financial advantages for the employer using outplacement services. Goodyear, for example, estimated it could save $14.50 in unemployment costs for every $1.00 invested in the outplacement program (Bailey, 1980). Employers may also benefit indirectly from an outplacement service. For example, if managers perceive the consequences of termination as less harmful to employees, they may be more willing to terminate subordinates for poor performance. The availability of the outplacement service may also help to maintain morale and productivity until a plant is actually closed. Terminated employees also may experience less shock and stress of job loss when outplacement services are provided. The firm that worked with Goodyear and others emphasizes the positive side of outplacement by calling their program "Career Continuation."

Outplacement programs appear to be an excellent solution to many of the problems and costs associated with involuntary organizational exit. Future research, however, must judge the true worth of this innovation.

RETIREMENT

This section will discuss retirement as a form of organizational exit, retirement trends, and both employer and employee retirement-related problems and ways of handling these problems.

Retirement Revolution

Employees who avoid disabling accidents and illnesses, terminations, and layoffs typically leave their employer through retirement. Retirement does not fall neatly into either voluntary or involuntary exit since employees often have the option of retiring earlier than the employer's mandatory retirement age. While the traditional retirement age has been sixty-five, the mandatory retirement age for most persons employed in private industry became seventy with passage in 1978 of an amendment (the Mandatory Retirement Act) to the Age Discrimination in Employment Act. This amendment is only one part of what has been called a "retirement revolution."

There are three major factors in the retirement revolution. First is the passage of the Mandatory Retirement Act, as mentioned. A second factor is the changing demographics of the labor force. Basically, the average age of the American worker is increasing and the proportion of older workers in the labor force and in the population is increasing. As the "baby boom" of the 1940s and 1950s gave way to the "baby bust" of the 1960s and 1970s, the number of new entrants to the labor force has dropped and will continue to do so. Additionally, the average life span has gone from sixty-eight years in 1950 to over seventy-two years in 1975, and is projected to go over seventy-three by 2000 (*Business Week*, June 19, 1978). Sheppard and Rix (1977), authors of *The Graying of Working America*, said that by the second decade of the next century, Americans now in their early to mid-thirties will have to either continue to work or accept retirement incomes substantially below their preretirement earnings. As Sheppard and Rix implied, the third major factor leading to a retirement revolution is inflation. The real discretionary income for persons aged sixty-five and over has declined from nearly $2,150 in 1972 to under $2,000 in 1978 (*Business Week*, 1978). Since 1978, this situation has worsened rather than improved. In summary, it appears that there will be increasing numbers of older workers in the labor force who, unless inflation dramatically slows or retirement incomes increase, must work past traditional retirement age. Congress has already acted to allow longer working lives, and industry is likely to need older workers if the "baby bust" continues.

The retirement revolution is regarded as a revolution because it runs counter to nearly a century of work by unions, employers, and Congress to lower retirement ages. The success of these efforts is reflected in labor force participation rates for persons aged sixty to sixty-four, which indicates a decline of approximately 20 percent for men from 1955 to 1977. For women, the trend is reversed, showing a small increase in participation rate (*Business Week,* June 19, 1978). The increase for women perhaps reflects a response to the inflation rate, the impact of the women's liberation movement, and the not uncommon phenomena of marital problems when the male retires (O'Meara, 1977).

Retirement Problems: Employee Perspective

Retirement is associated with a number of diverse problems even for retirees in good health and in sound financial condition. Retirement itself is rated at 45 points, only slightly less than involuntary termination, on the Holmes and Rahe (1967) social readjustment or stress scale. There are, however, other stress-causing events often associated with retirement, such as change in financial status (38 points), change in living conditions (25 points), change in residence (20 points), and change in social activities (18 points). If retirement is closely related to illness or health problems of the retiree or a family member, this is as stressful as retirement itself. Research by Holmes and Rahe and others suggests that when people experience stress-causing events totaling 150 or more points, the odds of serious illness increase substantially. Although retirement may be a stressful event, other factors may increase or decrease the degree of stress.

The major problem for most retirees is financial (O'Meara, 1977). While almost all retirees have Social Security and some have private pensions, these are often inadequate. Under OASDHI, both employers and employees contribute money to Social Security (FICA) for Old Age benefits upon retirement. This "public pension," which was established in 1935 under the Social Security Act, is inadequate financial support for a retiree. In 1979, the maximum monthly benefit an individual could draw was less than $500. Ironically, a person with millions of dollars in stocks and bonds might draw the maximum benefits, while a retired person would lose fifty cents in benefits for every dollar earned over $4,500 (the 1979 earning maximum). Many retirees also have private pensions as a source of retirement income. Private pensions are most commonly a benefit provided by the employer along with employee contributions. Some labor unions administer pensions for their members, and individuals may set up their pension plans through Individual Retirement Accounts (IRA) or a Keogh Plan. Individual pension plans decreased when ERISA requirements caused some employers to drop their pension programs. Qualified pension plans offer the financial advantages to the employee of not having to pay taxes on either pension contributions or interest and earnings from the pension fund until retirement. Despite the tax advantages, few private pensions have provisions for adjustment of benefits based upon the cost of living. The result is that many retirees face major financial problems soon after retirement. Unfortunately, the

Mandatory Retirement Act has not changed the *financial* standard retirement age of sixty-five. Social Security, many pension plans, and insurance policies still assume that contributions end and pay out of benefits begins at age sixty-five. Financial needs of future retirees must be met through more flexible retirement funding that allows part-time employment and accommodates cost of living changes.

A second major problem faced by retirees is health. While financial need and enjoyment of work lead many would-be retirees to continue working, poor health is a major cause of early retirement. One study of over 2,000 men and women found poor health to be a major factor leading to early retirement (Hall and Johnson, 1980). Poor health adds to existing financial problems by reducing ability to work and adding medical expenses. Thus, it would appear that health maintenance programs are an excellent investment for individuals, employers, and the economy.

Retirees also face many other problems. For example, they may also incur housing problems in moving to a smaller home or apartment in either a new community or the same one. Legal problems are also common as property is often sold, wills changed or made, and the tax status is changed. Retirees, especially younger ones in good health, may experience problems in beginning a second career. Loss of purpose in life, failing health, alcoholism, and marital problems are also common among retirees (O'Meara, 1977).

Retirement Problems: Employers' Perspective

For many decades, both employers' and employees' attitudes toward retirement were based upon three assumptions: (1) that work was physically demanding and gradually "wore people out"; (2) that there would always be an adequate supply of new, strong employees; and (3) that people would prefer not to work if they had a choice. Today, relatively few jobs are physically demanding, shortages of qualified employees are already occurring, and there are many people who prefer work to retirement. Unfortunately, many company policies still reflect the old assumptions despite the fact that few top-level managers accept the assumptions for their own jobs.

Specific retirement issues that must be addressed by employers include: (1) how to form a retirement policy that makes optimal use of human resources and is practical to administer, (2) how retirees should be identified, (3) how the company should aid pre-retirees, and (4) how retirement program costs can be controlled.

Retirement policies and identifying retirees.   Prior to the Mandatory Retirement Act, most employers had mandatory retirement ages of sixty-five years. Exceptions to this general pattern were typically to allow executive or professional level employees to work until sixty-eight years old, or to require earlier mandatory retirement for jobs involving substantial risks to public safety such as airline pilots. Some unions, including the United Auto Workers, United Steel Workers, and Teamsters, have negotiated pensions that permit an employee to retire after thirty years of service or less in some cases. Unfortunately, the Mandatory Retirement Act did not eliminate the discriminatory practice of retiring people based upon their age rather than their level of job performance. It merely provided an extra five years of nondiscrimination based upon age.

Some employers, such as Macy's in New York, Banker's Life and Casualty, Polaroid, and U.S. Steel, have had flexible retirement ages for at least some of their employees for some time (Sonnenfeld, 1978). The Mandatory Retirement Act has forced employers to either allow employees to work until they are seventy years old *or* document substandard performance in order to justify earlier mandatory retirement. Additionally, terminations, layoffs, denial of transfers, promotions, training opportunities, or other personnel changes to anyone in the forty- to seventy-year-old range is done at the risk of an age discrimination suit. As a larger proportion of the labor force approaches their mid- and late-sixties, the impact of the Mandatory Retirement Act will force employers to make better performance appraisals of older employees. This means that retirement policies must become more flexible and dependent upon valid assessment of employee job performance and health.

The administration of flexible retirement policies has many problems, including managerial stereotypes of older people, and performance appraisal systems that are often biased, unreliable, and invalid. A 1977 survey of *Harvard Business Review* readers showed that older workers were perceived as "rigid" and "resistant to change," and that older workers should be transferred rather than retrained, and were less likely to be promoted (Rosen and Jerdee, 1977). There is, however, little evidence of performance deterioration with age. The few problems associated with older workers are slower reaction times, longer time to make decisions among managers, and increased probability of chronic illness. The experience of companies such as Polaroid, Banker's Life, U.S. Steel, and Macy's, which have flexible retirement policies, is that performance and attendance of older employees is excellent (Sonnenfeld, 1977). Thus, it appears that flexible retirement policies must overcome managerial biases, and will require improved performance appraisal methods to identify older employees who need training or those who should retire.

Aiding Pre-Retirees and Controlling Retirement Costs.   The substantial problems and stress encountered by retirees, discussed earlier, may be reduced by employer-sponsored programs. Two recent surveys document retirement program activities and changes.

An ASPA-BNA survey of 267 employers found that over one-third have pre-retirement counseling programs, most of which include the spouse. The majority of these programs cover social security, company pensions, and other benefits or services provided by the employer after retirement (BNA, 1980). Some employers, for example, pay for membership in one of several retirement organizations, such as the American Association of Retired Persons (AARP) or Action for Independent Maturity (AIM), which is a division of AARP. AARP is an organization with over 12 million members and over 3,000 local chapters. It is for persons fifty-five years of age or older. Its activities include a bi-monthly magazine, news bulletins and guides, lobbying in Congress, health insurance, and a pharmacy service. AIM accepts slightly younger members, fifty years old, and emphasizes training and counseling programs. The ASPA-BNA survey also found that only 15 percent of respondents have "tapering off" programs whereby employees may work less as they approach retirement. Over half do have arrangements to retain employees as consultants or recall them for temporary work (BNA, 1980).

A 1979 American Management Association survey of 225 firms found that approximately one-third are conducting pre-retirement workshops and counseling programs, and another one-quarter are planning such services (Walker and Gutteridge, 1979). It would appear that some retirees are receiving help that should ease their transition from work to retirement. As more people reach retirement age and there is an inadequate supply of qualified new employees to replace them, it is likely that more employers will use "tapering off" programs. Employers could, for example, use a pool of near or recent retirees to cover absent or vacationing regular employees, or employees who did not want overtime work, rather than either remaining overstaffed or hiring temporary employees.

Employers today have a number of unique possibilities for reducing their retirement costs at a time when those costs have been rapidly increasing. First, the Mandatory Retirement Act makes it possible to retain willing and able employees longer. This could reduce retirement costs if: (1) life expectancy does not significantly increase, (2) pensions are revised so that employees continue to make contributions until actual retirement, and (3) a substantial proportion of employees choose to work beyond the traditional retirement age. Actual retirement-related cost savings are very complex, since costs of some benefits such as life insurance, disability benefits, and health care, increase as employees grow older. (See a 1979 article by Yaffe for a discussion of the effect on benefits of later retirement.)

There are, of course, other avenues for reducing pension and other retirement costs. For example, expert financial management of pension funds, a good medical care program that diagnoses and prevents health problems, safe and healthy working conditions, challenging and stimulating jobs, and excellent pre-retirement counseling can all lead to lower retirement costs. Retirement cost savings may also be realized by the use of "tapering off" programs, which allow employees to continue working part-time while their pension supplements their income. Such "tapering off" arrangements may not only reduce retirement-related costs, but may result in reducing costs associated with hiring new or temporary employees. Two or three retirees might share a job that would otherwise require hiring and training a new employee. Such an approach would not only reduce employer retirement costs, but it would help meet the forecast labor shortages of the next century. Finally, for "tapering off" or later retirement programs to work, work itself must change. Today, it is primarily managerial and professional employees who work beyond age sixty-five, while autoworkers, steel workers and other lower-level blue- and white-collar employees eagerly retire. When work seems as satisfying as, if not more satisfying than, leisure, retirement will be for only the ill and disabled.

SUMMARY AND CONCLUSIONS

This chapter has discussed and examined the implications of several types of organizational exit for both employers and employees. Generally, all types of organizational exit, except injuries, illness, and death, may have both positive and negative benefits for the employer and the employee. In this sense, the various forms of organizational exit are indicators of the relative effectiveness of the employer's personnel/human resources policies and programs. Organizations may function more efficiently and profitably if employers can achieve greater predictability and control of organizational exit.

This chapter has suggested that temporary, involuntary exits such as tardiness, absences, and short-term illnesses are the most difficult for employers to predict and control. Voluntary organizational exit is substantially related to employee commitment to the organization. Employers have, in large part, the ability to predict and control employee commitment via the many personnel and human resource policies affecting pay, promotional opportunities, nature of jobs, quality of supervision, working conditions, and so on. Of course, some voluntary turnover is both inevitable and beneficial for both employer and employee. Some of the greatest losses to employers, employees, and society occur in involuntary, permanent exit such as accidental death, disability or illness, mandatory retirement of productive employees, or termination of employees whose knowledge and/or skills are outdated.

The causes of organizational exit are many and often unique to specific industries and employers. For this reason, future research should begin by determining the proportion of organizational exits attributed to various causes. The next step would be to determine the costs, both to employers and employees, of various forms of exit. Finally, personnel and human resource programs must be directed toward predicting and controlling the most costly sources of organizational exit.

Discussion Questions

1. How might the causes of employee turnover and absenteeism differ between managerial and blue-collar workers? How widespread do you feel these problems may be?

2. What do you consider the most important things a manager can do to reduce turnover? Absenteeism?

3. Discuss the consequences—both negative and positive—of high turnover rates both for the individuals involved and for organizations.

4. What "price" should be paid to protect workers from harmful working conditions? In 1979, the U.S. Navy decided against removing all asbestos materials from older ships since removal would cost $2 billion. How should such cost-benefit decisions be made? How should managers decide how much to spend for worker protection versus compensating sick or injured workers?

5. With passage of the amendment to the Age Discrimination in Employment Act, most employees have the option to work until the age of seventy. While having this option is desirable, discuss the effects on older employees of a continued high inflation rate. Do employees have a right to leisure after years of work? How can adequate retirement income be provided?

PART EIGHT

OVERVIEW

The field of personnel management, with its various related components and activities, has been the focus of the foregoing sixteen chapters. The book began with some perspectives on the field, the practice of the personnel function in organizations, primarily in regard to the past and present, and personal research. An attempt was made to reconceptualize the field in light of recent trends. From that point on, a review and examination of the many different activities of the personnel function and selected issues for practice, theory-building, and research were presented. It seems important now to return to some broad perspectives on the field and speculate about the future.

What changes in the environment will impact on the field in the 1980s? How will the responsibilities and challenges of these changes be met? Will they alter or drastically shift the current philosophy regarding the employment relationship? Will the essentially positive and improving image and status of the personnel function and practitioners continue? If so, how? In Chapter 17, Strauss addresses these and other matters.

CHAPTER SEVENTEEN

PERSONNEL MANAGEMENT: PROSPECT FOR THE EIGHTIES

George Strauss

George Strauss is Professor of Business Administration and Associate Director of the Institute of Industrial Relations at the University of California, Berkeley. He received his Ph.D. from the Massachusetts Institute of Technology. Professor Strauss has served also as Associate Dean and Acting Dean of the School of Business Administration at Berkeley, as Managing Editor of the journal, *Industrial Relations,* and as Chairman of the Personnel Board, City of Berkeley. He is also the American editor of the *International Yearbook of Organizational Democracy.* He is the author and coauthor of six books and numerous articles dealing with industrial relations, organizational behavior, and personnel management.

This final chapter discusses the major personnel issues likely to concern organizations during the 1980s. A number of these were examined in earlier chapters, but this chapter will consider them in their broader social, political, and legal context.

In recent years, the personnel function has been affected by numerous developments. To name only a few: the growing movement for individual job rights and personal privacy; the minority and womens' rights movements; the discovery of long-range occupational health hazards and resultant federal regulations; an increasing concern for job security; and above all, the baby-boom generation, large in numbers and generally strong in its insistance on creative jobs and the freedom to determine *how* and *when* to work.

Together, these developments are greatly changing the personnel function. At one time its charge was simple: to provide the organization with enough trained workers to get the job done. The main constraints were economic—chiefly the labor market—and psychological—chiefly individual skills and motivation. How this personnel function was performed was definitely not the public's business as long as a few legal restrictions were observed. The only significant external interfering institution was the union.

Today, the personnel function most certainly is public business and is subject to elaborate regulation. As far as personnel is concerned, the organization is no longer simply a profit maximizer, operating in an economic environment. The social and political constraints are ever-growing.

All this is occurring at a time when American industry is subject to serious economic stress—inflation, declining productivity, and increasing foreign competition. Industry is being asked to do more and has less ability to respond. Given this dilemma, the 1980s will not be easy for personnel people.

This chapter attempts to deal with these problems. In accordance with the model suggested in Chapter 1, it begins with a forecast of the economic, legal, and social environment likely to impinge on personnel policies during the 1980s. With this introduction it then considers the basic issues likely to stir controversy in this environment. Finally, it assesses what all this means to the personnel function.

THE CHANGING PERSONNEL ENVIRONMENTS

This section ventures into the hazardous realm of forecasting, in an attempt to predict changes in six key organizational environments: economic, technological, demographic, legal, attitudinal, and union.

The Economic Environment

Turbulent as the 1950s and 1960s seemed at the time, economically they can be viewed as the "good old days." In only four years out of twenty during that period did consumer prices rise more than 3 percent. Similarly, there was an almost continuous increase in the standard of living, with money wages going up much faster than prices. Compared with this, the 1980s look bleak. Consider the following probabilities:

Not even the most optimistic economist expects inflation to disappear. At best it will moderate.

The energy and resource shortage will continue and intensify. The country may adjust to an "era of limits," but the adjustment will not be painless.

Foreign competition will continue to hit technologically mature industries such as textiles, steel, and autos (where—even ignoring differences in labor costs—the output per laborhour is lower than that of some major competitors). With regard to these industries, this country faces a difficult choice (Drucker, 1980). It can go the British route: protect and subsidize the traditional "sunset" industries in an effort to restore them to health or at least to maintain their employment (as done with Chrysler). Or it can go the route that many Japanese economists urge for their country: move as rapidly as possible into technologically more complex "sunrise" industries (such as information processing, bio-engineering, and computer-controlled manufacturing), which permit the use of comparative advantage in education. Either route is costly and risk prone. Taking the first may throw good money after bad. The

second requires us to accept substantial unemployment as mature industries are
run down.

A similar dilemma is faced with regards to the many "snowbelt" areas suffering
from high heating costs and technologically obsolete factories. Does the nation
passively sit by while jobs and population move south, or does it try to salvage
the enormous investment in the infrastructure of such dying communities as
Cleveland and Buffalo?

Other drains on our economy will occur as industry seeks to comply with
environmental and safety standards.

Offsetting these losses will be likely gains in productivity as the labor force grows
older and more sophisticated. On balance, our material standard of living will grow
much more slowly than it did in the past (already annual gains in productivity have fallen from 4.1 percent in 1957–1967 to 2.4 percent in 1973–1978). As an offset, our
environment should improve as we breathe purer air and work in safer places.

Perhaps the most important change may be the demise of our expectation of constant growth. We may be entering what Lester Thurow (1980) has called a "Zero-Sum
Society" in which every gain for one group means a loss for another. Tradeoffs will become increasingly necessary. Just as automotive engineers are finding that greater safety,
better mileage, and reduced polution emissions are hard to obtain simultaneously, so
society may learn that although safe environments, affirmative action, and increased
productivity are good things, to some extent getting one interferes with getting the
others.

On the other hand, there are some small grounds for optimism with regard to employment. The flow of new entrants into the labor force should decline, thus keeping
labor supply in check. The annual rate of labor force increase—2.3 percent during the
1970s—should drop to 1.1 percent during the 1980s, a figure more in line with the
1960s. In other words, the economy will have to grow only half as fast to maintain employment. Furthermore, the baby-boom generation, which caused much of the labor
force increase during the 1970s, is marrying late. The rate of family formation will continue to be high, thus generating demand for housing and furniture. Finally, adjustments to the energy shortage (e.g., synthetic fuel development) and foreign competition should create some jobs to counterbalance those which are lost. In the end, the
unemployment rate may depend on such uncertainties as fiscal policy and defense budgets.

Even if overall unemployment rates return to the pre-1970 levels of under 5 percent, conditions in northern manufacturing cities will be much worse, contributing to a
demand for job security at the very time it is in management's (and probably the economy's) interest to encourage mobility. The solution may be to persuade people to accept
job mobility through a combination of income guarantees and selective incentives—solutions the Reagan administration is unlikely to provide.

Even if unemployment slackens, social tensions are likely to be high, making life
harder for the personnel department. Not only will collective bargaining be complicated
when there are no gains to distribute, but the level of social tolerance overall may be
low. As Wall Street financier Felix Royhatan put it, "The disparities in our society, be-

tween classes and races, between sunbelt and frostbelt, are deep and getting deeper''
(*Economist,* September 19, 1981, p. 32), and the Reagan policy of reducing benefits for
the poor and taxes for the rich may do much to accentuate this. Under these circumstances, the personnel department's role, as a mediator between the organization and
the environment and among various internal pressure groups, will be much more difficult.

The Technological Environment

According to the U.S. Bureau of Labor Statistics (1979), the 1980s should see a continuation of the industrial shifts occurring during the 1970s. Employment in manufacturing should continue to drop, from 25 percent of the civilian employment in 1968 to
under 20 percent in 1990. Already there are more people selling goods (in wholesale and
retail trades) than making them, and this trend should continue. But it is in the service
industries that the biggest gain in employment should occur, especially as women work
rather than perform services at home.

On the other hand, the data on occupational distribution is surprising and somewhat upsetting. One of the great social safety valves for the last century has been the
upgrading of occupational distribution. First, there was the shift out of agricultural employment into manufacturing, and more recently out of manufacturing into various service occupations. The demand for managers and professionals grew by leaps and
bounds, and the fact that the job structure was being continually upgraded meant that
the majority of people in each generation held better jobs than their parents.

The data in Table 17–1 raise the question whether this process may have slowed
down. Note how the proportion of professional and technical employees in the labor
force grew more rapidly from 1960 to 1970 than from 1970 to 1979 and is expected to
grow still less rapidly until 1990. Employment of managers and administrators held constant from 1960 to 1976, climbed a bit to 1979, but is projected to decline. If the 1990

TABLE 17–1
Experienced Labor Force in Selected Years and Occupations, 1930–1979 and Projected 1990
Requirement

| | *Percent distribution* | | | | | | |
	1930	*1960*	*1970*	*1976*	*1979*	*1978*[a]	*1990*[ab]
Professional and technical	6.8	10.8	13.8	14.6	15.1	15.9	16.5
Managers and administrators	7.4	10.2	10.2	10.2	10.5	9.0	8.8

Sources: 1930: U.S. Bureau of the Census, *Historical Statistics of the United States,* 1960, 1970, 1976 and
1979: U.S. Bureau of Labor Statistics, *Handbook of Labor Statistics, 1980;* 1978 and 1990: Max Carey, ''Occupational Employment Growth Through 1990,'' *Monthly Labor Review* 104, no. 2 (August 1981): 45.

[a]Data for 1978 and 1990 not comparable with data for previous years.

[b]''High-trend I,'' the middle of three projections.

projections prove accurate, the demand for highly educated workers may have almost peaked, a quite disturbing prospect.

When one moves away from statistical projections, guessing becomes more hazardous. Two common predictions during the early 1960s were that (1) automation would eliminate most unskilled and semi-skilled work, and (2) computerization would lead to a radical reorganization of management, especially middle management (Leavitt and Whisler, 1958; Simon, 1960). Both proved premature if not exaggerated. At least as measured by productivity figures, technological change slowed down during the 1970s, while the changes introduced by computers occurred less rapidly than expected.

Possibly in the 1980s the computer's long-delayed impact will finally be felt at both blue-collar and managerial levels. Auto plants are now utilizing microcomputers to make robotization of manufacturing processes possible. Production workers will no longer have to work on each car as it moves down the assembly line. Instead, their job will be to monitor and repair equipment. In terms of its impact on the individual worker, the new technology will be closer to what Woodward (1965) called "process" than "batch"; nevertheless, robots can be programmed to make each successive item in a different way, so that each item is, in effect, custom-made. Thus, by contrast with the assembly line, which reduced manufacturing flexibility, robotization increases it.

The day will soon be here when it will be common for managers at all levels (including personnel managers) to have desk model microprocessors tied into main information sources. It may take some time for managers to become comfortable in using these; however, the widespread availability of information processing capability should make it *possible* to reverse the computer's original tendency toward organizational centralization. It should permit greater flexibility and decentralization in organizations that want this.

Thus, computerization should accelerate the spread of new organizational forms. Aside from this, there are other developments tending to make the organizational environment of the 1980s different from that of the 1960s. The big breakthroughs in electronics, information processing, and bio-engineering are occurring in small firms. Indeed, throughout the Western world small firms are creating much more new employment than are the industrial mammoths. Further, the mammoths themselves are changing. On the one hand, they buy up small firms as these show themselves successful. On the other hand, they are far more ready to live off low-profit or incompatible activities. Some of these activities are killed off altogether. Others are taken over by smaller operators. Thus, a product may be introduced by a small firm, carried through maturity by a larger one, and nursed through senility by a small firm once again. To the extent that an individual employee remains attached to a specific product, he or she should expect a variety of employers with a variety of personnel policies.

The Demographic Environment

By contrast with economic and technological forecasts, those regarding the labor force are relatively easy to make since, barring immigrants and a few visitors from outer space, all the people constituting the labor force of the 1980s are already with us. The critical issues relate to the post-war baby cohort, older workers, the female revolution, minority participation, and education.

The Post-War Baby Cohort.   The number of children born in the United States jumped from 2.9 million in 1945 to 3.8 million in 1947, climbed steadily to a peak of 4.3 million in 1957, after which it slowly dropped to a low of 3.1 million in 1975. (Since then, as the baby-boom generation began reproducing itself, there has been a renewed rise; however, the second baby-boom generation will not hit the labor market until after 1990.)

Each year the massive post-war cohort has its impact as it passes through the various stages of life. This phenomenon (which has been called the "watermelon passing through the boa constrictor") has occurred through much of the world, even China. The initial baby bulge led to overcrowded schools, then as the post-war babies became teen-agers, it contributed to college student riots, high teenage unemployment and crime, and (as untrained people entered the labor force) lowered productivity.

The population aged eighteen to twenty-four will rise from 15 million in 1956 to a peak of 29 million in 1983, and then should drop again to 25.2 million by 1990 (U.S. Bureau of Labor Statistics, 1979). In 1977, sixteen- to twenty-four-year-olds constituted over 24 percent of the labor force; by 1990, this figure may fall to 18 percent. Thus, during the 1980s there should be fewer teenagers available for entry level jobs. Youth unemployment (and possibly even total unemployment) may drop, and there will be less need to provide entry-level training. Youths entering the labor force in 1990 should have at least relatively better prospects than did their much older brothers and sisters ten or fifteen years earlier. On the other hand, there will be fewer young people willing to do dirty, manual jobs (Weber, 1979).

Meanwhile, the star-crossed post-war generation is moving into its thirties. By 1981, the 1947 baby was thirty-four years old and in many organizations he or she was in the lower ranks of management. Those born in the early years of the bulge were rather lucky, since the age groups before them were rather small and they filled a vacuum. The late-comers—those born from 1955 to 1960, especially—will have a harder time since the best jobs are already filled. Indeed, they will be up against stiff competition all their lives; some will find their promotions blocked until they are almost ready to retire. Further, the scramble for good jobs will be especially nasty because this extra-large cohort is much better educated than its predecessors and it includes, for the first time, large numbers of women and minority group members who also aspire to management positions.

Older Workers.   While the middle-aged group expands, the older labor force should contract. True, compulsory retirement before age seventy is no longer legal, but the new law has not substantially increased the number of older workers. As pensions and social security have become more liberal, the trend among both men and women has been to retire well before the previous legal age of sixty-five. At G.M. the average blue- and white-collar worker retires at fifty-six (Weber, 1979). The labor force participation of men aged fifty-five to sixty-four dropped from 87 percent in 1960 to 74 percent in 1978 and may fall as low as 59 percent in 1990 (U.S. Bureau of Labor Statistics,

1979). Female participation rates are even lower. On the other hand, continued infla-tion could affect this pattern, as more people worry about whether their pensions will prove adequate; many retirees are seeking part-time work.

One advantage of the older cohort's rapid retirement from full-time employment is that it should improve the promotional opportunities of those born immediately after World War II, but it will do little for the children born in the late 1950s and 1960s.

Education.   The growth in professional and managerial work has been matched by a skyrocketing increase in college enrollment. There were 3.6 million college students in 1960; by 1977 there were 11.5 million. Increased education has occurred not only at the college level: the average blue-collar worker had 9.0 years of education in 1948; today, he or she has 12.2 years.

But, in recent years, the number of highly educated workers grew faster than the jobs requiring such education, particularly since women now seek to use their education at work. As a consequence, there is today a surplus of well-educated people. One result is that many college graduates settle for jobs for which high school was traditionally enough. The difference in pay between the secondary school and college graduate has been declining. All this has contributed to making education less attractive. There has been a slight but real drop in the percentage of men who finish secondary school and a similar decline in those who receive college and university degrees. This decline has been largely balanced, so far, by a continued increase in female education. Further, since the BA—any old BA—is not worth much, there has been a growing demand for profes-sional degrees that prepare for specific jobs, as shown by the explosive development of MBA programs.

In the 1980s, this should change again. The declining number of young labor force entrants and the leveling out of their educational attainments should reduce the supply of educated youth. Meanwhile, the demand for educated workers will continue to grow, if more slowly than in the past. The economic return to education should rise once more.

The Female Revolution.   The post-war period has seen a revolution in the role of women, both on the job and in society generally. From 1947 to 1980, the number of males in the labor force went up by 37 percent, females by 151 percent—over four times as fast. Each year during the 1970s, a million new women entered the labor force, capped by a record-breaking influx of 1.9 million in 1978. By 1980, half of all adult women worked, a figure up from 33 percent in 1948. Predictions for 1990 range from a high of 60 percent to a low of 54 percent; by that time women may constitute 46 percent of the labor force. However, the *growth* in female participation may slacken; such par-ticipation is not likely to exceed that of males. Further, many women now approaching thirty may drop out of the labor market (at least partially) to have babies before it is too late. (Interestingly, this increase in female participation is not a worldwide phenome-non. It is happening in English-speaking countries and Sweden, but female participa-tion rates are declining in Italy, Germany, and Japan, and holding steady in France (U.S. Department of Commerce, 1977).)

The increase in employment in the United States occurred first among women aged thirty-five to sixty-four, then among those with children aged six to seventeen, and now it has extended to those with children under six, of whom 42 percent work. Smaller families and societal acceptance of working mothers mean that women intending to have children can still have almost the same working life as their male counterparts. Currently, in well over half of all U.S. marriages, both husband and wife work, at least part time. Half of U.S. children have working mothers.

The combined impact of the women's liberation movement and the civil rights laws has led to much progress. There are now female carpenters, plumbers, heavy equipment operators, locomotive engineers, telephone installers, and line repairmen. There are even 5,000 female miners. Still, the vast majority of women work in low-paying, low-skilled jobs with little hope for advancement.

Ever since the war, women have been graduated from high school in equal numbers to men. Now they earn almost as many bachelor's degrees and they have entered graduate work and professional work in great strength. Ten years ago, at Berkeley, only 4 percent of Business School master's level students were women; today the figure is over one-third. There has been a substantial increase in the number of female managers and professionals. In some banks, half the junior level managers are women, up from very low figures a few years ago—and these women are rising rapidly in the ranks.

The revolution has occurred amazingly, rapidly, and successfully. Ten years ago this writer predicted that it would be much easier to eliminate discrimination against minorities than against women. In the first place, I argued, a job was less important for married women than it was for minorities; second, women's family obligations were likely to conflict with their loyalties to their jobs; and finally, sexual attractions were bound to complicate on-the-job relations. Ten years' experience suggests that all three problems had been badly overestimated. The role of women changed faster than I had expected.

To make this change possible, many other changes had to occur—and not merely the addition of a second set of toilets in previously all-male domains, or the elimination of the old convention that if there is a woman on a committee she will automatically serve as secretary and make the coffee. Above all, it meant that many women, particularly middle-class women, had to decide for themselves that if men could combine marriage and a career, they could too—and that they were willing to make the sacrifices necessary to achieve this.

But the victory was not easy, and it is far, far from complete. Despite the fact that a few favored women have broken their way into managerial and professional jobs, women's wages are, on the average, still but 60 percent as much as men's. Part of the gap may be explained by differences in such factors as age, experience, education, and training (differences themselves, in part, explained by discrimination) and part by the fact that women are still concentrated in the so-called "girl ghettos," largely female (and relatively low-paid) jobs such as typist, salesclerk, and nurse. Further, female unemployment rates run 50 percent higher than those of males.

Minorities.   Minority emplo ment progress has been less dramatic than that of women. True, from 1959 to 19,8, nonwhite employment in sales occupations more than tripled, while that among professionals, managers, and clericals quadrupled. In 1959, only 14 percent of minority employees had white-collar jobs; by 1978, this figure had increased to 36 percent. Further, among young college graduates, the difference in earnings between the races had practically disappeared, and the same held true for young dual-career families.

Nevertheless, although some minority groups did well, black unemployment figures stubbornly remain twice as high as those of whites. The average black earns only 80 percent as much as the average white, and the average black family has an income only 60 percent as great. The differences in individual earnings in part reflect the fact that black employees tend to be relatively young and female; the differences in family incomes reflect these differences and also the relatively high proportion of black families without a husband present.

Equal employment policies have benefited many minorities, but a tragically large number remain unemployed or not even looking for work. One glimmer of hope: the coming shortage of white teenagers willing to take unskilled jobs may provide openings for minorities (particularly illegal immigrants) who now have no jobs at all. Indeed, the growing number of immigrants, both legal and illegal, should be a subject of increasing concern.

The Legal Environment

One of the major developments of the last twenty years has been the growing social and legal pressures on management. The days when free enterprise meant that managers could use their property as they wished are long gone. Public and governmental relations are getting to be as important to the organization as are finance and marketing. Some chief executives are spending two or three days a week on external affairs.

Nowhere has this escalating public concern with business behavior been shown as dramatically as in the personnel area. The liberal view at the turn of the century was that the economy should regulate itself. At one time, even the American Federation of Labor was opposed to unemployment insurance. Early laws protecting safety and outlawing child labor were declared unconstitutional.

Very gradually this view changed. Workman's compensation was introduced in some states about 1915, as were weak factory inspection laws. The Railway Labor Act, the first federal law regulating personnel administration, was passed in 1926; the National Labor Relations (Wagner) and Social Security Act in 1935; and the Fair Labor Standards Act in 1938. Then, for twenty-five years, the only new major federal laws regulating labor were the Taft-Hartley (1947) and Landrum-Griffin Acts (1959). On balance, these two laws reduced the Wagner Act's restrictions on management.

Beginning with World War II, there was increasing agitation for the elimination of discrimination against minorities. The federal government took some weak steps during the war and later some states passed laws. But the real breakthrough occurred with the passage of the Civil Rights Act of 1964. Although this outlawed discrimination against both minorities and women, the prohibition regarding women was introduced by a southern congressman almost as a joke, in hopes of defeating the bill.

Enforcement of the law regarding minorities started slowly (the law at first was rather weak), and the female issue was not taken seriously until 1970. Once the full effect of this law was felt, the aged, the handicapped, and Viet Nam veterans asked for and received similar protections.

Then, evidence as to the insidious long-term effects of certain workplace substances (especially asbestos) on employee health, and other evidence as to the mismanagement of pension funds, led to two more laws: the Occupational Safety and Health Act (OSHA) and the Employment Retirement Income Security Act (ERISA). Each provides for elaborate federal regulations of areas that were once lightly regulated, if at all, by the states.

Wages were placed under government controls during World War II and again during the Korean War. Then, in 1971–1973, came peace-time wage controls. In late 1978, President Carter introduced a "voluntary" wage-price program which was, in effect, compulsory for governmental contractors. Although wage-price controls quickly become unpopular after they are introduced, public memory is short. Once inflation mounts again, clamor to reintroduce them will grow. Thus, it is a safe bet that the 1980s will see a variety of Washington wage-control efforts.

All these new regulations came at a time when organizations were being restricted in other areas as well. Changes in the laws regarding product liability held companies to tighter standards of accountability. A Consumer Products Safety Commission began to regulate product safety. Environmental restrictions proliferated, especially regarding possible pollution of air, land, or water.

Together, these restrictions reflected a growing reliance on laws and adversary procedures as a means of resolving social problems, the seeming success of minorities in righting their wrongs, which led other groups to seek similar remedies, and a loss of faith in unions as protectors of workers' interests. One thing was clear: the American public no longer trusted organizational personnel policies. Not only were new laws passed, but there were strong pressure groups to police their enforcement. What organizations did was no longer their own private business.

The Reagan administration, of course, is trying to dismantle twenty years of regulatory mechanisms. As of this writing, it is far from clear how successful it will be. Over the long run, the trend toward greater legal regulation is more likely to be slowed than reversed. Despite Reagan, it is unlikely we will return to the 1920s.

The impact of government regulations will be discussed at greater length. Together, they have added to company costs, made personnel policies more legalistic, and greatly increased the importance of the personnel function.

Employee Values and Expectations

A major recent debate among personnel specialists has concerned work attitudes. Is there a revolt against work? Are people less willing to work hard? Is there a growing mismatch between what people demand from their jobs and what available jobs provide? Has job satisfaction dropped? Are there substantial groups of workers who are "turned off" of work altogether? Obviously, these issues are directly relevant to motivation, job design, and compensation. They constitute a key element of the social environment discussed in Chapter 1.

A good case can be made that work attitudes *should* have changed. Younger employees today are better educated, and they presumably have more skills and stronger expectations that they will be called upon to use. Women and minority groups are less willing to accept the "crumby" jobs that fell their way in the past. The baby-boom generation has presumably been raised according to permissive standards and therefore learned to reject the conventional values of authority and hard work for its own sake. Finally, despite recent setbacks, the standard of living and economic security of the average worker has risen considerably since the 1930s. Both economic and psychological theory predict that under such circumstances workers should give greater weight to nonpecuniary benefits. And since many families now consist of two breadwinners, holding a job may be less vital than it once was.

Daniel Yankelovich (1980) categorized American employees by job attitude. For 56 percent (mostly older workers), the old incentives still work. But for 44 percent (mostly younger workers), money and job security no longer motivate. Of these, one group (27 percent) is "hedonistic, live-for-today, turned-off, sensation seeking" (p. 71). The other group (17 percent), mostly young managers, is hungry for "responsibility, challenge, autonomy, informality," but frustrated because these are lacking on their jobs.

Certainly there is anecdotal evidence that blue-collar workers resist overtime, while white-collar and managerial employees are less willing to accept out-of-town transfers, to permit the organization to interfere with their personal lives, or to be pegged into an "Organization Man" mold. Both groups are showing less organizational loyalty; both are more anxious to do their own thing.

Have pecuniary incentives lost their motivating power, compared with nonpecuniary incentives, such as challenge? Measurement is difficult here and there are serious methodological and theoretical issues regarding the relationship between intrinsic and extrinsic rewards (Staw, 1976; Salancik and Pfeffer, 1977). According to some research, white- and blue-collar workers have quite different values. For example, a Michigan study (Quinn, Staines, and McCullough, 1974) found blue-collar workers placing pay first among factors "very important" to them, with interesting work coming fifth; by contrast, among white-collar workers pay came tenth and interesting work first. Despite such studies, there is little evidence that pay has lost its importance, particularly as inflation erodes real wages.

If job attitudes are massively shifting, this should show up on job satisfaction scales, yet the evidence is ambiguous. Table 17–2 presents data from the last three University of Michigan Quality of Employment Surveys. The first question taps global ("facet-free") attitudes toward the job as a whole. It should be noted that the proportion who are at least "somewhat satisfied" actually increased from 85 percent in 1969 to 89 percent in 1977. On the other hand, every one of the "facet-specific" items in the second question (only eight of which are presented) asked over the eight-year period declined, some quite substantially.

Other studies give similar results (Andrisani et al., 1977; Smith, Roberts, and Hulin, 1976). The vast majority of American employees report being satisfied with their jobs overall, but more subtle measures than the global question generally indicate significant declines occurring in most age and occupational groupings.

A conservative conclusion is that there is no immediate prospect of a revolt against work. People adjust to unsatisfactory work—though at the cost of frustration and reduced motivation—through lowering their expectations and turning their interests elsewhere (Strauss, 1974). On the other hand, there is evidence of declining satisfaction, re-

TABLE 17–2

Question: All in all, how satisfied would you say you are with your job?

Response Category	Percent Responding:		
	1969	1973	1977
Very satisfied	46	52	47
Somewhat satisfied	39	38	42
Not too satisfied	11	8	9
Not at all satisfied	3	2	3

Question: "How true . . . is this of your job?"

	Percent Answering "Very True"		
	1969	1973	1977
The pay is good.	40	41	27
The job security is good.	55	53	42
My fringe benefits are good.	42	44	33
The hours are good.	5⁻	51	43
The work is interesting.	63	61	53
I am given a chance to do the things I can do best.	45	41	31
I am not asked to do excessive amounts of work.	43	34	28
My supervisor is very concerned about the welfare of those under (him/her).	45	41	34

Source: R. P. Quinn, and G. L. Staines. *Quality of Employment Survey.* Ann Arbor: Institute of Social Research, University of Michigan, 1978.

duced organizational loyalty, and of growing interest in determining the conditions of one's work—for greater individual freedom, dignity, and opportunities for personal fulfillment and self-development. These new priorities, probably stronger among white-collar than blue-collar workers, are reflected in demands for flextime, privacy and freedom to determine the age at which one retires, as well as in a somewhat muted interest in job enrichment.

The Union Environment

Will workers look to unions as a means of obtaining greater freedom and control over the conditions under which they work? At the moment, this seems somewhat unlikely. Recent years have seen a steady decline in union power. From a peak of over 35 percent of nonagricultural employees after the war, union membership has dropped to about 23 percent. True, the number of members has grown, but not as fast as the labor force, and even total membership has remained stabilized at roughly 20 million since 1974 (plus about 2 million in occupational associations, such as the National Education Association).

For a while, in the late 1960s, the union decline seemed to be arrested as collective bargaining spread to the hitherto largely nonunion public sector, but even here organization has hardly grown since reaching roughly the 50-percent level in 1977. Manufacturing was long a union stronghold, but it is now but 45 percent organized, while in construction, once a bastion of union strength, less than half the work is done by union workers. Despite many efforts to organize white-collar workers, the percentage of the organized white-collar private sector labor force organized is probably less now than it was thirty years ago.

This decline in union strength makes the United States almost unique, since in almost every other democratic industrialized country unions have gained in both power and numbers. The 23 percent organization in the United States compares with 80 percent for Sweden (where even generals are organized), 67 percent for Austria, or 44 percent for Australia. Only France and Italy are below the United States.

A number of overlapping explanations can be offered for weak unions, although these are as much symptoms or results of loss of power, as explanations of why it has been lost. They are as follows:

> The traditionally unionized sectors, especially manufacturing, mining, transportation, and utilities, have grown much less rapidly than the nonunion sectors, such as trade and services. Factories have moved South and the number of blue-collar factory workers has declined.
>
> Managers of nonunion firms have increasingly adopted tougher, more sophisticated, and more effective techniques to keep their organizations "union free" with a whole new profession of union-prevention consultants to help them. Taking advantage of every technicality the law allows, they fend off unions as long as they can, and then, if they lose, they go only through the motions of bargaining. If charged with violating the law, their lawyers fight an endless delaying action.
>
> Arguably, unions, with their heavy emphasis on pecuniary benefits and *group* rights, no longer appeal to younger workers who are more interested in job challenge and opportunities for *individual* discretion.
>
> Unions have lost political clout and, as Chapter 15 describes, have been on the defensive on a number of legislative fronts. In 1978, even with a Democratic President and a heavily Democratic Congress, labor was unable to win passage of a so-called "Labor Reform Bill," which would have reduced the procedural barriers to NLRB action and strengthened the Board's penalties. Under the Reagan administration labor will have very little political clout.
>
> Unions have also lost some of their economic clout. Taxpayer revolts and budget cuts increased employer resistance in the government sector, and public employees lost a number of important strikes long before the air controllers' episode. Private firms, faced with foreign competition and declining profit margins, adopted tough stands against demands for substantial wage increases. Union wages barely kept up with the cost of living, and in some industries they fell well below it. (On the other hand, the differential between union and nonunion wage levels continues to widen.)
>
> Union jurisdictional lines and bargaining structure—developed for the most part during 1935-1945 or earlier—are becoming increasingly out of date.

What of the future? One scenario suggests that present trends will continue, leading to the substantial weakening and even crumbling of the labor movement as it is now known. It is not inconceivable that the 1980s will see a management offensive, forcing unions in a series of disastrous strikes, leaving some decertified and others reduced to impotence. Unions in some fields, such as the garment industry, may become so weakened that it may make little difference whether they disband.

The alternative scenario places its faith chiefly on women and the South. One reason for union weakness is the failure to organize women, particularly those who work part time. In the past, few women believed themselves permanently in the labor force and few had much hope of raising their wages to male levels. These beliefs are changing, but, so far, to achieve equality, women have been going to the Equal Employment Opportunity Commission and the courts. Union optimists argue that women will soon find that the union route is quicker and more effective. If so, one may see the unionization of offices, banks, and insurance companies (the so-called ''white-collar factories''), just as occurred in Sweden. Further, the lessened promotional opportunities for members of the baby-boom generation may increase desire for unionization among both men and women.

Unions' second great hope is the South. The expectation is that as the South becomes increasingly industrialized and as memories of racial segregation die off, the South's attitudes, behaviors, and laws will become increasingly like those of the rest of the country: Southern workers will reject paternalism, they will suffer from recessions, and they will demand benefits equal to those enjoyed by the rest of the country.

Optimists look also to the eventual passage of something like the 1978 Labor Reform Bill and to changes in union leadership itself. The men who founded the big unions in the 1930s—the George Meany generation—were themselves in their thirties and forties at the time. They controlled their unions for over thirty years, and few retired only recently. As a consequence, the orderly progression of younger men and women through increasingly higher offices never occurred. The new leadership in most unions is rather untried. It could make a big difference. Finally, optimists point to the recent poll in which 30 percent of nonunion workers indicated that they would vote for unionization were an election held in their workplace. Were this 30 percent actually organized, the union picture would change quite dramatically.

While the prospects for union growth are somewhat uncertain, so are the prospects for labor peace in the already unionized sector. A substantial portion of management is itching to give unionism a knockout blow. On the other hand, labor and management in steel and autos have been working closely together for a number of political objectives: approval of the Chrysler bail-out fund, protection against foreign competition, and reduced environmental regulation. We may be entering a period of "corporatism" (a British term) or "collusion" (as we Americans call it), during which the main parties work together in partnership with the government, with the unions trading moderation in wage demands for greater influence over corporate and governmental policies. Among the results of this cooperation may be trade protection, low-interest government loans for plant modernization, extended unemployment benefits for workers, and union input into company investment and plant-shutdown decisions. Everyone will be benefited, except perhaps the taxpayer and consumer.

One prediction seems reasonably safe: since major industrial relations policies are increasingly made in Washington, labor will be inevitably pushed toward greater political activity, thus following the example of labor movements in other countries.

All of this will impact organizational personnel policies, as will be discussed.

SOME SELECTED PERSONNEL ISSUES

Having sketched the major parameters for the personnel environment during the 1980s, eight potentially hot issues upon which this environment will impact will be briefly discussed. The first three issues—job redesign and human relations; new work schedules; and flexible work careers—gain significance because of employee demands for greater autonomy and self-determination. Security is the common theme for the next three: job security, fringe benefits, and occupational health and safety. The final two issues, equal employment and job rights, deal with group and individual rights.

The choice of issues reflects this writer's personal view that these will be the ones to receive major attention during the 1980s. Space limitations require the neglect of other issues which may prove to be equally critical, especially MBO (see Chapter 8), OD training (Chapter 11), the treatment of alcoholism, and the management of managers and professionals (see Sayles and Strauss, 1981).

Job Redesign and Human Relations

"Quality of Worklife" received much attention during the 1970s, and a number of firms experimented with various forms of job redesign such as job enrichment, "quality circles," and autonomous work groups. Among the best known of the experiments have taken place in Saab and Volvo in Sweden and at General Foods, AT&T, Texas Instruments, and Non-Linear Systems. Significantly, most of these changes occurred either in nonunion situations or were introduced with little union consultation. Unpublicized examples of job redesign appear especially common among small new manufacturing plants in such states as Oklahoma. On the other hand, GM and the UAW have been actively experimenting with job changes at a number of plants.

Taken as a whole, these projects introduce variety, autonomy, feedback, and task identity, all of which have been identified as contributing to motivation and satisfaction and also reducing job stress—a matter of much recent concern (Kahn, 1981). It should be noted, however, that the changes do more than provide what Herzberg (1966) calls "motivators." In the first place, many job redesign projects alter work flow and reduce friction-causing interfaces. Reported productivity increases may be more the result of better material flow than of harder work. Second, the best publicized experiments have been accompanied by important changes in the job environment ("hygienes") and in workers' status position. These changes help reduce what UAW Vice President Bluestone (1974) called

> the double standards that exist between workers and management. . . . Workers challenge the symbols of elitism traditionally taken for granted such as salary payments vs.

> hourly payments; time clocks for blue-collar workers; well-decorated dining rooms for white-collar workers versus plain Spartan-like cafeterias for blue-collar workers (p. 47).

At General Food's new Topeka dog food plant, for example, there were no reserved parking lots, no time clocks, and no differentiation between management offices and worker lounges. More important, perhaps, workers were given ample opportunity to break the monotony of the job and even, in one department, to make phone calls on company time.

The evidence suggests that demand for more challenging work is stronger among white-collar than among blue-collar workers. Nevertheless, job redesign is likely to be at least a minor priority, in both office and factory, through much of the decade to come. Just as during the 1920s every effort was made to deskill jobs by breaking them into their smallest components and making them as simple as possible, so during the 1980s there will be efforts to increase skill and provide opportunity for discretion. But this will occur chiefly when new factories are designed.

Parenthetically, it should be noted that job redesign is philosophically inconsistent with another 1970s fad—behavioral modification. The first encourages employee discretion and self-determination; the second, conformity to tightly programmed routines. The struggle between these rival panaceas should be dramatic (in the journals, if not on the plant and office floors). Nevertheless, job redesign should be the winner. Behavioral mod is simply too restrictive.

Other likely changes during the 1980s will make office architecture more cheerful and the work environment generally more pleasant. Further, if my earlier prediction proves accurate, and process technology becomes more common, there will be more jobs that require merely that workers stand by for emergencies. Such jobs will provide ample opportunities to "schmooze" (gossip) or read.

Greater stress will be placed on old-fashioned (1940s style) good "human relations." Supervisors will be trained to supervise less closely, to avoid punitive behavior where possible, to listen to workers' suggestions, and to hold regular meetings in which departmental problems can be freely discussed. As in the past, there will be considerable slippage between the personnel department's high-minded policy statements regarding these matters and actual shop-floor practice. Nevertheless, today's well-educated workforce has high expectations as to how it will be treated, and this should give good human relations greater urgency.

Technological change, especially computerization, will facilitate the development of functional workgroups in which professionals and quasi-professionals work together in a colleagial, rather than hierarchical, basis. To prevent functionalism from leading to suboptimization, there will be considerable use of temporary work teams and matrix organization, even though, as in the past, much matrix organization will fail to work as expected.

In Europe, there has been considerable agitation for various forms of "industrial democracy," including workers participation in plant-level managerial decisions and the addition of workers' representatives to company boards of directors. For reasons too complex to discuss here (Strauss, 1979), European style industrial democracy is unlikely to spread to the United States, although here and there a union director may be elected to a company board, as at Chrysler. Further, there may be an increasing number of worker-owned and controlled producers' cooperatives.

The personnel department should be in a position to contribute significantly to the redesign of jobs and structures, especially if technological change and computerization permit greater choice of organizational form.

Work Schedules

Many workers are more interested in *when* they work than in *how* they work. This is shown, for instance, by the increasing union demand that workers be free to turn down overtime. It is also evidenced by the growing interest in new approaches to work scheduling such as the compressed week, flextime, and job sharing, as well as the expansion of an older arrangement, part-time work.

What these plans have in common is that they are designed to permit employees to enjoy their life *off* the job, as opposed to *on* it. For some workers, these new schedules represent a changing life style, which downgrades work as a source of satisfaction. But for many women and some men it represents the opposite: an opportunity to combine work with family life. Indeed, work schedules have become a major issue for some women's groups.

Compressed Work Week.   The ten-hour, four-day week was the first of recent innovative approaches to work scheduling. The advantages of the plan are clear. By concentrating the work week into four days (or sometimes three), the plan provides an extra day to run errands, to engage in recreation, and even to hold a second job. Further, commuting time is reduced. This is an attractive package, and according to polls, a high percentage of workers state they prefer it to the conventional work week.

In practice, experience with the compressed week has been mixed. Some organizations report decreased absenteeism, reduced turnover, and higher productivity. Unmarried and childless younger workers find the new schedule attractive, especially if they engage in weekend recreation (in fact, attitudes toward recreation may determine attitudes toward the plan).

But other organizations experimented with the compressed workweek and then dropped it. Employees were enthusiastic at first, but later concluded that the gain of a three-day weekend was more than offset by the fatigue of a ten-hour day and loss of free evening time. Some (but not all) working couples find it harder to raise children under these conditions. Organizations that must operate five days a week find it difficult to schedule the fifth day. Further, unless supervisors put in a fifty-hour week, they must leave the job partly unsupervised. Finally, under many union and government contracts, work in excess of eight hours per day must be paid on an overtime basis. For all these reasons, it seems unlikely that the compressed work week will become more popular during the 1980s.

Flextime.   Unlike the compressed week, the virtue of flextime is lack of rigidity. First introduced in Europe, this new work scheduling procedure has spread widely through the United States, particularly among white-collar employees, and this trend should continue during the years ahead.

With flextime, each employee is free to choose his or her work schedule. Usually all employees are expected to be at work during a *core* period (e.g., 9–11 A.M. and 2–4 P.M.) and to pick their remaining hours from a *band* of other times (perhaps 7–9 A.M., 11 A.M.–2 P.M., and 4–6 P.M.). Some organizations allow employees to work less than eight hours on some days in exchange for more than eight hours on other days, and some allow employees to pick a different schedule each day, rather than sticking to one.

The advantages of flextime are many: it allows working parents to adjust their hours to their children's school schedules and also to their own psychological rhythms (some people prefer to start work early in the morning, others to sleep late). Workers can run errands during the day, thus requests for special leave are reduced. Since people set their own schedules, tardiness drops. Finally, by treating employees as adults who can set their own schedules, flextime boosts morale.

Organizations that have experimented with flextime generally report substantial benefits: increased productivity, reduced absenteeism and turnover, and less time spent on coffee breaks. But flextime is not without troubles: complex scheduling arrangements are often required, especially when minimum size crews are required at all times. Flextime creates many problems where teamwork is required, such as on an assembly line, or in such activities as nursing or police work, when one person cannot leave his or her post until relieved by another. In practice, flextime has been most successful in clerical and professional work.

Part-Time Work. Employees on flextime normally work a forty-hour week; part-time workers have greater flexibility yet. Both the growing number of women in the labor force (one-third of whom work part time) and the increasing number of workers who have retired from their original jobs contribute to the rapid rise in part-time employment. Today, 15 million Americans work exclusively on part-time schedules, with another 4 million moonlighting on part-time jobs in addition to their regular full-time employment.

Of the 15 million exclusive part-time workers, about one-fifth would prefer full-time jobs. The remainder prefer part-time work for a variety of reasons: school attendance, family responsibilities, physical limitations, and desire for leisure. Part-time work is attractive to many employers, too. It permits the hiring of workers who might not be available for full-time work. (Hospitals, for example, have found that nurses can be hired for four- or six-hour shifts who are not available for eight-hour ones.) In some cases, employees produce as much in six hours as they might in eight. Further, part-time work is especially useful in sales and service activities where work peaks at certain hours of the day.

Part-time work has its difficulties, too. Part-time workers are difficult to schedule and supervise. They cost as much to train as full-time workers, yet work less time. Further, the social security tax structure makes part-time employees more expensive than full-time ones (but many employers provide part-time workers relatively few benefits).

Job Sharing.   With job sharing, a single job is divided between two people, each of whom works part-time (say twenty hours a week or six months a year). In some cases, a husband and wife may share a single professional position. An advantage of job sharing is that the two individuals can be held jointly responsible for ensuring that the job is done on a full-time basis. A major difficulty is that it will work only if two individuals can be found who are willing to work a rather unusual schedule that directly complements each other's.

Work Schedules and the Future.   From 1901 to 1948, the average work week for nonstudent males dropped from fifty-eight to forty-three hours (including time spent moonlighting on second jobs). Since 1948, this figure has remained relatively unchanged. The total number of hours worked over a *year* has dropped, but, as shall be seen, this has been the result of longer vacations and more frequent holidays. Meanwhile, the number of women working part-time has multiplied many fold.

What of the future? There is some evidence that a substantial number of males—and even more females—would be willing to accept lower pay for extra time away from work. Unions also want to reduce the standard eight-hour day, forty-hour week, but there are many workers who, for a variety of reasons, want to supplement their income, either by working overtime or by taking a second job. So the movement may be toward a society in which regardless of the so-called standard work day or work week, only a minority work them.

Greater Career Flexibility

Along with greater control over their work schedules, employees are seeking greater freedom to shape their careers. (For another discussion of careers, see Chapter 13.) Again, these new demands are products of increased female labor force participation and the growing desire by both sexes for self-determination. Today, interest in career flexibility is strongest among professional and managerial employees; the future may see its spread throughout the workforce.

Open Personnel Systems.   The typical organization has a "closed" personnel system in which management unilaterally determines who will be transferred, promoted, fired, or receive training. To assist management in these decisions, many large organizations have a personnel planning unit. This unit predicts not merely future corporate needs for various kinds of employees (as discussed in Chapter 3), but also attempts to plan individual careers. Often there are secret card files or computer tapes that indicate that X is good material for vice president, but that Y is not likely to go beyond section chief. X, at least, is destined for a series of training programs and promotions that will provide him or her with varied experience in progressively more demanding functions. Very often these promotions are accompanied by transfers from one city to another.

For the most part, these critical decisions are made without significant input from the individual whose career is being planned; often the individual is kept completely uninformed as to his or her likely prospects. This closed system may satisfy organizational needs (though frequently it does not do that), but it ignores the individual's need for self-determination. The system is meeting growing resistance; for example, more and more managers are refusing transfers if these require uprooting families and requir-ing one's spouse to change jobs.

Given this resistance, a small number of organizations has been experimenting with "open" systems approaches that give individuals considerable opportunity to help plan their own careers. For example, prospective job openings are widely publicized with em-ployees being given the freedom to decide the jobs for which they would like to be con-sidered. Some employees may bid on high-risk jobs, where the chance of failure is sub-stantial (and which may require frequent transfer). Others may stay put and refuse to change at all. Similarly, employees are being permitted to choose for themselves whether they want training. They are less likely to be sent to training programs without advance consultation.

Realistic job previews (see Chapter 5) are consistent with open systems, so is giving workers the right to decide when they will retire. Some American companies have adopted what Scandinavians call the "glide," which means that as employees approach retirement, they may opt to gradually decrease the number of hours they work until finally they reach full retirement. This makes much more sense than plunging people into full retirement, all at once, against their will.

To assist employees in making the choices appropriate at various stages in their career, assessment centers and employee counseling programs may spread rapidly. As discussed earlier (Chapter 12), assessment centers are designed to provide employees with insights into their strengths and weaknesses. Armed with such insights, employees may enter career planning programs that are designed to help them reevaluate their career planning goals and alternatives. Increasingly, the employee's spouse is asked to join in the program.

Open career systems have the added advantage of reducing employment discrimi-nation charges. For example, one of the best ways to avoid age discrimination charges is to let older workers make their own decisions as to when to retire.

Multiple Careers. Recent years have seen a growing acceptance of the concept of midcareer change—a deliberate change in occupation as well as job. Midcareer change has become popular for a variety of reasons: (1) rapidly evolving technologies have made many jobs obsolete; (2) open personnel systems make job shifts easier to arrange; (3) many women seek new careers after raising their families; (4) career change helps reduce "burnout"—the phenomenon that, if one is on the job too long, one begins to lose his or her sensitivity, enthusiasm, and creativity; (5) since for those born near the end of the baby boom, opportunities for promotions will be lim-ited, career change allows lateral mobility; and, finally, (6) all of this is facilitated by the growth of continuing education programs (such as evening MBA courses that now enroll some 100,000 students).

Thus, open career systems expand employee options. Instead of spending a lifetime working full time on a single job, an employee might start a career by working several years as a student, then switch to full-time work until the first child comes along, work part time (or not at all) until the children are old enough to take care of themselves, move back to full time work (with perhaps a period off for full- or part-time school), and finally go to part time again a few years before full retirement. Each change in hours of work may (or may not) be accompanied by changes in employers or line of work.

Some people may even take top management positions for fixed terms and then switch back into less demanding responsibilities without the onus of having failed, much as do university deans and departments heads.

Dual-Career Families. Complicating matters further is the advent of two-career families in which husband and wife work. One spouse's career changes must mesh with the other's. If the employer offers one spouse a job in another city, it may also have to provide job-seeking help for the other.

Career Planning and the Organization. Much of the recent discussion has focused on employee needs. It has painted a glowing picture of career futures, largely ignoring employers' needs. Yet organizations cannot give employees complete freedom. Assessment centers and career planning programs sometimes encourage people to aspire for jobs beyond their reach, leading only to frustration. Frequent job changes require expensive training. Both long- and short-range planning become difficult when individuals are free to choose when to switch hours or to retire.

The 1980s will doubtless see an increase in nonstandard careers. Smart employers will learn to profit from this diversity of manpower. But the tension between personal and organizational needs will be difficult to resolve, and the utopia in which everyone does his or her own thing will still be far away. As yet, open personnel systems are more talked about than practiced.

Finally, *voluntary* career change for everyone can occur only in a full employment economy. At present, it is at most a middle-class luxury. The main concern for most workers is to obtain security from involuntary career change caused by unemployment.

Job Security

In the past, it was the employee who bore the risks of life's uncertainties. Declining company business or personal illness would result in a loss of work. Management could fire, layoff, and transfer people as it wished. But with the introduction of unions and written contracts, a balance of power and mutual obligations emerged. Fixed hours, seniority for layoffs, promotional ladders, and due process in disciplinary procedures all limited management's flexibility, especially with regard to blue-collar workers.

Now the balance may be shifting still further. Employees want management to assume most of the burden of adjusting to economic and personal risks; meanwhile, as has been seen, they wish greater freedom to determine their own work schedules and careers.

Step by step, employees have gained job security. First they won protection against unjust discipline or layoffs. Then, gradually, they won it against other forms of income interruption: sick leave when ill; pensions when old; other forms of payment when attending family funerals, when called for jury or national guard duty, or even when voting; and unemployment insurance and supplemental unemployment benefits (SUB) when work is not available. In companies with strong union contracts, employees have a guaranteed stream of income from the day they are hired to the day they die (and if they die before their spouse, until the day their spouse dies). To be sure, benefits when not working (especially sick leave, unemployment insurance, and pensions) may not be as high as pay while working. Nevertheless, this difference is being steadily reduced, especially in large, wealthy firms.

There is one gap left: plant closures and long-term layoffs. Elimination of this gap is high on the unions' agenda. Some contracts (e.g., steel) provide for up to two years' pay in case of plant shutdowns or long-term unemployment. Already, at least one steel company has decided it is cheaper to keep unprofitable mills open rather than incur these heavy shutdown costs. In newspapers, railroads, and the postal service, employers have had to promise lifetime employment for present employees (whether there is work or not) in return for freedom to introduce technological change.

Proposals to make plant shutdowns more difficult will become increasingly common as obsolete plants are abandoned in such cities as Youngstown, Ohio, which have come to rely upon these for a heavy proportion of their citizens' livelihood. Arguing that it is morally and economically unjustified to leave an entire community stranded simply because a large company can make more money elsewhere, unions have demanded that lengthy advance notice be given before commencing shutdowns. Considerable political steam is building to require such advance notice as a matter of law. Some proposals would force the employer to justify its action before an impartial third party.

The net impact of these proposals would be to make American personnel practice closer to that prevailing in much of Europe and Japan, where custom, law, and union contracts already guarantee regular employees almost the equivalent of lifetime employment. Employees will acquire what is in effect a property-right in their jobs.

Presumably, companies would behave very differently if they were forced to treat labor as they do equipment, as a fixed rather than a variable cost. As in Japan, they will be loath to hire permanent new employees. Instead, during periods of peak work, they will work overtime hours, subcontract some operations, and provide various forms of temporary employment—and during slack periods they will aggressively seek various forms of temporary work (including maintenance and nonprofit production) since they have to pay for their employees anyway. In return they may ask their unions to relax their contractual restrictions on the type of work their members can perform.

Another solution to the problem of obsolete jobs is to have the government bear the cost. Under the Trade Assistance Act, the federal government pays employees laid off as a result of foreign competition 70 percent of their gross pay for up to a year. The cost in 1980 was estimated at $1.44 billion. Other programs, some considerably more generous, provide special payments for postal employees, railroad workers, and lumber company employees displaced by the Redwood National Park. Some former railroad workers are guaranteed full pay, adjusted for industry-wide wage increases, until they reach age sixty-five, provided they do not work. The Reagan administration has cut back some of these benefits. Nevertheless, the 1980s should see general acceptance of the principle that individual employees should not bear the cost of economic disruption alone. The question remains: who will bear it, the employer or the government?

Finally, some serious problems may arise if the concept of lifetime employment becomes more fully accepted. In the first place, it will accentuate the distinction between the two segments of what has become known as the "dual labor market," with one segment working for large organizations and enjoying lifetime security and the other relegated to insecure, low-paying jobs. The second problem is that lifetime employment may reduce labor mobility. The concept of multiple careers will be less meaningful if it becomes economically risky to change employers. Job security programs should be designed to facilitate personal career renewal and the movement out of obsolete "sunset" jobs, industries, and communities.

Fringe Benefits

During the 1970s, the cost of fringe benefits—including such job security protections as unemployment insurance and SUB—rose half again as fast as wages. Already fringes comprise over 35 percent of total compensation, and some experts predict this figure will grow to 50 percent by 1990.

Certainly, fringes continue to be attractive. From the point of view of the employer, they serve as a "golden chain" ensuring employee loyalty. For example, employer-provided benefits provide tax and cost advantages and are more convenient for employees than buying them on their own. And, for unions, there are strong political advantages to be out with the latest model benefit. Thus, perhaps unconsciously, all parties seem to have decided to give higher priority to fringes than to equally costly wage increases.

Growing Costs.   Will the trend toward increasingly costly benefits continue? Even if present benefit formulae remain unchanged, there is reason to expect (as will be discussed) that fringe costs will rise faster than wages. Besides, all parties have learned to expect the benefit formulae to be made ever more generous. But in a "zero-sum" economy will fringes continue to grow in the face of relatively constant real take-home pay? Or will there be a renewed emphasis on immediate cash? The interests of younger workers, struggling to raise a family and to buy a home, may be very different than those of older workers who are more concerned with pensions and medical benefits.

It might seem that organizations have almost run out of benefits to give. Some more recent ones provide adoption expenses, legal insurance, and a paid day off on the first day of deer season. Some 70 million workers are now covered by dental plans. In some companies, guarantees of income security have received such a high priority that employees now enjoy something equivalent to Japanese lifetime employment (but with much better pensions). Union calls for a thirty-hour week or a four-day, eight-hour week have been largely rejected, but some unions have won so many holidays, vacations, and special paid days off (totaling over fifty days per year in many cases) that some workers have the equivalent of a four-day week. The last auto contract provides a full week off between Christmas and New Year's.

Pensions.   The costs of all benefits have been rising rapidly, but pension costs have grown especially fast. Workers are living longer and retiring earlier. Company contributions to pension funds have proven grossly inadequate for the level of benefits now anticipated, especially since the actuarial calculations that determine these contributions rarely take account of inflation. Pensions based on salaries prior to retirement have become cruelly unrealistic as prices increase. Many companies have increased the benefits paid employees who have already retired, but these increases have rarely matched the cost of living.

Most firms are strongly opposed to indexing their pensions (i.e., tying them to the cost of living). This is understandable when one realizes that indexing not only forces the company to pay more to those already retired, but also to set aside larger reserves to fund estimated future pension increases. An assumed annual 1 percent increase in the cost of living may increase the total pension cost by 10 percent (Berlin, 1980).

ERISA, which has elaborate provisions for vesting, funding, accountability, and recordkeeping, adds to company costs, especially in those firms whose pension plans are already shaky. ERISA has slowed down the introduction of new plans and has led some small companies to abandon old ones.

Although private pensions are often inadequate, less than half the private workforce has pensions at all. This unevenness of coverage has led to proposals that all employers be legally required to offer at least some pension protection. This, of course, might further proliferate the number of separate pension programs and (unless relieved by total portability) further reduce worker mobility. Neither would it solve the problems faced by declining industries that find it difficult to maintain their funds on an actuarially sound basis. An alternative, highly controversial solution would be to eliminate private pensions altogether and instead substantially expand social security benefits.

Meanwhile, the Social Security program is itself going through a crisis. Social Security benefits are protected against price increases through indexing, but the taxpayers—employers and employees—who finance them are not. Ever since Social Security was indexed in 1975, it has spent more than it has received; this, despite steadily increased taxes. The Social Security system operates on a pay-as-you-go basis, meaning in effect that present workers are paying the benefits of those who have retired. Already, there is something of a taxpayers' revolt against increased social security taxes and the Reagan administration has been seeking to cut back benefits.

In the years ahead, as the proportion of retirees to present workers increases, a war between the generations may break out (Kleiler, 1978). Old people are retiring earlier and increasing in number. Seventeen people were employed in 1950 for every pension recipient; during the 1980s, the ratio may drop to three-to-one (*Economist,* December 27, 1980, p. 26).

Still another hot issue for the 1980s relates to the investment of pension funds. Such funds, which now total $500 billion, may mount to $2 trillion by 1990. In most cases they are invested by company management, banks, or insurance companies. Now, unions are demanding a voice in how this money is used and are insisting that investments be made only in socially desirable activities—not in companies with South African ties, but in those with good labor relations records or in mortgages on union-built homes. Management naturally argues that since it puts up the money, it should determine its use; further, the sole criteria for investment should be safety and return, not the union's half-baked social objectives.

Medical Benefits.   Doctor and hospital bills are climbing faster than the cost of living, greatly increasing the cost of medical benefits. The problem is complicated by high administrative costs and some fraud and overuse. As with pensions, there is considerable unevenness of coverage, with those needing benefits most not getting them. Again, one highly controversial solution is to provide national health insurance. Given entrenched interests, however, only minor changes in the pension and medical benefit areas are likely during the 1980s.

Cafeteria Benefit Plans. The typical fringe program provides equal benefits for all employees, regardless of preference or need, yet the needs of a single, older woman, for example, may be very different from those of the parent of a growing family. Consistent with the spirit of self-determination, there has been much recent interest in cafeteria benefit plans that allow employees to choose among an assortment of equally expensive benefits. One employee, for example, might opt for high pensions and another for longer vacations or a company-paid life insurance policy. Cafeteria systems face a number of practical and legal difficulties, as well as some union opposition, hence are likely to spread only slowly during the 1980s.

Safety, Health, and Work Hazards

Health and safety became a major personnel issue in the 1970s. Occupational hazards had previously been regulated by weak state laws. Workman's compensation was designed to compensate workers for injuries incurred on the job, and incidentally, by transferring the costs of accidents to the employer, to encourage employers to take safety precautions. Progress was apparently being made since injury frequency fell dramatically from 24.2 in 1926 to 11.4 in 1958.

The late 1960s and early 1970s saw two developments. First, the accident rate stopped dropping. By statistics not directly comparable with those now used, the frequency rate actually increased to 15.2 in 1970. More important was the discovery of long-term occupational hazards, perhaps the most dramatic and tragic being the high incidence of lung cancer among those who had worked with asbestos twenty years earlier.

In 1970, Congress passed the Occupational Safety and Health Act. OSHA imposes on employers a general duty to provide employees a safe and healthy work environment. In addition, employers must live up to specific *standards* established after research and hearings. The standards and their enforcement have led to considerable controversy.

The following is an example. After much debate, a standard was promulgated, setting 90 decibels as the maximum permitted factory noise level (with the exception that up to 115 decibels was allowed for not more than fifteen minutes a day). Unions argued instead for 80 decibels since, at 90 decibels, some 15 percent of the population is likely to experience some hearing loss after twenty years of exposure. Industry representatives insisted that this was unduly restrictive, that the costs of maintaining such a low level would be prohibitive, and that in any case earmuffs could provide inexpensive hearing protection.

Note the issues here. Should the workplace be safe for everyone, or for only 85 percent of the people? Surely no employer has the right to risk another human being's life or health, and everything possible should be done to reduce illness-causing conditions. But what does "everything possible" mean in practice? There is no way to make the workplace absolutely safe without enormous costs and in some cases the sacrifice of other benefits. As standards become tighter, they impose rapidly increasing costs. Getting rid of the last 5 percent of the problem may be one hundred times more expensive than eliminating the first 95 percent. The typical worker is already less likely to suffer an accident on the job than at home or on the road.

Management argues that trade-offs are necessary. But how much is it worth to avoid a person's partial deafness? $100,000? $1,000,000? How much is a life worth? $100,000,000? Some companies argue that money spent on living up to some standards would be hundreds of times more cost-effective, in terms of saving lives, if it was spent enforcing traffic laws or in educating people not to smoke.

The Supreme Court has required the government to consider "the significance of the risk" before promulgating standards. But with regard to some questions—especially when one seeks to assess the long-term effects of new processes or substances—there are so many uncertainties that so-called statistics are little more than wild guesses. Unions are arguing that VDTs (visual display terminals) pose dangers of cataract and other visual problems and stress. Obviously, VDTs have not been in existence long enough to determine their long-run impact. How conservative should society be in guarding against as yet unmeasurable risks?

How are health hazards to be handled—through changing the job or instructing workers to work more safely? Since workers often violate instructions, changing the job is usually more effective, but also more expensive. With regard to noise abatement, employers argue that it would be less expensive to provide employees earmuffs than to eliminate the noise itself. Workers counter that really effective muffs are heavy and uncomfortable—and why should the employee be the one to suffer because management has a noisy workplace?

Occupational health impacts other social concerns. Unborn fetuses are considerably more prone to injury from some chemicals than are adults. Should companies be allowed to exclude pregnant women from processes making use of such chemicals? Since the risk may be highest during the first weeks of pregnancy (even before the woman is aware of her condition), can management exclude all women of child-bearing age from hazardous jobs? Suppose these women agree to be sterilized? Or does any exclusion constitute illegal sex discrimination? Women's groups argue that workplaces should be safe enough for everybody—or alternatively that women should be placed on nonhazardous jobs without loss of pay. Management responds that either policy would be prohibitively expensive and that the second is often impracticable.

Management argues that living up to OSHA's multitudinous rules (including keeping expensive records) is extremely expensive, especially for small businesses. Indeed, OSHA has become a prime target for conservative political opposition (much more so than equal opportunity rules, even through the latter may have more widespread impact). Management has lobbied hard for changes in the law to exempt companies with fewer than ten employees and those with low accident rates from some or all of the law's provisions, especially those requiring the keeping of records and permitting OSHA inspection of their premises.

As of this writing, these issues are still being hotly argued, with the Reagan administration moving rapidly toward substantial deregulation. Even under Carter, OSHA eliminated some trivial rules, for example, regarding the shape of toilet seats. OSHA insisted that it already concentrated its inspection efforts on industries with bad safety records. Further, it argued that, since small businesses often had the worst safety records, they should not be exempt; companies with few past accidents may be accumulating health hazards that may cause illness to appear ten to twenty years in the future.

With regard to these questions—and to many others discussed in this chapter—the tendency, until Reagan, had been to resolve questions of doubt in favor of the individual rather than the organization. Individual welfare was enhanced, but the cost to the employer was sometimes high and the cost was often passed on to the public in the form of higher prices. In the long run, having a healthy population pays off economically as well as socially. Nevertheless, the terms of the tradeoff are likely to be bitterly debated during the 1980s, with the personnel department again playing a key role.

Equal Employment Opportunity

Equal employment proved to be personnel's greatest challenge during the 1970s, and it may be so again during the 1980s. Chapter 7 dealt with legal issues concerned with personnel testing. This section will look at equal employment in a somewhat broader context.

At first, equal employment protection was concerned chiefly with minorities. Later it was extended to women, then, in turn, to older men, to Viet Nam veterans, to the handicapped, and (in some jurisdictions) to homosexuals. The focus originally was on hiring; today there is hardly an aspect of personnel policy that does not have equal employment implications. A few examples:

> May employers reimburse employees for business lunches in all-male private clubs?
>
> Can future promotability be considered a factor in determining who is to be laid off in a managerial cutback if this results in a disproportionate number of older managers being laid off?
>
> Certain products (e.g., coffee) are traditionally shipped in 100+ pound sacks, which are too heavy for most women and some men to tote, thus confining longshore employment to heavy-set males (particularly since the union insists that easier jobs be given to its longer service members). Should coffee-producing countries be required to ship their products in lighter sacks? Should women be exempted from their proportionate share of this heavy work? Or should shipowners be required to redesign their equipment so that cargo "manhandling" is completely eliminated?
>
> Overseas employment is particularly difficult for dual-career couples since it may be quite difficult for both parties to find jobs overseas. May a company require either its male or female managers to serve overseas as a condition for promotion into higher management?
>
> A hospital employee belongs to a religious group that requires its members not to work on Saturday. Previously all workers divided Saturday work equally. No one volunteers to take more than his or her share. Must this employee be given special privileges? The union insists that if only some employees are required to work Saturdays, these individuals be given premium pay.

Issues like these create innumerable problems for both lawyers and management. One of the stickiest areas, comparable work, will be discussed later. First, a basic issue still unresolved by either the U.S. Supreme Court or the court of public opinion should be considered: should the law require equal *opportunity* (or treatment) or should it require equal *achievement?*

The emphasis of government enforcement agencies has been on achievement, in part because discrimination with regard to treatment is so difficult to prove. EEOC rules require that if equal achievement is not obtained—that is, for example, only 5 percent of the company's employees are black, while 30 percent of the relevant labor force is black—then the company must prove the validity of its selection techniques. Yet as Chapter 7 argues, the standards of proof are quite tight, some say almost impossibly so. Indeed, a personnel director expresses a common view in saying, "The EEOC really doesn't care how you do your testing. They'll bug you till on the 'bottom line' you get the right number of women and minorities. And, if employers fail to achieve the appropriate results, they may be required to set goals and timetables indicating when and how these results will be obtained."

Aside from the law, two fundamental social issues seem involved. The first relates to the means by which equality is obtained, the second to the nature of the objective itself.

Discrimination against Whites.   Critics argue that affirmative action programs discriminate against white males, who are being made to suffer for the sins of previous generations. Although the law was designed to provide equal opportunities (an equal chance for every person to be considered on his or her merits, regardless of race or sex), in practice the whole administration of the law—its emphasis on counting people by race, its establishment of goals and timetables, and its stress on the "bottom line" concept—has been to require equal achievement. Therefore, according to critics, companies may no longer hire the best qualified candidate and are forced to discriminate against white males so as to meet their goals. In the press for instant equality among *groups,* it is argued, the rights of *individuals* have been trampled.

Supporters of the program have a number of answers. First, they insist that despite thirty years of equal employment effort, discrimination against women and minorities is still far greater than any possible problems suffered by white males. Second, they argue that any possible impact on white males will be trivial. "If 40 percent of the jobs are reserved for women and minorities, the white males still have their 60 percent." Finally, they suggest that the art of selection is so poorly developed that it is impossible to show any discrimination against whites now; what is easy to demonstrate is that selection systems worked tremendous hardships against women and minorities in the past.

All parties agree with the rhetoric that "qualifications should replace skin color as the basis for employment decisions." Personnel people argue that the impact of recent regulations has been to make skin color the all-important criterion. Minority representatives insist that the opposite is true: The regulations to date have received only token enforcement; widespread discrimination still exists, and much tighter controls are essential if freedom of opportunity is to become a reality.

How Equal Employment?   The second major question relates to the objective. Critics suggest that the goal of present national policy is for the racial and sexual composition of *every* job in *every* organization to mirror the racial and sexual composition of the population as a whole. If the labor force in a community is 10 percent black, 5 percent Spanish-American, 5 percent Asian, 85 percent white, 40 percent female, and 60 percent male, and if the company has twenty vice-presidents, present national policy requires the organization to establish a long-run goal in which at least two of the vice-presidents are black, one Spanish-American, one Asian, and eight female.

Once this balance is reached, what happens when a vice-president of one sex and ethnic group retires? Presumably, the goal would be to replace that individual with someone from the same sex and ethnic group; otherwise the balance is upset. To be sure, exceptions can be made if they are justified, but it is always administratively simpler to avoid trying to make justifications and to replace a black woman with another black woman. Thus, once a balance has been reached, there would be a considerable tendency to treat each job as if it were earmarked for a person of a given ethnic group and sex. In this way, an individual's chance for promotion would depend largely on whether vacancies occurred in jobs held by his or her own ethnic-sex group.

Critics argue that this policy carries things too far. Besides artificially restricting promotional opportunities and reducing flexibility in the use of personnel, it is based on the unrealistic assumption that abilities and preferences are evenly divided among races and sexes—that, for instance, the same proportion of men and women, blacks and whites want to be lawyers as want to be doctors, cooks, mathematicians, or jazz musicians. Yet organizations are required to make this their goal and to keep elaborate records indicating how close they come to reaching it.

Supporters of the program reply that all this wildly exaggerates the problem. Goals are required to give a sense of direction, and clearly the present imbalance needs to be reduced. Certainly, the wide distribution of races and sexes over all jobs is indeed a desirable national goal. Statistical measures are required to ensure progress; indeed, history shows that without some sort of measurement no progress is made.

The opportunities vs. achievement issue will undoubtedly be debated through much of the 1980s, with management arguing generally that equal opportunities are enough, while civil rights leaders insist that it is only achievement that counts. The Reagan administration and conservative congressmen are leaning heavily toward management's position. So far, the Supreme Court has not spoken definitively on the issue.

Aside from these basic questions relating to equal employment goals, there are numerous specific problems still requiring resolution during the 1980s. Many of these relate to the aged and the handicapped, two groups that have received protection only recently. Probably the most contentious issue is that of "comparable worth." Indeed, in the words of Eleanor Norton of the EEOC, it may be "the issue of the 1980s."

Comparable Worth.   There is a long tradition that "women's jobs" pay less than those held normally by men, even when women (for example, nurses) go through longer periods of education and training and exercise greater responsibilities than do men (for example, truck drivers). Today these traditional relationships are being challenged. The Equal Pay Act of 1963 makes it illegal not to give men and women the same pay when they hold the same job. But how about different jobs? As of this writing, there are several suits wending through the courts in which women's groups are arguing that it is a violation of the Civil Rights Act of 1964 not to pay men and women equally if their jobs are of *comparable* worth, even if the jobs themselves are very different.

How comparable worth is to be determined is still far from clear (and a special National Academy of Sciences committee made little progress in resolving the question). Possibly it would require some form of job evaluation that would set the basic relationships among jobs on a fairly rigid, nationwide basis. After all, if two jobs are of comparable worth in one company, presumably they will also be of comparable worth in another. So job *relationships* would have to be set uniformly everywhere. This would not necessarily mean that each employer would have exactly the same pay scale. Company A could pay truck drivers 10 percent more than Company B, but it would have to pay the same 10 percent differential to its nurses and secretaries (unless, of course, it could show that its truck drivers, nurses, or secretaries did work different from that of their counterparts in Company B).

The main trouble with such an approach is that it would require a complete revamping of the present system of setting wage differentials. Market forces and collective bargaining would be largely ignored, and in the last analysis wage structure would be determined by the government and the courts. Further, job evaluation itself suffers from many weaknesses. Many experts believe that a nationwide system of job evaluation would be totally impractical.

Market forces reflect supply and demand. Presumably if there are too few people in any given occupation, wages in that occupation will rise and people will move into it. Therefore, wage flexibility is required to achieve labor mobility—or so management argues. Women's groups respond that market forces operate imperfectly since discrimination prevents women from responding to wage changes by moving into higher paying occupations; instead they are "crowded" into lower paying jobs. In any case, there are other ways to encourage mobility besides the preservation of unjust differentials.

Management supporters reply once again that if there are discriminatory barriers restricting female mobility, it would be much simpler to eliminate these barriers than to undergo the turmoil that a complete revamping of the present wage system would entail. If women get a fair crack at becoming bricklayers, presumably those women who want bricklayers' high wages will become bricklayers rather than nurses. If shortages of nurses ensue, nurses' wages will go up; possibly men will become nurses, thus reducing the sexual imbalance in both jobs. Women's spokespersons respond that the process will take too long and assumes an unrealistic degree of responsiveness in the labor market.

Would comparable worth give the wrong signals? Would it increase the number of librarians when we already have too many? Computer personnel are already paid more than any "objective" job evaluation plan would allow them. Should these special, market induced differentials be disallowed?

Somewhat similar arguments arise regarding collective bargaining. Unions argue that workers themselves, through their unions, should participate in setting wage differentials. Women's groups respond that male-dominated unions inevitably are biased in favor of male jobs. Wages should be set on the basis of equity rather than supply scarcities or collective bargaining clout. Certainly, were the comparable worth principle to be accepted, the wages of many unionized truck drivers and bricklayers might drop, while those of many nonunion clericals might rise. There would be less reason to join a union, and union power and membership might decline.

Finally (as discovered in Chapters 4 and 9), job evaluation is far from an exact science. Perhaps the best that can be said for it is that it provides a systematic way of applying judgment. Possibly one can say that Job A requires more physical ability than Job B, so Job A should pay more. But, what if Job A requires a high amount of physical ability and Job B a high amount of mental ability? Which is worth more? There is no scientific way to determine whether a job that requires two years of college is worth more than one lifting eighty-pound sacks in zero-degree cold.

Job evaluation specialists generally agree that the greater the differences among the jobs compared, the less useful job evaluation becomes. Many organizations get around this problem by having separate job evaluation programs for managers, blue-collar workers, and white-collar workers, and some exclude whole sets of occupations (e.g., skilled trades). Women's groups complain that separate evaluation schemes merely preserve sex-biased differentials between white- and blue-collar workers.

Another common approach (described in Chapter 9) makes use of *key* jobs that are common enough in the labor market that competitive or *prevailing* wages can be determined. If, according to the market, the ability to lift eighty pounds is worth more than two years of college, wage differentials within the company are set to reflect this. Once again, women object that market-set differentials are based in discrimination.

It is still too early to predict how this comparable worth issue will be settled. "This is a case which is pregnant with the possibility of disrupting the entire economic system of the United States," one judge put it. "I'm not going to restructure the entire economy." But, as a lawyer replied, "The law bans discrimination in compensation, and discrimination should not be justified on the basis of the cost to correct it." In the end, perhaps nationwide job evaluation may not be required, and only the most blatant cases of salary inequity in large companies will be corrected. Certainly the issue is so complex that uniform national rules should not be introduced until there is considerable experimentation to determine what is workable (Milkovich, 1981).

Job Rights

Just as the rights for minorities and women were among the major personnel issues of the 1960s and the 1970s, so job rights may be the major new personnel issue for the 1980s. The demand is now for *individual* rights to due process, dignity, and self-expression, which go beyond economic job security and the *group* rights established by the civil rights legislation. Among the rights at issue are those involving unfair discharge, appeals from adverse management decisions, freedom of speech and dress, and protections from sexual harrassment and invasions of privacy.

Protection against Unfair Discharge. Traditionally, employment was at will. An employee could be discharged for any reason or none at all. As a corollary, an employee could be required to do anything the employer wanted—or be fired.

Gradually this concept has eroded away. Union contracts provide that discipline shall be for just cause only and that a disciplined employee may appeal to an impartial arbitrator. The National Labor Relations Act protects employees against discrimination because of union activity, while civil rights laws protect them against discrimination on the basis of race, ethnic background, sex, or age (if between forty and seventy years old). Thus, union members, women, members of ethnic and racial minorities, and older workers all have recourse to governmental agencies if they feel their discipline involves discrimination. The easiest way for the employer to protect not itself against such charges is to show that this discipline occurred for "just cause." This, in turn, means that employers must be prepared to document their reasons for disciplinary action. Particularly when older employees are discharged because they can no longer do the job, it becomes especially important to prove that discharge was caused by the workers' demonstrated inability to meet the minimum requirements of the job, not because of advanced age.

In addition, public employees enjoy protections under civil service laws and regulations; the Supreme Court has ruled that long-term government employees acquire a "property interest" in their jobs. In turn, this can entitle them to a hearing and other procedural protections against discharge or layoff. Some courts have held it illegal to use "a socially undesirable motive" to discharge a private-sector employee; for example, in Oregon, an employee may not be discharged for agreeing to serve on a jury.

Thus, due process has been creeping into large-scale organizations. However, due process rights are still somewhat sketchy and unsystematized. To avail themselves of these rights, private sector nonunion employees must go through the cumbersome process of alleging age, race, or sex discrimination and carrying their case to a government agency.

Private nonunion employers still have fairly considerable freedom to discharge at will, and the possibilities for abuse are still substantial. The nationwide discharge rate averages over 4 percent annually; some two million people suffer discharge each year. Even if 90 percent of these discharge cases would be held as justified, were they taken to arbitration, this would still leave 200,000 unfair discharges each year. As a consequence, there is increasing pressure to complete the job rights revolution by giving the 50,000,000 nonunion private sector employees the same protections against unfair discipline now enjoyed by unionized and governmental employees. At the least, it is suggested, management should be required to provide:

1. Written, uniform disciplinary rules, thus placing each employee on notice as to the standards to which he or she will be held
2. A written statement of charges before disciplinary action is taken
3. An opportunity for a hearing, perhaps with a representative (even a lawyer present); perhaps even the right to confront witnesses and to rebut testimony
4. An opportunity to appeal an adverse decision.

Some authorities argue that it is enough that these protections be provided by voluntary employer action, or that the right of appeal be only to the company president. Others believe that, since the worst offenders are unlikely to restrict their own freedom voluntarily, a right of appeal (either to an impartial arbitrator or to a governmental tribunal) should be established by law. Rights of this sort already exist in all major Western European countries.

Opponents argue, of course, that appeal rights will add an unneeded element of legalism and technicality to the employment process, require endless recordkeeping, and hamstring management attempts to maintain productivity and discipline. Further, they may be costly. The British system of public disciplinary appeals handles 45,000 cases annually and requires much of the time of 76 tribunals and 200 conciliation officers.

To restrict this volume, appeal rights need not be extended to all employees and cases. Supervisors and short-term employees may be exempted; employees may be required to bear part of the cost; and appeals may be allowed only against discharge, not lesser forms of discipline.

General Right to Appeal.   Unjust discipline is not the only form of ill treatment from which an employee may suffer. He or she may be unfairly denied a promotion, given an unfavorable vacation date, or placed on a nasty job. Numerous causes of dissatisfaction arise in nonunion organizations that might give rise to formal grievances were these organizations unionized.

Believing that not only should an organization *be* just, but should be *seen* as being just, an increasing number of nonunion firms now provide grievance procedures. Of course, a strong motivation here is the desire to eliminate the kinds of dissatisfaction that might lead to unionization.

Of the various forms of grievance procedures, the "open door policy" is perhaps the simplest. This policy permits individual employees to appeal decisions from their immediate boss to their boss's boss and then up the ladder to the company president. But "open doors" are often viewed as insufficient. In practice, higher ups may merely rubber-stamp their subordinate's decisions.

To provide a greater semblance of impartiality, some organizations provide independent appeals channels. The Army, for example, has Inspector-Generals to whom individual soldiers may appeal for justice. Xerox is one of a growing number of companies to use independent "ombudsmen," who typically are charged with investigating individual complaints, making recommendations for their settlement, and bringing these recommendations to top management's attention.

Some ombudsmen systems have worked with considerable success. But management is not required to accept the ombudsman's recommendation. Further, if the obudsman is seen as not being strictly impartial, the whole ombudsman system may be viewed as window dressing. A few companies (such as Northrup) now allow aggrieved nonunion employees to appeal their grievances to an independent review board (sometimes including their peers) or to an outside arbitrator. Appeals systems of this sort should spread during the 1980s.

Right to Privacy.   Recent years have seen the development of the concept that employees have the right to privacy (*Daily Labor Report,* July 3, 1979 and June 13, 1980; Ewing, 1977). The exact meaning of "privacy" is still evolving. The main rights claimed so far have been protection against the employer's prying excessively into employee's affairs, and greater opportunity for employees to inspect and correct their personnel records. Companies recently have been forced to give considerable thought to these issues, and some, such as AT&T, General Motors, and the Bank of America, have adopted tightened new privacy policies.

There is now considerable public support for protecting privacy, not solely on the job, but also in such areas as credit checks. In 1977, a presidentially appointed committee recommended that employers *voluntarily* agree to tell employees what records are maintained on them, to permit them to copy most of such material, and to let them add corrections to such records if justified. Two years later, President Carter endorsed the general concept of voluntarism, but urged legislation to ban lie detectors and to permit employees access to their medical records.

The polygraph issue is especially controversial. "Lie detectors" have been fairly widely used both during employment interviews and in investigating alleged dishonesty and stealing; on the other hand, unionists and civil libertarians claim that they are of limited value and may incriminate innocent people who may get emotionally upset when charged with acts they did not commit (Kahn, 1979). At least twelve states now prohibit their use for employment purposes and unions are seeking to outlaw their use elsewhere. There are also objections to the use of such techniques as voice or stress analyzers in employment interviews.

Other alleged violations of privacy include TV observation of washrooms (to insure that people are not malingering) or workplaces (to insure productivity), and the searching of workers' persons or clothes lockers (to find illegal drugs or stolen company property). The postal workers union objects to the use of concealed lookout galleries from which inspectors observe employees on the workroom floor. As their counsel argued, "The workplace isn't a prison. An employee has certain rights as a citizen—the freedom to come to work and do the job unimpeded and unspied on." The telephone workers union objects to "service monitoring" of employees' conversations (employers respond, of course, that telephone monitoring is no different from any other form of output inspection). Similar objections are voiced to the practice of hotel and restaurant chains that hire anonymous inspectors to assume the role of customers and to report confidentially to top management on employee misdeeds and the sloppiness they observe.

Other questions relate to personnel files. Should employees be allowed to read their own files, or should the employer be permitted to keep some or all of the material in them confidential? It is argued that the employees should be allowed to see, and to object to, anything placed in their file, especially if at some later date this material might be used against them. Management responds, naturally, that once these files are open, supervisors will be less candid in making assessments in promotional or transfer cases. At least seven states have resolved this question in favor of employee access to most records. Under the circumstances, employers have become much more circumspect as to what they put into the files.

Confidentiality is an especially critical issue in universities where tenure and promotional decisions are based heavily on letters of evaluation from professors in other institutions. If the person being considered for promotion can now see these letters, will the persons making the evaluations continue to be honest in their assessments, or will they hedge a bit to avoid causing animosity?

If files are to be open to the employee, who else should be allowed to see them? If an employee is seeking a new job, should the prospective employer be allowed to contact the old employer for a recommendation? What should the old employer say? A Presidential commission recommended that unless the employee permits full disclosure, the only information that might be provided should be the employee's salary, job title, and length of service.

> The Monsanto Company has a well developed privacy policy. It will disclose only the most basic employment information, such as dates of employment, last salary, and job title, to an interested third party, and will reveal the reason for an employee's termination only at the employee's written request. Supervisors are allowed to keep secret their temporary working notes for a six-month period between each employee's regular performance reviews but then the notes must be destroyed. Once information has been communicated to the employee, it can be added to the regular personnel file (*Daily Labor Report,* July 3, 1979, p. A-5).

Medical examinations also give rise to controversy. Can an employee be required to take a physical examination against his or her will? Can the company doctor withhold the results of such examinations from the employee involved? Suppose the information might distress the employee? To whom in the company (or outside the company) may the doctor reveal this information? Can the results of an involuntary physical examination be used to deny an individual a promotion, or to involuntarily transfer an individual from a dangerous high-paying job to a safer but lower-paying one?

There have been a number of abuses in the area; for example, doctors who have not told employees about actual or incipient occupational diseases, believing that their primary obligation was to the company that employed them, and that if they told the employees about their condition, these employees might sue the company. The medical profession has begun to reevaluate its responsibilities in matters such as this.

Free Speech.   Recent court decisions have given employees some rights to free speech, especially when they call attention to their employer's misdeeds (Westin, 1980). In contrast to the earlier legal doctrine that employees owe absolute loyalty to their employer, the new doctrine suggests that employees have the right to "blow the whistle" against their employer when, for example, the employer seeks to hide violations of the law. A California engineer won legal damages from an employer that had discharged him for "disloyalty" (he had reported that the company's new computer console violated the state safety code.) The NLRB held it a violation of the law for an airport servicing company to discharge an employee for writing a letter to the airlines that his company serviced charging that his employer's poor maintenance procedures jeopardized air safety (*Daily Labor Report,* March 17, 1980). Federal rules now protect employees against retaliation for reporting violations of safety and environmental protection regulations (*Daily Labor Report,* March 19, 1980). Five states have laws forbidding employers from infringing on their employees' political freedom.

Although protections against whistle blowing have become more common, there is less recognition of the right to use abusive language against one's own boss. Union contracts are making it increasingly clear that such language is grounds for discipline.

But suppose the subordinate merely disagrees politely with his or her boss (and carries out orders, though objecting to them)? Here the law is still developing. Governmental and unionized employees presumably enjoy this kind of free speech already.

Similar rights for private sector employees may be the subject of frequent personnel debates during the 1980s. On one side will be those who claim that free speech is good for the organization and essential for individual dignity; their opponents will argue that a company should not be a debating society.

Appearance and Dress.   For some employees, the essence of civil liberties is to be allowed to wear the dress and hairstyle they want. The rules have been changing rapidly here. Until the mid-1960s, it was an unwritten rule in most offices that men would wear suits and ties and women would wear dresses and high-heeled shoes. Within ten years, this custom had changed drastically. There was greater diversity all around. Many women shifted to slacks and sneakers. Blacks flaunted afros as signs of racial pride, and many white men adopted sports shirts, mustaches, beards, and long hair.

Employers resisted this with various degrees of tenacity. Complete dress freedom was permitted in some offices. In other situations, especially those where public contact was high, companies felt it necessary to adopt detailed attire codes (for example, men's hair should not cover the ears or extend below the earlobe, mustaches should be neatly trimmed, multicolored sport shirts would not be allowed, etc.). Despite the detail of these codes, they usually permitted considerably more freedom than ever was allowed during the 1950s.

Friction continues (and will continue) in many places, as companies seek to improve their appearance and employees argue that as long as they perform their job adequately they should be permitted to dress as they wish.

Attempts to establish a legal right of dress have met only mixed success. Some courts have extended free speech to include life styles and have held that employers may not impose "unreasonable" restrictions on clothing, hair style, and so forth. The predominant view, however, is that an organization may require its employees to adhere to common standards of grooming, provided these standards tend to enhance the organization's public image. The Supreme Court, for example, has held that policemen may be required to keep their hair reasonably short.

On the other hand, employers may not enforce a dress code that discriminates between the sexes. In 1980, the Supreme Court declined to review a lower court decision that indicated it was illegal for a company to require women to wear "career ensembles," consisting of five basic items (a color-coordinated skirt or slacks and a choice of jacket, tunic, or vest), while men were allowed to wear "customary business attire" of their own choice, either a suit or sports jacket and pants. The lower court majority called this dress code "demeaning" to women; the dissenting judge asserted that the majority opinion "ignores the fact of life that men's customary business attire has never really advanced beyond the stage of being a uniform" (*Daily Labor Report,* March 17, 1980, p. A-15).

Sexual Harassment.   Perhaps surprisingly, the concept that a woman should be free from sexual harassment is a relatively new one. There is still considerable disagreement as to what the term means and how extensively management should be held responsible for protecting it. As with other issues, changing standards create numerous problems for management.

At the least, sexual hasassment involves what might be called sexual extortion; for example, the boss makes it clear to his secretary that if she does not go to bed with him, she will lose her job. Recently, however, as women have begun moving out of "girl ghettos" they have been subjected to a variety of indignities from *fellow* workers, part of which are designed to make them quit. "Women coal miners report extremely high incidence of sexual harassment on the job including physical assault, verbal provocations and slurs, propositions and repeated incidents of male exposure in mine tunnels" (*Daily Labor Report*, June 17, 1980, p. E-6). To avoid such treatment, women seek legal protection against sexual harassment by fellow employees.

The EEOC has issued *Guidelines* outlawing sexual harassment, defining it as follows:

> Unwelcome sexual advances, requests for sexual favors, and other verbal and physical conduct of a sexual nature constitute sexual harassment when (1) submission to such conduct is made explicitly or implicitly a term . . . of employment, (2) submission or rejection of such conduct is . . . used as the basis of employment decisions, or (3) such conduct has the purpose or effect of substantially interfering with an individual's work performance or creating an intimidating, hostile, or offensive working environment. An employer should take all steps to prevent sexual harassment from occurring.

The *Guidelines* are fraught with numerous questions, including many relating to the definition itself (e.g., what is meant by "unwelcome," and "unreasonable"). Here are a few of them:

1. By contrast with discriminatory employment policy, sexual harassment is initiated by individuals for their own benefit and in most cases without the knowledge or approval of top management. To what extent should the organization be held responsible for the unauthorized behavior of individual lower-level managers? The *Guidelines* state that an employer is responsible for the acts of its supervisors "regardless of whether the specific acts complained of were authorized or even forbidden by the employer and regardless of whether the employer knew of or should have known of their occurrence." Thus, the employer is responsible for very personal acts of its supervisors, even those it "should (not) have known" about.

2. To what extent should management be responsible for the acts of nonmanagerial employees? Presumably management has the same obligation to protect its employees from harassment as it does to provide a safe working environment. But, in this case, to protect the rights of one group of employees, it must enforce discipline against another. Management's ability to discipline nonmanagerial employees is less than its ability to discipline managerial employees, especially if the former belong to unions. The *Guidelines* state: "An employer is responsible for acts of sexual harassment in the workplace where the employer, or its agents or supervisory employees, knows or should have known of the conduct, unless it can show that it took immediate and appropriate corrective action." Does "should have known" mean that the employers must increase their surveillance of employees? What does this do to other employee job rights? Suppose one member of an autonomous work group makes an unwelcome proposition to another? How much "should" the employer know about what happens in dark mine tunnels?

The issue presents dilemmas for unions, too. What should the union officer do when a female member charges a male member with harassment? Should the officer bring charges within the union structure (hardly an effective disciplinary technique)? Or should the officer request management to take disciplinary action? And, if management takes such action on its own, should the union suspend its normal function of defending a disciplined member? This is not an easy political decision, particularly since many members (and some officers) believe that "If a woman takes a man's job, she is asking for what she gets."

3. It is hard to eliminate boy meets girl. Where does one draw the line between sexual harassment and ardent wooing by a determined unrequited suitor? The *Guidelines* speak of "unwelcome . . . verbal . . . conduct of a sexual nature." Presumably a passionate declaration of love is "verbal conduct of a sexual nature." But when it is truly "unwelcome"? In novels, a lady's "No" frequently turns to "Yes." Obviously, there is much meat for the lawyer here unless all parties apply heavy (and unlawyer-like) doses of common sense.

4. A related point: sexual harassment often (normally?) occurs outside the sight and hearing of others. Proof is difficult since one person's word must be taken against that of another, and frequently the parties perceive the same situation differently. Since the test under the third criterion is "purpose or effect," the courts may be drawn fairly deeply into psychology.

5. Depending on how one broadly defines sexual harassment, its elimination will require substantial cultural changes (but so has affirmative action generally). The Working Woman's Institute has asked the EEOC specifically to outlaw: "making obscene gestures; placing nude . . . pictures of women in visible areas of the workplace; . . . showing stag movies on the job and/or in job related settings; and publically circulating jokes . . . which degrade women on the basis of their sexuality" (*Daily Labor Report,* June 17, 1980, p. E-5).

In parts of Italy it is fairly common for an attractive woman to receive admiring glances and low whistles as she walks down the street. Similar behavior occurs in some U.S. plants. Presumably this is a form of illegal sexual harassment (with the key question to be decided by the courts being whether the whistles are "unwelcome").

In the past, the standards of the shop were less refined than those of the office. As the National Labor Relations Board put it, "the use of vulgarities and obscenities is a reality of industrial life." Sexually-oriented banter is a common means of relieving boredom on the job (Schrank, 1978). It occurs even in mixed workgroups, with some women giving as well as they get. Status is measured in some U.S. male youth cultures by one's artistic use of four-lettered words and by the number of female conquests one can report. Changing this culture is difficult. On the other hand, many women have adjusted to it. As one put it, "Sure it's tough at first. They are trying you out. But once you make your position clear, they lay off you. And I can cuss back just as loud as they do."

But how about the woman who is less determined than this one? Or one less comfortable in cussing? Should women—or even men—be subjected to this kind of treatment? On the other hand, should federal regulations of labor relations extend to the elimination of obscene gestures, nudie pictures, and dirty jokes?

6. May an employer require a female employee (for instance, a cocktail waitress) to wear a scanty, revealing costume that may subject her to harassment by male customers? In 1980, a court ruled that under such circumstances she may sue her boss (*Daily Labor Report,* June 18, 1980). This reasoning may end Bunny uniforms.

CONCLUSION

The personnel function has never existed in a vacuum, but in recent years it has been buffeted by unprecedented pressures coming from all sides: from individual workers, from organized interest groups, and from the government in the form of laws and regulations. With stretching, one can group these pressures into three overlapping headings:

> For *self-determination,* especially greater freedom to determine *how* to do one's job (job enrichment, autonomous work groups) and *when* to do it (flextime, voluntary overtime, and retirement); career choice; and cafeteria benefits
> For *individual* and *group rights,* individual rights including privacy and freedom from sexual harrassment, and group rights encompassing protection against discrimination on the basis of age, sex, ethnic background, or handicap
> For *security,* both physical (especially occupational safety and health) and economic (guarantees against layoffs).

All these pressures impinge on the traditional personnel functions of recruitment, selection, training, compensation administration, performance evaluation, and the like. The day is long past when these functions could be handled in isolation from the larger environment. Indeed, new standards and expectations have been established for the personnel function. The entire selection process has been upgraded, for example, and performance appraisal has become more critical.

Nevertheless, these changes have not occurred without sharp debates, especially as to the impact of the various new government regulations. To conclude the chapter, the critical arguments may be summarized.

Criticism of the New Regulations. Critics argue that the government is increasingly dictating the details of personnel policy. ERISA and OSHA already state the fundamental rules in the pension and safety areas. Testing must conform to the EEOC-set *Uniform Guidelines.* If the plaintiff's position prevails with regard to "comparable worth," a standardized nationwide system of job evaluation may be imposed. Increasingly, too, the courts are reviewing disciplinary cases.

In the final analysis, according to the critics, personnel decisions are being made by the courts, with companies subject to heavy penalties if their initial decisions are found to be wrong. Regulation paperwork, and litigation are proliferating, contributing to America's reputation as the most legalistic country in the world.

Critics point also to rigid rules, developed on a national basis, which prevent flexibility or consideration of individual situations. These rules fail to recognize that, given the state of the art, many personnel decisions cannot help but be subjective; yet the rules require objectivity where objectivity is impossible. Uniform procedures are imposed on all industries, treating higher education exactly like trucking. Experimentation is discouraged, particularly since the courts give little weight to "good faith" as a defense against rule violation. Personnel directors, for example, claim that they feel forced to base their selection techniques not on what they feel is professionally best, but what they think meets the regulations. It is difficult to devise compensation or promotion plans that encourage excellence (unless excellence can be easily measured, say in units per hour).

Thus, personnel activity must be conducted with one eye on Washington, and organizations engage in "defensive personnel work" (somewhat equivalent to the "defensive medicine" practiced by doctors threatened by malpractice suits). The manager must always assume the possibility of an adversary proceeding. Records become increasingly important, for, once the matter gets in court, management must depend on these to defend its actions. Lawyers and professional psychologists are almost essential. Small firms find it difficult to keep abreast of the regulations, much less comply with them.

Finally, the cumulative costs of these regulations are quite high. Hiring lawyers and keeping records is very expensive (in 1979, AT&T had 750 people in its equal employment department). The costs of complying with OSHA have been estimated in the billions of dollars, if not tens of billions. Money spent on fringes and occupational health is not available for wages and consumption. All this contributes to higher costs (and prices), lowered productivity, and inability to meet competition from foreign countries that lack such restrictive rules—or so critics argue.

The Counterarguments. Supporters of the current programs insist that these arguments are exaggerated. The new programs are designed to deal with real evils: blatant discrimination, which relegated women and minority group members to low paid, insecure jobs; dangerous work sites, which condemned many workers to lingering, early deaths; patterns of sexual harrassment impossible to defend; and corruptly run pension plans that inevitably would have left workers without protections when they needed them most. Eliminating these evils will make a more humane society.

Further, the rules are reasonable. To be sure, they restrict company freedom, but no more than do union contracts, for example. The requirement that personnel policies be defendable merely forces companies to do what they should be doing anyway. There is little in the new rules that has not been advocated by progressive leaders of the personnel profession for some time. The regulations encourage innovation rather than the reverse. For example, most consent decrees and affirmative action agreements are carefully tailored to the needs of the individual employer.

As for costs, these may go up in the short run, but in the long run everyone will gain by unleashing the unused talents of people in menial jobs. Healthier people work more productively (and their hospital bills are less). Job security pays off in higher morale. And social justice is valuable in itself—beyond dollars-and-cents considerations.

A Balancing of Views. In the end, everyone must make up his or her own mind as to these issues. Certainly some tradeoffs are required. In one sense, the new rules do reduce organizational flexibility; on the other hand, all they really require is more effective personnel work. Probably the rules will increase costs, but the objectives are also probably worth the price. In the short run, affirmative action may be unfair to some white males; in the long run, a new standard of justice may be achieved. To be sure, some specific rules may be unjustified and unworkable, and some administrators may be insensitive to organizational needs. But the fact that many regulatory schemes need reform does not make them inherently defective. The various rules adopted during the Johnson, Nixon, Ford, and Carter administrations may have been too inflexible. On the other hand, the Reagan administration shows little sympathy for their objectives and has gone perhaps too far in seeking to dismantle them and preventing them from being effectively enforced. Twenty years of progress are under determined attack.

Similarly, growing demands for greater individual freedom to determine the nature of one's work, working hours, career path, and form of fringe benefits all create difficulties for management. Organizations must accommodate themselves to employees' desires, rather than the reverse. The end will almost certainly be greater individual satisfaction. It may also be more effective use of manpower.

Increased Role for Personnel.   Ever since this writer finished graduate school, he has been reading articles about personnel's increasing importance. To read these, one would believe that the personnel function has been enjoying forty years of logarithmically increasing status. Actually, the 1950s and 1960s were periods of relative decline. Most personnel functions—selection, training, wage administration, management development, and the like—were routinized. Even collective bargaining became rather tame. With reduced uncertainty came reduced power.

Things have been different since the early 1970s. However costly the new pressures may have been for the organization as a whole, they certainly have made the personnel function more important. One thing seems sure: for personnel people, the decade of the 1980s should be exciting.

Discussion Questions

1. On balance, is the trend toward providing greater job security (and compensating people if they are laid off) helpful or harmful to society? Should U.S. industry move toward Japanese-style lifetime employment?

2. It is widely argued that employees today prefer independence and self-determination to purely economic benefits. How valid is this argument? Assuming it were valid, what changes would be required in personnel practices?

3. Has governmental regulation of personnel practices gone too far? Where would you cut it back? Where whould you extend it? Why?

4. Assuming we are becoming a Zero-Sum Society, what pressures will this place on the personnel function?

5. It is argued that equal employment regulations (a) unrealistically assume that personnel is a science rather than an art, (b) require excessive rigidity and uniformity in

personnel practices, (c) discriminate against healthy young white males, and (d) set a socially undesirable goal that the proportions of each racial and sexual group be exactly the same on every job, regardless of its characteristics, thus among other things reducing social pluralism. Do you agree?

REFERENCES

Abodeely, J. E. *The NLRB and the appropriate bargaining unit* (Labor and Public Policy Series Report No. 3). Philadelphia: Industrial Research Unit, Wharton School of Finance and Commerce, University of Pennsylvania, 1971.

Ackerman, L. S. A human resource management control system. *Human Resource Planning 2* (1979): 197–204.

Adam, E. Behavior modification in quality control. *Academy of Management Journal 18* (1975): 662–679.

Adams, J. S. Inequity in social exchange. In L. Berkowitz (ed.), *Advances in experimental social psychology*. New York: Academic Press, 1965.

Ad Hoc Committee on Ethical Standards in Psychological Research. *Ethical principles in the conduct of research with human participants*. Washington: American Psychological Association, 1973.

Alabama v. *United States,* 304 F.2d 583, 586 (5th Cir.), 371 U.S. 37 (1962).

Albemarle Paper Co. v. *Moody,* 422 U.S. 405, 9 EPD #10,230, 10 FEP 1181 (1975).

Albright, L. E. Personal communication, 1980.

Alderfer, C. P. An empirical test of a new theory of human needs. *Organizational Behavior and Human Performance 4* (1969): 142–175.

Alderfer, C. P. *Existence, relatedness and growth: Human needs in organizational settings*. New York: Free Press, 1972.

Alderfer, C. P., and McCord, C. G. Personal and situational factors in the recruitment interview. *Journal of Applied Psychology 54* (1970): 377–385.

Aldrich, H. E. *Organizations and environments*. Englewood Cliffs, N.J.: Prentice-Hall, 1979.

Alexander, E. R. The design of alternatives in organizational contexts: A pilot study. *Administrative Science Quarterly 24* (1979): 382–404.

Allan, P. Career patterns of top executives in New York City government. *Public Personnel Review 33* (1972): 114–117.

Allen, R. 1967 school disputes in Michigan. *Public employee organization and bargaining*. Washington: Bureau of National Affairs, 1968.

Allen, R. E.; Keaveny, T. J.; and Jackson, J. H. *A reexamination of the preferred job characteristics of full-time and part-time workers*. Paper presented at the annual meeting of the National Academy of Management, San Francisco, August 1978.

American Psychological Association. *Standards for educational and psychological tests and manuals*. Washington: American Psychological Association, 1973.

American Society for Personnel Administration. *Occupational safety and health review.* Berea, Ohio: American Society for Personnel Administration, September 1978.

American Society for Personnel Administration. *Occupational safety and health review.* Berea, Ohio: American Society for Personnel Administration, September 1979.

American Society for Personnel Administration. *Occupational safety and health review.* Berea, Ohio: American Society for Personnel Administration, March 1980.

Anderson, C. W. The relation between speaking times and decision in the employment interview. *Journal of Applied Psychology 44* (1960): 267–268.

Anderson, J. C. Local union participation: A re-examination. *Industrial Relations 18* (1979): 18–31.

Anderson, J. C.; Busman, G.; and O'Reilly, C. A., III. What factors influence the outcome of union decertification elections? *Monthly Labor Review 102* (1979): 32–40.

Anderson, J. C., and Milkovich, G. Propensity to leave: A preliminary examination of March and Simon's model. *Relations Industrielles 35* (1980): 279–294.

Anderson, J. C.; Milkovich, G. T.; and Tsui, A. A model of intra-organizational mobility. *Academy of Management Review 6* (1981): 529–538.

Anderson, J. C.; O'Reilly, C. A.; and Busman, G. Union decertification in the U.S.: 1947–1977. *Industrial Relations 19* (1980): 100–107.

Andrisani, P.; Applebaum, E.; Keppel, R.; and Miljus, R. *Work attitudes and work experiences.* Philadelphia: Center for Labor and Human Resources, Temple University, 1977.

Andrisani, P. J., and Miljus, R. C. Individual differences in preferences for intrinsic versus extrinsic aspects of work. *Journal of Vocational Behavior 11* (1977): 14–30.

Archer, J. R., and Giorgia, M. J. Bibliography of the Occupational Research Division, Air Force Human Resources Laboratory (AFSC). *JSAS Catalog of Selected Documents in Psychology 5* (1977): 259.

Argyris, C. *Interpersonal competence and organizational effectiveness.* Homewood, Ill.: Dorsey Press, 1962.

Argyris, C. Problems and new directions for industrial psychology. In M. D. Dunnette (ed.), *Handbook of industrial and organizational psychology.* Chicago: Rand McNally, 1976.

Arnold v. *Ballard,* 390 F.Supp. 723, 9 EPD # 9921, 10 FEP 1363 (1975).

Arvey, R. D. *Fairness in selecting employees.* Reading, Mass: Addison-Wesley, 1979.

Arvey, R. D. Unfair discrimination in the employment interview: Legal and psychological aspects. *Psychological Bulletin 86* (1979): 736–765.

Arvey, R. D.; Gordon, M.; Massengill, O.; and Mussio, S. Differential dropout rates of minority and majority job candidates due to "time lags" between selection procedures. *Personnel Psychology 28* (1975): 175–180.

Arvey, R. D., and Ivancevich, J. M. Punishment in organizations: A review of propositions and research suggestions. *Academy of Management Review 5* (1980): 123–132.

Arvey, R. D., and Mossholder, K. M. A proposed methodology for determining similarities and differences among jobs. *Personnel Psychology 30* (1977): 363–374.

Arvey, R. D., and Mussio, S. J. Job expectations and valences of job rewards for culturally disadvantaged and advantaged clerical employees. *Journal of Applied Psychology 59* (1974): 230–232.

Astin, A. Criterion-centered research. *Educational and Psychological Measurement 24* (1964): 807–822.

Azrin, N. H.; Flores, T.; and Kaplan, S. J. Job-finding club: A group-assisted program for obtaining employment. *Behavior Research and Therapy 13* (1975): 17–27.

Babb, H. W., and Kopp, D. G. Applications of behavior modification in organization: A review and critique. *Academy of Management Review 3* (1978): 281–290.

Baehr, M. E. *Skills and attributes inventory.* Chicago: Industrial Relations Center, University of Chicago, 1971.

Baehr, M. E.; Lonergan, W. G.; and Potkay, C. R. *Work elements inventory.* Chicago: Industrial Relations Center, University of Chicago, 1967.

Bailey, T. Industrial outplacement at Goodyear, Part 1: The company's position. *Personnel Administrator 25* (1980): 42.

Bakke, E. W. Why workers join unions. *Personnel 22* (1945): 37–46.

Barbee, J. R., and Keil, E. C. Experimental techniques of job interview training for the disadvantaged: Videotape feedback, behavior modification, and microcounseling. *Journal of Applied Psychology 58* (1973): 209–213.

Barrett, G. V.; Alexander, R. A.; O'Connor, E. O.; Forbes, J. B.; Balascoe, L.; and Garver, T. *Public policy and personnel selection: Development of a selection program for patrol officers* (Technical Report 1). Akron, Ohio: University of Akron, Department of Psychology, April, 1975.

Barrett, R. S. *Performance rating.* Chicago: Science Research Associates, 1966.

Barron, J., and Gilley, D. W. The effect of unemployment insurance on the search process. *Industrial and Labor Relations Review 32* (1979): 363–366.

Barron, J., and Mellow, W. *The determinants of current search effort and subsequent labor force status.* Report prepared for the Employment and Training Administration, Department of Labor, September 1978.

Bartholomew, D. J., and Forbes, A. F. *Statistical techniques for manpower planning.* Chichester, England: Wiley, 1979.

Bartlett, T. E. *Career ladder analysis.* Mill Valley, Calif.: Syvern Research Associates, 1977.

Bartol, K. M. Expectancy theory as a predictor of female occupational choice and attitude toward business. *Academy of Management Journal 19* (1976): 669–675.

Baskett, C. D. Interview decisions as determined by competency and attitude similarity. *Journal of Applied Psychology 57* (1973): 343–345.

Bassett, G. A. PAIR records and information systems. In D. Yoder and H. G. Heneman, Jr. (eds.), *Planning and auditing PAIR.* Washington: Bureau of National Affairs, 1976.

Bassett, G. A. A study of the effects of task goal and schedule choice on work performance. *Organizational Behavior and Human Performance 24* (1979): 202–227.

Baum, J. F. Effectiveness of an attendance control policy in reducing chronic absenteeism. *Personnel Psychology 31* (1978): 71–77.

Baumgartel, H., and Jeanpierre, F. Applying new knowledge in the backhome setting: A study of Indian managers' adoptive efforts. *Journal of Applied Behavioral Science 8* (1972): 674–694.

Bayroff, A. G.; Haggerty, H. R.; and Rundquist, E. A. Validity of ratings as related to rating techniques and conditions. *Personnel Psychology 1* (1954): 93–112.

Beary, J. F., and Benson, H. A simple psychophysiologic technique which elicits the hypometabolic changes of the relaxation response. *Psychosomatic Medicine 36* (1977): 115–120.

Beatty, R. W., and Schneier, C. E. *Personnel administration: An experiential/skill-building approach.* Reading, MA: Addison-Wesley, 1977.

Becker, L. J. Joint effect of feedback and goal setting on performance: A field study of residential energy conservation. *Journal of Applied Psychology 63* (1978): 428–433.

Beehr, T. A. Perceived situational moderators of the relationship between subjective role ambiguity and role strain. *Journal of Applied Psychology 61* (1976): 35–40.

Beehr, T. A. *Monitoring job stress: A new human resources function.* Working paper, 1980.

Beehr, T. A., and Newman, J. E. Job stress, employee health, and organizational effectiveness: A facet analysis, model and literature review. *Personnel Psychology 31* (1978): 665–699.

Beehr, T. A.; Walsh, J. T.; and Taber, T. D. Relationship of stress to individually and organizationally valued states: Higher order needs as a moderator. *Journal of Applied Psychology 61* (1976): 41–47.

Beer, M. *Organization change and development: A systems view.* Santa Monica, Calif.: Goodyear, 1980.

Beer, M.; Ruh, R. A.; Dawson, J. A.; McCaa, B. B.; and Kavanagh, M. J. A performance management system: Research, design, introduction, and evaluation. *Personnel Psychology 31* (1978): 505–535.

Behling, O. The case for the natural science model for research in organizational behavior and organization theory. *Academy of Management Review 5* (1980): 483–490.

Behling, O.; Schreisheim, C.; and Tolliver, J. Alternatives to expectancy theories for work motivation. *Decisions Sciences 6* (1975): 449–461.

Bell, D. J. *Planning corporate manpower.* London: Longman, 1974.

Bell, F. O.; Hoff, A. L.; and Hoyt, K. B. A comparison of three approaches to criterion measurement. *Journal of Applied Psychology 47* (1963): 416–418.

Bem, D. J. Self-perception theory. In L. Berkowitz (ed.), *Advances in experimental social psychology,* vol. 6. New York: Academic Press, 1972.

Benson, H.; Beary, J. F.; and Carol, M. P. The relaxation response. *Psychiatry 37* (1974): 37–46.

Bentz, V. J. The Sears experience in the investigation, description, and prediction of executive behavior. In F. R. Wickert and D. F. McFarland (eds.), *Measuring executive success.* New York: Appleton-Century-Crofts, 1967.

Bentz, V. J. *Validity studies at Sears.* Paper presented at the annual meeting of the American Psychological Association, Washington, D.C., 1971.

Berger, C. J.; Cummings, L. L.; and Heneman, H. G. Expectancy theory and operant conditioning predictions under variable ratio and continuous schedules of reinforcement. *Organizational Behavior and Human Performance 14* (1975): 227–243.

Bergman, B. Occupational segregation, wages and profits when employers discriminate by race and sex. *Eastern Economic Journal 1* (1974): 103–110.

Berkowitz, M.; Goldstein, B.; and Indik, B. P. The state mediator: Background, self-image, and attitudes. *Industrial and Labor Relations Review 17* (1964): 257–275.

Berlew, D. C., and Hall, D. T. The socialization of managers: Effects of expectations on performance. *Administrative Science Quarterly 11* (1966): 207–223.

Berlin, B. Indexing pensions. *The Wall Street Journal,* June 19, 1980.

Berlyne, D. E. Arousal and reinforcement. In D. Levine (ed.), *Nebraska symposium on motivation.* Lincoln: University of Nebraska Press, 1967.

Bernardin, H. J. Effects of rater training on leniency and halo errors in student rating of instructors. *Journal of Applied Psychology 63* (1978): 301–308.

Bernardin, H. J. Rater training: A critique and reconceptualization. *Proceedings of the Academy of Management,* Atlanta, August 1979.

Bernardin, H. J. *Rater training: Where do we go from here?* Paper presented at the First Annual Scientist-Practitioner Conference in Industrial-Organizational Psychology, Old Dominion University, April 1980.

Bernardin, H. J.; LaShells, M. B.; Smith, P. C.; and Alvares, K. M. Behavioral expectation scales: Effect of developmental procedures and formats. *Journal of Applied Psychology 61* (1976): 75–79.

Bernardin, H. J., and Pence, E. C. The effects of rater training: Creating new response sets and decreasing accuracy. *Journal of Applied Psychology 65* (1980): 60–66.

Bernardin, H. J., and Walter, C. S. Effects of rater training and dairykeeping on psychometric error in ratings. *Journal of Applied Psychology 62* (1977): 64–69.

Bernardin, H. J.; LaShells, M. B.; Smith, P. C.; and Alvarez, K. M. Behavioral expectation scales: Effects of developmental procedures and formats. *Journal of Applied Psychology 61* (1976): 75–79.

Bernstein, V.; Hakel, M. D.; and Harlan, A. The college student as interviewer: A threat to generalizability? *Journal of Applied Psychology 60* (1975): 260–268.

Berwitz, C. J. *The job analysis approach to affirmative action.* New York: Wiley, 1975.

Bexton, W. H.; Heron, W.; and Scott, T. H. Effects of decreased variation in the sensory environment. *Canadian Journal of Psychology 8* (1954): 70–76.

Bills, M. Relation of mental alertness test scores to positions and permanency in company. *Journal of Applied Psychology 1* (1923): 154–156.

Blakeney, R. N., and MacNaughton, J. F. Effects of temporal placement of unfavorable information on decision making during the selection interview. *Journal of Applied Psychology 55* (1971): 138–142.

Blau, B. Understanding midcareer stress. *Management Review 67* (1978): 57–59.

Blau, P., and Duncan, O. *The American occupational structure.* New York: Wiley, 1967.

Block, R. H. The impact of seniority provisions on the manufacturing quit rate. *Industrial and Labor Relations Review 31* (1978): 474–488.

Bluestone, I. Comments on job enrichment. *Organizational Dynamics 2* (1974) 46–47.

Blumenfeld, W. S., and Holland, M. G. A model for the empirical evaluation of training effectiveness. *Personnel Journal 50* (1971): 637–640.

Blumrosen, R. G. Wage discrimination, job segregation, and Title VII of the Civil Rights Act of 1964. *University of Michigan Journal of Law Reform 12* (1979): 397–502.

Boche, A. Management concerns about assessment centers. In J. L. Moses and W. C. Byham (eds.), *Applying the assessment center method.* New York: Pergamon, 1977, 243–260.

Boehm, V. R. Changing career patterns for women in the Bell System. In L. D. Eyde (Chair), *Employment status of women in academia, business, government, and the military.* Symposium presented at the annual meeting of the American Psychological Association, New Orleans, 1974.

Boehm, V. R. *Establishing the validity of assessment centers* (Monograph V). Pittsburgh: Development Dimensions Press, 1981.

Boehm, V. R., and Hoyle, D. F. Assessment and management development. In J. L. Moses and W. C. Byham (eds.), *Applying the assessment center method.* New York: Pergamon, 1977, pp. 203–224.

Boese, R. R., and Cunningham, J. W. *Systematically derived dimensions of human work.* (Center Report, Ergometric Research and Development Series No. 14). Raleigh, N.C.: Center for Occupational Education, North Carolina State University, 1975.

Bolles, R. *What color is your parachute?* Berkeley, Calif.: Ten Speed Press, 1972.

Bolster, B. I., and Springbett, B. M. The reaction of interviews to favorable and unfavorable information. *Journal of Applied Psychology 45* (1961): 97–103.

Borman, W. C. Effects of instructions to avoid halo error on reliability and validity of performance evaluation ratings. *Journal of Applied Psychology 60* (1975): 556–560.

Borman, W. C. Format and training effects on rating accuracy and rater errors. *Journal of Applied Psychology 64* (1979): 410–421.

Borman, W. C. *Performance judgments: The quest for accuracy in ratings of performance effectiveness.* Paper presented at the First Annual Scientist-Practitioner Conference in Industrial-Organizational Psychology, Old Dominion University, April 1980.

Borman, W. C., and Dunnette, M. D. Behavior-based versus trait-oriented performance ratings: An empirical study. *Journal of Applied Psychology 60* (1975): 561–565.

Borman, W. C., and Vallon, W. R. A review of what can happen when behavioral expectation scales are developed in one setting and used in another. *Journal of Applied Psychology 59* (1974): 197–201.

Bouchard, T. J., Jr. Field research methods: Interviewing, questionnaires, participant observation, systematic observation, unobtrusive measures. In M. D. Dunnette (ed.), *Handbook of industrial and organizational psychology.* Chicago: Rand-McNally, 1976.

Bowey, A. M. Corporate manpower planning. *Management Decision 15* (1977): 421–469.

Bowin, R. Middle manager mobility patterns. *Personnel Journal 51* (1971): 878–882.

Box, G. E. P., and Jenkins, G. M. *Time series analysis forecasting and control* (rev. ed.). San Francisco: Holden-Day, 1976.

Bray, D. W. The management progress study. *American Psychologist 19* (1969): 419–420.

Bray, D. W.; Campbell, R. S.; and Grant, D. L. *Formative years in business: A long-term AT&T study of managerial lives.* New York: Wiley-Interscience, 1974.

Bray, D. W., and Grant, D. L. The assessment center in the measurement of potential for business management. *Psychological Monographs 80* (1966): (17, Whole No. 625).

Brayfield, A. H. Human effectiveness. *American Psychologist 20* (1965): 645–657.

Brett, J. M. Behavioral research on unions and union management systems. In B. M. Staw and L. L. Cummings (eds.), *Research in organizational behavior* (vol. 2). Greenwich, Conn.: JAI Press, 1980.

Brief, A. P.; Rose, G. L.; and Aldag, R. J. Sex differences in preferences for job attributes revisited. *Journal of Applied Psychology 62* (1977): 645–646.

Brief, A. P.; Schuler, R. S.; and Van Sell, M. *Managing stress.* Boston: Little, Brown, 1980.

Bright, W. E. How one company manages its human resources. *Harvard Business Review 54* (1976): 81–93.

Bright, W. E. Getting started in human resource planning. *Human Resource Planning 1* (1978): 49–52.

Broedling, L. A. The uses of the intrinsic-extrinsic distinction in explaining motivation and organizational behavior. *Academy of Management Review 2* (1977): 267–274.

Bronfenbrenner, M. Potential monopsony in labor markets. *Industrial and Labor Relations Review 9* (1956): 577–588.

Buck, V. *Working under pressure.* London: Staples, 1972.

Burack, E. H., and Mathys, N. J. *Human resource planning: A pragmatic approach to manpower staffing and development.* Lake Forest, Ill.: Brace-Park, 1979.

Bureau of Labor Statistics. *Directory of national unions and employee associations 1975.* Washington: Government Printing Office, 1976.

Bureau of Labor Statistics. *Employment projections for the 1980's* (Bulletin No. 2030). Washington: Government Printing Office, 1979.

Bureau of National Affairs. *Bulletin to management: BNA's quarterly report on job absence and turnover.* Washington: Bureau of National Affairs, September 1980.

Bureau of National Affairs. *Daily labor report.* Washington: Bureau of National Affairs, 1979 (July 3), 1980 (March 17, March 19, June 17).

Bureau of National Affairs. *Personnel activities, budgets, and staffs* (ASPA-BNA Survey No. 38). Washington: Bureau of National Affairs, July 1979.

Bureau of National Affairs. *Personnel activities, budgets, and staffs* (ASPA-BNA Survey No. 40). Washington: Bureau of National Affairs, June 1980.

Bureau of National Affairs. *Recruiting policies and practices.* Washington: Bureau of National Affairs, 1979.

Bureau of National Affairs. *Retirement policies and programs* (ASPA-BNA Survey No. 39). Washington: Bureau of National Affairs, January 1980.

Bureau of National Affairs Labor Report. General Electric Conciliation Agreement, *Fair Employment Practices Manual 431:53.* Washington: Bureau of National Affairs.

Bureau of National Affairs Labor Report. AT&T Discrimination Settlement, *Fair Employment Practices Manual 431:73.* Washington: Bureau of National Affairs.

Bureau of National Affairs Policy and Practice Series. *Compensation.* Washington: Bureau of National Affairs.

Bureau of National Affairs Special Report. *Alcoholism and employee relations.* Washington: Bureau of National Affairs, 1978.

Burke, D. R., and Rubin, L. Is contract rejection a major collective bargaining problem? *Industrial and Labor Relations Review 26* (1972): 820–833.

Burnaska, R. F., and Hollman, T. D. An empirical comparison of the relative effects of rater response biases on three rating scale formats. *Journal of Applied Psychology 59* (1974): 307–312.

Burrell, T., and Morgan, G. M. *Sociological paradigms and organizational analysis.* London: Heinemann, 1979.

Byham, W. C. Application of the assessment center method. In J. L. Moses and W. C. Byham (eds.), *Applying the assessment center method.* New York: Pergamon, 1977.

Byham, W. C. Starting an assessment center the correct way. *Personnel Administrator 25* (1980): 27–32.

Bylinsky, G. Those smart young robots on the production line. *Fortune 100* (1979): 90–96.

Calder, B. J., and Staw, B. M. The interaction of intrinsic and extrinsic motivation: Some methodological notes. *Journal of Personality and Social Psychology 31* (1975): 76–80.

Cameron, K. Measuring organizational effectiveness in institutions of higher education. *Administrative Science Quarterly 23* (1978): 604–632.

Campbell, D. T., and Fiske, D. W. Convergent and discriminant validation by the multitrait-multimethod matrix. *Psychological Bulletin 56* (1959): 81–105.

Campbell, D. T., and Stanley, J. C. *Experimental and quasi-experimental designs for research.* Chicago: Rand McNally, 1966.

Campbell, J. P. Personnel training and development. In P. H. Mussen and M. R. Rosenzweig (eds.), *Annual review of psychology,* vol. 22. Palo Alto, Calif.: Annual Reviews, 1971.

Campbell, J. P. Psychometric theory. In M. D. Dunnette (ed.), *Handbook of industrial and organizational psychology.* Chicago: Rand-McNally, 1976.

Campbell, J. P.; Dunnette, M. D.; Arvey, R. D.; and Hellervik, L. V. The development and evaluation of behaviorally based rating scales. *Journal of Applied Psychology 57* (1973): 15–22.

Campbell, J. P.; Dunnette, M. D.; Lawler, E. E., III; and Weick, K. E., Jr. *Managerial behavior, performance, and effectiveness.* New York: McGraw-Hill, 1970.

Campbell, J. P., and Pritchard, R. D. Motivation theory in industrial and organizational psychology. In M. C. Dunnette (ed.), *Handbook of industrial and organizational psychology.* Chicago: Rand McNally, 1976.

Cannell, C. F., and Kahn, R. L. Interviewing. In G. Lindzey and E. Aronson (eds.), *The handbook of social psychology,* vol. II. New York: Addison-Wesley, 1968.

Cannon, W. B. Organization for physiological homeostasis. *Physiological Review 9* (1929): 339–430.

Caplan, R. *Organizational stress and individual strain: A sociopsychological study of risk factors in coronary heart disease among administrators, engineers and scientists.* Unpublished doctoral dissertation, University of Michigan, 1971.

Caplan, R. D.; Cobb, S.; and French, J. R. P . Relationships of cessation of smoking with job stress, personality and social support. *Journal of Applied Psychology 60* (1975): 211–219.

Caplan, R. D.; Cobb, S.; French, J. R. P., Jr.; Harrison, R. U.; and Pinneau, S. R., Jr. *Job demands and worker health.* Cincinnati, Ohio: NIOSH Research Report, 1975.

Caplan, R. D., and Jones, K. W. Effects of workload, role ambiguity and Type A personality on anxiety, depression and heart rate. *Journal of Applied Psychology 60* (1975): 713–719.

Carey, M. Occupational employment growth through 1990. *Monthly Labor Review 104* (August 1981): 45.

Carlson, H. C. Personnel control systems. In D. Yoder and H. G. Heneman, Jr. (eds.), *Planning and auditing PAIR.* Washington: Bureau of National Affairs, 1976.

Carlson, R. E. Selection interview decisions: The effect of interviewer experience, relative quota situation, and applicant sample on interviewer decisions. *Personnel Psychology 20* (1967a): 259–280.

Carlson, R. E. The relative influence of appearance and factual written information on an interviewer's final rating. *Journal of Applied Psychology 51* (1967b): 461–468.

Carlson, R. E. Selection interview decisions: The effect of mode of applicant presentation on some outcome measures. *Personnel Psychology 21* (1968): 193–207.

Carlson, R. E. Effects of applicant sample on ratings of valid information in an employment setting. *Journal of Applied Psychology 54* (1970): 217–222.

Carlson, R. E. Effect of Interview information in altering valid impressions. *Journal of Applied Psychology 65* (1971): 66–72.

Carlson, R. E.; Schwab, D. P.; and Heneman, H. G. Agreement among selection interview styles. *Journal of Applied Psychology 5* (1970): 8–17.

Carlson, R. E.; Thayer, P. W.; Mayfield, E. C.; and Peterson, D. A. Research on the selection interview. *Personnel Journal 50* (1971): 268–275.

Carrell, M. R. A longitudinal field assessment of employee perceptions of equitable treatment. *Organizational Behavior and Human Performance 21* (1978): 108–118.

Carrell, M. R., and Dittrich, J. E. Equity theory: The recent literature, methodological considerations and new directions. *Academy of Management Review 3* (1978): 202–210.

Carroll, J. P., Jr., and Tosi, H. L., Jr. Goal characteristics and personality factors in an MBO program. *Administrative Science Quarterly 15* (1970): 295–305.

Carroll, S. J.; Paine, F. T.; and Ivancevich, J. J. The relative effectiveness of training methods—Expert opinion and research. *Personnel Psychology 25* (1972): 495–509.

Cartter, A. M. *Theory of wages and employment.* Homewood, Ill.: Irwin, 1959.

Cascio, W.F. *Applied psychology in personnel management.* Reston, Va.: Reston Publishing, 1978.

Cascio, W. F. *Impact of performance appraisal litigation on scientists and practitioners.* Paper presented at the First Annual Scientist-Practitioner Conference in Industrial-Organizational Psychology, Old Dominion University, April 1980.

Cascio, W. F., and Silbey, V. Utility of the assessment center as a selection device. *Journal of Applied Psychology 64* (1979): 107–118.

Cass, E. L., and Zimmer, F. G. *Man and work in society.* New York: Van Nostrand Reinhold, 1975.

Castaneda v. *Partida,* 430 U.S. 482 (1977).

Ceriello, V. R., and Frantzreb, R. B. A human resource planning model. *Human Factors 17* (1975): 35–41.

Certiorari denied by U.S. Supreme Court, 92 LRRM 2818 (1976).

Chafetz, I., and Fraser, C. R. P. Union decertification: An exploratory analysis. *Industrial Relations 18* (1979): 59–69.

Chamberlain, N. W., and Cullen, D. E. *The labor sector* (rev. ed.). New York: McGraw-Hill, 1971.

Cheek, L. Cost effectiveness comes to the personnel function. *Harvard Business Review 51* (1973): 96–105.

Cherrington, D. J.; Condie, S. J.; and England, J. L. Age and work values. *Academy of Management Journal 22* (1979): 617–623.

Cherrington, D. J., and England, J. L. The desire for an enriched job as a moderator of the enrichment-satisfaction relationship. *Organizational Behavior and Human Performance 25* (1980): 130–159.

Chew, W. B., and Justice, R. L. EEO modeling for large, complex organizations. *Human Resource Planning 2* (1979): 57–70.

Christal, R. E., and Weissmuller, J. J. *New Comprehensive Occupational Data Analysis Programs (CODAP) for analyzing task factor information* (AHFRL Interim Professional Paper No. 7R-76-3). Lackland Air Force Base, Texas: Air Force Human Resources Laboratory, 1976.

Churchill, N. C., and Shank, J. K. Affirmative action and guilt-edged goals. *Harvard Business Review 54* (1976): 111–116.

City of Los Angeles, Department of Water and Power v. *Manhart,* 16 EPD 8250 (1978).

Clark, J. B. *The distribution of wealth.* New York: MacMillan, 1900.

Clark, H. L., and Thurston, D. R. *Planning your staffing needs.* Washington: Bureau of Policies and Standards, U.S. Civil Service Commission, 1977.

Cobb, S. Physiologic changes in men whose jobs were abolished. *Journal of Psychosomatic Research 18* (1974): 245–258.

Cobb, S. Social support as a moderator of life stress. *Psychosomatic Medicine 38* (1976): 300–314.

Cobb, S., and Kasl, S. V. *Termination: The consequence of job loss.* Cincinnati, Ohio: Department of Health, Education and Welfare, 1977.

Cobb, S., and Rose, R. M. Hypertension, peptic ulcer, and diabetes in air traffic controllers. *Journal of the American Medical Association 224* (1973): 489–492.

Cohen, B. M.; Moses, J. L.; and Byham, W. C. *The validity of assessment centers: A literature review* (Monograph No. 2). Pittsburgh: Development Dimensions Press, 1974.

Cohen, S. L., and Bunker, K. A. Subtle effects on sex role stereotypes on recruiters' hiring decisions. *Journal of Applied Psychology 60* (1975): 566–572.

Cohen, S. L.; Groner, D. M.; Muxworthy, D. G.; and Glickman, E. I. Incorporating assessment center techniques into management training and development at Xerox. *Journal of Assessment Center Technology 2* (1979): 1–5.

Cohen, S. L., and Sands, L. The effects of order of exercise presentation on assessment center performance: One standardization concern. *Personnel Psychology 31* (1978): 35–46.

Colbert, G. A., and Taylor, L. R. Empirically derived job families as a foundation for the study of validity generalization. *Personnel Psychology 31* (1978): 355–364.

Colligan, M., and Smith, M. A methodological approach for evaluating outbreaks of mass psychogenic illness in industry. *Journal of Occupational Medicine 20* (1978): 6–15.

Commons, J. R. *Labor and administration.* New York: Macmillan, 1973.

Cone, J. D. *The overlapping worlds of behavioral assessment and performance appraisal.* Paper presented at the First Annual Scientist-Practitioner Conference in Industrial-Organizational Psychology, Old Dominion University, April 1980.

Connolly, T. Some conceptual and methodological issues in expectancy models of work performance motivation. *Academy of Management Review 1* (1976): 37–47.

Constantin, S. W. An investigation of information favorability in the employment interview. *Journal of Applied Psychology 61* (1976): 743–749.

Cook, T. D., and Campbell, D. T. The design and conduct of quasi-experiments and true experiments in field settings. In M. D. Dunnette (ed.), *Handbook of industrial and organizational psychology.* Chicago: Rand McNally, 1976.

Cooper, C. L. *Sources of managerial (di)stress.* Working paper, University of Manchester, England, 1979.

Cooper, C. L., and Marshall, J. Occupational sources of stress: A review of the literature relating to coronary heart disease and mental ill health. *Journal of Occupational Psychology 49* (1976): 11–28.

Cooper, M. J., and Aygen, M. M. A relaxation technique in the management of hypercholesterolemia. *Journal of Human Stress 5* (1979): 24–27.

Copus, D. *The numbers game is the only game in town: Statistical proofs and Title VII of the Civil Rights Act of 1964.* Unpublished manuscript, 1975.

Copus, D. Appellate court decisions involving use of statistics in job bias cases. *Daily Labor Report,* November 23, 1976.

Cornelius, E. T., III; Carron, T. J.; and Collins, M. N. Job analysis models and job classification. *Personnel Psychology 32* (1979): 693–708.

Costello, T. W., and Zalkind, S. S. *Psychology in administration.* Englewood Cliffs, N.J.: Prentice-Hall, 1963.

Cottrell, N. B. Social facilitation. In C. G. McClintock (ed.), *Experimental social psychology.* New York: Holt, Rinehart and Winston, 1972.

Cox, T. *Stress.* Baltimore: University Park Press, 1978.

Cozby, P. C. *Methods in behavioral research.* Palo Alto, Calif.: Mayfield, 1977.

Crawford, C. George Washington, Abraham Lincoln and Arthur Jensen: Are they compatible? *American Psychologist 34* (1979): 664–672.

Craypo, C. Collective bargaining in the conglomerate, multinational firm. *Industrial and Labor Relations Review 29* (1975): 3–25.

Crites, J. O. *Vocational psychology.* New York: McGraw-Hill, 1969.

Cronbach, L. J. The two disciplines of scientific psychology. *American Psychologist 12* (1957): 671–684.

Cronbach, L. J., and Meehl, P. E. Construct validity in psychological tests. *Psychological Bulletin 52* (1955): 281–302.

Crooks, L. A. The selection and development of assessment center techniques. In J. L. Moses and W. C. Byham (eds.), *Applying the assessment center method.* New York: Pergamon, 1977.

Crowell, A. H. Decision sequences in perception. Unpublished doctoral dissertation. McGill University, 1961.

Cummings, L. L. Toward organizational behavior. *Academy of Management Review 3* (1978): 90–98.

Cummings, L. L., and Dunham, R. B. (eds.), *Introduction to organizational behavior: Text and readings.* Homewood, Ill.: Irwin, 1980.

Cunningham, J. W.; Phillips, M. R.; and Spetz, S. H. *An exploratory study of a job component approach to estimating the human ability requirements of job classifications in a state competitive service system*. Raleigh, N.C.: North Carolina Office of State Personnel, 1976.

Dalton, D., and Todor, W. D. Turnover turned over: An expanded and positive perspective. *Academy of Management Review 4* (1979): 225–235.

Dalton, G. W.; Thompson, P. H.; and Price, R. L. The four stages of professional careers: A new look at performance by professionals. *Organizational Dynamics 6* (1977): 19–42.

Darlington, R. B. Multiple regression in psychological research and practice. *Psychological Bulletin 69* (1968): 161–182.

Davis, L. E., and Cherns, A. B. (eds.). *The quality of working life*. New York: Free Press, 1975.

Davis, L. E., and Taylor, J. C. (eds.). *Design of jobs* (2nd ed.). Santa Monica, Calif.: Goodyear, 1979.

Davis, T. C., and Pinto, P. R. A cost model for evaluating alternative manpower input strategies. *Human Factors 17* (1975): 42–51.

Dawes, R. M. A case study of graduate admissions: Application of three principles of human decision making. *American Psychologist 26* (1971): 180–188.

Deci, E. L. *Intrinsic motivation*. New York: Plenum, 1975.

Decker, P. J., and Cornelius, E. T., III. A note on recruiting sources and job survival rates. *Journal of Applied Psychology 64* (1979): 463–464.

DeCottis, T. A. An analysis of the external validity and applied relevance of three rating formats. *Organizational Behavior and Human Performance 19* (1977): 247–266.

Dendy v. *Washington Hospital Center,* 14 FEP Cases at 1774 (1977).

Denning, D. L., and Grant, D. L. Knowledge of the assessment process: Does it influence candidate ratings? *Journal of Assessment Center Technology 2* (1979): 7–12.

Department of Commerce. *Social indicators*. Washington: Government Printing Office, 1977.

Department of Employment Gazette. Employers, recruitment and the employment service *83* (1975): 1251–1257.

Department of Labor. *Dictionary of occupational titles* (vol. 2, 3rd ed.). Washington: Government Printing Office, 1965.

Department of Labor, Manpower Administration. *Handbook for analyzing jobs*. Washington: Government Printing Office, 1972.

Department of Labor. *Task analysis inventories: A method for collecting job information*. Washington: Government Printing Office, 1973.

Department of Labor. *Recruitment, job search, and the United States Employment Service* (R & D Monograph No. 43). Washington: Employment and Training Administration, Department of Labor, 1976.

Department of Labor. *Employment and training report of the President*. Washington: Government Printing Office, 1979.

Deslauriers, B. C., and Everett, P. B. Effects of intermittent and continuous token reinforcement on bus ridership. *Journal of Applied Psychology 62* (1977): 368–375.

DeVries, D. L., and McCall, M. M., Jr. *Performance appraisal: Is it tax time again?* Paper presented at Managerial Performance Appraisal Conference, Center for Creative Leadership, Greensboro, N.C., January 1976.

Dillman, D. A. *Mail and telephone surveys*. New York: Wiley, 1978.

Dipboye, R. L. A critical review of Korman's self-consistency theory of work motivation and occupational choice. *Organizational Behavior and Human Performance 18* (1977): 108–126.

Dipboye, R. L.; Arvey, R. D.; and Terpstra, D. E. Sex and physical attractiveness of raters and applicants as determinants of resume evaluations. *Journal of Applied Psychology 62* (1977): 288–294.

Dipboye, R. L., and Flannegan, M. F. Research settings in industrial and organizational psychology: Are findings in the field more generalizable than in the laboratory? *American Psychologist 34* (1979): 141–150.

Dipboye, R. L.; Fromkin, H. L.; and Wiback, K. Relative importance of applicant sex, attractiveness, and scholastic standing in evaluation of job applicant resumes. *Journal of Applied Psychology 60* (1975): 39–43.

Dipboye, R. L., and Wiley, J. W. Reactions of college recruiters to interviewee sex and self-presentation style. *Journal of Vocational Behavior 10* (1977): 1–12.

Dipboye, R. L., and Wiley, J. W. Reactions of male raters to interviewee self-presentation style and sex: Extensions of previous research. *Journal of Vocational Behavior 13* (1978): 192–203.

Dittman, A. T. The relationship between body movements and moods in interviews. *Journal of Applied Psychology 26* (1962): 480.

Dittrich, J. E., and Carrell, M. R. Organizational equity perceptions, employee job satisfaction and departmental absence and turnover rates. *Organizational Behavior and Human Performance 24* (1979): 29–40.

Division of Industrial/Organizational Psychology, American Psychological Association. *Principles for the validation and use of personnel selection procedures.* Washington: Author, 1975.

Dobmeyer, T. W. Modes of information utilization by employment interviewers in suitability ratings of hypothetical job applicants. Paper presented at Midwestern Psychological Convention, Cincinnati, 1970.

Dodd, W. E. Attitudes toward assessment center programs. In J. L. Moses and W. C. Byham (eds.), *Applying the assessment center method.* New York: Pergamon, 1977.

Doeringer, P. B., and Piore, M. *Internal labour markets and manpower analysis.* Lexington, Mass.: Heath, 1971.

Doeringer, P. B. Determinants of the structure of industrial type internal labor markets. *Industrial and Labor Relations Review 20* (1967): 206–220.

Donaldson, L., and Scannell, E. E. *Human resource development—The new trainer's guide.* Reading, Mass.: Addison-Wesley, 1978.

Donaldson, R. J. *Validation of the internal characteristics of an industrial assessment program using the multitrait-multimethod matrix approach.* Unpublished doctoral dissertation, Case Western Reserve University, 1969.

Dossett, D. L.; Latham, G. P.; and Mitchell, T. R. The effects of assigned versus participatively set goals and individual differences on employee behavior when goal difficulty is held constant. *Journal of Applied Psychology 64* (1979): 291–298.

Drandell, M. A composite forecasting methodology for manpower planning utilizing objective and subjective criteria. *Academy of Management Journal 18* (1975): 510–519.

Draper, J., and Merchant, J. R. Selecting the most appropriate manpower model. In D. T. Bryant and R. J. Niehaus (eds.), *Manpower planning and organization design.* New York: Plenum Press, 1978.

Driessnack, C. H. Outplacement: A benefit for both employee and company. *The Personnel Administrator 23* (1978): 24.

Drucker, P. F. Planning for redundant workers. *The Wall Street Journal,* September 25, 1974.

Drucker, P. F. The reindustrialization of America. *The Wall Street Journal,* June 13, 1980.

Drui, A. B. The use of regression equations to predict manpower requirements. *Management Science 8* (1963): 669–677.

Dulles, F. R. *Labor in America: A history* (3rd ed.). New York: Crowell, 1966.

Dunlop, J. Job vacancy measures and economic analysis. In National Bureau of Economic Research (eds.), *The measurement and interpretation of job vacancies.* New York: Columbia University Press, 1966.

Dunn, L. F. Measurement of internal income-leisure tradeoffs. *The Quarterly Journal of Economics 93* (1979): 373–393.

Dunnette, M. D. *Interpersonal perception in the employment interview.* Symposium paper presented at the annual meeting of the Midwestern Psychological Association, Chicago, 1966.

Dunnette, M. D. *Performance equals ability and what?* (Technical Report No. 4009). Center for the Study of Organizational Performance and Human Effectiveness, University of Minnesota, 1973.

Dunnette, M. D. *Handbook of industrial and organizational psychology.* Chicago: Rand McNally, 1976.

Dunnette, M. D., and Bass, B. M. Behavioral scientists and personnel management. *Industrial Relations 2* (1963): 115–130.

Dworkin, J. B., and Extejt, M. M. Why workers decertify their unions: A preliminary investigation. *Proceedings of the Academy of Management,* Atlanta, August 1979.

Dyer, L. Job search success of middle-aged managers and engineers. *Industrial and Labor Relations Review 26* (1973): 969–979.

Dyer, L. *Personnel policy theory and research.* Paper presented at the annual meeting of the Academy of Management, Detroit, August 1980.

Dyer, L. D.; Lipsky, D. B.; and Kochan, T. A. Union attitudes toward management cooperation. *Industrial Relations 16* (1977): 163–172.

Dyer, L.; Shafer, R. A.; and Regan, P. J. "Human Resource Planning at Corning Glass Works: A Field Study." Working paper. Ithaca, N.Y.: New York State School of Industrial and Labor Relations, Cornell University, December, 1980. *Integrating human resource planning with existing personnel programs.* Paper presented at the annual conference of the Human Resource Planning Society, Toronto, 1980.

Edwards, K. J. *Performance appraisal and the law: Legal requirements and practical guidelines.* Paper presented at Managerial Performance Feedback Conference, Center for Creative Leadership, Greensboro, N.C., January 1976.

EEOC v. E. I. duPont de Nemours & Co., 445 F. Supp. 223, 16 EPD #8146, 16 FEP 847 (1978).

EEOC v. United Virginia Bank/Seaboard National, 22 EPD 30,598 (1980).

Einhorn, H. J. Use of nonlinear, noncompensatory models as a function of task and amount of information. *Organizational Behavior and Human Performance 6* (1971): 1–27.

Ekman, P. Body position, facial expression, and verbal behavior during interviews. *Journal of Abnormal and Social Psychology 68* (1964): 295–301.

Elliott, D. K. Age and internal labor mobility of semi-skilled workers. *Occupational Psychology 40* (1966): 227–236.

Employers, recruitment and the employment service. *Department of Employment Gazette 83* (1975): 1251–1257.

England, G. W., and Patterson, D. G. Selection and placement—The past ten years. In H. G. Heneman, Jr. (Chairman) with L. C. Brown, M. K. Chandler, R. Kahn, H. S. Paines, and

G. P. Schultz (eds.), *Employment relations research: A summary and appraisal.* New York: Harper, 1960.

England, P. Assessing trends in occupational sex segregation, 1900–1976. In I. Berg (ed.), *Sociological perspectives on labor markets.* New York: Academic Press, 1981.

Ephlin, D. F. The union's role in job enrichment programs. *Proceedings of the Industrial Relations Research Association,* 1974.

Equal Employment Opportunity Commission. *Guidelines on employment testing procedures.* Washington: Author, 1966.

Equal Employment Opportunity Commission. Guidelines on employee selection procedures. *Federal Register 35* (1970): 12333–12336.

Equal Employment Opportunity Commission. *Minutes of commission meeting,* December 22, 1977.

Equal Employment Opportunity Commission. *EEOC announces criteria for selecting companies for major pattern and practice cases.* EEOC. Office of Public Affairs, March 20, 1978.

Equal Employment Opportunity Commission. Affirmative action guidelines: Technical amendments to the procedural regulations. *Federal Register 44* (1979): 4422.

Equal Employment Opportunity Commission. Adoption of questions and answers to clarify and provide a common interpretation of the Uniform Guidelines on Employee Selection Procedures. *Federal Register 44* (1979): 11996.

Equal Employment Opportunity Commission, Civil Service Commission, Department of Labor, Department of Justice. Uniform guidelines on employee selection procedures. *Federal Register 43* (August 25, 1978): 38290–38309.

Equal Employment Opportunity Commission, Office of Personnel Management, Department of Justice, Department of Labor, Department of the Treasury. Adoption of questions and answers to clarify and provide a common interpretation of the uniform guidelines on employee selection procedures. *Federal Register 44* (1979): 11996–12009.

Erdos, P. L. *Professional mail surveys.* New York: McGraw-Hill, 1970.

Erickson, E. *Childhood and society.* New York: Norton, 1950.

Ettelstein, M. S. Staffing guides: A tool for manpower forecasting. In R. B. Frantzreb (ed.), *Manpower Planning.* Sunnyvale, Calif.: Advanced Personnel Systems, August 1977.

Etzioni, A. *A comparative analysis of complex organizations* (rev. ed.). New York: Free Press, 1975.

Evans, M. G.; Kiggunda, M. M.; and House, R. J. A partial test and extension of the job characteristics model of motivation. *Organizational Behavior and Human Performance 24* (1979): 354–381.

Ewing, D. W. Freedom inside the organization. New York: McGraw-Hill, 1977.

Excelsior Underwear, Inc., 1956 NLRB 1236 (1966).

Fairbank, D. T., and Hough, R. L. Life event classifications and the event-illness relationship. *Journal of Human Stress 5* (1979): 41–47.

Farr, J. L. Response requirements and primacy-recency effects in a simulated selection interview. *Journal of Applied Psychology 57* (1973): 228–233.

Farr, J.; O'Leary, B.; and Bartlett, C. J. Effect of work sample test upon self-selection and turnover of job applicants. *Journal of Applied Psychologist 58* (1973): 283–285.

Farr, J. L., and York, C. M. Amount of information and primacy-recency effects in recruitment decisions. *Personnel Psychology 28* (1975): 233–238.

Feild, H. S., and Schoenfeldt, L. F. Ward and Hook revisited: A two-part procedure for overcoming a deficiency in the grouping of persons. *Educational and Psychological Measurement 35* (1975): 171–173.

Felder, H. E. *Job search: An empirical analysis of the search behavior of low income workers.* Menlo Park, Calif.: Stanford Research Institute, 1975.

Feldman, J. Considerations in the use of causal-correlational techniques in applied psychology. *Journal of Applied Psychology 60* (1975): 663–670.

Ferris, G. R.; Beehr, T. A.; and Gilmore, D. C. Social facilitation: A review and alternative conceptual model. *Academy of Management Review 3* (1978): 338–347.

Festinger, L. A theory of social comparison processes. *Human Relations 7* (1954): 117–140.

Fields, G. S. Direct labor market effects of unemployment insurance. *Industrial Relations 16* (1977): 1–14.

Filipowicz, C. A. The troubled employee: Whose responsibility? *The Personnel Administrator 24* (1979): 17–20, 21, 23.

Fine, S. A. *Functional job analysis scales: A desk aid.* Kalamazoo, Mich.: Upjohn Institute for Employment Research, 1973.

Fine, S. A., and Wiley, W. W. *An introduction to functional job analysis: Methods for manpower analysis* (Monograph No. 4). Kalamazoo, Mich.: Upjohn Institute for Employment Research, 1971.

Finkle, R. B., and Jones, W. S. *Assessing corporate talent.* New York: Wiley-Interscience, 1970.

Fischer, G. W. Multidimensional utility models for risky and riskless choice. *Organizational Behavior and Human Performance 17* (1976): 127–146.

Fischhoff, B. Attribution theory and judgment under uncertainty. In J. H. Harvey; W. J. Ickes; and R. F. Kidd (eds.), *New directions in attribution research.* Hillsdale, N.J.: Lawrence Erlbaum Associates, 1976.

Fitzroy, N. D. (ed.). Career guidance for women entering engineering. *Proceedings of Engineering Foundation Conference, 1973,* Henniker, N.H.

Flanagan, R. J., and Weber, A. R. (eds.). *Bargaining without boundaries.* Chicago: University of Chicago Press, 1974.

Flast, R. H. Taking the guesswork out of affirmative action planning. *Personnel Journal 56* (1977): 68–71.

Fleishman, E. A. *Structure and measurement of physical fitness.* Englewood Cliffs, N.J.: Prentice-Hall, 1964.

Fleishman, E. A. Toward a taxonomy of human performance. *American Psychologist 30* 1975, 1017–1032.

Fleishman, E. A. Evaluating physical abilities required by jobs. *The Personnel Administrator 24* (1979): 82–92.

Fogel, W. Occupational earnings: Market and institutional influences. *Industrial and Labor Relations Review 33* (1979): 24–35.

Follman, J. F. *Alcoholics and business.* New York: AMACOM, 1976.

Forbes, A. F. Markov chain models for manpower systems. In D. J. Bartholomew and A. R. Smith (eds.), *Manpower and management science.* London: D. C. Heath, 1971.

Fossum, J. A. Multiple dilemmas in testing: Professional standards, Griggs' requirements, and the duty to bargain. *Labor Law Journal 28* (1977): 102–108.

Fossum, J. A. *Labor relations: Development, structure, process.* Dallas: Business Publications, 1979.

Foulkes, F. K. Learning to live with OSHA. *Harvard Business Review 51* (1973): 57–67.

Frank, L. L., and Hackman, J. R. Effects of interviewer-interviewee similarity in interviewer objectivity in college admissions interviews. *Journal of Applied Psychology 60* (1975): 356–360.

Frankenhaeuser, M., and Gardell, B. Underload and overload in working life: Outline of a multidisciplinary approach. *Journal of Human Stress 2* (1976): 35–45.

Frantzreb, R. B. *Manpower planning.* Sunnyvale, Calif.: Advanced Personnel Systems, 1976 (November), 1977 (a/April, b/July, c/December), 1978 (January), 1979 (a/January, b/August, c/October), 1980 (September).

Frantzreb, R. B. Confessions of a manpower modeler. In L. F. Moore and L. Charach (eds.), *Manpower planning for Canadians* (2nd ed.). Vancouver, British Columbia: Institute of Industrial Relations, University of British Columbia, 1979.

French, J. R. P. Person role fit. In A. McLean (ed.), *Occupational stress.* Springfield, Ill.: Charles C. Thomas, 1974.

French, J. R. P., and Caplan, R. D. Organizational stress and individual strain. In A. J. Marrow (ed.), *The failure of success.* New York: AMACOM, 1972.

French, J. R. P., Jr.; Rogers, W.; and Cobb, S. Adjustment as a person-environment fit. In G. V. Coelho, D. A. Hamburg, and J. S. Adams (eds.), *Coping and adaptation: Interdisciplinary perspectives.* New York: Basic Books, 1974.

Friedlander, F., and Walter, E. Positive and negative motivations toward work. *Administrative Science Quarterly* 9 (1964): 194–207.

Friedman, M., and Rosenman, R. H. Association of a specific overt behavior pattern with blood and cardiovascular findings. *Journal of American Medical Association* 169 (1959): 1286–1296.

Friedman, M., and Rosenman, R. H. *Type A behavior and your heart.* New York: Knopf, 1974.

Fromkin, H. L., and Streufert, S. Laboratory experimentation. In M. D. Dunnette (ed.), *Handbook of industrial and organizational psychology.* Chicago: Rand-McNally, 1976.

Fry, F. L. More on the causes of quits in manufacturing. *Monthly Labor Review* 96 (1973): 48–49.

Furnco Construction Corp. v. *Waters,* 438 U.S. 567, 17 FEP Cases 1062, 1063 (1978).

Gandz, J., and Mikalachki, A. *Measuring absenteeism* (Working Paper No. 217). School of Business Administration, University of Western Ontario, 1979.

Gagne, R. M. Military training and principles of learning. *American Psychology* 18 (1962): 83–91.

Gagne, R. M. Behavioral objectives? Yes! *Educational Leadership* 29 (1972): 394–396.

Gal, R., and Lazarus, R. S. The role of activity in anticipating and confronting stressful situations. *Journal of Human Stress* 2 (1975): 4–20.

Gannon, M. J. Sources of referral and employee turnover. *Journal of Applied Psychology* 55 (1971): 226–228.

General Knit of California, Inc., 239 NLRB 101 (1978).

General Motors career development system: Supervisor's materials. Flint, Mich.: General Motors Corporation, 1977.

Getman, J. G.; Goldberg, S. B.; and Herman, J. B. *Union representation elections: Law and reality.* New York: Russell Sage, 1976.

Ghiselli, E. E. Dimensional problems of criteria. *Journal of Applied Psychology* 40 (1956): 1–4.

Ghiselli, E. E. Differentiation of individuals in terms of their predictability. *Journal of Applied Psychology* 40 (1956): 374–377.

Ghiselli, E. E. *The validity of occupational aptitude tests.* New York: Wiley, 1966.

Ghiselli, E. E. Comment on the use of moderator variables. *Journal of Applied Psychology* 56 (1972): 270.

Gillespie, J. F.; Leininger, W. E.; and Kahalas, H. A human resource planning and valuation model. *Academy of Management Journal* 19 (1976): 650–655.

Gitelman, H. Occupational mobility within the firm. *Industrial and Labor Relations Review* 20 (1966): 50–65.

Glueck, W. F. *Personnel: A diagnostic approach* (rev. ed.). Dallas: Business Publications, 1978.

Goldman, D. Managerial mobility motivations and central life interests. *American Sociological Review 38* (1973): 119–126.

Goldstein, A. P., and Sorcher, M. *Changing supervisory behavior.* New York: Pergamon, 1974.

Goldstein, I. L. *Training: Program development and application.* Monterey, Calif.: Brooks/Cole, 1974.

Goldstein, I. L. Training in work organizations. *Annual Review of Psychology 31* (1980): 229–272.

Gomberg, W. *Some observations on the problems of the relationships between union and management in the transportation industries* (mimeographed report). Washington: Department of Commerce, 1960.

Goodman, P. S. Social comparison process in organizations. In B. M. Staw and G. R. Salancik (eds.), *New directions in organizational behavior.* Chicago: St. Clair Press, 1977.

Gordon, M. E.; Kleiman, L. S.; and Hanie, C. A. Industrial-organizational psychology: Open thy ears o house of Israel. *American Psychologist 33* (1978): 893–905.

Gorman, C. D.; Clover, W. H.; and Doherty, M. E. Can we learn anything about interviewing real people from "interviews" of paper people? Two studies of the external validity of a paradigm. *Organizational Behavior and Human Performance 22* (1978): 165–192.

Gould, R. L. *Transformations: Growth and change in adult life.* New York: Simo . and Schuster, 1978.

Gould, S. *Correlates of organization identification and commitment.* Unpublished doctoral dissertation, Michigan State University, 1975.

Gould, S., and Hawkins, B. L. Organizational career stage as a moderator of the satisfaction-performance relationship. *Academy of Management Journal 21* (1978): 434–450.

Grant, D. L., and Bray, D. W. Contributions of the interview to assessment of management potential. *Journal of Applied Psychology 53* (1969): 24–34.

Gray, J. L. The myths of the myths about behavior mod in organizations. *Academy of Management Review 4* (1979): 121–130.

Green, S. G., and Mitchell, T. R. Attributional processes of leaders in leader-member interactions. *Organizational Behavior and Human Performance 23* (1979): 429–458.

Greenberger, R. S. *The Wall Street Journal,* July 22, 1980.

Greenhalgh, L., and Jick, T. D. The differential effect on employee quality level of the relationship between job insecurity and turnover. *Proceedings of the Academy of Management,* Atlanta, August 1979.

Greenwood, J. W. Management stressors. In *Reducing occupational stress.* Cincinnati, Ohio: NIOSH Research Report, 1978.

Greenwood, J. M., and McNamara, W. J. Interrater reliability in situational tests. *Journal of Applied Psychology 31* (1967): 101–106.

Greer, C. R., and Armstrong, D. C. *Human resource forecasting and planning: A state of the art investigation.* Paper presented at the annual meeting of the Academy of Management, Detroit, August 1980.

Greer, C. R., and Martin, S. A. Calculative strategy during union organizating campaigns. *Sloan Management Review 19* (1978): 61–74.

Griggs v. *Duke Power Co.,* 401 U.S. 424, 3 EPD #8137, 3 FEP 178 (1971).

Grimaldi, J. V., and Simonds, R. H. *Safety management* (3rd ed.). Homewood, Ill.: Irwin, 1975.

Grusky, O. Corporate size, bureaucratization, and managerial succession. *American Journal of Sociology 67* (1961): 261–269.

Grusky, O. Career mobility and organizational commitment. *Administrative Science Quarterly 10* (1966): 488–503.

Guilford, J. P. *Fundamental statistics in psychology and education* (4th ed.). New York: McGraw-Hill, 1965.

Guion, R. M. Criterion measurement and personal judgments. *Personnel Psychology 14* (1961): 141–149.

Guion, R. M. *Personnel testing.* New York: McGraw-Hill, 1965.

Gupta, N., and Beehr, T. A. Job stress and employee behaviors. *Organizational Behavior and Human Performance 23* (1979): 373–387.

Gurin, P. Psychological dimensions of minorities work force participation. *Sloan Management Review 15* (1974): 47–48.

Gutteridge, T. Commentary: A comparison of perspectives. In L. Dyer (ed.), *Careers in organizations.* Ithaca, N.Y.: New York State School of Industrial and Labor Relations, Cornell University, 1976.

Guzzo, R. A. Types of rewards, cognitions, and work motivation. *Academy of Management Review 4* (1979): 75–86.

Haccoun, R. R. *Weighting and order of cues as determiners of decisions in a simulated selection interview situation—a reformulation and empirical test of the concept of "gating."* Unpublished master's thesis, Ohio State University, 1970.

Hackman, J. R. Is job enrichment just a fad? In J. R. Hackman, E. E. Lawler, III, and L. W. Porter (eds.), *Perspectives on behavior in organizations.* New York: McGraw-Hill, 1977.

Hackman, J. R., and Oldham, G. R. The job diagnostic survey: An instrument for the diagnosis of jobs and the evaluation of job redesign projects. *Journal of Applied Psychology 60* (1975): 159–170.

Hackman, J. R., and Oldham, G. R. Motivation through the design of work: Test of a theory. *Organizational Behavior and Human Performance 16* (1976): 250–279.

Hackman, J. R., and Oldham, G. R. *Work redesign.* Reading, Mass. Addison-Wesley, 1980.

Hackman, J. R.; Pearce, J. L.; and Wolfe, J. C. Effects of changes in job characteristics on work attitudes and behaviors: A naturally occurring quasi-experiment. *Organizational Behavior and Human Performance 21* (1978): 289–304.

Hackman, J. R., and Suttle, J. L. *Improving life at work.* Santa Monica, Calif.: Goodyear, 1977.

Hader, J. J., and Lindeman, E. C. *Dynamic social research.* New York: Harcourt, 1933.

Haefner, J. E. Race, age, sex, and competence as factors in employer selection of the disadvantaged. *Journal of Applied Psychology 62* (1977): 199–200.

Hakel, M. D. Similarity of post-interview trait rating intercorrelations as a contributor to interrater agreement in a structured employment interview. *Journal of Applied Psychology 55* (1971): 443–448.

Hakel, M. D.; Dobmeyer, T. W.; and Dunnette, M. D. Relative importance of three content dimensions in overall suitability ratings of job applicants' resumes. *Journal of Applied Psychology 54* (1970): 65–71.

Hakel, M. D., and Dunnette, M. D. *Checklists for describing job applicants.* Minneapolis: University of Minnesota, 1970.

Hakel, M. D.; Hollman, T. D.; and Dunnette, M. D. Accuracy of interviewers, certified public accountants, and students in identifying the interests of accountants. *Journal of Applied Psychology 54* (1970): 115–119.

Hakel, M. D.; Leonard, R. L.; and Siegfried, W. D. *First-final impressions in interviews.* Unpublished paper, Ohio State University, 1972.

Hakel, M. D.; Ohnesorge, J. P.; and Dunnette, M. D. Interviewer evaluations of job applicants' resumes as a function of the qualification of the immediately preceding applicants. *Journal of Applied Psychology 54* (1970): 27–30.

Hakel, M. D., and Schuh, A. J. Job applicant attributes judged important across seven divergent occupations. *Personnel Psychology 24* (1971): 45–52.

Halaby, C. Bureaucratic promotion criteria. *Administrative Science Quarterly 23* (1978): 466–484.

Hall, A., and Johnson, T. R. The determinants of planned retirement age. *Industrial and Labor Relations Review, 53* (1980): 241–254.

Hall, D. T. *Careers in organizations.* Palo Alto, Calif.: Goodyear, 1976.

Hall, D. T., and Mansfield, R. Relationship of age and seniority with career variables of engineers and scientists. *Journal of Applied Psychology 60* (1975): 201–210.

Hall, D. T., and Nougaim, K. E. An examination on Maslow's need hierarchy in an organizational setting. *Organizational Behavior and Human Performance 3* (1968): 12–35.

Hall, D. T., and Schneider, B. Correlates of organizational identification as a function of career patterns and organizational type. *Administrative Science Quarterly 17* (1972): 340–350.

Hall, J. To achieve or not: The manager's choice. *California Management Review 18* (1976): 5–18.

Hamner, W. C. Reinforcement theory and contingency management in organizational settings. In H. Tosi and W. C. Hamner (eds.), *Organizational behavior: A contingency approach.* Chicago: St. Clair Press, 1974.

Hamner, W. C. Reinforcement theory and contingency management in organizational settings. In R. M. Steers and L. W. Porter (eds.), *Motivation and work behavior.* New York: McGraw-Hill, 1975.

Hamner, W. C., and Hamner, E. P. Behavior modification on the bottom line. *Organizational Dynamics 4* (1976): 8–21.

Hamner, W. C., and Smith, F. J. Work attitudes as predictors of unionization activity. *Journal of Applied Psychology 63* (1978): 415–421.

Harlan, A., Kerr, J.; and Kerr, S. Preference for motivator and hygiene factors in a hypothetical interview situation: Further findings and some implications for the employment interview. *Personnel Psychology 30* (1977): 557–566.

Harlow, D. Professional employees preference for upward mobility. *Journal of Applied Psychology 57* (1973): 137–141.

Harlow, H. F. The nature of love. *American Psychologist 13* (1958): 673–685.

Hazelwood School District v. *United States,* 15 FEP Cases 1, 10 (1977).

Hedges, J. N. Absence from work—A look at some national data. *Monthly Labor Review 96* (1973): 24–31.

Heilman, M. E., and Saruwatari, L. R. When beauty is beastly: The effect of appearance and sex on evaluations of job applicants for managerial and non-managerial jobs. *Organizational Behavior and Human Performance 23* (1979): 360–372.

Hemphill, J. K. *Dimensions of executive positions* (Research Monograph No. 98). Columbus, Ohio: Bureau of Business Research, Ohio State University, 1960.

Henderson, R. I. *Compensation management.* Reston, Va.: Reston Publishing, 1979.

Heneman, H. G., Jr., and Seltzer, G. *Manpower planning and forecasting in the firm: An exploratory probe.* Minneapolis: Industrial Relations Center, University of Minnesota, 1968.

Heneman, H. G., Jr. Quo vadis PAIR. *Personnel/Human Resources Division Newsletter 1* (1980): 2–4.

Heneman, H. G., III. Impact of test information and applicant sex on applicant evaluations in a selection simulation. *Journal of Applied Psychology 62* (1977): 524–526.

Heneman, H. G., III, and Sandver, M. G. Markov analysis in human resource administration: Applications and limitations. *Academy of Management Review 2* (1977): 535–542.

Heneman, H. G., III, and Schwab, D. P. An evaluation of research on expectancy theory predictions of employee performance. *Psychological Bulletin 78* (1972): 1–9.

Heneman, H. G., III; Schwab, D. P.; Fossum, J. A., and Dyer, L. *Personnel/Human resource management*. Homewood, Ill.: Irwin, 1980.

Heneman, H. G., III; Schwab, D. P.; Huett, D. L.; and Ford, J. J. Interviewer validity as a function of interview structure, biographical data, and interviewee order. *Journal of Applied Psychology 60* (1975): 748–753.

Herold, D. M. Improving the performance effectiveness of groups through a task contingent selection of intervention strategy. *Academy of Management Review 3* (1978): 315–325.

Herzberg, F. *Work and the nature of man*. Cleveland, Ohio: World Publishing, 1966.

Herzberg, F.; Mausner, B.; and Snyderman, B. *The motivation to work* (2nd ed.). New York: Wiley, 1959.

Hicks, J. R. *The theory of wages*. London: MacMillan, 1963.

Hickson, D. J.; Hinings, C. R.; Lee, C. A.; Schneck, R. E.; and Pennings, J. M. A strategic contingencies' theory of intraorganizational power. *Administrative Science Quarterly 16* (1971): 216–229.

Hildebrand, G. H. Cloudy future for coalition bargaining. *Harvard Business Review 48* (1968): 114–128.

Hill, R. E. New look at employee referrals. *Personnel Journal 49* (1970): 144–148.

Hill, R. E. An empirical comparison of two models for predicting preferences for standard employment offers. *Decision Sciences 5* (1974): 243–254.

Hills, S. M. Organizational politics and human resource planning. *Human Resource Planning 1* (1978): 31–38.

Hines v. *Anchor Motor Freight,* 424 U.S. 554 (1976).

Hinrichs, J. R. Personnel training. In M. D. Dunnette (ed.), *Handbook of industrial and organizational psychology*. Chicago: Rand McNally, 1976.

Hinrichs, J. R. An eight-year follow-up of a management assessment center. *Journal of Applied Psychology 63* (1978): 596–601.

Hinrichs, J. R., and Haanpera, S. Reliability of measurement in situational exercises. An assessment of the assessment center method. *Personnel Psychology 29* (1976): 31–40.

Hoffman, F. O. Identity crisis in the personnel function. *Personnel Journal 57* (1978): 126–132, 162.

Hogan, J. C., and Fleishman, E. A. An index of the physical effort required in human task performance. *Journal of Applied Psychology 64* (1979): 197–204.

Holland, J. L. Vocational preferences. In M. D. Dunnette (ed.), *Handbook of industrial and organizational psychology*. Chicago: Rand McNally, 1976.

Hollandsworth, J. G., Jr.; Kazelskis, R.; Stevens, J.; and Dressel, M. E. Relative contributions of verbal, articulative, and non-verbal communication to employment decisions in job interview settings. *Personnel Psychology 32* (1979): 359–368.

Holley, W. H., and Feild, H. S. Performance appraisal and the law. *Labor Law Review 26* (1975): 423–430.

Holley, W. H., and Jennings, K. M. *The labor relations process*. Hinsdale, Ill.: Dryden, 1980.

Hollman, T. D. Employment interviewers' errors in processing positive and negative information. *Journal of Applied Psychology 56* (1972): 130–134.

Hollywood Ceramics Co., 140 NLRB 221 (1962).

Holmes, T. H., and Rahe, R. H. Social readjustment rating scale. *Journal of Psychosomatic Research 11* (1967): 213–218.

Holmes, T. S., and Holmes, T. H. Short-term intrusions into the life style routine. *Journal of Psychosomatic Research 14* (1970): 121–132.

Holmstrom, V. L., and Beach, L. R. Subjective expected utility and career preferences. *Organizational Behavior and Human Performance 10* (1973): 201–207.

Holt, C., and David, M. The concept of job vacancies in a dynamic theory of the labour market. In National Bureau of Economic Research, *The measurement and interpretation of job vacancies.* New York: Columbia Press, 1966.

House, J. S. Occupational stress and coronary heart disease: A review and theoretical integration. *Journal of Health and Social Behavior 15* (1974): 12–27.

House, J. S. *Social support and stress.* Reading, Mass.: Addison-Wesley, 1980.

House, J. S.; McMichael, A. J.; Wells, J. A.; Kaplan, B. H.; and Landerman, L. R. Occupational stress and health among factory workers. *Journal of Health and Social Behavior 20* (1979): 139–160.

House, J. S., and Wells, J. A. Occupational stress and health. In *Reducing occupational stress.* Cincinnati, Ohio: NIOSH Research Report, 1978.

House, R. J., and Rizzo, J. R. Role conflict and ambiguity as critical variables in a model of organizational behavior. *Organizational Behavior and Human Performance 1* (1972): 467–505.

House, R. J., and Wigdor, L. A. Herzberg's dual factor theory of job satisfaction and motivation. *Personnel Psychology 20* (1967): 369–390.

Howard, A. An assessment of assessment centers. *Academy of Management Journal 17* (1974): 115–134.

Hoyer, D. T. A program for conflict management: An exploratory approach. *Proceedings of the Industrial Relations Research Association,* 1980.

Hoyle, D. F. AT&T complete assessment of nearly 1700 women under consent agreement. *Assessment and Development 2* (1975): 4–7.

Hoyle, D. F. Personal communication, 1979.

Huber, G. P.; Ullman, J.; and Leifer, R. Optimum organization design: An analytic-adoptive approach. *Academy of Management Review 4* (1979): 567–578.

Huck, J. R. The research base. In J. L. Moses and W. C. Byham (eds.), *Applying the assessment center method.* New York: Pergamon, 1977.

Huck, J. R., and Bray, D. W. Management assessment center evaluation and subsequent job performance of white and black females. *Personnel Psychology 29* (1976): 13–30.

Huffman, D. Oversight puts test guidelines in limbo. *Legal Times of Washington,* March 12, 1979.

Hulin, C. L. Effects of changes in job satisfaction levels on employee turnover. *Journal of Applied Psychology 32* (1968): 122–126.

Ilgen, D. R.; Fisher, C. D.; and Taylor, M. S. Consequences of individual feedback on behavior in organizations. *Journal of Applied Psychology 64* (1979): 349–371.

Ilgen, D. R., and Knowlton, W. A. Performance attributional effects on feedback from supervisors. *Organizational Behavior and Human Performance 25* (1980): 441–456.

Ilgen, D. R.; Martin, B. A.; and Peterson, R. B. *Reactions to performance feedback.* Paper presented at the First Annual Scientist-Practitioner Conference in Industrial-Organizational Psychology, Old Dominion University, April 1980.

Imada, A. S., and Hakel, M. D. Influence of nonverbal communication and rater proximity on impressions and decisions in simulated employment interviews. *Journal of Applied Psychology 62* (1977): 295–300.

Inkson, J. H. K. Self esteem as a moderator of the relationship between job performance and job satisfaction. *Journal of Applied Psychology 63* (1978): 243–247.

International Brotherhood of Teamsters v. *United States,* 14 FEP Cases at 1521 (1977), quoted in *Hazelwood School District* v. *United States,* 15 FEP Cases at 4 (1977).

Irish, R. K. *Go hire yourself an employer.* Garden City, N.J.: Anchor Press/Doubleday, 1973.

Ivancevich, J. M. Effects of goal setting on performance and job satisfaction. *Journal of Applied Psychology 61* (1976): 605–612.

Ivancevich, J. M. Different goal setting treatments and their effects on performance and job satisfaction. *Academy of Management 20* (1977): 406–419.

Ivancevich, J. M. A longitudinal study of the study of the effects of rater training on psychometric errors in ratings. *Journal of Applied Psychology 64* (1979): 502–508.

Ivancevich, J. M., and Donnelly, J. H. Job offer acceptance behavior and reinforcement. *Journal of Applied Psychology 55* (1971): 119–122.

Jackson, T. Industrial outplacement at Goodyear, Part 2: The consultant's viewpoint. *Personnel Administrator 25* (1980): 43.

Jaffee, C. L., and Sefcik, J. T., Jr. What is an assessment center? *Personnel Administrator 25* (1980): 40–43.

Jahoda, M. A. A social psychological approach to the study of culture. *Human Relations 14* (1961): 23–30.

Janger, A. R. *Personnel administration: Changing scope and organization* (Conference Board Report No. 203). New York: The Conference Board, 1966.

Janger, A. R. *The personnel function: Changing objectives and organization* (Conference Board Report No. 712). New York: The Conference Board, 1977.

Jaques, E. *Equitable payment.* New York: Wiley, 1961.

Jason, G. Ma Bell's daughters. *The Wall Street Journal,* February 28, 1978.

Jenkins, C. D. Psychologic and social precursors of coronary disease. *New England Journal of Medicine 284* (1971): 244–255, 307–319.

Jenkins, C. D. Psychosocial modifers of response to stress. *Journal of Human Stress 5* (1979): 3–15.

Jenkins, C. D.; Rosenman, R. H.; and Zyanski, S. J. Prediction of clinical coronary heart disease by a test for coronary-prone behavior pattern. *New England Journal of Medicine 290* (1974): 1271–1275.

Jennings, E. E. *The mobile manager: A study of the new generation of top executives.* Ann Arbor, Mich.: Bureau of Industrial Relations, University of Michigan, 1967.

Jeswald, T. A. Issues in establishing an assessment center. In J. L. Moses and W. C. Byham (eds.), *Applying the assessment center method.* New York: Pergamon, 1977.

Johns, G. Effects of informational order and frequency of applicant evaluation upon linear information-processing competence of interviewers. *Journal of Applied Psychology 60* (1975): 427–433.

Jones, M. *The evaluation of a performance measurement system: The state of Arkansas system.* Presented at the First Annual Scientist-Practitioner Conference in Industrial-Organizational Old Dominion University, April 1980.

Jurgenson, C. E. Job preferences (What makes a job good or bad?). *Journal of Applied Psychology 63* (1978): 267–276.

Kabanoff, B., and O'Brien, G. E. The effects of task type and cooperation upon group products and performance. *Organizational Behavior and Human Performance 23* (1979): 163–181.

Kahalas, H., and Key, R. A decisionally oriented manpower model for minority group hiring. *The Quarterly Review of Economics and Business 14* (1974): 71–84.

Kahn, A. The intimidation of job tests. *AFL-CIO Federationist 86* (1979): 1–8.

Kahn, R. L.; Wolfe, D. M.; Quinn, R. P.; Snoek, J. D.; and Rosenthal, R. A. *Organizational stress: Studies in role conflict and ambiguity.* New York: Wiley, 1964.

Kahn, R. Stress research and its implications: The United States. *Proceedings of the Industrial Relations Research Association,* 1981.

Kane, J. S. *Alternative approaches to the control of systematic error in appraisals.* Paper presented at the First Annual Scientist-Practitioner Conference in Industrial-Organizational Psychology, Old Dominion University, April 1980.

Kane, J. S., and Lawler, E. E., III. Performance appraisal effectiveness: Its assessment and determinants. In B. Staw (ed.), *Research in organizational behavior* (vol. 1). Greenwich, Conn.: JAI Press, 1979.

Kaplan, A. *The conduct of inquiry.* San Francisco: Chandler, 1964.

Kaplin, I. J. Catecholamines, adrenal hormones, and stress. *Hospital Practice,* (1976): 49–55.

Kasper, H. The asking price of labor and the duration of unemployment. *Review of Economics and Statistics 49* (1967): 165–172.

Katz, D. The motivational basis of organizational behavior. *Behavioral Science 9* (1964): 131–146.

Katz, D., and Kahn, R. L. *The social psychology of organizations.* New York: Wiley, 1966.

Katz, D., and Kahn, R. L. *The social psychology of organizations* (2nd ed.). New York: Wiley, 1978.

Katz, R. Time and work: Toward an integrative perspective. In B. M. Staw and L. L. Cummings (eds.), *Research in organizational behavior* (vol. 2). Greenwich, Conn.: JAI Press, 1980.

Katz, R., and VanMaanen, J. The loci of work satisfaction. In P. Warr (ed.), *Personal goals and work design.* New York: Wiley, 1976.

Katzell, R. A., and Dyer, F. J. Differential validity revived. *Journal of Applied Psychology 62* (1977): 137–145.

Kavanagh, M. J. The content issue in performance appraisal: A review. *Personnel Psychology 24* (1971): 653–668.

Kavanagh, M. J. *Evaluation of performance rating methods.* Working paper, School of Management, State University of New York, Binghamton, 1976.

Kavanagh, M. J.; MacKinney, A. C.; and Wolins, L. Issues in managerial performance: Multitrait-multimethod analyses of ratings. *Psychological Bulletin 75* (1971): 34–39.

Kavanagh, M. J., and Vaught, R. S. *The assessment of performance change: A time-series approach.* Working Paper Series #78–16, School of Management, State University of New York, Binghamton, 1978.

Keaveny, T. J., and McGann, A. F. A comparison of behavioral expectation scales and graphic rating scales. *Journal of Applied Psychology 60* (1975): 695–703.

Kelley, H. H. The processes of causal attribution. *American Psychologist 28* (1973): 107–128.

Kenny, D. A. *Correlation and causality.* New York: Wiley, 1979.

Kerlinger, F. N., and Pedhauzer, E. J. *Multiple regression in behavioral research.* New York: Holt, Rinehart and Winston, 1973.

Kerr, C., and Rosnow, J. M. (eds.). *Work in America: The decade ahead.* New York: Van Nostrand, 1979.

Keys, B. The management of learning grid for management development. *Academy of Management Review 2* (1977): 289–297.

Killian, R. A. *Human resource management: An ROI approach.* New York: AMACOM, 1976.

King, L. M., and Boehm, V. R. *Assessment center judgment stability across time periods and assessors.* Paper presented at the annual meeting of the American Psychological Association, Montreal, September 1980.

King, M. R., and Manaster, G. J. Body-image, self-esteem, expectations, self-assessments, and actual success in a simulated job interview. *Journal of Applied Psychology 62* (1977): 589–594.

Kipnis, D. *The powerholders.* Chicago: University of Chicago Press, 1976.

Kipnis, D. Mobility expectations and attitudes toward industrial structure. *Human Relations 17* (1964): 57–71.

Kipnis, D., and Cosentino, J. Use of leadership powers in industry. *Journal of Applied Psychology 53* (1969): 460–466.

Kleiler, F. *Can we afford early retirement?* Baltimore: Johns Hopkins University Press, 1978.

Klein, S. M. *Workers under stress.* Lexington: University of Kentucky Press, 1971.

Klimoski, R., and Strickland, W. Assessment centers: Valid or merely prescient. *Personnel Psychology 30* (1977): 353–363.

Kneller, G. A. Behavioral objectives? No! *Educational Leadership 29* (1972): 397–400.

Knowles, M. *The adult learner: A neglected species.* Houston: Gulf Publishing, 1978.

Knowles, M. C. Personal and job factors affecting labour turnover. *Personnel Practices Bulletin 20* (1964): 25–37.

Knowlton, W. A., and Mitchell, T. R. Effects of causal attributions on a supervisor's evaluation of subordinate performance. *Journal of Applied Psychology 65* (1980): 459–466.

Kochan, T. A. A theory of multilateral collective bargaining in city governments. *Industrial and Labor Relations Review 27* (1974): 525–542.

Kochan, T. A. How American workers view labor unions. *Monthly Labor Review 102* (1979): 23–31.

Kochan, T. A. *Collective bargaining and industrial relations: From theory to policy and practice.* Homewood, Ill.: Irwin, 1980a.

Kochan, T. A. Collective bargaining and organizational behavior and search. In B. M. Staw and L. L. Cummings (eds.), *Research in organizational behavior* (vol. 2). Greenwich, Conn.: JAI Press, 1980b.

Kochan, T. A. *Labor management relations research priorities for the 1980s.* Final report to the Secretary of Labor, Department of Labor, January 1980c.

Kochan, T. A., and Jick, T. A theory of the public sector mediation process. *Journal of Conflict Resolution 23* (1978): 209–240.

Kochan, T. A.; Mironi, M.; Ehrenberg, R. G.; Baderschneider, J.; and Jick, T. *Dispute resolution under factfinding and arbitration: An empirical analysis.* New York: American Atbitration Association, 1979.

Kolb, D. A. *Organizational psychology: An experimental approach.* Englewood Cliffs, N.J.: Prentice-Hall, 1971.

Kolb, D. A. *Learning style inventory.* Boston, Mass.: Mcber, 1976.

Komaki, J.; Waddell, W. M.; and Pearce, M. G. The applied behavioral analysis approach and individual employees: Improving performance in two small businesses. *Organizational Behavior and Human Performance 19* (1977): 337–352.

Kopelman, R. E. Across individual, within individual and return on effort versions of expectancy theory. *Decision Sciences 8* (1977): 651–662.

Korman, A. K. Hypothesis of work behavior revisited and an extension. *Academy of Management Review 1* (1976): 50–63.

Korman, A. K. An examination of Dipboye's "A critical appraisal of Korman's self-consistency theory of work motivation and occupational choice." *Organizational Behavior and Human Performance 18* (1977): 127–128.

Kovenklioglu, G., and Greenhaus, J. H. Causal attributions, expectations and task performance. *Journal of Applied Psychology 63* (1978): 698–705.

Krackhardt, D.; McKenna, J.; Porter, L. W.; and Steers, R. M. *Goal-setting, supervisory behavior, and employee turnover: A field experiment* (Technical Report No. 17). Graduate School of Management, University of Oregon, November 1978.

Kraut, A. I. Management assessment in international organizations. *Industrial Relations 12* (1973): 172–182.

Kraut, A. I. (Chairperson). Behavior modeling symposium. *Personnel Psychology 29* (1976): 325–370.

Krefting, L. A., and Brief, A. P. The impact of applicant disability on evaluative judgments in the selection process. *Academy of Management Journal 19* (1976): 675–680.

Krefting, L. A., and Mahoney, T. A. Determining the size of a meaningful pay increase. *Industrial Relations 16* (1977): 83–93.

Kriesberg, L. Careers, organizational size and succession. *American Journal of Sociology 68* (1962): 355–359.

Kuhn, J. W. *Bargaining in grievance settlement.* New York: Columbia University Press, 1961.

Kuhn, T. S. *The structure of scientific revolutions* (2nd ed.). Chicago: University of Chicago Press, 1970.

Landsberger, H. A. The behavior and personality of the labor mediator: The parties' perception of mediator behavior. *Personnel Psychology 13* (1960): 329–347.

Landy, F. J. The validity of the interview in police officer selection. *Journal of Applied Psychology 61* (1976): 193–198.

Landy, F. J., and Bates, F. Another look at contrast effects in the employment interview. *Journal of Applied Psychology 58* (1973): 141–144.

Landy, F. J., and Farr, J. L. Performance rating. *Psychological Bulletin 87* (1980): 72–107.

Langdale, J. A., and Weitz, J. Estimating the influence of job information on interviewer agreement. *Journal of Applied Psychology 57* (1973): 23–27.

Larwood, L., and Blackmore, J. Fair pay: Field investigations of the fair economic exchange. *Proceedings of the Academy of Management,* Orlando, Florida, August 1977.

Larwood, L.; Kavanagh, M.; and Levine, R. Perceptions of fairness with three alternative economic exchanges. *Academy of Management Journal 21* (1978): 69–83.

Larwood, L.; Levine, R.; Shaw, R.; and Hurwitz, S. Relations of objective and subjective inputs to exchange preference for equity of equality reward allocation. *Organizational Behavior and Human Performance 23* (1979): 60–72.

Latham, G. P. *The effect of various schedules of reinforcement on the productivity of tree planters.* Paper presented at the annual meeting of the American Psychological Association, New Orleans, September 1974.

Latham, G. P., and Baldes, J. J. The practical significance of Locke's theory of goal setting. *Journal of Applied Psychology 60* (1975): 122–124.

Latham, G. P., and Dossett, D. L. Designing incentive plans for unionized employees: A comparison of continuous and variable ratio reinforcements. *Personnel Psychology 31* (1978): 47–61.

Latham, G. P., and Kinne, S. B. Improving job performance through training in goal setting. *Journal of Applied Psychology 59* (1974): 187–191.

Latham, G. P.; Mitchell, T. R.; and Dossett, D. L. The importance of participative goal setting and anticipated rewards on goal difficulty and job performance. *Journal of Applied Psychology 63* (1978): 163–171.

Latham, G. P., and Saari, L. M. Importance of supportive relationships in goal setting. *Journal of Applied Psychology 64* (1979): 151–156.

Latham, G. P.; Saari, L. M.; Pursell, E. D.; and Campion, M. A. The situational interview. *Journal of Applied Psychology 65* (1980): 422–426.

Latham, G. P.; Wexley, K. N.; and Pursell, E. D. Training managers to minimize rating errors in the observation of behavior. *Journal of Applied Psychology 60* (1975): 550–555.

Latham, G. P., and Yukl, G. A. A review of research on the application of goal setting in organizations. *Academy of Management Journal 18* (1975a): 824–825.

Latham, G. P., and Yukl, G. A. Assigned versus participative goal setting with educated and uneducated wood workers. *Journal of Applied Psychology 60* (1975b): 299–302.

Latham, G. P., and Yukl, G. A. The effects of assigned and participative goal setting on performance and job satisfaction. *Journal of Applied Psychology 61* (1976): 166–171.

Lawler, E. E., III. Job design and employee motivation. *Personnel Psychology 22* (1969): 426–435.

Lawler, E. E., III. *Pay and organizational effectiveness.* New York: McGraw-Hill, 1971.

Lawler, E. E., III. Secrecy and the need to know. In H. Tosi, R. House, and M. D. Dunnette (eds.), *Managerial motivation and compensation.* East Lansing, Mich.: Michigan State University Press, 1972.

Lawler, E. E., III. Should the quality of work life be legislated? In K. M. Rowland; M. London; G. R. Ferris; and J. L. Sherman (eds.), *Current issues in personnel management.* Boston: Allyn and Bacon, 1980.

Lawler, E. E., III. *Motivation in work organizations.* Belmont, Calif.: Brooks/Cole, 1973.

Lawler, E. E., III. Control systems in organizations. In M. D. Dunnette (ed.), *Handbook of industrial and organizational psychology.* Chicago: Rand McNally, 1976.

Lawler, E. E., III. Should the quality of working life be legislated? *The Personnel Administrator 21* (1976): 17–21.

Lawler, E. E., and Hackman, J. R. Impact of employee participation in the development of pay incentive plans: A field experiment. *Journal of Applied Psychology 53* (1969): 467–471.

Lawler, E. E., III; Kuleck, W. J., Jr.; Rhode, J. G.; and Sorensen, J. E. Job choice and post decision dissonance. *Organizational Behavior and Human Performance 13* (1975): 133–145.

Lazarsfeld, P. F., and Menzel, H. On the relation between individual and collective properties. In A. Etzioni (ed.), *A sociological reader on complex organizations.* New York: Holt, Rinehart and Winston, 1961.

Lazarus, R. S. *Psychological stress and the coping process.* New York: McGraw-Hill, 1966.

Lazarus, R. S. Positive denial: The case for not facing reality. *Psychology Today* (1979): 48, 51, 52, 57, 60.

Lazer, R. I. The discrimination danger in performance appraisal. *The Conference Board Review 13* (1976): 60–64.

Leavitt, H. J. Applied organizational change in industry. In J. G. March (ed.), *Handbook on organizations.* Chicago: Rand McNally, 1965.

Leavitt, H. J., and Whisler, T. L. Management in the 1980's. *Harvard Business Review 36* (1958): 41–48.

Ledvinka, J. Race of interviewer and the language elaboration of black interviewees. *Journal of Social Issues 27* (1971): 185–197.

Ledvinka, J. The intrusion of race: Black responses to a white observer. *Social Science Quarterly 52* (1972): 907–920.

Ledvinka, J. Race of employment interviewer and reasons given by job seekers for leaving their jobs. *Journal of Applied Psychology 58* (1973): 362–364.

Ledvinka, J., and LaForge, R. L. A staffing model for affirmative action planning. *Human Resource Planning 1* (1978): 135–150.

Lee, R. J., and Hecht, R. M. *Understanding your workstyle.* New York: Lee-Hecht & Associates, 1977.

Lehman, E. *Mobility and satisfaction in an industrial organization.* Unpublished doctoral dissertation, Columbia University, 1966.

LeSieur, F. G. (ed.). *The Scanlon plan.* Cambridge, Mass.: MIT Press, 1958.

Lesser, P. J. The legal viewpoint. In A. McLean (ed.), *To work is human.* New York: Macmillan, 1967.

Levi, T. *Stress and distress in response to psychosocial stimuli.* Elmsford, N.Y.: Pergamon Press, 1972.

Levinson, B. Bureaucratic succession. In A. Etzoni (ed.), *Complex organizations.* New York: Holt, Rinehart and Winston, 1961.

Levinson, D. J. The mid-life transition: A period in adult psychosocial development. *Psychiatry 40* (1977): 99–112.

Levinson, D. J.; Darrow, C.; Klein, E.; Levinson, M.; and McKee, B. *The seasons of a man's life.* New York: Knopf, 1978.

Levinson, H. *Executive stress.* New York: Harper and Row, 1970.

Levinson, H. *Psychological man.* Cambridge, Mass.: The Levinson Institute, 1976.

Likert, R. *The human organization.* New York: McGraw-Hill, 1967.

Lindblom, C. E. The science of muddling through. *Public Administration Review 19* (1959): 79–88.

Linn, R. L. Single group validity, differential validity, and differential prediction. *Journal of Applied Psychology 63* (1978): 507–512.

Lippman, S., and McCall, J. The economies of job search: A survey (Pt. 1). *Economic Inquiry 14* (1976): 155–190.

Livernash, E. R. The internal wage structure. In G. W. Taylor and F. W. Pierson (eds.), *New concepts in wage determination.* New York: McGraw-Hill, 1957.

Livingstone, E. Attitudes of women operatives to promotion. *Occupational Psychology 27* (1953): 191–199.

Locke, E. A. Toward a theory of task motivation and incentives. *Organizational Behavior and Human Performance 3* (1968): 157–189.

Locke, E. A. The case against legislating the quality of working life. *The Personnel Administrator 21* (1976): 19–21.

Locke, E. A. The nature and causes of job satisfaction. In M. D. Dunnette (ed.), *Handbook of industrial and organizational psychology.* Chicago: Rand McNally, 1976.

Locke, E. A. The myths of behavior mod in organizations. *Academy of Management Review 2* (1977): 543–553.

Locke, E. A. The ubiquity of the technique of goal setting in theories and approaches to employee motivation. *Academy of Management Review 3* (1978): 594–601.

Locke, E. A. Myths in "The myths about behavior mod in organizations." *Academy of Management Review 4* (1979): 131–136.

London, M., and Hakel, M. D. Effects of applicant stereotypes, order, and information on interview impressions. *Journal of Applied Psychology 69* (1974): 157–162.

London, M., and Poplawski, J. R. Effects of information on stereotype development in performance appraisal and interview contexts. *Journal of Applied Psychology 61* (1976): 199–205.

Long, G., and Feuille, P. Final offer arbitration: "Sudden death" in Eugene. *Industrial and Labor Relations Review 27* (1974): 186–203.

Lord, R. G., and Hohenfeld, J. A. A longitudinal field assessment of equity effects on the performance of major league baseball players. *Journal of Applied Psychology 64* (1979): 19–26.

Lowe, M. Union leaders suspect bonus hinders safety. *Toronto Globe and Mail,* September 18, 1980.

Lowin, A. Participative decision making: A model, literature critique, and prescriptions for research. *Organizational Behavior and Human Performance 8* (1968): 68–106.

Lubben, G. L.; Thompson, D. E.; and Klasson, C. R. Performance appraisal: The legal implications of Title VII. *Personnel 28* (1980): 12–21.

Lublin, J. S. *The Wall Street Journal,* September 2, 1980.

Luthans, F. *An organizational modification (O.B.MOD.) approach to O.D.* Paper presented at the annual meeting of the Academy of Management, Seattle, August, 1974.

Lyons, T. F. Role clarity, need for clarity, satisfaction, tension, and withdrawal. *Organizational Behavior and Human Performance 6* (1971): 99–110.

Lytle, C. W. *Job evaluation methods.* New York: Ronald Press, 1954.

Maas, J. B. Patterned scaled expectation interview: Reliability studies on a new technique. *Journal of Applied Psychology 49* (1965): 431–433.

Maccoby, M. *Changing work.* Working paper, 1975.

McAdams, T. Dismissal: A decline in employer autonomy. *Business Horizons 21* (1978): 67–72.

McAfee, B., and Green, B. Selecting a performance appraisal method. *The Personnel Administrator 76* (1977): 61–64.

McClelland, D. C. *The achieving society.* Princeton, N.J.: Van Nostrand, 1961.

McClelland, D. C. Managing motivation to expand human freedom. *American Psychologist 33* (1978): 201–210.

McClelland, D. C., and Burnham, D. H. Power is the great motivator. *Harvard Business Review 54* (1976): 100–110.

McCormick, E. J. Job information: Its development and applications. In D. Yoder and H. G. Heneman, Jr. (eds.), *ASPA handbook of personnel and industrial relations.* Washington: Bureau of National Affairs, 1979.

McCormick, E. J. *Job analysis.* New York: AMACOM, 1979.

McCormick, E. J.; DeNisi, A. S.; and Shaw, J. B. Use of the Position Analysis Questionnaire for establishing the job component validity of tests. *Journal of Applied Psychology 64* (1979): 51–56.

McCormick, E. J.; Jeanneret, P. R.; and Mecham, R. C. A study of job characteristics and job dimensions as based on the Position Analysis Questionnaire (PAQ). *Journal of Applied Psychology 56* (1972): 347–368.

McCormick, E. J., and Mecham, R. C. Job analysis data as a basis for synthetic test validity. *Psychology Annual 4* (1970): 30–35.

McCormick, E. J., and Tiffin, J. *Industrial psychology* (6th ed.). Englewood Cliffs, N.J.: Prentice-Hall, 1974.

MacCrimmon, K. R. Improving decision making with manpower management systems. *The Business Quarterly 36* (1971): 29–41.

MacCrimmon, K. R., and Taylor, D. N. Decision making and problem solving. In M. D. Dunnette (ed.), *Handbook of industrial and organizational psychology.* Chicago: Rand McNally, 1976.

McGehee, W., and Thayer, P. W. *Training in business and industry.* New York: Wiley, 1961.

McGovern, T. V., and Tinsley, E. A. Interviewer evaluations on interviewee nonverbal behavior. *Journal of Vocational Behavior 13* (1978): 163–171.

McGrath, J. E. Stress and behavior in organizations. In M. D. Dunnette (ed.), *Handbook of industrial and organizational psychology.* Chicago: Rand McNally, 1976.

McGregor, D. An uneasy look at performance appraisal. *Harvard Business Review 35* (1957): 89–94.

McGregor, D. *The human side of enterprise.* New York: McGraw-Hill, 1960.

McKelvey, J. T. Fact-finding in public employment disputes: Promise or illusion. *Industrial and Labor Relations Review 22* (1969): 528–543.

McKersie, R. B., and Shropshire, W. W., Jr. Avoiding written grievances: A successful program. *Journal of Business 34* (1962): 135–152.

MacKinney, A. C. The assessment of performance change: An inductive example. *Organizational Behavior and Human Performance 2* (1967): 56–72.

MacKinnon, D. W. From selecting spies to selecting managers—The OSS assessment program. In J. L. Moses and W. C. Byham (eds.), *Applying the assessment center method.* New York: Pergamon, 1977.

McLean, A. A. *Work stress.* Reading, Mass.: Addison-Wesley, 1979.

McNenly, P. Workers promising more strikes. *Toronto Star,* September 20, 1980.

Macy, B. A., and Mirvis, P. H. A methodology for assessment of quality of work life and organizational effectiveness in behavioral-economic terms. *Administrative Science Quarterly 21* (1976): 212–226.

Mahler, W. R. An experimental study of two methods of rating employees. *Personnel 25* (1948): 211–220.

Mahoney, T. Compensation preferences of managers. *Industrial Relations 3* (1964): 135–144.

Mahoney, T. A. Another look at job satisfaction and performance. In T. A. Mahoney (ed.), *Compensation and reward perspectives.* Homewood, Ill.: Irwin, 1979a.

Mahoney, T. A. Economic constraints and the ability to pay. In T. A. Mahoney (ed.), *Compensation and reward perspectives.* Homewood, Ill.: Irwin, 1979b.

Mahoney, T. A. Organizational hierarchy and position worth. *Academy of Management Journal 22* (1979c): 726–737.

Mahoney, T. A., and Milkovich, G. T. *Techniques for application of Markov analysis to manpower analysis.* Minneapolis: Industrial Relations Center, University of Minnesota, 1971.

Mahoney, T. A., and Milkovich, G. T. *Internal labor markets: An empirical investigation.* Minneapolis: Industrial Relations Center, University of Minnesota, 1972.

Mahoney, T. A., and Milkovich, G. T. An empirical investigation of the internal labor market concept. *Proceedings of the Academy of Management,* Minneapolis, August 1972.

Maloney, W. F. *Experimental negotiating agreement: Development and impact.* Unpublished paper, Graduate School of Business Administration, University of Michigan, 1974.

Maniha, J. Universalism and particularism in bureaucratized organizations. *Administrative Science Quarterly 20* (1975): 177–190.

March, J. C., and March, J. G. Almost random careers: The Wisconsin school superintendency, 1940–1972. *Administrative Science Quarterly 22* (1977): 377–409.

March, J. G., and Simon, H. A. *Organizations.* New York: Wiley, 1958.

Mardon, J., and Hopkins, R. M. The eight year career development plan. *Training and Development Journal 23* (1969): 10–15.

Marrow, A. J. *The practical theorist: The life and works of Kurt Lewin.* New York: Basic Books, 1969.

Marshall, F. R., King, A. G.; and Briggs, V. M. *Labor economics: Wages, employment and trade unionism* (4th ed.). Homewood, Ill.: Irwin, 1980.

Martin, J. *The best practice of business (vol. 6): Manpower planning.* London: John Martin, 1978.

Martin, N., and Strauss, A. Patterns of mobility within industrial organizations. *Journal of Business 29* (1956): 107–110.

Martin, R. A. Employment advertising—Hard sell, soft sell, or what? *Personnel 48* (1971): 33–40.

Martindale, D. Sweaty palms in the control tower. *Psychology Today 10* (February 1977): 70–75.

Maslow, A. H. A theory of human motivation. *Psychological Review 50* (1943): 370–396.

Maslow, A. H. *Motivation and personality.* New York: Harper, 1954.

Maslow, A. H. *Eupsychian management.* Homewood, Ill.: Dorsey Press, 1965.

Mass, N. J. Managerial recruitment and attrition: A policy analysis model. *Behavioral Science 23* (1978): 49–60.

Massey, R. H.; Mullins, C. J.; and Earles, J. A. *Performance appraisal ratings: The content issue* (AFHRL-TR-78-69). Brooks Air Force Base, Texas: Air Force Human Resources Laboratory, 1978.

Matarazzo, J. D.; Weins, A. N.; and Saslow, G. Studies of interview speech behavior. In L. Krasner and L. P. Ullman (eds.), *Research in behavior modification.* New York: Holt, 1965.

Matteson, M. T., and Ivancevich, J. M. Organizational stressors and heart disease: A research model. *Academy of Management Review 4* (1979): 347–358.

Mawhinney, T. C. Operant terms and concepts in the description of individual work behavior: Some problems of interpretation, application and evaluation. *Journal of Applied Psychology 60* (1975): 704–712.

Mawhinney, T. C. Intrinsic x extrinsic work motivation: Perspectives from behaviorism. *Organizational Behavior and Human Performance 24* (1979): 411–440.

Mayfield, E. C. The selection interview—A re-evaluation of published research. *Personnel Psychology 17* (1964): 239–260.

Mayfield, E. C., and Carlson, R. E. Selection interview decisions: First results from a long-term research project. *Personnel Psychology 19* (1966): 41–53.

Medalie, J. H.; Kahn, H. A.; Neufeld, H. N.; Riss, E.; and Goldbourt, U. Five-year myocardial infarction incidence—II: Association of single variables to age and birthplace. *Journal of Chronic Diseases 26* (1973): 329–340.

Merton, R. *Social theory and social structure.* Glencoe, Ill.: Free Press, 1957.

Meyer, H. E. Personnel directors are the new corporate heroes. *Fortune 93* (1976): 84–88.

Meyer, H. H.; Kay, E.; and French, R. P., Jr. Split roles in performance appraisal. *Harvard Business Review 43* (1965): 123–129.

Middlemist, R. D., and Peterson, R. B. Test of equity theory by controlling for comparison co-worker efforts. *Organizational Behavior and Human Performance 15* (1976): 335–354.

Miles, R. C. Learning in kittens with manipulatory, exploratory and food incentives. *Journal of Comparative and Physiology Psychology 51* (1958): 39–42.

Miles, R. H. A comparison of the relative impacts of role perceptions of ambiguity and conflict by role. *Academy of Management Journal 19* (1976): 25–35.

Milkovich, G. Comparable worth, job evaluation and wage discrimination. *Proceedings of the Industrial Relations Research Association,* 1981.

Milkovich, G. T.; Anderson, J. C.; and Greenhalgh, L. Organizational careers: Environmental, organization, and individual determinants. In L. Dyer (ed.), *Careers in organizations.* Ithaca, N.Y.: New York State School of Industrial and Labor Relations, Cornell University, 1976.

Milkovich, G. T.; Annoni, A. J.; and Mahoney, T. A. The use of the Delphi procedure in manpower forecasting. *Management Science 19* (1972): 381–388.

Milkovich, G., and Dyer, L. *Affirmative action planning concepts.* New York: Human Resources Planning Society, 1979.

Milkovich, G. T., and Krzystofiak, F. Simulation and affirmative action planning. *Human Resource Planning 2* (1979): 71–80.

Milkovich, G. T., and Mahoney, T. A. Human resource planning and PAIR policy. In D. Yoder and H. G. Heneman, Jr. (eds.), *Planning and auditing PAIR.* Washington: Bureau of National Affairs, 1976.

Milkovich, G. T., and Mahoney, T. A. Human resource planning models: A perspective. *Human Resource Planning 1* (1978): 19–30.

Mills, T. Altering the social structure in coal mining: A case study. *Monthly Labor Review 100* (1976): 3–10.

Miller, D., and Form, W. *Industrial sociology.* New York: Harper, 1951.

Miner, M. G. Safety policies and the impact of OSHA. *Personnel Policies Forum* (Survey No. 117). Washington: Bureau of National Affairs, 1977.

Mintzberg, H. *The nature of managerial work.* New York: Harper and Row, 1973.

Mintzberg, H. An emerging strategy of "direct" research. *Administrative Science Quarterly 24* (1979): 582–589.

Mintzberg, H.; Raisinghani, D.; and Theoret, A. The structure of "unstructured" decision processes. *Administrative Science Quarterly 21* (1976): 246–275.

Mirvis, P. H., and Lawler, E. E., III. Measuring the financial impact of employee attitudes. *Journal of Applied Psychology 62* (1977): 1–8.

Mitchel, J. O. Assessment center validity. *Journal of Applied Psychology 60* (1975): 573–579.

Mitchell, T. R. Expectancy models of job satisfaction, occupational preference and effort: A theoretical, methodological, and empirical appraisal. *Psychological Bulletin 81* (1974): 1053–1077.

Mitchell, T. R. Cognitions and Skinner: Some questions about behavioral determinism. *Organization and Administrative Sciences 6* (1976): 63–72.

Mitchell, T. R. Organizational behavior. *Annual Review of Psychology 30* (1979): 243–281.

Mitchell, T. R. Expectancy-value models in organizational psychology. In N. Feather (ed.), *Expectancy, incentive and action.* Hillsdale, N.J.: Lawrence Erlbaum Associates, 1980.

Mitchell, T. R., and Beach, L. R. A review of occupational preference and choice research using expectancy theory and decision theory. *Journal of Occupational Psychology 99* (1976): 231–248.

Mitchell, T. R., and Biglan, A. Instrumentality theories: Current uses in psychology. *Psychological Bulletin 76* (1971): 432–454.

Mitchell, T. R., and Knudsen, B. W. Instrumentality theory predictions of students' attitudes towards business and their choice of business as an occupation. *Academy of Management Journal 16* (1973): 41–52.

Mobley, W. H. Intermediate linkages in the relationship between job satisfaction and employee turnover. *Journal of Applied Psychology 62* (1977): 237–240.

Mobley, W. H.; Horner, S. O.; and Hollingsworth, A. T. An evaluation of precursors of hospital employee turnover. *Journal of Applied Psychology 63* (1978): 408–414.

Moch, M. K., and Fitzgibbons, D. E. *Absenteeism and efficiency: An empirical assessment.* Working paper, University of Illinois at Urbana-Champaign, 1980.

Moore, G. Steel industry consent decrees—A model for the future. *Employee Relations Law Journal 3* (1977): 214–239.

Moore, M.; Miller, R.; and Fossum, J. Predictors of managerial career expectations. *Journal of Applied Psychology 59* (1974): 90–92.

Moore, M. L., and Dutton, P. Training needs analysis: Review and critique. *Academy of Management Review 3* (1978): 532–545.

Morano, R. Determining organizational training needs. *Personnel Psychology 26* (1973): 479–487.

Morgan, G., and Smircich, L. The case for qualitative research. *Academy of Management Review 5* (1980): 491–500.

Morgan, H., and Cogger, J. *The interviewer's manual.* New York: Psychology Corporation, 1972.

Morris, F. *Current trends in the use (and misuse) of statistics in employment discrimination litigation.* Washington: Equal Employment Advisory Council, 1977.

Moser, M. Hypertension: A major controllable public health problem—Industry can help. *Occupational Health Nursing* (1977): 19–26.

Moses, J. L. Assessment center performance and management progress. *Studies in Personnel Psychology 4* (1972): 7–12.

Moses, J. L. The development of an assessment center for the early identification of supervisory potential. *Personnel Psychology 26* (1973): 569–580.

Moses, J. L. The assessment center method. In J. L. Moses and W. C. Byham (eds.), *Applying the assessment center method.* New York: Pergamon, 1977.

Moses, J. L., and Boehm, V. R. Relationships of assessment center performance to management progress of women. *Journal of Applied Psychology 60* (1975): 527–529.

Mossberg, W. S. Labor agency to revoke job-safety rules it believes are burdensome, ineffective. *The Wall Street Journal,* December 2, 1977.

Movement for Opportunity and Equality v. *Detroit Diesel Allison Division of General Motors Corporation, et al.* 622 FZD 1235 (1979).

Muchinsky, P. M., and Harris, S. L. The effect of applicant sex and scholastic standing on the evaluation of job applicant resumes in sex-typed occupations. *Journal of Vocational Behavior 11* (1977): 95–108.

Muchinsky, P. M., and Taylor, M. S. Intrasubject predictions of occupational preference: The effect of manipulating components of the valence model. *Journal of Vocational Behavior 8* (1976): 185–196.

Munsterberg, H. *The psychology of industrial efficiency.* Boston: Houghton Mifflin, 1913.

Munsterberg, H. *Psychology: General and applied.* New York: Appleton, 1914.

Murphy, L. R., and Colligan, M. J. Mass psychogenic illness in a shoe factory. *International Archives of Occupational and Environmental Health 44* (1979): 133–138.

Murray, V. V., and Dimick, D. E. Contextual influences on personnel policies and programs: An explanatory model. *Academy of Management Review 3* (1978): 750–761.

Murrell, K.; Griew, S.; and Tucker, W. A. Age structure in the engineering industry: A preliminary study. *Occupational Psychology 31* (1957): 150–168.

Myers, C. A., and Shultz, G. P. *The dynamics of a labor market*. New York: Prentice-Hall, 1951.

NLRB v. Babcock & Wilcox, Inc., 351 U.S. 105 (1956).

NLRB v. General Electric Co., 418 F.2d 766 (1969).

NLRB v. Gissel Packing Co., 395 U.S. 575 (1969).

NLRB v. Truitt Mfg. Co., 351 U.S. 149 (1956).

Nadler, D. A. The effects of feedback on task group behavior: A review of the experimental research. *Organizational Behavior and Human Performance 23* (1979) 309–338.

Nash, A. W.; Muczyk, J. P.; and Vettori, F. L. The relative practical effectiveness of programmed instruction. *Personnel Psychology 24* (1971): 397–418.

National Academy of Sciences. *Job evaluation: An analytic review*. Washington: National Academy of Science, 1979.

National Labor Relations Board. *Forty-fifth annual report of the National Labor Relations Board*. Washington: Government Printing Office, 1980.

National Safety Council. *Accident facts* (1978 ed.). Chicago: National Safety Council, 1979.

Nealey, S. M. Pay and benefit preferences. *Industrial Relations 3* (1963): 17–28.

Nemeroff, W. F., and Cosentino, J. Utilizing feedback and goal setting to increase performance appraisal interviewer skills of managers. *Academy of Management Journal 22* (1979): 566–576.

Newman, J. E., and Beehr, T. A. Personal and organizational strategies for handling job stress: A review of research and opinion. *Personnel Psychology 32* (1979): 1–43.

NH court rules on wc stress case. *The National Underwriter,* May 11, 1979.

Niehaus, R. J. *Computer-Assisted human resource planning*. New York: Wiley, 1979.

Nirtaut, D. J. Assessment centers: An examination of the process, participant reaction, and adverse effects. *Journal of Assessment Center Technology 1* (1978): 18–23.

Nisbett, R. E., and Wilson, J. D. The halo effect: Evidence for unconscious alteration of judgements. *Journal of Personality and Social Psychology 35* (1977): 250–256.

Notz, W. W. Work motivation and the negative effects of extrinsic rewards: A review with implications for theory and practice. *American Psychologist 30* (1975): 884–891.

Nunnally, J. C. *Psychometric theory*. New York: McGraw-Hill, 1967.

Obradovic, J. Modification of the forced-choice method as a criterion of job proficiency. *Journal of Applied Psychology 54* (1970): 228–233.

O'Connell, J.; Fragner, B. N.; and Huberman, J. Employees' cafeteria offers insurance options. *Harvard Business Review 53* (1975): 7–10.

Odiorne, G. Personnel management in the '80s. *The Personnel Administrator 22* (1977): 21–24.

Oettinger, M. P. Nation-wide job evaluation in the Netherlands. *Industrial Relations 4* (1964): 45–59.

Office of Strategic Services (OSS) Assessment Staff. *Assessment of men*. New York: Rinehart, 1948.

Oldham, G. R. Organizational choice and some correlates of individuals' expectancies. *Decision Sciences 7* (1976): 873–884.

Olson, C. A. *Scaling union member preferences for bargaining outcomes*. Unpublished manuscript, Krannert Graduate School of Management, Purdue University, 1979.

Olson, C. A. *Informal presentation of research*. Los Angeles: Graduate School of Management, University of California, Los Angeles, 1980.

O'Meara, J. R. *Retirement: Reward or rejection* (Report No. 713). New York: The Conference Board, 1977.

Opsahl, R. L., and Dunnette, M. D. The role of financial compensation in industrial motivation. *Psychologial Bulletin 66* (1966): 94–118.

O'Reilly, C. A.; Bretton, G.; and Roberts, K. Professional employees' preference for upward mobility: An extension. *Journal of Vocational Behavior 5* (1974): 139–145.

O'Reilly, C. A., and Caldwell, D. F. Informational influence as a determinant of perceived task characteristics and job satisfaction. *Journal of Applied Psychology 64* (1979): 57–165.

Organ, D. W. *The applied psychology of work behavior: A book of readings.* Dallas, Texas: Business Publications, 1978.

Organizational Dynamics. Job redesign on the assembly line: Farewell to blue-collar blues, vol. 2 (1973): 51–67.

Orne, M. T. The nature of hypnosis: Artifact and essence. *Journal of Abnormal Social Psychology 58* (1959): 277–299.

Paperman, J. B., and Martin, D. D. Human resource accounting: A managerial tool? In K. M. Rowland, M. London, G. R. Ferris, and J. L. Sherman (eds.), *Current issues in personnel management.* Boston: Allyn and Bacon, 1980.

Parker, J. Interactions of external and internal labor markets for engineers and scientists. *Proceedings of the Industrial Relations Research Association,* 1965.

Parker, T. C. Assessment centers: A statistical study. *Personnel Administrator 25* (1980): 65–67.

Parmerlee, M., and Schwenk, C. Radical behaviorism in organizations: Misconceptions on the Locke-Gray debate. *Academy of Management Review 4* (1979): 601–608.

Parnes, H. *Research on labor mobility.* New York: Social Science Research Council, 1954.

Parnes, H. S., and Kohen, A. I. Occupational information and labor market status: The case of young men. *Journal of Human Resources 10* (1975): 44–55.

Pass, J. J., and Cunningham, J. W. *Occupational clusters based on systematically derived work dimensions: Final report.* Raleigh, N.C.: Center for Occupational Education, North Carolina State University, 1977.

Pate, L. E. Cognitive versus reinforcement views of intrinsic motivation. *Academy of Management Review 3* (1978): 505–514.

Patten, T. H., Jr. Human resource planning and organization development. *Human Resource Planning 1* (1978): 179–184.

Patz, A. L. Linear programming applied to manpower management. *Industrial Management Review 2* (1970): 31–38.

Payne, S. L. *The art of asking questions.* Princeton, N.J.: Princeton University Press, 1951.

Pearlman, K. Job families: A review and discussion of their implications for personnel selection. *Psychological Bulletin 87* (1980): 1–28.

Peerless Plywood Co., 197 NLRB 247 (1953).

Pennings, J. Work value systems of white collar workers. *Administrative Science Quarterly 15* (1970): 397–405.

Personnel/Human Resources Division Domain Statement. *P/HR Newsletter,* 1979.

Peters, L. H., and Terborg, J. R. The effects of temporal placement of unfavorable information and of attitude similarity on personnel selection decisions. *Organizational Behavior and Human Performance 13* (1975): 279–293.

Peters, R., and Atkin, R. The effect of open pay systems on allocation of salary increases. *Proceedings of the Academy of Management,* Detroit, August 1980.

Peterson, R. B., and Tracy, L. Testing a behavioral model of labor negotiations. *Industrial Relations 16* (1977): 35–50.

Pfeffer, J. Power and resource allocation in organizations. In B. M. Staw and G. R. Salancik (eds.), *New directions in organizational behavior.* Chicago: St. Clair Press, 1977.

Pfeffer, J., and Salancik, G. R. *The external control of organizations.* New York: Harper and Row, 1978.

Pieters, G. R.; Hundert, A. T.; and Beer, M. Predicting organizational choice: A post hoc analysis. *Proceedings of the 76th Annual Convention of the American Psychological Association,* 1968.

Pinneau, S. R., Jr. *Effects of social support on psychological and physiological strains.* Unpublished doctoral dissertation, University of Michigan, 1975.

Pinto, P. R. Commentary: Neglected issues, unanswered questions. In L. Dyer (ed.), *Careers in organizations.* New York State School of Industrial and Labor Relations, Cornell University, 1976.

Pinto, P. R.; Gutteridge, T.; and Tsui, A. *Career planning and career management: Perspectives of the individual and the organization* (Bulletin No. 62). Minneapolis: Industrial Relations Center, University of Minnesota, 1975.

Porter, L. W. *Organizational patterns of managerial job attitudes.* New York: American Foundation for Management Research, 1964.

Porter, L. W., and Lawler, E. E., III. *Managerial attitudes and performance.* Homewood, Ill.: Dorsey, 1968.

Porter, L. W.; Lawler, E. E.; and Hackman, J. R. *Behavior in organizations.* New York: McGraw-Hill, 1975.

Porter, L. W., and Roberts, K. H. Communication in organizations. In M. D. Dunnette (ed.), *Handbook of industrial and organizational psychology.* Chicago: Rand McNally, 1976.

Porter, L. W., and Steers, R. M. Organizational, work, and personal factors in employee turnover and absenteeism. *Psychological Bulletin 80* (1973): 151–176.

Porter, L. W.; Steers, R. M.; Mowday, R. T.; and Boulian, P. V. Organizational commitment, job satisfaction, and turnover among psychiatric technicians. *Journal of Applied Psychology 59* (1974): 603–609.

Price, J. L. *The study of turnover.* Ames: Iowa State University Press, 1977.

Prien, E. P., and Ronan, W. W. Job analysis: A review of research findings. *Personnel Psychology 24* (1971): 371–396.

Primoff, E. S. *Summary of job-element principles: Preparing a job-element standard.* Washington: Personnel Measurement and Development Center, Civil Service Commission, 1971.

Primoff, E. S. *The J-coefficient procedure.* Washington: Personnel Measurement and Development Center, Civil Service Commission, 1972.

Pritchard, R. D.; Campbell, K. M.; and Campbell, D. J. Effects of extrinsic financial rewards on intrinsic motivation. *Journal of Applied Psychology 62* (1977): 9–15.

Pritchard, R. D.; Leonard, D. W.; Von Begen, C. W., Jr.; and Kirk, R. J. The effects of varying schedules of reinforcement on human task performance. *Organizational Behavior and Human Performance 16* (1976): 205–230.

Pruden, H. The upward mobile, indifferent and ambivalent typology of managers. *Academy of Management Journal 16* (1973): 454–464.

Putt, A. M. One experiment in nursing adults with peptic ulcers. *Nursing Research 19* (1970): 484–494.

Quigley, R. C. Management aptitude program. The FBI assessment center. *FBI Law Enforcement Bulletin,* June 1976.

Quinn, R. P., and Staines, G. L. *Quality of employment survey.* Ann Arbor, Mich.: Institute of Social Research, University of Michigan, 1978.

Quinn, R. P.; Staines, G. L.; and McCullough, M. *Job satisfaction: Is there a trend?* (Manpower Research Monograph No. 30). Washington: Department of Labor, 1974.

Rahe, R. H. The pathway between subjects' recent life changes and their near-future illness reports. In B. Dohrenwend and B. Dohrenwend (eds.), *Stressful life events: Their nature and effects.* New York: Wiley, 1974.

Rahe, R. H. Epidemiological studies of life change and illness. *International Journal of Psychiatric Medicine 6* (1975): 133–146.

Rahe, R. H. Life change events and mental illness: An overview. *Journal of Human Stress 5* (1979): 2–10.

Rand, T. M., and Wexley, K. N. A demonstration of the Byrne similarity hypothesis in simulated employment interviews. *Psychological Reports 36* (1975): 535–544.

Randolph, D. A. Easing the exit. *The Wall Street Journal,* May 22, 1980.

Rayback, J. G. *A history of American labor.* New York: Free Press, 1966.

Rees, A. Information networks in labor markets. *American Economic Review 56* (1966): 559–566.

Rees, A. *The economics of work and pay.* New York: Harper and Row, 1973.

Rees, A., and Shultz, G. P. *Workers and wages in an urban labor market.* Chicago: University of Chicago Press, 1970.

Reid, G. L. Job search and the effectiveness of job-finding methods. *Industrial and Labor Relations Review 25* (1972): 479–495.

Reilly, R.; Tenopyr, M.; and Sperling, S. Effects of job previews on job acceptance and survival of telephone operator candidates. *Journal of Applied Psychology 64* (1979): 218–220.

Renwick, P. A., and Tosi, H. The effects of sex, marital status, and educational background on selection decisions. *Academy of Management Journal 21* (1978): 93–103.

Republic Aviation Corp. v. *NLRB,* 324 U.S. 793 (1945).

Results of the assessment center return on investment survey. *Journal of Assessment Center Technology 2* (1979): 19–26.

Reynolds, L. G. *The structure of labor markets.* New York: Harper, 1951.

Rice, B. Midlife encounters: The Menninger seminars for businessmen. *Psychology Today 12* (1979): 66ff.

Richardson, R. C. *Collective bargaining by objectives: A positive approach.* Englewood Cliffs, N.J.: Prentice-Hall, 1977.

Richardson, R. C. Positive collective bargaining. In D. Yoder and H. G. Heneman, Jr. (eds.), *ASPA handbook of personnel and industrial relations.* Washington: Bureau of National Affairs, 1979.

Rinefort, F. C. A new look at occupational safety. *The Personnel Administrator 22* (1977): 29–36.

Ritchie, R. J., and Boehm, V. R. *Screening for assessment centers using biographical data and paper-and-pencil tests.* Paper presented at the International Congress on the Assessment Method, New Orleans, June 1979.

Ritchie, R. J. *Selecting commission sales people with an assessment center.* Paper presented at the International Congress on the Assessment Center Method, Toronto, June 1980.

Robertson, G., and Humphreys, J. *Labour turnover and absenteeism in selected industries.* Northwestern Manpower Adjustment Study (Component Study No. 10), Toronto, 1978.

Robinson, D. D.; Wahlstrom, O. W.; and Mecham, R. C. Comparison of job evaluation methods: A "policy capturing" approach using the Position Analysis Questionnaire (PAQ). *Journal of Applied Psychology 59* (1974): 633–637.

Rockwell v. *Board of Education,* Michigan Supreme Court, 89 LRRM 2017 (1975).

Rogers, D. P., and Sincoff, M. Z. Favorable impression characteristics of the recruitment interviewer. *Personnel Psychology 31* (1978): 495–504.

Rogosa, D. A critique of cross-lagged correlation. *Psychological Bulletin 88* (1980): 245–258.

Ronan, W. A study of some concepts concerning labor turnover. *Occupational Psychology 51* (1967): 193–202.

Ronan, W. W., and Prien, E. P. *Perspective on the measurement of human performance.* New York: Appleton-Century-Crofts, 1971.

Rose, G. L., and Andiappan, P. Sex effects on managerial hiring decisions. *Academy of Management Journal 21* (1978): 104–112.

Rose, G. L., and Brief, A. P. Effects of handicap and job characteristics on selection evaluations. *Personnel Psychology 32* (1979): 385–392.

Rosen, B., and Jerdee, T. H. Too old or not too old. *Harvard Business Review 55* (1977): 97–106.

Rosen, B., and Jerdee, T. H. Influence of sex role stereotypes on personnel decisions. *Journal of Applied Psychology 59* (1974): 9–14.

Rosen, B., and Mericle, M. F., Influence of strong versus weak fair employment policies and applicant's sex on selection decisions and salary recommendations in a management simulation. *Journal of Applied Psychology 64* (1979): 435–439.

Rosenberg, M. J. The conditions and consequences of evaluation apprehension. In R. Rosenthal and R. L. Rosnow (eds.), *Artifacts in behavioral research.* New York: Academic Press, 1969.

Rosenfeld, C. Job seeking methods used by American workers. *Monthly Labor Review 98* (1975): 39–42.

Ross, A. M. The external wage structure. In G. W. Taylor and F. C. Pierson (eds.), *New concepts in wage determination.* New York: McGraw-Hill, 1957.

Ross, I. C., and Zander, A. Need satisfactions and employee turnover. *Personnel Psychology 10* (1957): 327–338.

Roth, J. The study of career timetables. In B. Glaser (ed.), *Organizational careers.* Chicago: Adeline, 1968.

Rothstein, M., and Jackson, D. N. Decision making in the employment interview: An experimental approach. *Journal of Applied Psychology 63* (1980): 271–283.

Rottenberg, S. On choice in labor markets. *Industrial and Labor Relations Review 9* (1956): 183–199.

Rotter, J. B. Generalized expectancies for internal versus external control of reinforcement. *Psychological Monographs 80* (1966): (Whole No. 609).

Rowe, P. M. Individual differences in selection decisions. *Journal of Applied Psychology 47* (1963): 304–307.

Rowe, P. M. Order effects in assessment decisions. *Journal of Applied Psychology 51* (1967): 13–22.

Rowland, K. M.; London, M.; Ferris, G. R.; and Sherman, J. *Current issues in personnel management.* Boston: Allyn and Bacon, 1980.

Rowland, K. M., and Sovereign, M. G. Markov chain analysis of internal manpower supply. *Industrial Relations 9* (1969): 88–99.

Rubin, J. Z., and Brown, B. R. *The social psychology of bargaining and negotiation.* New York: Academic Press, 1975.

Rummel, R. M., and Rader, J. W. Coping with executive stress. *Personnel Journal 57* (1978): 305–307, 332.

Rush, J., and Peacock, A. *A review and integration of theories of life/career stages.* Working Paper, University of Western Ontario, London, Ontario, 1980.

Rush, J.; Peacock, A.; and Milkovich, G. Career stages: A partial test of Levinson's model of life/career stages. *Journal of Vocational Behavior 16* (1980): 347–359.

Ryder, M. S.; Rehmus, C. M.; and Cohen, S. *Management preparation for collective bargaining.* Homewood, Ill.: Dow-Jones-Irwin, 1966.

Rynes, S. L.; Heneman, H. G., III; and Schwab, D. P. Individual reactions to organizational recruiting: A review. *Personnel Psychology 33* (1980): 529–542.

Saal, F. E.; Downey, R. G.; and Lahey, M. A. Rating the ratings: Assessing the psychometric quality of rating data. *Psychological Bulletin 88* (1980): 413–428.

Saal, F. E., and Landy, F. J. The mixed standard rating scale: An evaluation. *Organizational Behavior and Human Performance 18* (1977): 19–35.

Sackett, P. R. *The interviewer as hypothesis tester: The effects of impressions of an applicant on subsequent interviewer behavior.* Unpublished doctoral dissertation, Ohio State University, 1979.

Sackett, P. R., and Hakel, M. D. Temporal stability and individual differences in using assessment information to form overall ratings. *Organizational Behavior and Human Performance 23* (1979): 120–137.

Saklad, D. A. Manpower planning and career development at Citicorp. In L. Dyer (ed.), *Careers in organizations.* Ithaca, N.Y.: New York State School of Industrial and Labor Relations, Cornell University, 1976.

Salancik, G. R. Commitment and control of organizational behavior and belief. In B. M. Staw and G. R. Salancik (eds.), *New directions in organizational behavior.* Chicago: St. Clair Press, 1977.

Salancik, G. R., and Pfeffer, J. An examination of need satisfaction models of job attitudes. *Administrative Science Quarterly 22* (1977): 427–456.

Salancik, G. R., and Pfeffer, J. A social information processing approach to job attitudes and task design. *Administrative Science Quarterly 23* (1978): 224–253.

Saleh, S. D.; Lee, R.; and Prien, E. Why nurses leave their jobs—An analysis of female turnover. *Personnel Administration 28* (1965): 25–28.

Sales, S. M. Organizational roles as a risk factor in coronary heart disease. *Administrative Science Quarterly 14* (1969): 325–336.

Sales, S. M. Some effects of role overload and role underload. *Organizational Behavior and Human Performance 5* (1970): 592–608.

Salvendy, G., and Seymour, W. D. *Prediction and development of industrial work performance.* New York: Wiley, 1973.

Sands, W. A. A method for evaluating alternative recruiting-selection strategies: The CAPER model. *Journal of Applied Psychology 57* (1973): 222–227.

Sandver, M. H. *Regional differentials in outcomes in NLRB certification elections.* Paper presented at the annual meeting of the Academy of Management, Detroit, August 1980.

Sarason, I. G.; Smith, R. E.; and Diener, E. Personality research: Components of variance attributable to the person and the situation. *Journal of Personality and Social Psychology 32* (1975): 199–204.

Sattler, J. M. Racial "experimenter effects" in experimentation, testing, interviewing, and psychotherapy. *Psychological Bulletin 73* (1970): 137–160.

Sawyer, J. Measurement and prediction, clinical, and statistical. *Psychological Bulletin 66* (1966): 178–200.

Sayles, L. R., and Strauss, G. *The local union* (rev. ed.). New York: Harcourt, Brace, & World, 1967.

Sayles, L., and Strauss, G. *Managing human resources* (2nd ed.). Englewood Cliffs, N.J.: Prentice-Hall, 1981.

Scandura, J. M. Structural approach to instructional problems. *American Psychologist 32* (1977): 33–53.

Schachter, S. *The psychology of affiliation.* Stanford, Calif.: Stanford University Press, 1959.

Schachter, S.; Ellertson, N.; McBride, D.; and Gregory, P. An experimental study of cohesiveness and productivity. *Human Relations 4* (1951): 229–238.

Schein, E. H. *Organizational psychology* (rev. ed.). Englewood Cliffs, N.J.: Prentice-Hall, 1971.

Schein, E. G. *Career dynamics: Matching individual and organizational needs.* Reading, Mass.: Addison-Wesley, 1978.

Schelling, T. C. An essay on bargaining. *American Economic Review 46* (1956): 281–306.

Schiller, B. R. Job search media: Utilization and effectiveness. *The Quarterly Review of Economics and Business 15* (1975): 55–63.

Schmidt, F.; Greenthal, A.; Hunter, J.; Berner, J.; and Seaton, F. Job sample vs. paper-and-pencil trades and technical tests: Adverse impact and examinee attitudes. *Personnel Psychology 30* (1977): 187–197.

Schmidt, F. L.; Berner, J. G.; and Hunter, J. E. Racial differences in validity of employment tests: Reality or illusion? *Journal of Applied Psychology 58* (1973): 5–9.

Schmidt, F. L., and Kochan, L. B. Composite vs. multiple criteria: A review and resolution of the controversy. *Personnel Psychology 24* (1972): 419–434.

Schmitt, N. Social and situational determinants of interview decisions: Implications for the employment interview. *Personnel Psychology 29* (1976): 79–101.

Schmitt, N. Interrater agreement in dimensionality and combination of assessment center judgments. *Journal of Applied Psychology 62* (1977): 171–176.

Schmitt, N., and Coyle, B. W. Applicant decisions in the employment interview. *Journal of Applied Psychology 61* (1976): 184–192.

Schmitt, N.; Coyle, B. W.; and Rauschenberger, J. A. Monte Carlo evaluation of three formula estimates of cross-validated multiple correlation. *Psychological Bulletin 84* (1977): 751–758.

Schmitt, N., and Hill, T. E. Sex and race composition of assessment center groups as a determinant of peer and assessor ratings. *Journal of Applied Psychology 62* (1977): 261–264.

Schneider, J., and Locke, E. A. A critique of Herzberg's incident classification system and a suggested revision. *Organizational Behavior and Human Performance 6* (1971): 441–457.

Schrank, R. *Ten thousand working days.* Cambridge, Mass.: MIT Press, 1978.

Schreisheim, C. A. Job satisfaction, attitude towards unions and voting in a union representation election. *Journal of Applied Psychology 63* (1978): 548–552.

Schuler, R. S. Role perceptions, satisfaction, and performance: A partial reconciliation. *Journal of Applied Psychology 60* (1975): 683–687.

Schuler, R. S. Role conflict and ambiguity as a function of the task—structure—technology interaction. *Organizational Behavior and Human Performance 20* (1977): 66–74.

Schuler, R. S. Definition and conceptualization of stress in organization. *Organizational Behavior and Human Performance 25* (1980): 184–215.

Schuler, R. S. *Personnel and human resource management.* St. Paul, Minn.: West, 1980.

Schwab, D. P. Construct validity in organizational behavior. In B. M. Staw and L. L. Cummings (eds.), *Research in organizational behavior* (vol. 2). Greenwich, Conn.: JAI Press, 1980.

Schwab, D. P., and Heneman, H. G. Relationship between interview structure and interview-er reliability in an employment situation. *Journal of Applied Psychology 53* (1969): 214–217.

Schwab, D. P., and Olian, J. D. *Gate keeping in organizations.* Unpublished paper, Center for Personnel/Human Resource Management, University of Wisconsin-Madison, 1980.

Schwab, D. P.; Olian-Gottlieb, J. D.; and Heneman, H.G., III. Between-subjects expectancy theory research: A statistical review of studies predicting effort and performance. *Psychological Bulletin 86* (1979): 139–147.

Schwab, D. P.; Rynes, S. L.; and Aldag, R. J. *Theories and research on organizational participation.* Unpublished paper, Center for Human Resource Management, University of Wisconsin-Madison, 1980.

Scott, W. D. The scientific selection of salesmen. *Advertising and Selling XXV* (1915): 5–6, 94–96.

Scott, W. D. Selection of employees by means of quantitative determinations. *Annals of the American Academy of Political and Social Science 65* (1916).

Scott, W. E., Jr. The behavioral consequences of repetitive task design: Research and theory. In L. L. Cummings and W. E. Scott (eds.), *Readings in organizational behavior and human performance.* Homewood, Ill.: Irwin, 1969.

Scott, W. E., Jr. The effects of extrinsic rewards on intrinsic motivation. *Organizational Behavior and Human Performance 15* (1976): 117–129.

Scott, W. E., Jr., and Erskine, J. A. *The effects of variations in task design and monetary reinforcers on task behavior.* Unpublished manuscript, Indiana University, 1977.

Scott, W. G., and Hart, D. K. The moral nature of man in organizations. *Academy of Management Journal 14* (1971): 241–255.

Seashore, S. *Group cohesiveness in the industrial work group.* Ann Arbor, Mich.: Institute for Social Research, University of Michigan, 1954.

Seashore, S. E.; Lawler, E. E., III; Mirvis, P. H.; and Cammann, C. (eds.), *Observing and measuring organizational change: A guide to field practice.* New York: Wiley-Interscience, 1980.

Seltzer, R. A. Computer-assisted instruction—What it can and cannot do. *American Psychologist 26* (1971): 373–377.

Selye, H. *The stress of life.* New York: McGraw-Hill, 1956.

Sharf, J. The *prima facie* case: Keeping Title VII honest. In McGovern (ed.), *Equal Employment Practice Guide.* Washington: Committee on Equal Employment and Collective Bargaining of the Council on Labor Law and Labor Relations, Federal Bar Association, 1978.

Sharon, A. T. *The effects of instructional conditions in producing leniency on two types of rating scales.* Unpublished doctoral dissertation, University of Maryland, 1968.

Shartle, C. L. *Occupational information* (3rd ed.). Englewood Cliffs, N.J.: Prentice-Hall, 1959.

Sheard, J. L. Intrasubject prediction of preferences for organization types. *Journal of Applied Psychology 54* (1970): 248–252.

Sheppard, H. L., and Belitsky, A. H. *The job hunt.* Baltimore: Johns Hopkins Press, 1966.

Sheppard, H. L., and Rix, S. E. *The graying of working America.* New York: Free Press, 1977.

Sheth, J. N. Recent developments in organizational buying behavior. In A. G. Woodside; J. N. Sheth; and P. D. Bennet (eds.), *Consumer and industrial buying behavior.* New York: North-Holland, 1977.

Shiller, B. R. Job search media: Utilization and effectiveness. *The Quarterly Review of Economics and Business 15* (1975): 55–63.

Shirley, S. A. Stress management at TRW. In *Reducing occupational stress.* Cincinnati: NIOSH Research Report, 1978.

Shoben, E. Differential pass-fail rates in employment testing: Statistical proof under Title VII. *Harvard Law Review 91* (1978): 793.

Shopping Kart Food Market, Inc., 228 NLRB 190 (1977).

Shostak, A. B. *Blue collar stress.* Reading, Mass.: Addison-Wesley, 1980.

Sigelman, C. K.; Elias, S. F.; and Danker-Brown, P. Interview behaviors of mentally retarded adults as predictors of employability. *Journal of Applied Psychology 65* (1980): 67–73.

Silverman, D., and Jones, J. *Organizational work.* London: Collier Macmillan, 1976.

Simas, K., and McCarrey, M. Impact of recruiter authoritarianism and applicant sex on evaluation and selection decisions in a recruitment interview analogue study. *Journal of Applied Psychology 64* (1979): 483–491.

Simkin, W. E. *Mediation and the dynamics of collective bargaining.* Washington: Bureau of National Affairs, 1971.

Simon, H. A. Rational decision making in business organizations. *American Economic Review 69* (1979): 493–513.

Simon, H. A. Management by machines. In M. Anshen and G. L. Bach (eds.), *Management of the corporation in 1985.* New York: McGraw-Hill, 1960.

Simon, H. L., and Kirschenbaum, H. *Values clarification: A handbook of practical strategies for teachers and students.* New York: Hart, 1972.

Singer, J. N. Sex differences—Similarities in job preference factors. *Journal of Vocational Behavior 5* (1974): 357–365.

Skinner, B. F. *Beyond freedom and dignity.* New York: Knopf, 1971.

Slivinski, L. W.; Grant, K. W.; Bourgeois, R. P.; Pederson, L. D.; and McCloskey, J. L. Longitudinal follow-up of a first level management assessment centre. *Journal of Assessment Center Technology 1* (1978): 6–12.

Slivinski, L. W.; McCloskey, J. L.; and Bourgeois, R. P. *Comparison of different methods of assessment.* Paper presented at the International Congress on the Assessment Center Method, New Orleans, June 1979.

Slivinski, L. W.; McDonald, V. S.; and Bourgeois, R. P. Immediate and long-term reactions to an assessment centre. *Journal of Assessment Center Technology 2* (1979): 13–18.

Smith v. *Hussman Refrigerator Co. & Local 13889, United Steelworkers of America,* 619 F.2d 1229 (1980).

Smith, A. *The wealth of nations: Inquiry into the nature and causes of the wealth of nations.* New York: Random House, 1937.

Smith, A. *The wealth of nations* (vol. 1). Homewood, Ill.: Irwin, 1963.

Smith, L. "Equality Opportunity" rules are getting tougher. *Fortune 97* (1978a): 152–156.

Smith, L. The EEOC's bold foray into job evaluation. *Fortune 98* (1978b): 58–64.

Smith, M. J.; Colligan, M. J.; and Harrell, J. J., Jr. *A review of psychological stress research of the National Institute for Occupational Safety and Health, 1971 to 1976.* Cincinnati, Ohio: NIOSH Research Report, 1978.

Smith, P.; Roberts, K.; and Hulin, C. Ten year job satisfaction trends in a stable organization. *Academy of Management Journal 19* (1976): 462–468.

Smith, R. A., and Jones, D. L. The Supreme Court and labor arbitration: The emerging federal law. *Michigan Law Review 63* (1965): 7.

Smock, D. B., and Holt, B. G. Children's reactions to novelty: An experimental study of curiosity motivation. *Child Development 33* (1962): 631–642.

Soelberg, P. O. Unprogrammed decision making. *Industrial Management Review 8* (1967): 19–29.

Solomon, S. The asbestos fallout at Johns-Manville. *Fortune 99* (1979): 196–209.

Somers, G. G. (ed.). *The next twenty-five years of industrial relations.* Madison, Wisc.: Industrial Relations Research Association, 1973.

Sonnenfeld, J. Dealing with the aging work force. *Harvard Business Review 56* (1978): 81–92.

Sparacino, J. The type A behavior pattern: A critical assessment. *Journal of Human Stress 5* (1975): 37–51.

Springbett, B. M. Factors affecting the final decision in the employment interview. *Canadian Journal of Psychology 12* (1958): 13–22.

Standing, T. E. Assessment and management selection. In J. L. Moses and W. C. Byham (eds.), *Applying the assessment center method.* New York: Pergamon, 1977.

Starbuck, W. Organizational growth and development. In J. March (ed.), *Handbook on organizations.* Chicago: Rand-McNally, 1965.

Staw, B. M. Motivation in organizations: Toward synthesis and redirection. In B. M. Staw and G. R. Salancik (eds.), *New directions in organizational behavior.* Chicago: St. Clair Press, 1977.

Staw, B. M. The consequences of turnover. *Journal of Occupational Behavior 1* (1980): 253–273.

Staw, B. *Intrinsic and extrinsic motivation.* Morristown, N.J.: General Learning Press, 1976.

Staw, B. M., and Oldham, G. R. Reconsidering our dependent variables: A critique and empirical study. *Academy of Management Journal 21* (1978): 539–559.

Steers, R. M. Antecedents and outcomes of organizational commitment. *Administrative Science Quarterly 22* (1977): 46–56.

Steers, R. M. *Organizational effectiveness.* Santa Monica, Calif.: Goodyear, 1977.

Steers, R., and Mowday, R. T. The motivational properties of tasks. *Academy of Management Review 2* (1977): 645–658.

Steers, R. M., and Mowday, R. T. Employee turnover and post-decision accommodation processes. In L. L. Cummings and B. M. Staw (eds.), *Research in Organizational Behavior* (vol. 3). Greenwich, Conn.: JAI Press, 1981.

Steers, R. M., and Porter, L. W. *Motivation and work behavior* (2nd ed.). New York: McGraw-Hill, 1979.

Steers, R. M., and Porter, L. W. The role of task-goal attributes in employee performance. *Psychological Bulletin 81* (1974): 434–452.

Steers, R. M., and Rhodes, S. R. Major influences on employee attendance: A process model. *Journal of Applied Psychology 63* (1978): 391–407.

Stephens, T. A., and Burroughs, W. A. An application of operant conditioning to absenteeism in a hospital setting. *Journal of Applied Psychology 63* (1978): 518–521.

Stephenson, G. M., and Brotherton, C. J. (eds.). *Industrial relations: A social psychological approach.* New York: Wiley, 1979.

Stern, J. L. The Wisconsin public employee fact-finding procedure. *Industrial and Labor Relations Review 20* (1966): 3–29.

Stern, J. L.; Rehmus, C. M.; Loewenberg, J. J.; Kasper, H.; and Dennis, B. D. *Final offer arbitration.* Lexington, Mass.: Heath, 1975.

Sterrett, J. H. The job interview: Body language and perceptions of potential effectiveness. *Journal of Applied Psychology 63* (1978): 388–390.

Stevens, D. W. *Assisted job search for the insured unemployed.* Kalamazoo, Mich.: Upjohn Institute for Employment Research, 1974.

Stevens, D. W. *A reexamination of what is known about job seeking behavior in the United States.* Paper presented at the Conference on Labor Market Intermediaries, The National Commission for Manpower Policy, November 1977.

Stigler, G. Information in the labor market. *Journal of Political Economy* (Supplement) 70 (1962): 94–105.

Stogdill, R. *The handbook of leadership.* New York: Free Press, 1974.

Stoikov, V., and Raimon, R. Determinants of differences in quit rates among industries. *American Economic Review 58* (1968): 1283–1298.

Stoltz, R. E. Development of a criterion of research productivity. *Journal of Applied Psychology 42* (1958): 308–310.

Stone, C. H., and Yoder, D. *Job analysis.* Los Angeles: California State College, 1970.

Stone, C. I., and Sawatzki, B. Hiring bias and the disabled interviewee: Effects of manipulating work history and disability information of the disabled job applicant. *Journal of Vocational Behavior 16* (1980): 96–104.

Stone, R. C. Factory organization and vertical mobility. *American Sociological Review 18* (1953): 28–35.

Storey, W. *Career action planning.* Croton, N.Y.: General Electric Company, 1976.

Strang, H. R.; Lawrence, E. C.; and Fowler, P. C. Effects of assigned goal level and knowledge of results on arithmetic computation: A laboratory study. *Journal of Applied Psychology 63* (1978): 446–450.

Strauss, G. Organizational behavior and personnel relations. *A Review of Industrial Relations Research 1* (1970): 145–206.

Strauss, G. Can social psychology contribute to industrial relations? In G. M. Stephenson and C. J. Brotherton (eds.), *Industrial relations: A social psychological approach.* New York: Wiley, 1979.

Strauss, G. Workers: Attitudes and adjustments. In J. M. Rosow (ed.), *The worker and the job: Coping with change.* Englewood Cliffs, N.J.: Prentice-Hall, 1974.

Strauss, G. Quality of worklife and participation as bargaining issues. In H. A. Juris and M. Roomkin (eds.), *The shrinking perimeter: Unionism and labor relations in the manufacturing sector.* Lexington, Mass.: Lexington Books, 1979.

Summers, C. W. The individual employee's rights under the collective bargaining agreement: What constitutes fair representation? In J. T. McKelvey (ed.), *The duty of fair representation.* Ithaca, N.Y.: New York State School of Industrial and Labor Relations, Cornell University, 1977.

Super, D.; Crites, J.; Hummel, R.; Moser, H.; Overstreet, P.; and Wernath, C. *Vocational development: A framework for research.* New York: Teachers College Press, 1957.

Super, D., and Hall, D. T. Career development: Exploration and planning. In M. R. Rosenzweig and L. W. Porter (eds.), *Annual review of psychology* (vol. 29). Palo Alto, Calif.: Annual Reviews, 1978.

Sweet, D. H. Something new in personnel: "Out-placement." *Personnel Journal 50* (1971): 559–563.

Sydiaha, D. On the equivalence of clinical and statistical methods. *Journal of Applied Psychology 43* (1959): 395–401.

Sydiaha, D. Bales' interaction process analysis of personnel selection interviews. *Journal of Applied Psychology 45* (1961): 393–401.

Taber, T. D.; Beehr, T. A., and Walsh, J. T. The relationship between objective and perceived job characteristics. *Proceedings of the Academy of Management,* San Francisco, August 1978.

Taber, T. D.; Walsh, J. T.; and Cooke, R. A. Developing a community-based program for reducing the social impact of a plant closing. *Journal of Applied Behavioral Science 15* (1979): 133–155.

Taft, P. *Organized labor in American history.* New York: Harper and Row, 1964.

Taft, P. Internal union structure and functions. In G. G. Somers (ed.), *The next twenty-five years of industrial relations.* Madison, Wisc.: Industrial Relations Research Association, 1973.

Taft, R. Use of the "group situation observation" method in the selection of trainee executives. *Journal of Applied Psychology 32* (1948): 587–594.

Task Force on Assessment Center Standards. *Standards and ethical considerations for assessment center operations.* Paper presented at the International Congress of the Assessment Center Method, New Orleans, June 1979.

Tausky, C., and Dubin, R. Career anchorage: Managerial mobility motivations. *American Sociological Review 30* (1965): 725–735.

Taylor, F. W. *Principles of scientific management.* New York: Harper, 1911.

Taylor, L. R. The construction of job families based on the component and overall dimensions of the PAQ. *Personnel Psychology 31* (1978): 325–340.

Taylor, L. R., and Colbert, G. A. The construction of job families based on company-specific PAQ job dimensions. *Personnel Psychology 31* (1978): 341–354.

Tead, O., and Metcalf, H. C. *Personnel administration.* New York: McGraw-Hill, 1920.

Telly, C. S.; French, W. L.; and Scott, W. G. The relationship of inequity to turnover among hourly workers. *Administrative Science Quarterly 16* (1971): 164–172.

Tessler, R., and Sushelsky, L. Effects of eye-contact and social status on the perception of a job applicant in an employment interviewing situation. *Journal of Vocational Behavior 13* (1978): 338–347.

Theorell, T. Workload, life change and myocardial infarction. In *Reducing occupational stress.* Cincinnati: NIOSH Research Report, 1978.

Theorell, T., and Rahe, R. H. Psychosocial characteristics of subjects with myocardial infarction in Stockholm. In E. K. E. Gunderson and R. H. Rahe (eds.), *Life stress and illness.* Springfield, Ill.: Charles C. Thomas, 1973.

Thompsen, D. J. Eliminating pay discrimination caused by job evaluation. *Personnel 55* (1978): 11–22.

Thompson, A., and Carlson, W. *Occupations, personnel and careers.* Pittsburgh: University of Pittsburgh, 1962.

Thompson, J. D. *Organizations in action.* New York: McGraw-Hill, 1967.

Thomson, H. A. Comparison of predictor and criterion judgments on managerial performance using the multitrait-multimethod approach. *Journal of Applied Psychology 54* (1970): 496–502.

Thorndike, R. L. *Personnel selection.* New York: Wiley, 1949.

Thornton, G. C., III. Professional issues in assessment center applications. *Journal of Assessment Center Technology 2* (1979): 1–6.

Thornton, G. C., III, and Zorich, S. Training to improve observer accuracy. *Journal of Applied Psychology 65* (1980): 351–354.

Thurow, L. *Generating inequality: Mechanisms of distribution in the U.S. economy.* New York: Basic Books, 1975.

Thurow, L. *The zero-sum society.* New York: Basic Books, 1980.

Title VII of the Civil Rights Act of 1964, pp. 703(a), 42 U.S.C. pp. 2000e.

Toops, H. A. A research utopia in industrial psychology. *Personnel Psychology 12* (1959): 189–225.

Tornow, W. W., and Pinto, P. R. The development of a managerial job taxonomy: A system for describing, classifying, and evaluating executive positions. *Journal of Applied Psychology 61* (1976): 410–418.

Torpey, W. Promotion from within. *Public Personnel Review 13* (1952): 176–178.

Townsend, R. *Up the organization.* New York: Fawcett, 1970.

Trattner, M. H. Task analysis in the design of three concurrent validity studies of the Professional and Administrative Career Examination. *Personnel Psychology 32* (1979): 109–119.

Treiman, D. J. *Job evaluation: An analytic review* (Interim Report to the Equal Employment Opportunity Commission). Washington: National Academy of Sciences, 1979.

Trice, H. M.; Belasco, J.; and Alutto, J. A. The role of ceremonials in organizational behavior. *Industrial and Labor Relations Review 23* (1969): 40–51.

Truesdale, J. C. From General Shoe to General Knit: A return to Hollywood Ceramics. *Labor Law Journal 30* (1979): 67–75.

Tryon, R. C., and Bailey, D. E. *Cluster analysis.* New York: McGraw-Hill, 1970.

Tucker, D. H., and Rowe, P. M. Consulting the application form prior to interview: An essential step in the selection process. *Journal of Applied Psychology 62* (1977): 283–287.

Tucker, D. H., and Rowe, P. M. Relationship between expectancy, causal attributions, and final hiring decisions in the employment interview. *Journal of Applied Psychology 64* (1979): 27–34.

Tullar, W. L.; Mullins, T. W.; and Caldwell, S. A. Effects of interview length and applicant quality on interview decision time. *Journal of Applied Psychology 64* (1979): 669–674.

Uhrbrock, R. S. Job analysis in industry. *Occupations 12* (1934): 69–74.

Ullman, J. C. Employee referrals: Prime tool for recruiting workers. *Personnel 43* (1966): 30–35.

Ullman, J. C., and Gutteridge, T. G. The job search. *Journal of College Placement 33* (1973): 67–72.

Ulrich, L., and Trumbo, D. The selection interview since 1949. *Psychological Bulletin 63* (1965): 100–116.

Umstot, D. D.; Bell, C. H.; and Mitchell, T. R. Effects of job enrichment and task goals on satisfaction and productivity: Implications for job design. *Journal of Applied Psychology 61* (1976): 379–394.

Uniform Guidelines on Employee Selection Procedures. *Federal Register 43* (1978): 38295–38309.

United States v. *State of New York,* 21 EPD 30, 314 (1979).

United States v. *State of South Carolina,* 15 FEP Cases at 1196 (1977).

Uyar, K. M. Markov chain forecasts of employee replacement needs. *Industrial Relations 11* (1972): 96–106.

Vaca v. *Sipes,* 386 U.S. 171 (1967).

Valenzi, E., and Andrews, I. R. Individual differences in the decision process of employment interviewers. *Journal of Applied Psychology 58* (1973): 49–53.

Vance, R. J.; Kuhnert, K. W.; and Farr, J. L. Interview judgments: Using external criteria to compare behavioral and graphic scale ratings. *Organizational Behavior and Human Performance 22* (1978): 279–294.

Vardi, Y., and Hammer, T. Intraorganizational mobility and career perceptions among rank and file employees. *Academy of Management Journal 20* (1977): 622–634.

Vecchiotti, D. I., and Korn, J. H. Comparison of student and recruiter values. *Journal of Vocational Behavior 16* (1980): 43–50.

Venardos, M. G., and Harris, M. B. Job interview training with rehabilitation clients: A comparison of videotape and role playing procedures. *Journal of Applied Psychology 58* (1973): 365–367.

Vetter, E. *Manpower planning for high talent personnel.* Ann Arbor, Mich.: Bureau of Industrial Relations, University of Michigan, 1967.

Vroom, V., and MacCrimmon, K. Toward a stochastic model of managerial careers. *Administrative Science Quarterly 12* (1968): 26–36.

Vroom, V. H. *Work and motivation.* New York: Wiley, 1964.

Vroom, V. H. Organizational choice: A study of pre- and postdecision processes. *Organizational Behavior and Human Performance* (1966): 212–225.

Vroom, V. H., and MacCrimmon, K. R. Toward a stochastic model of managerial careers. *Administrative Science Quarterly 13* (1968): 24–46.

Vroom, V. H., and Yetton, P. W. *Leadership and decision making.* Pittsburgh: University of Pittsburgh Press, 1973.

Wachter, M. Primary and secondary labor markets: A critique of the dual approach. *Brookings Paper on Economic Activity 3* (1974): 637–681.

Wachter, M. L. Cyclical variation in the interindustry wage structure. *American Economic Review 60* (1970): 75–84.

Wagner, J. A., III. *The organizing dilemma: Individualism and collectivism in organizations.* Unpublished doctoral dissertation, University of Illinois at Urbana-Champaign, 1982.

Wagner, R. The employment interview: A critical summary. *Personnel Psychology 2* (1949): 17–46.

Wahba, M. A., and Bridwell, L. G. Maslow reconsidered: A review of research on the need hierarchy theory. *Organizational Behavior and Human Performance 15* (1976): 212–240.

Wahba, M. A., and House, R. J. Expectancy theory in work and motivation: Some logical and methodological issues. *Human Relations 27* (1974): 121–147.

Wahlund, I., and Nerell, G. Stress factors in the working environments of white-collar workers. In *Reducing occupational stress.* Cincinnati, Ohio: NIOSH Research Report, 1978.

Walker, J. W. Evaluating the practical effectiveness of human resource planning applications. *Human Resource Management 13* (1974): 19–27.

Walker, J. W. Human resource planning: An odyssey to 2001 and beyond. *Pittsburgh Business Review 47* (1978): 2–8.

Walker, J. W. *Human resource planning.* New York: McGraw-Hill, 1980.

Walker, J. W. Lets get realistic about careers. *Human Resources Management 15* (1976): 2–7.

Walker, J. W., and Gutteridge, T. G. *Career planning practices.* New York: AMACOM, 1979.

Walker, J. W., and Wolfe, M. N. Patterns in human resource planning practices. *Human Resource Planning 1* (1978): 189–198.

Wall, J. A., Jr. *Mediation: A categorical analysis and a proposed framework for future research.* Paper presented at the annual meeting of the Academy of Management, Detroit, August 1980.

Wallace, S. R. *Criteria for what?* Presidential address, Division 14, American Psychological Association, 1964.

Walton, R. E., and McKersie, R. B. *A behavioral theory of labor negotiations.* New York: McGraw-Hill, 1965.

Wanous, J. *Organizational entry.* Reading, Mass. Addison-Wesley, 1980.

Wanous, J. P. Occupational preferences: Perceptions of valence and instrumentality, and objective data. *Journal of Applied Psychology 56* (1972): 152–155.

Wanous, J. P. Effects of a realistic job preview on job acceptance, job attitudes, and job survival. *Journal of Applied Psychology 58* (1973): 327–332.

Wanous, J. P. Organizational entry: Newcomers moving from outside to inside. *Psychological Bulletin 84* (1977): 601–618.

Wanous, J. P. *Organizational entry: Recruitment, selection, and socialization of newcomers.* Reading, Mass.: Addison-Wesley, 1980.

Ward, D., and Eastman, R. Force adjustment cost analysis. In R. B. Frantzreb (ed.), *Manpower planning.* Sunnyvale, Calif.: Advanced Personnel Systems, October 1979.

Ward, J. H. Jr., and Hook, M. E. Application of an hierarchical grouping procedure to a problem of grouping profiles. *Educational and Psychological Measurement 23* (1963): 69–81.

Warner, H. A., and Rubin, I. W. Motivation of research and development entrepreneurs. *Journal of Applied Psychology 53* (1969): 178–184.

Warshaw, L. J. *Stress management.* Reading, Mass.: Addison-Wesley, 1979.

Washburn, P. V., and Hakel, M. D. Visual cues and verbal content as influences on impressions after simulated employment interviews. *Journal of Psychology 58* (1973): 137–140.

Weaver, C. N. Job preferences of white collar and blue collar workers. *Academy of Management Journal 18* (1975): 167–175.

Webb, E. J.; Campbell, D. T.; Schwartz, R. D.; and Sechrest, L. *Unobtrusive measures.* Chicago: Rand-McNally, 1966.

Weber, A. R. (ed.). *The structure of collective bargaining.* New York: Free Press, 1961.

Weber, A. Conflict and compression: The labor market environment of the 1980's. In C. Kerr and J. Rosow (eds.), *Work in America: The decade ahead.* New York: Van Nostrand, 1979.

Weber, W. L. Manpower planning in hierarchical organizations: A computer simulation approach. *Management Science 18* (1971): 119–144.

Webster, E. C. *Decision making in the employment interview.* Montreal, Canada: Eagle, 1964.

Weick, K. E. Middle range theories of social systems. *Behavioral Science 19* (1974): 357–367.

Weick, K. E.; Bougon, M. C.; and Maruyama, G. The equity context. *Organizational Behavior and Human Performance 15* (1976): 32–65.

Weick, K. E. *The social psychology of organizing* (2nd ed.). Reading, Mass.: Addison-Wesley, 1979.

Weis, W. L. Profits up in smoke. *Personnel Journal,* 1981, in press.

Weiss, D. J. Multivariate procedures. In M. D. Dunnette (ed.), *Handbook of industrial and organizational psychology.* Chicago: Rand-McNally, 1976.

Weiss, H. M., and Shaw, J. B. Social influences on judgments about tasks. *Organizational Behavior and Human Performance 24* (1979): 126–140.

Welch, F. What have we learned from empirical studies of unemployment insurance. *Industrial and Labor Relations Review 30* (1977): 451–461.

Westin, A. (ed.). *Whistle-Blowing: Loyalty and dissent in the organization.* New York: McGraw-Hill, 1980.

Wexley, K. N., and Nemeroff, W. F. Effects of racial prejudice, race of applicant, and biographical similarity on interviewer evaluations of job applicants. *Journal of Social and Behavioral Sciences 20* (1974): 66–78.

Wexley, K. N.; Sanders, R. E.; and Yukl, G. A. Training interviews to eliminate control effects in employment interviews. *Journal of Applied Psychology 57* (1973): 233–236.

Wexley, K. N.; Yukl, G. A.; Kovacs, S. Z.; and Sanders, R. E. Importance of contrast effects in employment interviews. *Journal of Applied Psychology 56* (1972): 45–48.

Wheeler, H. N. Compulsory arbitration: A "narcotic" effect? *Industrial Relations 14* (1975): 117–120.

Wheeler, H. N. Closed offer: Alternative to final offer selection. *Industrial Relations 16* (1977): 298–305.

White, J. K. Individual differences and the job quality-workers response relationships: Review, integration and comments. *Academy of Management Review 3* (1978): 267–280.

594

REFERENCES

White, R. W. Motivation reconsidered: The concept of competence. *Psychological Review 66* (1959): 297–333.
White, S. E., and Mitchell, T. R. Job enrichment versus social cues: A comparison and competitive test. *Journal of Applied Psychology 64* (1979): 1–9.
White, S.; Mitchell, T. R.; and Bell, C. H. Goal setting, evaluation apprehension and social cues as determinants of job performance and job satisfaction in a simulated organization. *Journal of Applied Psychology 62* (1977): 665–673.
White, T. Production workers and perceptions of intraorganizational mobility. *Sociological Inquiry 44* (1974): 121–129.
Whitla, D. K., and Tirrell, J. E. The validity of ratings of several levels of supervisors. *Personnel Psychology 6* (1953): 461–466.
Whyte, W. F. *Money and motivation.* New York: Harper, 1955.
Wiener, Y., and Schneiderman, M. L. Use of job information as a criterion in employment decisions of interviewers. *Journal of Applied Psychology 59* (1974): 699–704.
Wiggins, J. S. *Personality and prediction: Principles of personality assessment.* Reading, Mass.: Addison-Wesley, 1973.
Wikstrom, W. S. *Manpower planning: Evolving systems.* New York: The Conference Board, 1971.
Wilensky, H. L. Work careers, and social integration. *International Social Science Journal 12* (1960): 543–560.
Wilkinson, I., and Kipnis, D. Interfirm use of power. *Journal of Applied Psychology 63* (1978): 315–320.
Winpisinger, W. Job satisfaction: A union response. *American Federationist 80* (1973): 8–10.
Winter, F. W., and Rowland, K. M. Personnel decisions: A Bayesian approach. *California Management Review 22* (1980): 33–41.
Witte, E. Field research on complex decision-making processes: The phase theorem. *International Studies of Management and Organization 2* (1972): 156–182.
Witte, R., and Cannon, M. Employee assistance programs: Getting top management's support. *The Personnel Administrator 24* (1979): 23–26, 44.
Wood, G. *Fundamentals of psychological research* (2nd ed.). Boston: Little, Brown, 1977.
Woodward, J. *Industrial organization: Theory and practice.* London: Oxford University Press, 1965.
Wright, O. R., Jr. Summary of research on the selection interview since 1964. *Personnel Psychology 22* (1969): 391–413.
Yaffe, R. M. Changing retirement patterns: Their effect on employee benefits. *The Personnel Administrator 24* (1979): 29–34.
Yankelovich, D. Yankelovich on today's workers. *Best of Business 2* (1980): 67–72.
Yolles, S. F.; Carone, P. A.; and Krinsky, L. W. *Absenteeism in industry.* Springfield, Ill.: Charles C. Thomas, 1975.
Youngman, M. B.; Oxtoby, R.; Monk, J. D.; and Heywood, J. *Analysing jobs.* West Mead, England: Gower Press, Teakfield Ltd., 1978.
Yukl, G. A., and Latham, G. P. Consequences of reinforcement schedules and incentive magnitudes for employee performance: Problems encountered in an industrial setting. *Journal of Applied Psychology 60* (1975): 294–298.
Yukl, G. A.; Latham, G. P.; and Purcell, E. D. The effectiveness of performance incentives under continuous and variable ratio schedules of reinforcement. *Personnel Psychology 29* (1976): 221–231.

Yukl, G. A., and Latham, G. P. Interrelationships among employee participation, individual differences, goal difficulty, goal acceptance, instrumentality and performance. *Personnel Psychology 31* (1978): 305–324.

Yukl, G.; Wexley, K. N.; and Seymore, J. P. Effectiveness of pay incentive under variable ratio and continuous reinforcement schedules. *Journal of Applied Psychology 56* (1972): 19–23.

Zadny, J. J.; and James, L. F. A review of research on job placement. *Rehabilitation Counseling Bulletin 21* (1977): 150–158.

Zajonc, R. B. Social facilitation. *Science 149* (1965): 269–274.

Zalusky, J. Arbitration: Updating a vital process. *American Federationist 83* (1976): 1–8.

Zedeck, S. An information processing model and approach to the study of motivation. *Organizational Behavior and Human Performance 18* (1977): 47–77.

Zedeck, S. Problems with the use of moderator variables. *Psychological Bulletin 70* (1971): 293–310.

Zerga, J. E. Job analysis: A resume and bibliography. *Journal of Applied Psychology 27* (1943): 249–267.

Zeuthen, F. *Problems of monopoly and economic warfare.* London: Routledge and Kegan Paul, 1930.

Zikmund, W. G.; Hitt, M. A.; and Pickens, B. A. Influence of sex and scholastic performance on reactions to job applicant resumes. *Journal of Applied Psychology 63* (1978): 252–254.

AUTHOR INDEX

SUBJECT INDEX